INDEX TO *POETRY* *for* CHILDREN *and* YOUNG PEOPLE

1970–1975

VOLUMES IN THIS SERIES

INDEX TO CHILDREN'S POETRY *(1942)*

INDEX TO CHILDREN'S POETRY: FIRST SUPPLEMENT *(1954)*

INDEX TO CHILDREN'S POETRY: SECOND SUPPLEMENT *(1965)*

INDEX TO POETRY FOR CHILDREN AND YOUNG PEOPLE: 1964-1969

INDEX TO POETRY FOR CHILDREN AND YOUNG PEOPLE: 1970-1975

INDEX TO *POETRY* *for* CHILDREN *and* YOUNG PEOPLE

1970–1975

A TITLE, SUBJECT, AUTHOR, AND FIRST LINE INDEX

TO POETRY IN COLLECTIONS

FOR CHILDREN AND YOUNG PEOPLE

Compiled by
John E. Brewton
and
G. Meredith Blackburn III
and
Lorraine A. Blackburn

THE H. W. WILSON COMPANY • NEW YORK 1978

International Standard Book Number: 0-8242-0621-5

Printed in the United States of America

Library of Congress Cataloging in Publication Data

Main entry under title:

Index to poetry for children and young people.
1970-1975.
"First supplement to Index to poetry for children and young people, 1964-1969."
Bibliography: p.
1. Children's poetry—Indexes. I. Brewton, John Edmund, 1898-
PN1023.B722 821'.001'6 77-26036
ISBN 0-8242-0621-5

CONTENTS

INTRODUCTION

The INDEX TO POETRY FOR CHILDREN AND YOUNG PEOPLE: 1970-1975, inclusive, is a dictionary index to 110 collections of poems for children and young people published from 1970 through 1975, with title, subject, author, and first line entries. More than 10,000 poems by approximately 2,500 authors and translators are classified under more than 2,000 subjects.

The INDEX TO POETRY FOR CHILDREN AND YOUNG PEOPLE: 1970-1975 is the first supplement to INDEX TO POETRY FOR CHILDREN AND YOUNG PEOPLE: 1964-1969.

Scope. The carefully selected list of books of poetry for children and young people which are indexed includes collections for the very young child (e.g., books such as those classed in "Easy Books" in the *Children's Catalog,* Mother Goose, etc.); collections for the elementary school grades (e.g., the range of collections in class 821.08 in the *Children's Catalog*); and collections suitable for junior and senior high school age (e.g., such collections as those found in class 821.08 in the *Junior High School Library Catalog* and in the *Senior High School Library Catalog).* In addition to anthologies or collections of poetry by more than one poet, volumes by individual poets (e.g., books by David McCord, Eve Merriam), and collections of selected poems by a single author (e.g., *The Pinnacled Tower,* poems by Thomas Hardy, selected by Helen Plotz and *Don't You Turn Back,* poems by Langston Hughes, selected by Lee Bennett Hopkins) are also included. Books partly in prose and partly in verse (e.g., *The Sandburg Treasury, Prose and Poetry for Young People* by Carl Sandburg) are indexed; as well as collections of poems on a single subject (e.g., *Sing Hey for Christmas Day,* compiled by Lee Bennett Hopkins). The inclusion of comprehensive collections (e.g., *The Poetry of Black America,* compiled by Arnold Adoff and *A Flock of Words,* edited by David MacKay) gives the index a wide range.

Selection of Collections Included. Selection of the 110 collections included is based on a list of titles voted on by consulting librarians and teachers in various parts of the United States. A comprehensive list of anthologies and volumes of poetry by individual authors was sent to the selected consultants, their advice secured, and the final selection made. A list of consultants follows this Introduction.

Entries. Entries are of four types: title, subject, author, and reference from first line to title. The addition of collection symbols to title, subject, and author entries makes these complete within themselves, thus obviating the necessity for cross references.

1. TITLE ENTRY. The fullest information is given in this entry. Although the symbols designating the books in which the poems are to be found are given in author and subject entries as well as in the title entries, the title entry is the only one which gives full name of author, when known, and full name of translator. Refer-

ences to the title entry have been made (a) from variant titles (e.g., Cure for a pussy cat. See That little black cat); (b) from titles of selections to the source title (e.g., The little doll. See The water babies); and (c) from first lines (e.g., "The way a crow." See Dust of snow).

The title entry includes:

(a) Title, followed by first line in parentheses when needed to distinguish between poems with the same title.

(b) Variant titles, indented under the main title. When the same poem appears in different books with different titles, one title, generally the one appearing in the most collections, has been chosen as the title entry and all variations have been indented and listed under this title.

(c) Full name of author, when known.

(d) Full name of translator.

(e) Symbols for collections in which the poem is to be found.

In order to bring together selections from a single source, selections are listed under source titles. An example follows:

The **water** babies, sels. Charles Kingsley
  Young and old.—OpOx
    The old song.—RoIt

All entries subordinated under source titles are entered in their alphabetical position and referred to the source entry. Examples follow:

The **old** song. See The water babies—Young and old
Young and old. See The water babies

A group title (e.g., Limericks, Nonsense verses, Rhyming riddles) under which several poems appear has been subordinated as a variant to a title under which the poem appears in another book. Otherwise it has been subordinated to its own first line. Examples follow:

"A **man** who was fond of his skunk." David McCord
  Three limericks.—McS
"**There** is a young lady, whose nose (continually prospers)." Edward Lear
  Limericks.—JoA-4
  Nonsenses.—OpOx

2. Subject Entry. Entries are grouped by specific subjects. For example, under **Animals** are listed the poems about animals in general, while poems about specific animals are grouped under names of animals, as **Dogs.** A single poem is often classified under a number of subject headings (e.g., I have seen black hands, is listed under the subject headings **Blacks, Hands, Life, Race relations**).

Both *See* and *See also* references have been made freely to and from related subjects. These are filed at the beginning of the entries for the subject. Examples follow:

Prayers. See also Grace, Hymns
Reptiles. See Crocodiles, Lizards, Snakes

In order that individual poems or selections from longer poems which have been subordinated to source titles in the title entries may be classified according to subject and may also be readily identified as to sources, they have been entered under subject headings as follows:

Spring
"The flowers that bloom in the spring." From The Mikado. W. S. Gilbert.—RoIt

Variant titles and titles of selections subordinate to source titles are treated in the same way as under the title and author entries.

The subject entry gives:

(a) Title, followed by first line in parentheses when needed to distinguish between poems with the same title.

(b) Name, including initials, of author.

(c) Symbols for collections in which the poem is to be found.

3. AUTHOR ENTRY. All titles are listed alphabetically under the name of the author. Variant titles and titles of selections subordinated under source titles are entered in their proper alphabetical place and referred to the main title or source title.

The author entry gives, under the full name of the author:

(a) Title, followed by first line in parentheses when needed to distinguish between poems with the same title.

(b) Symbols for collections in which the poem is to be found.

(c) Cross references from variant titles to main titles.

(d) Cross references from titles of selections to source titles.

4. FIRST LINE REFERENCES. The first line is always given in quotation marks, even when it is also the title. When the title differs from first line, reference is made from first line to title.

Arrangement. The arrangement is alphabetical. Articles are always retained at the beginning of title and first line, but the articles (except articles in dialect and foreign articles) are disregarded in the alphabeting. Such entries are alphabeted by the word following the article and this word is printed in boldface (e.g., The **cat,** is filed under C). Articles in dialect and foreign articles are filed under the dialect or foreign article (e.g., "**D** blues" is filed under D and **La** belle dame sans merci, is filed under L). Abbreviations are filed as if spelled in full (e.g., **St** is filed as Saint). Contractions are filed as one word (e.g., **I'd** is filed as Id). Hyphenated words are filed as separate words. An exception is made if the hyphen is part of the word (e.g., **A-ha**). To facilitate quick use the entries beginning with **O** and **Oh** have been filed together, under O. Likewise, names beginning **Mac** and **Mc** have been filed together as Mac. Punctuation has been disregarded in filing. Where the wording is the same, entries have been arranged in the following order: author, subject, first line, first line used as title, title.

Grades. The books have been graded and the grades are given in parentheses in the Analysis of Books Indexed and in the Key to Symbols. The grading is only approximate and is given to indicate in general the grades for which each book is suitable. A book that is comprehensive in nature and is suitable for a wide range of grades up to and beyond the twelfth grade is designated (r), reference.

Uses. THE INDEX TO POETRY FOR CHILDREN AND YOUNG PEOPLE should serve as a practical reference book for all who desire to locate poems for children and young people by subject, author, title, or first line. It should prove especially useful to librarians, teachers in elementary and secondary schools, teachers and students of literature for children and young people, radio and television artists, parents, young people, and children. The variety of subject classifications should be particularly useful to anyone preparing programs for special occasions, to teachers planning activities around interests of children and young people, to parents who desire to share poetry, and to anyone searching for poems on a given topic. The Analysis of Books Indexed, which gives in detail the contents of each book, number of poems included, number of authors represented, and number of poems in each group or classification, should prove valuable in the selection of collections for purchase or use. The comprehensiveness of the books indexed insures the usefulness of the INDEX to those interested in poetry from the nursery through the secondary school and beyond.

Acknowledgments. The compilers thank the consultants who cooperated in checking lists of titles to be included. Grateful recognition is given to Sara Westbrook Brewton who collaborated on the early preparation of this INDEX and on all four previous editions. Evelyn Stephenson has given invaluable assistance on this and previous editions. Thanks are also due the publishers who generously supplied copies of the books which are included in the Index and Bruce Carrick, Editor of General Publications of The H. W. Wilson Company, and his staff for their painstaking work.

JOHN EDMUND BREWTON
G. MEREDITH BLACKBURN III
LORRAINE A. BLACKBURN

CONSULTANTS

James M. Bray
Director of Children's Services
Public Library
Rochester, Minnesota

Elizabeth Breting
Director of Children's Services
Public Library
Kansas City, Missouri

Annie Jo Carter
Coordinator of School Library Services
Metropolitan Public Schools
Nashville, Tennessee

Laurie Dudley
Special Services Librarian
Public Library
Abilene, Texas

Edith Edmonds
Former Elementary School Librarian
Winnetka Public School Libraries
Winnetka, Illinois

Beth Greggs
Area Children's Supervisor
King County Library System
Seattle, Washington

Amy Kellman
Head, Children's Department
Carnegie Library
Pittsburgh, Pennsylvania

Kathlyn King Lundgren
Audio-Visual Librarian
Nebraska Western College
Scottsbluff, Nebraska

Anne Pellowski
Director-Librarian
U. S. Committee for UNICEF, Information Center on Children's Cultures
New York, New York

Donald B. Reynolds, Jr.
Media Consultant
SEMBCS
Littleton, Colorado

Marylett R. Robertson
Librarian
West Hills Elementary School
Knoxville, Tennessee

Marian R. Schroether
Children's Librarian
Public Library
Waukegan, Illinois

Della Thomas
Former Director, Curriculum Materials Laboratory
Oklahoma State University
Stillwater, Oklahoma

Helen Tyler
Media Services Specialist
Eugene School District
Eugene, Oregon

Caroljean L. Wagner
Librarian Grade 3
Public Library
Milwaukee, Wisconsin

Jane B. Wilson
Private Consultant on Children's Services
Chapel Hill, North Carolina

ANALYSIS OF BOOKS OF POETRY INDEXED

Grades are given in parentheses at the end of each entry: (k), kindergarten or preschool grades; (1), first grade; (2), second grade, etc. Comprehensive general collections are designated (r), reference.

Abdul, Raoul, ed. Magic of Black poetry, edited with commentaries by Raoul Abdul; il. by Diane Burr. Dodd 1972 (5-up)

Contents. 95 poems by 48 poets grouped as follows: Beginning, 9; Springtime, 8; Love, 7; Nonsense, 12; Creatures, 8; Places, 7; Singing words, 10; Ballads & legends, 2; Christmas, 8; Heroes, 10; Like it is, 6; Night, 4; Tomorrows, 3; and Epilogue, 1. Also Introduction by Raoul Abdul; and About the poets.

Adams, Adrienne, comp. and il. Poetry of earth. Scribner 1972 (r)

Contents. 33 poems by 27 poets ungrouped. Illustrations on each page. Table of contents but no index.

Adoff, Arnold, ed. Black out loud; an anthology of modern poems by Black Americans; drawings by Alvin Hollingsworth. Macmillan 1970 (k-3)

Contents. 68 poems by 38 poets grouped as follows: Introductory poem, 1; Black all day, 11; I am a poet, 10; Perhaps you will remember, 11; Right on: white America, 12; But here I am, 11; and You are loved, awake or dreaming, 12. Also Preface, Biographical notes. Indexed by authors, first lines, and titles.

Adoff, Arnold, ed. My Black me; a beginning book of Black poetry. Dutton 1974 (k-3)

Contents. 50 poems by 25 poets grouped as follows: I, 9; II, 10; III, 9; IV, 6; V, 8; and VI, 8. Also brief biographical sketches of the poets; and introduction, This book of Black. Indexed by authors and first lines.

Adoff, Arnold, ed. Poetry of Black America; anthology of the 20th century. Harper 1973 (r)

Contents. 618 poems by 145 poets grouped by authors chronologically. Also Preface, Use the words to raise the children singing with their power by Arnold Adoff; Introduction by Gwendolyn Brooks; and Biographical notes. Indexed by authors, first lines, and titles.

Alderson, Brian, comp. Cakes and custard; children's rhymes chosen by Brian

Alderson; il. by Helen Oxenbury. Morrow, published in the United States in 1975 (k-4)
Contents. 148 traditional nursery rhymes and one rhyme by Robert Graves and 2 by James Reeves. Also Foreword: Where the rhymes come from. Indexed by first lines.

Allen, Samuel, comp. Poems from Africa, selected by Samuel Allen; drawings by Romare Bearden. Crowell 1973 (r)
Contents. 128 poems by 46 poets and 41 translators grouped as follows: Prologue, 1; Oral tradition, 48; West Africa (in English), 36; West Africa (translated from the French), 21; South Africa, 9; East Africa, 10; and Epilogue, 3. Also Introduction and Biographies of the poets. Indexed by authors, translators, first lines, and titles.

Allen, Terry, ed. Whispering wind; poetry by young American Indians. Doubleday 1972 (r)
Contents. 104 poems grouped by 14 young American Indians as follows: Alonzo Lopez, 14; Liz Sohappy, 4; Grey Cohoe, 6; Janet Campbell, 2; Ramona Carden, 2; Ted Palmanteer, 6; Donna Whitewing, 7; Calvin O'John, 14; King D. Kuka, 2; Patricia Irving, 8; Ronald Rogers, 3; Emerson Blackhorse "Barney" Mitchell, 4; Agnes T. Pratt, 15; and Phil George, 17. Introduction by Mae J. Durham. Preface by T. D. Allen. Brief introductions of each author.

Atwood, Ann. My own rhythm; an approach to haiku; photographs in color by the author. Scribner 1973 (r)
Contents. Discussion of haiku with selections and color photographs. Includes 25 haiku by Atwood, Buson, Issa, and Bashō.

Baron, Virginia Olsen, ad. Sunset in a spider web; Sijo poetry of ancient Korea, adapted by Virginia Olsen Baron from translations by Chung Seuk Park; il. by Minja Park Kim. Holt 1974 (7-12)
Contents. 74 poems by 45 ancient Korean poets ungrouped. Also Introduction by Virginia Olsen Baron.

Behn, Harry, comp. and tr. More cricket songs; Japanese haiku translated by Harry Behn, il. with pictures by Japanese masters. Harcourt 1971 (4-up)
Contents. 84 haiku by 29 Japanese poets and 1 haiku by Harry Behn.

Belting, Natalia. Summer's coming in; il. by Adrienne Adams. Holt 1970 (5-up)
Contents. 8 poems ungrouped.

Belting, Natalia. Whirlwind is a ghost dancing; il. by Leo and Diane Dillon. Dutton 1974 (5-up)
Contents. 23 poems ungrouped.

Bierhorst, John, ed. In the trail of the wind; American Indian poems and ritual orations; il. with period engravings. Farrar 1971 (5-up)
Contents. 126 poems of 40 tribes of American Indians grouped as follows:

The beginning, 12; In the trail of the wind, 7; Give us many good roads, 10; Home, 7; The deer, 5; The words of war, 10; Among flowers that enclose us, 11; Of death, 12; Of rain and birth, 10; Dreams, 11; Omens and prophecies, 5; The arrival of the whites, 13; and We shall live again, 13. Also Introduction, Notes, Glossary of tribes, cultures, and languages, and Suggestions for further reading.

Bierhorst, John, comp. and ad. Songs of the Chippewa, adapted from the collections of Frances Densmore and Henry Rowe Schoolcraft, and arranged for piano and guitar by John Bierhorst; il. by Joe Servello. Farrar 1974 (5-up)
Contents. 17 songs of the Chippewa ungrouped. Also Introduction and Notes.

Blegvad, Lenore, comp. Mittens for kittens and other rhymes about cats chosen by Lenore Blegvad; pictures by Erik Blegvad. A Margaret K. McElderry book. Atheneum 1974 (k-3)
Contents. 25 rhymes ungrouped.

Bodecker, N. M., tr. and il. It's raining said John Twaining; Danish nursery rhymes. A Margaret K. McElderry book. Atheneum 1973 (k-3)
Contents. 13 Danish nursery rhymes ungrouped.

Bodecker, N. M. Let's marry said the cherry and other nonsense poems; il. by the author. A Margaret K. McElderry book. Atheneum 1974 (4-up)
Contents. 33 poems ungrouped.

Brewton, Sara and John E. and Blackburn, G. Meredith III, comps. My tang's tungled and other ridiculous situations; il. by Graham Booth. Crowell 1973 (4-up)
Contents. 120 poems by 61 poets grouped as follows: Introductory poem, 1; My tang's tungled, 22; The folk who live in Backward town, 12; This little morsel, 13; Family fun, 14; Animal adventures, 16; Don't ever seize a weasel by the tail, 8; The ways of animals, 18; All schools have rules, 7; How foolish, 8; and Concluding poem, 1. Indexed by authors, first lines, and titles.

Bryan, Ashley, comp. and il. Walk together children; Black American spirituals. Atheneum 1975 (5-up)
Contents. 24 Black American spirituals with words and music.

Causley, Charles. Figgie hobbin; il. by Trina Schart Hyman. Walker 1973 (5-up)
Contents. 13 poems ungrouped. Also Introduction by Ethel L. Heins.

Chute, Marchette. Rhymes about us; il. by the author. Dutton 1974 (k-3)
Contents. 60 poems ungrouped.

Ciardi, John. Fast and slow; poems for advanced children and beginning parents; il. by Becky Gaver. Houghton 1975 (3-up)
Contents. 34 poems ungrouped.

Clifton, Lucille. Everett Anderson's Christmas coming; il. by Evaline Ness. Holt 1971 (k-2)
Contents. 9 poems ungrouped.

Clifton, Lucille. Everett Anderson's year; il. by Ann Grifalconi. Holt 1974 (k-2)
Contents. 12 poems, one for each month of the year, reflect the major and minor events in the life of a young boy.

Clifton, Lucille. Some of the days of Everett Anderson; il. by Evaline Ness. Holt 1970 (k-2)
Contents. 9 poems ungrouped.

Clymer, Theodore, comp. Four corners of the sky; poems, chants, and oratory selected by Theodore Clymer; il. by Marc Brown. An Atlantic Monthly Press book; Little, Brown and Company. Little 1975 (4-up)
Contents. 56 poems and chants of the American Indians of 26 tribes. Also brief Preface and Bibliography.

Cole, William, comp. Oh, how silly; il. by Tomi Ungerer. Viking 1970 (3-5)
Contents. 55 poems by 20 poets ungrouped. Also Introduction. Indexed by authors and titles.

Cole, William, comp. Oh, that's ridiculous; drawings by Tomi Ungerer. Viking 1972 (3-5)
Contents. 52 poems by 29 poets ungrouped.

Cole, William, ed. Pick me up; a book of short short poems. Macmillan 1972 (7-12)
Contents. 241 poems by 153 poets grouped as follows: Beginnings, 17; The wit of poets, 26; The poetry of wit, 24; The things of nature, 23; The nature of things, 34; Creatures of earth and water, 23; Flyers and leapers, 21; Portraits, 22; Pictures, 23; and Ends, 28. Also Introduction. Indexed by authors, first lines, and titles.

Cole, William, ed. Poems from Ireland; selected by William Cole; drawings by William Stobbs. Crowell 1972 (r)
Contents. 175 poems by 84 poets. Poems are arranged alphabetically by authors. Also Introduction by William Cole and brief Biographies of the poets. Indexed by authors, first lines, and titles. One of the Poems of the world series prepared under the general editorship of Lillian Morrison.

Cole, William, ed. Poets' tales, a new book of story poems; il. by Charles Keeping. World Publishing 1971 (7-12)
Contents. 147 poems by 107 poets grouped as follows: Strange and mysterious, 27; Characters and individualists, 23; Birds, beasts, and bugs, 16; Adventures and disasters, 13; Love stories, 13; Fighting men, 18; At sea, 15; and Odd and funny, 22. Also Introduction by William Cole. Indexed by authors, first lines, and titles.

Emrich, Duncan, ed. Nonsense book of riddles, rhymes, tongue twisters, puzzles, and jokes from American folklore; il. by Ib Ohlsson. Four winds 1970 (3-up)
Contents. Riddles, including true riddles; puzzles, or problem questions; and conundrums, or trick questions; Game rhymes, including Counting out, Hide and seek, Skip rope, Ball bouncing, and Teasing; Autograph album and Memory book rhymes; Tongue-twisters; Nonsense and funsense. Also Introduction, Notes, and Bibliography.

Fisher, Aileen. Do bears have mothers, too; il. by Eric Carle. Crowell 1973 (k-3)
Contents. 12 short poems about baby animals.

Fisher, Aileen. Feathered ones and furry; il. by Eric Carle. Crowell 1971 (3-5)
Contents. 55 poems ungrouped.

Fisher, Aileen. My cat has eyes of sapphire blue; pictures by Marie Angel. Crowell 1973 (3-5)
Contents. 24 short poems ungrouped about cats and kittens.

Fleming, Alice, comp. Hosannah the home run; poems about sports; il. with photographs. Little 1972 (5-up)
Contents. 34 poems by 29 poets ungrouped.

Froman, Robert. Street poems. McCall 1971 (4-up)
Contents. 56 poems ungrouped.

Hanaka Fukuda, tr. Wind in my hand; with the editorial assistance of Mark Taylor, Haiku translations by Hanaka Fukuda; il. by Lydia Cooley. Golden Gate Junior Books, San Carlos, California 1970 (5-up)
Contents. Wind in my hand is a story based on the autobiographical notes in Issa's own diary. The poems included are not in chronological order of their writing but were chosen for their appropriateness to the story. Included are 42 haikus, 40 by Issa, one by Bashō, and one by an unknown writer. Also included is a Foreword.

Hannum, Sara and Chase, John Terry, comps. Wind is round, il. by Ronald Bowen. Atheneum 1970 (7-12)
Contents. 69 poems by 45 poets ungrouped. Also Introduction. Indexed by authors and titles.

Hill, Helen and Perkins, Agnes, comps. New coasts & strange harbors, Discovering poems; il. by Clare Romano and John Ross. Crowell 1974 (r)
Contents. 206 poems by 84 poets grouped as follows: Of song and dance, 12; Balance and skill, 9; Looking at people, 15; Listening to people, 12; Still lifes and moving pictures, 16; The swift seasons roll, 28; Father of the man, 13; When I was a child, 15; A beautiful brief moment, 9; A kiss for Eve, 13; The buzzing doubt, 11; Taking wing, 10; That dark other mountain, 14; and Nightmares, 15. Also Foreword. Indexed by authors, first lines, and titles.

Hoban, Russell. Egg thoughts and other Frances songs; pictures by Lillian Hoban. Harper 1972 (k-3)
Contents. 22 songs ungrouped.

Hoberman, Mary Ann. Little book of little beasts; pictures by Peter Parnall. Simon 1973 (k-4)
Contents. 19 poems ungrouped.

Hoberman, Mary Ann. Nuts to you & nuts to me; an alphabet of poems; il. by Ronni Solbert. Knopf 1974 (k-1)
Contents. 26 poems alphabetically arranged.

Hoberman, Mary Ann. Raucous auk; a menagerie of poems; il. by Joseph Low. Viking 1973 (k-3)
Contents. 34 poems ungrouped.

Hogrogian, Nonny, il. One I love, two I love and other loving Mother Goose rhymes. Dutton 1972 (k-3)
Contents. 17 Mother Goose rhymes.

Holman, Felice. I hear you smiling and other poems; il. by Laszlo Kubinyi. Scribner 1973 (3-5)
Contents. 40 poems ungrouped.

Hopkins, Lee Bennett, comp. The city spreads its wings; il. by Moneta Barnett. Watts 1970 (3-5)
Contents. 21 poems by 15 poets ungrouped.

Hopkins, Lee Bennett, comp. City talk, photographs by Roy Arenella. Knopf 1970 (4-up)
Contents. 42 cinquains written by 39 children, and an introductory one by Lee Bennett Hopkins, grouped as follows: Spring, 12; Summer, 13; Fall, 9; and Winter, 8. Also Introduction.

Hopkins, Lee Bennett, ed. Don't you turn back, Poems by Langston Hughes; woodcuts by Ann Grifalconi. Knopf 1970 (5-9)
Contents. 45 poems by Langston Hughes grouped as follows: My people, 17; Prayers and dreams, 11; Out to sea, 10; and I am a Negro, 7. Also An Introduction by Arna Bontemps, and A note from the editor. Indexed by first lines and titles.

Hopkins, Lee Bennett, comp. Hey-how for Halloween, il. by Janet McCaffery. Harcourt 1974 (2-5)
Contents. 22 poems by 20 poets ungrouped. Indexed by authors and titles.

Hopkins, Lee Bennett, comp. Poetry on wheels; drawings by Frank Aloise. Garrard 1974 (2-5)
Contents. 49 poems by 30 poets grouped as follows: Riding on land, 27;

Sailing on the sea, 8; and Flying in the air, 14. Indexed by authors and titles.

Hopkins, Lee Bennett, comp. Sing hey for Christmas day; il. by Laura Jean Allen. Harcourt 1975 (2-5)
Contents. 21 poems by 16 poets ungrouped. Indexed by authors and titles.

Hughes, Ted. Meet my folks; il. by Mila Lazarevich. Bobbs-Merrill 1973 (5-up)
Contents. 11 poems ungrouped.

Jacobs, Leland B., comp. Poetry of witches, elves, and goblins; drawings by Frank Aloise. Garrard 1970 (2-5)
Contents. 48 poems by 23 poets grouped as follows: Introductory poems, 3; About witches, 5; About elves, 6; About brownies, 4; About goblins, 5; About giants, 2; About fairies, 15; About leprechauns, 2; About other wee folk, 4; and Closing poems, 2. Indexed by authors and titles.

Johnson, Edna; Sickels, Evelyn R; and Sayers, Frances Clarke, eds. Anthology of children's literature, Fourth revised edition, with black and white illustrations by Fritz Eichenberg, and full color paintings by N. C. Wyeth. Houghton 1970 (r)
Contents. Three sections are devoted to poetry. The first section, Around the world in nursery rhymes, contains 178 traditional rhymes. The second section, Nonsense verses, contains 46 verses by 12 poets. The third section, Poetry, includes 234 poems by 103 poets grouped as follows: Fairies, fay, and far away, 12; "Bring the day," 42; Wind and weather, 23; "The lamb white days," 16; Sown upon the fields, 9; The lovely diminutives, 31; A delirium of birds, 11; Creatures that comfort and console, 10; Surge of the sea, 7; Christmas, Christmas, 13; Ballads, tales, and echoes of time, 18; Aye, my dear and tender, 9; and The grace of understanding, 33. All sections have introductions and bibliographies. Indexed by authors, first lines, and titles.

Jones, Hettie, comp. Trees stand shining, poetry of the North American Indians; paintings by Robert Andrew Parker. Dial 1971 (4-up)
Contents. 32 poems or songs of 15 North American Indian tribes. Also Introduction.

Jordan, June and Bush, Terri, comps. Voice of the children. Holt 1970 (1-8)
Contents. 63 poems and prose selections written by 26 Black and Puerto Rican children, grouped as follows: Politics, 17; Observations, 16; Blackness, 13; Love and nature, 11; and Very personal, 15. Also Foreword by Vanessa Howard and Afterword by June Jordan. Indexed by authors and titles.

Kennedy, X. J. One winter night in August and other nonsense jingles; il. by David McPhail. A Margaret K. McElderry book. Atheneum 1975 (2-up)
Contents. 51 poems ungrouped.

Kuskin, Karla. Any me I want to be; il. by the author. Harper 1972 (2-6)
Contents. 30 poems ungrouped. Also Introduction by Karla Kuskin.

Kuskin, Karla. Near the window tree, poems and notes; il. by the author. An Ursula Nordstrom book. Harper 1975 (2-6)

Contents. 32 poems with accompanying notes on where one gets ideas for poems. Also Children may skip this introduction.

Langstaff, John, comp. Season for singing; American Christmas songs and carols with music harmonized and arranged by Seymour Barab for piano or guitar accompaniment; il. by John Johnson. Doubleday 1974 (5-up)

Contents. 50 American Christmas songs and carols grouped as follows: Folk carols, 10; Shaker, Moravian, Indian, 4; Black tradition, spirituals and gospel, 11; Shape-note hymns and composed songs, 16; and Part songs, 9. Also Introduction. Indexed by first lines.

Larrick, Nancy, comp. More poetry for holidays; drawings by Harold Berson. Garrard 1973 (2-5)

Contents. 50 poems by 29 poets grouped as follows: New year's day, 1; Ground hog day, 1; Pancake day, 1; Lincoln's birthday, 2; Valentine's day, 3; Washington's birthday, 2; St. Patrick's day, 3; Purim, 1; Passover, 1; April fool's day, 1; Good Friday, 1; Easter, 2; Arbor day, 2; Bird day, 3; May day, 2; Summer reading, 1; Fourth of July, 1; End of vacation, 1; Rosh Hashanah, 2; Halloween, 5; Children's book week, 1; Sukkot, 2; Thanksgiving, 2; Hanukkah, 3; Christmas, 5; and End of a year, 1. Also Special days have special meaning. Indexed by authors and titles.

Lee, Dennis. Alligator pie; il. by Frank Newfeld. Houghton 1975 (k-4)

Contents. 37 poems ungrouped. Also Hockey sticks and high-rise: A postlude.

Lenski, Lois. City poems; il. by the author. Walck 1971 (k-3)

Contents. 120 poems for young children, grouped as follows: I like the city, 19; Places in the city, 18; People in the city, 19; Fun in the city, 21; Our block in the city, 21; and My home in the city, 22. Also Foreword by Charlotte S. Huck and Preface by the author. Indexed by first lines and titles.

Lewis, Richard, ed. I breathe a new song; poems of the Eskimo; il. by Oonark, with an introduction by Edmund Carpenter. Simon 1971 (r)

Contents. 81 poems of the Eskimo, grouped as follows: Part one, With the dawning light, 11; Part two, You great long-tails, 8; Part three, Harpoon of my making, 9; Part four, Do not weep, little one, 6; Part five, I failed, indeed, in my hunting, 13; Part six, I see your face, 8; Part seven, Fear was about me, 7; Part eight, I am tired of watching and waking, 12; and Part nine, The dead who climb up to the sky, 7. Also Life as it was, an introduction by Edmund Carpenter; Editor's note; and Bibliography.

Livingston, Myra Cohn, ed. Listen, children, listen; an anthology of poems for the very young; il. by Trina Schart Hyman. Harcourt 1972 (k-3)

Contents. 81 poems by 46 poets ungrouped. Indexed by authors and titles.

Livingston, Myra Cohn. The Malibu and other poems; il. by James J. Spanfeller. A Margaret K. McElderry book. Atheneum 1972 (5-up)
Contents. 40 poems ungrouped.

Livingston, Myra Cohn, ed. Poems of Lewis Carroll selected by Myra Cohn Livingston, with illustrations by John Tenniel, Harry Furnias, Henry Holiday, Arthur B. Frost, and Lewis Carroll from the original editions. Crowell 1973 (5-up)
Contents. 42 poems grouped as follows: Poems from Alice's adventures in wonderland, 9; Poems from Through the looking-glass and what Alice found there, 6; Poems from Sylvie and Bruno, 3; Poems from Sylvie and Bruno concluded, 4; More parodies and other humorous verse, 6; Puzzles, acrostics, dedications, and riddles, 13; and The hunting of the snark—an agony in eight fits, 1. Also Introduction, Notes on the poems. Indexed by first lines and titles. One of the Poems of the world series prepared under the general editorship of Lillian Morrison.

Livingston, Myra Cohn, ed. Speak roughly to your little boy; a collection of parodies and burlesques, together with the original poems, chosen and annotated for young people; il. by Joseph Low. Harcourt 1971 (5-up)
Contents. 135 poems by 73 poets grouped in two sections. In Section I is presented the original poems in italics, arranged alphabetically as to author, and followed by the parody or burlesque. In Section II is presented a collection of parodies on anonymous poems, nursery rhymes, literary fashions, authors' general works, together with one self-parody. Also Notes on the original poems and parodies. Indexed by authors, original poems and parodies separated; first lines; and titles, original poems and parodies separated.

Livingston, Myra Cohn, ed. What a wonderful bird the frog are, an assortment of humorous poetry and verse. Harcourt 1973 (3-up)
Contents. 141 poems by 82 poets and 5 translators ungrouped. Indexed by authors, translators, first lines, and titles.

Mackay, David, ed. Flock of words; an anthology of poetry for children and others collected and annotated by David Mackay; drawings by Margery Gill. Harcourt (First American edition) 1970 (r)
Contents. 297 poems by 149 poets ungrouped. Also Preface by Professor Benjamin DeMott; Introduction by David Mackay. Indexed by authors, first lines, and titles.

Manning-Sanders, Ruth, comp. Festivals; il. by Raymond Briggs. Dutton 1973 (4-up)
Contents. Prose text and poems arranged by months and the festivals and holidays therein.

McCord, David. Away and ago; rhymes of the never was and always is; drawings by Leslie Morrill. Little 1975 (3-7)
Contents. 63 poems ungrouped.

McCord, David. For me to say, rhymes of the never was and always is; drawings by Henry B. Kane. Little 1970 (3-7)
Contents. 99 poems ungrouped.

McCord, David. Star in the pail; il. by Marc Simont. Little 1975 (3-7)
Contents. 31 poems ungrouped.

Merriam, Eve. Finding a poem; il. by Seymour Chwast. Atheneum 1970 (6-up)
Contents. 38 poems ungrouped and an essay, Writing a poem.

Merriam, Eve. Out loud; designed by Harriet Sherman. Atheneum 1973 (5-up)
Contents. 41 poems ungrouped.

Mezey, Robert, comp. Poems from the Hebrew; etchings by Moishe Smith. Crowell 1973 (r)
Contents. 108 poems grouped as follows: The ancient poems, 25; The poets of moorish Spain, 16; and The modern poets, 67. Also Introduction. Indexed by poets and translators, first lines, and titles. One of the Poems of the world series under the general editorship of Lillian Morrison.

Miller, Mitchell, il. One misty moisty morning; rhymes from Mother Goose; pictures by Mitchell Miller. Farrar 1971 (k-3)
Contents. 21 nursery rhymes ungrouped.

Moore, Lilian. Sam's place, poems from the country; drawings by Talivaldis Stubis. Atheneum 1973 (k-3)
Contents. 20 poems ungrouped.

Moore, Lilian. See my lovely poison ivy and other verses about witches, ghosts and things; pictures by Diane Dawson. Atheneum 1975 (1-5)
Contents. 35 poems ungrouped.

Moore, Lilian and Thurman, Judith, comps. To see the world afresh. Atheneum 1974 (7-12)
Contents. 66 poems by 46 poets and 9 translators grouped as follows: Part one, The muscle in your heart, 8; Part two, How deep the earth can be, 11; Part three, A human face, 14; Part four, Leaving the roots on, 8; Part five, All things innocent, 13; Part six, Is that how it is with poetry, 9; and Part seven, A place for the genuine, 3. Also Introduction and Section notes. Indexed by authors and titles.

Morrison, Lillian, comp. Best wishes, amen; a new collection of autograph verses; il. by Loretta Lustig. Crowell 1974 (3-up)
Contents. 311 verses grouped as follows: This is page one, 29; Sitting in the schoolroom, 25; City of love, state of wishes, 32; I've seen prettier girls, 34; Friendship is like china, 26; Boys are humbugs, 18; All the girls are marrying, 27; Lincoln, Lincoln, I've been thinkin', 33; Be kind in all you say and do, 29; Think of me sometimes, 22; May your life be like spaghetti, 18; and ? Escribo yo en tu libro?, 18. Also Preface and Acknowledgments.

Morse, David, ed. Grandfather rock; the new poetry and the old. Delacorte 1972 (7-12)

Contents. 59 poems by 34 poets grouped as follows: Ancient voices, 6; Loneliness and love, 8; Death, 4; Tigers of wrath, 10; Prophetic voices, 6; Anthems of the New Republic, 10; and Spaces, 15. Also introduction, The new poetry and the old; commentaries; and Final notes. Indexed by authors, performers, first lines, and titles.

Morton, Miriam, comp. and trans. Moon is like a silver sickle; a celebration of poetry by Russian children; il. by Eros Keith. Simon and Schuster 1972 (5-up)

Contents. 92 poems by Russian children, 46 poems by girls and 46 by boys grouped as follows: Discoveries and delights, 28; A sense of self, 11; Family and friends, 18; Loving, 10; War and peace, 6; and Thoughts and hopes, 19. Also Translator's note, Introduction, and Sources and acknowledgments.

Ness, Evaline, comp. and il. Amelia mixed the mustard and other poems. Scribner 1975 (4-up)

Contents. 20 poems by 15 poets ungrouped.

Opie, Iona and Peter, eds. Oxford book of children's verse, chosen and edited with notes by Iona and Peter Opie. Oxford 1973 (r)

Contents. 332 poems by 124 poets, grouped as follows: Medieval and sixteenth century, 16; Seventeenth century, 25; Eighteenth century, 57; Nineteenth century, First half, 91; Nineteenth century, Second half, 109; and Twentieth century, 34. Also Authors and sources. Indexed by authors, first lines and familiar titles.

Parker, Elinor, ed. Four seasons five senses; il. by Diane DeGroat. Scribner 1974 (4-up)

Contents. 101 poems by 55 poets grouped as follows: Introductory poem, 1; Winter, 25; Spring, 25; Summer, 25; and Autumn, 25. Indexed by authors, first lines, and titles.

Parker, Elinor, comp. Poets and the English scene; il. with photographs. Scribners 1975 (r)

Contents. 66 poems by 49 poets grouped as follows: London and surrounding countryside, 14; South from London to the Channel, 9; To Land's End and beyond, 8; Welsh border country, 5; The Lake country, 5; Yorkshire and the Midlands, 8; East Anglia, 3; Cambridge and Oxford, 8; and The heart of England, 6. Also Glossary, Sources, and commentaries. Indexed by authors and first lines.

Peck, Richard, ed. Sounds & silences; poetry for now. Dell 1970 (7-12)

Contents. 103 poems by 66 poets grouped as follows: The family, 11; Childhood, 8; Isolation, 6; Identity, 11; Realities, 11; Illusion, 9; Dissent, 11; Communication, 5; Love, 8; War, 10; Pain, 6; and Recollections, 7. Also Introduction. Indexed by authors, first lines, and titles.

Plotz, Helen, ed. Marvelous light; poets and poetry. Crowell 1970 (7-12)
Contents. 117 poems by 101 poets and translators grouped as follows: Making of the sun, 28; While we two walked, 33; Each age a lens, 39; and They told me you were dead, 17. Also Introduction. Indexed by authors, first lines, and titles.

Plotz, Helen, ed. Pinnacled tower; selected poems of Thomas Hardy; wood engravings by Clare Leighton. Macmillan 1975 (7-12)
Contents. 110 poems by Thomas Hardy grouped as follows: Introduction, 1; The year's awakening, The world of nature, 17; Past things retold, Friends and family, 10; In time of the breaking of nations, Men and women, 32; The spinner of the years, Man and the universe, 16; When I set out for Lyonnesse, Love and marriage, 34. Also Introduction. Indexed by titles and first lines.

Prelutsky, Jack. Circus; pictures by Arnold Lobel. Macmillan 1974 (k-4)
Contents. 18 poems ungrouped.

Prelutsky, Jack. Packrat's day and other poems; il. by Margaret Bloy Graham. Macmillan 1974 (k-4)
Contents. 15 poems ungrouped.

Prelutsky, Jack. Toucans two and other poems; pictures by Jose Arvego. Macmillan 1970 (k-4)
Contents. 17 poems ungrouped.

Ross, David, ed. Illustrated treasury of poetry for children; with commentary and an introduction by Mark Van Doren; il. by Burmah Burris, Mel Klapholz, Ursula Landshoff, Gyo Fujikawa, Sir John Tenniel, W. S. Gilbert, Edward Lear, and others. Grosset 1970 (r)
Contents. 438 poems by 71 poets grouped as follows: The seasons, 42; Christmas, 14; The tide falls, the tide rises, 22; Creatures of the sea and sky, 37; In search of the horizon, 20; Spells and enchantments, 8; Miracles, 28; Miniature, 26; Music, 30; Nonsense, 16; Limericks, 21; Present mirth, 28; Creatures on land, 44; Cast of characters, 31; Love poems, 6; Men at arms, 10; Recollections, 31; and Wisdom, 24. Also Introduction. Indexed by authors, first lines, and titles.

Sandburg, Carl. Sandburg treasury: Prose and poetry, including Rootabaga stories, Early moon, Wind song, Abe Lincoln grows up, and Prairie-town boy. il. by Paul Bacon. Harcourt 1970 (r)
Contents. 165 poems grouped as follows: Early moon, 70, grouped as follows: Pictures of today, 11; Children, 10; Wind and sea, 11; Portraits, 12; Birds and bugs, 12; Night, 10; and End thoughts, 4; and Wind song, 95, grouped as follows: New poems, 16; Little people, 14; Little album, 15; Corn belt, 14; Night, 12; Blossom themes, 12; and Wind, sea, and sky, 12. Also Introduction by Paula Sandburg. Indexed by titles.

Serwadda, W. Moses, comp. Songs and stories from Uganda; transcribed and edited by Hewitt Pantaleoni; il. by Leo and Diane Dillon. Crowell 1974 (4-up)

Contents. 13 songs with accompanying stories retold from Ugandan folklore. Also A note from the author, Editor's preface, and How to pronounce words in Ugandan.

Silverstein, Shel. Where the sidewalk ends; the poems and drawings of Shel Silverstein. Harper 1974 (3-up)
Contents. 127 poems ungrouped. Indexed by titles.

Thomas, Marlo, conceived by. Free to be . . . you and me. McGraw 1974 (k-4)
Contents. 16 poems by 10 poets ungrouped.

Thurman, Judith, ed. I became alone, Five women poets; decorations by James and Ruth McCrea. Atheneum 1975 (7-12)
Contents. 62 poems by 5 women poets grouped as follows: Sappho, 13; Louise Labe, 9; Anne Bradstreet, 13; Juana Inez de la Cruz, 8; and Emily Dickinson, 19. Also Preface, brief biographies of each poet, and Notes.

Townsend, John Rowe, ed. Modern poetry; a selection by John Rowe Townsend; il. with photographs by Barbara Pfeffer. Lippincott 1971 (r)
Contents. 136 poems by 71 poets ungrouped. Also Foreword. Indexed by authors, first lines, and titles.

Tripp, Wallace, comp. and il. A great big ugly man came up and tied his horse to me; a book of nonsense verse. Little 1973 (k-3)
Contents. 41 nonsense verses by 3 known poets and many unknown.

Tucker, Nicholas, comp. Mother Goose abroad; nursery rhymes collected by Nicholas Tucker; pictures by Trevor Stubley. Crowell 1975 (k-3)
Contents. 19 nursery rhymes from France, Spain, Belgium, Holland, Germany, and Sweden.

Tucker, Nicholas, comp. Mother Goose lost; nursery rhymes collected by Nicholas Tucker; pictures by Trevor Stubley. Crowell 1971 (k-3)
Contents. 31 nursery rhymes. Also Introduction.

Untermeyer, Louis, comp. Golden book of poems for the very young; pictures by Joan Walsh Anglund. Golden Press, Inc. 1971 (k-3)
Contents. 40 poems by 27 poets ungrouped.

Watson, Clyde. Father Fox's pennyrhymes; il. by Wendy Watson. Crowell 1971 (k-4)
Contents. 31 verses ungrouped.

Wilbur, Richard. Opposites; il. by author. Harcourt 1973 (5-up)
Contents. 39 poems ungrouped.

Worth, Valerie. Small poems; with pictures by Natalie Babbitt. Farrar 1972 (4-up)
Contents. 24 poems ungrouped.

KEY TO SYMBOLS FOR BOOKS INDEXED

Grades are given in parentheses at the end of each entry: (k), kindergarten or preschool grade; (1), first grade; (2) second grade, etc. Comprehensive general collections are designated (r), reference.

Space is left under each symbol where the library call number may be inserted.

AbM Abdul, R. ed. Magic of Black poetry. Dodd 1972 (5-up)

AdB Adoff, A. ed. Black out loud. Macmillan 1970 (k-3)

AdM Adoff, A. ed. My Black me. Dutton 1974 (k-3)

AdP Adams, A. comp. and il. Poetry of earth. Scribner 1972 (r)

AdPb Adoff, A. ed. Poetry of Black America. Harper 1973 (r)

AlC Alderson, B. comp. Cakes and custard. Morrow 1975 (k-4)

AlPa Allen, S. comp. Poems from Africa. Crowell 1973 (r)

AlW Allen, T. ed. Whispering wind. Doubleday 1972 (r)

AtM Atwood, A. My own rhythm. Scribner 1973 (r)

BaSs Baron, V. O. ad. Sunset in a spider web. Holt 1974 (7-12)

BeM Behn, H. tr. More cricket songs. Harcourt 1971 (4-up)

BeSc Belting, N. Summer's coming in. Holt 1970 (5-up)

BeWi Belting, N. Whirlwind is a ghost dancing. Dutton 1974 (5-up)

BiI Bierhorst, J. ed. In the trail of the wind. Farrar 1971 (5-up)

BiS Bierhorst, J. comp. and ad. Songs of the Chippewa. Farrar 1974 (5-up)

BlM Blegvad, L. comp. Mittens for kittens and other rhymes about cats. Atheneum 1974 (k-3)

BoI Bodecker, N. M. tr. and il. It's raining said John Twaining. Atheneum 1973 (k-3)

BoL Bodecker, N. M. Let's marry said the cherry and other nonsense poems. Atheneum 1974 (4-up)

BrM Brewton, S. and J. E. and Blackburn III, G. M. comps. My tang's tungled and other ridiculous situations. Crowell 1973 (4-up)

BrW Bryan, A. comp. and il. Walk together children. Atheneum 1975 (5-up)

CaF Causley, C. Figgie hobbin. Walker 1973 (5-up)

ChRu Chute, M. Rhymes about us. Dutton 1974 (k-3)

CiFs Ciardi, J. Fast and slow. Houghton 1975 (3-up)

ClE Clifton, L. Everett Anderson's year. Holt 1974 (k-2)

ClEa Clifton, L. Everett Anderson's Christmas coming. Holt 1971 (k-2)

LiLc Livingston, M. C. ed. Listen, children, listen. Harcourt 1972 (k-3)

LiM Livingston, M. C. The Malibu and other poems. Atheneum 1972 (5-up)

LiPc Livingston, M. C. ed. Poems of Lewis Carroll. Crowell 1973 (5-up)

LiS Livingston, M. C. ed. Speak roughly to your little boy. Harcourt 1971 (5-up)

LiWw Livingston, M. C. ed. What a wonderful bird the frog are. Harcourt 1973 (3-up)

MaF Manning-Sanders, R. comp. Festivals. Dutton 1973 (4-up)

MaFw Mackay, D. ed. Flock of words. Harcourt 1970 (r)

McAa McCord, D. Away and ago. Little 1975 (3-7)

McFm McCord, D. For me to say. Little 1970 (3-7)

McS McCord, D. Star in the pail. Little 1975 (3-7)

MeF Merriam, E. Finding a poem. Atheneum 1970 (6-up)

MeO Merriam, E. Out loud. Atheneum 1973 (5-up)

MeP Mezey, R. comp. Poems from the Hebrew. Crowell 1973 (r)

MiMg Miller, M. One misty moisty morning. Farrar 1971 (k-3)

MoBw Morrison, L. comp. Best wishes, amen. Crowell 1974 (3-up)

MoG Morse, D. ed. Grandfather rock. Delacorte 1972 (7-12)

MoM Morton, M. comp. and tr. Moon is like a silver sickle. Simon 1972 (5-up)

MoSm Moore, L. See my lovely poison ivy. Atheneum 1975 (1-5)

MoSp Moore, L. Sam's place. Atheneum 1973 (k-3)

MoT Moore, L. and Thurman, J. comps. To see the world afresh. Atheneum 1974 (7-12)

NeA Ness, E. comp. and il. Amelia mixed the mustard and other poems. Scribner 1975 (4-up)

OpOx Opie, I. A. and P. eds. Oxford book of children's verse. Oxford 1973 (r)

PaF Parker, E. comp. Four seasons five senses. Scribner 1974 (4-up)

PaP Parker, E. ed. Poets and the English scene. Scribner 1975 (r)

PeS Peck, R. comp. Sounds & silences. Dell 1970 (7-12)

PlM Plotz, H. ed. Marvelous light. Crowell 1970 (7-12)

PlP Plotz, H. ed. Pinnacled tower. Macmillan 1975 (7-12)

PrC Prelutsky, J. Circus. Macmillan 1974 (k-4)

PrP Prelutsky, J. Packrat's day and other poems. Macmillan 1974 (k-4)

PrT Prelutsky, J. Toucans two and other poems. Macmillan 1970 (k-4)

RoIt Ross, D. ed. Illustrated treasury of poetry for children. Grosset 1970 (r)

SaT Sandburg, C. Sandburg treasury: Prose and poetry. Harcourt 1970 (r)

SeS Serwadda, W. M. comp. Songs and stories from Uganda. Crowell 1974 (4-up)

SiW Silverstein, S. Where the sidewalk ends. Harper 1974 (3-up)

ThF Thomas, M. comp. Free to be . . . you and me. McGraw 1974 (k-4)

ThI Thurman, J. ed. I became alone. Atheneum 1975 (7-12)

ToM Townsend, J. R. ed. Modern poetry. Lippincott 1971 (r)

TrG Tripp, W. A great big ugly man came up and tied his horse to me. Little 1973 (k-3)

TucMg Tucker, N. comp. Mother Goose abroad. Crowell 1975 (k-3)

TucMgl Tucker, N. comp. Mother Goose lost. Crowell 1971 (k-3)

UnGb Untermeyer, L. comp. Golden book of poems for the very young. Golden press 1971 (k-3)

WaF Watson, C. Father Fox's pennyrhymes. Crowell 1971 (k-4)

WiO Wilbur, R. Opposites. Harcourt 1973 (5-up)

WoS Worth, V. Small poems. Farrar 1972 (4-up)

KEY TO ABBREVIATIONS

ad. adapted
at. attributed
bk. book
comp. compiler, compiled
comps. compilers
ed. edition, editor
eds. editors
il. illustrated, illustrator
ils. illustrators
jt. auth. joint author
jt. auths. joint authors
k kindergarten or preschool grade
pseud. pseudonym
pseuds. pseudonyms
r reference
rev. revised
rev ed revised edition
sel. selection
sels. selections
tr. translator
tr. fr. translated from
trs. translators
wr. at. wrongly attributed

DIRECTIONS FOR USE

SEE KEY TO SYMBOLS, PAGE xxvii, AND KEY TO ABBREVIATIONS, PAGE XXX.

The TITLE ENTRY is the main entry and gives the fullest information, including title (with the first line in parentheses when needed to distinguish between poems with the same title); variant titles; full name of author; translator; and symbols for collections in which the poem is to be found. VARIANT TITLES and titles with variant first lines are also listed in their alphabetical order, with *See* references to the main title.

Africa. David Diop, tr. fr. the French by Ulli Beier.—AlPa
Cradle hymn ("Hush, my dear, lie still and slumber") Isaac Watts.—OpOx
Hush my babe.—LaS
Hush my babe. See Cradle hymn ("Hush, my dear, lie still and slumber")
"Hush, my dear, lie still and slumber." See Cradle hymn—Hush my babe

Titles of poems are grouped according to subject, in alphabetical order under a subject heading. The SUBJECT ENTRY gives the title of poem; name of author with initials only; first line where needed for identification; variant titles; source title for subordinate selections; and the symbols for the collections in which the poem is to be found.

Cats
Cat ("The black cat yawns") M. B. Miller.—HoH—LiLc
The kitten playing with the falling leaves. W. Wordsworth.—UnGb
The kitten and the falling leaves.—RoIt
"Pussy-cat, pussy-cat, where have you been." Mother Goose.—AlC
"Pussy cat, pussy cat."—BlM—JoA-4

The AUTHOR ENTRY gives the full name of the author; title of poem with its variants (first line in parentheses when needed for identification); and the symbols for the collections in which the poem is to be found. Included under the author entry are references from variant titles, and from titles of selections to the source title.

Carryl, Charles Edward
Davy and the goblin, sels.
Robinson Crusoe's island.—RoIt
The walloping window-blind.—RoIt
Robinson Crusoe's island. See Davy and the goblin
The walloping window-blind. See Davy and the goblin

FIRST LINES of poems, enclosed in quotation marks, are listed in their alphabetical order with references to the title entry where all the information may be found. First lines are enclosed in quotation marks even when used as titles.

"A **century** and eight more years." See The
  four directions
"**Something** went crabwise." See The presence
"**There** was a girl in our town." Unknown.—EmN

When the source of a poem is more familiar than the title of the poem, or when only selections from a longer work are given, such titles are grouped under the source title. All titles subordinated to SOURCE TITLES are also entered in their alphabetical order with references to the source title.

As you like it, sels. William Shakespeare
  "Blow, blow, thou winter wind."—PaF—RoIt
  "Under the greenwood tree."—RoIt
    In Arden forest.—JoA-4
"**Blow**, blow, thou winter wind." See As you
  like it
In Arden forest. See As you like it—"Under
  the greenwood tree"
"**Under** the greenwood tree." See As you like
  it

INDEX TO POETRY FOR CHILDREN AND YOUNG PEOPLE

A

A., F. P., pseud. See Adams, Franklin P.
"**A.**" See Sliding
"**A,** b, c, d, e, f, g." Unknown.—EmN
"**A,** B, C, tumble down D." See "A, B, C, tumble down dee"
"**A,** B, C, tumble down dee." Mother Goose.—BlM
  "A, B, C, tumble down D."—AlC
A. E., pseud. See Russell, George William
"**A** was an apple pie." Unknown.—EmN
A was an archer. Unknown.—OpOx
"**A** was an archer, and shot at a frog." See A was an archer
"**A** was once an apple pie." See An alphabet
The **aardvark** ("The aardvark knows a lot of things") Jack Prelutsky.—PrT
Aardvark ("Since") Julia Fields.—AdB—AdM
"The **aardvark** knows a lot of things." See The aardvark
Aardvarks
  The aardvark ("The aardvark knows a lot of things") J. Prelutsky.—PrT
  Aardvark ("Since") J. Fields.—AdB—AdM
Abandoned. Vanessa Howard.—JoV
The **ABC.** Spike Milligan.—CoOh
Abdul Abulbul Amir. Unknown.—RoIt
Abdul, Raoul
  Call to prayer. tr.—AbM
  Humorous verse. tr.—AbM
  Lament of the slave. tr.—AdM
Abeita, Louise
  See E-Yeh-Shuré
"**Abiding** in the shadow of the Almighty." See Psalms—Psalm 91
Abigail. Kaye Starbird.—NeA
"**Abigail** knew when she was born." See Abigail
Abou Ben Adhem. Leigh Hunt.—RoIt
"**Abou** Ben Adhem, may his tribe increase." See Abou Ben Adhem
About a monster-ous toothache. Lilian Moore.—MoSm
"**About** an excavation." Charles Reznikoff.—CoPu
"**About** suffering they were never wrong." See Musée des beaux arts
"**About** the time that taverns shut." See The ballad of Minepit Shaw
Above Penmaenmawr. Tony Connor.—ToM
Above the bright blue sky. Albert Midlane.—OpOx
"**Above** the meadow." Chiyo, tr. fr. the Japanese by Harry Behn.—BeM
"**Above** the mist." Unknown, fr. Ammassalik Eskimo.—LeIb
"**Above** the place where the minnow maiden sleeps while her fins move gently in the water." See Dream song
"**Above** the quiet valley and unrippled lake." See Spring oak
"**Above** the river that is east." See Look, Hart, that horse you ride is wood
"**Above** the tree." Felice Holman.—HoI
"**Abracadabra.**" Unknown.—MoBw
Abraham ibn Ezra
  Born without a star.—MeP
  I have a garment.—MeP
  My stars.—MeP
Abraham (about)
  Story of Isaac. L. Cohen.—MoG
Abraham and Isaac. See The Chester miracle play
Abraham Lincoln walks at midnight. Vachel Lindsay.—JoA-4
Absence
  "From you I have been absent in the spring."—W. Shakespeare
    Sonnet.—PaF
  Song for an absent chief. Unknown.—AlPa
The **absent-minded** man. Georgia H. MacPherson.—BrM
"An **absolute.**" See The breathing
Academic. James Reeves.—ToM
Acceptance
  From riot rimes U.S.A. #79. R. R. Patterson.—AdM
  On learning to adjust to things. J. Ciardi.—CiFs
  Verses. W. Cowper.—RoIt
Accident. Lois Lenski.—LeC
Accidents
  Accident. L. Lenski.—LeC
  "As I was falling down the stair." H. Mearns.—BrM
  Aunt Eliza. H. Graham.—LiWw
  Daddy fell into the pond. A. Noyes.—BrM
  "A decrepit old gasman, named Peter." Unknown.—LiWw
  Fast and far. J. Ciardi.—CiFs
  Framed in a first-story winder. Unknown.—CoOh
  George. H. Belloc.—CoOh
  Hallelujah. A. E. Housman.—CoOr
    "Hallelujah, was the only observation."—CoPu—LiWw

Advice ("Here's a nice advice") A. Resnikoff.—CoOh
Advice ("If you're sleepy in the jungle") M. A. Hoberman.—HoR
"Backward running porcupines." M. A. Hoberman.—HoR
Don't ever seize a weasel by the tail. J. Prelutsky.—BrM
"Don't worry if your job is small." Unknown.—BrM
Glowworm. D. McCord.—BrM
"If you should meet a crocodile." Unknown.—BrM
The panther. O. Nash.—BrM—CoOh
Rising in the morning. H. Rhodes.—OpOx
Sources of good counsel. P. Idley.—OpOx
Staying alive. D. Wagoner.—MoT
To Henrietta, on her departure for Calais. T. Hood.—OpOx
Advice ("Come along, come along") Marchette Chute.—ChRu
Advice ("Here's a nice advice") Alexander Resnikoff.—CoOh
Advice ("If you're sleepy in the jungle") Mary Ann Hoberman.—HoR
Advice from an elderly mouse. Elizabeth Jane Coatsworth.—BrM
Advice to a knight. T. Harri Jones.—MaFw
Advice to grandsons. Unknown.—CoOh
Aeneas (about)
Aeneid, sels. Virgil
The boat race.—FlH
The boxing match.—FlH
Aeneid, sels. Virgil
The boat race, tr. fr. the Latin by Rolfe Humphries.—FlH
The boxing match, tr. fr. the Latin by Rolfe Humphries.—FlH
Aeroplane. Mary McB. Green.—HoP
Aeroplanes. See Airplanes
Affection. See Friendship; Kindness; Love
Affinities. Adrien Stoutenburg.—MoT
Affliction. See Blind; Cripples
"**Aforetime,** by the waters wan." See Carmina Burana—Roast swan song
"**Afraid** of the dark." See Thursday evening: Bedtime
Afraid of the dark. Shel Silverstein.—SiW
Africa
Africa. D. Diop.—AlPa
African dream. B. Kaufman.—AdPb
Black warrior. N. Jordan.—AdPb
Blue Tanganyika. L. Bethune.—AdPb
Bwagamoyo. L. Bethune.—AdPb
Etta Moten's attic. From Far from Africa: Four poems. M. Danner.—AdPb
For Koras and Balafong. L. S. Senghor.—AlPa (sel.)
Heritage. C. Cullen.—AdPb
Long, long you have held between your hands. L. S. Senghor.—AlPa
My name is Afrika. K. Kgositsile.—AdPb
Our history. M. S. Dipoko.—AlPa
The renegade. D. Diop.—AlPa
Sand hill road. M. Grosser.—PeS
The sea. M. Mongameli.—AlPa
A sense of coolness. Q. Troupe.—AdPb
Shaka Zulu. F. M. Mulikita.—AlPa
Song of Lawino: An African lament. O. P'Bitek.—AlPa (sel.)
Stanley meets Mutesa. D. Rubadiri.—AlPa (sel.)
"We're an African people." From African poems. D. L. Lee.—AdM
Young Africa's plea. D. Osadebay.—AlPa
Africa. David Diop, tr. fr. the French by Ulli Beier.—AlPa
"**Africa** my Africa." See Africa
The **African** affair. Bruce McM. Wright.—AdPb
African China. Melvin B. Tolson.—AdPb
African dream. Bob Kaufman.—AdPb
African poems, sel. Don L. Lee
"We're an African people."—AdM
After. Ralph Hodgson.—JoA-4
After a fire. See Pencil stubs
After a game of squash. Samuel L. Albert.—FlH
After a journey. Thomas Hardy.—PlP
After dinner. Marchette Chute.—ChRu
"**After** each quake." See Crack in the wall holds flowers
After ever happily; or, The princess and the woodcutter. Ian Seraillier.—MaFw
"**After** it snows." See Lying on things
After many a summer. Alfred Tennyson.—RoIt
"**After** many strange thoughts." See After working
"**After** my wake, oh people of my lodge." See Proviso
"**After** night's thunder far away had rolled." See Haymaking
"**After** one more grandiloquent effort he slips back." See The beetle in the country bathtub
"**After** our fierce loving." See The profile on the pillow
After rain. Edward Thomas.—HiN
"**After** scanning its face again and again." See Burning—John Muir on Mt Ritter
After school. Aileen Fisher.—FiFo
"**After** she eats." See Cat bath
After snow. Walter Clark.—HiN
"**After** supper." See Do fishes go to school
"**After** the darkness has come." See Disturbances
"**After** the dreadful Flood was past." See The tower of Babel
After the fair. Thomas Hardy.—PlP
"**After** the First Communion." See Sunday afternoon
"**After** the first powerful, plain manifesto." See The Express
"**After** the goddess." Onitsura, tr. fr. the Japanese by Harry Behn.—BeM
"**After** the good fairy." See The birth of the poet
"**After** the last red sunset glimmer." See Plowboy

"**After** the murder." See The last quatrain of the ballad of Emmett Till
After the rain. Yannis Ritsos, tr. fr. the Greek by Nikos Stangos.—MoT
"**After** the rain, the chirping of the birds sounds more emphatic." See After the rain
"**After** the red leaf and the gold have gone." See A spell before winter
"**After** the sunburn of the day." See Prairie—Haystacks
"**After** the usual rounds at night." See A sense of property
After the visit. Thomas Hardy.—PlP
After the winter. Claude McKay.—AdPb
"**After** the yellow-white." See Pie
"**After** they passed I climbed." See A story
"**After** thunder goes." Shiki, tr. fr. the Japanese by Harry Behn.—BeM
After winter. Sterling A. Brown.—AdPb
After working. Robert Bly.—HaWr
"**After** yesterday." A. R. Ammons.—MoT
Afternoon
  Afternoon. D. O'Grady.—CoPi
  Afternoon: Amagansett beach. J. H. Wheelock.—HaWr
  Sunday afternoon. D. Levertov.—PeS
Afternoon. Desmond O'Grady.—CoPi
Afternoon: Amagansett beach. John Hall Wheelock.—HaWr
Afternoon and his unfinished poem. Calvin O'John.—AlW
"**Afternoon,** and the houses are quiet as dust at the foot of a wall." See Afternoon
"**Afternoon** sits down on an old rocking chair." See Afternoon and his unfinished poem
Afton water. Robert Burns.—RoIt
"**Again.**" See Dry spell
Again. Carl Sandburg.—SaT
"**Again** the day." See If the stars should fall
"**Again** tonight I read Before Disaster." See A letter to Yvor Winters
Against idleness and mischief. Isaac Watts.—LiS—OpOx
Against quarrelling and fighting. Isaac Watts.—OpOx
"**Against** sudden needle-pains. Feverfew and red-nettle which." See A charm against the stitch
"**Against** the broad sky." Takahama Kyoshi, tr. fr. the Japanese by Geoffrey Bownas and Anthony Thwaite.—MaFw
"**Against** the rubber tongues of cows and the hoeing hands of men." See Thistles
"**Against** the stone breakwater." See The storm
"**Agatha** Fry, she made a pie." See Helping
Age. See also Birthdays; Old age; Youth; Youth and age
  Barney. Unknown.—EmN
  Chard Whitlow. H. Reed.—PlM
  The conventionalist. S. Smith.—CoPu
  Eleven. A. MacLeish.—HiN
  Fifteen. W. Stafford.—PeS
  "I was born in a frying pan." Unknown.—EmN
  "The little girl I used to be." M. Harris.—RoIt
  Monday morning: Good morning. L. Clifton.—ClS
  Poem at thirty. S. Sanchez.—AdPb
  Portrait of a girl with comic book. P. McGinley.—PeS
  Rising five. N. Nicholson.—ToM
  Ten years old. N. Giovanni.—AdM
  "What a day." S. Silverstein.—SiW
  "Wild goose, O wild goose." Issa.—HaW
Age. Walter Savage Landor.—CoPu
The **aged** aged man. See Through the looking-glass
Aghadoe. John Todhunter.—CoPi
Agincourt, Battle of, 1415
  King Henry's speech before Agincourt. From King Henry V. W. Shakespeare.—MaF
Ago love. Jerome Holland.—JoV
"**Agonies** confirm His hour." See Bahá'u'lláh in the garden of Ridwan
"**Agonies** of change." See Death takes only a minute
Agriculture. See Farm life; Harvests
Aguinaldo: "Mary," said Saint Joseph. Unknown, ad. fr. the Puerto Rican by Seymour Barab.—LaS
"**Ah,** are you digging on my grave." Thomas Hardy.—PlP
"**Ah,** brother, good-day." See Tartuffe
"**Ah,** but a good wife." See Late abed
"**Ah,** captain." See The surrender speech of Cuarihtémoc
"**Ah,** cherry blossoms." Issa, tr. fr. the Japanese by Hanako Fukuda.—HaW
"**Ah,** did you once see Shelley plain." See Memorabilia
"**Ah** Faustus." See The tragical history of Doctor Faustus
"**Ah,** flowers that we wear." See And yet the earth remains unchanged
"**Ah,** good evening, my dear." See Father Goose tells a story
"**Ah,** lovely Devon." Unknown.—TrG
"**Ah,** my first-slain deer." See Make me a man
"**Ah-nee-nen-way-way** ah-nee-nen-way-way." See Song of a boy growing up
"**Ah** swallow . . . swallow—what a beautiful word." See What a beautiful word
"**Ah,** what pleasant visions haunt me." See The secret of the sea
"**Ah,** you should see Cynddylan on a tractor." See Cynddylan on a tractor
"**Ah,** your slow and brutal stare." See Rama Kam
A-ha. Dorothy Aldis.—LaM
"**Ahab's** gaily clad fisher friends." See Evil is no black thing
"**Ahem.**" See Euphemistic
The **Ahkond** of Swat. Edward Lear.—RoIt
Aidoo, Christina Ama Ata
  Sebonwoma.—AlPa (sel.)
Aiken, Conrad
  And in the hanging gardens.—CoPt

The argument, sel.
"Do not believe your Shakespeare's grief."—CoPu
Crickets.—RoIt
Discordants, sel.
Music I heard with you.—RoIt
"Do not believe your Shakespeare's grief." See The argument
The frog.—JoA-4
The grasshopper.—JoA-4
Music I heard with you. See Discordants
Aikin, John
Tit for tat: A tale.—OpOx
Aikin, Lucy
The beggar man.—OpOx
The swallow.—OpOx
"**Aim** get your sights and its sound." See Canto 7
Aimless. Robert Froman.—FrSp
"**Ain't** no trees." See Star in the sky
"**Ain't** she sweet, ain't she sweet." Unknown.—EmN
Air
Hail, polluters. R. Froman.—FrSp
Air heaves at matter." See Night wind in fall
"The **air** is damp." See Song of ships
"The **air** is dirty." Glen Thompson.—JoV
Air pilots. See Fliers and flying
"The **airplane** taxis down the field." See Taking off
Airplane trip. Bobbi Katz.—HoP
Airplanes. See also Fliers and flying
Aeroplane. M. McB. Green.—HoP
Airplane trip. B. Katz.—HoP
The crescent boat. From Peter Bell. W. Wordsworth.—RoIt
Darius Green and his flying machine. J. T. Trowbridge.—OpOx
The elfin plane. R. B. Bennett.—JaP
"The engingines." P. Goodman.—HoP
From an airplane. H. Behn.—HoP
Geography lesson. Z. Ghose.—ToM
Glider. R. Froman.—FrSp
Night travel. M. Chute.—ChRu
The plane. C. Uhrman.—HoP
Power dive. N. MacCaig.—CoPu
Roofer. R. Froman.—FrSp
Sky's nice. S. J. Johnson.—HoP
Spider Snyder. X. J. Kennedy.—KeO
"Take off." J. Oppenheim.—HoP
Taking off. Unknown.—HoP
Airships. See Airplanes; Balloons; Fliers and flying
"**Aja,** I am joyful, this is good." See Utitiaq's song
"**Ajaja-aja-jaja.**" See improvised song of joy
Akanji, Sangodore
The renegade. tr.—AlPa
Akanyonyi. Unknown, tr. fr. the Luganda by W. Moses
Serwadda.—SeS
Akhenaton, Pharaoh of Egypt
Hymn to the sun.—AbM
Akhmatova, Anna
The Muse.—PlM
Akhmatova, Anna (about)
The Muse. A. Akhmatova.—PlM
Akjartoq's song of the olden days. Unknown, fr. Caribou Eskimo.—LeIb
Alabama
Alabama. J. Fields.—AdPb
Alabama earth. L. Hughes.—HoD
Christ in Alabama. L. Hughes.—AdPb
Daybreak in Alabama. L. Hughes.—HoD
Alabama. Julia Fields.—AdPb
Alabama earth. Langston Hughes.—HoD
Aladdin. James Russell Lowell.—RoIt
Alarm. David McCord.—McAa
"**Alarm** and time clock still intrude too early." See And on this shore
"**Alarm** clock." See The alarm clock
Alarm clock. Eve Merriam.—MeF
The **alarm** clock. Mari Evans.—AdB
An **alarming** sandwich. X. J. Kennedy.—KeO
Alas, alack. Walter De La Mare.—OpOx
"**Alas,** alas, for Miss Mackay." Mother Goose.—TucMgl
"**Alas,** poor Mungo." See Epitaph
"**Alas,** what use to me if perfectly." Louise Labé, tr. fr. the French by Judith Thurman.—ThI
Alaska
Dance song. Unknown.—LeIb
"Somebody saw a crow flying by and asked him where he was going." Unknown.—LeIb
Alaverdoshvili, Liuda
The brook.—MoM
The watermelon.—MoM
Alba, Nanina
Be Daedalus.—AdPb
For Malcolm X.—AdPb
Albatross. Judy Collins.—MoG
Albatrosses
Albatross. J. Collins.—MoG
Albert, Samuel L.
After a game of squash.—FlH
"**Albert.**" See Baby
Albert Ayler, eulogy for a decomposed saxophone player. Stanley Crouch.—AdPb
"**Albert,** have you a turtle." See Lmntl
Alberti, Rafael
The collegiate angels.—MaFw
Aldis, Dorothy (Keeley)
A-ha.—LaM
Blum.—LiLc
A dreadful sight.—CoOr
Hiding.—JoA-4
A riddle: What am I.—HoH
Snow.—CoPu
Train ride.—HoP
Windy wash day.—JoA-4
Aldrich, Thomas Bailey
Kriss Kringle.—RoIt
Memory.—RoIt
Aleksandrovsky, Sasha
"I might repeat in every line."—MoM

"**All** saddled, all bridled, all ready to go." Unknown.—EmN
All Saints' day
Souling song. Unknown.—MaF
"**All** schools." See All schools have rules
All schools have rules. Eleanor Farjeon.—BrM
"**All** silence says music will follow." See Onion bucket
"**All** that are not hid." Unknown.—EmN
"**All** that I have." See Handfuls of wind
"**All** that I ran from." See The mood
All that's past. Walter De La Mare.—RoIt
"**All** the bells were ringing." Christina Georgina Rossetti.—LiLc
"**All** the long school-hours, round the irregular hum." See A snowy day in school
"**All** the people on our street." Lois Lenski.—LeC
"**All** the sandwich cookies sweet." See Lorna Doone: Last cookie song
"**All** the smoke." Eli Siegel.—CoPu
All the world moved. June Jordan.—AdPb
"**All** the world moved next to me strange." See All the world moved
"**All** their lives in a box, what generations." See The silkworms
"**All** there was of men was the smoke above their houses." See Upon an image from Dante
"**All** things bright and beautiful." Cecil Frances Alexander.—OpOx
All things can tempt me. William Butler Yeats.—CoPi
"**All** things can tempt me from this craft of verse." See All things can tempt me
All things come alike to all. Ecclesiastes.—MeP
"**All** things come to pass." See My name is Afrika
"**All** things uncomely and broken, all things worn out and old." See The lover tells of the rose in his heart
"**All** things within this fading world hath end." See Before the birth of one of her children
"**All** those who see my children say." See Unselfishness
"**All** through October." See Indian summer: Vermont
"**All** through the backwater." See The wind in the willows—Duck's ditty
"**All** unexpected I came and took by surprise." See Caribou hunting
"**All** was quiet in this park." See Pain
"**All** ye woods, and trees, and bowers." See The god of sheep
"**All** year the flax-dam festered in the heart." See Death of a naturalist
"**All** you violated ones with gentle hearts." See For Malcolm X
"**All** your dumb jokes." See The new one
Allah
El-Hajj Malik El-Shabazz. R. Hayden.—AdPb
"**Allah** is the Most High." See Call to prayer
Allen, Samuel
Dylan, who is dead.—AdPb
If the stars should fall.—AdPb
A moment please.—AdPb
Rama Kam. tr.—AlPa
Requiem for a black girl. tr.—AlPa (sel.)
Souffles. tr.—AlPa
The staircase.—AdPb
To Satch.—AbM—AdPb
Allen-a-Dale. Walter Scott.—CoPt
"**Allen-a-Dale** has no fagot for burning." See Allen-a-Dale
Alleyway. Salvatore Quasimodo, tr. fr. the Italian by Jack Bevan.—MaFw
Allie. Robert Graves.—JoA-4
"**Allie,** call the birds in." See Allie
Alligator children. Aileen Fisher.—FiD
Alligator/crocodile. Mary Ann Hoberman.—HoR
Alligator pie. Dennis Lee.—LeA
"**Alligator** pie, alligator pie." See Alligator pie
Alligators
Alligator children. A. Fisher.—FiD
Alligator/crocodile. M. A. Hoberman.—HoR
Alligator pie. D. Lee.—LeA
The cantankerous 'gator. O. Herford.—BrM
Mr 'Gator. N. M. Bodecker.—BoL
The purist. O. Nash.—LiWw
Allingham, William
A dream.—CoPi—CoPt
The fairies.—JaP (sel.)—JoA-4—LiLc—OpOx
The lepracaun; or, Fairy shoemaker.—RoIt
A memory.—PaF—RoIt
Riding.—OpOx
Robin Redbreast.—OpOx
A swing song.—RoIt
Wishing.—OpOx
Alma-Tadema, Laurence (or Lawrence)
"If no one ever marries me."—NeA—OpOx
An **almanac.** William Sharp.—JoA-4
Almanacs
An almanac. W. Sharp.—JoA-4
"The **Almighty** has dealt bitterly with me." See The great sad one
Almond trees
Bare almond-trees. D. H. Lawrence.—MaFw
"**Aloft,** lightly on fingertips." See Burial
Alomías, Robles D.
On the death of Atahualpa. tr.—BiI
Alone ("The leaves shudder, the branch shakes") Kostya Raikin, tr. fr. the Russian by Miriam Morton.—MoM
Alone ("The wind took them, light swept them all away") Chaim Nachman Bialik, tr. fr. the Hebrew by A. C. Jacobs.—MeP
"**Alone** on the roof." See Roofer
"**Alone** on the shore in the pause of the nighttime." See The full heart
Alone together. Grey Cohoe.—AlW
"**Along** the shore the tall thin grass." See In memory of Colonel Charles Young
Alphabet
"A was an apple pie." Unknown.—EmN
A was an archer. Unknown.—OpOx
The ABC. S. Milligan.—CoOh

Alphabet—*Continued*
An alphabet. E. Lear.—OpOx
Nonsense alphabet.—JoA-4
"Apple-pie, pudding and pancake." Mother Goose.—AlC
"Great A, little a." Mother Goose.—EmN—JoA-4
"I am not found on the ground." Unknown.—EmN
Inside information. D. McCord.—McAa
"It's in the church." Unknown.—EmN
A learned song. Mother Goose.—JoA-4
The likes and looks of letters. D. McCord.—McAa
More or less. D. McCord.—McFm
"O is open." M. A. Hoberman.—HoN
A riddle ("The beginning of eternity") Unknown.—RoIt
A riddle ("'Twas in heaven pronounced, and 'twas muttered in hell") C. M. Fanshawe.—RoIt
Snake. M. A. Hoberman.—HoLb
Winter alphabet. E. Merriam.—MeO
"X." M. A. Hoberman.—HoN
"Zebra starts with Z—just look." M. A. Hoberman.—HoN
An **alphabet.** Edward Lear.—OpOx
Nonsense alphabet.—JoA-4
"**Alphonso,** Alphonso, Alphonso and Arabella." See The gingham umbrella
Alps
Presence of mind. H. Graham.—LiWw
"**Also** an old image has a moment of birth." See Moon
Alterman, Natan
Beyond melody.—MeP
Moon.—MeP
The olive tree.—MeP
The silver tray.—MeP
Song to the wife of his youth.—MeP
"**Although** he's only asked to spend." See Thoughtless guest
"**Although** I shelter from the rain." See The lamentation of the old pensioner
"**Although** I'd be pretty." See I'd not be a robin
"**Although** she feeds me bread of bitterness." See America
"**Although** we argue." Unknown.—MoBw
Alton Locke, sel. Charles Kingsley
The sands of Dee.—JoA-4—RoIt
"**Always.**" Lisa Pepper.—HoC
"**Always** be happy." Unknown.—MoBw
"**Always,** or nearly always, on old apple trees." See Somewhere around Christmas
"**Am** I happy or sad that I cry inside." See Old man's plea
"**Am** I really old, as people say." Kim Jung-ku, tr. fr. the Korean by Chung Seuk Park and ad. by Virginia Olsen Baron.—BaSs
"**Am** I to tell you next of the storms and stars of autumn." See The Georgics
The **amateur** flute. Unknown.—LiS
The **ambiguous** dog. Arthur Guiterman.—BrM
Ambition. See also Conduct of life; Success
Ambition. P. George.—AlW
Excelsior. H. W. Longfellow.—LiS
Higher. Unknown.—LiS
Watering the horse. R. Bly.—HiN
You too. P. Irving.—AlW
Ambition. Phil George.—AlW
Ambulance. Lois Lenski.—LeC
Ambulances
Ambulance. L. Lenski.—LeC
Auto wreck. K. Shapiro.—MaFw—PeS
"**Amelia** mixed the mustard." Alfred Edward Housman.—LiWw—NeA
Amen. Richard W. Thomas.—AdPb
"**Amen,** Brother Ben." Unknown.—EmN
Amends to nature. Arthur Symons.—PaF
America. See also names of countries, as Mexico; United States
"America." B. Hamilton.—AdB
America ("Although she feeds me bread of bitterness") C. McKay.—AdPb
America ("If an eagle be imprisoned") H. Dumas.—AdB—AdPb—CoPu
America bleeds. A. Lewis.—AdPb
Blue Ruth, America. M. S. Harper.—AdPb
Brown river, smile. J. Toomer.—AdPb
Do nothing till you hear from me. D. Henderson.—AdPb
Elephant rock. Primus St John.—AdPb
The feral pioneers. I. Reed.—AdPb
The gangster's death. I. Reed.—AdPb
I hear America singing. W. Whitman.—RoIt
In memoriam, Martin Luther King, Jr. J. Jordan.—AdPb
"Man flies through the universe." M. Goode.—JoV
"My blackness is the beauty of this land." L. Jeffers.—AdPb
"Next to of course god America i." E. E. Cummings.—HiN—PeS
Right on: white America. S. Sanchez.—AdB—AdPb
Walt Whitman at Bear mountain. L. Simpson.—PlM
America—Discovery and exploration. See also names of explorers, as Columbus, Christopher
"This boy think he bad to get." C. Pass.—JoV
"**America.**" Bobb Hamilton.—AdB
America ("Although she feeds me bread of bitterness") Claude McKay.—AdPb
America ("If an eagle be imprisoned") Henry Dumas.—AdB—AdPb—CoPu
America bleeds. Angelo Lewis.—AdPb
American Indians. See Indians of the Americas
American revolution. See United States—History—Revolution
Amichai, Yehuda
"As for the world."—MeP
I was the moon.—MeP
In the middle of this century.—MeP
"Leaves without trees."—MeP
Mayor.—MeP
National thoughts.—MeP

On my birthday.—MeP
"The place where I have not been."—MeP
They call me.—MeP
To my mother.—MeP
Amichai, Yehuda (about)
On my birthday. Y. Amichai.—MeP
"**Amidst** the mists and coldest frosts." Unknown.—EmN
Amini, Johari
Positives.—AdPb
Signals.—AdPb
To a poet I knew.—AdPb
Ammons, A. R.
"After yesterday."—MoT
Saying.—MoT
Small song.—CoPu
Amoebas
The microbe. H. Belloc.—LiWw
Ode to the amoeba. A. Guiterman.—LiWw
"**Among** boy-crawling bamboo." See Of bombs and boys
"**Among** twenty snowy mountains." Wallace Stevens.—MoT
"**Among** your many playmates here." See Fascination
Amos
Amos, sels. Bible, Old Testament
The basket of summer fruit.—MeP
The prophecies against Moab, Judah, and Israel.—MeP
The basket of summer fruit. See Amos
The prophecies against Moab, Judah, and Israel. See Amos
Anatomy. See Body, Human; also names of parts of the body, as Hands
Ancestors. Grey Cohoe.—AlW
Ancestral faces. Kwesi Brew.—AlPa
Ancestry. See also Heritage
Ancestors. G. Cohoe.—AlW
Ancestral faces. K. Brew.—AlPa
The fall of J. W. Beane. O. Herford.—CoPt
The folding fan. G. Cohoe.—AlW
For Koras and Balafong. L. S. Senghor.—AlPa (sel.)
The hairy dog. H. Asquith.—BrM
Having New England fathers. J. Holmes.—RoIt
"I shall bring honour to my blood." I. Diaw.—AlPa
"My ancestors can't see me." Yi Hwang.—BaSs
Night of Sine. L. S. Senghor.—AlPa
On buying a dog. E. Klauker.—CoPu
Prayer to masks. L. S. Senghor.—AlPa
The sea. M. Mongameli.—AlPa
Souffles. B. Diop.—AlPa
Stark boughs on the family tree. M. Oliver.—PeS
"The **ancient** armadillo." See The armadillo
Ancient music. Ezra Pound.—LiS—MaFw
"**And** as I have said before and elsewhere, If I." See Ogden Nash gets all the cash
"**And** dawn shall trail after me to the shore." See Parting
"**And** death shall have no dominion." Dylan Thomas.—ToM
"**And** down the road she wambled slow." See Bessie Bobtail
"**And** God stepped out on space." See The creation
"**And** Gwydion said to Math, when it was spring." See The wife of Llew
"**And** he is risen? Well be it so . . . ." See A drizzling Easter morning
"**And** here, on my breast, have I bled." Unknown, tr. fr. the Chippewa.—ClFc
"**And** here we see the invisible boy." See Invisible boy
"**And** I have loved thee, Ocean, and my joy." See The sea
"**And** I said, Hear, I pray you, O heads of Jacob." See Micah—A denunciation of the princes and prophets
"**And** I say nothing—no, not a word." See My sister Jane
"**And** I think over again." See Song
"**And** I thought of how impossibly alone we were." See After a game of squash
"**And** in the frosty season, when the sun." See The prelude
And in the hanging gardens. Conrad Aiken.—CoPt
"**And** in the hanging gardens there is rain." See And in the hanging gardens
"**And** it came to pass in those days." See Gospel according to Luke—Christ's nativity
"**And** now for the Dancing Pants." See Dancing Pants
"**And** now to God the Father, he ends." See In church
And on some days I might take less. John Ciardi.—CiFs
And on this shore. M. Carl Holman.—AdPb
"**And** one morning while in the woods I stumbled suddenly on the thing." See Between the world and me
And other poems. R. S. Morgan.—MaFw
"**And** returning at last to his birthplace he found the ocean." See Odysseus
"**And** several strengths from drowsiness campaigned." See The sermon on the warpland
"**And** so it happened in the morningtide." See The Canterbury tales—The Franklin's tale
"**And** some are sulky, while some will plunge." See Horses
And son. Eve Merriam.—MeF
"**And** summer mornings the mute child, rebellious." See Eleven
"**And** the country is quiet. The red eye of heaven." See The silver tray
"**And** the days are not full enough." Ezra Pound.—MaFw
"**And** the old women gathered." Mari Evans.—AdPb
"**And** the waves arrived." See Our history
"**And** then I pressed the shell." See The shell

"**And** then there was the time I was formed." See This is real
"**And** they both lived happily ever after." See After ever happily; or, The princess and the woodcutter
And they lived happily ever after for a while. John Ciardi.—CiFs
"**And** they were there in the city of fire, enflamed." See Ju Ju
And was not improved. Lerone Bennett, Jr.—AdPb
"**And** we conquered." Rob Penny.—AdPb
And what about the children. Audre Lorde.—AdPb
"**And** what is so rare as a day in June?" See The vision of Sir Launfal—June
And what shall you say. Joseph Seaman Cotter, Jr.—AdPb
"**And** when." See Query
"**And** when that ballad lady went." See A road in Kentucky
And when the green man comes. John Haines.—HiN
"**And** where are the graves, so many graves." See Graves
"**And** who shall separate the dust." See Common dust
And yet the earth remains unchanged. Unknown, tr. fr. the Aztec by Angel Garibay.—BiI
Anderson, Ethel
  The clipper Dunbar to the clipper Cutty Sark.—CoPt
Anderson, S. E.
  Junglegrave.—AdPb
  The sound of Afroamerican history chapt I.—AdPb
  The sound of Afroamerican history chapt II.—AdPb
Andrade, Jorge Carrera
  Walnut.—CoPu
"**Andrew** Airpump asked his aunt her ailment." Unknown.—EmN
Androzejewski, B. W. and Lewis, I. M.
  The limits of submission. trs.—AdM (sel.)—AlPa (sel.)
  Modern song. trs.—AbM
Anecdotes of four gentlemen. See "As a little fat man of Bombay"
Anecdotes of four gentlemen. See "There was a sick man of Tobago"
Anecdotes of four gentlemen. See "There was an old miser at Reading
Anecdotes of four gentlemen. See "There was an old soldier of Bicester"
Aneirin
  Odes of the months.—MaFw (sel.)
"An **angel** came as I lay in bed." Unknown, tr. fr. the Hebrew by Rose Fyleman.—JoA-4
"An **angel** of cinnamon." See Two Spanish gypsy lullabies
Angels
  Abou Ben Adhem. L. Hunt.—RoIt
  "An angel came as I lay in bed." Unknown.—JoA-4
  Blind angel. D. Rokeah.—MeP
  Epigram addressed to an artist. R. Burns.—CoPu
  "It came upon a midnight clear." E. H. Sears.—LaS
  "May the angels round." Unknown.—EmN
  Night. W. Blake.—OpOx
  Rise up shepherd, and follow. Unknown.—LaS
  Shepherds in Judea. J. Ingalls.—LaS
  They call me. Y. Amichai.—MeP
  Witness. E. Merriam.—MeF
The **angels** are stooping. See A cradle song
Anger
  The angry man. P. McGinley.—PeS
  Angry old men. B. Payne.—CoPi
  The Cuisitaws come east. Unknown.—BiI
  Mad. R. Froman.—FrSp
  The sad tale of Mr Mears. Unknown.—CoPt
  Temper. R. Fyleman.—OpOx
Angina pectoris. W. R. Moses.—HiN
"**Angled** sunbeam lowered." See Question
The **angler's** song. Izaak Walton.—FlH
Angoff, Charles
  Song for boys and girls.—RoIt
The **angry** man. Phyllis McGinley.—PeS
Angry old men. Basil Payne.—CoPi
Animal crackers. See From the kitchen
"**Animal** crackers, I ate them years." See From the kitchen—Animal crackers
Animal fair. See "I went to the animal fair"
Animal tracks
  Footprints ("In summertime") A Fisher.—FiFo
  Footprints ("It was snowing") L. Moore.—MoSm
  I'll let you know if I find her. J. Ciardi.—CiFs
  Invisible tree. R. Tamara.—MoT
  Merry Christmas. A. Fisher.—FiFo—HoS—LaM
  The presence. M. W. Kumin.—MoT
  Rabbit tracks. A. Fisher.—FiFo
  Trinity place. D. McCord.—McAa
Animal trainers
  "I tame the very fiercest beast." J. Prelutsky.—PrC
  "My trainer steps into the ring." J. Prelutsky.—PrC
"**Animal** willows of November." See The willows of Massachusetts
Animals. See also Circus; Fables; also names of classes of the animal kingdom, as Birds; also names of animals, as Elephants
  Alarm. D. McCord.—McAa
  All lives, all dances and all is loud. Unknown.—AbM
  Allie. R. Graves.—JoA-4
  At the zoo ("First I saw the white bear") W. M. Thackeray.—OpOx
  At the zoo ("I like the zebra") A. Fisher.—FiFo
  "Beast of the sea." Unknown.—LeIb

Beasts and birds. A. O'Keefe.—OpOx
Bed-time story. M. Cane.—RoIt
The bloath. S. Silverstein.—SiW
"The bull's in the barn threshing the corn." Mother Goose.—TucMgl
The butterfly's ball. W. Roscoe.—OpOx
"Calico pie." E. Lear.—LiLc—UnGb
Chant. D. McCord.—McS
Chorus of the years. From The dynasts. T. Hardy.—PlP
Crocodile. W. J. Smith.—BrM
Direction. A. Lopez.—AlW
Disaster. C. S. Calverley.—CiS
"Don't dress your cat in an apron." D. Greenburg.—ThF
Enter this deserted house. S. Silverstein.—SiW
The farmer and the queen. S. Silverstein.—SiW
Footprints. A. Fisher.—FiFo
Fred. S. Silverstein.—SiW
The friendly beasts. Unknown.—RoIt
Funeral. R. Hoban.—HoE
The furry ones. A. Fisher.—FiFo
The heaven of animals. J. Dickey.—HiN
"Hey, diddle, diddle." Mother Goose.—AlC—JoA-4
The history of the flood. J. Heath-Stubbs.—MaFw
"I found a silver dollar." D. Lee.—LeA
"I think I could turn and live with animals." From Song of myself. W. Whitman.—RoIt
"I went to the animal fair." Unknown.—EmN
  Animal fair.—RoIt
"If only I were able." B. Lapin.—MoM
If you should meet. D. Lee.—LeA
I'm no animal. C. Minor.—JoV
J. Prior, Esq. N. M. Bodecker.—BoL
Johnny Crow's garden. L. L. Brooks.—JoA-4
A kitten. A. Fisher.—FiFo
Laughing time. W. J. Smith.—BrM
A little book of little beasts. M. A. Hoberman.—HoLb
Low tides. M. C. Livingston.—LiM
The marsh. W. D. Snodgrass.—HaWr
Mechanical menagerie. X. J. Kennedy.—KeO
The migration of the grey squirrels. W. Howitt.—RoIt
"Mr Zookeeper." L. B. Hopkins.—HoCs
The moon. Unknown.—RoIt
My brother Bert. T. Hughes.—HuMf
My Uncle Mick. T. Hughes.—HuMf
Off to Yakima. L. F. Jackson.—BrM
Old Shellover. W. De La Mare.—LiLc—OpOx
One more river. Unknown.—RoIt
Ookpik. D. Lee.—LeA
Procyonidae. M. A. Hoberman.—HoR
"Quack, said the billy goat." C. Causley.—CaF
The sleepyheads. A. Fisher.—FiFo
Some natural history. D. Marquis.—LiWw
"The squirrel has a bushy tail." Unknown.—EmN
That's not. D. McCord.—McAa
"Those game animals, those long-haired caribou." Unknown.—LeIb
"Three young rats with black felt hats." Mother Goose.—BlM—JoA-4
Twilight at the zoo. A. Rodger.—HiN
The unicorn. S. Silverstein.—SiW
Up and down. N. M. Bodecker.—BoL
Variation on a sentence. L. Bogan.—RoIt
What's their names. M. A. Hoberman.—HoR
"Where in the world are the animals from." M. A. Hoberman.—HoR
The worst. S. Silverstein.—SiW
The Yipiyuk. S. Silverstein.—SiW
The zoo. B. Pasternak.—MaFw
Zoogeography. M. A. Hoberman.—HoR

Animals—Care
Auguries of innocence. W. Blake.—RoIt (sel.)
Beau's reply. W. Cowper.—RoIt
The bells of Heaven. R. Hodgson.—JoA-4
The burial of the linnet. J. H. Ewing.—OpOx
Dapple Gray. Unknown.—RoIt
Donkeys. Edward Field.—RoIt
The early purges. S. Heaney.—AdP
"The fawn." Issa.—AtM
Four little foxes. L. Sarett.—RoIt
Hymn for Saturday. C. Smart.—OpOx
"I had a little pony." Mother Goose.—AlC—JoA-4—TrG
"I love little pussy." Jane Taylor.—BlM
  "I like little pussy."—JoA-4
  Pussy.—OpOx
"If I had a donkey that wouldn't go." Mother Goose.—JoA-4
If I were president. I. Veley.—JoV
The little animal. J. Tusiami.—RoIt
Little things. J. Stephens.—AlP—CoPu—JoA-4
"Little tiny puppy dog." S. Milligan.—CoOh
Mary's lamb. S. J. Hale.—OpOx
The meadow mouse. T. Roethke.—AdP—MoT
"Mrs Malone." E. Farjeon.—OpOx
The mouse's petition. A. L. Barbauld.—OpOx
"My mother saw a dancing bear." C. Causley.—CaF
That little black cat. D'Arcy W. Thompson.—OpOx
  Cure for a pussy cat.—RoIt
The pet lamb. W. Wordsworth.—OpOx
The puzzled game-birds. T. Hardy.—PlP
The snare. J. Stephens.—AdP
Still life; Lady with birds. Q. Prettyman.—AdPb
To Christ our Lord. G. Kinnell.—HaWr
Traveling through the dark. W. Stafford.—HiN—MaFw—MoT—PeS

Animals—Prehistoric. See Dinosaurs
"Ann, Ann." See Alas, alack
Annabel Lee ("It was many and many a year ago") Edgar Allan Poe.—JoA-4—LiS—RoIt
Annabel Lee ("'Twas more than a million years ago") Stanley Huntley.—LiS
Anne Rutledge. See The Spoon River anthology

"**Anne** stood on the balcony." Unknown.—MoBw
"**Announced** by all the trumpets of the sky." See The snow-storm
"**Anonymous** as cherubs." See Two voices in a meadow
Another grace. Robert Herrick.—OpOx
Another on her. Robert Herrick.—LiS
"**Another** room." See Not mine
"**Another** way to spell Chicago is." Unknown.—EmN
The **answer.** John Hall Wheelock.—HaWr
Answer to a child's question. Samuel Taylor Coleridge.—OpOx—RoIt
"An **ant.**" Felice Holman.—HoI
Ant and eleph-ant. Spike Milligan.—CoOr
Antar
The romance of Antar (sel.).—AbM
Antar (about)
The romance of Antar (sel.). Antar.—AbM
"The **anteater.**" See Anteater
Anteater. Mary Ann Hoberman.—HoR
Anteaters
Anteater. M. A. Hoberman.—HoR
Antelopes
Fast and slow. D. McCord.—McFm—McS
Gazelle. M. A. Hoberman.—HoR
The gnat and the gnu. O. Herford.—BrM
The gnu ("G stands for gnu, whose weapons of defence") H. Belloc.—CoPu
The gnu ("There's this to remember about the gnu") T. Roethke.—BrM—LiWw
The gnu family. I. Orleans.—BrM
Lalla Rookh. T. Moore.—LiS (sel.)
"A yak who was new to the zoo." D. Ross.—RoIt
"**Antennas.**" See Catchers
Antes, John
Christ the Lord most glorious.—LaS
Anthem for doomed youth. Wilfred Owen.—MaFw
Anthropoids. Mary Ann Hoberman.—HoR
Antigone I. Herbert Martin.—AdPb
Antigone VI. Herbert Martin.—AdPb
Antiquity. See Time
"**Anton** Leeuwenhoek was Dutch." See The microscope
Ants
"All my legs were very tired." K. Kuskin.—KuA
"An ant." F. Holman.—HoI
Ant and eleph-ant. S. Milligan.—CoOr
Anteater. M. A. Hoberman.—HoR
"Ants are always all around." M. A. Hoberman.—HoN
The bee, the ant, and the sparrow. N. Cotton.—OpOx
The dove and the ant. J. De La Fontaine.—JoA-4
The odyssey of a snail. F. García Lorca.—MaFw
Question. M. A. Hoberman.—HoLb
"**Ants** are always all around." Mary Ann Hoberman.—HoN
Any author to any friend. Martial, tr. fr. the Latin by Dudley Fitts.—PlM
"**Any** of the several names." See Eulogy for populations
Anya
"My mama has been clever."—MoM
"**Anything** does for a ship if it floats." See Boating
"**Anywhere** I look." See Dingman's marsh
Apache Indians. See Indians of the Americas—Apache
Apartment house. Lois Lenski.—LeC
Apartments and apartment life. See also City life
Apartment house. L. Lenski.—LeC
December 21: Snow. L. Clifton.—ClEa
December 24: A tree in an elevator. L. Clifton.—ClEa
December 25: Christmas night. L. Clifton.—ClEa
Home in the sky. L. Lenski.—LeC
"I live upstairs." L. Lenski.—LeC
"Pigeons on the rooftop." L. Lenski.—LeC
Two-room flat. L. Lenski.—LeC
Apes. See Gorillas
Aphrodite
"You know the place, then." Sappho.—ThI
Appetizer. Robert Froman.—FrSp
The **apple.** Judah Halevi, tr. fr. the Hebrew by Robert Mezey.—MeP
"**Apple** core." Unknown.—EmN
An **apple** for Isaac. Solomon ibn Gabirol, tr. fr. the Hebrew by David Goldstein.—MeP
"**Apple-pie,** pudding and pancake." Mother Goose.—AlC
An **apple-tree** rhyme. Unknown.—JoA-4
Apple trees
An apple-tree rhyme. Unknown.—JoA-4
Patriarchs. L. Moore.—MoSp
Silence. W. J. Turner.—PaF
Somewhere around Christmas. J. Smith.—MaFw
Apples
The apple. J. Halevi.—MeP
"Apple core." Unknown.—EmN
An apple for Isaac. Solomon ibn Gabirol.—MeP
Apples. From Market women's cries. J. Swift.—CoPi
"I saw an apple." Borya.—MoM
Moonlit apples. J. Drinkwater.—PaF
Only seven. H. S. Leigh.—LiS
Apples. See Market women's cries
"**Apples** for the little ones." Clyde Watson.—WaF
"**Apples,** peaches, cream, and butter." Unknown.—EmN
"**Apples,** peaches, peanut butter." Unknown.—EmN
"**Apples,** peaches, pumpkin pie." Unknown.—EmN
Appoggiatura. Donald Jeffrey Hayes.—AdPb
April
"April." J. Stancher.—HoC

April ("The little goat") Yvor Winters.—CoPu—JoA-4
April ("Rain is good") L. Clifton.—ClE
April ("Two little clouds one April day") Unknown.—RoIt
April and May. R. W. Emerson.—JoA-4
April landscape. A. L. Rowse.—PaP
April rain song. L. Hughes.—HoD—LiLc
April rise. L. Lee.—MaFw—ToM
April snow. F. Holman.—HoI
April 23. N. Belting.—BeSc
April 24. N. Belting.—BeSc
April 30. N. Belting.—BeSc
Home thoughts from abroad. R. Browning.—JoA-4—RoIt
Song. W. Watson.—JoA-4
Thaw. W. Gibson.—CoPu
"**April.**" Mark Stancher.—HoC
April ("The little goat") Yvor Winters.—CoPu—JoA-4
April ("Rain is good") Lucille Clifton.—ClE
April ("Two little clouds one April day") Unknown.—RoIt
April and May. Ralph Waldo Emerson.—JoA-4
"**April,** April." See Song
"**April** cold with dropping rain." See April and May
April Fool's day
"The first of April, some do say." Unknown.—MaF
"Oh did you hear." S. Silverstein.—LaM
Oh have you heard. S. Silverstein.—SiW
One day only. M. Chute.—ChRu
April 4, 1968. Michael Goode.—JoV
April landscape. A. L. Rowse.—PaP
April rain song. Langston Hughes.—HoD—LiLc
April rise. Laurie Lee.—MaFw—ToM
April snow. Felice Holman.—HoI
April 23. Natalia Belting.—BeSc
April 24. Natalia Belting.—BeSc
April 30. Natalia Belting.—BeSc
Aqalàni. Unknown, tr. fr. the Navajo by Washington Matthews.—BiI
Aquarium. Valerie Worth.—WoS
Aquariums
Aquarium. V. Worth.—WoS
Arabesque. Fred Johnson.—AdPb
Arapaho Indians. See Indians of the Americas—Arapaho
Araucanian Indians. See Indians of the Americas—Araucanian
Arberry, A. J.
Concert. tr.—AbM
The radish. tr.—AbM
Arbor day. Marchette Chute.—ChRu
Archaeology. Richard Church.—PaP
Archery. See Bows and arrows
Arctic regions. See also Eskimos
A North Pole story. M. B. Smedley.—OpOx
"**Are** you awake, Gemelli." See Star-talk
"**Are** you deaf, Father William, the young man said." Lewis Carroll.—LiPc
"**Are** you flying through the night." See The fire-fly
Arenstein, Philip
"Thunder."—HoC
The **argument,** sel. Conrad Aiken
"Do not believe your Shakespeare's grief." CoPu
Argument. Eve Merriam.—MeO
Argumentation
Argument. E. Merriam.—MeO
The nose and the eyes. W. Cowper.—RoIt
Reason. J. Miles.—HiN
"**Ariel** was glad he had written his poems." See The planet on the table
Ariel's song. See The tempest
Arise, my love. See The song of Solomon
Arithmetic. See also Mathematics
Arithmetic. C. Sandburg.—MaFw—SaT
Child Margaret. C. Sandburg.—MaFw—SaT
Exit x. D. McCord.—McFm
"Is six times one a lot of fun." K. Kuskin.—KuN
"May your life be like arithmetic." Unknown.—EmN
A mortifying mistake. A. M. Pratt.—BrM
Numbers. E. M. Roberts.—LiL
Smart. S. Silverstein.—SiW
Unearned increment. C. Morley.—LiWw
Who hasn't played gazintas. D. McCord.—McFm
"Yonder comes the teacher." Unknown.—EmN
Arithmetic. Carl Sandburg.—MaFw—SaT
"**Arithmetic** is where numbers fly like pigeons in and out of your head." See Arithmetic
Arkansas
Bear with me and you may learn. J. Ciardi.—CiFs
"Wish I was in Arkansas." Unknown.—EmN
The **Armada,** 1588. John Wilson.—OpOx
The **armadillo** ("The ancient armadillo") Jack Prelutsky.—PrT
The **armadillo** ("While walking in the woods") N. M. Bodecker.—BoL
Armadillos
Advice. M. A. Hoberman.—HoR
The armadillo ("The ancient armadillo") J. Prelutsky.—PrT
The armadillo ("While walking in the woods") N. M. Bodecker.—BoL
Instructions. S. Silverstein.—SiW
Armagh, Ireland
Armagh. W. R. Rodgers.—CoPi
Armagh. W. R. Rodgers.—CoPi
Armattoe, R. E. G.
The lonely soul.—AlPa
Armistice day. See Veteran's day
Armor. See Arms and armor
Armour, Richard
Fish story.—FlH
Money.—JoA-4
Arms and armor
Bronzeville man with a belt in the back. G. Brooks.—AdPb

Arms and armor—*Continued*
"In that dark cave." S. Silverstein.—CoPu
Armstrong, Mildred Bowers
City fairies.—JaP
Arnold, Matthew
Dover beach.—MaFw (sel.)—MoG—PaP (sel.)—RoIt
"How changed is here each spot man makes or fills." See Thyrsis
"So, some tempestuous morn in early June." See Thyrsis
Thyrsis, sels.
"How changed is here each spot man makes or fills."—PaP
"So, some tempestuous morn in early June."—PaF
Aronin, Ben
Rosh Hashanah.—LaM
"**Around** and over and under the stump." Unknown.—EmN
"**Around,** around the sun we go." See Mother Goose's garland
"**Around** the fire one wintry night." See The beggar man
"**Around** the house the flakes fly faster." See Birds at winter nightfall
"**Around** the rough and rugged rocks." Unknown.—EmN
Arriving in the country again. James Wright.—CoPu
Arrows. See Bows and arrows
Arroyo. Tom Weatherly.—AdPb
Arson. Lilian Moore.—MoSp
Art and artists
The artist. W. Raleigh.—LiLw
Before a saint's picture. W. S. Landor.—OpOx
Crayons. M. Chute.—ChRu
The egg boiler. G. Brooks.—AdPb
Epigram addressed to an artist. R. Burns.—CoPu
Fortunatus the R. A. Nikarchos.—LiWw
The makers. R. Kell.—CoPi
The messed damozel. C. H. Towne.—LiS
Mousemeal. H. Nemerov.—HiN
Musée des beaux arts. W. H. Auden.—ToM
Museum piece. R. Wilbur.—LiWw
My Uncle Mick. T. Hughes.—HuMf
Poem for Aretha. N. Giovanni.—AdPb
PSI. M. B. Tolson.—AdPb
"Remarkable truly, is art." G. Burgess.—CoOr
Sadie's playhouse. M. Danner.—AdPb
"**Art** thou poor, yet hast thou golden slumbers." See Pleasant comedy of patient Grissell—Sweet content
Arthur, King (about)
"When good King Arthur ruled this land." Mother Goose.—AlC—JoA-4
"The **artisan** didn't collect his gear and say." See The makers
The **artist.** Walter Raleigh.—LiWw
"The **artist** and his luckless wife." See The artist
Artiuschanko, Yura
Lenin.—MoM
An **Arundel** tomb. Philip Larkin.—ToM
"**As** a beauty I'm not a great star." See My face
"**As** a child." See Four sheets to the wind
"**As** a child I was." See Woman
"**As** a friend to the children commend me the yak." See The yak
"**As** a little fat man of Bombay." Unknown
Anecdotes of four gentlemen.—OpOx
"**As** a rule, man is a fool." See Man is a fool
"**As** beautiful Kitty one morning was tripping." See Kitty of Coleraine
"**As** deep as the deep blue sea." Unknown.—EmN—MoBw
As dew in Aprille. Unknown.—MaFw
"**As** for the world." Yehuda Amichai, tr. fr. the Hebrew by Assia Gutmann.—MeP
As he lay dying. Randolph Stow.—MaFw
"**As** he lay dying, two fat crows." See As he lay dying
"**As** he trudged along to school." See The story of Johnny Head-in-air
"**As** I came over the humpbacked hill." See The green fiddler
"**As** I drive to the junction of lane and highway." See At Castle Boterel
As I float. David Ross.—RoIt
As I grew older. Langston Hughes.—HoD
"**As** I in hoary winter's night stood shivering in the snow." See The burning babe
"**As** I lie in bed I hear." See Winter night
"**As** I looked out one May morning." See The princess and the gypsies
"**As** I sat on a sunny bank." See I saw three ships
"**As** I talk with learned people." See A spade is just a spade
"**As** I walked down the lane." Unknown.—EmN
"**As** I walked with my friend." See Columbus
"**As** I was crossing London bridge." Unknown.—EmN
"**As** I was dashing down Cutting hill." Unknown.—EmN
"**As** I was falling down the stair." Hughes Mearns.—BrM
"**As** I was going o'er London bridge." Unknown.—TrG
"**As** I was going to Banbury." Mother Goose.—JoA-4—TucMgl
"**As** I was going to Derby." See The ram
"**As** I was going to St Ives." Mother Goose.—BlM—EmN—JoA-4
"**As** I was going to sell my eggs." Mother Goose.—JoA-4
"**As** I was going up Pippen-hill." Mother Goose.—AlC
"**As** I was going up the hill." Mother Goose.—AlC
"**As** I was going up the stair." See I met a man
"**As** I was sailing down the coast." See The High Barbaree
"**As** I was sitting." See What I think

"**As** I was sitting in my chair." See The perfect reactionary
"**As** I was standing in the street." Unknown.—BrM—CoOh—TrG
"**As** I was walking all alane." See The twa corbies
"**As** I went down the country road." Unknown.—EmN
"**As** I went down to Dymchurch Wall." See In Romney marsh
"**As** I went down Zig Zag." Charles Causley.—CaF
"**As** I went into the city, clattering chimes." See December music
"**As** I went out a crow." See The last word of a bluebird
"**As** I went over London bridge." Unknown.—TrG
"**As** I went over the water." Mother Goose.—AlC
"**As** I went through a field of wheat." Unknown.—EmN
"**As** I went up October street." See The wave
"**As** I were a-walking upon a fine day." See Because I were shy
"**As** imperceptibly as grief." Emily Dickinson.—PaF
As into the garden. Alfred Edward Housman.—CoPt
"**As** into the garden Elizabeth ran." See As into the garden
"**As** inward love breeds outward talk." See The angler's song
"**As** it fell out upon a day." See Dives and Lazarus
As long as I live. M. Kunene.—AlPa
"**As** long as people." See On wearing ears
"**As** my eyes." See Dream song
"**As** my eyes." Unknown, tr. fr. the Chippewa by Frances Densmore.—JoT
"**As** New Year's day dawns." Ransetsu, tr. fr. the Japanese by Harry Behn.—BeM
"**As** rain to holiday." See The happy cynic to his love
"**As** round as an apple, as deep as a cup." Mother Goose.—JoA-4
"**As** round their dying father's bed." See The father and his children
"**As** sad and salt as tears." See The sea is melancholy
"**As** she jumped up to open the door." See Motionless swaying
"**As** shepherds in Jewry were guarding their sheep." See Shepherds in Judea
"**As** simple an act." See Way out West
"**As** soon as I'm in bed at night." See Mrs Brown
"**As** still as a flower." Ann Atwood.—AtM
"**As** sure as you get married." Unknown.—EmN
"**As** surely as I hold your hand in mine." See Brown boy to brown girl
"**As** the candle light and fire light." See Cottage
"**As** the corn becomes higher." See Cricket march
"**As** the holly groweth green." See Song
"**As** the leaves say." See Free will
"**As** the racing circle closed in like a lasso." See Ceremonial hunt
"**As** the train rattles along the bumpety rails." See The trains
"**As** the wind blows sharply." See Far-off things
"**As** the words dissolve from the fading page." See The mother
"**As** things be/come." See Word poem (perhaps worth considering)
"**As** Tommy Snooks and Bessy Brooks." Mother Goose.—AlC—JoA-4
"**As** we get older we do not get any younger." See Chard Whitlow
As you like it, sels. William Shakespeare
"Blow, blow, thou winter wind."—PaF—RoIt
"Under the greenwood tree."—RoIt
In Arden forest.—JoA-4
Asayasu
"A breeze stirs at dawn."—BeM
Ash, C. B.
Adbaston, sel.
The Wrekin.—PaP
The Wrekin. See Adbaston
Ash Wednesday. See Lent
"**Ashes** to ashes." Unknown.—MoBw
"**Ashes** to ashes and dust to dust." Unknown.—EmN
Asia. See also names of countries, as India
An importer. R. Frost.—LiWw
Asia's song. Percy Bysshe Shelley.—MoG
"**Ask** for another name for Santa Claus." See A Christmas package
Ask the mountains. Phil George.—AlW
"**Asking** his sister for paper and pencil." See Something peaceful
"**A-sleepin'** at length on the sand." See The sea serpant
Aspiration. See Ambition
Asquith, Herbert
Aunt Jane.—BrM
The hairy dog.—BrM
Assassination. Don L. Lee.—AdB—AdPb
Assassinations
Assassination. D. L. Lee.—AdB—AdPb
Asses. See Donkeys
Astrology
Born without a star. Abraham ibn Ezra.—MeP
My stars. Abraham ibn Ezra.—MeP
Astronauts
Only a little litter. M. C. Livingston.—LiM
When I'm an astronaut. L. B. Jacobs.—BrM
Astronomy. See also Moon; Planets; Stars; Sun; Tides; World
Rhyme for astronomical baby. From Boston nursery rhymes. J. Cook.—LiS
"When I heard the learn'd astronomer." W. Whitman.—RoIt

Asturias, Miguel Angel
"The Indians come down from Mixco."—MoT
Aswelay. Norman Henry Pritchard II.—AdPb
"**Aswell** within her billowed skirts." See The mad-woman
"**At** a certain time the Earth opened in the West, where its mouth is." See The Cussitaws come east
At breakfast. May Swenson.—PeS
At Castle Boterel. Thomas Hardy.—PlP
At Dunwick. Anthony Thwaite.—ToM
"**At** dusk." See If the owl calls again
"**At** dusk the muskrat quits his den." See Muskrat
"**At** evening when the lamp is lit." See The land of story-books
"**At** first nothing is." See Nothing is
At first sight. Lillian Morrison.—JoA-4
At flock Mass. F. R. Higgins.—CoPi
At grass. Philip Larkin.—HaWr
"**At** his writing lesson." Issa, tr. fr. the Japanese by Hanako Fukuda.—HaW
At home. Unknown, tr. fr. the Russian by Miriam Morton.—MoM
"**At** home it's It's me." See Grammar
"**At** Mrs Tyson's farmhouse, the electricity is pumped." See The force
"**At** night may I roam." Unknown, tr. fr. the Sioux by Frances Densmore and Robert P. Higheagle.—JoT
"**At** night the city shows its treasures." See Hidden treasure
"**At** night, when all the feet have fled." See Theatre mouse
"**At** night when planets light the sky." See Planets
"**At** night while." See Black warrior
"**At** nine of the night I opened my door." Charles Causley.—CaF
"**At** noontime." Sappho, tr. fr. the Greek by Mary Barnard.—ThI
"**At** school." Diane Marstiller.—HoC
At sea. Eve Merriam.—MeO
"**At** sunset when the night-dews fall." See The snail
"**At** Tara in this fateful hour." See The rune of Saint Patrick
At that moment. Raymond Richard Patterson.—AdPb
At the Creche. See En el portal de Belen
At the draper's. Thomas Hardy.—PlP
"**At** the edge of the world." Unknown, tr. fr. the Papago.—JoT
"**At** the feet o' Jesus." See Feet o' Jesus
"**At** the field's end, in the corner missed by the mower." See The far field
"**At** the first sign of my horse's fright." Unknown, tr. fr. the Korean by Chung Seuk Park and ad. by Virginia Olsen Baron.—BaSs
At the grave of John Clare. Charles Causley.—MaFw (sel.)
At the library. Marchette Chute.—ChRu
At the ocean. Eve Merriam.—MeO
At the pool. X. J. Kennedy.—KeO
At the railway station, Upway. Thomas Hardy.—MaFw—PlP
"**At** the rainbow spring." Unknown, tr. fr. the Zuñi by Frances Densmore.—JoT
At the rink. Lois Lenski.—LeC
"**At** the round earth's imagined corners, blow." See Holy sonnet VII
At the scorpions' ascent. Omer Hillel, tr. fr. the Hebrew by Sholom J. Kahn.—MeP
At the sea-side. See At the seaside
At the seaside. Robert Louis Stevenson.—LiLc—OpOx
At the sea-side.—JoA-4
"**At** the time of the White Dawn." See Song of the fallen deer
"**At** the top of the house." See Moonlit apples
At the wood's edge. Unknown, tr. fr. the Iroquois by Horatio Hale.—BiI
At the word *farewell.* Thomas Hardy.—PlP
At the zoo ("First I saw the white bear, then I saw the black") W. M. Thackeray.—OpOx
At the zoo ("I like the zebra") Aileen Fisher.—FiFo
"**At** the zoo I saw: A long-necked, velvety giraffe." See Giraffe
"**At** times when we're walking." See Underground rumbling
"**At** twilight a bell." Shiki, tr. fr. the Japanese by Harry Behn.—BeM
Atavism. Richard Lake.—HiN
Athletes and athletics. See also names of sports, as Baseball
Plunger. C. Sandburg.—SaT
Atkins, Russell
Christophe.—AbM
It's here in the.—AdPb—PeS
Narrative.—AdPb
Night and a distant church.—AdPb
On the fine arts garden, Cleveland.—AdPb
Atlanta, Georgia
An old woman remembers. S. A. Brown.—AdPb
Atlantic Charter. See The island: 1620-1942
Atomic age
"Geiger, geiger, ticking slow." P. Dehn.—LiS
"O nuclear wind, when wilt thou blow." P. Dehn.—LiS
Respectful request. R. Durem.—AbM
"Ring-a-ring o' neutrons." P. Dehn.—LiS
Sonic boom. J. Updike.—PeS
Atoms. See Atomic age
Attah, Ernest
Spring blossom.—AbM
"**Attention,** architect." See Message from a mouse, ascending in a rocket
"**Attentive** eyes, fantastic heed." See A poet
Attics
Etta Moten's attic. From Far from Africa: Four poems. M. Danner.—AdPb
Atwood, Ann
"All day the kite pinned."—AtM
"As still as a flower."—AtM

"Clouds shadow the stream."—AtM
"From the dark canoe."—AtM
"Knighted by the sun's."—AtM
"Luminous silence. . . . "—AtM
"Mingled with the wild."—AtM
"The moon almost full."—AtM
"An ocean of clouds."—AtM
"Primitive paintings. . . . "—AtM
"A reckless morning. . . . "—AtM
" . . . the sea fanning out."—AtM
"So slowly, you come."—AtM
"Spring in the river."—AtM
"Spring on the river."—AtM
"A stairway of light."—AtM
"Staring at the field."—AtM
"The straight strokes of reeds."—AtM
"The tree after Christmas."—AtM
"The trees' reflection."—AtM

Atwood, Margaret
Carrying food home in winter.—MoT

Au jardin des plantes. John Wain.—MaFw

Auctioneer ("Now I go down here and bring up a moon") Carl Sandburg.—SaT

Auctioneer ("What am I bid, what am I bid") Eve Merriam.—MeO

Auctioneers
Auctioneer ("Now I go down here and bring up a moon") C. Sandburg.—SaT
Auctioneer ("What am I bid, what am I bid") E. Merriam.—MeO
For sale. S. Silverstein.—CoOr—SiW

Auden, W. H.
"Deep in earth's opaque mirror." See Symmetries and asymmetries
Edward Lear.—PlM
Elegy for J. F. K.—MaFw
In memory of W. B. Yeats.—PlM
"Leaning out over." See Symmetries and asymmetries
Musée des beaux arts.—ToM
O what is that sound.—MaFw—ToM
On this island.—MaFw—ToM
Postscript.—MaFw
Surgical ward.—PeS
Symmetries and asymmetries, sels.
"Deep in earth's opaque mirror."—MaFw
"Leaning out over."—MaFw
To T. S. Eliot on his sixtieth birthday.—PlM
The Unknown Citizen.—PeS

Auden, W. H. (about)
To Auden on his fiftieth birthday. R. Eberhart.—PlM
To W. H. Auden on his fiftieth birthday. B. Howes.—PlM

Auguries of innocence. William Blake.—RoIt (sel.)

August
August ("Mike says") Myra Cohn Livingston.—LiM
August ("Now I am seven mama can stay") L. Clifton.—ClE
An August midnight. T. Hardy.—JoA-4—PlP
August weather. K. Tynan.—PaF
Mid-August at Sourdough mountain lookout. G. Snyder.—HiN

August ("Mike says") Myra Cohn Livingston.—LiM

August ("Now I am seven mama can stay") Lucille Clifton.—ClE

An **August** midnight. Thomas Hardy.—JoA-4—PlP

August 2. Norman Jordan.—AdPb

August 8. Norman Jordan.—AdM

August 24, 1963—1:00 a.m.—Omaha. Donna Whitewing.—AlW

August weather. Katharine Tynan.—PaF

"**Augustus** was a chubby lad." See The story of Augustus who would not have any soup

Auk talk. Mary Ann Hoberman.—HoR

Auks
Auk talk. M. A. Hoberman.—HoR
The great auk's ghost. R. Hodgson.—LiWw

Auld Daddy Darkness. James Ferguson.—OpOx

"**Auld** Daddy Darkness creeps frae his hole." See Auld Daddy Darkness

"The **auld** wife sat at her ivied door." See Ballad

Aunt Eliza. Harry Graham.—LiWw

Aunt Helen. T. W. Eliot.—PeS

Aunt Jane. Herbert Asquith.—BrM

Aunt Jane Allen. Fenton Johnson.—AdPb

"**Aunt** Jane's in such a hurry." See Aunt Jane

"**Aunt** Jemima ate cake." Unknown.—EmN

"**Aunt** Jemima climbed a tree." Unknown.—EmN

Aunt Jemima of the ocean waves. Robert Hayden.—AdPb

Aunt Julia. Norman MacCaig.—ToM

"**Aunt** Julia spoke Gaelic." See Aunt Julia

"**Aunt** Sue has a head full of stories." See Aunt Sue's stories

Aunt Sue's stories. Langston Hughes.—HoD

Aunts
Aunt Eliza. H. Graham.—LiWw
Aunt Helen. T. S. Eliot.—PeS
Aunt Jane. H. Asquith.—BrM
Aunt Jane Allen. F. Johnson.—AdPb
"Aunt Jemima ate cake." Unknown.—EmN
"Aunt Jemima climbed a tree." Unknown.—EmN
Aunt Jemima of the ocean waves. R. Hayden.—AdPb
Aunt Julia. N. MacCaig.—ToM
Aunt Sue's stories. L. Hughes.—HoD
Aunts watching television. J. Pudney.—ToM
By her aunt's grave. T. Hardy.—PlP
Great-aunts. S. O'Criadáin.—CoPi
Lizards and snakes. A. Hecht.—HiN
My Aunt Dora. T. Hughes.—HuMf
My Aunt Flo. T. Hughes.—HuMf
"My aunt kept turnips in a flock." R. Jarrell.—LiWw

Aunts watching television. John Pudney.—ToM

"The **aunts** who knew not Africa." See Aunts watching television

Aurora borealis. See Northern lights

Austin, Mary
Grizzly bear.—RoIt
"Neither spirit nor bird."—RoIt
The sandhill crane.—AdP
A song of greatness. tr.—JoA-4
Australia
Bandicoot. M. A. Hoberman.—HoR
The bushrangers. E. Harrington.—CoPt
Up from down under. D. McCord.—JoA-4
Waltzing Matilda. Unknown.—CoPt
The **author** to her book. Anne Bradstreet.—ThI
Authors and authorship. See Writers and writing
Auto wreck. Karl Shapiro.—MaFw—PeS
Autobiographical note. Vernon Scannell.—ToM
Autobiography ("In my childhood trees were green") Louis MacNeice.—MaFw
An **autobiography** ("Wales England wed, so I was bred. 'Twas merry London gave me breath") Ernest Rhys.—CoPu
Autograph album verses
"Abracadabra." Unknown.—MoBw
"Adam and his better half." Unknown.—MoBw
"Although we argue." Unknown.—MoBw
"Always be happy." Unknown.—MoBw
"Anne stood on the balcony." Unknown.—MoBw
"As deep as the deep blue sea." Unknown.—EmN—MoBw
"As sure as you get married." Unknown.—EmN
"Ashes to ashes." Unknown.—MoBw
"Autographs are finger kisses." Unknown.—EmN
"Be kind to all." Unknown.—MoBw
"Before you journey to the end of life." Unknown.—MoBw
"Best wishes to you." Unknown.—MoBw
"Blue is the sky." Unknown, tr. fr. the Spanish.—MoBw
"The boy stood on the burning deck (eating peanuts by the peck)." Unknown.—CoOh—MoBw
"The boy stood on the burning deck (his feet were full of blisters)." Unknown.—MoBw
"The boy stood on the railroad track." Unknown.—MoBw
"Boys are humbugs." Unknown.—MoBw
"Boys are mean." Unknown.—MoBw
"Bread and butter." Unknown.—MoBw
"Butter is butter." Unknown.—MoBw
"By hook or by crook." Unknown.—EmN
"Can't keep a squirrel on the ground." Unknown.—MoBw
"City of love." Unknown.—MoBw
"Coca-cola came to town." Unknown.—MoBw
"Come when you are called." Unknown.—EmN
"A corkscrew drowns more people." Unknown.—MoBw
"Debbie and Mark." Unknown.—MoBw
"Deck the halls with poison ivy." Unknown.—MoBw
"Dewey was an admiral down on Manila bay." Unknown.—MoBw
"Did you ever stop to think." Unknown.—MoBw
"Do you love me or do you not." Unknown.—CoPu
"Do you love me."—MoBw
"Doctor Bell fell down the well." Unknown.—MoBw
"Donna, Donna." Unknown.—MoBw
"Don't be crooked." Unknown.—EmN
"Don't make love by the garden gate." Unknown.—EmN
"Don't try to be an angel." Unknown.—MoBw
"Don't worry, the Liberty Bell is cracked too." Unknown.—MoBw
"Ducks on the mill pond." Unknown.—MoBw
"Early to bed and early to rise." Unknown.—MoBw
"East is east." Unknown.—MoBw
"Eeeeeeeeeeeeee." Unknown.—MoBw
"Every day in your life." Unknown.—EmN
"Everything has an end and a piece of string has two." Unknown.—MoBw
"Excuse the writing." Unknown.—MoBw
"Fall from a steamer's burning deck." Unknown.—MoBw
"Fall from an apple tree." Unknown.—EmN
"A fool and his money soon part at the carnival." Unknown.—MoBw
For a blue page. Unknown.—MoBw
For a green page. Unknown.—MoBw
For a white page. Unknown.—MoBw
"For 120 years of happiness." Unknown.—MoBw
"A friend in need." Unknown.—MoBw
"Friendship is like china." Unknown.—MoBw
"Get the ladder." Unknown.—MoBw
"The girl of my choice." Unknown.—MoBw
"Girls who chatter." Unknown.—MoBw
"Gloria is your name." Unknown.—MoBw
"God made the rivers." Unknown.—MoBw
"Good little girls love their brothers." Unknown.—EmN
"The grapes hang green upon the vine." Unknown.—EmN
"Grass grows low." Unknown.—MoBw
"Green is green." Unknown.—MoBw
"Grow up, grow up." Unknown.—MoBw
"Hang on." Unknown.—MoBw
"Happiness." Unknown.—MoBw
"He that takes but never gives." Unknown.—MoBw
"He took her in the garden." Unknown.—MoBw
"He who takes what isn't his'n." Unknown.—MoBw
"Health and happiness." Unknown.—MoBw
"Health and long life to you." Unknown.—MoBw
"Henry's in the White House." Unknown.—MoBw

"Here I stand all nice and clean." Unknown.—MoBw
"Here I stand on two little chips." Unknown.—MoBw
"Here's luck and hoping you sit on a tack." Unknown.—EmN
"The higher the mountains." Unknown.—MoBw
"Holland." Unknown.—MoBw
"I dip my pen into the ink." Unknown.—MoBw
"I don't know who tells me." Unknown.—MoBw
"I don't want any money." Unknown.—MoBw
"I had a television set." Unknown.—MoBw
"I know that I'm a runt." Unknown.—MoBw
"I looked your album o'er and o'er." Unknown.—MoBw
"I love cake, I love pie." Unknown.—EmN
"I love cookies." Unknown.—MoBw
"I love to go fishing." Unknown.—MoBw
"I love you a little." Unknown.—EmN
"I love you once." Unknown.—MoBw
"I said it." Unknown.—MoBw
"I saw you in the ocean." Unknown.—MoBw
"I see you in the ocean." Unknown.—EmN
"I see you want." Unknown.—MoBw
"I want you to live as long as you want." Unknown.—EmN
"I went into the garden." Unknown.—MoBw
"I went to your house for a piece of cheese." Unknown.—MoBw
"I wish I was a head of cabbage." Unknown.—EmN
"I wish I were a china cup." Unknown.—EmN
"I wish I were a graham cracker." Unknown.—MoBw
"I wish you health." Unknown.—EmN
"I wish you love." Unknown.—EmN
"I wish you luck, I wish you joy." Unknown.—EmN
"I wish you were a little mouse." Unknown.—MoBw
"If a fellow tries to win your heart." Unknown.—MoBw
"If apart we two must be." Unknown.—EmN
"If Cupid shoots." Unknown.—EmN
"If ever I go to Paradise." Unknown.—MoBw
"If Richard were king." Unknown.—MoBw
"If the ocean was milk." Unknown.—MoBw
"If you could look into my heart." Unknown.—MoBw
"If you ever go to France." Unknown.—MoBw
"If you get a husband." Unknown.—EmN
"If you have a friend." Unknown, tr. fr. the Spanish.—MoBw
"If you love me as I love you." Unknown.—EmN
"If you think you are in love." Unknown.—MoBw
"If you want to be happy." Unknown, tr. fr. the Spanish.—MoBw
"If you wish to be happy." Unknown, tr. fr. the Spanish.—MoBw
"If your shoe is in a knot." Unknown.—MoBw
"I'm a cute little girl." Unknown.—MoBw
"I'm not much for lines." Unknown.—MoBw
"In curve, out curve." Unknown.—MoBw
"In the dark, dark world." Unknown.—MoBw
"In the golden chain of friendship." Unknown.—EmN
"In the storm of life you may need an umbrella." Unknown.—EmN
"In the woodbox of memory." Unknown.—EmN
"In this world, you can do as you please." Unknown.—MoBw
"Into a closed mouth no flies will enter." Unknown, tr. fr. the Spanish.—MoBw
"Into a golden chest." Unknown, tr. fr. the Spanish.—MoBw
"It takes a cool cool boy." Unknown.—MoBw
"It tickles me." Unknown.—EmN
"It's a long way to Easy Street." Unknown.—MoBw
"It's nice to be natural." Unknown.—MoBw
"It's not the man who knows the most." Unknown.—MoBw
"I've been eating onions." Unknown.—MoBw
"Jake, Jake, open the gate." Unknown.—EmN
"Judge not your friends from outward show." Unknown.—EmN
"Just because your head is shaped like an air conditioner." Unknown.—MoBw
"Just like a puzzle, always mixed up." Unknown.—MoBw
"Ladies and gentlemen." Unknown.—MoBw
"Ladies and gentlemen, I come before you to." Unknown.—MoBw
"Leaves may wither." Unknown.—EmN
"Like London, always in a fog." Unknown.—MoBw
"Lincoln, Lincoln, I've been thinkin'." Unknown.—MoBw
"Little Miss Muffet (. . . and she picked up a spoon and beat the hell out of it)." Unknown.—MoBw
"Lots of." Unknown.—MoBw
"Love and a cough cannot be hid." Unknown.—MoBw
"Love many, trust few." Unknown.—EmN
"The man who has plenty of good peanuts." Unknown.—MoBw
"Many a ship was lost at sea." Unknown.—EmN
"Mary had a little lamb (its fleece was white as snow, Mary passed a butcher shop)." Unknown.—MoBw
"Mary had a little lamb (whose fleece was white as snow; she took it down to Pittsburgh)." Unknown.—MoBw

"Roses are red (violets are blue, please shut the door)." Unknown.—MoBw
"Roses are red (violets are blue, St Joseph's is glad)." Unknown.—MoBw
"Roses are red (violets are blue, sugar is sweet, and good in your coffee)." Unknown.—MoBw
"Roses are red (violets are blue, umbrellas get lost)." Unknown.—MoBw
"Roses are red (violets are blue, unless you have a garden)." Unknown.—MoBw
"Roses are red (violets are blue, what you need)." Unknown.—MoBw
"Roses are red (violets are blue, you vote for me)." Unknown.—MoBw
"Roses are red (violets are green, I think you're in love)." Unknown.—MoBw
"Roses are red (violets are green, take my advice)." Unknown.—MoBw
"Roses are red, violets are green (you have a shape)." Unknown.—MoBw
"Roses are red (Washington's dead)." Unknown.—MoBw
"Roses on my shoulders." Unknown.—MoBw
"Rots of ruck." Unknown.—MoBw
"Save your money." Unknown.—MoBw
"Say it." Unknown.—MoBw
"Shame on you." Unknown.—MoBw
"She turns the pages through and through." Unknown.—EmN
"She who weddeth keeps God's letter." Unknown.—MoBw
"Should old acquaintance be forgot." Unknown.—MoBw
"Snow White gave a party." Unknown.—MoBw
"Some kiss behind a lily." Unknown.—EmN
"Some write for pleasure." Unknown.—EmN
"Sometimes a tie is round your neck." Unknown.—MoBw
"Sugar, sugar." Unknown.—MoBw
"Sweet is the girl who reads this line." Unknown.—MoBw
"There are rocks in the ocean." Unknown.—MoBw
"There are three kinds of friends." Unknown.—MoBw
"There is a word in English spoken." Unknown.—EmN
"There is free cheese in every trap." Unknown.—MoBw
"There is many a kiss to remember." Unknown.—MoBw
"There once was a grizzly bear." Unknown.—MoBw
"There was once a young man named Paul." Unknown.—MoBw
"There's an autograph book in heaven." Unknown.—EmN
"Think of me early." Unknown.—EmN
"Think of me now." Unknown.—MoBw
"This is a free country." Unknown.—MoBw
"This is page one." Unknown.—MoBw
"Though days be dark." Unknown.—MoBw
"Though they scold and nag and argue." Unknown.—MoBw
" 'Tis sweet to kiss." Unknown.—MoBw
"To achieve a good life." Unknown, tr. fr. the Spanish.—MoBw
"To be written after someone who has written." Unknown.—MoBw
"To the prettiest girl in the world." Unknown.—MoBw
"Top." Unknown.—MoBw
"True friends are like diamonds." Unknown.—EmN
"Turn to the next page and see a man." Unknown.—MoBw
"2 big U R." Unknown.—EmN
"2 good." Unknown.—MoBw
"2 skinny." Unknown.—MoBw
"U R 2 good." Unknown.—EmN
Vera had a little light." Unknown.—EmN
"Violets are blue (roses are red, I'm your friend)." Unknown.—MoBw
"The waves of life flow on forever." Unknown.—MoBw
"Way back here and out of sight." Unknown.—EmN
"Way up on the hill." Unknown.—MoBw
"What eyes, what a nose." Unknown, tr. fr. the Spanish.—MoBw
"When a task is once begun." Unknown.—MoBw
"When all your friends have deserted you." Unknown.—EmN
"When distant lands divide us." Unknown.—EmN
"When folks like you are far away." Unknown.—MoBw
"When I am gone out of your mind." Unknown.—MoBw
"When in my lonely grave I sleep." Unknown.—EmN
"When months and years have glided by." Unknown.—MoBw
"When night folds its curtain." Unknown.—EmN
"When nothing is left to say." Unknown.—MoBw
"When on this page." Unknown.—EmN
"When on this page your eyes do bend." Unknown.—MoBw
"When the dusk of twilight's falling." Unknown.—MoBw
"When the golden sun is setting (and your feet)." Unknown.—EmN
"When the golden sun is setting (and your mind)." Unknown.—EmN
"When the golden sun is sinking." Unknown.—MoBw
"When you are married." Unknown.—EmN
"When you are old and cannot see." Unknown.—EmN
"When you are twenty and able to dress." Unknown.—EmN
"When you bake your first cherry pie." Unknown.—MoBw

B

The **ballad** of Chocolate Mabbie. Gwendolyn Brooks.—PeS
The **ballad** of Hagensack. Wallace Irwin.—CoPt
The **ballad** of Minepit Shaw. Rudyard Kipling.—CoPt
The **ballad** of Mrs Noah. Robert Duncan.—ToM
The **ballad** of red fox. Melvin Walker La Follette.—AdP
A **ballad** of remembrance. Robert Hayden.—AdPb
The **ballad** of Sir Patrick Spens. See Sir Patrick Spens
Ballad of the bread man. Charles Causley.—ToM
The **ballad** of the fox. Unknown.—RoIt
The **ballad** of the harp-weaver. Edna St Vincent Millay.—CoPt—RoIt
The **ballad** of the light-eyed little girl. Gwendolyn Brooks.—PeS
The **ballad** of William Sycamore. Stephen Vincent Benét.—JoA-4—RoIt
The **ballade** ("A ballade rhymes with 'odd' and it is odd, and not") David McCord.—McFm
Ballade ("Fountains that frisk and sprinkle") William Ernest Henley.—PaF
Ballade: An easy one. David McCord.—McFm
"A **ballade** rhymes with 'odd' and it is odd, and not." See A ballade
Ballades (about)
  The ballade. D. McCord.—McFm
  Ballade: An easy one. D. McCord.—McFm
Ballads—Old English and Scottish
  The daemon lover. Unknown.—MaFw
  Get up and bar the door. Unknown.—CoPt—JoA-4
  Green broom. Unknown.—CoPt
  How Robin Hood rescued the widow's sons. Unknown.—CoPt
  The riddling knight. Unknown.—JoA-4—RoIt
  Robin Hood and Little John. Unknown.—JoA-4
  Sir Patrick Spens. Unknown.—JoA-4—MaFw
    The ballad of Sir Patrick Spens.—RoIt
  True Thomas. Unknown.—CoPt
    Thomas Rymer.—MaFw
  Twa corbies. Unknown.—CoPt—MaFw
Balloons
  Balloons ("Kate's on for two, Elise is three") D. McCord.—McAa
  Balloons ("Since Christmas they have lived with us") S. Plath.—HiN—ToM
  "Balloons to blow." M. A. Hoberman.—HoN
  Five cent balloons. C. Sandburg.—SaT
  "In just." From Chanson innocente. E. E. Cummings.—RoIt
    In just-spring.—JoA-4
  Multi-colored balloon. H. D. Greggs.—AbM
  "What's the news of the day." Mother Goose.—AlC—MiMg
Balloons ("Kate's on for two, Elise is three") David McCord.—MaAa
Balloons ("Since Christmas they have lived with us") Sylvia Plath.—HiN—ToM
"**Balloons** to blow." Mary Ann Hoberman.—HoN
"**Balls** of string or little bits." See String
Bamboo
  "A father deer." Issa.—HaW
  "I like you, bamboo." Kim Kwang-wuk.—BaSs
  "Let's be off to the bamboo." Issa.—HaW
  "Peach and plum blossoms of spring." Kim Yu-ki.—BaSs
"**Banana** leaves are burning." See Containing communism
Bananas
  Lament of the banana man. E. Jones.—ToM
  Song of the banana man. E. Jones.—ToM
"**Bananas** ripe and green, and ginger root." See The tropics in New York
Band-aids
  Band-aids. S. Silverstein.—SiW
Band-aids. Shel Silverstein.—SiW
"A **band** is playing." See Parade
"The **bandicoot.**" See Bandicoot
Bandicoot. Mary Ann Hoberman.—HoR
Bandicoots
  Bandicoot. M. A. Hoberman.—HoR
"**Bang** bang bang." See The history of the flood
Bang-klang. Shel Silverstein.—SiW
Bangs, John Kendrick
  The little elf.—JaP—UnGb
"**Banners** flying." See Fake
"A **bantam** rooster." Kikaku, tr. fr. the Japanese by Harry Behn.—BeM
Barab, Seymour
  The season for singing.—LaS
Baraka, Imamu Amiri. See Jones, LeRoi
Barannikov, Kostya
  "Let there always be a sky."—MoM
"**Barbara,** Barbara." Unknown.—EmN
"**Barbara's** eyes are blue as azure." See Won't you
Barbauld, Anna Laetitia
  The mouse's petition.—OpOx
"**Barber,** barber, shave a pig." Mother Goose.—AlC—JoA-4
"The **barber** shaved the mason." Mother Goose.—AlC
Barber shop. Lois Lenski.—LeC
Barbers and barbershops
  "Barber, barber, shave a pig." Mother Goose.—AlC—JoA-4
  "The barber shaved the mason." Mother Goose.—AlC
  Barber shop. L. Lenski.—LeC
  The barber's. W. De La Mare.—JoA-4
  "A clergyman told from his text." Unknown.—RoIt
  "Good guys, bad guys." Unknown.—MoBw
  "Hippity hop." Unknown.—EmN
The **barber's.** Walter De La Mare.—JoA-4
Barbershops. See Barbers and barbershops
Barcelona, Spain
  Barcelona. C. McKay.—AbM
Barcelona. Claude McKay.—AbM
Bare almond-trees. D. H. Lawrence.—MaFw

"**Bare** branches of trees." See Winter alphabet
"**Barely** did the dust settle." See Taking off
Barham, Richard Harris. See Ingoldsby, Thomas, pseud.
Baring-Gould, Sabine
"Now the day is over."—OpOx
Barker, George
The Cutty Sark. See Dreams of a summer night, part VI
Dreams of a summer night, part VI, sel.
The Cutty Sark.—MaFw
On a friend's escape from drowning off the Norfolk coast.—ToM
Sonnet of fishes.—MaFw
Sonnet to my mother. See To my mother
To my mother.—HiN—MaFw
Sonnet to my mother.—PeS
Barnard, Mary
"At noontime." tr.—ThI
"But you, monkey face." tr.—AdPb
"Don't ask me what to wear." tr. ThI
"He is more than a hero." tr.—ThI
"I have had not one word from her." tr.—ThI
"It was you, Atthis, who said." tr.—ThI
"Prayer to my lady of Paphos." tr.—ThI
"Sleep darling." tr.—ThI
"Tonight I've watched." tr.—ThI
"We know this much." tr.—ThI
"Without warning." tr.—ThI
"You know the place, then." tr.—ThI
Barnes, Colin (about)
From jazz for five. J. Smith.—ToM (sel.)
Barnes, William (about)
The last signal. T. Hardy.—PlM—PlP
Barnouw, Adriaan J.
Such is Holland. tr.—MaFw
Barns
Prairie barn. From The people, yes. C. Sandburg.—SaT
She opens the barn door every morning. C. Sandburg.—SaT
Barrax, Gerald W.
Black Narcissus.—AdPb
Efficiency apartment.—AdPb
For Malcolm: After Mecca.—AdPb
Fourth dance poem.—AdPb
To a woman who wants darkness and time.—AdPb
Your eyes have their silence.—AdPb
"A **barrel** of water." Unknown.—EmN
Barrels
"Niddy, niddy, noddy." Unknown.—EmN
Barricades. Michael S. Harper.—AdPb
Barricades hammered into place." See Barricades
Barrows, Marjorie
Finding fairies.—JaP
Baruch, Dorothy W.
Funny the way different cars start.—HoP
The **base** stealer. Robert Francis.—FlH—HiN
Baseball
"April." J. Stancher.—HoC
The base stealer. R. Francis.—FlH—HiN
"Baseball." J. Wagner.—HoC
Catch. R. Francis.—HiN
Dorlan's home walk. A. Guiterman.—CoPt
The double-play. R. Wallace.—FlH
Dream of a baseball star. G. Corso.—FlH
Hits and runs. C. Sandburg.—FlH—SaT
Little league. D. McCord.—McAa
Little-league baseball fan. W. R. Moses.—HiN
"These are." J. Vitale.—HoC
To Satch. S. Allen.—AbM—AdPb
The umpire. W. Gibson.—FlH
"**Baseball.**" Joel Wagner.—HoC
Bashō
"The best I have to."—BeM
"A dry leaf drifting."—BeM
"The first winter rain."—AtM
"Has a drift of snow."—BeM
"Hidden by darkness."—BeM
"Low clouds are shattered."—BeM
"Nothing in the voice of the cicada."—MaFw
"The old pond."—HaW
"On a bare branch."—MaFw
"Scattered on the sand."—BeM
"Swallows, spare those bees."—BeM
"There goes my best hat."—BeM
"This unimportant."—BeM
"Trapped in a helmet."—BeM
"Wandering, dreaming."—BeM
"The waves are so cold."—BeM
"When a cuckoo sings."—BeM
Basic for better living. Eve Merriam.—MeF
Basic for further irresponsibility. Eve Merriam.—MeF
Basic for irresponsibility. Eve Merriam.—MeF
Basket. Carl Sandburg.—SaT
The **basket** of summer fruit. See Amos
Basketball
Basketball: A love song because it is. T. Meschery.—FlH
Foul shot. E. A. Hoey.—FlH
Basketball: A love song because it is. Tom Meschery.—FlH
Baskets
"I see a star." A. Lopez.—AlW
To the cedar tree. Unknown.—JoT
Bat-Miriam, Kocheved. See also Mezey, Robert and Bat-Miriam, Kocheved, jt. trs.
Distance spills itself.—MeP
Parting.—MeP
The **bat.** Theodore Roethke.—JoA-4—MaFw—PeS
"A **bat** is born." See Bats
Batchelor, Tanya
"The snow."—HoC
Bateman, Thomas
Sister awake.—MaF
Bates, David
Speak gently.—LiS
Bates, G. E.
Pentagonia.—LiS
Bates, Scott
Fable of the transcendent Tannenbaum.—CoPt

"The bear went over the mountain." Unknown.—EmN—JoA-4
Bear with me and you may learn. J. Ciardi.—CiFs
Bears. A. Rich.—HiN
"Benjy met a bear, the bear met Benjy. Unknown.—EmN
"A big black bug bit a big black bear." Unknown.—EmN
The black bear. J. Prelutsky.—PrP
"The common cormorant or shag." Unknown.—TrG
"Eight big black bears six feet tall." J. Prelutsky.—PrC
Father Goose tells a story. A. Resnikoff.—CoOh
Grizzly bear. M. Austin.—RoIt
"I am the Grizzly Bear." Unknown.—ClFc
I am writing this at sea. J. Ciardi.—CiFs
"I remember the white bear." Unknown.—LeIb
"Koala means the world to her." K. Kuskin.—KuN
The marvellous bear shepherd. Unknown.—MaFw
"My mother saw a dancing bear." C. Causley.—CaF
My teddy bear. M. Chute.—ChRu
The polar bear. J. Prelutsky.—PrT
"Robert Rutter dreamt a dream." Unknown.—EmN
Signal song on capture of polar bear. Unknown.—LeIb
"Teddy bear, Teddy bear." Unknown.—EmN
"There was an old person of Ware." E. Lear.—LiLc
Limericks.—JoA-4
Us two. A. A. Milne.—OpOx
Waiting. H. Behn.—JoA-4
Bears. Adrienne Rich.—HiN
"**Beast** of the sea." Unknown, fr. the Iglulik Eskimo.—LeIb
The **beast** section. Welton Smith.—AdPb
Beasts. See Animals
Beasts and birds. Adelaide O'Keefe.—OpOx
The **Beatles**
Lucy in the sky with diamonds.—PeS
Beaumont, Francis
Pining for love.—CoPu
— and Fletcher, John
Jolly red nose.—RoIt
"Nose, nose, jolly red nose."—TrG
"Nose, nose, jolly red nose." See Jolly red nose
The river-god's song
Song.—RoIt
Song. See The river-god's song
Beau's reply. William Cowper.—RoIt
The **beautiful.** William Henry Davies.—CoPu
"**Beautiful** as a star hanging in the sky." See Beautiful is our lodge
"**Beautiful** heights, city of a great King." See Jerusalem
Beautiful is our lodge. Unknown, ad. by John Bierhorst from the collections of Frances Densmore.—BiS
"A **beautiful** lady named Pysche." Unknown.—LiWw
"**Beautiful** soup, so rich and green." See Alice's adventures in wonderland—Turtle soup
"**Beautiful** star in heav'n so bright." See Star of the evening
"**Beautiful** you rise upon the horizon of heaven." See Hymn to the sun
"**Beautifully** Janet slept." See Janet waking
Beauty
At flock Mass. F. R. Higgins.—CoPi
"Back from the country." O. St J. Gogarty.—CoPi
The beautiful. W. H. Davies.—CoPu
Beauty. E-Yeh-Shure.—JoA-4
Black woman. L. S. Senghor.—AlPa
Blue girls. J. C. Ransom.—RoIt
An epitaph. W. De La Mare.—CoPu
"The fair maid who, the first of May." Mother Goose.—AlC
I tell her she is lovely. M. Gibbon.—CoPi
July 31. N. Jordan.—AdPb
Last lines—1916. P. Pearse.—CoPi
"Look below you. The river is a thousand fathoms deep." Yi Hyun-bo.—BaSs
Manhole covers. K. Shapiro.—HiN—JoA-4
My face. A. Euwer.—LiWw
My people. L. Hughes.—AdM—HoD
Night. S. Teasdale.—JoA-4—PaF
The noble nature. From To the immortal memory and friendship of that noble pair, Sir Lucius Cary and Sir Henry Morison. B. Jonson.—RoIt
"Now a spring rain falls." Chiyo.—BeM
On getting a natural. D. Randall.—AdPb
"On the small table, the early mellowed." Park In-ro.—BaSs
Pied beauty. G. M. Hopkins.—MaFw—RoIt
The planter's daughter. A. Clarke.—CoPi
Poem for Flora. N. Giovanni.—AdM—AdPb—NeA
Prayer. Unknown.—BiI
Rhodora. R. W. Emerson.—RoIt
She walked unaware. P. MacDonogh.—CoPi
The sleeping beauty. E. Sitwell.—MaFw (sel.)
Sonnet IV. Unthrifty loveliness. W. Shakespeare.—MoG
Spring. G. M. Hopkins.—PaF
Spring blossom. E. Attah.—AbM
The swans. A. Fisher.—FiD
Taught me purple. E. T. Hunt.—PeS
A thing of beauty. J. Keats.—RoIt
Through dawn's pink aurora. P. George.—AlW
A valentine for a lady. Lucilius.—LiWw
When Sue wears red. L. Hughes.—JoA-4
"Where are you going, my pretty maid." Mother Goose.—JoA-4
Beauty, personal
Black magic. D. Randall.—AdPb
"It was you, Atthis, who said." Sappho.—ThI

Beechwoods at Knole. V. Sackville-West.—PaP
Beehive. Jean Toomer.—AdPb
Beeny cliff. Thomas Hardy.—PlP
Beer, Patricia
A dream of hanging.—ToM
"**Beer** can in the gutter." See Friendly
Bees. See also Honey
Against idleness and mischief. I. Watts.—LiS—OpOx
"Bee, a bee, a bumble bee." Unknown.—EmN
Bee song. C. Sandburg.—SaT
The bee, the ant, and the sparrow. N. Cotton.—OpOx
"A bee thumps against the dusty window." R. Sund.—CoPu
Beehive. J. Toomer.—AdPb
Bees ("Every bee") J. Prelutsky.—BrM—PrT
Bees ("Honeybees are very tricky") R. Hoban.—HoE
The buzzing doubt. D. L. Hill.—HiN
By chance I walk. Yüan Mei.—MaFw
The castaways. E. V. Rieu.—CoPt
For a good and sweet New Year. S. R. Weilerstein.—LaM
Hammock. D. McCord.—McS
How. A. Fisher.—FiFo
The humble-bee. R. W. Emerson.—PaF
Invitation to a bee. C. Smith.—OpOx
Julius Caesar and the honey-bee. C. T. Turner.—RoIt
"Next I come to the manna, the heavenly gift of honey." From The Georgics. Virgil.—MaFw
Opportunity. H. Graham.—LiWw
Question. M. A. Hoberman.—HoLb
"Resting from the noon." Gonsui.—BeM
Robbing the tree hive. E. G. Moll.—CoPt
Solomon and the bees. J. G. Saxe.—RoIt
"Swallows, spare those bees." Bashō.—BeM
"A swarm of bees in May." Mother Goose.—AlC
"There was an old man in a tree (who was horribly bored)." E. Lear.—RoIt
Limericks.—JoA-4
Nonsenses.—OpOx
Waiting. H. Behn.—JoA-4
"What does the bee do." C. G. Rossetti.—OpOx
Where the bee sucks. From The tempest. W. Shakespeare.—JoA-4—LiLc
Who am I? (I). M. A. Hoberman.—HoLb
Bees ("Every bee") Jack Prelutsky. BrM—PrT
Bees ("Honeybees are very tricky") Russell Hoban.—HoE
"**Bees,** bees." See For a good and sweet New Year
"**Bees** in the late summer sun." See Bee song
"**Beeston,** the place, near Nottingham." See Autobiographical note
Beethoven, Ludwig van (about)
"Higgledy-piggledy." E. W. Seaman.—LiWw
Wrath. J. Hollander.—LiWw
"A **beetle,** a bat, and a bee." See The castaways
The **beetle** in the country bathtub. John Hall Wheelock.—HaWr
The **beetle** in the wood. Byron Herbert Reece.—CoPt
Beetles
The beetle in the country bathtub. J. H. Wheelock.—HaWr
The beetle in the wood. B. H. Reece.—CoPt
"Bless you, bless you, burnie-bee." Mother Goose.—JoA-4
The castaways. E. V. Rieu.—CoPt
Clock-a-clay. J. Clare.—RoIt
Forgiven. A. A. Milne.—BrM
I don't like beetles. R. Fyleman.—OpOx
Lady-bird. C. Southey.—UnGb
Lady bug. Unknown.—JoA-4
"Lady bug, lady bug (fly away)." Unknown.—EmN
"Lady bug, lady bug (go home)." Unknown.—EmN
"Lady bug, lady bug (your house)." Unknown.—EmN
"Ladybird, ladybird, fly away home." Mother Goose.—AlC
"Ladybug, ladybug, turn around." Unknown.—EmN
"Puva, puva, puva." Unknown.—ClFc
Tea party. H. Behn.—LiLc
"Then said the blowfly." Unknown.—LeIb
Before a saint's picture. Walter Savage Landor.—OpOx
"**Before** I melt." See The snow-flake
"**Before** men came up from below the earth to live." Natalia Belting.—BeWi
"**Before** my door the box-edg'd border lies." See Rural scenery
"**Before** she has her floor swept." See Portrait by a neighbor
Before the birth of one of her children. Anne Bradstreet.—ThI
"**Before** the bright sun rises over the hill." See The gleaner
Before the summer downpour. Sveta Kolosova, tr. fr. the Russian by Miriam Morton.—MoM
"**Before** you journey to the end of life." Unknown.—MoBw
The **beggar** boy. Cecil Frances Alexander.—OpOx
The **beggar** man. Lucy Aikin.—OpOx
Beggars
The beggar boy. C. F. Alexander.—OpOx
The beggar man. L. Aikin.—OpOx
Blind old woman. C. Major.—AdPb
Dives and Lazarus. Unknown.—MaFw
"Hark, hark." Mother Goose.—JoA-4
"I am a little beggar girl." Mother Goose.—AlC
"If wishes were horses." Mother Goose.—AlC—EmN
The little cart. Ch'ên Tsû-lung.—MaFw
"There goes a beggar." Kikaku.—BeM
"The **beginning** of eternity." See A riddle

To my youngest kinsman. R. L. A. Chear.—OpOx
"Tom was a bad boy." Unknown.—EmN
Tony the turtle. E. V. Rieu.—BrM
"Trip upon trenchers, and dance upon dishes." Mother Goose.—AlC
Twelve articles. J. Swift.—LiWw
Two little kittens. Unknown.—OpOx
The two little Miss Lloyds. E. Turner.—OpOx
Two men. E. A. Robinson.—LiWw
"We laughed and talked together." Unknown.—EmN
What Johnny told me. J. Ciardi.—CiFs
When happy little children play. J. Ciardi.—CiFs
"When Jacky's a very good boy." Mother Goose.—AlC
"When little Fred was called to bed." Mother Goose.—TucMgl
Where's Mary. I. O. Eastwick.—NeA
Whole duty of children. R. L. Stevenson.—OpOx
The wrong start. M. Chute.—ChRu
"**Behind** his dinner jacket." See He's doing natural life
"**Behind** the bush, behind the thorn." Unknown.—EmN
"**Behind** the mountain ledge." See Looking at the moon on putting out from the shore at Nagato
Behn, Harry
"Above the meadow." tr.—BeM
"After the goddess." tr.—BeM
"After thunder goes." tr.—BeM
All kinds of time.—JoA-4
"As New Year's day dawns." tr.—BeM
"At twilight a bell." tr.—BeM
"Back in my home town." tr.—BeM
"A bantam rooster." tr.—BeM
"The best I have to." tr.—BeM
"Beyond stillness, a." tr.—BeM
"A breeze stirs at dawn." tr.—BeM
"Butterflies, beware." tr.—BeM
"The chiming river." tr.—BeM
Circles.—LiLc
"Climbing a steep hill." tr.—BeM
"Clouds of morning mist." tr.—BeM
"The crickets are saying." tr.—BeM
"Cuckoo, if you must." tr.—BeM
"Deep in a windless." tr.—BeM
"Drifting, feathery." tr.—BeM
"A drowsy breeze." tr.—BeM
"A dry leaf drifting." tr.—BeM
"Eleven horsemen." tr.—BeM
"Even a wise man." tr.—BeM
Evening.—CoPu—JoA-4
"Flapping into fog." tr.—BeM
From an airplane.—HoP
"A full moon comes up." tr.—BeM
The gnome.—JaP
Hallowe'en.—JoA-4
"Hands flat on the ground." tr.—BeM
"Has a drift of snow." tr.—BeM
"Here comes our noble." tr.—BeM
"Hidden by darkness." tr.—BeM
"Hills have disappeared." tr.—BeM
"A horsefly mutters." tr.—BeM
"Hovering above." tr.—BeM
"How can a creature." tr.—BeM
"A hundred mountains." tr.—BeM
"I called to the wind." tr.—BeM
"If my complaining." tr.—BeM
"If things were better." tr.—HaW—LiWw
"In my house this spring." tr.—BeM
"Into a forest." tr.—BeM
"It's not so easy." tr.—BeM
The kite.—JoA-4
"Late summer evening." tr.—BeM
Listening.—UnGb
"Look at that strutting." tr.—BeM
"Low clouds are shattered." tr.—BeM
"Moon moves down the sky." tr.—BeM
"My tired old nag shakes." tr.—BeM
Near and far.—JoA-4—LiLc
The new little boy.—LiLc
"Now a spring rain falls. tr.—BeM
"Now that night is gone." tr.—BeM
"O moon, why must you." tr.—LiWw
"O that moon last night." tr.—BeM
"Once upon a time." tr.—BeM
"One star lingering."—BeM
"Our old family dog." tr.—BeM
"Parched by the shrill song." tr.—BeM
"Perch in my plum tree." tr.—BeM
"Pilgrims plod slowly." tr.—BeM
"Please don't go, I called." tr.—BeM
"The ragged phantom." tr.—BeM
"Resting from the noon." tr.—BeM
"Restless little flea." tr.—BeM
"Scattered on the sand." tr.—BeM
"Slanting, windy rain. . . . " tr.—BeM
"Small bird, forgive me." tr.—BeM
"Snow, softly, slowly." tr.—BeM
"Swallows, spare those bees." tr.—BeM
"Swinging, swaying grass." tr.—BeM
"Tangled over twigs." tr.—BeM
Tea party.—LiLc
"There goes a beggar." tr.—BeM
"There goes my best hat." tr.—BeM
"There, where the skylark's." tr.—BeM
"This unimportant." tr.—BeM
"Tides of a spring sea." tr.—BeM
"Trapped in a helmet." tr.—BeM
Trees.—LaM—UnGb
"Under a small, cold." tr.—BeM
"Under a spring mist." tr.—BeM
Waiting.—JoA-4
"Wandering, dreaming." tr.—BeM
"Warbler, wipe your feet." tr.—BeM
"Watching a petal." tr.—BeM
"Waterfall, only." tr.—BeM
"The waves are so cold." tr.—BeM
"When cherry trees bloom." tr.—BeM
"When nightingales burst." tr.—BeM
"White and wise and old." tr.—BeM
"Who can stay indoors." tr.—BeM
"Who goes there, drifting." tr.—BeM
"A wintry blizzard." tr.—BeM

"Before men came up from below the earth to live."—BeWi
"The chief of the world."—BeWi
"Dew Eagle, at night."—BeWi
"Digger Boy was hunting clams."—BeWi
"First man and first woman."—BeWi
"Flint Boy tied his dog."—BeWi
"Glooscap's wigwam."—BiWi
"Icicles are the walking sticks of the winter winds."—BeWi
"In the beginning there was no earth."—BeWi
"Lightning is a great giant."—BeWi
"A man sits in the ice."—BeWi
May day.—BeSc
May 1.—BeSc
May 8.—BeSc
May 14.—BeSc
"Moon sits smoking his pipe."—BeWi
"North Wind dresses her daughter winds."—BeWi
"The northern lights are the flames of the smoke."—BeWi
"Not long after the earth was made."—BeWi
"The sky is a bowl of ice."—BeWi
"Springs do not freeze in the cold of winter."—BeWi
"The stars are night birds with bright breasts."—BeWi
"The sun is a yellow-tipped porcupine."—BeWi
"Sun rays shining through the dusty air."—BeWi
"Wind is a ghost."—BeWi
"The winds are people dwelling."—BeWi
"Winter breaks."—BeSc
"Winter is an old man walking in the woods."—BeWi

Ben. Thomas Wolfe.—HiN
"**Ben** Hall was out on the Lachlan side." See The death of Ben Hall
Bench in the park. Lois Lenski.—LeC
"**Bend** low again, night of summer stars." See Summer stars
Bendix. John Updike.—PeS
"**Beneath** this yew, the shadow of a shade." Unknown.—CoPu

Benét, Laura
The witch's house.—RoIt

Benét, Stephen Vincent.
The ballad of William Sycamore.—JoA-4—RoIt
The general public.—PlM
The mountain whippoorwill.—CoPt

— and Carr, Rosemary
Nancy Hanks.—JoA-4

Benét, Stephen Vincent (about)
Love to Stephen. E. Wylie.—PlM

Benign neglect / Mississippi, 1976. Primus St John.—AdPb
Benjamin Bunnn. Shel Silverstein.—SiW
"**Benjy** met a bear, the bear met Benjy." Unknown.—EmN

Bennett, Gwendolyn B.
Hatred.—AdPb
Heritage.—AdPb
Sonnet I.—AdPb
Sonnet II.—AdPb
To a dark girl.—AdPb

Bennett, John
The ingenious little old man.—BrM—CoOr

Bennett, Lerone, Jr
And was not improved.—AdPb
Blues and bitterness.—AdPb

Bennett, Peggy
Plain talk for a pachyderm.—LiWw

Bennett, Rodney
Peter Tatter.—BrM

Bennett, Rowena Bastin
The elfin plane.—JaP
Fairy washing.—JaP
Motor cars.—HoP
The power shovel.—HoP
The witch of Willowby wood.—LeM (sel.)

Bennington. N. M. Bodecker.—BoL

Beowulf
Beowulf's voyage to Denmark. Unknown.—MaFw (sel.)

Beowulf's voyage to Denmark. Unknown, tr. fr. the Anglo-Saxon by Michael Alexander.—MaFw (sel.)

Berchan
The Fort of Rathangan.—CoPi

Beresford, Anne
The Romanies in town.—ToM
Saturday in New York.—ToM

Bergengren, Ralph
The worm.—BrM

Bernard, Oliver
The bridges. tr.—MaFw
Flowers. tr.—MaFw
Phrases. tr.—MaFw (sel.)

Berries. See names of berries, as Blackberries

Berrigan, Daniel
To a dead poet, his book.—Plm
To Wallace Stevens.—PlM

Berryman, John
Note to Wang Wei.—PlM

Beseeching the breath. Unknown, tr. fr. the Zuñi by Ruth Bunzel.—BiI
"**Beseeching** the breath of the divine one." See Beseeching the breath

Beshenkovskaya, Olya
The radiance of creativity.—MoM

"**Beside** the drums my dusty moccasins." See Until then
Bessie Bobtail. James Stephens.—CoPi
"The **best** game the fairies play." Rose Fyleman.—JaP
"The **best** I have to." Bashō, tr. fr. the Japanese by Harry Behn.—BeM
Best loved of Africa. Margaret Danner.—AdPb
"**Best** wishes too you." Unknown.—MoBw

Bethlehem
Christmas morning. E. M. Roberts.—JoA-4
"O little town of Bethlehem." P. Brooks.—JoA-4—LaS

"The Lord is my shepherd." See Psalms—Psalm 23
"Lord, thou hast been our dwelling place." See Psalms—Psalm 90
A meditation on Providence. See Psalms—Psalm 104
On the gifts of God. See Psalms—Psalm 127
"Praise ye the Lord." See Psalms—Psalm 150
A prayer to be delivered from liars and warmongers. See Psalms—Psalm 120
A prayer to be restored to the sanctuary. See Psalms—Psalm 84
The prophecies against Moab, Judah, and Israel. See Amos
Psalm 1. See Psalms
Psalm 23. See Psalms
Psalm 24. See Psalms
Psalm 30. See Psalms
Psalm 46. See Psalms
Psalm 84. See Psalms
Psalm 90. See Psalms
Psalm 91. See Psalms
Psalm 104. See Psalms
Psalm 107. See Psalms
Psalm 120. See Psalms
Psalm 121. See Psalms
Psalm 124. See Psalms
Psalm 126. See Psalms
Psalm 127. See Psalms
Psalm 137. See Psalms
Psalm 150. See Psalms
A psalm of thanksgiving. See Psalms—Psalm 124
"Rejoice not, O Israel, for joy." See Hosea
"Remember now thy Creator." See Ecclesiastes
They that go down. See Psalms—Psalm 107
The tree and the chaff. See Psalms—Psalm 1
The two paths. See Proverbs
"When God set about to create heaven." See Genesis
The writing of Hezekiah King of Judah, when he had been sick, and was recovered by his sickness. See Isaiah
Bible characters. See also names of Bible characters, as Adam and Eve
Abraham and Isaac. From The Chester miracle play. Unknown.—MaFw
An apple for Isaac. Solomon ibn Gabirol.—MeP
The ballad of Mrs Noah. R. Duncan.—ToM
"Didn't my Lord deliver Daniel." Unknown.—BrW
Innocent's song. C. Causley.—ToM
Judas. Unknown.—MaFw
Mary passed this morning. O. Dodson.—AdPb
The parable of the old man and the young. W. Owen.—MaFw—MoG
Song for unbound hair. Unknown.—RoIt
Story of Isaac. L. Cohen.—MoG
The vision of Belshazzar. Lord Byron.—RoIt
Bickerstaffe, Isaac
An expostulation.—CoPi—LiWw—RoIt
Love in a village, sel.
Song.—CoPi
"There was a jolly miller."—AlC
Song. See Love in a village
"There was a jolly miller." See Love in a village—Song
Bicycles and bicycling
"Come out and ride around the block with me." K. Kuskin.—KuA
My bicycle and me. L. Kulichkova.—MoM
"A **bicycle's** fine for a little trip." See Preferred vehicles
"The **bicycles** go by in twos and threes." See Inniskeen road, July evening
Bierhorst, John
The face of my mountains. tr.—BiI
"With rejoicing mouth." tr.—BiI
"**Big.**" See Hardrock
"**Big** A, little a, ron." Unknown.—EmN
"**Big** at the bottom." Unknown.—EmN
The **big** baboon. Hilaire Belloc.—CoOh
"The **big** baboon is found upon." see The big baboon
"A **big** black bug bit a big black bear." Unknown.—EmN
"**Big** bus at the bus stop." See Superstink
"A **big** buzz." See Who am I (I)
"**Big** clocks go tick." See Tick-tock talk
"The **big** cranes come." See Ghosts
"**Big** old billboard." See Blah-blah
"**Big** pile." See Greedy
Big question. David McCord.—McFm
The **big** Rock Candy mountain. Unknown.—CoOh
The big Rock Candy mountains.—PeS
The **big** Rock Candy mountains. See The big Rock Candy mountain
"**Big** trucks for steel beams." See Trucks
"**Big** trucks with apples." See Country trucks
Big wind. Theodore Roethke.—HiN
"The **bigger** the box the more it holds." See Boxes and bags
Bilen, Max
"Tomorrow belongs to God." tr.—AlPa
Billings, William
A Virgin unspotted.—LaS
"Wake ev'ry breath."—LaS
When Jesus wept.—LaS
"**Billy** Batter." Dennis Lee.—LeA
"**Bimbo,** bombo, tomkin pie." Clyde Watson.—WaF
Bimbo's pome. Paul Klee, tr. fr. the Swiss by Anselm Hollo.—MaFw
"The **binocular** owl." See The woods at night
Binsey poplars felled 1879. Gerard Manley Hopkins.—MaFw
Binyon, Laurence
The burning of the leaves.—PaF
Birago, Diop
Omen.—MaFw
Birch trees
"Three little birches." M. Nikogosian.—MoM
"A **bird** came down the walk." Emily Dickinson.—RoIt

"A **bird** doesn't grow sorghum." See Nuyonyi
Bird gardens. Aileen Fisher.—FiFo
"The **bird** is lost." See Yardbird's skull
The **bird** of night. Randall Jarrell.—AdP—HiN—MoT
"A **bird** sings the selfsame song." See The selfsame song
"A **birdie** with a yellow bill." See Time to rise
Birds. See also names of birds, as Robins
"After the goddess." Onitsura.—BeM
Akanyonyi. Unknown.—SeS
"All the bells were ringing." C. G. Rossetti.—LiLc
Allie. R. Graves.—JoA-4
And other poems. R. S. Morgan.—MaFw
Answer to a child's question. S. T. Coleridge.—OpOx—RoIt
As he lay dying. R. Stow.—MaFw
Aswelay. N. H. Pritchard II.—AdPb
Back again. A. Fisher.—FiFo
Beau's reply. W. Cowper.—RoIt
"A bird came down the walk." E. Dickinson.—RoIt
Bird gardens. A. Fisher.—FiFo
"The birds." K. Finnell.—HoC
The birds ("From out of the wood did a cuckoo fly") P. Dearmer.—MaF
Birds ("Of all the forms of life that still dwell in man as in a living ark") St J. Perse. —JoA-4
Birds at winter nightfall. T. Hardy.—CoPu—JoA-4—PlP
"Birds, do not blame the blossoms." Song Soon.—BaSs
"The birds in the feeder." D. McCord
Two triolets.—McS
Birds in the rain. D. McCord.—McFm
"Birds of a feather flock together." Mother Goose.—AlC
Birdsongsingsong. M. A. Hoberman.—HoLb
Cape Ann. T. S. Eliot.—JoA-4
The carol of the birds. J. J. Niles.—LaS
Daedalus. A. Reid.—HiN
Dingman's marsh. J. Moore.—HiN
The dinkey-bird. Eugene Field.—RoIt
Dream song. Unknown.—BiS
Early bird. S. Silverstein.—SiW
"Eggs are laid by turkeys." M. A. Hoberman.—HoN
"The fawn." Issa.—AtM
Feathers and moss. J. Ingelow.—LiS
Friendship. Unknown.—BiI
From the shore. C. Sandburg.—SaT
Garnishing the aviary. From Far from Africa: Four poems. M. Danner.—AdPb
"Haik, the white bird of omen." Unknown.—ClFc
"Hail, Bishop Valentine, whose day this is." J. Donne.—MaF
A health to the birds. S. MacManus.—CoPi
The High Barbaree. L. E. Richards.—JoA-4
"I circle around." Unknown.—ClFc
"I go forth to move about the earth." A. Lopez.—AlW
"I heard a bird sing." O. Herford.—LiLc
"I like them feathery, too." A. Fisher.—FiFo
I watched a blackbird. T. Hardy.—PlP
In Glencullen. J. M. Synge.—CoPi—CoPu
Kaleeba. Unknown.—SeS
Like a summer bird. A. Fisher.—FiFo
Little. D. McCord.—McFm—McS
Little dead. M. C. Livingston.—LiM
Looking for feathers. A. Fisher.—FiFo
Maybe the birds. J. Jordan.—MoT
"My home is a white dome." K. Kuskin.—KuA
Nnyonyi. Unknown.—SeS
Of the child with the bird on the bush. J. Bunyan.—OpOx
Off they flew. A. Fisher.—FiFo
On a spaniel called Beau killing a young bird. W. Cowper.—RoIt
Overlooking the River Stour. T. Hardy.—PaP—PlP
The peacock at home. C. A. Dorset.—OpOx
"Perch in my plum tree." Onitsura.—BeM
The pig tale. From Sylvie and Bruno. L. Carroll.—LiPc
Pipes and drums. L. Holmes.—JaP (sel.)
"Poor bird." W. De La Mare.—MaFw
Practical concerns. W. J. Harris.—AdPb
Proud songsters. T. Hardy.—MaFw
Purrrrr ce. Unknown.—SeS
The puzzled game-birds. T. Hardy.—PlP
The red cockatoo. Po Chü-i—CoPu
Requiem for a personal friend. E. Boland.—CoPi
The rivals. J. Stephens.—RoIt
River roads. C. Sandburg.—SaT
The rooks. J. E. Browne.—OpOx
Runover rhyme. D. McCord.—McFm—McS
Saint Francis and the birds. S. Heaney.—MaFw
Sea change. J. Masefield.—CoPt
Sea-hawk. R. Eberhart.—HaWr
The selfsame song. T. Hardy.—PlP
Sleepyheads. C. Sandburg.—SaT
"Small bird, forgive me." Unknown.—BeM
Snow. E. Thomas.—CoPu
Songs of birds. Unknown.—BiI
Spring morning. A. Fisher.—FiFo
"The stars are night birds with bright breasts." N. Belting.—BeWi
Still life: Lady with birds. Q. Prettyman.—AdPb
Streamside exchange. J. P. Clark.—AlPa
"There was an old man in a tree (whose whiskers were)." E. Lear
Limericks.—JoA-4
"There was an old man on whose nose." E. Lear
Limericks.—JoA-4
"There was an old man who said, Hush." E. Lear
Limericks.—JoA-4
Nonsenses.—OpOx
"These are the days when birds come back." E. Dickinson.—PaF

Three birds flying. E. Merriam.—MeO
To a waterfowl. W. C. Bryant.—RoIt
"To cheer our minds." W. Ronksley.—OpOx
To paint the portrait of a bird. J. Prévert.—MaFw
"The tree after Christmas." A. Atwood.—AtM
"Tree birds." K. Kuskin.—KuN
Twerüre. Unknown.—SeS
Waiting. A. Fisher.—FiFo
"Warbler, wipe your feet." Issa.—BeM
"A wee bird sat upon a tree." Unknown.—JoA-4
What a beautiful word. W. Cole.—CoOr
"What does little birdie say." From Sea dreams. A. Tennyson.—RoIt
Cradle song.—OpOx
"What there is of me to see." K. Kuskin.—KuA
The wheatear and the snowbird. Unknown.—LeIb
Where's Mary. I. O. Eastwick.—NeA
Wings. V. Hugo.—JoA-4
Winter birds. A. Fisher.—FiFo—LaM
The woods at night. M. Swenson.—JoA-4
Word bird. E. Merriam.—MeF
Words spoken by a mother to her newborn son as she cuts the umbilical cord. Unknown.—BiI
The year's awakening. T. Hardy.—PlP
The yellow bird. J. W. Thompson.—AdPb
Birds—Eggs and nests
Feathers and moss. J. Ingelow.—LiS
"Look at six eggs." C. Sandburg.—RoIt
The raven's song. Unknown.—LeIb
The thrush's nest ("Bramble, like barbed wire") R. Ryan.—CoPi
The thrush's nest ("Within a thick and spreading hawthorn bush") J. Clare.—MaFw—RoIt
Winter nests. A. Fisher.—FiFo
Winter surprise. A. Fisher.—FiFo
The wrens. A. Fisher.—FiFo
Birds—Migration
Flight. L. Moore.—MoSp
The geese. R. Peck.—PeS
How. A. Fisher.—FiFo
The last word of a bluebird. R. Frost.—JoA-4—LiLc
Stork story. M. A. Hoberman.—HoR
"**Birds.**" See Birdsongsingsong
"The **birds.**" Kelli Finnell.—HoC
The **birds** ("From out of the wood did a cuckoo fly") Percy Dearmer.—MaF
Birds ("Of all the forms of life that still dwell in man as in a living ark") St John Perse, tr. by Robert Fitzgerald.—JoA-4
Birds and sunlight." See Yellow
Birds at winter nightfall. Thomas Hardy.—CoPu—JoA-4—PlP
"**Birds,** do not blame the blossoms." Song Soon, tr. fr. the Korean by Chung Seuk Park and ad. by Virginia Olsen Baron.—BaSs
"The **birds** in the feeder." David McCord
Two triolets.—McS
Birds in the rain. David McCord.—McFm
"**Birds** of a feather flock together." Mother Goose.—AlC
Birdsongsingsong. Mary Ann Hoberman.—HoLb
Birmingham, Alabama
Birmingham. M. Walker.—AdPb
Birmingham 1963. R. R. Patterson.—AdPb
Poems: Birmingham 1962-1964. J. Fields.—AdPb
Birmingham. Margaret Walker.—AdPb
Birmingham 1963. Raymond Richard Patterson.—AdPb
"A **birr,** a whirr, a salmon's on." See The taking of the salmon
Birth. See also Birthdays
Birth. A. Gilboa.—MeP
The birth of the poet. Q. Prettyman.—AdB
Born without a star. Abraham ibn Ezra.—MeP
Christ's nativity. From Gospel according to Luke, Bible, New Testament.—RoIt
The cicadas. Judith Wright.—MaFw
The circle of weeping. A. Gilboa.—MeP
Conception. W. Cuney.—AbM
"Father, the year is fallen." A. Lorde.—AdPb
"Fear have I when it comes." L. Curry.—JoV
"I was born upon thy bank, river." H. D. Thoreau.—CoPu
Just born pig. F. Lape.—CoPu
Little brand new baby. T. Paxton.—PeS
My stars. Abraham ibn Ezra.—MeP
Now that I am forever with child. A. Lorde.—AdPb
On the birth of my son, Malcolm Coltrane. J. Lester.—AdPb
Prayer before birth. L. MacNeice.—CoPi—PeS—ToM
Song. Unknown.—BiI
Song of a new cradleboard. P. George.—AlW
This is real. T. Palmanteer.—AlW
Birth. Amir Gilboa, tr. fr. the Hebrew by Robert Mezey and Shula Starkman.—MeP
The **birth** of the poet. Quandra Prettyman.—AdB
Birthday cake. Lois Lenski.—LeC
"The **birthday** cake was beautiful." See Birthday cake
Birthday verses written in a child's album. James Russell Lowell.—OpOx
Birthdays
Birthday cake. L. Lenski.—LeC
Birthday verses written in a child's album. J. R. Lowell.—OpOx
Birthdays. M. Chute.—BrM
Chard Whitlow. H. Reed.—PlM
"Eena meena dixie dan." Unknown.—EmN
For K. R. on her sixtieth birthday. R. Wilbur.—PlM
"Happy birthday, silly goose." C. Watson.—WaF
July. L. Clifton.—ClE
A long life. L. Lenski.—LeC
A monstrous mouse. X. J. Kennedy.—KeO

Black is what the prisons are." See The African affair
Black jam for dr negro. Mari Evans.—AdPb
Black magic. Dudley Randall.—AdPb
Black majesty. Countee Cullen.—AdPb
"A **black** man." Sam Cornish.—AdPb
A **black** man talks of reaping. Arna Bontemps.—AdPb
Black man's feast. Sarah Webster Fabio.—AdPb
Black Narcissus. Gerald W. Barrax.—AdPb
A **black** November turkey. Richard Wilbur.—HiN
"The **black** one, last as usual, swings her head." See Fetching cows
The **black** panther. Kostya Raikin, tr. fr. the Russian by Miriam Morton.—MoM
Black people ("I see black people") Ted Joans.—AdM
Black people ("Who are they") Juanita Bryant.—JoV
"**Black** people think." See Awareness
A **black** poetry day. Alicia Loy Johnson.—AdB
"**Black** poets should live, not leap." See For black poets who think of suicide
Black power. Alvin Saxon.—AdPb
"**Black** reapers with the sound of steel on stones." See Reapers
"The **black** Snake Wind came to me." Unknown, tr. fr. the Pima by Frank Russell.—JoT
Black star line. Henry Dumas.—AdPb
Black-tailed deer song. Unknown, tr. fr. the Pima by Frank Russell.—BiI
Black trumpeter. Henry Dumas.—AdPb
Black warrior. Norman Jordan.—AdPb
"**Black** we are and much admired." Unknown.—EmN
"**Black** within and red without." Mother Goose.—EmN—JoA-4
Black woman ("My hair is springy like the forest grasses") Naomi Long Madgett.—AdPb
Black woman ("Naked woman, black woman") Léopold Sédar Senghor, tr. fr. the French by John Reed and Clive Wake.—AlPa
"**Black** woman, African woman, O my mother, I think of you." See To my mother
"**Black** woman I have." Linda Curry.—JoV
Blackberries
  The blackberry thicket. A. Stanford.—HaWr
  Blackberrying. S. Plath.—ToM
  Eating out in autumn. M. Chute.—ChRu
Blackberry street. Dudley Randall.—AdB—HiN
The **blackberry** thicket. Ann Stanford.—HaWr
Blackberrying. Sylvia Plath.—ToM
The **blackbird.** Humbert Wolfe.—JoA-4
A **blackbird** singing. R. S. Thomas.—MaFw
Blackbirds
  "As I went over the water." Mother Goose.—AlC
  The blackbird. H. Wolfe.—JoA-4
  A blackbird singing. R. S. Thomas.—MaFw
  I watched a blackbird. T. Hardy.—PlP
  "The little blackbirds are singing this song." Unknown.—ClFc
  "Sally over the water." Unknown.—EmN
  "Sing a song of sixpence." Mother Goose.—AlC—EmN—JoA-4—LiS
  The spring call. T. Hardy.—PlP
  Thirteen ways of looking at a blackbird. W. Stevens.—MoT
Blackfeet Indians. See Indians of the Americas—Blackfeet
Blackfriars. Eleanor Farjeon.—OpOx
Blackie, the electric Rembrandt. Thom Gunn.—MaFw
Blackie thinks of his brothers. Stanley Crouch.—AdPb
Blacks
  The African affair. B. M. Wright.—AdPb
  African China. M. B. Tolson.—AdPb
  African dream. B. Kaufman.—AdPb
  The alarm clock. M. Evans.—AdB
  "Ali." Lloyd Corbin, Jr.—AdB—AdM—AdPb
  All of us a family. C. Meyer.—JoV
  Amen. R. W. Thomas.—AdPb
  "America." B. Hamilton.—AdB
  And was not improved. L. Bennett, Jr.—AdPb
  And what shall you say. J. S. Cotter, Jr.—AdPb
  Arroyo. T. Weatherly.—AdPb
  As I grew older. L. Hughes.—HoD
  Aunt Jane Allen. F. Johnson.—AdPb
  Aunt Sue's stories. L. Hughes.—HoD
  Award. R. Durem.—AdPb
  Awareness. D. L. Lee.—AdB—AdM—AdPb
  A ballad of remembrance. R. Hayden.—AdPb
  Be cool, baby. R. Penny.—AdPb
  Beyond the nigger. S. Plumpp.—AdPb
  Black all day. R. R. Patterson.—AdB—AdPb
  The black finger. A. W. Grimké.—AdPb
  Black humor. A. MacLeish.—HiN
  Black is a soul. J. White.—AdPb
  "Black is best." L. Thompson.—AdB—AdM—AdPb
  Black magic. D. Randall.—AdPb
  Black majesty. C. Cullen.—AdPb
  "A black man." S. Cornish.—AdPb
  A black man talks of reaping. A. Bontemps.—AdPb
  Black man's feast. S. W. Fabio.—AdPb
  Black Narcissus. G. W. Barrax.—AdPb
  Black people ("I see black people") T. Joans.—AdM
  Black people ("Who are they") J. Bryant.—JoV
  Black power. A. Saxon.—AdPb
  Black star line. H. Dumas.—AdPb
  Black trumpeter. H. Dumas.—AdPb
  Black warrior. N. Jordan.—AdPb
  Black woman ("My hair is springy like the forest grasses") N. L. Madgett.—AdPb
  Black woman ("Naked woman, black woman") L. S. Senghor.—AlPa
  "Black woman I have." L. Curry.—JoV
  Blackberry street. D. Randall.—AdB—HiN

Blacks—*Continued*
Blackie thinks of his brothers. S. Crouch.—AdPb
Blues and bitterness. L. Bennett, Jr.—AdPb
Bottled: New York. H. Johnson.—AdPb
Brown boy to brown girl. C. Cullen.—AdPb
But he was cool. D. L. Lee.—AdPb
Canto 4. T. Weatherly.—AdPb
Carol of the brown king. L. Hughes.—HoS—LiLc
Cathexis. F. J. Bryant, Jr.—AdPb
Children's rhymes. L. Hughes.—AdB
Christ in Alabama. L. Hughes.—AdPb
Coal. A. Lorde—AdPb
Color. L. Hughes.—AdB—HoD
Crack in the wall holds flowers. A. D. Miller.—AdPb
Cross over the river. S. Cornish.—AdM
A dance for militant dilettantes. A. Young.—AdPb
Dark girl. A. Bontemps.—PeS
Dark people. K. M. Cumbo.—AdB
The days of my people. M. Gill.—JoV
Death in Yorkville. L. Hughes.—AdPb
Dedication to the final confrontation. L. Corbin, Jr.—AdPb
Definition for blk/children. S. Sanchez.—AdPb
Determination. D. Randall.—AdPb
"Do not think." C. Freedom.—AdM
Dream deferred. L. Hughes.—AdM—AdPb
Dream variation. L. Hughes.—AdM—AdPb—HoD
The Easter bunny blues or all I want for Christmas is the Loop. Ebon (Dooley).—AdPb
El-Hajj Malik El-Shabazz. R. Hayden.—AdPb
Elephant rock. Primus St John.—AdPb
The emancipation of George Hector. M. Evans.—AbM
Enchantment. L. Alexander.—AdPb
Floodtide. A. M. Touré.—AdPb
Florida road workers. L. Hughes.—PeS
Flowers of darkness. F. M. Davis.—AdPb
For a lady I know. C. Cullen.—AbM—LiWw
Four epitaphs.—AdPb
For Angela. Z. Gilbert.—AdPb
For Bill Hawkins, a black militant. W. J. Harris.—AdPb
For black poets who think of suicide. E. Knight.—AdPb
For de Lawd. L. Clifton.—AdM—AdPb
For Malcolm: After Mecca. G. W. Barrax.—AdPb
For Malcolm X. M. Walker.—AdPb
For my people. M. Walker.—AdPb
For real. J. Cortez.—AdPb
For Sammy Younge. C. Cobb.—AdPb
For some poets. M. Jackson.—AdB—AdPb
For Stephen Dixon. Z. Gilbert.—AdPb
From blackwoman poems. D. L. Lee.—AdM
From riot rimes U.S.A. #78. R. R. Patterson.—AdM
From riot rimes U.S.A. #79. R. R. Patterson.—AdM
From the dark tower. C. Cullen.—AdPb
Georgia dusk. J. Toomer.—AdPb
Ghetto. V. Howard.—JoV
Ginger bread mama. D. Long.—AdPb
Good morning. L. Hughes.—AdM
Good Saint Benedict. Unknown.—AbM
"A grandfather poem." W. J. Harris.—AdM—AdPb
"Grief streams down my chest." L. Jeffers.—AdPb
Half black half blacker. S. Plumpp.—AdPb
Harlem freeze frame. L. Bethune.—AdPb
"He sees through stone." E. Knight.—AdPb
Here where Coltrane is. M. S. Harper.—AdPb
Heritage ("I want to see the slim palm trees") G. B. Bennett.—AdPb
Heritage ("What's Africa to me") C. Cullen.—AdPb
He's doing natural life. Conyus.—AdPb
Homecoming. S. Sanchez.—AdPb
Honky. C. Cooper.—AdPb
Hospital/poem. S. Sanchez.—AdPb
How high the moon. L. Jeffers.—AdPb
The hungry black child. A. D. Miller.—AdPb
I have seen black hands. R. Wright.—AdPb
"I know I'm not sufficiently obscure." R. Durem.—AdPb
"I told Jesus." S. Plumpp.—AdPb
I, too. L. Hughes.—HoD—RoIt
"I, too, sing America."—AdPb
"I used to wrap my white doll up in." M. Jackson.—AdB—AdPb
"I was jus." B. O'Meally.—AdM
The idea of ancestry. E. Knight.—AdPb
Idle chatter. H. Dumas.—AdB
If blood is black then spirit neglects my unborn son. C. K. Rivers.—AdPb
"If I ride this train." J. Johnson.—AdPb
Image. H. Dumas.—AdB
Imperial thumbprint. T. Weatherly.—AdPb
In bondage. C. McKay.—AdPb
In defense of black poets. C. K. Rivers.—AdB
"In Orangeburg my brothers did." A. B. Spellman.—AdPb
In Texas grass. Q. Troupe.—AdPb
Incident. C. Cullen.—AbM—AdPb—JoA-4
Initiation. J. Cortez.—AdPb
An invitation to Madison county. Jay Wright.—AdPb
"It aint no." B. O'Meally.—AdM
Its curtains. T. Joans.—AdPb
Jesus was crucified or: It must be deep. C. M. Rodgers.—AdPb
Jitterbugging in the streets. C. C. Hernton.—AdPb
Ju Ju. A. M. Touré.—AdPb
Judeebug's country. J. Johnson.—AdPb
A Juju of my own. L. Bethune.—AdPb
Junglegrave. S. E. Anderson.—AdPb
Keep on pushing. D. Henderson.—AdPb
"Last night somebody called me a darky." N. Guillén.—AbM
The last riot. V. Howard.—JoV

Lead. J. Cortez.—AdPb
Leroy. LeRoi Jones.—AdPb
"Listen children." L. Clifton.—AdM—AdPb
The little black boy. W. Blake.—OpOx
Lullaby. L. Hughes.—HoD
Man I thought you was talking another language that day. V. H. Cruz.—AdB
Martin's blues. M. S. Harper.—AdPb
Memorial wreath. D. Randall.—AdPb
Middle passage. R. Hayden.—AdPb
Migration. C. G. Clemmons.—AdPb
Mister Banjo. Unknown.—AbM
Mr Roosevelt regrets. P. Murray.—AdPb
A moment please. S. Allen.—AdPb
Montgomery. S. Cornish.—AdM—AdPb
Monument in black. V. Howard.—AdM—JoV
Morning light (the dew-drier). E. L. Newsome.—AdPb
"My blackness is the beauty of this land." L. Jeffers.—AdPb
"My brother is homemade." S. Cornish.—AdM
My name is Afrika. K. Kgositsile.—AdPb
My own hallelujahs. Z. Gilbert.—AdPb
My people. L. Hughes.—AdM—HoD
Nation. C. Cobb.—AdPb
The Negro. L. Hughes.—HoD
"Negro dreams." D. Long.—AdPb
A Negro labourer in Liverpool. D. Rubadiri.—AlPa
A Negro love song. P. L. Dunbar.—AbM
The Negro speaks of rivers. L. Hughes.—AdPb—HoD—MoT—PeS
Negro woman. L. Alexander.—AdPb
The new integrationist. D. L. Lee.—AdB
The new math. V. Howard.—JoV
New York. L. S. Senghor.—AlPa
Nikki-Rosa. N. Giovanni.—AdPb
#4. H. D. Long.—AdM—AdPb
Number 5—December.—D. Henderson.—AdB
O black and unknown bards. J. W. Johnson.—AdPb
O Daedalus, fly away home. R. Hayden.—AdPb—HiN
Oh, freedom. Unknown.—AbM
Old black men. G. D. Johnson.—AdPb
Old black men say. J. A. Emanuel.—AdM—AdPb
An old woman remembers. P. A. Brown.—AdPb
On getting a natural. D. Randall.—AdPb
On seeing two brown boys in a Catholic church. F. Horne.—AdPb
One thousand nine-hundred & sixty-eight winters. . . . J. Earley.—AbM—AdM
Othello Jones dresses for dinner. E. Roberson.—AdPb
Our black people. K. Grosvenor.—AdM
Outcast. C. McKay.—AdPb
Poem ("Little brown boy") H. Johnson.—AdPb
Poem ("Look at me 8th") S. Sanchez.—AdPb
Poem (No name No. 2). N. Giovanni.—AdB
A poem for a poet. D. L. Lee.—AdPb
A poem for black hearts. LeRoi Jones.—AdPb
Poem for Flora. N. Giovanni.—AdM—AdPb—NeA
Poll. E. Roberson.—AdPb
Portrait. E. Rodgers.—AdM
Positives: For Sterling Plumpp. D. L. Lee.—AdPb
Prime. L. Hughes.—AdPb
PSI. M. B. Tolson.—AdPb
Query. Ebon (Dooley).—AdPb
The question. V. Howard.—JoV
Reincarnation. M. Jackson.—AdPb
Requiem for a black girl. Y. Ouologuem.—AlPa (sel.)
The return. A. Bontemps.—AdPb
Riding across John Lee's finger. S. Crouch.—AdPb
Riots and rituals. R. W. Thomas.—AdPb
Robert Whitmore. F. M. Davis.—AdPb
Roses and revolutions. D. Randall.—AdPb
Rubin. C. Cooper.—AdPb
Sadie's playhouse. M. Danner.—AdPb
Sam's world. S. Cornish.—AdM
The scarlet woman. F. Johnson.—AdPb
Scenery. T. Joans.—AdPb
Scottsboro, too, is worth its song. C. Cullen.—AdPb
The second sermon on the warpland. G. Brooks.—AdPb
The sermon on the warpland. G. Brooks.—AdPb
Seventh son. E. Roberson.—AdPb
Sing me a new song. J. H. Clarke.—AdPb
"Sitting on the dock." C. Meyer.—JoV
Snapshots of the cotton South. F. M. Davis.—AdPb
Sometimes I go to Camarillo and sit in the lounge. K. C. Lyle.—AdPb
The song of the smoke. W. E. B. DuBois.—AdPb
Songs for the Cisco Kid or singing. K. C. Lyle.—AdPb
Sonnet to Negro soldiers. J. S. Cotter, Jr—AdPb
"Sorrow is the only faithful one." O. Dodson.—AdPb
SOS. LeRoi Jones.—AdM—AdPb
The sound of Afroamerican history chapt I. S. E. Anderson.—AdPb
The sound of Afroamerican history chapt II. S. E. Anderson.—AdPb
Southern road ("Swing dat hammer—hunh") S. A. Brown.—AdPb
The southern road ("There the black river, boundary to hell") D. Randall.—AdPb
A spade is just a spade. W. E. Hawkins.—AdPb
Special bulletin. L. Hughes.—AdPb
Spirits unchained. K. Kgositsile.—AdPb
The still voice of Harlem. C. K. Rivers.—AdPb
Strange legacies. S. A. Brown.—AdPb
Strategies. W. Smith.—AdPb

Blacks—*Continued*
Strong men. S. A. Brown.—AdPb
Summertime and the living. R. Hayden.—AdPb—HiN
The sun came. E. Knight.—AdPb
Sun song. L. Hughes.—AdM—HoD
Sunday morning: Lonely. L. Clifton.—ClS
Taxes. D. L. Lee.—AdB
Telephone conversation. W. Soyinka.—MaFw
Ten years old. N. Giovanni.—AdM
Theme one: The variations. A. Wilson.—AdPb
"Those boys that ran together." L. Clifton.—AdPb
Tired. F. Johnson.—AdPb
To a dark girl. G. B. Bennett.—AdPb
To all sisters. S. Sanchez.—AdPb
To Dinah Washington. E. Knight.—AdPb
To L. J. Perry.—AdPb
To my mother. C. Laye.—AlPa
To Richard Wright. C. K. Rivers.—AdPb
To some millions who survive Joseph E. Mander, Senior. S. E. Wright.—AdPb
To the white fiends. C. McKay.—AdPb
Tony get the boys. D. L. Graham.—AdPb
The true import of present dialogue, Black vs. Negro. N. Giovanni.—AdPb
12 gates to the city. N. Giovanni.—AdPb
Umamina. B. W. Vilakazi.—AlPa (sel.)
Until they have stopped. S. E. Wright.—AdPb
Us. J. Lester.—AdPb
Vive noir. M. Evans.—AdB—AdPb
Wake-up niggers. D. L. Lee.—AdPb
Walk with de Mayor of Harlem. D. Henderson.—AdPb
Washiri (Poet). K. M. Cumbo.—AdB
We can't always follow the white man's way. D. Clarke, Jr.—JoV
We have been believers. M. Walker.—AdPb
We own the night. LeRoi Jones.—AdB—AdPb
We walk the way of the new world. D. L. Lee.—AdPb
". . . We want." LeRoi Jones.—AdB
We wear the mask. P. L. Dunbar.—AdPb
Wednesday night prayer meeting.—Jay Wright.—AdPb
Wednesday noon: Adventure. L. Clifton.—ClS
"We're an African people." From African poems. D. L. Lee.—AdM
"Where is my head going." K. Grosvenor.—AdM
The west ridge is menthol cool. D. L. Graham.—AdPb
What color is black. B. Mahone.—AdM
What's black power. L. Baez.—JoV
"When black people are." A. B. Spellman.—AdPb
When I heard dat white man say. Z. Gilbert.—AdPb
The white house. C. McKay.—AdPb
Will I make it. J. Holland.—JoV
Word poem (perhaps worth considering). N. Giovanni.—AdB—AdPb
You are the brave. R. R. Patterson.—AdPb
You're nothing but a Spanish colored kid. F. Luciano.—AdPb
Youth. L. Hughes.—HoD—JoA-4

Blacksmiths and blacksmithing
The forge. S. Heaney.—CoPi
Riddle. Unknown.—RoIt
"What shoemaker makes shoes without leather." Unknown.—EmN

"The **blacksmith's** boy went out with a rifle." See Legend
The **blacksmith's** serenade. Vachel Lindsay.—CoPt
The **Blackstone** Rangers. Gwendolyn Brooks.—AdPb

Blackwell, Arlene
"Four walls to talk to me."—JoV
Sands junior high school.—JoV
"There's a certain illness within you."—JoV

Blackwoman poems. Don L. Lee.—AdM
Blah-blah. Robert Froman.—FrSp

Blaikley, Howard
From the underworld.—MoG

Blair, Lee
Beware.—JaP
Ghost weather.—JaP
Jamboree.—JaP
The leprechaun.—JaP
The treat.—JaP
What I think.—JaP

Blake, William
Auguries of innocence.—RoIt (sel.)
The book of Thel, sel.
The worm.—MaFw
The chimney sweeper.—OpOx
Cradle song.—JoA-4
The echoing green.—JoA-4—PaF
Happy songs. See The piper
The lamb.—JoA-4—LiLc—OpOx—RoIt
Laughing song.—JoA-4—OpOx—RoIt
The little black boy.—OpOx
London.—MoG
The mental traveller. See The Pickering manuscript
Night.—OpOx
Nurse's song.—JoA-4—OpOx
"O why was I born with a different face."—CoPu
"The only man that e'er I knew."—CoPu
The Pickering manuscript, sel.
The mental traveller.—MoG
The piper.—LiLc—OpOx
Happy songs.—UnGb
The school boy.—MaFw
The shepherd.—RoIt
Sir Joshua Reynolds.—CoPu
Soft snow.—PaF
Spring.—JoA-4—LiLc—PaF—RoIt—UnGb
The tiger.—LiS—RoIt
To autumn.—PaF
The worm. See The book of Thel

"**Blanaid** loves roses." See Blanaid's song

Blanaid's song. Joseph Campbell.—CoPi
"**Blank** faces full of eyes." See Bremerton, January 18, 1969
Blast off. Joanne Oppenheim.—HoP
Bleek, W. H. I.
Giraffe. tr.—AbM
"**Bless** you, bless you, burnie-bee." Mother Goose.—JoA-4
Blessed are they that sow. Avraham Ben Yitzhak, tr. fr. the Hebrew by Robert Mezey.—MeP
"**Blessed** are they that sow and shall not reap." See Blessed are they that sow
The **blessed** damozel. Dante Gabriel Rossetti.—LiS (sel.)
"The **blessed** damozel leaned out." See The blessed damozel
"**Blessed** is the man that walketh not in the counsel of the ungodly." See Psalms—Psalm 1
"**Blessed** is today." Kim Koo, tr. fr. the Korean by Chung Seuk Park and ad. by Virginia Olsen Baron.—BaSs
A **blessing.** James Wright.—MaFw
A **blessing** on the cows. Seumas O'Sullivan.—CoPi
Blessings
A blessing. James Wright.—MaFw
A blessing on the cows. S. O'Sullivan.—CoPi
House blessing. Unknown.—BiI
Night blessing. P. George.—AlW
Blight, John
Cormorants.—MaFw
Blind
The blind boy. C. Cibber.—OpOx
The blind men and the elephant. J. G. Saxe.—CoPt—JoA-4—RoIt
Blind old woman. C. Major.—AdPb
Charles. L. Clark.—MaFw
Haec fabula docet. R. Frost.—LiWw
On his blindness. J. Milton.—MaFw
"The train." Unknown.—AlPa
"You will always find me." Unknown.—ClFc
Blind angel. David Rokeah, tr. fr. the Hebrew by Robert Mezey and Shula Starkman.—MeP
The **blind** boy. Colley Cibber.—OpOx
Blind man's buff. Unknown, tr. fr. the Chinese by I. T. Headland.—JoA-4
The **blind** men and the elephant. John Godfrey Saxe.—CoPt—JoA-4—RoIt
Blind old woman. Clarence Major.—AdPb
"A **blindman** by the name of LaFontaine." See Haec fabula docet
Blizzards
"Eleven horsemen." Shiki.—BeM
"A wintry blizzard." Kyoruko.—BeM
The **bloath.** Shel Silverstein.—SiW
Blocks. See Toys
"**Blood** thudded in my ears. I scuffed." See First confession
"**Blossom** on the plum." See March
Blossom themes. Carl Sandburg.—MaFw—SaT
"The **blossoms** fall like snow flakes." See Butterflies
"**Blow,** blow, thou winter wind." See As you like it
"**Blow** out the candles of your cake." See To K. R. on her sixtieth birthday
"**Blow** out the light, they said, they said." See Temper
Blow up. Robert Froman.—FrSp
"**Blow,** winds, and crack your cheeks, rage, blow." See King Lear
Blue (color)
Cheap blue. C. Sandburg.—SaT
Like it should be. M. C. Livingston.—LiM
November blue. A. Meynell.—PaP
Variation on a sentence. L. Bogan.—RoIt
Blue and red poem. Amir Gilboa, tr. fr. the Hebrew by Robert Mezey and Shula Starkman.—MeP
The **blue** and the gray. Francis Miles Finch.—RoIt
The **blue** gift. David Perkins.—HiN
Blue girls. John Crowe Ransom.—RoIt
Blue horses. Ed Roberson.—AdPb
"**Blue** is the sky." Unknown, tr. fr. the Spanish.—MoBw
Blue jays. See Jays
"A **blue-middied** girl." See City street
"The **blue** mountains are what they are." Kim In-hu, tr. fr. the Korean by Chung Seuk Park and ad. by Virginia Olsen Baron.—BaSs
Blue Ruth, America. Michael S. Harper.—AdPb
Blue Tanganyika. Lebert Bethune.—AdPb
"The **blue** wings." Andrei Karlov, tr. fr. the Russian by Miriam Morton.—MoM
"**Bluebells,** cockle shells." Unknown.—EmN
Blueberries
The secret. R. P. T. Coffin.—PaF
"**Bluebird,** what do you feed on." Carl Sandburg.—SaT
Bluebirds
"Bluebird, what do you feed on." C. Sandburg.—SaT
The last word of a bluebird. R. Frost.—JoA-4—LiLc
Blues (music)
Adrian Henri's talking after Christmas blues. A. Henri.—ToM
Black is a soul. J. White.—AdPb
Blues. H. Mungin.—AdB
Blues and bitterness. L. Bennett, Jr.—AdPb
Blues note. B. Kaufman.—AdPb
The blues today. M. Jackson.—AdB—AdPb
Canto 7. T. Weatherly.—AdPb
Come back blues. M. S. Harper.—AdPb
"D blues." C. C. Hernton.—AdPb
Get up, blues. J. A. Emanuel.—AdB—AdPb
"Go 'way from my window." Unknown.—AbM
Homage to the Empress of the Blues. R. Hayden.—AdPb
"I remember how she sang." R. Penny.—AdPb

Bodecker, N. M.
The armadillo.—BoL
Bennington.—BoL
Booteries and fluteries and flatteries and things.—BoL
The fly in Rye.—BoL
The geese in Greece.—BoL
Getting together.—BoL
Gluk.—BoL
"If I were an elephant."—BoL
"The island of Llince."—BoL
"The island of Lundy."—BoL
"The island of Mull."—BoL
"The island of Murray."—BoL
"The island of Rum."—BoL
"The island of Yarrow."—BoL
"The island of Yorrick."—BoL
"It's raining, said John Twaining." tr.—BoI
J. Prior, Esq.—BoL
John.—BoL
The lark in Sark.—BoL
"Lazy Lucy."—BoL
"Let's marry, said the cherry."—BoL
"Little Jack Sander of Dee." tr.—BoI
"Little Miss Price." tr.—BoI
"Me and I and you." tr.—BoI
Miss Bitter.—BoL
Mr Beecher.—BoL
Mr Docer.—BoL
Mr 'Gator.—BoL
Mr Melter.—BoL
Mr Skinner.—BoL
Mr Slatter.—BoL
Mr Weller.—BoL
"My little dad had five little piggies." tr.—BoI
"On a green, green hill." tr.—BoI
"Pat-a-cake." tr.—BoI
Perfect Arthur.—BoL
The porcupine.—BoL
"Quail." tr.—BoI
"Row, row, row." tr.—BoI
The snail at Yale.—BoL
"Squire McGuire." tr.—BoI
"There once was a king." tr.—BoI
"Three little guinea pigs." tr.—BoI
"Two cats were sitting in a tree." tr.—BoI
Up and down.—BoL
"Who." tr.—BoI
Boden, Frederick
Mining places.—PaP
Body, Human. See also names of parts of body, as Hands
The confession. T. Ingoldsby.—RoIt
Counting small-boned bodies. R. Bly.—MoT
Gentleman to lady. From Quatrains. T. Carmi.—MeP
Gone away. D. Levertov.—PeS
Mrs Snipkin and Mrs Wobblechin. L. E. Richards.—JoA-4—OpOx
Question. M. Swenson.—JoA-4
"**Body** my house." See Question
The **body** politic. Donald Hall.—PeS
Bogan, Louise
Variation on a sentence.—RoIt
Bokusui
"A dry leaf drifting."—BeM
"A horsefly mutters."—BeM
Boland, C. J.
The two travellers.—CoPi
Boland, Eavan
Requiem for a personal friend.—CoPi
"**Bold** Lanty was in love, you see, with lively Rosie Carey." See Lanty Leary
The **bold** unbiddable child. Winifrid M. Letts.—CoPi
Bolio, Antonio Mediz
"The moon and the year." tr.—BiI
Bombers and bombing
Kid stuff. F. Horne.—AbM—AdPb
My spoon was lifted. N. Replansky.—CoPu
Of bombs and boys. R. Corbin.—PeS
Vapor trail reflected in the frog pond. G. Kinnell.—PeS
You know, Joe. R. Durem.—AdB
Boncho
"The ragged phantom."—BeM
"With a whispering."—BeM
Bone, Gavin
A charm against the stitch. tr.—MaFw
Bones
"Here lies old Jones." Unknown.—LiWw
Monument in bone. P. George.—AlW
Perfect. G. Jones.—MaFw
Yardbird's skull. O. Dodson.—AdPb
Bonny George Campbell. Unknown.—RoIt
Bontemps, Arna
A black man talks of reaping.—AdPb
Close your eyes.—AdPb
Dark girl.—PeS
The day-breakers.—AdPb
The return.—AdPb
Southern mansion.—AdPb
A **book.** See "There is no frigate like a book"
A **book.** Myra Cohn Livingston.—LiM
"A **book** can tell how it's going." See A book
The **book** of Thel, sel. William Blake
The worm.—MaFw
Booker T. and W. E. B. Dudley Randall.—AbM
Books. David McCord.—McAa
Books and reading
Aardvark. J. Fields.—AdB—AdM
Abigail. K. Starbird.—NeA
The adventure of Chris. D. McCord.—McAa
After a fire. From Pencil stubs. J. Ciardi.—LiWw
Any author to any friend. Martial.—PlM
At the library. M. Chute.—ChRu
A book. M. C. Livingston.—LiM
Books. D. McCord.—McAa
"Books fall open." D. McCord.—JoA-4
"Books make me feel like." Fourth graders, Springfield elementary school, Pleasant Valley, Pa.—LaM
The bookworms. R. Burns.—CoPu
A classic waits for me. E. B. White.—LiS

Books and reading—*Continued*
The day is done. H. W. Longfellow.—RoIt
Fay folks. Unknown.—JaP
"Go, little booklet, go." B. Nye.—CoPu
"I pity the river." Unknown.—EmN
"If perchance this book should roam." Unknown.—EmN
If you have seen. T. Moore.—LiWw
Introduction ("This book you hold") W. Cole.—CoOr
Introduction ("This skinny poem will introduce") W. Cole.—CoOh
Invitation. S. Silverstein.—SiW
"It aint no." Bob O'Meally.—AdM
The King of Hearts. W. J. Smith.—BrM
The King of Spain. W. J. Smith.—BrM
The land of story-books. R. L. Stevenson.—RoIt—UnGb
Lao-Tsu. From The philosophers. Po Chü-i.—LiWw
Library. L. Lenski.—LeC
A little book of little beasts. M. A. Hoberman.—HoLb
"My teddy stands in the nook." Olga.—MoM
Ogden Nash gets all the cash. D. McCord.—PlM
On first looking into Chapman's Homer. J. Keats.—PlM
Picture people. M. C. Livingston.—JoA-4
Public library. R. Froman.—FrSp
Reading. M. Chute.—ChRu
"Reading Yeats I do not think." L. Ferlinghetti.—PlM
"The rose is red, the grass is green." Mother Goose.—AlC
Sam at the library. C. C. Hole.—BrM
Shut not your doors. W. Whitman.—PlM
Summer doings. W. Cole.—LaM
Temper. R. Fyleman.—OpOx
"There is no frigate like a book." E. Dickinson
A book.—RoIt
"This book is one thing." Unknown.—EmN
"Three wishes." K. Kuskin.—KuN
To a reviewer who admired my book. From Pencil stubs. J. Ciardi.—LiWw
To the author of Hesperides and Noble Numbers. M. Van Doren.—PlM
The visit of the professor of aesthetics. From Far from Africa: Four poems. M. Danner.—AdPb
The way that it's going. M. C. Livingston.—LiM
When I would travel. D. McCord.—McFm
Why. P. Irving.—AlW
"Why don't I send my books to you." Martial.—PlM
Word bird. E. Merriam.—MeF
A word or two on Levinia. D. McCord.—McAa
"**Books** collide." See To W. H. Auden on his fiftieth birthday
"**Books** fall open." David McCord.—JoA-4
"**Books** make me feel like." Fourth graders, Springfield elementary school, Pleasant Valley, Pa.—LaM
The **bookworms.** Robert Burns.—CoPu
"The **boom** above my knees lifts, and the boat." See Sailing to an island.
"The **boomerang** and kangaroo." See Up from down under
Boomerangs
Image. H. Dumas.—AdB
Booteries and fluteries and flatteries and things. N. M. Bodecker.—BoL
Booth, Philip
Cider.—HaWr
Ego.—PeS
"If it comes."—HiN
The round.—HiN
The total calm.—HaWr
Was a man.—HiN
Boots and shoes. See also Shoemakers
Choosing shoes. F. Wolfe.—BrM
"Cinderella, dressed in blue." Unknown.—EmN
An event. M. Chute.—ChRu
Fairy shoes. A. Wynne.—JaP
"I'm scratched and scuffed." K. Kuskin.—KuA
"It walks east, west, north, and south." Unknown.—EmN
The man who had shoes. J. Ciardi.—CiFs
"Me and I and you." Unknown.—BoI
The moccasins of an old man. R. Carden.—AlW
"Old lady, old lady." Unknown.—EmN
The old woman who lived in a shoe. J. Johnson.—ThF
Opportunity. M. Chute.—ChRu
Shoeshine boy. L. Lenski.—LeC
"There was an old man from Peru." Unknown.—RoIt
"There was an old woman who lived in a shoe." Mother Goose.—AlC—JoA-4
"Two brothers we are." Unknown.—EmN
Unusual shoelaces. X. J. Kennedy.—KeO
"What is the opposite of a *shoe.*" R. Wilbur.—WiO
"What is the opposite of *hat.*" R. Wilbur.—WiO
"What will I wear on my feet." Unknown.—EmN
Borders. Sveta Mosova, tr. fr. the Russian by Miriam Morton.—MoM
Boredom
Ennui. L. Hughes.—HoD
The Land of Happy. S. Silverstein.—SiW
Story of Reginald. H. Phillips.—CoOr
Tartuffe. Molière.—LiWw (sel.)
To the reader. C. Baudelaire.—MoG
"When I heard the learned astronomer." W. Whitman.—RoIt
Borges, Jorge Luis
To a Saxon poet.—BlM
"**Born** of the sorrowful heart." See For Paul Laurence Dunbar

Born without a star. Abraham ibn Ezra, tr. fr. the Hebrew by Meyer Waxman.—MeP

Borya

"I saw an apple."—MoM

Boston harbor

Islands in Boston harbor. D. McCord.—McFm

Boston nursery rhymes, sels. Joseph Cook.—LiS

Rhyme for a chemical baby

Rhyme for a geological baby

Rhyme for astronomical baby

Rhyme for botanical baby

Botany

Rhyme for botanical baby. From Boston nursery rhymes. J. Cook.—LiS

"A **bottle** of pop, big banana." Unknown.—MoBw

Bottled: New York. Helene Johnson.—AdPb

Bottles

"Cinderella, dressed in silk." Unknown.—EmN

"Johnny over the ocean." Unknown.—EmN

Song of the pop-bottlers. M. Bishop.—BrM

"The **boughs** do shake and the bells do ring." Mother Goose.—JoA-4

Bounce ball rhymes. See Ball bouncing rhymes

"**Bounce** buckram, velvet's dear." Mother Goose.—AlC

"**Bouncie,** bouncie, ballie." Unknown.—EmN

Bouncing song. Dennis Lee.—LeA

"**Bow** down my soul in worship very low." See St Isaac's church, Petrograd

Bow harp. Tchicaya U Tam'si, tr. fr. the French by Gerald Moore.—AlPa

"**Bow,** wow, wow." Mother Goose.—AlC—JoA-4—TrG

Bowen, Lord (Edward Ernest)

The rain it raineth.—CoPu—LiWw

The rain.—RoIt

Bowles, Caroline Anne

Lady-bird.—UnGb

Bowles, W. L.

Avenue in Savernake forest.—PaP

Bowls

"You are like an old wooden bowl." Unknown.—LeIb

Bowman, Isa (about)

"Is all our life, then, but a dream." L. Carroll.—LiPc

Bownas, Geoffrey and Thwaite, Anthony

"Against the broad sky." trs.—MaFw

"The chicken wants." trs.—MaFw

"Disturbed, the cat." trs.—MaFw

Folk song from Fukushima. trs.—MaFw

"A heavy cart rumbles." trs.—MaFw

"In the old man's eyes." trs.—MaFw

"I've seen everything." trs.—MaFw

"Judging from the pictures." trs.—MaFw

Late summer. trs.—MaFw

Looking at the moon on putting out from the shore at Nagato. trs.—MaFw

"The noisy cricket." trs.—MaFw

"Now the man has a child." trs.—MaFw

"Oh, do not swat the fly." trs.—HaW

"Stop, don't swat the fly." trs.—MaFw

"On a bare branch." trs.—MaFw

"On far hills." trs.—MaFw

Poems of solitary delights. trs.—MaFw

Rain on Castle island. trs.—MaFw

"Red sky in the morning." trs.—MaFw

"Scampering over saucers." trs.—MaFw

"Sheltering from the rain." trs.—MaFw

Silent, but. . . . trs.—MaFw

"The snake fled." trs.—MaFw

"Snow melting." trs.—MaFw

"Then settle, frost." trs.—MaFw

"The wind blows grey." trs.—MaFw

"Winter withering." trs.—MaFw

"With his apology." trs.—MaFw

Bowra, C. M.

All lives, all dances and all is loud. tr.—AbM

Bows and arrows

"He constantly bends it, he constantly sends it straight." Unknown.—LeIb

Image. H. Dumas.—AdB

"Through the woods." Unknown.—EmN

"A **box** of biscuits." Unknown.—EmN

Boxes

Boxes. A. Fisher.—FiM

Boxes and bags. C. Sandburg.—SaT

"Cinderella, dressed in rose." Unknown.—EmN

Little boxes. M. Reynolds.—PeS

Two boxes. S. Silverstein.—SiW

Boxes. Aileen Fisher.—FiM

Boxes and bags. Carl Sandburg.—SaT

Boxing

The boxing match. From Aeneid. Virgil.—FlH

My Lord, what a morning. W. Cuney.—AbM

On Apis the prizefighter. Lucilius.—LiWw

On Hurricane Jackson. A. Dugan.—HiN

The **boxing** match. See Aeneid

The **boy** and the geese. Padraic Fiacc.—CoPi

The **boy** and the parrot. John Hookham Frere.—OpOx

The **boy** and the snake. Charles and Mary Lamb.—OpOx

Boy at the window. Richard Wilbur.—PeS

"The **boy** climbed up into the tree." See The rescue

Boy down the hall. Lois Lenski.—LeC

"**Boy** heart of Johnny Jones, aching today." See Buffalo Bill

Boy in the Roman zoo. Archibald MacLeish.—HiN

"A **boy** on a bike." See Accident

"The **boy** sat listening closely." See Borders

The **boy** serving at table. John Lydgate.—OpOx

"The **boy** stood on the burning deck (eating peanuts by the peck)." Unknown.—CoOh—MoBw

"The **boy** stood on the burning deck (his feet were full of blisters)." Unknown.—MoBw

"The **boy** stood on the railroad track." Unknown.—MoBw

"The **boy** that is good." See The description of a good boy
"The **boy** wasn't ready for a hat." See The trouble was simply that
The **boy** who laughed at Santa Claus. Ogden Nash.—CoPt
Boyhood. See Boys and boyhood
Boys and boyhood. See also Babies; Childhood recollections; Children and childhood
Boy at the window. R. Wilbur.—PeS
Boy in the Roman zoo. A. MacLeish.—HiN
Boys' names. E. Farjeon.—JoA-4
Buffalo Bill. C. Sandburg.—SaT
The cave. G. W. Dresbach.—PeS
The companion. Y. Yevtushenko.—MaFw
Farm child. R. S. Thomas.—CoPu—MaFw
February. L. Clifton.—ClE
Invisible boy. S. Silverstein.—SiW
Is this someone you know. J. Ciardi.—UnGb
"Knighted by the sun's." A. Atwood.—AtM
Legend. Judith Wright.—MaFw
The long-haired boy. S. Silverstein.—SiW
Midnight on the Great Western. T. Hardy.—PlP
Monday morning: Good morning. L. Clifton.—ClS
The new little boy. H. Behn.—LiLc
Of bombs and boys. R. Corbin.—PeS
"Those boys that ran together." L. Clifton.—AdPb
What are little boys made of . . . (love and care). E. Laron.—ThF
"What are little boys made of, made of." Mother Goose.—AlC—EmN—JoA-4
"When I was a little boy." Unknown.—TrG
"Where have all the flowers gone." P. Seeger.—PeS
"**Boys** and girls come out to play." Mother Goose.—JoA-4
"**Boys** are humbugs." Unknown.—MoBw
"**Boys** are mean." Unknown.—MoBw
A **boy**'s head. Miroslav Holub, tr. fr. the Czech by Ian Milner.—MaFw
Boys' names. Eleanor Farjeon.—JoA-4
A **boy**'s song. James Hogg.—OpOx
"**Boys** with lots." See December 25: Christmas morning
Bradstreet, Anne
The author to her book.—ThI
Before the birth of one of her children.—ThI
Contemplations.—ThI (sel.)
Epitaph.—ThI
An epitaph on my dear and ever honoured mother Mrs Dorothy Dudley.—ThI
The four seasons of the year, sel.
Spring.—ThI
In memory of my dear grandchild Anne Bradstreet.—ThI
In memory of my dear grandchild Elizabeth Bradstreet.—ThI
In reference to her children, 23 June, 1656.—ThI
A letter to her husband, absent upon publick employment.—ThI
Meditations divine and morall.—ThI (sel.)
Spring. See The four seasons of the year
To my dear and loving husband.—ThI
Upon the burning of our house, July 10th, 1666.—ThI
Brady, John (about)
Brady's bend. M. Keller.—CoPt
Brady's bend. Martha Keller.—CoPt
Brahmins
Cossimbazar. H. S. Leigh.—LiWw
Brains
The dinosaur. B. L. Taylor.—LiWw
"Doctor Emmanuel Harrison-Hyde." J. Reeves.—AlC
Doctor Emmanuel.—CoPu
"John Wesley Gaines." Unknown.—CoPu
Brainstorm. Howard Nemerov.—HiN
Braithwaite, William Stanley
Golden moonrise.—AdPb
In a grave-yard.—AdPb
To ——. —AdPb
"**Bramble,** like barbed wire." See The thrush's nest
The **branch.** Elizabeth Madox Roberts.—JoA-4
The **brass** serpent. T. Carmi, tr. fr. the Hebrew by Dom Moraes.—MeP (sel.)
Brathwaite (or Braithwaite), Edward
Chad.—ToM
Leopard.—AbM
Mmenson.—ToM
Timbuctu.—ToM
The twist.—AbM
"**Brave** Buffalo." Unknown, tr. fr. the Teton Sioux by Frances Densmore.—JoT
"**Brave** news is come to town." Mother Goose.—AlC
"**Brave** weathercock, I see thou'lt set thy nose." See Upon the weathercock
Bravery. See Courage
Brawne, Fanny (about)
Lines supposed to have been addressed to Fanny Brawne. J. Keats.—CoPu
Bread
"Cinderella, dressed in red." Unknown.—EmN
"Jack, Jack, the bread's a-burning." Mother Goose.—AlC
Ripeness. R. Whitman.—MoT
"**Bread** and butter." Unknown.—MoBw
"**Bread** and milk for breakfast." See Winter
The **bread-knife** ballad. Robert Service.—CoOr
Breakfast
At breakfast. M. Swenson.—PeS
Bobby Boaster and his toaster. X. J. Kennedy.—KeO
Breakfast. D. McCord.—McFm
The king's breakfast. A. A. Milne.—OpOx
Morning. M. Chute.—ChRu
Sit up when you sit down. J. Ciardi.—BrM
To Thomas Moore. Lord Byron.—PlM—RoIt
Winter. C. G. Rossetti.—RoIt
Breakfast. David McCord.—McFm
"**Breasts** small as shells from the sea." See Quatrains—Gentleman to lady

Breath and breathing
Beseeching the breath. Unknown.—BiI
Cold morning. F. Holman.—HoI
My breath became. Unknown.—BiI
"**Breathe** on him." Unknown, tr. fr. the Pawnee by Alice Fletcher.—BiI
"**Breathes** there a bard who isn't moved." See On being chosen poet of Vermont
"**Breathes** there the man with soul so dead." See The lay of the last minstrel—Patriotism
The **breathing.** Denise Levertov.—HaWr
Breek, Lily
Thank you.—MoM
"A **breeze** stirs at dawn." Asayasu, tr. fr. the Japanese by Harry Behn.—BeM
Bremerton, January 18, 1969. Agnes T. Pratt.—AlW
Brennan, Eileen
One kingfisher and one yellow rose.—CoPi
Brew, Kwesi
Ancestral faces.—AlPa
Dry season.—AlPa
The mesh.—AlPa
Brian Boy Magee. Ethna Carbery.—CoPi
"**Bricks** stacked up." See Castles
Bridal songs. See Brides and bridegrooms
Brides and bridegrooms
"Bless you, bless you, burnie-bee." Mother Goose.—JoA-4
The erl-king's daughter. J. G. Herder.—CoPt
"I saw three ships come sailing by." Mother Goose.—JoA-4
A lady comes to an inn. E. J. Coatsworth.—CoPt
"Let's marry, said the cherry." N. M. Bodecker.—BoL
My newest bride. Y. S. Chemba.—AlPa
The streets of Laredo. L. MacNeice.—ToM
Tailor. E. Farjeon.—OpOx
"The **bridge** says: Come across, try me; how good I am." See Potomac town in February
Bridges, Robert
First spring morning.—JoA-4
The idle flowers.—JoA-4
London snow.—PaF
North wind in October.—PaF
Screaming tarn.—CoPt
"Spring goeth all in white." JoA-4—PaF
Bridges, Robert (about)
To R. B. G. M. Hopkins.—PlM
Bridges
"As I was going o'er London bridge." Unknown.—TrG
The bridges. J. N. A. Rimbaud.—MaFw
Coca cola sunset. F. Holman.—HoI
First Monday Scottsboro Alabama. T. Weatherly.—AdPb
Horatius at the bridge. From Lays of ancient Rome. T. B. Macaulay.—RoIt
"London Bridge is broken down." Mother Goose.—JoA-4
"On the bridge of Avignon." Mother Goose.—TucMg
The toll taker. P. Hubbell.—HoCs
"Tommy o'Lin, and his wife, and wife's mother." Mother Goose.—MiMg
The troll bridge. L. Moore.—MoSm
"When a shadow appeared on the water." Unknown.—BaSs
The **bridges.** Jean-Nicolas-Arthur Rimbaud, tr. fr. the French by Oliver Bernard.—MaFw
"A **brief** goodbye." See Goodbye and run
Brief lines in not so brief. Ogden Nash.—PlM
Brigands. See Crime and criminals
"**Bright.**" See Watermaid
"**Bright** drips the morning from its trophied nets." See Sonnet of fishes
"The **bright** light of the stars is dimmed." See Standing at the foot of the steps at night
"**Bright** was the summer's noon when quickening steps." See The prelude
"**Bring** back some bric-a-brac." Unknown.—EmN
Bring home some ice, not some mice." Unknown.—EmN
"**Bring** me all of your dreams." See The dream keeper
"**Bring** me now the bright flower." See Nightsong
"**Bring** on the clowns." Jack Prelutsky.—PrC
"**Bring** out your hair ornaments." Unknown, fr. the Iglulik Eskimo.—LeIb
Bring the day, sel. Theodore Roethke
"O small bud wakening."—JoA-4
"**Bring** your shovel." See Cleaning up the block
Bringing him up. Lord Dunsany.—CoPu—LiWw
Brinton, D. G.
Hymn. tr.—BiI
Over the water. tr.—BiI
Prophecy. tr.—BiI
Song. tr.—BiI
Who are they. tr.—BiI
Bristol, England
In the dim city. A. Salmon.—PaP
"A **Briton** who swore at his king." David Ross.—RoIt
"The **broad** beach." See Afternoon: Amagansett beach
"**Broad** met Stout." See Too polite
"The **broad** woods." Unknown, tr. fr. the Iroquois.—JoT
Brock, Edwin
Evolution.—ToM
5 ways to kill a man.—MoT
Song of the Battery hen.—ToM
Brody, Sylvia
"Sea way."—HoC—HoP
A **broken** gull. John Moore.—HiN
Broken heart, broken machine. Richard E. Grant.—AdPb
"The **broken** pillar of the wings jags from the clotted shoulder." See Hurt hawks
Broken sky. Carl Sandburg.—SaT
Brontë, Emily
Fall, leaves, fall.—PaF

Brontë, Emily—*Continued*
How still, how happy.—PaF
"How still, how happy! Those are words.—PaP
"How still, how happy! Those are words." See How still, how happy
The night-wind.—PaF
"There is a spot, 'mid barren hills."—PaP
Brontë, Emily (about)
Haworth in May. W. R. Childe.—PaP
"There is a spot, 'mid barren hills." E. Brontë.—PaP
Bronzeville man with a belt in the back. Gwendolyn Brooks.—AdPb
The **brook.** Linda Alaverdoshvili, tr. fr. the Russian by Miriam Morton.—MoM
Brooke, L. Leslie
Johnny Crow's garden.—JoA-4
Brooke, Rupert
"I only know that you may lie." See The old vicarage, Grantchester
The old vicarage, Grantchester, sel.
"I only know that you may lie."—PaP
Brooklyn, New York
Number 7. L. Ferlinghetti.—PeS
Brooks, Gwendolyn
The ballad of Chocolate Mabbie.—PeS
The ballad of the light-eyed little girl.—PeS
The bean eaters.—AdPb
The Blackstone Rangers.—AdPb
Bronzeville man with a belt in the back.—AdPb
The Chicago *Defender* sends a man to Little Rock.—AdPb
The crazy woman.—AbM
Cynthia in the snow.—LiLc
The egg boiler.—AdPb
The empty woman.—PeS
Hunchback girl: She thinks of heaven.—PeS
Keziah.—UnGb
The last quatrain of the ballad of Emmett Till.—AdPb
Malcolm X.—AbM—AdPb
Martin Luther King, Jr.—AdB—AdPb
Medgar Evers.—AdPb
The old-marrieds.—AdPb
Otto.—HoS
Paul Robeson.—AdPb
Riot.—AdPb
Rudolph is tired of the city.—UnGb
The second sermon on the warpland.—AdPb
The sermon on the warpland.—AdPb
A song in the front yard.—AdPb
The sonnet-ballad.—PeS
Strong men, riding horses.—AdPb
"To be in love."—PeS
Two dedications.—AdPb (sel.)
Vern.—HoCs
We real cool.—AdM—AdPb
Brooks, Gwendolyn (about)
When I heard dat white man say. Z. Gilbert.—AdPb
Brooks, Phillips
"O little town of Bethlehem."—JoA-4—LaS
Brooks
The branch. E. M. Roberts.—JoA-4
The brook. L. Alaverdoshvili.—MoM
The resolve. D. Levertov.—HaWr
Thank you. L. Breek.—MoM
"The **broom,** the shovel, the poker and the tongs." Edward Lear.—JoA-4
Brooms
"My world is an enormous room." K. Kuskin.—KuA
On guard. A. Fisher.—FiM
Witch's broom notes. D. McCord.—McAa
"**Brother,** come." See And what shall you say
"**Brother** John, Brother John." Mother Goose, tr. fr. the French.—TucMg
"**Brother** to the firefly." See Morning light (the dew drier)
Brotherhood
Outwitted. E. Markham.—CoPu
Sisters and brothers. B. Hart.—ThF
Three old brothers. F. O'Connor.—CoPi
To Malcom X. J. Thompson.—AdM
When I peruse the conquer'd fame. W. Whitman.—CoPu
Brothers. See also Brothers and sisters
Ben. T. Wolfe.—HiN
"Bishop Cody's last request." T. Paxton.—MoG
Brothers. L. Hughes.—HoD
A dream of hanging. P. Beer.—ToM
"Gloria, my little sister." R. Hoban.—HoE
My brother Bert. T. Hughes.—HuMf
"My brother is homemade." S. Cornish.—AdM
My little brother. M. Chute.—ChRu
The pain and the great one. J. Blume.—ThF
Poem for my brother Kenneth. O. Dodson.—AdPb
Sisters and brothers. B. Hart.—ThF
"These are." J. Vitale.—HoC
The twins. H. S. Leigh.—BrM—RoIt
"You are like a friend of mine." Unknown.—ClFc
Brothers. Langston Hughes.—HoD
Brothers and sisters
"Bouncie, bouncie, ballie." Unknown.—EmN
"Brothers and sisters have I none." Unknown.—EmN
Choosing a name. C. and M. Lamb.—OpOx
Death of a sister. Unknown.—BiI
For sale. S. Silverstein.—CoOr—SiW
"Gloria, my little sister." R. Hoban.—HoE
"Mister Lister sassed his sister." C. Watson.—WaF
My sister Jane. T. Hughes.—HuMf—MaFw
The pain and the great one. J. Blume.—ThF
The riddling knight. Unknown.—JoA-4—RoIt
Sisters and brothers. B. Hart.—ThF
The sitter and the butter and the better batter fritter. D. Lee.—LeA
Triolet against sisters. P. McGinley.—LiWw
"Trip upon trenchers, and dance upon dishes." Mother Goose.—AlC

We are seven. W. Wordsworth.—LiS—OpOx—RoIt
"**Brothers** and sisters have I none." Unknown.—EmN
Brough, Robert Barnabas
My Lord Tomnoddy.—CoPu
Brown, John (about)
Narrative. R. Atkins.—AdPb
October 16: The raid. L. Hughes.—AdB—AdPb
Brown, Palmer
"The spangled pandemonium."—CoOr
Brown, Pete
Not again.—CoPu
Brown, Sterling A.
After winter.—AdPb
Foreclosure.—AdPb
Old Lem.—AdPb
An old woman remembers.—AdPb
Remembering Nat Turner.—AdPb
Sister Lou.—AdPb
Southern road.—AdPb
Strange legacies.—AdPb
Strong men.—AdPb
Brown, Susan
The house of the goblin.—HoH
Brown, Thomas (or Tom)
"I do not love thee, Doctor Fell." tr.—MiMg—TrG
"**Brown** and furry." Christina Georgina Rossetti.—RoIt
Caterpillar.—OpOx
The caterpillar.—JoA-4—UnGb
Brown boy to brown girl. Countee Cullen.—AdPb
Brown gold. Carl Sandburg.—SaT
"**Brown** I am and much admired." Unknown.—EmN
"**Brown** leaf." See Glides
"**Brown** lived at such a lofty farm." See Brown's descent or The willy-nilly slide
"A **brown** old man with a green thumb." See He was
"The **brown** owl sits in the ivy bush." See The great brown owl
"**Brown** owls come here in the blue evening." Unknown, tr. fr. the Papago.—ClFc
Brown penny. William Butler Yeats.—CoPi
Brown river, smile. Jean Toomer.—AdPb
Browne, Jane Euphemia (Aunt Effie)
The great brown owl.—OpOx
Little raindrops.—OpOx
Pleasant changes.—OpOx
The rooks.—OpOx
Browne, Michael Dennis
Song for Joey.—CoOr
"A **brownie** child." See Fay folks
Brownies. See Fairies
"The **brownies** are a happy folk." See The brownies' year
"**Brownies** on the hillside." See Where brownies are
The **brownies**' year. Unknown.—JaP
Browning, Elizabeth Barrett
The little cares.—RoIt
Browning, Robert
The bishop orders his tomb at Saint Praxed's church.—MoG
Home thoughts from abroad.—JoA-4—RoIt
How they brought the good news from Ghent to Aix.—LiS
The lost leader.—PlM
Memorabilia.—PlM
The Pied Piper of Hamelin.—OpOx
Pippa passes, sels.
Pippa's song.—LiLc—MoG—RoIt
Song ("The year's at the spring")—MoG
Pippa's song. See Pippa passes
Song ("The year's at the spring"). See Pippa passes
Brownjohn, Alan
The rabbit.—ToM
Brown's descent or The willy-nilly slide. Robert Frost.—CoPt
"**Bruadar** and Smith and Glinn." Unknown, tr. fr. the Irish by Douglas Hyde.—CoPi
Bruchac, Joseph
The drum-maker.—MoT
Brutus, Dennis
Nightsong city.—AlPa
Poem.—AlPa (sel.)
"**Bryan** O'Lin had no breeches to wear." Mother Goose.—TrG—TucMgl
Bryant, F. J., Jr
Cathexis.—AdPb
Bryant, George S.
How Bill went East.—CoPt
Bryant, Juanita
Black people.—JoV
My life.—JoV
"No friends nor enemies."—JoV
Bryant, Veronica
"I am waiting to hear from the president, to ask."—JoV
Bryant, William Cullen
To a waterfowl.—RoIt
To the fringed gentian.—PaF
Bubbles. Carl Sandburg.—SaT
"**Buck** horn." See Weeds: A hex
The **buck** in the snow. Edna St Vincent Millay.—AdP—RoIt
Buchanan, Robert
The green gnome.—CoPt
Buckingham palace
Buckingham palace. A. A. Milne.—OpOx
Malice at Buckingham palace. S. Milligan.—CoOh
Buckingham palace. A. A. Milne.—OpOx
Buddha
"An icicle hangs." Issa.—HaW
"Watching a petal." Kubutsu.—BeM
"The **buds** on the trees at this time of the year." See The beginning of spring
Buffalo. Henry Dumas.—AdPb
Buffalo Bill. Carl Sandburg.—SaT
"**Buffalo** Bill's." E. E. Cummings.—MoG
Buffalo dusk. Carl Sandburg.—AdP—SaT

Buffaloes
"Brave Buffalo." Unknown.—JoT
Buffalo. H. Dumas.—AdPb
Buffalo dusk. C. Sandburg.—AdP—SaT
Efon (Buffalo). Unknown.—AdPa
The flower-fed buffaloes. V. Lindsay.—JoA-4
Monument in bone. P. George.—AlW
"What is life." Unknown.—ClFc
"The **buffaloes** are gone." See Buffalo dusk
"Bug." Karla Kuskin.—KuN
"A **bug** sat in a silver flower." Karla Kuskin.—KuN
Bug spots. Carl Sandburg.—SaT
Bugakova, Natasha
To Leningrad.—MoM
"Buggity." Karla Kuskin.—KuN
Bugle song. See The princess
Bugles
Bugle song. From The princess. A. Tennyson.—RoIt
Bugs. See Insects
"Bugs never speak." Karla Kuskin.—KuN
Build-on rhymes
"Can you make a cambric shirt." Mother Goose.—JoA-4
"Children, go where I send thee." Unknown.—LaS
"A frog he would a-wooing go." Mother Goose.—JoA-4
"I went downtown to see Mrs Brown." Unknown.—EmN
"If all the seas were one sea." Mother Goose.—JoA-4
"London Bridge is broken down." Mother Goose.—JoA-4
"A man of words and not of deeds." Mother Goose.—AlC
Pentagonia. G. E. Bates.—LiS
"There is a hill (And on that hill)." Unknown.—EmN
"There is a mill with seven corners." Unknown.—EmN
"There was a crooked man." Mother Goose.—AlC—BlM
"There was a crooked man, and he went a crooked mile."—JoA-4
"There was a monkey climb'd up a tree." Mother Goose.—AlC
"There were three jovial Welshmen." Mother Goose.—AlC—JoA-4
"This is the house that Jack built." Mother Goose.—JoA-4
The house that Jack built.—LiS
"The twelve days of Christmas." Mother Goose.—JoA-4
"Who killed Cock Robin." Mother Goose.—JoA-4
Builders and building. See also Construction; Work; also types of builders, as Carpenters
Again. C. Sandburg.—SaT
The builders. S. H. Hay.—LiWw
Buildings. M. C. Livingston.—JoA-4
The ceiling. T. Roethke.—LiLc
Chant of the awakening bulldozers. P. Hubbell.—HoP
The concrete mixer. T. Langley.—HoCs
The deacon's masterpiece; or, The wonderful one-hoss shay. O. W. Holmes.—RoIt
Homemade boats. S. Silverstein.—SiW
Little girl. Unknown.—JoA-4
Making a home. M. Chute.—ChRu
On Sir John Vanbrugh, architect. A. Evans.—LiWw
Recycled. L. Moore.—MoSp
Roofer. R. Froman.—FrSp
Solid. R. Froman.—FrSp
A time for building. M. C. Livingston.—HoCs
Two dedications. G. Brooks.—AdPb (sel.)
The **builders.** Sara Henderson Hay.—LiWw
Buildings. Myra Cohn Livingston.—JoA-4
"Buildings are a great surprise." See Buildings
"The **buildings** are tall." See In the city
Bukhteyeva, Natasha
My gift.—MoM
A **bulb.** Richard Kendall Munkittrick.—CoPu
Bulbs
A bulb. R. K. Munkittrick.—CoPu
Bulldozers
Chant of the awakening bulldozers. P. Hubbell.—HoP
Bullfrog. Ted Hughes.—MoT
Bullmer, Jerce
That head.—CoOr
Bullock. See Ch'ên and Bullock
Bullokar, William
To his child.—OpOx
"The **bull's** in the barn threshing the corn." Mother Goose.—TucMgl
Bumi. LeRoi Jones.—AdPb
A **bummer.** Michael Casey.—MoT
Bump on your thumb. Dennis Lee.—LeA
"Bums, on waking." James Dickey.—MoT
Bunches of grapes. Walter De La Mare.—LiLc—OpOx
"Bunches of grapes, says Timothy." See Bunches of grapes
"A **bundle** is a funny thing." See Bundles
Bundles. John Farrar.—HoS
Bunner, Henry Cuyler
Grandfather Watt's private Fourth.—CoPt
One, two, three.—RoIt
Bunthorne's song. See Patience
Bunyan, John
Of the boy and butterfly.—OpOx
Of the child with the bird on the bush.—OpOx
Upon a snail.—OpOx
Upon the horse and his rider.—OpOx
Upon the swallow.—OpOx
Upon the weathercock.—OpOx
Bunyan, Paul (about)
Paul Bunyan. S. Silverstein.—SiW
Bunzel, Ruth
Beseeching the breath. tr.—BiI
How the days will be. tr.—BiI
Offering. tr.—BiI
Presenting an infant to the sun. tr.—BiI

"The **buoy** clangs offshore, indolently." See The cry
Burdette, Robert J.
My first cigar.—CoPt
Sisyphus.—CoPt
Burgess, Gelett
Glue.—CoOh
My house.—BrM
"Remarkable truly, is art."—CoOr
The roof.—CoOr
Burial. Robert Francis.—HiN
The **burial** of the linnet. Juliana Horatia Ewing.—OpOx
Burials. See Funerals
"**Burly,** dozing humble-bee." See The humble-bee
Burning, sel. Gary Snyder
John Muir on Mt Ritter.—MaFw
The **burning** babe. Robert Southwell.—MaFw
The **burning** of the leaves. Laurence Binyon.—PaF
Burns, Robert
Afton water.—RoIt
The bookworms.—CoPu
Comin' thro' the rye.—LiS
Epigram addressed to an artist.—CoPu
John Anderson, my jo.—RoIt
On Andrew Turner.—CoPu
Wee Willie Gray.—OpOx
Burr, Gray
"Robin Hood."—HiN
"**Bury** her deep, down deep." See Cat's funeral
"**Bury** me on a Sunday." See Farmer Dunman's funeral
"**Bury** this old Illinois farmer with respect." See Illinois farmer
Bus noises. Melanie Ray.—HoP
Bus stop. Leland B. Jacobs.—HoP
"**Bus** stop at the corner." See Let's ride the bus
"The **bus** stop is a special place." See Bus stop
Buses. See Busses
"A **bushel** of wheat (a bushel of clover)." Unknown.—EmN
"A **bushel** of wheat (a bushel of corn)." Unknown.—EmN
"A **bushel** of wheat (a bushel of cotton)." Unknown.—EmN
"A **bushel** of wheat (a bushel of hay)." Unknown.—EmN
"A **bushel** of wheat (a bushel of rye)." Unknown.—EmN
"A **bushel** of wheat (and a bottle of rum)." Unknown.—EmN
The **bushrangers.** Edward Harrington.—CoPt
"**Bushy** forelock." See The young Cossack
Buson
"Clouds of morning mist."—BeM
"Deep in a windless."—BeM
"Moon moves down the sky."—BeM
"Now that night is gone."—BeM
"Scampering over saucers."—MaFw
"Slanting, windy rain. . . . "—BeM
"Tides of a spring sea."—BeM
"White and wise and old."—BeM
"The winter storm."—AtM
Busses
Bus noises. M. Ray.—HoP
Bus stop. L. B. Jacobs.—HoP
Good green bus. R. Field.—HoP (sel.)
Let's ride the bus. L. Lenski.—LeC
People on the bus. L. Lenski.—LeC
Signs. L. B. Hopkins.—HoP
Superstink. R. Froman.—FrSp
"The wheels of the bus go round and round." Unknown.—HoP
"**Busy,** curious, thirsty fly." See On a fly drinking from his cup
"**Busy** in study be thou, child." See Demeanour
But he was cool. Don L. Lee.—AdPb
"**But** I must gather knots of flowers." See The May queen
"**But** in the crowding darkness not a word did they say." See The old-marrieds
"**But** instead of looking south in the direction in which he was going he looked to the north." See Aqalàni
"**But** please walk softly as you do." See Enter this deserted house
But then. Ben King.—CoPt
"**But** this little morsel of morsels here." See A child's day—This little morsel
"**But** you, monkey face." Sappho, tr. fr. the Greek by Mary Barnard.—ThI
Butchers
"Rub-a-dub dub." Mother Goose.—JoA-4
Butler, Hazel Parker
I cannot forget you. tr.—BiI
Butter
"Betty Botts bought some butter." Unknown.—EmN—JoA-4
"Betty bought a bit of butter to put into her batter." Unknown.—EmN
"Bitty Batter bought some butter." Unknown.—EmN
"Come, butter, come." Unknown.—EmN
The pat of butter.—T. Hardy.—PlP
"**Butter** is butter." Unknown.—MoBw
"The **buttercup** in the meadow." See The treat
Buttercups
"Buttercups and daisies." M. Howitt.—OpOx
The treat. L. Blair.—JaP
"**Buttercups** and daisies." Mary Howitt.—OpOx
"The **buttercups** in May." See Things to remember
Butterflies
"Above the tree." F. Holman.—HoI
"Brown and furry." C. G. Rossetti.—RoIt
Caterpillar.—OpOx
The caterpillar.—JoA-4—UnGb
Butterflies. Chu Miao Tuan.—MaFw
"Butterflies, beware." Shosen.—BeM
"Butterflies playing happily." Unknown.—BaSs
"Butterfly, butterfly, butterfly, butterfly." Unknown.—JoT
Butterfly song.—BiI
Butterfly in the fields. Joseph Campbell.—CoPi

C

"**Cabbages** catch at the moon." See Nocturn cabbage
The **caboose** who wouldn't come last. X. J. Kennedy.—KeO
Cactus tree. Joni Mitchell.—MoG
Cactuses
Cactus tree. J. Mitchell.—MoG
Caeiro, Alberto, pseud. (Fernando Pessoa)
XIV.—MoT
Caesar, Gaius Julius (about)
"Caesar sighed and seized the scissors." Unknown.—EmN
Julius Caesar and the honey-bee. C. T. Turner.—RoIt
"Julius Caesar made a law." Mother Goose.—TucMgl
"**Caesar** sighed and seized the scissors." Unknown.—EmN
Cakchiquel Indians. See Indians of the Americas—Cakchiquel
Cake. See From the kitchen
Cakes and cookies
April 24. N. Belting.—BeSc
Bakery shop. L. Lenski.—LeS
Baking a hamantash. S. G. Levy.—LaM
Birthday cake. L. Lenski.—LeC
"Cookie cutters." M. A. Hoberman.—HoN
Cookies. M. Chute.—ChRu
May 14. N. Belting.—BeSc
"Mix a pancake." C. G. Rossetti.—LaM—LiLc
"The moon's the north wind's cooky." V. Lindsay.—JoA-4—LiLc—UnGb
My birthday cake. X. J. Kennedy.—KeO
"Pat-a-cake." Unknown.—BoI
Self. N. H. Pritchard II.—AdPb
Souling song. Unknown.—MaF
"Teacher, teacher, made a mistake." Unknown.—EmN
Calais, France
To Henrietta, on her departure for Calais. T. Hood.—OpOx
"**Caleb** likes a good sad clown." See Circus
A **calendar** ("January brings the snow") See The garden year
Calendar ("Someday wooed a peacock") Eve Merriam.—MeF
Calendars
Calendar. E. Merriam.—MeF
"Deep in the mountains we have no calendar." Unknown.—BaSs
The garden year. Sara Coleridge.—RoIt
A calendar.—UnGb
The months.—OpOx
Caliban in the coal mines. Louis Untermeyer.—PeS
"**Calico** pie." Edward Lear.—LiLc—UnGb
California
Sand hill road. M. Grosser.—PeS
"The **caliph** shot a gazelle." See Humorous verse
"**Call** down the hawk from the air." See The hawk
"**Call** it neither love nor spring madness." See Without name
The **call** of the fells. Herbert Palmer.—PaP
Call to prayer. Unknown, tr. fr. the Arabic by Raoul Abdul.—AbM
A **call** to the wild. Lord Dunsany.—CoPi
Callanan, Jeremiah John
The convict of Clonmel. tr.—CoPi
The outlaw of Loch Lene. tr.—CoPi
Callimachus
Heraclitus.—PlM
"**Calling** black people." See SOS
"The **calm.**" See Suicide's note
Calverley, Charles Stuart
Ballad.—LiS
Changed.—RoIt
Disaster.—LiS
Lovers, and a reflection.—LiS
Morning.—RoIt
Calves. See also Cattle; Cows
Fur coat. E. Blunden.—CoPu
"I would like you for a comrade." E. A. Parry.—NeA—OpOx
The pasture. R. Frost.—JoA-4—LiLc
"There was an old man (and he had a calf)." Mother Goose.—JoA-4
"There was an old woman sat spinning." Mother Goose.—AlC
Cambridge, England
Cambridgeshire. F. Cornford.—PaP
The devourers. R. Macaulay.—PaP
"I only know that you may lie." From The old vicarage, Grantchester. R. Brooke.—PaP
In the backs. F. Cornford.—PaP
Travelling home. From In the fruitful flat land. F. Cornford.—PaP
Cambridge town is a beleaguered city." See The devourers
Cambridgeshire. Frances Cornford.—PaP
Camel. Mary Ann Hoberman.—HoR
The **camel** and the flotsam. Jean De La Fontaine, tr. fr. the French by Marianne Moore.—JoA-4
"The **camel** has a heavy bump." See Camel
Camels
Camel. M. A. Hoberman.—HoR
The camel and the flotsam. J. De La Fontaine.—JoA-4
The camel's complaint. From The admiral's caravan. C. E. Carryl.—JoA-4—OpOx
"A dromedary standing still." J. Prelutsky.—PrT
The hump. From Just-so stories. R. Kipling.—OpOx
The pig tale. From Sylvie and Bruno. L. Carroll.—LiPc
The **camel's** complaint. See The admiral's caravan
"The **camel's** hump is an ugly lump." See Just-so stories—The hump
Campbell, Janet
Nespelim man.—AlW
"Red Eagle."—AlW

Campbell, Joseph (Seosamh MacCathmhaoil, pseud.)
Blanaid's song.—CoPi
Butterfly in the fields.—CoPi
"Three colts exercising in a six-acre."—CoPi
Campbell, Myrna
"It's fall."—HoC
Campbell, Roy
The odyssey of a snail. tr.—MaFw
To the reader. tr.—MoG
Campbell, Thomas
The soldier's dream.—RoIt
Camping and hiking
Eat-it-all Elaine. K. Starbird.—NeA
Off for a hike. A. Fisher.—FiFo
"Tents and teepees." M. A. Hoberman.—HoN
Campion, Thomas
"Now winter nights enlarge."—MaFw—RoIt
"**Can** anyone lend one." See Drats
"**Can** anything avail." See The husband's view
"**Can-I-poet.**" See For some poets
"**Can** u walk away from ugly." See Positives: For Sterling Plumpp
Can you can't. Donna Whitewing.—AlW
"**Can** you Con." Unknown.—EmN
Can you copy. Mary Ann Hoberman.—HoR
"**Can** you make a cambric shirt." Mother Goose.—JoA-4
Canada
Canada geese. F. Holman.—HoI
Canada geese. Felice Holman.—HoI
Canaries
The canary. E. Turner.—OpOx
The canary's flight. J. R. Jiménez.—JoA-4
To a young brother. M. J. Jewsbury.—OpOx
The **canary**. Elizabeth Turner.—OpOx
"**Canary**-birds feed on sugar and seed." See The admiral's caravan—The camel's complaint
The **canary's** flight. Juan Ramón Jiménez, tr. fr. the Spanish by Eloise Roach.—JoA-4
The **candle** indoors. Gerard Manley Hopkins.—MaFw
Candlemas day. See Ground hog day
Candles
The candle indoors. G. M. Hopkins.—MaFw
"Candles.—" A. Coor.—HoC
"Color yellow, color coral." F. Holman.—HoI
"Little Nancy Etticoat." Mother Goose.—EmN—JoA-4
"Rub-a-dub dub." Mother Goose.—JoA-4
"**Candles.**" Ann Coor.—HoC
Candy
Chocolate. R. Hoban.—HoE
Gumballs. X. J. Kennedy.—KeO
The licorice fields at Pontefract. J. Betjeman.—ToM
"Miss Quiss." C. Watson.—WaF
Number 20. L. Ferlinghetti.—PeS
The sugar-plum tree. Eugene Field.—OpOx
Well, yes. R. Froman.—FrSp
"**Candy** bar." See Well, yes
Cane, Melville
Bed-time story.—RoIt
The **cannibal** flea. Tom Hood, Jr.—LiS
Cannibalee: A po'em of passion. Charles Fletcher Lummis.—LiS
Cannibals
The cannibal flea. T. Hood, Jr.—LiS
Cannibalee: A po'em of passion. C. F. Lummis.—LiS
"A thousand hairy savages." S. Milligan.—CoPu
The yarn of the Nancy Bell. W. S. Gilbert.—RoIt
Canning, George
The elderly gentleman.—RoIt
Canoes and canoeing. See also Kayaks
"The chief of the world." N. Belting.—BeWi
"From the dark canoe." A. Atwood.—AtM
"**Can't** catch me." Unknown.—EmN
"**Can't** keep a squirrel on the ground." Unknown.—MoBw
"**Can't** you hear that rooster crowin'." See New morning
The **cantankerous** 'gator. Oliver Herford.—BrM
The **Canterbury** tales, sels. Geoffrey Chaucer
The Franklin's tale, ad. by Anne Malcolmson.—JoA-4
The Manciple's tale
Controlling the tongue.—OpOx
The prologue.—MaFw
Canto 4. Tom Weatherly.—AdPb
Canto 5. Tom Weatherly.—AdPb
Canto 7. Tom Weatherly.—AdPb
The **cap** and bells. William Butler Yeats.—MaFw
Cape Ann. T. S. Eliot.—JoA-4
Cape Horn
Cape Horn gospel. J. Masefield.—CoPt
Cape Horn gospel. John Masefield.—CoPt
Capital punishment. See Punishment
"A **capital** ship for an ocean trip." See Davy and the goblin—The walloping window-blind
Caprice. Dorothy Stott Shaw.—CoPt
Caps. See Hats
"**Captain** Fox was paddling along sociably." See The fox and the goat
Captain Hook. Shel Silverstein.—SiW
"**Captain** Hook must remember." See Captain Hook
Captain Spud and his First Mate, Spade. John Ciardi.—CiFs
"The **captain** stood on the carronade: First Lieutenant, says he." See The old navy
Carbery, Ethna, pseud. (Anna Johnston)
Brian Boy Magee.—CoPi
The love-talker.—CoPi—CoPt
Carden, Ramona
The moccasins of an old man.—AlW
Tumbleweed.—AlW
Cardinal. Jim Harrison.—HaWr
Cardinals (birds). See Red birds
Carentan O Carentan. Louis Simpson.—ToM

"A **caressing** breeze touched." Unknown, tr. fr. the Russian by Miriam Morton.—MoM
Cargoes
Country trucks. M. Shannon.—HoP
Trucks. J. S. Tippett.—HoP—JoA-4
Caribou hunting. Unknown, fr. Iglulik Eskimo.—LeIb
Caribous
Caribou hunting. Unknown.—LeIb
"First they shot a female caribou." Unknown.—LeIb
"Glorious it is to see." Unknown.—LeIb
"I wanted to use my weapon." Unknown.—LeIb
Magic words to bring luck when hunting caribou. Unknown.—LeIb
"O warmth of summer sweeping over the land." Unknown.—LeIb
"Over there I could think of nothing else." Unknown.—LeIb
Ulivfak's song of the caribou. Unknown.—LeIb
Carleton, Will M.
The doctor's story.—CoPt
Carman, Bliss
A vagabond song.—RoIt
Carmel, California
Moonlight night: Carmel. L. Hughes.—HoD
Carmen. Victor Hernandez Cruz.—AdPb
Carmi, T.
The brass serpent.—MeP (sel.)
The condition.—MeP
Gentleman to lady. See Quatrains
Quatrains, sels.
Gentleman to lady.—MeP
Shell to gentleman.—MeP
Shell to gentleman. See Quatrains
Snow in Jerusalem.—MeP
Carmina Burana, sel. The Goliard poets
Roast swan song, tr. by George F. Whicher.—LiWw—MaFw
"**Carnelian** tips the maple tree." See March jewels
Carney, Julia A.
Little things.—OpOx
Carol ("Deep in the fading leaves of light") W. R. Rodgers.—MaFw
Carol ("In the bleak mid-winter") Christina Georgina Rossetti
"What can I give Him."—HoS—LiLc
Carol ("There was a Boy bedded in bracken") John Short.—ToM
The **carol** of the birds. John Jacob Niles.—LaS
Carol of the brown king. Langston Hughes.—HoS—LiLc
The **carousel.** Gloria C. Oden.—AdPb
Carousels. See Merry-go-rounds
Carpenters and carpentry
The carpenter's Son. From A Shropshire lad. A. E. Housman.—LiS
My hammer. Alesha.—MoM
The walrus and the carpenter. From Through the looking-glass. L. Carroll.—JoA-4—LiPc—OpOx
The **carpenter's** Son. See A Shropshire lad
"**Carpets** cover many floors where I come from." See To Vietnam
Carr, Rosemary. See Benét, Stephen Vincent and Carr, Rosemary, jt. auths.
Carriages and carts
The deacon's masterpiece; or, The wonderful one-hoss shay. O. W. Holmes.—RoIt
"It can run and it can walk." Unknown.—EmN
Carrington, Andre
"It's hot."—HoC
"A **carrion** crow sat on an oak." Mother Goose.—JoA-4
Carroll, Lewis, pseud. (Charles Lutwidge Dodgson)
The aged aged man. See Through the looking-glass
Alice's adventures in wonderland, sels.
Alice's recitation.—LiS
The lobster.—OpOx
'Tis the voice of the lobster.—JoA-4
"'Tis the voice of the lobster, I heard him declare."—LiPc
The voice of the lobster.—RoIt
"All in the golden afternoon."—LiPc
The duchess's lullaby.—LiS
"Speak roughly to your little boy."—LiPc
"Fury said to."—LiPc
"How doth the little crocodile."—LiLc—LiPc
The crocodile.—JoA-4
How doth.—LiS
The lobster quadrille.—OpOx
The mad hatter's song.—LiS
"Twinkle, twinkle, little bat."—LiLc
"They told me you had been to her."—LiPc
The white rabbit's verses.—JoA-4
Turtle soup.—LiPc—LiS
"You are old, Father William, the young man said."—LiPc
Father William.—LiS
You are old, Father William.—OpOx
Alice's recitation. See Alice's adventures in wonderland
"All in the golden afternoon." See Alice's adventures in wonderland
"Are you deaf, Father William, the young man said."—LiPc
The beaver's lesson. See The hunting of the Snark
"A boat beneath a sunny sky." See Through the looking-glass
"A child of the pure unclouded brow." See Through the looking-glass
The crocodile. See Alice's adventures in wonderland—"How doth the little crocodile"
Disillusionised.—LiPc
The duchess's lullaby. See Alice's adventures in wonderland

Carrying food home in winter. Margaret Atwood.—MoT
"**Carrying** my world." See Father
Carryl, Charles Edward
The admiral's caravan, sel.
The camel's complaint.—JoA-4—OpOx
The camel's complaint. See The admiral's caravan
Davy and the goblin, sels.
Robinson Crusoe's island.—RoIt
The walloping window-blind.—RoIt
Robinson Crusoe's island. See Davy and the goblin
The walloping window-blind. See Davy and the goblin
Carryl, Guy Wetmore
The embarrassing episode of little Miss Muffet.—CoPt
The sycophantic fox and the gullible raven.—LiWw
"**Cars** and trucks at the red light." See The go-go goons
Carson, Kit (about)
The four directions. E. B. Mitchell.—AlW
Carter, Russell Gordon
Jungle incident.—BrM
Carter, Sydney
The Lord of the Dance.—LaS
Casey Jones. Robert Hunter.—MoG
Casey, Michael
A bummer.—MoT
Cashel of Munster. Unknown, tr. fr. the Irish by Samuel Ferguson.—CoPi
Cassady, Neal (about)
Joseph Mica. Unknown.—MoG
Cassowaries
The cassowary. Unknown.—CoOr
The **cassowary.** Unknown.—CoOr
The **castaways.** E. V. Rieu.—CoPt
Castles
Castles. M. Ridlon.—HoCs
"Castles and candlelight." J. Reeves.—CoPt
Colonel Fazackerley. C. Causley.—CaF
"North wind blows hard through the trees." Kim Jong-su.—BaSs
Castles. Marci Ridlon.—HoCs
"**Castles** and candlelight." James Reeves.—CoPt
Casual lines. Si Shih, tr. fr. the Chinese by Teresa Li.—MaFw
"**Cat.**" Lilian Moore.—MoSm
Cat ("The black cat yawns") Mary Britton Miller.—HoH—LiLc
Cat ("The spotted cat hops") Valerie Worth.—WoS
"**Cat** and I." See Fight
The **cat** and the moon. William Butler Yeats.—CoPi—MaFw
Cat & the weather. May Swenson.—HaWr
Cat bath ("After she eats") Aileen Fisher.—FiFo
Cat bath ("She always tries") Aileen Fisher.—FiM
"A **cat** came fiddling out of a barn." Mother Goose.—AlC—JoA-4
"The **cat** goes out." See Our cat
"**Cat** in the cold, so eager to come in." See Will you, won't you
Cat in the long grass. Alan Dixon.—MaFw
Cat in the snow. Aileen Fisher.—FiM
Cat of cats. William Brighty Rands.—CoPu—OpOx
Cat on couch. Barbara Howes.—HiN
Cat play. Aileen Fisher.—FiM
"The **cat** ran over the roof of the house." Unknown.—EmN
"A **cat** said." See Vietnam #4
"The **cat** sat asleep by the side of the fire." Mother Goose.—AlC
"A **cat** sits on the pavement by the house." See The lonely man
"**Cat** takes a look at the weather." See Cat & the weather
"The **cat** that comes to my window sill." See That cat
Cat ways. Aileen Fisher.—FiM
"The **cat** went here and there." See The cat and the moon
The **cataract** at Lodore, July 31, 1936. Helen Bevington.—LiS
The **cataract** of Lodore. Robert Southey.—LiS—OpOx
Catch. Robert Francis.—HiN
"**Catch** him coming off the thing after a state of the Union." See Strategies
Catchers. Robert Froman.—FrSp
Caterpillar. See "Brown and furry"
The **caterpillar.** See "Brown and furry"
Caterpillar on a pillar. X. J. Kennedy.—KeO
Caterpillars
"Brown and furry." C. G. Rossetti.—RoIt
Caterpillar.—OpOx
The caterpillar.—JoA-4—UnGb
Caterpillar on a pillar. X. J. Kennedy.—KeO
Cocoon. D. McCord.—JoA-4
"Now that night is gone." Buson.—BeM
Standing. S. Silverstein.—SiW
The word beautiful. M. Swenson.—JoA-4
Cathexis. F. J. Bryant, Jr.—AdPb
Cats
"A, B, C, tumble down dee." Mother Goose.—BlM
"A, B, C, tumble down D."—AlC
Acrobat. A. Fisher.—FiM
Advice from an elderly mouse. E. J. Coatsworth.—BrM
Affinities. A. Stoutenberg.—MoT
"As I was going to St Ives." Mother Goose.—BlM—EmN—JoA-4
"As still as a flower." A. Atwood.—AtM
Bimbo's pome. P. Klee.—MaFw
Boxes. A. Fisher.—FiM
"Cat." L. Moore.—MoSm
Cat ("The black cat yawns") M. B. Miller.—HoH—LiLc
Cat ("The spotted cat hops") V. Worth.—WoS
The cat and the moon. W. B. Yeats.—CoPi—MaFw
Cat & the weather. M. Swenson.—HaWr

Cats—*Continued*
Cat bath ("After she eats") A. Fisher.—FiFo
Cat bath ("She always tries") A. Fisher.—FiM
"A cat came fiddling out of a barn." Mother Goose.—AlC—JoA-4
Cat in the long grass. A. Dixon.—MaFw
Cat in the snow. A. Fisher.—FiM
Cat of cats. W. B. Rands.—CoPu—OpOx
Cat on couch. B. Howes.—HiN
Cat play. A. Fisher.—FiM
"The cat ran over the roof of the house." Unknown.—EmN
"The cat sat asleep by the side of the fire." Mother Goose.—AlC
Cat ways. A. Fisher.—FiM
Cat's funeral. E. V. Rieu.—JoA-4
The cats of Kilkenny. Unknown.—RoIt
Chitterabob. Unknown.—BlM
"There was a man, and his name was Dob."—TrG
Country cat. E. J. Coatsworth.—UnGb
Curves. A. Fisher.—FiM
Dame Trot. Mother Goose.—BlM
Dame Wiggins of Lee. Unknown.—OpOx
"Ding, dong, bell." Mother Goose.—AlC—BlM—JoA-4
"Disturbed, the cat." Karai Senryū.—MaFw
A dog and a cat. Mother Goose.—BlM
"A dog and a cat went out together."—TucMgl
Drats. S. Silverstein.—SiW
The early purges. S. Heaney.—HiN
"Examining the breeze." K. Kuskin.—KuN
A fable. O. Herford.—MaF
"Feedum, fiddledum, fee." Mother Goose.—AlC
Fight. J. Jaszi.—BrM
Five little pussy cats. Unknown.—BlM
Fourteen ways of touching the Peter. G. MacBeth.—MaFw
French Persian cats having a ball. E. Morgan.—ToM
"Fur of cats." A. Fisher.—FiM
Game for autumn. A. Fisher.—FiM
"Great A, little a." Mother Goose.—EmN—JoA-4
Half-asleep. A. Fisher.—FiM
The High Barbaree. L. E. Richards.—JoA-4
Hoddley, Poddley. Unknown.—BlM
The house mouse. J. Prelutsky.—PrP
The hunter. A. Fisher.—FiM
"Hush-a-bye, baby (pussy is a lady)." Mother Goose.—BlM
"I do not wish I were a cat." K. Kuskin.—KuN
I doot, I doot. Unknown.—BlM
"I love little pussy." Jane Taylor.—BlM
"I like little pussy." JoA-4
Pussy.—OpOx
"If you." K. Kuskin.—KuA
Ignored. R. Froman.—FrSp
In and out. A. Fisher.—FiM
"In the spring rain." Issa.—HaW
"Jean, Jean, Jean." Unknown.—BlM
"Julia loves her Rosalie." K. Kuskin.—KuN
A kitten. A. Fisher.—FiFo
Kitten capers. A. Fisher.—FiM
The kitten playing with the falling leaves. W. Wordsworth.—UnGb
The kitten and the falling leaves.—RoIt
Kitten talk. A. Fisher.—FiM
The kittens. A. Fisher.—FiM
Kitty cornered. E. Merriam.—MeO
Lady feeding the cats. D. Stewart.—MaFw (sel.)
The lavender kitten.—A. Lopez.—AlW
Lingle, lingle. Unknown.—BlM
Listening. A. Fisher.—FiM
The lonely man. R. Jarrell.—ToM
Macavity: The mystery cat. T. S. Eliot.—OpOx
"Me, ray, doh." Unknown.—JoA-4
Milk for the cat. H. Monro.—JoA-4
Miss Jane. Unknown.—BlM
Mittens for kittens. Unknown.—BlM
Mother Tabbyskins. E. A. Hart.—OpOx
"A mouse in her room woke Miss Dowd." Unknown.—TrG
My cat. A. Fisher.—FiM
My cat Jeoffry. C. Smart.—RoIt
"My kitten." A. Fisher.—FiFo
My kitten. M. Chute.—ChRu
The mysterious cat. V. Lindsay.—JoA-4
The naming of cats. T. S. Eliot.—LiWw
New kittens. A. Fisher.—FiM
"Old Mother Shuttle." Mother Goose.—MiMg
On guard. A. Fisher.—FiM
"One, two, three . . . I like cats." Unknown.—EmN
Our cat ("Our cat goes out") M. Chute.—ChRu
Our cat ("Though it is New Year's Eve") V. Lapin.—MoM
The owl and the pussy-cat. E. Lear.—JoA-4—OpOx—UnGb
Pangur Bán. Unknown.—CoPi
Pat-cat. A. Fisher.—FiFo
Pockets. A. Fisher.—FiM
Purring song. Unknown.—BlM
Pussy. Unknown.—OpOx
"Pussy-cat, pussy-cat, where have you been." Mother Goose.—AlC-JoA-4
"Pussy cat, pussy cat." BlM—JoA-4
Rat a tat tat. Unknown.—BlM
The rescue. H. Summers.—CoPt
"Rindle, randle." Unknown.—BlM
The Rum Tum Tugger. T. S. Eliot.—BrM—RoIt
"Six little mice sat down to spin." Mother Goose.—BlM—JoA-4—TrG
"Sleeping, waking," Issa.—MaFw
Song. O. Herford.—LiS
The song of the Jellicles. T. S. Eliot.—LiLc—OpOx
"Stillness is my secret." K. Kuskin.—KuA
Substitute. A. Fisher.—FiM
"Take a word like cat." K. Kuskin.—KuN

"The terrible cat of black velvet fur." K. Kuskin.—KuN
That cat. B. King.—RoIt
"That cat is crazy." K. Kuskin.—KuN
That little black cat. D'Arcy W. Thompson.—OpOx
Cure for a pussy cat.—RoIt
"There's music in a hammer." Unknown.—RoIt
"This cat." K. Kuskin.—KuN
"This is the cat." Unknown.—BlM
"Three little kittens." Mother Goose.—BlM
Three wishes. Unknown.—RoIt
Tom. A. Fisher.—FiM
"Two cats were sitting in a tree." Unknown.—BoI
Two little kittens. Unknown.—OpOx
Ways and purrs. A. Fisher.—FiM
"When a cat is asleep." K. Kuskin.—KuN
"Who's that ringing." Unknown.—BlM
Will you, won't you. M. Van Doren.—HiN
Your cat and mine. A. Fisher.—FiM
Cat's funeral. E. V. Rieu.—JoA-4
"**Cats** have secret pockets." See Pockets
The **cats** of Kilkenny. Unknown.—RoIt
"**Cattail.**" See Kitten talk
Cattle. See also Calves; Cows
Deer among cattle. J. Dickey.—MoT
The even sea. M. Swenson.—HaWr
The herdboy. Li Yu.—MaFw
The ox-tamer. W. Whitman.—RoIt
The oxen. T. Hardy.—PlP
The sands of Dee. From Alton Locke. C. Kingsley.—JoA-4—RoIt
"What is the opposite of *fox*." R. Wilbur.—WiO
Catullus, Gaius Valerius
"I must, Varus, tell you."—PlM
"**Caught** therefore in this case." See Leopard
The **caulker.** M. A. Lewis.—CoPt
"**Cause** nobody deals with Aretha, a mother with four children, having to hit the road." See Poem for Aretha
Causley, Charles
"As I went down Zig Zag."—CaF
"At nine of the night I opened my door."—CaF
At the grave of John Clare.—MaFw (sel.)
Ballad of the bread man.—ToM
Colonel Fazackerley.—CaF
Figgie hobbin.—CaF
"A fox came into my garden."—CaF
"I saw a jolly hunter."—CaF
Innocent's song.—ToM
Keats at Teignmouth.—PlM
King Foo Foo.—CaF
Logs of wood.—CaF
"My mother saw a dancing bear."—CaF
"Old Mrs Thing-um-e-bob."—CaF
" 'Quack,' said the billy goat."—CaF
Riley.—CaF
"Tell me, tell me, Sarah Jane."—CaF
Timothy Winters.—ToM
Cautionary verses to youth of both sexes. Theodore Hook.—OpOx
Cavafy, Constantine
The first step.—PlM
Cavalry
Cavalry crossing a ford. W. Whitman.—CoPu
Cavalry crossing a ford. Walk Whitman.—CoPu
The **cave.** Glenn W. Dresbach.—PeS
Caves
The cave. G. W. Dresbach.—PeS
The child who cried. F. Holman.—HoI
The echo. P. Solomon.—JoV
Cayley, G. J.
An epitaph.—CoPu
Cecil county. Ron Wellburn.—AdPb
Cedar waxwing. William H. Matchett.—HaWr
The **ceiling.** Theodore Roethke.—LiLc
Celebration ("I shall dance tonight") Alonzo Lopez.—AlW
A **celebration** ("With songs and dances, a celebration") Volodimir Shepelev, tr. fr. the Russian by Miriam Morton.—MoM
Celebrations of the day. Felice Holman.—HoI
Celia. Unknown.—BrM
"**Celia** sat beside the seaside." See Celia
Cell song. Etheridge Knight.—AdPb
Cellars
John Mouldy. W. De La Mare.—HiN—OpOx
Cemeteries. See also Epitaphs; Tombs
The dead at Clonmacnoise. Unknown.—CoPi
Dorset. J. Betjeman.—ToM
Dunbarton. R. Lowell.—ToM
Elegy written in a country churchyard. T. Gray.—PaP (sel.)
In a grave-yard. W. S. Braithwaite.—AdPb
The levelled churchyard. T. Hardy.—PlP
Memo. C. Lynch.—AdPb
Trinity place. C. Sandburg.—SaT
"Where have all the flowers gone." P. Seeger.—PeS
Census nonsense. X. J. Kennedy.—KeO
Centaurs
Census nonsense. X. J. Kennedy.—KeO
The centaurs. J. Stephens.—CoPi
The **centaurs.** James Stephens.—CoPi
Centipede. David McCord.—McAa
"The **centipede** has fifty legs." See Centipede
"A **centipede** was happy quite." See The puzzled centipede
Centipedes
Centipede. D. McCord.—McAa
"A mathematician named Lynch." Unknown.—BrM
The puzzled centipede. Unknown.—BrM
"A centipede was happy quite."—RoIt
Central park, New York
Local note. A. Guiterman.—CoPu
"A **century** and eight more years." See The four directions
Ceremonial hunt. Elizabeth Jane Coatsworth.—JoA-4
"**Certainly** Adam in Paradise had not more sweet." See Meditation
Chad. Edward Brathwaite.—ToM

"**Chaff** is in my eye." See Preoccupation
The **chair.** Theodore Roethke.—RoIt
Chairs
The chair. T. Roethke.—RoIt
"Chairs." V. Worth.—WoS
"If I'd as much money as I could spend." Mother Goose.—AlC—JoA-4
The perfect reactionary. H. Mearns.—LiWw
The table and the chair. E. Lear.—JoA-4—UnGb
"Three wishes." K. Kuskin.—KuN
"**Chairs.**" Valerie Worth.—WoS
Chaka. Léopold Sédar Senghor, tr. fr. the French by John Reed and Clive Wake.—AlPa (sel.)
Chamber music, sels. James Joyce
"Lean out of the window."—RoIt
The noise of waters.—RoIt
Chamber music (XXXV).—MaFw
"Strings in the earth and air"
Chamber music (I).—MaFw
Chambers, Theodore
"A time."—HoC
The **chameleon.** Jack Prelutsky.—PrP
Chameleons. See Lizards
Chamisso, Adelbert von
A tragic story.—LiWw
Chang Mann
"A fisherman discouraged by a storm."—BaSs
Change
Blue girls. J. C. Ransom.—RoIt
The chameleon. J. Prelutsky.—PrP
Changed. C. S. Calverley.—RoIt
Customs change. Unknown.—OpOx
"How changed is here each spot man makes or fills." From Thyrsis. M. Arnold.—PaP
Nothing gold can stay. R. Frost.—HiN—MoT
Pleasant changes. J. E. Browne.—OpOx
The poet of Bray. J. Heath-Stubbs.—PlM
Suspense. A. Stoutenburg.—HaWr
When we grow up. S. Miller.—ThF
"**Change-up.**" Don L. Lee.—AdPb
"The **changeable** chameleon." See The chameleon
Changed. Charles Stuart Calverley.—RoIt
Chanson innocente, sel. E. E. Cummings
"In just."—HiN—RoIt
In just-spring.—JoA-4
Chant. David McCord.—McS
Chant of the awakening bulldozers. Patricia Hubbell.—HoP
A **chant** out of doors. Marguerite Wilkinson.—JoA-4
Chants
Chant. D. McCord.—McS
Chant of the awakening bulldozers. P. Hubbell.—HoP
A chant out of doors. M. Wilkinson.—JoA-4
"Comes the deer to my singing." Unknown.—ClFc
"Do not touch me." Unknown.—ClFc
"Early this morning the coming of the sun." Unknown.—ClFc
"The evening glow yet lingers." Unknown.—ClFc
"Toward calm and shady places." Unknown.—ClFc
Chanukah. See Hanukkah
Chanukah poem. E-l class, Jewish children's school of Philadelphia.—LaM
Chaplin, Charlie (about)
"Charlie Chaplin sat on a pin." Unknown.—EmN
"Charlie Chaplin went to France." Unknown.—EmN
Patriotic ode on the fourteenth anniversary of the persecution of Charlie Chaplin. B. Kaufman.—AdPb
Chapman, Arthur
The surrender speech of Chief Joseph. tr.—BiI
Chapter two. Winfield Townley Scott.—RoIt
Character. See Conduct of life
The **character** of a happy life. Henry Wotton.—RoIt
Chard Whitlow. Henry Reed.—PlM
The **charge** of the Light Brigade. Alfred Tennyson.—RoIt
Charity
The beggar boy. C. F. Alexander.—OpOx
Christmas is coming. Unknown.—HoS
Christmas is a-comin'.—RoIt
Charles. Leonard Clark.—MaFw
Charles, Ray (about)
Blues note. G. Kaufman.—AdPb
"**Charley** Wag, Charley Wag." Mother Goose.—JoA-4
"**Charlie** Chaplin sat on a pin." Unknown.—EmN
"**Charlie** Chaplin went to France." Unknown.—EmN
A **charm** against the stitch. Unknown, tr. fr. Old English by Gavin Bone.—MaFw
A **charm** against toothache.—John Heath-Stubbs.—MaFw
A **charm** for our time. Eve Merriam.—MeO
"**Charm** me asleep, and melt me so." See To music to becalm his fever
Charms
A charm against the stitch. Unknown.—MaFw
A charm against toothache. J. Heath-Stubbs.—MaFw
A charm for our time. E. Merriam.—MeO
Charms. Unknown.—BiI
"Come, butter, come." Unknown.—EmN
"The fair maid who, the first of May." Mother Goose.—AlC
"Fishy, fishy, bite." Unknown.—EmN
"I went to the toad that lies under the wall." Mother Goose.—MiMg
I've got a home in that rock. R. R. Patterson.—AdM—AdPb
"Orpheus with his lute made trees." From Henry VIII. W. Shakespeare
Music.—RoIt
The protective grigri. T. Joans.—AdPb

A talisman. M. Moore.—HiN
Charms. Unknown, tr. fr. the Crow by Robert Lowie.—BiI
The **chase.** Lois Lenski.—LeC
"**Chat.**" See French Persian cats having a ball
Chataway, Gertrude (about)
"Girt with a boyish garb for boyish task." L. Carroll.—LiPc
"**Chatter** of birds two by two raises a night song joining a litany of." See Prairie water by night
Chaucer, Geoffrey
The Canterbury tales, sels.
The Franklin's tale, ad. by Anne Malcolmson.—JoA-4
The manciple's tale
Controlling the tongue.—OpOx
The prologue.—MaFw
Controlling the tongue. See The Canterbury tales—The manciple's tale
The Franklin's tale. See The Canterbury tales
The manciple's tale. See The Canterbury tales
The prologue. See The Canterbury tales
To my empty purse.—LiWw
Chaucer, Geoffrey (about)
Chaucer. H. W. Longfellow.—PlM
The lyf so short. W. Stafford.—PlM
Chaucer. Henry Wadsworth Longfellow.—PlM
Cheap blue. Carl Sandburg.—SaT
Chear, Abraham
To my youngest kinsman, R.L.—OpOx
"**Cheep,** cheep, cheep." See Sparrows
Cheese
"What is the opposite of *cheese.*" R. Wilbur.—WiO
The **cheetah.** Jack Prelutsky.—PrP
Cheetahs
The cheetah.—J. Prelutsky.—PrP
Chelsea morning. Joni Mitchell.—MoG
Chemba, Y. S.
My newest bride.—AlPa
The **chemist** to his love. Unknown.—LiWw
Chemistry
The chemist to his love. Unknown.—LiWw
Rhyme for a chemical baby. From Boston nursery rhymes. J. Cook.—LiS
Ch'ên and Bullock
Fifteen poems of my heart. trs.—MaFw (sel.)
The ruined city. trs.—MaFw
Ch'ên Tzû-lung
The little cart.—MaFw
Cherokee Indians. See Indians of the Americas—Cherokee
Cherries
"Riddle cum riddle cum rawley." Unknown.—EmN
The riddle song. Unknown.—EmN
"Un, deux, trois, j'irai dans le bois." Mother Goose.—JoA-4
"When I went through the garden gap." Unknown.—EmN
"**Cherries** and roses." See Seasons
The **cherry** tree carol. Unknown.—LaS
Cherry trees
"Ah, cherry blossoms." Issa.—HaW
The cherry tree carol. Unknown.—LaS
In a town garden. D. Mattam.—CoPu
"Loveliest of trees, the cherry now." From A Shropshire lad. A. E. Housman.—MaFw
Loveliest of trees.—JoA-4—PaF
"No one could be. . . . " Issa.—HaW
When cherry trees bloom." Joso.—BeM
"**Cherub** in armor." See Love to Stephen
Chester. Shel Silverstein.—SiW
"**Chester** come to school and said." See Chester
The **Chester** miracle play, sel. Unknown
Abraham and Isaac.—MaFw
"**Chesterfield** cigarettes fill the light-colored room as I enter." Michael Goode.—JoV
Chesterton, Gilbert Keith
The fat white woman speaks.—LiS
The song of Quoodle.—JoA-4
Triolet.—LiLc
Chestnuts
The chestnuts are falling. L. Moore.—MoSp
For children if they'll take them. X. J. Kennedy.—RoIt
The **chestnuts** are falling. Lilian Moore.—MoSp
Cheyenne Indians. See Indians of the Americas—Cheyenne
Chicago
"Another way to spell Chicago is." Unknown.—EmN
"Chicken in the car." Unknown.—EmN
The Easter bunny blues or all I want for Christmas is the Loop. Ebon (Dooley).—AdPb
I am Chicago. From The windy city. C. Sandburg.—SaT
The **Chicago** *Defender* sends a man to Little Rock. Gwendolyn Brooks.—AdPb
Chicago poet. Carl Sandburg.—SaT
Chickadees
Titwillow. From The Mikado. W. S. Gilbert.—RoIt
"**Chicken** in the car." Unknown.—EmN
"The **chicken** wants." Karai Senryū, tr. fr. the Japanese by Geoffrey Bownas and Anthony Thwaite.—MaFw
Chickens
"Aunt Jemima climbed a tree." Unknown.—EmN
"A bantam rooster." Kikaku.—BeM
"Behind the bush, behind the thorn." Unknown.—EmN
A call to the wild. Lord Dunsany.—CoPi
"The chicken wants." K. Senryū.—MaFw
The chickens. Unknown.—RoIt
Five little chickens.—UnGb
"A fox came into my garden." C. Causley.—CaF
"Had a little chicky." Unknown.—EmN
The hen and the carp. I. Serraillier.—LiWw
The hens. E. M. Roberts.—LiLc—UnGb
"Hickety, pickety, my black hen." Mother Goose.—AlC—JoA-4

Chickens—*Continued*
"I had me a little hen, the prettiest ever seen." Mother Goose.—JoA-4
"I knew a man." C. Watson.—WaF
I won't hatch. S. Silverstein.—SiW
Janet waking. J. C. Ransom.—HiN—PeS
Near and far. H. Behn.—JoA-4—LiLc
"Once I had a rooster." Unknown.—EmN
"Once upon a time." Unknown.—EmN
"Out in the garden pickin' peas." Unknown.—EmN
Plymouth rocks. D. McCord.—McFm
Point of view. S. Silverstein.—SiW
The poultries. O. Nash.—CoOr
The poultry show. D. McCord.—McAa
"The Reverend Henry Ward Beecher." R. W. Holmes.—RoIt
The riddle song. Unknown.—EmN
Song of the Battery hen. E. Brock.—ToM
"This is the cat." Unknown.—BlM
Three hens. H. Johnstone.—CoOr
Well, I never. Unknown.—JoA-4
"What's the use, said the rooster." Unknown.—EmN
"When three hens go out to feed." Mother Goose.—TucMg
Who. A. Fisher.—FiFo
The **chickens.** Unknown.—RoIt
Five little chickens.—UnGb
"The **chief** of the world." Natalia Belting.—BeWi
"**Chief** they are bringing it." See Drum chant
Chiefs
Drum chant. Unknown.—AlPa
"If everyone were a chief." Kim Chang-up.—BaSs
Song. Unknown.—AlPa
Song for an absent chief. Unknown.—AlPa
Child, Lydia Maria
Thanksgiving day.—RoIt
The **child** ("He lives among a dog") Donald Hall.—HiN
Child ("Your clear eye is the one absolutely beautiful thing") Sylvia Plath.—MaFw
The **child** and the fairies. Unknown.—JaP
"The **child** at winter sunset." Mark Van Doren.—HiN
"**Child** I warn thee in all wise." See Symon's lesson of wisdom for all manner of children; or, how to become a bishop
"A **child** is like a rare bird." See Praise of a child
"The **child** is on my shoulders." See Three spring notations on bipeds—Laughing child
Child Margaret. Carl Sandburg.—MaFw—SaT
"The **child** Margaret begins to write numbers on a Saturday." See Child Margaret
Child moon. Carl Sandburg.—SaT
"A **child** need not be very clever." See Grandpa is ashamed
"**Child** of patient industry." See Invitation to the bee
"**Child** of the pure unclouded brow." See Through the looking-glass
Child on top of a greenhouse. Theodore Roethke.—HiN
Child rest. Phil George.—AlW
"A **child** said What is the grass, fetching it to me with full hands." See Song of myself—What is the grass
"A **child** should always say what's true." See Whole duty of children
A **child** that has a cold. Thomas Dibdin.—CoPu
"A **child** that has a cold we may suppose." See A child that has a cold
The **child** who cried. Felice Holman.—HoI
Childe, Wilfred Rowland
Haworth in May.—PaP
Childhood. See Childhood recollections; Children and childhood
Childhood ("When I was a child I knew red miners") Margaret Walker.—AdB—AdPb
Childhood ("When legs beneath kilts grow sturdy and strong") Unknown, tr. fr. the Scottish by G. R. D. McLean.—MaFw
Childhood recollections
Aladdin. J. R. Lowell.—RoIt
Alleyways. S. Quasimodo.—MaFw
Autobiographical note. V. Scannell.—ToM
Autobiography. L. MacNeice.—MaFw
Baking day. R. Joseph.—ToM
Bears. A. Rich.—HiN
Beechwoods at Knole. V. Sackville-West.—PaP
Cambridgeshire. F. Cornford.—PaP
Cathexis. F. J. Bryant, Jr.—AdPb
Childhood. M. Walker.—AdB—AdPb
Crystal moment. R. P. T. Coffin.—PeS
December music. W. T. Scott.—RoIt
The early purges. S. Heaney.—HiN
The elementary scene. R. Jarrell.—PeS
"Far in a western brookland." From A Shropshire lad. A. E. Housman.—PaP
Fern hill. D. Thomas.—JoA-4—PaF—PeS
First confession. X. J. Kennedy.—HiN
Fishing. A. T. Pratt.—AlW
I, Icarus. A. Nowlan.—HiN
"I remember, I remember." T. Hood.—RoIt
"I used to wrap my white doll up in." M. Jackson.—AdB—AdPb
In school-days. J. G. Whittier.—OpOx
In the kitchen of the old house. D. Hall.—ToM
In these dissenting times. A. Walker.—AdPb
Incident. C. Cullen.—AbM—AdPb—JoA-4
Invocation. V. Miller.—HiN
I've watched you now. W. Wordsworth.—RoIt
Kindergarten. R. Rogers.—AlW
"The little girl I used to be." M. Harris.—RoIt
Love and age. From Gryll Grange. T. L. Peacock.—RoIt
Man is nothing but. S. Tchernichovsky.—MeP
Manners. E. Bishop.—HiN
May. L. Clifton.—ClE
Meditation. T. Traherne.—RoIt
Memory of a porch. D. Justice.—HiN

Mountain road. M. Oliver.—RoIt
My early home. J. Clare.—RoIt
My lost youth. H. W. Longfellow.—RoIt
My mother. A. Taylor.—OpOx
Nikki-Rosa. N. Giovanni.—AdPb
The old familiar faces. C. Lamb.—MoG
"On Wenlock Edge the wood's in trouble." From A. Shropshire lad. A. E. Housman.—PaP
Only for me. M. Van Doren.—HiN
Out into Essex. J. Betjeman.—PaP
Recollection. D. Donnelly.—HiN
The remorse for time. H. Nemerov.—HiN
"Robin Hood." G. Burr.—HiN
Running. R. Wilbur.—HiN
The rustling of grass. A. Noyes.—PaF
The sea. Lord Byron.—RoIt
Sing me a song. R. L. Stevenson.—RoIt
The south country. H. Belloc.—PaP
Stay near me. W. Wordsworth.—RoIt
A storm in childhood. T. H. Jones.—MaFw
A terrible infant. F. Locker-Lampson.—CoPu
" 'Tis time, I think, by Wenlock town." From A Shropshire lad. A. E. Housman.—PaP
To the cuckoo. W. Wordsworth.—RoIt
U name this one. C. M. Rodgers.—AdPb
Uncle Roderick. N. MacCaig.—ToM
Virginia. E. Loftin.—AdPb
Woman. E. Loftin.—AdPb
Young. A. Sexton.—HiN—ToM
"You're a joy to behold." Unknown.—MoBw
"**Childhood** remembrances are always a drag." See Nikki-Rosa
Children and childhood. See also Babies; Boys and boyhood; Childhood recollections; Girls and girlhood
Allie. R. Graves.—JoA-4
And on some days I might take less. J. Ciardi.—CiFs
And what about the children. A. Lorde.—AdPb
The ballad of Chocolate Mabbie. G. Brooks.—PeS
The child ("He lives among a dog") D. Hall—HiN
Child ("Your clear eye is the one absolutely beautiful thing") S. Plath.—MaFw
"The child at winter sunset." M. Van Doren.—HiN
Child on top of a greenhouse. T. Roethke.—HiN
Child rest. P. George.—AlW
A child that has a cold. T. Dibdin.—CoPu
The child who cried. F. Holman.—HoI
Childhood ("When I was a child I knew red miners") M. Walker.—AdB—AdPb
Childhood ("When legs beneath kilts grow sturdy and strong") Unknown.—MaFw
Children are slaves. I. Velez.—JoV
"Children, go where I send thee." Unknown.—LaS
"Children of the city." L. Lenski.—LeC
The children of Vietnam. O. Teitelman.—MoM
The children's hour. H. W. Longfellow.—RoIt
Clear. A. Lewis.—AdPb
The collier. V. Watkins.—MaFw—ToM
Declaration of independence. W. Gibbs.—PeS
The dreamer. W. Childress.—PeS
The dying child. J. Clare.—MaFw
Early supper. B. Howes.—HiN
Eleven. A. MacLeish.—HiN
Fantasia.—E. Merriam.—MeF
Father and child. W. B. Yeats.—CoPu
Five cent balloons. C. Sandburg.—SaT
For a junior school poetry book. C. Middleton.—MaFw
For my unborn and wretched children. A. B. Spellman.—AdPb
The fragment. H. Belloc.—CoPu
The goodnight. L. Simpson.—ToM
Grandpa is ashamed. O. Nash.—CoPu
The gypsies are coming. S. Silverstein.—SiW
Heart's needle. W. D. Snodgrass.—HiN (sel.)
"Here we come a-wassailing." Unknown.—MaF
In reference to her children, 23 June, 1656. A. Bradstreet.—ThI
Japanese children. J. Kirkup.—MaFw
The knowledgeable child. L. A. G. Strong.—CoPi
Laughing child. From Three spring notations on bipeds. C. Sandburg.—SaT
Life in our village. Matei Markwei.—AbM
"Mingled with the wild." A. Atwood.—AtM
"Monday's child is fair of face." Unknown.—JoA-4
"A motherless child—see." Issa.—HaW
My own true family. T. Hughes.—HuMf
"My parents kept me from children who were rough." S. Spender.—PeS
My parents.—MaFw
Navajo children, Canyon de Chelly, Arizona. C. Middleton.—MaFw
Nonsense. N. Koralova.—MoM
Nurse's song. W. Blake.—JoA-4—OpOx
An old story. H. Nemerov.—CoPu
The old woman who lived in a shoe. J. Johnson.—ThF
On the death of friends in childhood. D. Justice.—HiN
Praise of a child. Unknown.—AlPa
Questioning faces. R. Frost.—CoPu—HiN
A refusal to mourn the death, by fire, of a child in London. D. Thomas.—ToM
Reincarnation. M. Jackson.—AdPb
"Ride your red horse down Vinegar lane." C. Watson.—WaF
Rising five. N. Nicholson.—ToM
Rites of passage. A. Lorde.—AdPb
Saturday's child. C. Cullen.—AdPb
"A skylark circles." Issa.—HaW
The sleeping giant. D. Hall.—HiN
Some kids I know. R. Hoban.—HoE
A song in the front yard. G. Brooks.—AdPb
The special person. D. Lee.—LeA
"A step-child beats straw." Issa.—HaW

A kitten. A. Fisher.—FiFo
Minnie. E. Farjeon.—UnGb
New kittens. A. Fisher.—FiM
Pancake. S. Silverstein.—SiW
The road not taken. R. Frost.—RoIt
Choosing a name. Charles and Mary Lamb.—OpOx
Choosing shoes. Ffrida Wolfe.—BrM
Chopsticks. Yüan Mei, tr. fr. the Chinese by Kotewill and Smith.—MaFw
Choric song. See The lotos eaters
"**Chorus:** O suitably-attired-in-leather-boots." See Fragment of a Greek tragedy
Chorus of the years. See The dynasts
"**Chris** met a toad." See The adventure of Chris
Christ. See Jesus Christ
Christ in Alabama. Langston Hughes.—AdPb
"**Christ** is a nigger." See Christ in Alabama
Christ the Lord most glorious. John Antes.—LaS
"**Christ** the Lord, the Lord most glorious." See Christ the Lord most glorious
Christenings
Better come quietly. From Six theological cradle songs. P. Viereck.—LiWw
"When I was christened." From Perambulator poems. D. McCord.—LiWw
Christianity
Inspection. Unknown.—AlPa
They came from the east. Unknown.—BiI
Christmas. See also Christmas trees; Santa Claus
Adrian Henri's talking after Christmas blues. A. Henri.—ToM
Aguinaldo: "Mary," said Saint Joseph. Unknown.—LaS
All hail to the morning. S. Wakerfield.—LaS
"Apples for the little ones." C. Watson.—WaF
"At nine of the night I opened my door." C. Causley.—CaF
The babe of Bethlehem. Unknown.—LaS
Behold that star. Unknown.—LaS
The birds. P. Dearmer.—MaF
Bobby's first poem. N. Gale.—CoPu
"Bounce buckram, velvet's dear." Mother Goose.—AlC
Bundles. J. Farrar.—HoS
The burning babe. R. Southwell.—MaFw
Carol ("Deep in the fading leaves of light") W. R. Rodgers.—MaFw
Carol ("There was a Boy bedded in bracken") J. Short.—ToM
The carol of the birds. J. J. Niles.—LaS
Carol of the brown king. L. Hughes.—HoS—LiLc
The cherry tree carol. Unknown.—LaS
"Children, go where I send thee." Unknown.—LaS
Christ the Lord most glorious. J. Antes.—LaS
"Christmas (a season we)." O. Lermand.—HoC
"Christmas (Virgin offspring)." A. Fair.—HoC
Christmas at sea. R. L. Stevenson.—CoPt—RoIt
Christmas eve ("My stocking's where") D. McCord.—McS
Christmas eve ("On a winter night") M. Edey.—HoS
Christmas eve rhyme. C. McCullers.—HoS
The Christmas exchange. A. Guiterman.—BrM
A Christmas folk-song. L. W. Reese.—JoA-4
A Christmas hymn. R. Wilbur.—ToM
"Christmas in the city." L. Lenski.—LeC
Christmas is coming. Unknown.—HoS
Christmas is a-comin'.—RoIt
Christmas landscape. L. Lee.—MaFw
A Christmas lullaby. M. Hillert.—HoS
Christmas morning. E. M. Roberts.—JoA-4
"Christmas morning I." C. Freeman.—AdPb
Christmas: 1924. T. Hardy.—PlP
A Christmas package, sels. D. McCord.—McAa (Complete)
1. "I hung up a stocking"
2. "Here's that little girl who wraps up each gift"
3. "Asked for another name for Santa Claus"
4. "Rock candy: hard sweet crystals on a string"
5. "Alert live reindeer galloping on air"
6. Though holly halos hang from many a nail"
7. "That broken star"
8. "My stocking's where"
9. "A collar for Sokko"
Christmas shoppers. A. Fisher.—LaM
Christmas star. B. Pasternak.—MaFw
Christmas time. L. B. Hopkins.—HoS
Christus natus est. C. Cullen.—AbM
The computer's first Christmas card. E. Morgan.—ToM
Counting the days. J. S. Tippett.—HoS
Country Christmas. A. Fisher.—HoS
Cradle hymn ("Away in a manger, no crib for a bed") M. Luther.—JoA-4
Away in a manger.—LaS
Cradle hymn ("Hush, my dear, lie still and slumber") I. Watts.—OpOx
Hush, my babe.—LaS
"Dame, get up and bake your pies." Mother Goose.—JoA-4
Day before Christmas. M. Chute.—HoS—LaM
December. A. Fisher.—HoS
December music. W. T. Scott.—RoIt
December 20: 5 more days. L. Clifton.—ClEa
December 22: Window shopping. L. Clifton.—ClEa
December 23: Early. L. Clifton.—ClEa
December 23: Late. L. Clifton.—ClEa
December 24: Christmas eve. L. Clifton.—ClEa
December 25: Christmas morning. L. Clifton.—ClEa

Christmas is coming. Unknown.—HoS
Christmas is a-comin'.—RoIt
"**Christmas** is coming, the geese are getting fat." See Christmas is coming
Christmas landscape. Laurie Lee.—MaFw
A **Christmas** lullaby. Margaret Hillert.—HoS
Christmas morning. Elizabeth Madox Roberts.—JoA-4
"**Christmas** morning i." See Gift
"**Christmas** morning I." Carol Freeman.—AdPb
Christmas: 1924. Thomas Hardy.—PlP
A **Christmas** package, sels. David McCord.—McAa (Complete)
1. "I hung up a stocking"
2. "Here's that little girl who wraps each gift"
3. "Asked for another name for Santa Claus"
4. "Rock candy: hard sweet crystals on a string"
5. "Alert live reindeer galloping on air"
6. "Though holly halos hang from many a nail"
7. "That broken star"
8. "My stocking's where"
9. "A collar for Sokko"
Christmas shoppers. Aileen Fisher.—LaM
Christmas star. Boris Pasternak, tr. fr. the Russian by Lydia Pasternak.—MaFw
Christmas time. Lee Bennett Hopkins.—HoS
Christmas trees
December 24: A tree in an elevator. L. Clifton.—ClEa
"Fir tree tall." J. Hanson.—HoS—LaM
"Little tree." E. E. Cummings.—HoS—LiLc—MaFw
Merry. S. Silverstein.—SiW
The outdoor Christmas tree ("Little winter cottontails") A. Fisher.—FiFo
The outdoor Christmas tree ("Suet chunks and popcorn strings") M. Chute.—ChRu
Christophe, Henri (about)
Christophe. R. Atkins.—AbM
Christophe. Russell Atkins.—AbM
Christopher Robin (about)
Now we are sick. J. B. Morton.—CoPu
Christ's nativity. See Gospel according to Luke
Christus natus est. Countee Cullen.—AbM
A **chronicle.** Unknown.—RoIt
The **chronometer.** A. M. Sullivan.—JoA-4
"**Chrysanthemum,** why don't you bloom." Yi Jung-bo, tr. fr. the Korean by Chung Seuk Park and ad. by Virginia Olsen Baron.—BaSs
Chrysanthemums
"Chrysanthemum, why don't you bloom." Yi Jung-bo.—BaSs
The last chrysanthemum. T. Hardy.—RoIt
Mom's mums. D. McCord.—McAa
"Then settle, frost." Ōtomo Ōemaru.—MaFw
Chu Miao Tuan
Butterflies.—MaFw
"**Chug.** Puff. Chug." See Tugs
Chuilleanáin, Eiléan Ni
Swineherd.—CoPi
Chun Keum
"When darkness covers the mountain village."—BaSs
Chung Chui
"Old man weighed down with a bundle on your head."—BaSs
Chung Chul
"I'd like to carve a moon."—BaSs
"While your parents are here."—BaSs
Chung On
"I close my book and open the window."—BaSs
Chung Seuk Park
"Am I really old, as people say." tr.—BaSs
"At the first sign of my horse's fright." tr.—BaSs
"Birds, do not blame the blossoms." tr.—BaSs
"Blessed is today." tr.—BaSs
"The blue mountains are what they are." tr.—BaSs
"Butterflies playing happily." tr.—BaSs
"Butterfly, let's fly to the green mountains." tr.—BaSs
"Chrysanthemum, why don't you bloom." tr.—BaSs
"Deep in the mountains we have no calendar." tr.—BaSs
"Do not blow in the garden, wind." tr.—BaSs
"Do not delight in what you own." tr.—BaSs
"Don't bring out the straw mat." tr.—BaSs
"Dragonflies and heron fly together." tr.—BaSs
"Even the thousand-sprayed green willow." tr.—BaSs
"A fisherman discouraged by a storm." tr.—BaSs
"A flock of sparrows, chattering." tr.—BaSs
"A frosty dawn, a waning moon." tr.—BaSs
"The Great Bear has moved across the sky." tr.—BaSs
"Hey there, white seagull." tr.—BaSs
"How I'd like to live." tr.—BaSs
"I close my book and open the window." tr.—BaSs
"I have lived up half my life already." tr.—BaSs
"I hold a rod in one hand." tr.—BaSs
"I left home without my umbrella." tr.—BaSs
"I like you, bamboo." tr.—BaSs
"I'd like to carve a moon." tr.—BaSs
"If everyone were a chief." tr.—BaSs
"If teardrops were pearls." tr.—BaSs
"If you talk too much, you are a swindler." tr.—BaSs
"In a hermit's cottage, silent, still." tr.—BaSs
"In a valley where a stream flows." tr.—BaSs
"In this faraway village where the snow has melted." tr.—BaSs
"Is that a cuckoo singing." tr.—BaSs
"It rained." tr.—BaSs
"Let me ask you, Mind." tr.—BaSs
"Long and lonely December night." tr.—BaSs

Presents.—BrM
A problem.—ChRu
Pussy willows.—ChRu
Rabbits.—ChRu
Reading.—ChRu
Reasons.—ChRu
Refuge.—ChRu
School concert.—ChRu
Seasons.—ChRu
Showers.—ChRu
Sleeping outdoors.—ChRu
Spring Saturday.—ChRu
The surprise.—ChRu
The swing.—ChRu
Valentine.—ChRu
The visitor.—ChRu
Wanting.—ChRu
Winter night.—ChRu
Words.—ChRu
The wrong start.—ChRu

Ciardi, John
After a fire. See Pencil stubs
And on some days I might take less.—CiFs
And they lived happily ever after for a while.—CiFs
Bear with me and you may learn.—CiFs
Captain Spud and his First Mate, Spade.—CiFs
The family reunion.—CiFs
Fast and far.—CiFs
Fast and slow.—CiFs
A fine fat fireman.—CiFs
Flowers.—CiFs
A fog full of apes.—CiFs
He lived, alas, in a house too big.—CiFs
I am writing this at sea.—CiFs
I hate to wait.—CiFs
I should never have trusted that bird.—CiFs
I'll let you know if I find her.—CiFs
Is this someone you know.—UnGb
Letter from a death bed.—HiN
A long hard day.—CiFs
The man in the onion bed.—BrM
The man who had shoes.—CiFs
On being too right to be polite.—CiFs
On going to Hohokus (and why I live in New Jersey).—CiFs
On learning to adjust to things.—CiFs
Pencil stubs, sels.
After a fire.—LiWw
To a reviewer who admired my book.—LiWw
Pets.—CiFs
Questions, questions, questions.—CiFs
Read this with gestures.—CiFs
Riddle.—CiFs
Romping.—HiN
The shark.—CiFs
Sit up when you sit down.—BrM
Some cook.—BrM
Some sound advice from Singapore.—CiFs
Someone slow.—UnGb
Susie's new dog.—CiFs
Thanks anyhow.—CiFs
To a reviewer who admired my book. See Pencil stubs
We all have thought a lot about you.—CiFs
Well, welcome, now that you're here.—CiFs
What Johnny told me.—CiFs
What night would it be.—HoH
When happy little children play.—CiFs
Why Noah praised the whale.—CiFs
Why the sky is blue.—CiFs

Cibber, Colley
The blind boy.—OpOx

Cicadas
The cicadas. Judith Wright.—MaFw
Invocation. V. Miller.—HiN
"Late summer evening." Shiki.—BeM
"Parched by the shrill song." Soseki.—BeM

The **Cicadas.** Judith Wright.—MaFw

Cider
Cider. P. Booth.—HaWr
Great things. T. Hardy.—PlP

Cider. Philip Booth.—HaWr

"Cin, Cinn." Unknown.—EmN

Cincinnati, Ohio
"Cin, Cinn." Unknown.—EmN

Cinderella
"Cinderella, dressed in black." Unknown.—EmN
"Cinderella, dressed in blue." Unknown.—EmN
"Cinderella, dressed in brown." Unknown.—EmN
"Cinderella, dressed in green (died)." Unknown.—EmN
"Cinderella, dressed in green (married)." Unknown.—EmN
"Cinderella, dressed in pink." Unknown.—EmN
"Cinderella, dressed in red." Unknown.—EmN
"Cinderella, dressed in rose." Unknown.—EmN
"Cinderella, dressed in silk." Unknown.—EmN
"Cinderella, dressed in yellow." Unknown.—EmN
Interview. S. H. Hay.—LiWw

"Cinderella, dressed in black." Unknown.—EmN
"Cinderella, dressed in blue." Unknown.—EmN
"Cinderella, dressed in brown." Unknown.—EmN
"Cinderella, dressed in green (died)." Unknown.—EmN
"Cinderella, dressed in green (married)." Unknown.—EmN
"Cinderella, dressed in pink." Unknown.—EmN
"Cinderella, dressed in red." Unknown.—EmN
"Cinderella, dressed in rose." Unknown.—EmN
"Cinderella, dressed in silk." Unknown.—EmN
"Cinderella, dressed in yellow." Unknown.—EmN
The **cinquain.** David McCord.—McFm

Cinquains (about)
The cinquain. D. McCord.—McFm
Cipher poems
"Jgmu gjl vgrv x ugemdt pupdeto? Wxxl x ugmh vj f jji." L. Carroll.—LiPc
The **circle** of weeping. Amir Gilboa, tr. fr. the Hebrew by Ruth Finer Mintz.—MeP
Circles
Circles ("The thing to draw with compasses") H. Behn.—LiPc
Circles ("The white man drew a small circle in the sand") From The people, yes. C. Sandburg.—MaFw—SaT
Discovery. M. C. Livingston.—LiLc
Circles. See The people, yes
Circles. Harry Behn.—LiLc
Circus. See also Animals; Clowns; also names of circus animals, as Lions
The acrobats. S. Silverstein.—SiW
"Bring on the clowns." J. Prelutsky.—PrC
Circus. D. McCord.—McFm
Circus lion. C. Day-Lewis.—ToM
Circus time. E. Merriam.—MeO
"Eight big black bears six feet tall." J. Prelutsky.—PrC
"The famed sword-swallower, looking bored." J. Prelutsky.—PrC
"The famous human cannonball." J. Prelutsky.—PrC
"Four furry seals, four furry fat seals." J. Prelutsky.—PrC
"The great fire-eater, befitting his name." J. Prelutsky.—PrC
"Here come the elephants, ten feet high." J. Prelutsky.—PrC
"The high-diver climbs to the ladder's top." J. Prelutsky.—PrC
"Hooray. Here comes the great parade." J. Prelutsky.—PrC
"I tame the very fiercest beast." J. Prelutsky.—PrC
In memory of the circus ship Euzkera, wrecked in the Caribbean sea, 1 September 1948. W. Gibson.—HiN
"Listen to the music, listen to the din." J. Prelutsky.—PrC
"The mightiest strong man on all of the planet." J. Prelutsky.—PrC
"My trainer steps into the ring." J. Prelutsky.—PrC
"Over and over the tumblers tumble." J. Prelutsky.—PrC
"Two horses race into the ring." J. Prelutsky.—PrC
"The wiggling, wriggling, jiggling juggler." J. Prelutsky.—PrC
Circus. David McCord.—McFm
"The **circus** is coming to town." See Circus time
Circus lion. C. Day-Lewis.—ToM
Circus time. Eve Merriam.—MeO
Cisco Kid (about)
Songs for the Cisco Kid. K. C. Lyle.—AdPb
Citadels. Richard Kell.—CoPi
Cities and city life. See also names of cities, as San Francisco; also Urban renewal
Afternoon. D. O'Grady.—CoPi
"All the people on our street." L. Lenski.—LeC
Apartment house. L. Lenski.—LeC
August. M. C. Livingston.—LiM
Birthday cake. L. Lenski.—LeC
The Blackstone Rangers. G. Brooks.—AdPb
Boy down the hall. L. Lenski.—LeC
A call to the wild. Lord Dunsany.—CoPi
The chase. L. Lenski.—LeC
"Children of the city." L. Lenski.—LeC
"Christmas in the city." L. Lenski.—LeC
Cities #8. V. H. Cruz.—AdB (sel.)
City, sels. L. Hughes
"In the evening the city."—HoCs
"In the morning the city."—HoCs—LiLc
The city ("A city is tall buildings, and streets, and parks") V. Pitt.—HoCs
The city ("If flowers want to grow") D. Ignatow.—CoPu
City blockades. L. B. Hopkins.—HoCs
The city child ("Dainty little maiden, whither would you wander") A. Tennyson.—OpOx
City child ("The sidewalk is my yard") L. Lenski.—LeC
City city city. L. Lenski.—LeC
City fairies. M. B. Armstrong.—JaP
City lights. L. Lenski.—LeC
City market. L. Lenski.—LeC
The city mouse and the garden mouse. C. G. Rossetti.—UnGb
The city mouse.—JoA-4—RoIt
The city question. R. Froman.—FrSp
City street ("A blue-middied girl") F. Holman.—HoI
City street ("Honk-honk-honk") L. Lenski.—LeC
Cleaning up the block. L. Lenski.—LeC
Clothesline. L. Lenski.—LeC
The country mouse and the city mouse. R. S. Sharpe.—OpOx
Crowd. E. Merriam.—MeO
Dark people. K. M. Cumbo.—AdB
Dear country witch. L. Moore.—MoSm
Definition of nature. E. Redmond.—AdPb
Dress me, dear mother. A. Shlonsky.—MeP
Early astir. H. Read.—CoPu
Erevan is my city. M. N. Kogosian.—MoM
Factory. L. Lenski.—LeC
Fake. R. Froman.—FrSp
Falling. B. Kaufman.—AdPb
Far-off things. L. Lenski.—LeC
The flattered lightning bug. D. Marquis.—CoPt
Fog. C. Sandburg.—HoCs—JoA-4—MaFw—SaT—UnGb
Gang. L. Lenski.—LeC
Get 'em here. L. B. Hopkins.—HoCs
Going. L. Lenski.—LeC
Good green bus. R. Field.—HoP (sel.)
Hidden treasure. B. Katz.—HoCs
"High-rise project." L. Lenski.—LeC

"Home in the basement." L. Lenski.—LeC
Home in the sky. L. Lenski.—LeC
The homecoming singer. Jay Wright.—AdPb
Homesick. L. Lenski.—LeC
"I live upstairs." L. Lenski.—LeC
I love the city. L. Lenski.—LeC
"I sat on the stoop." L. Lenski.—LeC
"I took a walk." L. Lenski.—LeC
"I wonder how many people in this city." L. Cohen.—CoPu
In the city. L. Lenski.—LeC
In the dim city. A. Salmon.—PaP
In the inner city. L. Clifton.—MoT
In this year of grace. J. Hewitt.—CoPi
"Johnny, come home." L. Lenski.—LeC
"J's the jumping jay-walker." From All around the town. P. McGinley.—BrM
Judeebug's country. J. Johnson.—AdPb
Keep on pushing. D. Henderson.—AdPb
Knock on wood. H. Dumas.—AdPb
Landscape in concrete. L. Lenski.—LeC
Litter. L. Lenski.—LeC
A little green thing. L. Lenski.—LeC
Lonesome place. L. Lenski.—LeC
Look out the window. L. Lenski.—LeC
Manhole covers. K. Shapiro.—HiN—JoA-4
Mike 65. L. Raphael.—AdPb
Milk-stand. L. Lenski.—LeC
Motor cars. R. B. Bennett.—HoP
"Mumbo Jumbo." D. Lee.—LeA
Murphy in Manchester. J. Montague.—CoPi
"My heart is in the city." L. Lenski.—LeC
The nature of jungles. W. R. Moses.—HiN
Never a tree. L. Lenski.—LeC
No heat today. L. Lenski.—LeC
Number 7. L. Ferlinghetti.—PeS
On Homer's birthplace. T. Heywood.—PlM
On the avenue. R. Froman.—FrSp
125th street. L. Hughes.—HoCs
Our block. L. Lenski.—LeC
Our court. L. Lenski.—LeC
"Our flat is hot." L. Lenski.—LeC
The park. L. Lenski.—LeC
Peep show. J. R. Jiménez.—JoA-4
Penthouse. L. Lenski.—LeC
People in the city. L. Lenski.—LeC
Pictures of a city. R. Fripp and P. Sinfield.—MoG
"Pigeons on the rooftop." L. Lenski.—LeC
Playtime. L. Lenski.—LeC
Rain in the city. L. Lenski.—LeC
Rain rain on the splintered girl. I. Reed.—AdPb
Rehabilitation. L. Lenski.—LeC
Review from Staten island. G. C. Oden.—AdPb
Riot. L. Lenski.—LeC
The Romanies in town. A. Beresford.—ToM
Rudolph is tired of the city. G. Brooks.—UnGb
The ruined city. Pao Chao.—MaFw
A rumble. V. Schonborg.—HoP
Shower bath. L. Lenski.—LeC
"Sing a song of people." L. Lenski.—LeC
The skyscraper. L. Lenski.—LeC
Snow in the suburbs. T. Hardy.—JoA-4
Sometimes on my way back down to the block. V. H. Cruz.—AdB
Spring in the city. L. Lenski.—LeC
Star in the sky. L. Lenski.—LeC
Stories of the street. L. Cohen.—MoG
"Street closed." L. Lenski.—LeC
Suburban madrigal. J. Updike.—PeS
Summer festival. L. Lenski.—LeC
Sunday in the city. L. Lenski.—LeC
The sunset city. H. S. Cornwell.—RoIt
Surgery. R. Froman.—FrSp
Swallow the lake. C. Major.—AdPb
Taxi driver. L. Lenski.—LeC
Thaw in the city. L. Lipsitz.—HiN
Things to do if you are a subway. B. Katz.—HoCs—HoP
To nowhere. D. Ignatow.—HiN
To the new annex to the Detroit county jail. R. W. Thomas.—AdPb
The toll taker. P. Hubbell.—HoCs
Two-room flat. L. Lenski.—LeC
Urban renewal. L. Lenski.—LeC
A walk in the city. L. Lenski.—LeC
Watching the wrecking crane. B. Katz.—HoP
What is a city. L. Lenski.—LeC
Where the sidewalk ends. S. Silverstein.—SiW
Windows with faces. L. Lenski.—LeC
Wonderful New York. C. Meyer.—JoV
Cities #8. Victor Hernandez Cruz.—AdB (sel.)
Citizens
The Unknown Citizen. W. H. Auden.—PeS
City, sels. Langston Hughes
"In the evening the city."—HoCs
"In the morning the city."—HoCs—LiLc
The **city** ("A city is tall buildings, and streets, and parks") Valerie Pitt.—HoCs
The **city** ("If flowers want to grow") David Ignatow.—CoPu
City blockades. Lee Bennett Hopkins.—HoCs
The **city** child ("Dainty little maiden, whither would you wander") Alfred Tennyson.—OpOx
City child ("The sidewalk is my yard") Lois Lenski.—LeC
City city city. Lois Lenski.—LeC
City fairies. Mildred Bowers Armstrong.—JaP
City fire. Lois Lenski.—LeC
"The **city** gleams in crimson red." See The October anniversary
"The **city** is a lonesome place." See Lonesome place
"A **city** is a place laid out." See In the city
"A **city** is tall buildings, and streets, and parks." See The city
City life. See Cities and city life; Ghettoes; also names of cities, as New York
City lights. Lois Lenski.—LeC
"The **city** lights shine." See City lights
City market. Lois Lenski.—LeC
The **city** mouse. See The city mouse and the garden mouse

The **city** mouse and the garden mouse. Christina Georgina Rossetti.—UnGb
The city mouse.—JoA-4—RoIt
"The **city** mouse lives in a house." See The city mouse and the garden mouse
"**City** of clanging bells." See In the dim city
"**City** of love." Unknown.—MoBw
"**City** of weathered cloister and worn court." See Oxford
"**City** planners." See To the new annex to the Detroit county jail
The **city** question. Robert Froman.—FrSp
City school. Lois Lenski.—LeC
City street ("A blue-middied girl") Felice Holman.—HoI
City street ("Honk-honk-honk") Lois Lenski.—LeC
City thunder. Robert Froman.—FrSp
Civil war. See United States—History—Civil war
Civil war song. Unknown, tr. fr. the Hottentot by Leonard Doob and Leonhard Schultze.—AlPa
Civilization
Tired. F. Johnson.—AdPb
Clapton, Eric and Sharp, Martin
Tales of brave Ulysses.—MoG
Clare, John
Adieu.—MaFw
Clock-a-clay.—RoIt
The dying child.—MaFw
July.—PaF (sel.)
My early home.—RoIt
November ("The landscape sleeps in mist from morn to noon")—MaFw (sel.)
November ("Sybil of months, and worshipper of winds")—PaF
The old year.—RoIt
Sheep in winter.—MaFw
Snow storm.—MaFw (sel.)
Song's eternity.—RoIt
"There's not a hill in all the view."—PaP
The thrush's nest.—MaFw—RoIt
To a primrose.—MaFw
Winter in the fens.—MaFw
Clark, Ann Nolan
In my mother's house, sel.
"Yucca."—JoA-4
"Yucca." See In my mother's house
Clark, Badger
The glory trail.—CoPt
Clark, John Pepper
"Ibadan."—AbM
Night rain.—AlPa
Night song.—AlPa (sel.)
The Ozidi saga, sel.
A lament. tr.—AlPa
Skulls and cups.—AlPa
Song.—AlPa
Streamside exchange.—AlPa
Clark, Leonard
Charles.—MaFw
Clark, Walter
After snow.—HiN
Free will.—HiN
"The morning after."—HiN
Uncle Death.—HiN
Clarke, Austin
Irish-American dignitary.—CoPi
The planter's daughter.—CoPi
A strong wind.—CoPi
Clarke, David, Jr
We can't always follow the white man's way.—JoV
Who are you—who are you.—JoV
Clarke, John Henrik
Sing me a new song.—AdPb
Clarke, Peter
In air.—AbM
Play song.—AbM
"A **class** of thirty engineers." See The pay is good
A **classic** waits for me. E. B. White.—LiS
"A **classic** waits for me, it contains all, nothing is lacking." See A classic waits for me
Clayoquot Indians. See Indians of the Americas—Clayoquot
Cleaning house. X. J. Kennedy.—KeO
Cleaning up the block. Lois Lenski.—LeC
Cleanliness. See also Bathing
Cleanliness. C. and M. Lamb.—OpOx
Desperate Dan. Mother Goose.—AlC
The dirtiest man in the world. S. Silverstein.—SiW
King Foo Foo. C. Causley.—CaF
No sale. R. Froman.—FrSp
Roll, river, roll. R. Froman.—FrSp
"There was a young lady of Crete." Unknown.—RoIt
"Who are you." Mother Goose.—TucMgl
Cleanliness. Charles and Mary Lamb.—OpOx
"**Cleanly,** sir, you went to the core of the matter." See A correct compassion
Clear. Angelo Lewis.—AdPb
"**Clear** and cool, clear and cool." See The water babies—The tide river
"The **clear** cool note of the cuckoo which has ousted the legitimate nest holder." See Sincere flattery of W. W. (Americanus)
"**Clear** the way." See War song
Cleator Moor. Norman Nicholson.—ToM
Clemmons, Carole Gregory
I'm just a stranger here, Heaven is my home.—AdPb
Love from my father.—AdPb
Migration.—AdPb
Spring.—AdPb
"**Cleopatra** ruled the Nile." Unknown.—MoBw
"A **clergyman** told from his text." Unknown.—RoIt
"The **clerihew.**" David McCord.—McFm
Clerihews (about)
"The clerihew." D. McCord.—McFm
Clerk-Maxwell, J. See Maxwell, James Clerk
Cleveland, Ohio
On the fine arts garden, Cleveland. R. Atkins.—AdPb
"**Clickety**-clock." See Song of the train

Cliffs
At Dunwich. A. Thwaite.—ToM
Cornish cliffs. J. Betjeman.—ToM
Clifton, Lucille
April.—ClE
August.—ClE
December.—ClE
December 20: 5 more days.—ClEa
December 21: Snow.—ClEa
December 22: Window shopping.—ClEa
December 23: Early.—ClEa
December 23: Late.—ClEa
December 24: Christmas eve.—ClEa
December 24: A tree in an elevator.—ClEa
December 25: Christmas morning.—ClEa
December 25: Christmas night.—ClEa
The discoveries of fire.—MoT
February.—ClE
The 1st.—MoT
For de Lawd.—AdM—AdPb
Friday: Mom is home—Payday.—ClS
Friday: Waiting for mom.—ClS
Good times.—AdM—AdPb—HiN
"In the inner city."—MoT
January.—ClE
July.—ClE
June.—ClE
"Listen children."—AdM—AdPb
March.—ClE
May.—ClE
Miss Rosie.—AdPb
Monday morning: Good morning.—ClS
"My mama moved among the days."—AdPb
November.—ClE
October.—ClE
Saturday night: Late.—ClS
September.—ClE
Sunday morning: Lonely.—ClS
Sunday night: Goodnight.—ClS
"Those boys that ran together."—AdPb
Thursday evening: Bedtime.—ClS
To Bobby Seale.—AdM—AdPb
Tuesday all day: Rain.—ClS
Wednesday noon: Adventure.—ClS
Climbing
Finding a poem. E. Merriam.—MeF
Jacob's ladder. Unknown.—BrW
John Muir on Mt Ritter. From Burning. G. Snyder.—MaFw
"Mount Taishan is high and steep." Sa Eun Yang.—BaSs
Presence of mind. H. Graham.—LiWw
The rescue. H. Summers.—CoPt
A story. W. Stafford.—CoPt
"Two cats were sitting in a tree." Unknown.—BoI
Uncle Simon and Uncle Jim. A. Ward.—BrM
"**Climbing** a steep hill." Kwaso, tr. fr. the Japanese by Harry Behn.—BeM
"**Climbing** the last steps to your house, I knew." See Light dying
The **clipper** Dunbar to the clipper Cutty Sark. Ethel Anderson.—CoPt
"The **clock.**" See Clock
Clock. Valerie Worth.—WoS
Clock-a-clay. John Clare.—RoIt
The **clock** ticks. Eve Merriam.—MeO
Clocks and watches
After the rain. Y. Ritsos.—MoT
"The alarm clock." M. Evans.—AdB
Alarm clock. E. Merriam.—MeF
"As I went down Zig Zag." C. Causley.—CaF
Clock. V. Worth.—WoS
The clock ticks. E. Merriam.—MeO
Eight o'clock. A. E. Housman.—CoPu
"Hickory dickory dock." Mother Goose.—JoA-4
On a sundial. H. Belloc.—CoPu—LiWw
On the job. R. Froman.—FrSp
"Round as a biscuit (busy as a bee)." Unknown.—EmN
The sad tale of Mr Mears. Unknown.—CoPt
The slow starter. L. MacNeice.—ToM
Someone slow. J. Ciardi.—UnGb
"Tick . . . tock." K. Kuskin.—KuA
Tick-tock talk. D. McCord.—McAa—McS
Time. F. Holman.—HoI
Wanting. M. Chute.—ChRu
The watch. M. Swenson.—CoPt—RoIt
Ways of winding a watch. E. Merriam.—MeF
Why. L. Moore.—MoSm
"**Close** by the margin of the brook." See Dame Duck's lecture
Close your eyes. Arna Bontemps.—AdPb
Clothesline. Lois Lenski.—LeC
Clothing and dress. See also names of clothing, as Boots and shoes
"As I was going up the hill." Mother Goose.—AlC
At the draper's. T. Hardy.—PlP
The ballad of the harp-weaver. E. St V. Millay.—CoPt—RoIt
Benjamin Bunnn. S. Silverstein.—SiW
The big baboon. H. Belloc.—CoOh
"The boy stood on the burning deck (eating peanuts by the peck)" Unknown.—CoOh—MoBw
"Bryan O'Lin had no breeches to wear." Mother Goose.—TrG—TucMgl
"Can you make a cambric shirt." Mother Goose.—JoA-4
The chameleon. J. Prelutsky.—PrP
Chocolate. R. Hoban.—HoE
"Cinderella, dressed in black." Unknown.—EmN
"Cinderella, dressed in blue." Unknown.—EmN
"Cinderella, dressed in brown." Unknown.—EmN
"Cinderella, dressed in green (died)." Unknown.—EmN
"Cinderella, dressed in green (married)." Unknown.—EmN
"Cinderella, dressed in pink." Unknown.—EmN
"Cinderella, dressed in silk." Unknown.—EmN

Clothing and dress.—*Continued*
"Cinderella, dressed in yellow." Unknown.—EmN
A coat. W. B. Yeats.—PlM
Cocoa skin coat. X. J. Kennedy.—KeO
The colour. T. Hardy.—PlP
Dance of the Abakweta. From Far from Africa: Four poems. M. Danner.—AdPb
Dancing pants. S. Silverstein.—SiW
"Diddle, diddle, dumpling, my son John." Mother Goose.—JoA-4
"Deedle, deedle, dumpling, my son John."—AlC
The dolls' wash. J. H. Ewing.—OpOx
"Don't ask me what to wear." Sappho.—ThI
"Don't dress your cat in an apron." D. Greenburg.—ThF
Dress me, dear mother. A. Shlonsky.—MeP
Fur coat. E. Blunden.—CoPu
Going into breeches. C. and M. Lamb.—OpOx
"Goody, goody, gout." Unknown.—EmN
"Had a little girl dressed in blue." Unknown.—EmN
"Hark, hark." Mother Goose.—JoA-4
"Hector Protector was dressed all in green." Mother Goose.—AlC
"Heigh-ho Silver everywhere." Unknown.—EmN
"His shirt soon shrank in the suds." Unknown.—EmN
"The house of snail upon his back." K. Kuskin.—KuN
The hungry moths. R. McCuaig.—CoPu
I have a garment. Abraham ibn Ezra.—MeP
"I see London, I see France." Unknown.—EmN
"If I'd as much money as I could spend." Mother Goose.—AlC—JoA-4
"If the world was crazy." S. Silverstein.—SiW
"It chanced to be our washing day." O. W. Holmes.—RoIt
Itinerant. E. Merriam.—MeO
"It's raining, it's raining." Mother Goose.—TucMgl
John. N. M. Bodecker.—BoL
"King Dagobert, they say." Mother Goose.—TucMg
"Lazy sheep, pray tell me why." Mother Goose.—TucMgl
"Little Polly Flinders." Mother Goose.—AlC
Love in a space-suit. J. Kirkup.—ToM
"Mary Mack, dressed in black." Unknown.—EmN
"Mother, mother, what is that." Unknown.—EmN
My beard. S. Silverstein.—SiW
"My grandmother sent me a new-fashioned." Unknown.—EmN
The new muffler. M. Chute.—ChRu
"Old Abram Brown is dead and gone." Mother Goose.—AlC
"One misty moisty morning." Mother Goose.—AlC—JoA-4—MiMg
Othello Jones dresses for dinner. E. Roberson.—AdPb
"A pant hunter, pantless, is panting for pants." Unknown.—EmN
The perils of invisibility. W. S. Gilbert.—CoPt
Poor Angus. S. Silverstein.—SiW
A problem. M. Chute.—ChRu
The robins. F. Holman.—HoI
Routine. A. Guiterman.—CoOh
"She wore her stockings inside out." Unknown.—BrM
"Snow is white and coal is black." Unknown.—EmN
"Step on a rock." Unknown.—EmN
"Sun suits suit." M. A. Hoberman.—HoN
"Susan shineth shoes and socks." Unknown.—EmN
Tailor. E. Farjeon.—OpOx
"They say shoes and socks." Unknown.—EmN
"Three young rats with black felt hats." Mother Goose.—BlM—JoA-4
Upon Julia's clothes. R. Herrick.—LiS
The vesture of the soul. G. W. Russell.—CoPi
Wee Willie Gray. R. Burns.—OpOx
"Well I never." Mother Goose.—AlC—JoA-4
"What will I be married in." Unknown.—EmN
When Sue wears red. L. Hughes.—JoA-4
"You leap out of bed; you start to get ready." From Poems in praise of practically nothing. S. Hoffenstein.—LiWw
Clouds. See also Weather
April. Unknown.—RoIt
Broken sky. C. Sandburg.—SaT
Clouds. C. G. Rossetti.—RoIt
"Clouds shadow the stream." A. Atwood.—AtM
Cold morning. F. Holman.—HoI
"Don't you ever." Unknown.—JoT
"Downy white feathers are moving beneath the sunset." Unknown.—ClFc
"Hovering above." Onitsura.—BeM
"I marvel at the ways of God." E. B. White.—LiWw
In winter sky. D. McCord.—McFm
The jigsaw puzzle in the sky. F. Holman.—HoI
"Low clouds are shattered." Bashō.—BeM
"Moon sits smoking his pipe." N. Belting.—BeWi
"Nicely, nicely, nicely, nicely, there away in the east." Unknown.—ClFc
"An ocean of clouds." A. Atwood.—AtM
"The opposite of a *cloud* could be." R. Wilbur.—WiO
"The ragged phantom." Boncho.—BeM
Rolling clouds. From Sky talk. C. Sandburg.—SaT
Song for the sun that disappeared behind the rain clouds. Unknown.—AlPa
"The temple cannot be far." Unknown.—BaSs
Clouds. Christina Georgina Rosseti.—RoIt

"The **clouds** are bunched roses." See Two songs
"The **clouds** are full of new blue sky." See Sometimes
"**Clouds** are swirling, clouds are straying." See Phantoms of the steppe
"**Clouds,** clouds." See Weather incantation
"**Clouds** of morning mist." Busōn, tr. fr. the Japanese by Harry Behn.—BeM
"**Clouds** shadow the stream." Ann Atwood.—AtM
"**Clouds** spout upon her." See Rain on a grave
"**Cloudy** days." Ann Coor.—HoC
"**Clownlike,** happiest on your hands." See You're
Clowns. See also Circus
"Bring on the clowns." J. Prelutsky.—PrC
Circus. D. McCord.—McFm
"One winter afternoon." E. E. Cummings.—HiN
Coal
"Black we are and much admired." Unknown.—EmN
Caliban in the coal mines. L. Untermeyer.—PeS
Coal. A. Lorde.—AdPb
"Guess a riddle now you must." Unknown.—EmN
"Old Mother Shuttle." Mother Goose.—MiMg
Coal. Audre Lorde.—AdPb
A **coat.** William Butler Yeats.—PlM
Coatsworth, Elizabeth Jane
Advice from an elderly mouse.—BrM
Ceremonial hunt.—JoA-4
Country cat.—UnGb
In Walpi.—JoA-4
A lady comes to an inn.—CoPt
The maple.—LaM
The mouse.—JoA-4
Much nicer people.—CoPu
The Navajo.—JoA-4
The storm.—CoPu
Sudden storm.—HoCs
The swallows.—LiLc
To poor Pygmalion.—CoPu
"Violets, daffodils."—CoPu
"The warm of heart shall never lack a fire."—CoPu
"What is once loved."—CoPu
Cobb, Charlie
Containing communism.—AdPb
For Sammy Younge.—AdPb
Nation.—AdPb
To Vietnam.—AdPb
Cobwebs
A bit of cobweb. L. Sarchuk.—MoM
Fog. L. Moore.—MoSm
Pearl cobwebs. From Smoke and steel. C. Sandburg.—SaT
Sitting in the woods: A contemplation. W. R. Moses.—HiN
"Tangled over twigs." Onitsura.—BeM
"There was an old woman toss'd (tossed) up in a basket." Mother Goose.—AlC—JoA-4—MiMg
"**Coca-cola** came to town." Unknown.—MoBw
Coca cola sunset. Felice Holman.—HoI
Cochiti Pueblo Indians. See Indians of the Americas—Cochiti Pueblo
"**Cock** a doodle doo." Mother Goose.—JoA-4
"The **cock** and the hen." Unknown, tr. fr. the Scottish by Norah and William Montgomerie.—JoA-4
"The **cock** crows." See Depression before spring
"The **cock** is crowing." See Written in March
"The **cock:** Lock the dairy door." Mother Goose.—AlC
Cockatoos
The red cockatoo. Po Chü-i.—CoPu
Cockles and mussels. Unknown.—RoIt
Cocks. See Chickens
Cocoa skin coat. X. J. Kennedy.—KeO
Coconuts
Locked in. I. Gustafson.—CoPt
Cocoon. David McCord.—JoA-4
Codes
Me and my giant. S. Silverstein.—SiW
Cody, William Frederick (about)
Buffalo Bill. C. Sandburg.—SaT
"Buffalo Bill's." E. E. Cummings.—MoG
The continuing story of Bungalow Bill. J. Lennon and P. McCartney.—MoG
Coffee
"Coffee hot, coffee cold." Unknown.—EmN
"A cup of proper coffee in a copper coffee cup." Unknown.—EmN
"While grinding coffee at the store." W. E. Engel.—CoOh
"**Coffee** hot, coffee cold." Unknown.—EmN
Coffin, Robert P. Tristram
Crystal moment.—PeS
The secret.—PaF
Coghill, Neville
The Canterbury tales, sel.
The prologue. tr.—MaFw
Cohen, Leonard
For Anne.—PeS
"I wonder how many people in this city."—CoPu
Song.—PeS
Stories of the street.—MoG
Story of Isaac.—MoG
Suzanne.—MoG
Cohoe, Grey
Alone together.—AlW
Ancestors.—AlW
The folding fan.—AlW
Mom.—AlW
Snowflakes.—AlW
Thirst.—AlW
Coins. Valerie Worth.—WoS
"**Coins** are pleasant." See Coins
"**Cold,** cold." See A song of winter
"**Cold,** cold." See Weather chant

"**Come** buy my fine wares." See Market women's cries—Apples
"**Come,** come, you naughty scamp." Mother Goose.—TucMg
"**Come** down from the moon." See Descent
"**Come** fleetly, come fleetly, my hookabadar." See Cossimbazar
"**Come,** follow me by the smell." See Market women's cries—Onions
"**Come** here, my beloved." See Modern concert song
"**Come** in kayaks." Unknown, fr. the Caribou Eskimo.—LeIb
"**Come,** it is late in the day." See Girl's song
"**Come,** let us draw the curtains." See Autumn
"**Come,** let's play on the jungle gym." See Jungle gym
"**Come,** let's to bed." Mother Goose.—AlC
"**Come,** little cub." See Bear cubs
"**Come** live with me and be my love." See The passionate shepherd to his love
"**Come** Mamina." See Umamina
"**Come,** my little Robert, near." See Cleanliness
"**Come** on out of there with your hands up, Chaplin." See Patriotic ode on the fourteenth anniversary of the persecution of Charlie Chaplin
"**Come** out and ride around the block with me." Karla Kuskin.—KuA
"**Come** picture this lovely and frightening scene." Karla Kuskin.—KuA
"**Come** play with me." See To a squirrel at Kyle-na-no
"**Come,** said Old Shellover." See Old Shellover
"**Come** soon." See Letter to a friend
"**Come** take up your hats, and away let us haste." See The butterfly's ball
"**Come** to me broken dreams and all." See The still voice of Harlem
"**Come** to my party." Unknown.—EmN
"**Come** try our." See Dear country witch
"**Come** unto these yellow sands." See The tempest
"**Come** unto these yellow sands." Paul Dehn.—LiS
"**Come.** What shall it be." See The Indian market
"**Come** when you are called." Unknown.—EmN
"**Come** with your shining white fire." See Light my way to bed
"**Come** you masters of war." See Masters of war
"**Comes** the deer to my singing." Unknown, tr. fr. the Navajo.—ClFc
The **comic** adventures of Old Mother Hubbard and her dog. Sarah Catherine Martin.—OpOx
Comin' thro' the rye. Robert Burns.—LiS
The **coming** fall. Denise Levertov.—MoT (sel.)
"**Coming** from the South." See Six ten sixty-nine
"**Coming** up Buchanan street, quickly, on a sharp winter evening." See Trio
"**Coming** up the stairs." See Night encounter
Commercials
  Housework. S. Harnick.—ThF
  No sale. R. Froman.—FrSp
"The **committee** is at the school." See Inspection
"The **common** cormorant or shag." Unknown.—TrG
Common dust. Georgia Douglas Johnson.—AdPb
Communication. See also Mail service; Radio; Railroads; Rides and riding; Roads and trails; Telegraph; Telephones
  Hot line to the nursery. D. McCord.—McFm
  How she resolved to act. M. Moore.—PeS
  These days. C. Olsen.—MoT
The **companion.** Yevgeny Yevtushenko, tr. fr. the Russian by Robin Milner-Gulland and Peter Levi.—MaFw
Companions. Adrien Stoutenburg.—HaWr
Company manners. Eve Merriam.—MeO
Comparisons. Christina Georgina Rossetti.—OpOx
Complaint over bad hunting. Unknown, fr. the Ammassalik Eskimo.—LeIb
The **complaint** to God. See Job
Complaints
  Caliban in the coal mines. L. Untermeyer.—PeS
  The camel's complaint. From The admiral's caravan. C. E. Carryl.—JoA-4—OpOx
  Complaint over bad hunting. Unknown.—LeIb
  The complaint to God. From Job, Bible, Old Testament.—MeP
  The first step. C. Cavafy.—PlM
  "If my complaining." Issa.—BeM
  The little house. Alesha.—MoM
  The mouse. E. J. Coatsworth.—JoA-4
  To my empty purse. G. Chaucer.—LiWw
  A woman's complaint. Unknown.—BiI
Composed on a May morning, 1838. William Wordsworth.—PaF
Composed upon Westminster bridge. William Wordsworth.—PaP
Compozishun—to James Herndon and others. Ronald J. Goba.—HiN
Computers
  The computer's first Christmas card. E. Morgan.—ToM
  Neuteronomy. E. Merriam.—MeF
The **computer's** first Christmas card. Edwin Morgan.—ToM
Conceit
  Ego swamp. K. D. Kuka.—AlW
  Who. S. Silverstein.—SiW
Conception. Waring Cuney.—AbM
Concert. Ibn Sharaf, tr. fr. the Spanish by A. J. Arberry.—AbM
Concrete
  The concrete mixer. T. Langley.—HoCs
"**Concrete** cold face cased in steel." See Pictures of a city
The **concrete** mixer. Timothy Langley.—HoCs

Sources of good counsel. P. Idley.—OpOx
Spanish music in winter. D. Avidan.—MeP (sel.)
The suppliant. G. D. Johnson.—AdPb
Surview. T. Hardy.—PlP
Symon's lesson of wisdom for all manner of children; or, how to become a bishop. Unknown.—OpOx
The ten commandments. Unknown.—OpOx
There. R. Mezey.—MoT
There lived a king. W. S. Gilbert.—CoPt
A thing of beauty. J. Keats.—RoIt
A thought. S. Ukachev.—MoM
To a child five years old. N. Cotton.—OpOx
"To fling songs into the air." Y. Grizlov.—MoM
To get thine ends. R. Herrick.—RoIt
To his child. W. Bullokar.—OpOx
To his little son Benedict from the Tower of London. J. Hoskyns.—OpOx
To his son, Vincent Corbet, on his birthday, November 10, 1630, being then three years old. R. Corbet.—OpOx
"To infinite heights will the roads of life." V. Lapin.—MoM
Tom and Joe. D. McCord.—McAa
Upon boys diverting themselves in the river. T. Foxton.—OpOx
Upon the horse and his riders. J. Bunyan.—OpOx
We wear the mask. P. L. Dunbar.—AdPb
What shall he tell that son. C. Sandburg.—PeS
"While your parents are here." Chung Chul.—BaSs
Young soul. LeRoi Jones.—MoT
Confederate States of America. See United States—History—Civil War
The **confession.** Thomas Ingoldsby.—RoIt
Confession overheard in a subway. Kenneth Fearing.—PeS
Confession stone. Owen Dodson.—AbM
Confessions
The confession. T. Ingoldsby.—RoIt
Confession overheard in a subway.—K. Fearing.—PeS
Confession stone. O. Dodson.—AbM
First confession. X. J. Kennedy.—HiN
Confidence
I may, I might, I must. M. Moore.—JoA-4
Song. Unknown.—BiI
Wings. V. Hugo.—JoA-4
Conflict. Mable Segun.—AlPa
"**Confucius** say." Unknown.—MoBw
Congo
Mmenson. E. Brathwaite.—ToM
Conkling, Hilda
Dandelion.—JoA-4
Little snail.—JoA-4
Connecticut
Me and I and you." Unknown.—BoI
"A **connoisseur** of pearl." See African China
Connor, Tony
Above Penmaenmawr.—ToM
Elegy for Alfred Hubbard.—ToM
Conquerors. Henry Treece.—ToM
Conscience. See also Duty
The conscientious objector. K. Shapiro.—PeS
The **conscientious** objector. Karl Shapiro.—PeS
Conservation
The field, revisited. F. Holman.—HoI
A **considerable** speck. Robert Frost.—AdP
Consideration for others. Christopher Smart.—OpOx
Considering the snail. Thom Gunn.—HaWr—MaFw
Constable, Thomas
Old October.—RoIt
Constantinople
"Can you Con." Unknown.—EmN
"C N O." Unknown.—EmN
"With a c and a si and a constanti." Unknown.—EmN
Constellations. See also Stars
"The Great Bear has moved across the sky." Yi Jung-jin.—BaSs
Constrictor restricter. X. J. Kennedy.—KeO
Containing communism. Charlie Cobb.—AdPb
Contemplations. Anne Bradstreet.—ThI (sel.)
Contemporary nursery rhyme. Unknown.—LiS
"**Contend** in a sea which the land partly encloses." See The yachts
Content. Robert Greene.—RoIt
Contention of Ajax and Ulysses, sel. James Shirley
"The glories of our blood and state."—RoIt
Contentment
After the winter. C. McKay.—AdPb
Content. R. Greene.—RoIt
Contentment ("I would like to be wise") M. Chute.—ChRu
Contentment ("Those my friendships most obtain") N. Cotton.—OpOx
The harper. Unknown.—CoPi
Heart's content. Unknown.—RoIt
Man is a fool. Unknown.—RoIt
Sweet content. From Pleasant comedy of patient Grissell. T. Dekker.—RoIt
"Touch me not, for I am fragile." P. Solomon.—JoV
Contentment ("I would like to be wise") Marchette Chute.—ChRu
Contentment ("Those my friendships most obtain") Nathaniel Cotton.—OpOx
The **continuing** story of Bungalow Bill. John Lennon and Paul McCartney.—MoG
Controlling the tongue. See The Canterbury tales—The manciple's tale
Conundrums. See Riddles
The **convent.** Seumas O'Sullivan.—CoPi
The **conventionalist.** Stevie Smith.—CoPu
Convents
The convent. S. O'Sullivan.—CoPi
The **convergence** of the twain. Thomas Hardy.—PlP
Conversation
Conversation with a giraffe at dusk in the zoo. D. Livingstone.—ToM

Corncrakes
The corncrake. J. H. Cousins.—CoPi
"**Corner** stand." See Appetizer
"The **cornered** and trapped." See For Mack C. Parker
Cornfield ridge and stream. Carl Sandburg.—SaT
Cornfields. See Corn and cornfields
Cornford, Frances
Cambridgeshire.—PaP
Country idyll.—CoPu
In the backs.—PaP
In the fruitful flat land, sel.
Travelling home.—PaP
The princess and the gypsies.—CoPt
A recollection.—CoPu
To a fat lady seen from the train.—CoPu—LiS
Travelling home. See In the fruitful flat land
Village before sunset.—CoPu
Youth.—CoPu
Cornhuskers. See Prairie
Cornish, Sam
"A black man."—AdPb
Cross over the river.—AdM
Death of Dr King.—AdPb
Death of Dr King #1.—AdM (sel.)
Frederick Douglass.—AdPb
Montgomery.—AdM—AdPb
"My brother is homemade."—AdM
One-eyed black man in Nebraska.—AdPb
Panther.—AdPb
The river.—AdPb
Sam's world.—AdM
To a single shadow without pity.—AdPb
"Your mother."—AdM
Cornish cliffs. John Betjeman.—ToM
Cornwall, Barry, pseud. (Bryan Waller Procter)
The owl.—RoIt
The sea.—RoIt
Cornwall, England
April landscape. A. L. Rowse.—PaP
Autumn in Cornwall. A. C. Swinburne.—PaP
Cornish cliffs. J. Betjeman.—ToM
Sunday afternoon in St Enodoc church, Cornwall. J. Betjeman.—PaP
Cornwell, Henry Sylvester
The sunset city.—RoIt
A **correct** compassion. James Kirkup.—MaFw
Corso, Gregory
Dream of a baseball star.—FlH
Nature's gentleman.—LiWw
Cortez, Jayne
For real.—AdPb
Initiation.—AdPb
Lead.—AdPb
Cory, William (Johnson) (William Johnson-Cory)
A ballad for a boy.—OpOx
Heraclitus. tr.—CoPu—PlM
Cossimbazar. Henry Sambrooke Leigh.—LiWw
Cottage. Seumas O'Sullivan.—CoPi
The **cottager** to her infant. Dorothy Wordsworth.—OpOx
Cottages
Cottage. S. O'Sullivan.—CoPi
"Ten years it took." Song Soon.—BaSs
"What if a rafter is too short or too long." Shin Heum.—BaSs
Cotter, Joseph Seaman, Jr
And what shall you say.—AdPb
Sonnet to Negro soldiers.—AdPb
Cotton, Nathaniel
The bee, the ant, and the sparrow.—OpOx
Contentment.—OpOx
Early thoughts of marriage.—OpOx
To a child five years old.—OpOx
Cotton
Snapshots of the cotton South. F. M. Davis.—AdPb
"A **coughdrop** lies in my doghouse." X. J. Kennedy.—KeO
"**Could** be, they were broken." See Choice
Could it have been a shadow. Monica Shannon.—JaP
Councils. Marge Piercy.—MoT
The **counsels** of O'Riordan, the rann maker. T. D. O'Bolger.—CoPi
"**Count** this among my heartfelt wishes." See Fish story
Counter service. Robert Froman.—FrSp
Counting
Counting the days. J. S. Tippett.—HoS
"1, 2, 3, 4, 5." Mother Goose.—AlC
"Twelve huntsmen with horns and hounds." Mother Goose.—AlC
"Un, deux, trois, j'irai dans le bois." Mother Goose.—JoA-4
When I'm an astronaut. L. B. Jacobs.—BrM
Counting out. Unknown.—EmN
Counting out rhyme. See "Round about, round about"
Counting-out rhymes
"A, b, c, d, e, f, g." Unknown.—EmN
"Acka backa soda cracker." Unknown.—EmN
"Bee, a bee, a bumble bee." Unknown.—EmN
Counting out. Unknown.—EmN
"Eena meena dixie dan." Unknown.—EmN
"Eeny meeny mony my." Unknown.—EmN
"Eeny meeny tipsy teeny." Unknown.—EmN
"Eins, zwei, Polizei." Mother Goose.—JoA-4
"Engine, engine, Number Nine." Unknown.—EmN
"Hinty, minty, cuty, corn." Unknown
Counting out rhymes.—RoIt
"Ibiddy, bibiddy, sibiddy sab." Unknown.—EmN
"Ibiddy, bibiddy, sibiddy sail." Unknown.—EmN
"I-N spells in." Mother Goose.—AlC
"Intery, mintery, cutery, corn." Mother Goose.—EmN—JoA-4
"Itty mitty tippity tab." Unknown.—EmN
"Knickerbocker knock about." C. Watson.—WaF
"Mary Mack, dressed in black." Unknown.—EmN

Counting-out rhymes—*Continued*
"Monkey, monkey, bottle of beer." Unknown.—EmN
"My mother and your mother." Unknown.—EmN
"My mother, your mother." Unknown.—EmN
Nursery song in pidgin English. Unknown.—LiS
"One little, two little, three little Indians." Unknown.—EmN
"One, two (buckle my shoe)." Mother Goose.—AlC—EmN
"1, 2 buckle my shoe."—JoA-4
"One, two, sky blue." Unknown.—EmN
"One, two three (spells)." Unknown.—EmN
"One, two, three, four, five, six, seven . . . (all bad children)." Unknown.—EmN
"One, two, three, four, five, six, seven (all good children)." Unknown.—EmN
"One, two, three . . . out in the middle." Unknown.—EmN
"Onery, twoery, ickary, Ann." Unknown.—EmN
"Out goes the cat." Unknown.—EmN
"Penny on the water." Mother Goose.—AlC—EmN
"Red, white, and blue (all out but you)." Unknown.—EmN
"Riggedy, higgedy, wiggedy, rig." Unknown.—LaM
"Roses are red . . . when I choose." Unknown.—EmN
"Rosy apple, lemon or pear." Unknown.—RoIt
"Round about, round about." Unknown
Counting out rhyme.—LiS
"Teacups and saucers." Unknown.—EmN
"Up town, down town." C. Watson.—WaF
"You can stand." Unknown.—EmN
Counting small-boned bodies. Robert Bly.—MoT
Counting the days. James S. Tippett.—HoS
Countries. See names of countries, as Mexico
Country. See Country life
"**Country** bumpkin." Clyde Watson.—WaF
Country cat. Elizabeth Jane Coatsworth.—UnGb
Country Christmas. Aileen Fisher.—HoS
Country idyll. Frances Cornford.—CoPu
Country life. See also Farm life; Village life
"Am I to tell you next of the storms and stars of autumn." From The Georgics. Virgil.—MaFw
Arriving in the country again. James Wright.—CoPu
Binsey poplars felled 1879. G. M. Hopkins.—MaFw
Bitter summer thoughts. C. Sandburg.—SaT
Blue horses. E. Roberson.—AdPb
The boy and the snake. C. and M. Lamb.—OpOx
A boy's song. J. Hogg.—OpOx
City fairies. M. B. Armstrong.—JaP
The city mouse and the country mouse. R. S. Sharpe.—OpOx
Country cat. E. J. Coatsworth.—UnGb
Country Christmas. A. Fisher.—HoS
Dear country witch. L. Moore.—MoSm
Fetching cows. N. MacCaig.—MaFw
Haymaking. E. Thomas.—PaP
Hoddesdon. A. S. Wilson.—PaP
Life in the country. M. Silverton.—CoPu
Midsummer jingle. N. Levy.—CoPu
O country people. J. Hewitt.—CoPi
On a little boy's endeavouring to catch a snake. T. Foxton.—OpOx
"Only a bold man ploughs the Weald for corn." From The land. V. Sackville-West.—PaP
Out into Essex. J. Betjeman.—PaP
The Romanies in town. A. Beresford.—ToM
Rudolph is tired of the city. G. Brooks.—UnGb
Rural scenery. J. Scott.—PaP
Simon Soggs' Thanksgiving. W. A. Croffut.—CoPt
Summer. C. G. Rossetti.—PaF
"There's not a hill in all the view." J. Clare.—PaP
To a fat lady seen from the train. F. Cornford.—LiS
Where the sidewalk ends. S. Silverstein.—SiW
The **country** mouse and the city mouse. Richard Scrafton Sharpe.—OpOx
Country trucks. Monica Shannon.—HoP
The **County** Mayo. Anthony Rafter, tr. fr. the Irish by James Stephens.—CoPi
Courage. See also Conduct of life; Heroes and heroines; Perseverance
Abdul Abulbul Amir. Unknown.—RoIt
Close your eyes. A. Bontemps.—AdPb
Feigned courage. C. and M. Lamb.—OpOx
"Friends." Unknown.—ClFc
The friends. D. Lee.—LeA
"I go forth to move about the earth." A. Lopez.—AlW
If we must die. C. McKay.—AdPb
Invictus. W. E. Henley.—RoIt
Legend. Judith Wright.—CoPt—MaFw
A North Pole story. M. B. Smedley.—OpOx
The pay is good. R. Kell.—ToM
Snow in Jerusalem. T. Carmi.—MeP
Strong men, riding horses. G. Brooks.—AdPb
The tale of Custard the Dragon. O. Nash.—UnGb
You are the brave. R. R. Patterson.—AdPb
Courlander, Harold
Work song. tr.—AbM
Court trials
"Fury said to." From Alice's adventures in wonderland. L. Carroll.—LiPc
Courtesy. See Etiquette
Courting. Alexander Resnikoff.—CoOh
Courtship. See also Love
"As I was going up Pippen-hill." Mother Goose.—AlC

The blacksmith's serenade. V. Lindsay.—CoPt
"Can you make a cambric shirt." Mother Goose.—JoA-4
Cashel of Munster. Unknown.—CoPi
The choice. W. M. Letts.—CoPi
"Country bumpkin." C. Watson.—WaF
Courtship. A. Resnikoff.—CoOh
The courtship of the Yonghy-Bonghy-Bo. E. Lear.—JoA-4
"Curly locks, curly locks, wilt thou be mine." Mother Goose.—AlC
"Curly locks, curly locks."—HoMg—JoA-4
"Eight o'clock is striking." Mother Goose.—AlC
The fair Circassian. R. Garnett.—CoPt
Fantasia. W. M. Letts.—CoPi
"A frog he would a-wooing go." Mother Goose.—JoA-4
"Here's a song of Tinker & Peter." Clyde Watson.—WaF
"I am a pretty wench." Unknown.—TrG
"I had a little castle upon the sea sand." Mother Goose.—TucMgl
"I had a young man." Mother Goose.—AlC
"In the month of February." Mother Goose.—TucMgl
"It's once I courted as pretty a lass." Unknown.—TrG
"John and Mary." Unknown.—EmN
The keys to Canterbury. Unknown.—JoA-4
"King Fisher courted Lady Bird." From Sylvie and Bruno concluded. L. Carroll.—LiPc
Like a sparkling bead. I. Bedniakov.—MoM
Lying. T. Moore.—CoPi
"Penny candy." C. Watson.—WaF
The picnic. J. Logan.—HiN
"Sukey, you shall be my wife." Mother Goose.—TucMgl
"The time I've lost in wooing." T. Moore.—CoPi
A tree toad. Unknown.—BrM
"Vera had a little light." Unknown.—EmN
The visit of the professor of aesthetics. From Far from Africa: Four poems. M. Danner.—AdPb
The wheatear and the snowbird. Unknown.—LeIb
The whistling thief. Unknown.—CoPt
"Young Roger came tapping at Dolly's window." Mother Goose.—AlC
The **courtship** of the Yonghy-Bonghy-Bo. Edward Lear.—JoA-4
"**Cousin** Reg is a charming boy." See Story of Reginald
Cousins, James H.
The corncrake.—CoPi
A curse on a closed gate. tr.—CoPi
Cover my earth mother. Unknown, tr. fr. the Zuñi by M. C. Stevenson.—BiI
"**Cover** my earth mother four times with many flowers." See Cover my earth mother
Cover up. Robert Froman.—FrSp
Covetousness. Peter Idley.—OpOx
"**Covetousness** hath never end." See Covetousness
"The **cow.**" See Cow
Cow ("The cow") Valerie Worth.—WoS
The **cow** ("The cow mainly moos as she chooses to moo") Jack Prelutsky.—PrP
The **cow** ("The friendly cow, all red and white") Robert Louis Stevenson.—OpOx—RoIt
Cow ("Hide of milk-and-honey") Harold Massingham.—MaFw
The **cow** ("Thank you, pretty cow that made") Ann and Jane Taylor.—OpOx
"The **cow** has a cud." See Chant
"The **cow** mainly moos as she chooses to moo." See The cow
"**Cow** sounds heavy." Karla Kuskin.—KuN
Cowan, Margaret
If I was president.—JoV
Cowboys
The glory trail. L. B. Clark.—CoPt
I am a cowboy in the boat of Ra. I. Reed.—AdPb
Strong men, riding horses. G. Brooks.—AdPb
The Zebra Dun. Unknown.—CoPt
Cowell, Sam
Villikins and his Dinah.—CoPt
Cowley, Malcolm
A smoke of birds.—MoT
Cowper. Norman Nicholson.—PlM
Cowper, William
Beau's reply.—RoIt
The nightingale and glow-worm.—RoIt
The nose and the eyes.—RoIt
On a spaniel called Beau killing a young bird.—RoIt
The poplar field.—MaFw
The snail.—RoIt
Squirrel in sunshine.—CoPu
Verses.—RoIt
The woodman's dog.—CoPu—JoA-4
Cowper, William (about)
Cowper. N. Nicholson.—PlM
Cows. See also Calves; Cattle
A blessing on the cows. S. Sullivan.—CoPi
Caprice. D. S. Shaw.—CoPt
Country idyll. F. Cornford.—CoPu
Cow ("The cow") V. Worth.—WoS
The cow ("The cow mainly moos as she chooses to moo") J. Prelutsky.—PrP
The cow ("The friendly cow, all red and white") R. L. Stevenson.—OpOx—RoIt
Cow ("Hide of milk-and-honey") H. Massingham.—MaFw
The cow ("Thank you, pretty cow that made") A. and J. Taylor.—OpOx
"Cow sounds heavy." K. Kuskin.—KuN
Cows ("The cows that browse in pastures") X. J. Kennedy.—KeO
Cows ("When I look at cows and think") A. Fisher.—FiFo

Cows.—*Continued*
"Cushy cow, bonny, let down thy milk." Mother Goose.—JoA-4
Drinking time. D. J. O'Sullivan.—CoPi
"East is east and west is west." Unknown.—CoOh
A farmer's boy. Unknown.—RoIt
Fence. V. Worth.—WoS
Fetching cows. N. MacCaig.—MaFw
The five toes. Unknown.—JoA-4
Jonathan. Unknown.—JoA-4
"Ladies and gentlemen." Unknown.—EmN
Life in the country. M. Silverton.—CoPu
"Milk-white moon, put the cows to sleep." C. Sandburg.—SaT
Milkmaid. L. Lee.—ToM
"Moo, moo, moo." Issa.—HaW
An old man's herd—On the Friday before Christmas. F. Holman.—HoI
Plymouth rocks. D. McCord.—McFm
"There was a piper, he'd a cow." Mother Goose.—AlC
"There was an old man who said, How" Nonsenses.—OpOx
"Two lookers." Unknown.—EmN
The woman of three cows. Unknown.—CoPi
Cows ("The cows that browse in pastures") X. J. Kennedy.—KeO
Cows ("When I look at cows and think") Aileen Fisher.—FiFo
"The **cows** that browse in pastures." See Cows
Coyotes
Coyote's night. P. George.—AlW
"I know everything in the bottom of my heart." Unknown.—ClFc
"Mad coyote." Unknown.—JoT
"My tail rattles." Unknown.—ClFc
Coyote's night. Phil George.—AlW
Crabapples
Crabapples. C. Sandburg.—SaT
Crabapples. Carl Sandburg.—SaT
Crabbe, George
"When next appeared a dam—so call the place—."—PaP
Crabbe, George (about)
George Crabbe. E. A. Robinson.—PlM
Crabs
Old Chang the crab. Unknown.—JoA-4
Crack in the wall holds flowers. Adam David Miller.—AdPb
"The **cracked** bell rings to Lenten service over." See April landscape
Crackers. See Cakes and cookies
The **crackling** twig. James Stephens.—CoPu
Cradle hymn ("Away in a [the] manger, no crib for a bed") Martin Luther.—JoA-4
Away in a manger.—LaS
Cradle hymn ("Hush, my dear, lie still and slumber") Isaac Watts.—OpOx
Hush, my babe.—LaS
A **cradle** song ("The angels are stooping") William Butler Yeats.—LiLc
A **cradle** song ("Golden slumbers kiss your eyes") See Lullaby
Cradle song ("Sleep, sleep, beauty bright") William Blake.—JoA-4
Cradle song ("What does little birdie say") See Sea dreams
Cradle songs. See Lullabies
Cradlesong. Tchicaya U Tam'si, tr. fr. the French by Gerald Moore.—AlPa (sel.)
Craik, Dinah Maria. See Mulock, Dinah Maria
Crane, Hart
To Emily Dickinson.—PlM
Crane, Hart (about)
Look, Hart, that horse you ride is wood. P. Viereck.—PlM
Crane, Stephen
"I saw a man pursuing the horizon."—RoIt
Cranes (birds)
"My dame had a tame lame crane." Unknown.—EmN
Recollection. D. Donnelly.—HiN
The sandhill crane. M. Austin.—AdP
Cranes (machines)
The death of the craneman. A. Hayes.—HiN
Near and far. H. Behn.—JoA-4—LiLc
Sunday sculpture. B. Katz.—HoP
Watching the wrecking crane.—B. Katz.—HoP
"**Crash** goes the trashcan, clatter and clacket." See Raccoon
Crashaw, Richard
The shepherds' hymn.—MaF
Craveirinha, José
Poem of the future citizen.—AbM
"**Crawl** into bed." Quandra Prettyman.—AdB
"**Crawling** to the edge to drool." See At the pool
Crayons. Marchette Chute.—ChRu
"A **crazy** kangaroo I knew." See Kangaroo and kiwi
The **crazy** woman. Gwendolyn Brooks.—AbM
"A **creak** out of the marsh in the dark hollow." See Facing up
Creation
"All things bright and beautiful." C. F. Alexander.—OpOx
The creation. J. W. Johnson.—AdPb—JoA-4
The creation of man. Unknown.—AbM
Emergence song. Unknown.—BiI
Genesis. E. Sewell.—PlM
He wove the strands of our life. Unknown.—BiI
"In the beginning there was no earth." N. Belting.—BeWi
Invitation of the Creator. Unknown.—AlPa
Nothing is. Sun Ra.—AdPb
Pied beauty. G. M. Hopkins.—MaFw—RoIt
Proud songsters. T. Hardy.—MaFw
Some days/out walking above. De Leon Harrison.—AdPb
Song of creation. Unknown.—BiI
"Then are the trackless copses alive with the trilling of birds." From The Georgics. Virgil.—MaFw
"Then he descended." Unknown.—BiI

They stooped over and came out. Unknown.—BiI
This newly created world. Unknown.—BiI
Thus it is told. Unknown.—BiI
Upward going. Unknown.—BiI
"When God set about to create heaven." From Genesis, Bible, Old Testament.—MaFw
The **creation.** James Weldon Johnson.—AdPb—JoA-4
The **creation** of man. Unknown, ad. by Zora Neale Hurston.—AbM
"**Creator,** you who dwell at the ends of the earth unrivaled." See Prayer
Credo. Georgia Douglas Johnson.—AdPb
Creek Indians. See Indians of the Americas—Creek
Creeley, Robert
Like they say.—CoPu
The name.—PeS
Please.—PlM
Creepy. Keith Hall, Jr.—HoH
The **cremation** of Sam McGee. Robert W. Service.—CoPt
The **crescent** boat. See Peter Bell
Cricket march. Carl Sandburg.—SaT
"**Cricket,** my boy." Issa, tr. fr. the Japanese by Hanako Fukuda.—HaW
Crickets
Cricket march. C. Sandburg.—SaT
"Cricket, my boy." Issa.—HaW
"Crickets." V. Worth.—WoS
Crickets ("All busy punching tickets") D. McCord.—JoA-4
Crickets ("Creak creak a wicker rocker") E. Merriam.—MeO
Crickets ("One cricket said to another") C. Aiken.—RoIt
"The crickets are saying." Kikaku.—BeM
Incidents in the life of my Uncle Arly. E. Lear.—LiWw—RoIt
"A little yellow cricket." Unknown.—JoT
"The noisy cricket." Watanabe Suiha.—MaFw
"Nothing in the voice of the cicada." Bashō.—MaFw
On the grasshopper and cricket. J. Keats.—JoA-4—PaF
Splinter. C. Sandburg.—SaT
"Trapped in a helmet." Bashō.—BeM
"**Crickets.**" Valerie Worth.—WoS
Crickets ("All busy punching tickets") David McCord.—JoA-4
Crickets ("Creak creak a wicker rocker") Eve Merriam.—MeO
Crickets ("One cricket said to another") Conrad Aiken.—RoIt
"The **crickets** are saying." Kikaku, tr. fr. the Japanese by Harry Behn.—BeM
Crime and criminals. See also Murder
The ballad of Minepit Shaw. R. Kipling.—CoPt
Confession overheard in a subway. K. Fearing.—PeS
From the underworld. H. Blaikley.—MoG
Macavity: The mystery cat. T. S. Eliot.—OpOx
Orpheus and Eurydice. From Metamorphoses. Ovid.—MoG
The outlaw of Loch Lene. Unknown.—CoPi
Outlaws. R. Graves.—HaWr
Paddy O'Rafther. S. Lover.—CoPi
"Pinky Pauper picked my pocket." C. Watson.—WaF
Porches. V. Worth.—WoS
A ruffian. T. L. Beddoes.—CoPu
To a rogue. J. Addison.—CoPu
"We can be together." P. Kantnea.—MoG
Cripples
Disabled. W. Owen.—CoPt
One, two, three. H. C. Bunner.—RoIt
"**Crispy,** salty, fry bread, smoked, dried, deer meat." See Child rest
Crisscross. Carl Sandburg.—SaT
"**Cristofo** Colombo was a hungry man." See Mysterious biography
Criticism. See Critics and criticism
Critics and criticism
His answer to the critics. Solomon ibn Gabirol.—MeP
The owl critic. J. T. Fields.—CoPt
The poet's fate. T. Hood.—CoPu
The scholars. W. B. Yeats.—PlM
To a captious critic. P. L. Dunbar.—AbM
To a friend: constructive criticism. Trajan, Emperor of Rome.—LiWw
To Christopher North. A. Tennyson.—CoPu
"The **critics** cry unfair." See In defense of black poets
"**Croak,** said the toad, I'm hungry, I think." Mother Goose.—TucMgl
"The **crocodile.**" See Alligator/Crocodile
"The **crocodile.**" See The crocodile's toothache
The **crocodile.** See Alice's adventures in wonderland—"How doth the little crocodile"
Crocodile. William Jay Smith.—BrM
"The **crocodile** wept bitter tears." See Crocodile
Crocodiles
Alligator/Crocodile. M. A. Hoberman.—HoR
"Come picture this lovely and frightening scene." K. Kuskin.—KuA
Crocodile. W. J. Smith.—BrM
The crocodile's toothache. S. Silverstein.—SiW
"How doth the little crocodile." From Alice's adventures in wonderland. L. Carroll.—LiLc—LiPc
The crocodile.—JoA-4
How doth.—LiS
"If you should meet a crocodile." Unknown.—BrM
The monkeys and the crocodile. L. E. Richards.—JoA-4
The purist. O. Nash.—LiWw
Said a long crocodile. L. Moore.—MoSm
The **crocodile's** toothache. Shel Silverstein.—SiW

The man in the onion bed. J. Ciardi.—BrM
A small discovery. J. A. Emanuel.—LiLc
"A tear rolled down my cheek." C. O'John.—AlW
Wailing song. Unknown.—BiI
"The weeping spreads." Unknown.—BiI
When Jesus wept. W. Billings.—LaS
Why is happy. D. Whitewing.—AlW
Winifred Waters. W. B. Rands.—OpOx
Crystal moment. Robert P. Tristram Coffin.—PeS
Cuccu song. See "Sumer is icumen in"
The **cuckoo** ("The cuckoo is a pretty bird") Unknown.—RoIt
The **cuckoo** ("If the cuckoo were") Kodo, tr. fr. the Japanese by Kenneth Yasuda.—MaFw
"The **cuckoo** and the donkey." Mother Goose, tr. fr. the German.—TucMg
"**Cuckoo,** if you must." Soseki, tr. fr. the Japanese by Harry Behn.—BeM
"The **cuckoo** is a pretty bird." See The cuckoo
Cuckoo song. See "Sumer is icumen in"
Cuckoos
The cuckoo ("The cuckoo is a pretty bird") Unknown.—RoIt
The cuckoo ("If the cuckoo were") Kodo.—MaFw
"The cuckoo and the donkey." Mother Goose.—TucMg
"Cuckoo, if you must." Soseki.—BeM
"O the cuckoo she's a pretty bird." Mother Goose.—AlC
"Repeat that, repeat." G. M. Hopkins.—MaFw
"Sumer is icumen in." Unknown.—RoIt
Cuccu song.—MaFw
Cuckoo song.—LiS
"Summer is a-coming in." Unknown.—RoIt
"There, where the skylark's." Kyorai.—BeM
To the cuckoo. W. Wordsworth.—RoIt
Weathers. T. Hardy.—PlP
"When a cuckoo sings." Bashō.—BeM
"**Cucumbers** always give me squirms." See From the kitchen—Cucumbers vs. pickles
Cucumbers vs. pickles. See From the kitchen
Cullen, Countee
Black majesty.—AdPb
Brown boy to brown girl.—AdPb
Christus natus est.—AbM
For a lady I knew.—AbM—LiWw
Four epitaphs.—AdPb
For a mouthy woman.—AbM—AdPb
For a poet.—AbM
For John Keats, apostle of beauty
Four epitaphs.—AdPb
For my grandmother
Four epitaphs.—AdPb
For Paul Laurence Dunbar
Four epitaphs.—AdPb
From the dark tower.—AdPb
Heritage.—AdPb
In memory of Colonel Charles Young.—AdPb
Incident.—AbM—AdPb—JoA-4
The lost zoo, sel.
The wakeupworld.—JoA-4
Saturday's child.—AdPb
Scottsboro, too, is worth its song.—AdPb
Sonnet.—PeS
Tableau.—AdPb
The wakeupworld. See The lost zoo
Yet do I marvel.—AdPb—PeS
Cult. Eve Merriam.—MeF
Cultural exchange. Langston Hughes.—AdPb
The **cumberbunce.** Paul West.—CoOh
Cumbo, Kattie M.
Dark people.—AdB
Malcolm.—AdB
Washiri (poet).—AdB
The **cummerbund.** Edward Lear.—LiWw
Cummings, E. (Edward) E. (Estlin)
"All in green went my love riding."—JoA-4—MaFw
"Buffalo Bill."—MoG
"Buy me an ounce and I'll sell you a pound."—HiN
Chanson innocente, sel.
"In just."—HiN—RoIt
In just-spring.—JoA-4
"Hist whist."—HoH
"In just." See Chanson innocente
In just-spring. See Chanson innocente—"In just"
"Little tree."—HoS—LiLc—MaFw
"My sweet old etcetera."—PeS
"Next to of course god america i."—HiN—PeS
"Nobody loses all the time."—LiWw—MaFw
"One winter afternoon."—HiN
"Pity this busy monster, manunkind."—PeS
"Rain or hail."—LiWw
Somewhere I have never travelled.—PeS
"Spring is like a perhaps hand."—MaFw
"Sweet spring is your."—HiN
"Who are you, little I."—LiLc
Cuney, Waring
Conception.—AbM
My Lord, what a morning.—AbM
Cunningham, Allan
"A wet sheet and a flowing sea."—RoIt
"A **cup** of proper coffee in a copper coffee cup." Unknown.—EmN
Cupid
If Cupid shoots. Unknown.—EmN
"What is the opposite of *Cupid.*" R. Wilbur.—WiO
Cups without wine. Judah Halevi, tr. fr. the Hebrew by Robert Mezey.—MeP
"**Cups** without wine are low things." See Cups without wine
The **curate's** kindness. Thomas Hardy.—PlP
The **cure.** William Carlos Williams.—PlM
Cure for a pussy cat. See That little black cat
"The **curfew** tolls the knell of parting day." See Elegy written in a country churchyard
Curiosity
Pandora. M. C. Livingston.—LiM—NeA
Warning to children. R. Graves.—MaFw

"**Curly** locks, curly locks." See "Curly locks, curly locks, wilt thou be mine"
"**Curly** locks, curly locks, wilt thou be mine." Mother Goose.—AlC
"Curly locks, curly locks."—HoM—JoA-4
Currey, R. N.
Unseen fire.—ToM
Curry, Linda
"Black woman I have."—JoV
"Death prosecuting life born."—JoV
"Fear have I when it comes."—JoV
Find my father with freedom.—JoV
For Nina Simone wherever you are.—JoV
"The grey sky."—JoV
No way out.—JoV
A **curse** on a closed gate. Unknown, tr. fr. the Irish by James H. Cousins.—CoPi
Curse on people that wish one ill. Unknown, tr. fr. the Yana by Edward Sapir.—BiI
Curses
"Bruadar and Smith and Glinn." Unknown.—CoPi
A curse on a closed gate. Unknown.—CoPi
Curse on people that wish one ill. Unknown.—BiI
A glass of beer. J. Stephens.—HiN
Irish curse on the occupying English. Unknown.—CoPi
Magic formula against disease. Unknown.—BiI
Traveller's curse after misdirection. R. Graves.—HiN—LiWw
"**Curses** on the snake of creation." See Magic formula against disease
"A **curve** came winding in the road." See On a bike
Curves
Curves. A. Fisher.—FiM
Curves. Aileen Fisher.—FiM
"**Cushy** cow, bonny, let down thy milk." Mother Goose.—JoA-4
The **Cussitaws** come east. Unknown, tr. fr. the Creek by A. S. Gatschet.—BiI
Customs
April 23. N. Belting.—BeSc
April 24. N. Belting.—BeSc
April 30. N. Belting.—BeSc
Customs change. Unknown.—OpOx
May day. N. Belting.—BeSc
May 1. N. Belting.—BeSc
May 14. N. Belting.—BeSc
Song of Lawino: An African lament. O. p'Bitek.—AlPa (sel.)
Customs change. Unknown.—OpOx
The **Cutty** Sark. See Dreams of a summer night, part VI
"**Cygnets,** you must practice early." See The swans
Cymbeline, sel. William Shakespeare
A morning song.—JoA-4
Cynddylan on a tractor. R. S. Thomas.—ToM
Cynic's epitaph. Thomas Hardy.—LiWw
Cynthia in the snow. Gwendolyn Brooks.—LiLc
Cypress trees
The black finger. A. W. Grimké.—AdPb
Last laugh. D. Young.—CoPu

D

D., H., pseud. (Hilda Doolittle; Mrs Richard Aldington)
Heat. H. D.—PaF
"**D** blues." Calvin C. Hernton.—AdPb
D. M. See M., D.
"**Daddy** drinks." See Idle chatter
Daddy fell into the pond. Alfred Noyes.—BrM
"**Daddy** how does an elephant feel." See Questions, quistions & quoshtions
Daddy-longlegs
Harvestman. D. McCord.—McFm—McS
"**Daddy's** back." See Sunday morning: Lonely
Daedalus. See also Icarus
Be Daedalus. N. Alba.—AdPb
Daedalus. A. Reid.—HiN
Daedalus. Alastair Reid.—HiN
The **daemon** lover. Unknown.—MaFw
Daffodils
Daffodils. W. Wordsworth.—JoA-4
"I wandered lonely as a cloud."—LiS
"Daffy-down-dilly has come up to town." Mother Goose.—AlC
"Daffy-down-dilly is new come to town."—HoMg
The Lent lily. From A Shropshire lad. A. E. Housman.—PaF
To daffadills. R. Herrick.—PaF
To daffodils.—JoA-4
Daffodils. William Wordsworth.—JoA-4
"I wandered lonely as a cloud."—LiS
"**Daffy**-down-dilly has come up to town." Mother Goose.—AlC
"Daffy-down-dilly is new come to town."—HoMg
"**Daffy**-down-dilly is new come to town." See "Daffy-down-dilly has come up to town"
"**Dainty** little maiden, whither would you wander." See The city child
The **dairymaid** and her milk-pot. Jean De La Fontaine, tr. fr. the French by Marianne Moore.—JoA-4
Daisies
"Buttercups and daisies." M. Howitt.—OpOx
Daisies. V. Worth.—WoS
Easter daisies. A. Fisher.—LaM
"The sun is today so enchanting." I. Muller.—MoM
Daisies. Valerie Worth.—WoS
"**Daisy** Deborah Delilah Dean." Unknown.—CoOr
Dakota Indians. See Indians of the Americas—Dakota
Dalcour, Pierre
Verse written in the album of mademoiselle.—AbM

Dalgliesh, Alice and Rhys, Ernest
Gretchen. trs.—JoA-4
Tradja of Norway. trs.—JoA-4
"**Dallán** Dé, Dallán Dé." See Butterfly in the fields
The **dalliance** of the eagles. Walt Whitman.—CoPu
Dalven, Rae
The first step. tr.—PlM
The **dam.** Patric Dickinson.—CoPt
Dame Duck's lecture. Unknown.—RoIt
"**Dame,** get up and bake your pies." Mother Goose.—JoA-4
"**Dame** Kangaroo is well-equipped." See Marsupial transportation
Dame Trot. Mother Goose.—BlM
"**Dame** Trot and her cat." See Dame Trot
Dame Wiggins of Lee. Unknown.—OpOx
"**Dame** Wiggins of Lee was a worthy old soul." See Dame Wiggins of Lee
Dan. Carl Sandburg.—SaT
The **dance** ("In Breughel's great picture, The Kermess") William Carlos Williams.—HiN
Dance ("Washing on the line") Robert Froman.—FrSp
A **dance** for militant dilettantes. Al Young.—AdPb
"**Dance,** little baby, dance up high." See The baby's dance
Dance of the Abakweta. See Far from Africa: Four poems
Dance of the infidels. Al Young.—AdPb
Dance song ("Eastward I was idle") Unknown, fr. the Copper Eskimo.—LeIb
Dance song ("I am quite unable") Unknown, fr. the Copper Eskimo.—LeIb
Dance song ("My song, that one, it begins to want to come out") Unknown, fr. Point Hope, Alaska.—LeIb
"**Dance** there upon the shore." See To a child dancing in the wind
"**Dance** to your daddy." Unknown, tr. fr. the Scottish by Iona and Peter Opie.—JoA-4
The **dancer.** Al Young.—AdPb
Dancers. See Dances and dancing
Dances and dancing
Bottled: New York. H. Johnson.—AdPb
"Buy me an ounce and I'll sell you a pound." E. E. Cummings.—HiN
Canto 5. T. Weatherly.—AdPb
Celebration. A. Lopez.—AlW
"Charlie Chaplin went to France." Unknown.—EmN
"Come unto these yellow sands." From The tempest. W. Shakespeare.—LiS—RoIt
Cordelia Brown. Unknown.—AbM
The dance. W. C. Williams.—HiN
Dance of the Abakweta. From Far from Africa: Four poems. M. Danner.—AdPb
Dance song ("Eastward I was idle") Unknown.—LeIb
Dance song ("I am quite unable") Unknown.—LeIb
Dance song ("My song, that one, it begins to want to come out") Unknown.—LeIb
"Dance to your daddy." Unknown.—JoA-4
Dancing pants. S. Silverstein.—SiW
"Dancing teepees." C. O'John.—AlW
Dark girl. A. Bontemps.—PeS
"Dry and parched." A. Lopez.—AlW
Enchantment. L. Alexander.—AdPb
Fourth dance poem. G. W. Barrax.—AdPb
Good times. L. Clifton.—AdM—AdPb—HiN
Great things. T. Hardy.—PlP
"In the spring rain." Issa.—HaW
Juba dance. Unknown.—AbM
"The king said to Salome." Unknown.—CoOh
Lines written for Gene Kelly to dance to. C. Sandburg.—SaT
"Little Martha piggy-wig." C. Watson.—WaF
The lobster quadrille. From Alice's adventures in wonderland. L. Carroll.—OpOx
The Lord of the Dance. S. Carter.—LaS
The lost dancer. J. Toomer.—AdPb
My papa's waltz. T. Roethke.—HiN—MaFw—PeS
Off the ground. W. De La Mare.—CoPt
Phrases. Jean-Nicolas-Arthur Rimbaud.—MaFw
A piper. S. O'Sullivan.—CoPi—CoPu
The round. P. Booth.—HiN
Sea horse. Unknown.—AbM
Song. Unknown.—BiI
Song of the deer dancing. Unknown.—BiS
Song of the ghost dance. Unknown.—BiI
The song of the Jellicles. T. S. Eliot.—LiLc—OpOx
"Spanish dancer, do the split." Unknown.—EmN
"Sun dancers." P. Irving.—AlW
Tarantella. H. Belloc.—LiS
Tarantula. M. A. Hoberman.—HoR
Theme one: The variations. A. Wilson.—AdPb
"There was a man and he stayed within." Mother Goose.—TucMg
To a child dancing in the wind. W. B. Yeats.—CoPi
Twerüre. Unknown.—SeS
The twist. E. Brathwaite.—AbM
We dance like Ella riffs. C. M. Rodgers.—AdPb
We spirits dance. Unknown.—BiI
Zalka Peetruza. R. G. Dandridge.—AdPb
Dancing. See Dances and dancing
Dancing pants. Shel Silverstein.—SiW
"**Dancing,** prancing." See Signs of Christmas
"**Dancing** teepees." Calvin O'John.—AlW
"**Dandelion.**" See No pretending
Dandelion. Hilda Conkling.—JoA-4
Dandelions
Dandelion. H. Conkling.—JoA-4
The first dandelion. W. Whitman.—RoIt
"First you see me in the grass." Unknown.—EmN
No pretending. R. Froman.—FrSp

Dawn ("Quick cold hands") Octavio Paz.—MoT
"**Dawn** an unsympathetic yellow." See Electrical storm
"The **dawn** breaks over the mooring." Mikhail Lukonin, tr. fr. the Russian by Miriam Morton.—MoM
Dawn is a feeling. Mike Pinder.—MoG
"**Dawn** is a feeling, a beautiful ceiling." See Dawn is a feeling
Day. See also Afternoon; Bed-time; Evening; Morning; Night
The clock ticks. E. Merriam.—MeO
"Days that the wind takes over." K. Kuskin.—KuN
First sight of her and after. T. Hardy.—PlP
Hidden treasure. B. Katz.—HoCs
"I look out of my window." Olga.—MoM
"Luminous silence. . . . " A. Atwood.—AtM
"O small bird wakening." From Bring the day. T. Roethke.—JoA-4
Problems. C. O'John.—AlW
Query. L. McKee.—CoPu
Song. D. Justice.—HiN
This day is over. C. O'John.—AlW
"What a day." S. Silverstein.—SiW
"Who are you, little I." E. E. Cummings.—LiLc
"Who can stay indoors." Kikaku.—BeM
"**Day** after day, alone on a hill." See The fool on the hill
"**Day** and night I scan the horizon." Nar-gad Diack, tr. fr. the Senegal by Lamine Diakhaté.—AlPa
"**Day** arises." See Magic song for him who wishes to live
Day before Christmas. Marchette Chute.—HoS—LaM
The **day-breakers.** Arna Bontemps.—AdPb
"The **day** broke with slender rain." See My breath became
"**Day** by day I float my paper boats one by one down the running stream." See Paper boats
Day, Doris (about)
"Doris Day, the movie star." Unknown.—EmN
"The **day** frolics through the village." See A bit of cobweb
"The **day** has risen." Unknown, tr. fr. the Hopi by H. R. Voth.—BiI
"The **day** he discovered a mother and child in the river, he wrote." See A Negro soldier's Viet Nam diary
The **day** is done. Henry Wadsworth Longfellow.—RoIt
"The **day** is done, and the darkness." See The day is done
"A **day** is drawing to its fall." See First sight of her and after
"The **day** is full of mischief." See Like a sparkling bead
"The **day** is past, the sun is set." See Evening
Day-Lewis, Cecil
"Am I to tell you next of the storms and stars of autumn." See The Georgics
Circus lion.—ToM
The Georgics, sels. tr.—MaFw
"Am I to tell you next of the storms and stars of autumn"
"Next I came to the manna, the heavenly gift of honey"
"Then are the trackless copses alive with the trilling of birds"
Jig.—CoPi
"Next I came to the manna, the heavenly gift of honey." See The Georgics
"Then are the trackless copses alive with the trilling of birds." See The Georgics
Watching post.—ToM
Day of the wolf. Keith Wilson.—HaWr
"**Day** unto day bequeaths its trembling sun." See The lonely say
"The **day** when Charmus ran with five." See A mighty runner
"The **day** will come." See All of us a family
Daybreak. Carl Sandburg.—SaT
"**Daybreak** comes first." See Daybreak
Daybreak in Alabama. Langston Hughes.—HoD
"**Daylight** falls upon the path, the forest falls behind." See I think I understand
Dayre, Sydney (Mrs Cochran)
A lesson for mamma.—OpOx
Morning compliments.—OpOx
Days. See Days of the week
"The **days** are cold, the nights are long." See The cottager to her infant
"The **days** grow ever shorter." See A schoolboy's lament
"The **days** grow long, the mountains." See South wind
The **days** of my people. Michael Gill.—JoV
"The **days** of my people, lonely, sad; hiding behind." See The days of my people
Days of the week
"If you sneeze on Monday, you sneeze for danger." Mother Goose.—AlC
"Monday's child is fair of face." Unknown.—JoA-4
Days of the week—Saturday
At home. Unknown.—MoM
"On Saturday night (shall be)." Mother Goose.—AlC
Saturday in New York. A. Beresford.—ToM
Saturday's child. C. Cullen.—AdPb
Spring Saturday. M. Chute.—ChRu
Days of the week—Sunday
Going to church. L. Lenski.—LeC
"On Saturday night (shall be)." Mother Goose.—AlC
Ploughing on Sunday. W. Stevens.—HiN
Sabbath stars. A. Shlonsky.—MeP
Sunday afternoon. D. Levertov.—PeS
Sunday in the city. L. Lenski.—LeC
Sunday morning. W. Moreland.—AdPb
Sunday morning song. Unknown.—AbM
Sunday street, downtown. R. Froman.—FrSp

The cremation of Sam McGee. R. W. Service.—CoPt
"The crickets are saying." Kikaku.—BeM
Crossing the bar. A. Tennyson.—RoIt
Dark girl. A. Bontemps.—PeS
The dead at Clonmacnoise. Unknown.—CoPi
"The dead man dragged from the sea." C. Gardner.—AdPb
"The dead who climb up to the sky." Unknown.—LeIb
Death. Unknown.—AlPa
Death as history. Jay Wright.—AdPb
Death in Yorkville. L. Hughes.—AdPb
Death of a friend. P. Murray.—AdPb
Death of a naturalist. S. Heaney.—HiN
Death of a peasant. R. S. Thomas.—MaFw
Death of a sister. Unknown.—BiI
Death of a son. Unknown.—BiI
The death of Ben Hall. W. H. Ogilvie.—CoPt
The death of Dr King. S. Cornish.—AdPb
The death of Dr King #1.—AdM (sel.)
The death of Keats. V. Watkins.—PlM
The death of kings. From King Richard II. W. Shakespeare.—MoG
The death of Robin Hood ("Give me my bow, said Robin Hood") Eugene Field.—CoPt
The death of Robin Hood ("When Robin Hood and Little John") Unknown.—MaFw
The death of the ball turret gunner. R. Jarrell.—PeS
The death of the craneman. A. Hayes.—HiN
Death songs. L. V. Mack.—AdPb
Death takes only a minute. A. T. Pratt.—AlW
"Death will come." Unknown.—ClFc
Deathwatch. M. S. Harper.—AdPb
The discovery. M. Gibbon.—CoPi
Do nothing till you hear from me. D. Henderson.—AdPb
A dream ("I heard the dogs howl in the moonlight night") W. Allingham.—CoPi
The dream (Part I) ("Our life is twofold, sleep hath its own world") Lord Byron.—MoG
The dug-out. S. Sassoon.—MaFw
The dying child. J. Clare.—MaFw
Dylan Thomas. S. Spender.—PlM
The early purges. S. Heaney.—HiN
Endless deep. C. Minier.—JoV
The erl-king's daughter. J. G. Herder.—CoPt
Eulogy for populations. R. Wellburn.—AdPb
Euphemistic. E. Merriam.—MeO
Evil is no black thing. S. W. Fabio.—AdPb
Excelsior. H. W. Longfellow.—LiS
Exit Molloy. D. Mahon.—CoPi
"Exultation is the going." E. Dickinson.—ThI
Fall down. C. C. Hernton.—AdPb
The far field. T. Roethke.—JoA-4 (sel.)
Farewell. M. Kunene.—AlPa
The father and his children. Unknown.—OpOx
Father Son and Holy Ghost. A. Lorde.—AdPb
Final curve. L. Hughes.—AdM
First death in Nova Scotia. E. Bishop.—HiN
Flannan isle. W. W. Gibson.—CoPt
For a lamb. R. Eberhart.—PeS
For real. J. Cortez.—AdPb
The fox. K. Patchen.—ToM
"From the middle." Unknown.—ClFc
The gangster's death. I. Reed.—AdPb
Glimpse. P. C. Lomax.—AdPb
"The glories of our blood and state." From Contention of Ajax and Ulysses. J. Shirley.—RoIt
Go down death. J. W. Johnson.—AdPb
The Golden Vanity. Unknown.—RoIt
Gone away. D. Levertov.—PeS
"Had a little girl dressed in blue." Unknown.—EmN
Heraclitus. Callimachus.—CoPu—PlM
Here where Coltrane is. M. S. Harper.—AdPb
Hospital/poem. S. Sanchez.—AdPb
The hour. U. Z. Greenberg.—MeP
How Bill went East. G. S. Bryan.—CoPt
How's my boy. S. Dobell.—RoIt
"I heard a fly buzz—when I died." E. Dickinson.—ThI
"I may not know them all by name." Unknown.—MoM
I saw. N. Sach.—MeP
"If a man who turnips cries." S. Johnson.—MiMg
If we must die. C. McKay.—AdPb
Illinois farmer. C. Sandburg.—SaT
Imperial thumbprint. T. Weatherly.—AdPb
In memory of my dear grandchild Anne Bradstreet. A. Bradstreet.—ThI
In tenebris. T. Hardy.—PlP
In the backs. F. Cornford.—PaP
Incident in a rose garden. D. Justice.—HiN
The invention of comics. LeRoi Jones.—AdPb
It's here in the. R. Atkins.—AdPb—PeS
Janet waking. J. C. Ransom.—HiN—PeS
John Muir on Mt Ritter. From Burning. G. Snyder.—MaFw
Joseph Mica. Unknown.—MoG
Julie-Jane. T. Hardy.—PlP
Junglegrave. S. E. Anderson.—AdPb
The king must die. B. Taupin.—MoG
The knight's leap. C. Kingsley.—CoPt
Lacrimas or there is a need to scream. K. C. Lyle.—AdPb
"Ladies and gentlemen." Unknown.—EmN
Lalla Rookh. T. Moore.—LiS
Last rites. C. G. Rossetti.—OpOx
The last signal. T. Hardy.—PlM—PlP
The last soldier. S. Morozov.—MoM
The lesson. E. Lucie-Smith.—HiN—ToM
Letter from a death bed. J. Ciardi.—HiN
Lines for a dead poet. D. Ferry.—PlM
Lingle, lingle. Unknown.—BlM
"Little General Monk." Mother Goose.—MiMg
The lonely say. Avraham Ben Yitzhak.—MeP
Longing for death. Unknown.—AlPa
The love-talker. E. Carbery.—CoPi—CoPt

"When black people are." A. B. Spellman.—AdPb
When I awoke. R. R. Patterson.—AdPb
"Who comes." Unknown.—LeIb
The widow of Drynam. P. MacDonogh.—CoPi
A woman mourned by daughters. A. Rich.—HiN
The workbox. T. Hardy.—PlP
The wreck of the Hesperus. H. W. Longfellow.—RoIt
Ye hasten to the grave. P. B. Shelley.—MoG
You and I shall go. Unknown.—BiI
Death. Unknown, tr. fr. the Kuba by Ulli Beier.—AlPa
Death and immortality. See also Immortality
In memoriam, sels. A. Tennyson
"Now fades the last long streak of snow."—PaF
Ring out, wild bells.—MaF—RoIt
"Tonight the winds begin to rise."—PaF
"Red Eagle." J. Campbell.—AlW
Death as history. Jay Wright.—AdPb
Death in Yorkville. Langston Hughes.—AdPb
Death of a friend. Pauli Murray.—AdPb
Death of a naturalist. Seamus Heaney.—HiN
Death of a peasant. R. S. Thomas.—MaFw
Death of a sister. Unknown, tr. fr. the Fox by William Jones.—BiI
Death of a son. Unknown, tr. fr. the Iroquois by Ely S. Parker.—BiI
The **death** of Ben Hall. Will H. Ogilvie.—CoPt
Death of Dr King. Sam Cornish.—AdPb
Death of Dr King #1.—AdM (sel.)
The **death** of justice. Walter Everette Hawkins.—AdPb
The **death** of Keats. Vernon Watkins.—PlM
The **death** of kings. See King Richard II
The **death** of Robin Hood ("Give me my bow, said Robin Hood") Eugene Field.—CoPt
The **death** of Robin Hood ("When Robin Hood and Little John") Unknown.—MaFw
The **death** of the ball turret gunner. Randall Jarrell.—PeS
The **death** of the craneman. Alfred Hayes.—HiN
"**Death** prosecuting life born." Linda Curry.—JoV
Death songs. L. V. Mack.—AdPb
Death takes only a minute. Agnes T. Pratt.—AlW
"**Death,** tho I see him not, is near." See Age
"**Death** will come." Unknown, tr. fr. the Omaha.—ClFc
Deathwatch. Michael S. Harper.—AdPb
"**Debbie** and Mark." Unknown.—MoBw
"**Debbie** is in DEBt." See Inside information
Deborah Delora. Unknown.—CoOh
"**Deborah** Delora, she liked a bit of fun." See Deborah Delora
Deceit
Grandpa is ashamed. O. Nash.—CoPu
A word of encouragement. J. R. Pope.—CoPu
December
December ("The end of a thing") L. Clifton.—ClE
December ("I like days") A. Fisher.—HoS
December music. W. T. Scott.—RoIt
December ("The end of a thing") Lucille Clifton.—ClE
December ("I like days") Aileen Fisher.—HoS
December music. Winfield Townley Scott.—RoIt
December 20: 5 more days. Lucille Clifton.—ClEa
December 21: Snow. Lucille Clifton.—ClEa
December 22: Window shopping. Lucille Clifton.—ClEa
December 23: Early. Lucille Clifton.—ClEa
December 23: Late. Lucille Clifton.—ClEa
December 24: Christmas eve. Lucille Clifton.—ClEa
December 24: A tree in an elevator. Lucille Clifton.—ClEa
December 25: Christmas morning. Lucille Clifton.—ClEa
December 25: Christmas night. Lucille Clifton.—ClEa
Deciduous. Eve Merriam.—MeO
"**Deciduous** deciduous." See Deciduous
"**Deck** the halls with poison ivy." Unknown.—MoBw
Declaration of independence. Wolcott Gibbs.—PeS
"A **decrepit** old gasman, named Peter." Unknown.—LiWw
Dedication to the final confrontation. Lloyd Corbin, Jr.—AdPb
"**Deedle,** deedle, dumpling, my son John." See "Diddle, diddle, dumpling, my son John"
Deeds
Crickets. C. Aiken.—RoIt
"A man of words and not of deeds." Mother Goose.—AlC
"**Deep** and dark is ocean's mystery." See Villanelle of the sea
"**Deep** in a windless." Busōn, tr. fr. the Japanese by Harry Behn.—BeM
"**Deep** in Alabama earth." See Alabama earth
"**Deep** in earth's opaque mirror." See Symmetries and asymmetries
"**Deep** in the fading leaves of light." See Carol
"**Deep** in the mountains we have no calendar." Unknown, tr. fr. the Korean by Chung Seuk Park and ad. by Virginia Olsen Baron.—BaSs
"**Deep** in the stable tied with rope." See Country idyll
"**Deep** in the woods is a blackberry bush." See Eating out in autumn
"**Deep** in your cheeks." See Origins
"**Deep** river." Unknown.—BrW
Deer
"All in green went my love riding." E. E. Cummings.—JoA-4—MaFw
The baby tigers. K. Raikin.—MoM

Delany, Clarissa Scott
Solace.—AdPb
Delaware Indians. See Indians of the Americas—Delaware
Delicatessen. Lois Lenski.—LeC
De Magalhães, J. V. Conto
Love song. tr.—BiI
Demeanour. Unknown.—OpOx
Demetracopoulou, D.
Dream song ("Above the place where the minnow maiden sleeps while her fins move gently in the water") tr.—BiI
Dream song ("Where will you and I sleep") tr.—BiI
Spirits. tr.—BiI
We spirits dance. tr.—BiI
You and I shall go. tr.—BiI
De Molina, Christóbal
Prayer. tr.—BiI
"**Denied** the shelter of air and the power." See A broken gull
Denmark. See also Nursery rhymes—Danish
Beowulf's voyage to Denmark. Unknown.—MaFw (sel.)
Densmore, Frances
"As my eyes." tr.—JoT
"At the rainbow spring." tr.—JoT
"Brave Buffalo." tr.—JoT
"Butterfly, butterfly, butterfly, butterfly." tr.—JoT
"The deer, the deer, here he went." tr.—JoT
"Don't you ever." tr.—JoT
Dream song ("Sometimes") tr.—BiI
Dream song ("Where the mountain crosses") tr.—BiI
"An eagle feather I see." tr.—JoT
"Father." tr.—JoT
"Friend." tr.—JoT
"Here am I." tr.—JoT
"The old men." tr.—JoT
"The Sioux women." tr.—JoT
Song ("Mine is a proud village, such as it is") tr.—BiI
Song ("Whence does he spring") tr.—BiI
Song of reproach. tr.—BiI
"They are sailing on the breeze." tr.—JoT
"A voice." tr.—JoT
War song. tr.—BiI
The wind blows from the sea. tr.—BiI
"A wolf." tr.—JoT
"You, whose day it is." tr.—JoT
"A young man going to war." tr.—JoT
—and Higheagle, Robert P.
"At night may I roam." trs.—BiI
Dentists
The crocodile's toothache. S. Silverstein.—SiW
Tooth trouble. D. McCord.—McS
A **denunciation** of the princes and prophets. See Micah
Department store. Lois Lenski.—LeC
Depreciation
To Pi Ssu Yao. Tu Fu.—PlM
Depression before spring. Wallace Stevens.—HaWr
Der arme poet. Michael Roberts.—PlM
Deranged. Padraic Fiacc.—CoPi
De Sahagún, Bernardino
Omen ("By daylight a fire fell") tr.—BiI
Omen ("By night a voice was heard in the air") tr.—BiI
Prayer. tr.—BiI
Supplication to the rain god and the spirits of water. tr.—BiI
Words spoken by a mother to her newborn son as she cuts the umbilical cord. tr.—BiI
"**Descend,** silent spirit." See Prayer to the snowy owl
Descent. Eve Merriam.—MeO
Descents
Brown's descent or The willy-nilly slide. R. Frost.—CoPt
Descent. E. Merriam.—MeO
The **description** of a good boy. Henry Dixon.—OpOx
Desert places. Robert Frost.—HiN
The **deserted** village, sel. Oliver Goldsmith
The village schoolmaster.—RoIt
Deserts
Children of the desert. From The people, yes. C. Sandburg.—SaT
Desert places. R. Frost.—HiN
Rain in the desert. J. G. Fletcher.—HiN
The **design.** Clarence Major.—AdPb
"**Desolate** and lone." See Lost
Despair
Bessie Bobtail. J. Stephens.—CoPi
On slaughter. C. N. Bialik.—MeP
On the death of Atahualpa. Unknown.—BiI
The unfortunate grocer. L. E. Richards.—CoOr
"**Desperate** Dan." Mother Goose.—AlC
Destruction
Filling the marsh. F. Holman.—HoI
The house on a hill. E. A. Robinson.—RoIt
Walt Whitman at Bear mountain. L. Simpson.—PlM
Determination. Dudley Randall.—AdPb
Detroit, Michigan
To the new annex to the Detroit county jail. R. W. Thomas.—AdPb
Deutsch, Babette
July in Dutchess county.—HaWr
Morning workout.—FlH
No moon, no star.—HaWr
De Veaux, Michael
"Two days."—HoC
Devil
The daemon lover. Unknown.—MaFw
The devil's bag. J. Stephens.—CoPi—CoPt
Epigram. A. Lanusse.—AbM
Epigram addressed to an artist. R. Burns.—CoPu
"It did not last: the Devil, howling Ho." J. C. Squire.—LiWw
The love-talker. E. Carbery.—CoPi—CoPt
On Andrew Turner. R. Burns.—CoPu

Devil—*Continued*
"St Dunstan, as the story goes." Mother Goose.—MiMg—TrG
"Tom was a bad boy." Unknown.—EmN
Twilight piece. C. N. Bialik.—MeP
The **devil's** bag. James Stephens.—CoPi—CoPt
The **devourers.** Rose Macaulay.—PaP
Dew
"A breeze stirs at dawn." Asayasu.—BeM
"Dew Eagle, at night." N. Belting.—BeWi
"Grasshopper, take care." Issa.—HaW
"I washed my hands in water that never rained nor run." Unknown.—EmN
Morning light (the dew-drier). E. L. Newsome.—AdPb
"Now that night is gone." Busōn.—BeM
"This dewdrop world." Issa.—AtM
"**Dew** Eagle, at night." Natalia Belting.—BeWi
"The **dew** was falling fast, the stars began to blink." See The pet lamb
"**Dewey** was an admiral down on Manila bay." Unknown.—MoBw
"**Dewy** drops." See You too
d'Harcourt, R. and M.
Song. tr.—BiI
Diack, Nar-gad
"Day and night I scan the horizon."—AlPa
Diakhaté, Lamine
"Day and night I scan the horizon." tr.—AlPa
"I shall bring honour to my blood." tr.—AlPa
Dialect—American—Blacks
"D blues." C. Hernton.—AdPb
Little brown baby. P. L. Dunbar.—AbM
A Negro love song. P. L. Dunbar.—AbM
Positives. J. Amini.—AdPb
Signals. J. Amini.—AdPb
Sister Lou. S. A. Brown.—AdPb
Southern road. S. A. Brown.—AdPb
When I heard dat white man say. Z. Gilbert.—AdPb
When Malindy sings. P. L. Dunbar.—AdPb
Dialect—Scottish. See also entries under Burns, Robert
"Hogmanay." Unknown.—MaF
"It's the nicht atween the saints and souls." Unknown.—MaF (sel.)
Last laugh. D. Young.—CoPu
The mither's lament. S. G. Smith.—CoPu
Diamonds
"Spring in the river." A. Atwood.—AtM
"**Diana** Fitzpatrick Mauleverer James." A. A. Milne.—CoPu
Diaries
Not again. P. Brown.—CoPu
Diaw, Ibra
"I shall bring honour to my blood."—AlPa
Dibdin, Charles
The sailor's consolation.—RoIt
Dibdin, Thomas
A child that has a cold.—CoPu
"**Dick** and Will and Charles and I." See Autumn
Dick Szymanski. Ogden Nash.—FlH
"**Dickery,** dickery, dare." Mother Goose.—AlC—TrG
Dickey, James
"Bums, on waking."—MoT
Deer among cattle.—MoT
The dusk of horses.—JoA-4
The heaven of animals.—HiN
The lifeguard.—PeS
Listening to foxhounds.—HaWr
Dickinson, Emily
"As awful tempest mashed the air."—ThI
"As imperceptibly as grief."—PaF
Autumn. See "The morns are meeker than they were"
"Because I could not stop for death."—MaFw—ThI
"A bird came down the walk."—RoIt
A book. See "There is no frigate like a book"
"Dear March, come in."—PaF
"Exultation is the going."—ThI
"I can wade grief."—ThI
"I heard a fly buzz—when I died."—ThI
"I like to see it lap the miles."—ThI
"I lost a world, the other day."—ThI
"I never hear the word *escape.*"—ThI
"I never saw a moor."—JoA-4—LiLc
"I stepped from plank to plank."—ThI
"If you were coming in the fall."—ThI
I'm nobody. See "I'm nobody, who are you"
"I'm nobody, who are you."—ThI
I'm nobody.—CoPu
"A light exists in spring."—PaF
Morning. See "Will there really be a morning"
"The morns are meeker than they were."—JoA-4—PaF
Autumn.—RoIt
"A narrow fellow in the grass."—AdP—MaFw—ThI
The snake.—UnGb
"Of all the souls that stand create."—ThI
"Our journey had advanced."—MoG
"The poets light but lamps."—PlM
"Presentiment—is that long shadow—on the lawn."—ThI
"A route of evanescence."—ThI
"The sky is low, the clouds are mean."—PaF
The snake. See "A narrow fellow in the grass"
"Success is counted sweetest."—RoIt
"That love is all there is."—ThI
"There is no frigate like a book"
A book.—RoIt
"There's a certain slant of light."—PaF—ThI
"These are the days when birds come back."—PaF
This was a poet.—PlM
"The way I read a letter's—this."—ThI
"Will there really be a morning"
Morning.—RoIt
"The wind, tapped like a tired man."—ThI
Dickinson, Emily (about)
I am in danger—Sir. A. Rich.—PlM
To Emily Dickinson. H. Crane.—PlM

Dickinson, Patric
The dam.—CoPt
"**Did** they catch as it were in a Vision at shut of the day." See Jezreel
"**Did** they dare, did they dare, to slay Eoghan Ruadh." See Lament for death of Eoghan Ruadh O'Neill
"**Did** you ever." See Acrobat
"**Did** you ever ever ever think." See Question
"**Did** you ever see the catfish." Unknown.—EmN
"**Did** you ever see the chimney-sweep." Unknown.—EmN
"**Did** you ever see the cowslip." Unknown.—EmN
"**Did** you ever see the moonbeam." Unknown.—EmN
"**Did** you ever see the ocean-wave." Unknown.—EmN
"**Did** you ever see the peanut-stand." Unknown.—EmN
"**Did** you ever see the toothpick." Unknown.—EmN
"**Did** you ever stop to think." Unknown.—MoBw
"**Did** you hear of the curate who mounted his mare." See The priest and the mulberry tree
"**Did** you say *a notion* or *an ocean.*" Unknown.—EmN
"**Diddle,** diddle, dumpling, my son John." Mother Goose.—JoA-4
"Deedle, deedle, dumpling, my son John."—AlC
"**Didn't** my Lord deliver Daniel." Unknown.—BrW
"**Didrum** drum." See Purring song
Differences
For Hettie. LeRoi Jones.—PeS
"**Digger** Boy was hunting clams." N. Belting.—BeWi
Digging ("Children my finger and my thumb") Seamus Heaney.—ToM
Digging ("Today I think") Edward Thomas.—JoA-4—PaF
Digging for China. Richard Wilbur.—HiN
"A **diller,** a dollar." Mother Goose.—AlC—JoA-4
"**Dilly** dilly piccalilli." Clyde Watson.—WaF
Dinesen, Isak
Zebra.—AdP
"**Ding,** dong." Clyde Watson.—WaF
"**Ding,** dong, bell." Mother Goose.—AlC—BlM—JoA-4
Dingman's marsh. John Moore.—HiN
The **dinkey-bird.** Eugene Field.—RoIt
Dinky. Theodore Roethke.—LiWw
Dinner
Dinnertime. M. Chute.—ChRu
The feckless dinner party. W. De La Mare.—CoPt
Get up, get up. Unknown.—CoPu
Othello Jones dresses for dinner. E. Roberson.—AdPb
Point of view. S. Silverstein.—SiW
Dinnertime. Marchette Chute.—ChRu
The **dinosaur.** Bert Leston Taylor.—LiWw
Dinosaurs
"Bellowed the ogre." L. Moore.—MoSm
The dinosaur. B. L. Taylor.—LiWw
The ichthyosaurus. J. F. Bellows.—CoOr
"If I had a brontosaurus." S. Silverstein.—CoOr—SiW
Natural history. W. J. Smith.—LiWw
The power shovel. R. B. Bennett.—HoP
Steam shovel. C. Malam.—HoP
"The trouble with a dinosaur." X. J. Kennedy.—KeO
"The **dinosaurs** are not dead." See Steam shovel
Dinsburg, Tanya
In autumn.—MoM
Diop, Birago
Souffles.—AlPa
Diop, David
Africa.—AlPa
Defiance against force.—AlPa
Rama Kam.—AlPa
The renegade.—AlPa
Dipoko, M'bella Sonne
Our history.—AlPa
Pain.—AlPa
Direction. Alonzo Lopez.—AlW
Dirge ("I see it") Unknown, tr. fr. the Dahomean by Frances Herskovits.—AlPa
Dirge ("It is the endless dance of the dead") Quincy Troupe.—AdPb
A **dirge** ("Rough wind, that moanest loud") Percy Bysshe Shelley.—MoG
Dirge for the year. Percy Bysshe Shelley.—PaF
Dirges. See Laments
Dirt road. Calvin O'John.—AlW
The **dirtiest** man in the world. Shel Silverstein.—SiW
The **dirty** word. Eve Merriam.—MeF
Disabled. Wilfred Owen.—CoPt
Disappointment. See Failure; Misfortune; Pessimism
Disaster. Charles S. Calverley.—LiS
Disasters. See also kinds of disasters, as Shipwrecks
Disaster. C. S. Calverley.—LiS
Discontent. See Contentment
Discordants, sel. Conrad Aiken
Music I heard with you.—RoIt
The **discoveries** of fire. Lucille Clifton.—MoT
The **discovery** ("Adam, who thought himself immortal still") Monk Gibbon.—CoPi
Discovery ("Round and round and round I spin") Myra Cohn Livingston.—LiLc
Disease. See Sickness
Disgrace. Unknown.—AbM
"A **dish** full of all kinds of flowers." Unknown.—EmN
Dishes. See Pottery
Dishonesty. See Truthfulness and falsehood
Disillusionised. Lewis Carroll.—LiPc
Dislikes. See Likes and dislikes

Dismal observations. John Hall Wheelock.—PlM
Disneyland
The pilgrimage. M. C. Livingston.—LiM
Disobedience. See Obedience
Distance spills itself. Yocheved Bat-Miriam, tr. fr. the Hebrew by Robert Mezey and Shula Starkman.—MeP
"**Distance** spills itself and grows dazzling and blue." See Distance spills itself
Distances
The camel and the flotsam. J. De La Fontaine.—JoA-4
Distance spills itself. Y. Bat-Miriam.—MeP
The **distant** drum. Calvin C. Hernton.—AdB
Disturbances. Anthony Thwaite.—ToM
"**Disturbed,** the cat." Karai Senryū, tr. fr. the Japanese by Geoffrey Bownas and Anthony Thwaite.—MaFw
The **dive.** Cornelia Brownell Gould.—FlH
"**Diver** on the board." See Markings: The semicolon
Dives (about)
Dives and Lazarus. Unknown.—MaFw
Dives and Lazarus. Unknown.—MaFw
Divided. Jean Ingelow.—LiS
Diving. See Swimming and diving
"**Diving** into the movie dark." See Screen
The **division.** Thomas Hardy.—PlP
Dixon, Alan
Cat in the long grass.—MaFw
Dixon, Henry
The description of a good boy.—OpOx
Djangatolum. See Corbin, Lloyd, Jr
Do fishes go to school. Ruth Whitman.—RoIt
"**Do** ghouls." Lilian Moore.—MoSm
"**Do** I love you." See A love song
"**Do** not believe your Shakespeare's grief." See The argument
"**Do** not blow in the garden, wind." Unknown, tr. fr. the Korean by Chung Seuk Park and ad. by Virginia Olsen Baron.—BaSs
Do not cry. Unknown, ad. by John Bierhorst from the collections of Frances Densmore.—BiS
"**Do** not delight in what you own." Yi Jung-bo, tr. fr. the Korean by Chung Seuk Park and ad. by Virginia Olsen Baron.—BaSs
"**Do** not let any woman read this verse." See Deirdre
"**Do** not think." Carol Freeman.—AdM
"**Do** not touch me." Unknown, tr. fr. the Yokut.—ClFc
"**Do** not weep, little one." See Sung by a little girl to soothe a crying baby
Do nothing till you hear from me. David Lawrence.—AdPb
"**Do** the Russians want war." Yevgeny Yevtushenko, tr. fr. the Russian by Miriam Morton.—MoM
"**Do** you ask me what I think of." See What I think of Hiawatha
"**Do** you ask what the birds say, the sparrow, the dove." See Answer to a child's question
"**Do** you carrot all for me." Unknown.—EmN
"**Do** you know." See Thunder
Do you know the man. Shel Silverstein.—CoOh
"**Do** you know the man with the flowers growing." See Do you know the man
"**Do** you like beer." Unknown.—EmN
"**Do** you like butter." Unknown.—EmN
"**Do** you like chicken." Unknown.—EmN
"**Do** you like jelly." Unknown.—EmN
"**Do** you like pie." Unknown.—EmN
"**Do** you love me." See "Do you love me or do you not"
"**Do** you love me or do you not." Unknown.—CoPu
"Do you love me."—MoBw
"**Do** you not wish to renounce the Devil." See Epigram
"**Do** you prefer." See Getting together
"**Do** you remember an inn." See Tarantella
"**Do** you remember that night." Unknown, tr. fr. the Irish by Eugene O'Curry.—CoPi
"**Do** you want a dollar." Unknown.—EmN
"**Do** you want a nickel." Unknown.—EmN
"**Do** you want a penny." Unknown.—EmN
Do you want affidavits. Carl Sandburg.—SaT
Dobell, Sydney
How's my boy.—RoIt
Docks. Carl Sandburg.—SaT
Doctor. Lois Lenski.—LeC
"**Doctor** Bell fell down the well." Unknown.—MoBw
"**Doctor,** doctor, it fits real fine." See Vet's rehabilitation
"**Doctor** Emmanuel Harrison-Hyde." James Reeves.—AlC
Doctor Emmanuel.—CoPu
"**Doctor** Foster went to Gloucester." Mother Goose.—JoA-4
Dr Ping and Mr Pong. David McCord.—McAa
Doctors
A correct compassion. J. Kirkup.—MaFw
Doctor. L. Lenski.—LeC
"Doctor Emmanuel Harrison-Hyde." J. Reeves.—AlC
Doctor Emmanuel.—CoPu
The doctor's story. W. M. Carleton.—CoPt
Gentle Doctor Brown. B. L. Taylor.—CoOh
"If a doctor is doctoring a doctor." Unknown.—BrM
"If everyone were a chief." Kim Chang-up.—BaSs
"If one doctor doctors another doctor." Unknown.—EmN
"Mother, mother, I am sick, sick, sick." Unknown.—EmN
Mother Tabbyskins. E. A. Hart.—OpOx
On Dr Lettsom, by himself. J. C. Lettsom.—CoPu
"One, two, three a nation." Unknown.—EmN
The prologue. From The Canterbury tales. G. Chaucer.—MaFw
The **doctor's** story. Will M. Carleton.—CoPt
The **dodo.** Hilaire Belloc.—CoOh
"The **dodo** used to walk around." See The dodo

Dodoes
The dodo. H. Belloc.—CoOh
Dodona's oaks were still. Patrick MacDonogh.—CoPi
Dodson, Owen
Confession stone.—AbM
I break the sky.—AdPb
Mary passed this morning.—AdPb
Poems for my brother Kenneth.—AdPb (sel.)
"Sorrow is the only faithful one."—AdPb
Yardbird's skull.—AdPb
"**Does** she want." See Cat play
The **dog** ("The truth I do not stretch or shove") Ogden Nash.—CoOr—CoPu
Dog ("Under a maple tree") Valerie Worth.—WoS
A **dog** and a cat. Mother Goose.—BlM
"A dog and a cat went out together."—TucMgl
"A **dog** and a cat went out together." See A dog and a cat
Dog and fox. David Ferry.—CoPu
"The **dog** beneath the cherry-tree." See The ambiguous dog
Dog-days
Dog-days. A. Lowell.—PaF
Dog-days. Amy Lowell.—PaF
"**Dog** means dog." See Blum
"A **dog** starved at his master's gate." See Auguries of innocence
"The **dog** will come when he is called." See Beasts and birds
Dog with schoolboys. Jean Follain, tr. fr. the French by Keith Waldrop.—CoPu
Dogs
An addition to the family: for M. L. E. Morgan.—ToM
After school. A. Fisher.—FiFo
"Ah, are you digging on my grave." T. Hardy.—PlP
The ambiguous dog. A. Guiterman.—BrM
The ballad of Minepit Shaw. R. Kipling.—CoPt
Beau's reply. W. Cowper.—RoIt
"Bow, wow, wow." Mother Goose.—AlC—JoA-4—TrG
Chitterabob. Unknown.—BlM
"There was a man, and his name was Dob."—TrG
The comic adventures of Old Mother Hubbard and her dog. S. C. Martin.—OpOx
"A coughdrop lies in my doghouse." X. J. Kennedy.—KeO
Cruel Frederick. H. Hoffman.—LiS
Dan. C. Sandburg.—SaT
The dog ("The truth I do not stretch or shove") O. Nash.—CoOr—CoPu
Dog ("Under a maple tree") V. Worth.—WoS
A dog and a cat. Mother Goose.—BlM
"A dog and a cat went out together."—TucMgl
Dog and fox. D. Ferry.—CoPu
Dog with schoolboys. J. Follain.—CoPu
The dog's cold nose. A. Guiterman.—CoPt
Doldrums. C. O'John.—AlW
Double-tail dog. S. Silverstein.—SiW
Dream dog. L. Lenski.—LeC
An elegy on the death of a mad dog. O. Goldsmith.—LiWw—RoIt
Epigram engraved on the collar of a dog which I gave to his Royal Highness. A. Pope.—RoIt
"I am His Highness' dog at Kew."—TrG
Epitaph to a Newfoundland dog. Lord Byron.—RoIt
"Flint Boy tied his dog." N. Belting.—BeWi
German shepherd. M. C. Livingston.—LiM
Gone. D. McCord.—McFm—McS
Gretchen. Unknown.—JoA-4
The hairy dog. H. Asquith.—BrM
"Hark, hark." Mother Goose.—JoA-4
Hoddley, poddley. Unknown.—BlM
Howard. A. A. Milne.—CoOr
"I do not understand." K. Kuskin.—KuA
I doot, I doot. Unknown.—BlM
"I had a little dog (and his color)." Unknown.—EmN
"I had a little dog (and his name was Harry)." Unknown.—EmN
"I had a little dog (and his name was Jack)." Unknown.—EmN
"I had a little dog (and his name was Rover)." Unknown.—EmN
"I had a little dog (his name was Joanna)." Unknown.—EmN
"I had a little dog (his name was Nickel)." Unknown.—EmN
Ignored. R. Froman.—FrSp
I'll let you know if I find her. J. Ciardi.—CiFs
I'm skeleton. L. Moore.—MoSm
"I've got a dog as thin as a rail." Unknown.—CoOr
The kill. D. Hall.—HaWr
Listening to foxhounds. J. Dickey.—HaWr
"The little dog ran around the engine." Unknown.—EmN
"Little tiny puppy dog." S. Milligan.—CoOh
The lonely man. R. Jarrell.—ToM
Meditatio. E. Pound.—LiWw
Miss Jane. Unknown.—BlM
"Mother, a dog is at the door." X. J. Kennedy.—KeO
Mother Tabbyskins. E. A. Hart.—OpOx
Motto for a dog house. A. Guiterman.—CoPu
My dog is a plumber. D. Greenburg.—ThF
My little dog. M. Chute.—ChRu
New puppy. A. Fisher.—FiFo
The night hunt. T. MacDonagh.—CoPi
Off for a hike. A. Fisher.—FiFo
"Old Farmer Giles." Mother Goose.—TucMgl
"Old Mother Hubbard." Mother Goose.—JoA-4
"Old Mother Shuttle." Mother Goose.—MiMg
On a spaniel called Beau killing a young bird. W. Cowper.—RoIt
On buying a dog. E. Klauber.—CoPu

Dogs—*Continued*
"Once a farmer had a dog." Unknown.—EmN
"Our old family dog." Issa.—BeM
A personal experience. O. Herford.—BrM
"Rin Tin Tin." Unknown.—EmN
"See saw." C. Watson.—WaF
Sniffing. A. Fisher.—FiFo
The song of Quoodle. G. K. Chesterton.—JoA-4
The span of life. R. Frost.—MaFw
Special delivery. X. J. Kennedy.—KeO
Susie's new dog. J. Ciardi.—CiFs
The tale of a dog. J. S. Lambert, Jr.—BrM
"There was an old woman, as I've heard tell." Mother Goose.—JoA-4
Three signs of spring. D. McCord.—McS
"Through a wide field of stubble." R. Sund.—CoPu
"Under the willow." Issa.—MaFw
Vern. G. Brooks.—HoCs
Wags and purrs. A. Fisher.—FiM
We were not like dogs. U. Z. Greenberg.—MeP
A week after the first Sputnik. Unknown.—MoM
"When darkness covers the mountain village." Chun Keum.—BaSs
"With a twitching nose." R. Wright
Hokku poems.—AdPb
The wolf and the dog. C. Rosario.—JoV
The woodman's dog. W. Cowper.—CoPu—JoA-4
"**Dogs** can wag." See Wags and purrs
The **dog's** cold nose. Arthur Guiterman.—CoPt
Dolama, Abu
Humorous verse.—AbM
Doldrums. Calvin O'John.—AlW
Dolls
"Baby, my dolly, oh, she never cries." Mother Goose.—TucMgl
Can you can't. D. Whitewing.—AlW
The dolls' wash. J. H. Ewing.—OpOx
"I do not laugh or sing or smile or talk." K. Kuskin.—KuA
The little doll. From The water babies. C. Kingsley.—OpOx
A mortifying mistake. A. M. Pratt.—BrM
Na-na doll. R. Hoban.—HoE
William's doll. S. Harnick.—ThF
"Yes, rain is leaking." Issa.—HaW
The **dolls'** wash. Juliana Horatia Ewing.—OpOx
"**Dolphin** daughter." Aileen Fisher.—FiD
Dolphins
"Dolphin daughter." A. Fisher.—FiD
Dolphy, Eric (about)
Fall down. C. C. Hernton.—AdPb
"The **dome** of the capitol looks to the Potomac." See Smoke rose gold
Don Juan, sel. Lord Byron
"A mighty mass of brick, and smoke, and shipping."—PaP
Donald Oge: Grief of a girl's heart. Unknown, tr. fr. the Irish by Lady Gregory.—CoPi
Donkey. Vasko Popa, tr. by Anne Pennington.—MoT
"The **donkey** sat down on the roadside." See Time out
Donkeys
"The cuckoo and the donkey." Mother Goose.—TucMg
Donkey. V. Popa.—MoT
Donkeys. Edward Field.—RoIt
"If I had a donkey that wouldn't go." Mother Goose.—JoA-4
Platero. J. R. Jiménez.—JoA-4
"Said the monkey to the donkey." Unknown.—TrG
"See saw." C. Watson.—WaF
A surprise. M. Douglas.—CoOr
"Though there is still quite a way to go." Unknown.—BaSs
Time out. J. Montague.—CoPi
Donkeys. Edward Field.—RoIt
"A **donkey's** tail is very nice." See The monotony song
Donleavy, J. P.
When I brought the news.—CoPt
"**Donna,** Donna." Unknown.—MoBw
Donne, John
"Hail, Bishop Valentine, whose day this is."—MaF
Holy sonnet V.—MaFw (sel.)
Holy sonnet VII.—MaFw
Donnelly, Dorothy
Chinese baby asleep.—HiN
Glass world.—HiN
Leaflight.—HiN
Recollection.—HiN
Serenade.—HiN
"**Don't** ask me what to wear." Sappho, tr. fr. the Greek by Mary Barnard.—ThI
"**Don't** be crooked." Unknown.—EmN
"**Don't** bring out the straw mat." Han Hwak, tr. fr. the Korean by Chung Seuk Park and ad. by Virginia Olsen Baron.—BaSs
"**Don't** Care didn't care." Mother Goose.—AlC
"**Don't** cross the street." Lois Lenski.—LeC
"**Don't** dress your cat in an apron." Dan Greenburg.—ThF
Don't ever seize a weasel by the tail. Jack Prelutsky.—BrM
"**Don't** let them die out." See Now poem. For us
"**Don't** make love by the garden gate." Unknown.—EmN
"**Don't** make love in an onion patch." Unknown.—MoBw
"**Don't** mind my small hut." Issa, tr. fr. the Japanese by Hanako Fukuda.—HaW
"**Don't** preserve my customs." See Young Africa's plea
"**Don't** run along the wrong lane." Unknown.—EmN
"**Don't** run when you see." See October
"**Don't** try to be an angel." Unknown.—MoBw
"**Don't** walk." See Orders

Dream song ("Above the place where the minnow maiden sleeps while her fins move gently in the water") Unknown.—BiI
Dream song ("As my eyes") Unknown.—BiI
Dream song ("High in the sky I go") Unknown.—BiS
Dream song ("Walk with the sun") L. Alexander.—AdPb
Dream song ("Where the mountain crosses") Unknown.—BiI
Dream variation. L. Hughes.—AdM—AdPb—HoD
Dream voyage to the center of the subway. E. Merriam.—MeF
The dreamer. W. Childress.—PeS
Dreaming in the Shanghai restaurant. D. J. Enright.—ToM
Dreams ("Crooked") C. Cooper.—AdPb
Dreams ("Hold fast to dreams") L. Hughes.—HoD
Dreams ("In my younger years") N. Giovanni.—AdPb
Fantasia. E. Merriam.—MeF
The fly-away horse. Eugene Field.—UnGb
For a poet. C. Cullen.—AbM
The garden. S. Silverstein.—SiW
Good morning. L. Hughes.—AdM
He wishes for the cloths of heaven. W. B. Yeats.—JoA-4
Her story. N. L. Madgett.—AdPb
The heroes. L. Simpson.—PeS
"I am waiting." M. Goode.—JoV
"I close my book and open the window." Chung On.—BaSs
"I had a dream last night . . . of a thousand mothers." C. Meyer.—JoV
"If it comes." P. Booth.—HiN
Incident on a journey. T. Gunn.—ToM
Invocation. V. Miller.—HiN
John-John. T. Macdonagh.—CoPi—CoPt
Kubla Khan. S. T. Coleridge.—RoIt
La belle dame sans merci. J. Keats.—JoA-4—RoIt
The little land. R. L. Stevenson.—JoA-4
Loneliness. A. Young.—AdPb
Lord Chancellor's song. From Iolanthe. W. S. Gilbert.—RoIt
"The morning after." W. Clark.—HiN
"My first dream of the year." Issa.—HaW
My intrigue. J. Holland.—JoV
My own true family. T. Hughes.—HuMf
"Negro dreams." D. Long.—AdPb
Ode. A. O'Shaughnessy.—CoPi—RoIt
On torpid Marcus. Lucilius.—LiWw
"One time Henry dreamed the number." D. Long.—AdPb
Pamela. D. McCord.—McFm
Poems for my brother Kenneth. O. Dodson.—AdPb (sel.)
Postscript. W. H. Auden.—MaFw
The question. P. B. Shelley.—PaF
"Rain, shivering, wreaked the earth." The Group.—JoV
Reincarnation. M. Jackson.—AdPb
"Robert Rutter dreamt a dream." Unknown.—EmN
Sixteen months. C. Sandburg.—SaT
Snail. L. Hughes.—AbM—HoD—JoA-4
The snail's dream. O. Herford.—BrM
"The snow flakes sail gently." Gabriel Okara.—AlPa
The soldiers dream. T. Campbell.—RoIt
The spring will come. H. D. Lowry.—CoPu
Such stuff as dreams. F. P. Adams.—LiS
"There was an old man from Peru." Unknown.—RoIt—TrG
Three birds flying. E. Merriam.—MeO
Truly my own. V. Howard.—JoV
"Wandering, dreaming." Bashō.—BeM
Winter milk. C. Sandburg.—SaT
Word poem (perhaps worth considering). N. Giovanni.—AdB—AdPb
Wynken, Blynken, and Nod. Eugene Field.—OpOx

Dreams ("Crooked") Charles Cooper.—AdPb
Dreams ("Hold fast to dreams") Langston Hughes.—HoD
Dreams ("In my younger years") Nikki Giovanni.—AdPb
"**Dreams**, graves, pools, growing." See So to speak
Dreams of a summer night, part VI, sel. George Barker
The Cutty Sark.—MaFw
Dreidel song. Efraim Rosenzweig.—LaM
Dresback, Glenn W.
The cave.—PeS
Dress. See Clothing and dress
Dress me, dear mother. Avraham Shlonsky, tr. fr. the Hebrew by Robert Mezey.—MeP
"**Dress** me, dear mother, in splendor, a coat of many colors." See Dress me, dear mother
"**Drifting**, feathery." Shiki, tr. fr. the Japanese by Harry Behn.—BeM
"**Drifting** night in the Georgia pines." See O Daedalus, fly away home
Drinking. See Drinks and drinking
Drinking time. D. J. O'Sullivan.—CoPi
Drinks and drinking
Alice. S. Silverstein.—SiW
Casual lines. Su Shih.—MaFw
Cedar waxwing. W. H. Matchett.—HaWr
Civil war song. Unknown.—AlPa
Drinking time. D. J. O'Sullivan.—CoPi
Drum chant. Unknown.—AlPa
Friday: Mom is home—Payday. L. Clifton.—ClS
A glass of beer. J. Stephens.—HiN
Heather ale. R. L. Stevenson.—CoPt
"If all the world was apple pie." Mother Goose.—EmN—JoA-4
"If all the land were apple pie."—RoIt
Jazz Jane. S. Silverstein.—SiW
The Kentucky wassail song. Unknown.—JoA-4
Love from my father. C. G. Clemmons.—AdPb

Drinks and drinking—*Continued*
The luck of Edenhall. H. W. Longfellow.—CoPt
Miniver Cheevy. E. A. Robinson.—LiS
Minnow Minnie. S. Silverstein.—SiW
Mr Flood's party. E. A. Robinson.—CoPt
My papa's waltz. T. Roethke.—HiN—MaFw—PeS
Off to Yakima. L. F. Jackson.—BrM
"Round about, round about." Unknown
Counting out rhyme.—LiS
"Said the monkey to the donkey." Unknown.—TrG
Song of encouragement. Unknown.—BiI
Song of the pop-bottler. M. Bishop.—BrM
The treat. L. Blair.—JaP
Uncle Bull-boy. J. Jordan.—AdPb
Witch, witch. R. Fyleman.—JaP
Drinkwater, John
Moonlit apples.—PaF
Snail.—LiLc
The sun.—LiLc
"**Drip** drips the kitchen faucet." See Leak
Drippy weather. Aileen Fisher.—FiFo
"The **driver** rubbed at his nettly chin." See To the four courts, please
Drivers and driving
Driving. M. C. Livingston.—HoP—LiM
Driving toward the Lac Qui Parle river. R. Bly.—HiN
Lines for a night driver. P. K. Dufault.—HaWr
To the four courts, please. J. Stephens.—CoPi
Driving. Myra Cohn Livingston.—HoP—LiM
"**Driving** that train, high on cocaine." See Casey Jones
Driving to the beach. Joanna Cole.—HoP
Driving to town late to mail a letter. Robert Bly.—MoT
Driving toward the Lac Qui Parle river. Robert Bly.—HiN
A **drizzling** Easter morning. Thomas Hardy.—PlP
Droit de seigneur. Richard Murphy.—CoPi
"A **dromedary** standing still." Jack Prelutsky.—PrT
Drouth
"Dry and parched." A. Lopez.—AlW
Dry season. K. Brew.—AlPa
Dry spell. L. Moore.—MoSp
A **drover.** Padraic Colum.—CoPi
Drowning
By the Exeter river. D. Hall.—ToM
"Ding, dong, bell." Mother Goose.—AlC—BlM—JoA-4
An inscription by the sea. E. A. Robinson.—CoPu
Look Hart, that horse you ride is wood. P. Viereck.—PlM
On a friend's escape from drowning off the Norfolk coast. G. Barker.—ToM
Politeness. H. Graham.—CoOh
The sands of Dee. From Alton Locke. C. Kingsley.—JoA-4—RoIt
Star night. F. Holman.—HoI
Suicide's note. L. Hughes.—HoD
"There was an old woman, her name it was Peg." Mother Goose.—AlC
"Three wise men of Gotham." Mother Goose.—AlC—JoA-4
"The tide rises, the tide falls." H. W. Longfellow.—RoIt
Drowsy. Carl Sandburg.—SaT
"A **drowsy** breeze sighs." Onitsura, tr. fr. the Japanese by Harry Behn.—BeM
Drugs. See also Medicine
The idea of ancestry. E. Knight.—AdPb
To mother and Steve. M. Evans.—AdPb
Drum chant. Unknown, tr. fr. the Akan by J. H. Kwabena Nketia.—AlPa
The **drum**-maker. Joseph Bruchac.—MoT
"**Drum** on your drums, batter on your banjoes." See Jazz fantasia
"A **drumdrumdrum.**" See Two dedications
Drummer Hodge. Thomas Hardy.—PlP
Drummers and drums
The distant drum. C. C. Hernton.—AdB
Drum chant. Unknown.—AlPa
The drum-maker. J. Bruchac.—MoT
Drummer Hodge. T. Hardy.—PlP
Drums of freedom. G. Thompson.—JoV
From jazz for five. J. Smith.—ToM (sel.)
Lament of the drums. C. Okigbo.—AlPa (sel.)
Piano and drums. G. Okara.—AlPa
The rustling of grass. A. Noyes.—PaF
Talking to his drum. E. B. Mitchell.—AlW
Ttimba. Unknown.—SeS
"Two heads I have, and when my voice." Unknown.—EmN
Until then. P. George.—AlW
"You will always find me." Unknown.—ClFc
Drummond, William Henry
The wreck of the Julie Plante.—CoPt
Drums. See Drummers and drums
Drums of freedom. Glen Thompson.—JoV
"**Drunk** on sour cherries, the harlequin of birds." See Cedar waxwings
Drury, Misses (about)
"Maidens, if you love the tale." L. Carroll.—LiPc
"**Dry** and parched." Alonzo Lopez.—AlW
"A **dry** leaf drifting (down to an icy)." Bokusui, tr. fr. the Japanese by Harry Behn.—BeM
"A **dry** leaf drifting (down to earth)." Bashō. tr. fr. the Japanese by Harry Behn.—BeM
The **dry** season. Kwesi Brew.—AlPa
Dry spell. Lilian Moore.—MoSp
Dryads. See Fairies
Dryden, John
The fire of London.—MaFw (sel.)
Dublin, Ireland
Cockles and mussels. Unknown.—RoIt
Dublin. L. MacNeice.—CoPi
Dublin made me. D. MacDonagh.—CoPi
"If ever you go to Dublin town." P. Kavanagh.—ToM
Dublin. Louis MacNeice.—CoPi
Dublin made me. Donagh MacDonagh.—CoPi

"Dublin made me and no little town." See Dublin made me
Du Bois, William Edward Burghardt
The song of the smoke.—AdPb
Du Bois, William Edward Burghardt (about)
Booker T. and W. E. B. D. Randall.—AbM
For William Edward Burghardt Du Bois on his eightieth birthday. B. D. Latimer.—AdPb
On the death of William Edward Burghardt Du Bois by African moonlight and forgotten shores. C. K. Rivers.—AdPb
The **duchess's** lullaby. See Alice's adventures in wonderland
Duck ("When the neat white") Valerie Worth.—WoS
A **duck** ("With legs so short and far apart") Aileen Fisher.—FiFo
The **duck** and the kangaroo. Edward Lear.—JoA-4—OpOx
"A **duck** who had got such a habit of stuffing." See The notorious glutton
Duckett, Alfred A.
Sonnet.—AdPb
"Ducklings." See Green
Ducks
Dame Duck's lecture. Unknown.—RoIt
Duck ("When the neat white") V. Worth.—WoS
A duck ("With legs so short and far apart") A. Fisher.—FiFo
The duck and the kangaroo. E. Lear.—JoA-4—OpOx
"Ducks are lucky." M. A. Hoberman.—HoN
Duck's ditty. From The wind in the willows. K. Grahame.—JoA-4—OpOx
"Ducks on the mill pond." Unknown.—MoBw
Duck's walking. D. McCord.—McAa
"Green head." Unknown.—EmN
"How God hath labored to produce the duck." D. Hall.—CoPu
"I saw a ship a-sailing." Mother Goose.—AlC—JoA-4—MiMg
"In stature the manlet was dwarfish." From Sylvia and Bruno concluded. E. Lear.—LiPc
"I've seen everything." Jōsō.—MaFw
A memory. W. Allingham.—PaF—RoIt
The notorious glutton. A. Taylor.—OpOx
The prayer of the little ducks. C. B. de Gasztold.—AdP
The ptarmigan sings to the long-tailed duck. Unknown.—LeIb
Railroad ducks. F. Frost.—HoP
"There was a little man, and he had a little gun." Mother Goose.—JoA-4
"There was an old lady of France." E. Lear.—LiLc
"With his apology." Karai Senryū.—MaFw
"Ducks are lucky." Mary Ann Hoberman.—HoN
Duck's ditty. See The wind in the willows
"Ducks on the mill pond." Unknown.—MoBw
Ducks walking. David McCord.—McAa
Duerr, Jody
"A dream."—HoC
Dufault, Peter Kane
Lines for a night driver.—HaWr
The **dug-out.** Siegfried Sassoon.—MaFw
Dugan, Alan
On Hurricane Jackson.—HiN
Dumas, Henry
America.—AdB—AdPb—CoPu
Black star line.—AdPb
Black trumpeter.—AdPb
Buffalo.—AdPb
Image.—AdB
Knock on wood.—AdPb
The **dumb** soldier. Robert Louis Stevenson.—OpOx
Dumbbell. William Cole.—CoOh
Dunbar, Paul Laurence
Frederick Douglass.—AdPb
Little brown baby.—AbM
A Negro love song.—AbM
The paradox.—AdPb
Sympathy.—AdPb
To a captious critic.—AbM
We wear the mask.—AdPb
When Malindy sings.—AdPb
Dunbar, Paul Laurence (about)
For Paul Laurence Dunbar. C. Cullen
Four epitaphs.—AdPb
Dunbar, William
"Empresse of townes, exalt in honour." See In honour of the city of London
In honour of the city of London, sel.
"Empresse of townes, exalt in honour."—PaP
Lament for the makers.—PlM (sel.)
Dunbarton. Robert Lowell.—ToM
Duncan, Robert
The ballad of Mrs Noah.—ToM
The **dunce.** Jacques Prévert, tr. fr. the French by John Dixon Hunt.—MaFw
Duns Scotus's Oxford, sel. Gerard Manley Hopkins
"Towery city and branchy between towers."—PaP
Dunsany, Lord (Edward John Moreton Drax Plunkett)
Bringing him up.—CoPu—LiWw
A call to the wild.—CoPi
Dunwich, England
At Dunwich. A. Thwaite.—ToM
Durem, Ray
Award.—AdPb
Friends.—AdPb
"I know I'm not sufficiently obscure."—AdPb
Problem in social geometry—the inverted square.—AdPb
Respectful request.—AbM
Vet's rehabilitation.—AdPb
You know, Joe.—AdB
"During the season of cut organs we." See Initiation
"Dusk." See No dawns

Easter
Bobby's first poem. N. Gale.—CoPu
A drizzling Easter morning. T. Hardy.—PlP
The Easter bunny blues or all I want for Xmas is the Loop. Ebon (Dooley).—AdPb
Easter daisies. A. Fisher.—LaM
Easter morning, sels. D. McCord.—McAa (Complete)
1. "Question: What kind of rabbit can an Easter rabbit be"
2. "Mr Rabbit, a basket on his arm"
3. "Is Easter just a day of hats"
"Loveliest of trees the cherry now." From A Shropshire lad. A. E. Housman.—MaFw
Loveliest of trees.—JoA-4—PaF
There is a green hill. C. F. Alexander.—OpOx
Were you there. Unknown.—BrW
The **Easter** bunny blues or all I want for Xmas is the Loop. Ebon (Dooley).—AdPb
Easter daisies. Aileen Fisher.—LaM
Easter morning, sels. David McCord.—McAa (Complete)
1. "Question: What kind of rabbit can an Easter rabbit be"
2. "Mr Rabbit, a basket on his arm"
3. "Is Easter just a day of hats"
The **eastern** gate. Unknown, tr. fr. the Chinese by Arthur Waley.—MaFw
"**Eastward** I was idle." See Dance song
Eastwick, Ivy O.
"Bittersweet."—JaP
"Stay, Christmas."—HoS
Where's Mary.—NeA
Easy diver. Robert Froman.—FrSp
"**Easy** on your drums." See Dark girl
"**Eat** a tomato and you'll turn red." See Vegetables
"**Eat,** eat, thou hast bread." See Prophecy
Eat-it-all Elaine. Kaye Starbird.—NeA
Eating. See Food and eating
Eating at the restaurant of How Chow Now. David McCord.—McFm
Eating out in autumn. Marchette Chute.—ChRu
"**Eaves** moan." See In the farmhouse
Eberhart, Richard
For a lamb.—PeS
On a squirrel crossing the road in autumn, in New England.—JoA-4—RoIt
Sea-hawk.—HaWr
To a poet who has had a heart attack.—PlM
To Auden on his fiftieth.—PlM
Ebon (Dooley)
The Easter bunny blues or all I want for Xmas is the Loop.—AdPb
The prophet's warning or shoot to kill.—AdPb
Query.—AdPb
Ecclesiastes
All things come alike to all. See Ecclesiastes
Ecclesiastes, sels. Bible, Old Testament
All things come alike to all.—MeP
The light is sweet.—RoIt
"Remember now thy Creator."—MeP
The light is sweet. See Ecclesiastes
"Remember now thy Creator." See Ecclesiastes
Ecclesiasticus
Gladness of heart.—RoIt
The **echo.** Phillip Solomon.—JoV
Echoes
Bugle song. From The princess. A. Tennyson.—RoIt
The echo. P. Solomon.—JoV
The echoing green. W. Blake.—JoA-4—PaF
"A hundred mountains." Issa.—BeM
The **echoing** green. William Blake.—JoA-4—PaF
Ecology
Ecology. L. Moore.—MoSp
Ecology. Lilian Moore.—MoSp
The **Eddystone** light. Unknown.—CoPt
Eden, Garden of
Eden. D. M. Thomas.—HiW
Eve. Y. Fichman.—MeP
To the garden the world. W. Whitman.—MoG
Woodstock. J. Mitchell.—MoG
Eden. D. M. Thomas.—HiN
Edey, Marion
Christmas eve.—HoS
The **edge** of the world. Shel Silverstein.—SiW
The **educators.** D. M. Black.—ToM
Edward Lear. W. H. Auden.—PlM
"**Eeeeeeeeeeeee.**" Unknown.—MoBw
The **eel.** Ogden Nash.—JoA-4
Eels
The eel. O. Nash.—JoA-4
Eels. S. Milligan.—CoOr
Electric eels. J. Prelutsky.—PrP
Eels. Spike Milligan.—CoOr
"**Eena** meena dixie dan." Unknown.—EmN
"**Eentsie** weentsie spider." Unknown.—EmN
"**Eeny** meeny mony my." Unknown.—EmN
"**Eeny** meeny tipsy teeny." Unknown.—EmN
Effendi. Michael S. Harper.—AdPb
Efficiency apartment. Gerald W. Barrax.—AdPb
Efon (Buffalo). Unknown, tr. fr. the Yoruba by Ulli Beier and Bakare Gbadamosi.—AlPa
The **egg** boiler. Gwendolyn Brooks.—AdPb
Egg thoughts. Russell Hoban.—HoE
Eggs. See also Birds—Eggs and nests
"As I went through a field of wheat." Unknown.—EmN
The egg boiler. G. Brooks.—AdPb
Egg thoughts. R. Hoban.—HoE
"Eggs are laid by turkeys." M. A. Hoberman.—HoN
The friends. D. Lee.—LeA
The hen and the carp. I. Serraillier.—LiWw
"Hickety, pickety, my black hen." Mother Goose.—AlC—JoA-4
The hot day. M. Chute.—ChRu
"Humpty Dumpty sat on a wall." Mother Goose.—EmN—JoA-4
I won't hatch. S. Silverstein.—SiW
"In marble halls as white as milk." Mother Goose.—EmN—JoA-4
The ostrich. O. Nash.—CoOh
The poultry. O. Nash.—CoOr

Eggs.—*Continued*
Riddle. Unknown.—RoIt
"There's more than one way to be right." R. Wilbur.—WiO
"**Eggs** are laid by turkeys." Mary Ann Hoberman.—HoN
Egita, Charles J.
Passing by the junkyard.—HoP
Ego. Philip Booth.—PeS
Ego swamp. King D. Kuka.—AlW
Egotists. See Pride and vanity
Egrets. See Herons
Egrets. Judith Wright.—AdP—HiN—JoA-4
Egypt
From the prophecy against Egypt. From Isaiah.—MeP
I am a cowboy in the boat of Ra. I. Reed.—AdPb
"King Tut." X. J. Kennedy.—KeO—LiWw
Ozymandias. P. B. Shelley.—LiS—RoIt
Ozymandias revisited. M. Bishop.—LiS
"**Eh-nee-wek** kah-yea neen." See Very much afraid
"**Eight** are the lights." Ilo Orleans.—LaM (sel.)
"**Eight** big black bears six feet tall." Jack Prelutsky.—PrC
"**Eight** gray geese grazing gaily into Greece." Unknown.—EmN
Eight oars and a coxswain. Arthur Guiterman.—FlH
"**Eight** oars compel." See Eight oars and a coxswain
Eight o'clock. Alfred Edward Housman.—CoPu
"**Eight** o'clock is striking." Mother Goose.—AlC
Eight witches. B. J. Lee.—HoH
"**Eight** witches rode the midnight sky." See Eight witches
Eighteen flavors. Shel Silverstein.—SiW
"**Eighteen** luscious, scrumptious flavors." See Eighteen flavors
1867. Joseph Mary Plunkett.—CoPi
"**Eileen** Carroll." See Eels
"**Eins,** zwei, Polizei." Mother Goose.—JoA-4
Einstein, Albert (about)
"It did not last: the Devil, howling Ho." J. C. Squire.—LiWw
Ekwere, John
Rejoinder.—AlPa
El-Hajj Malik El-Shabazz. Robert Hayden.—AdPb
The **elderly** gentleman. George Canning.—RoIt
Eldorado. Edgar Allan Poe.—RoIt
The **electric** cop. Victor Hernandez Cruz.—AdPb
Electric eels. Jack Prelutsky.—PrP
"**Electric** eels are rather rude." See Electric eels
Electrical storm. Elizabeth Bishop.—HaWr
Electricity
Electric eels. J. Prelutsky.—PrP
The force. P. Redgrove.—ToM
"Fur of cats." A. Fisher.—FiM
Elegies. See Laments
Elegy ("Her face like a rain-beaten stone on the day she rolled off") Theodore Roethke.—HiN
Elegy ("The jackals prowl, the serpents hiss") Arthur Guiterman.—LiWw
Elegy for Alfred Hubbard. Tony Connor.—ToM
Elegy for J. F. K. W. H. Auden.—MaFw
Elegy for Jane. Theodore Roethke.—PeS
Elegy for minor poets. Louis MacNeice.—PlM
An **elegy** on the death of a mad dog. Oliver Goldsmith.—LiWw—RoIt
Elegy written in a country churchyard. Thomas Gray.—PaP (sel.)
The **elementary** scene. Randall Jarrell.—PeS
An **elementary** school classroom in a slum. Stephen Spender.—ToM
Elephant. Mary Ann Hoberman.—HoR
"**Elephant** child." Aileen Fisher.—FiD
The **elephant,** or the force of habit. Alfred Edward Housman.—LiWw
Elephant rock. Primus St John.—AdPb
Elephants
Ant and eleph-ant. S. Milligan.—CoOr
The blind men and the elephant. J. G. Saxe.—CoPt—JoA-4—RoIt
The continuing story of Bungalow Bill. J. Lennon and P. McCartney.—MoG
"East is east and west is west." Unknown.—CoOh
Elephant. M. A. Hoberman.—HoR
"Elephant child." A. Fisher.—FiD
The elephant, or the force of habit. A. E. Housman.—LiWw
Eletelephony. L. E. Richards.—BrM—JoA-4—OpOx
"Here come the elephants, ten feet high." J. Prelutsky.—PrC
The hockey game. D. Lee.—LeA
"I asked my mother for fifty cents." Unknown.—JoA-4
In the middle. D. McCord.—McS
Making friends. V. Lapin.—MoM
Mmenson. E. Brathwaite.—ToM
Oliphaunt. From The adventures of Tom Bombadil. J. R. R. Tolkien.—LiLc
Plain talk for a pachyderm. P. Bennett.—LiWw
Questions, quistions & quoshtions. S. Milligan.—CoOr
Thoughtless guest. V. Hobbs.—BrM
Tit for tat: A tale. J. Aikin.—OpOx
We must be polite. C. Sandburg.—SaT
Why Noah praised the whale. J. Ciardi.—CiFs
"The **elephant's** a bulky beast." See Elephant
"The **elephants** on Noah's ark." See Why Noah praised the whale
Eletelephony. Laura E. Richards.—BrM—JoA-4—OpOx
Elevator. Felice Holman.—HoI
Elevator boy. Lois Lenski.—LeC
"The **elevator** car in the elevator shaft." See A modern ballad, The ups and downs of the elevator car

An **epitaph** ("A lovely young lady I mourn in my rhymes") G. J. Cayley.—CoPu
Epitaph ("Mr Heath-Stubbs, as you must understand") John Heath-Stubbs.—ToM
Epitaph ("This is the grave of Mike O'Day") Unknown.—RoIt
Epitaph ("Within this tomb a patriot lyes") Anne Bradstreet.—ThI
An **epitaph** and a reply. Unknown.—RoIt
Epitaph for a lighthouse-keeper's horse. J. B. Morton.—CoPu
Epitaph for a postal clerk. X. J. Kennedy.—LiWw
Epitaph in Elgin cathedral. Unknown.—LiWw
Epitaph intended for Sir Isaac Newton. Alexander Pope.—RoIt
 Intended for Sir Isaac Newton.—LiWw
Epitaph on a dormouse, which some children were to bury. Unknown.OpOx
Epitaph on Charles II. John Wilmot.—LiWw
An **epitaph** on my dear and ever honoured mother Mrs Dorothy Dudley. Anne Bradstreet.—ThI
Epitaph to a Newfoundland dog. Lord Byron.—RoIt
Epitaphs
 Anne Rutledge. From The Spoon River anthology. E. L. Masters.—RoIt
 "Beneath this yew, the shadow of a shade." Unknown.—CoPu
 Cynic's epitaph. T. Hardy.—LiWw
 Epitaph ("Alas, poor Mungo") B. Franklin.—RoIt
 An epitaph ("Here lies a most beautiful lady") W. De La Mare.—CoPu
 An epitaph ("A lovely young lady I mourn in my rhymes") G. J. Cayley.—CoPu
 Epitaph (Mr Heath-Stubbs as you must understand") J. Heath-Stubbs.—ToM
 Epitaph ("This is the grave of Mike O'Day") Unknown.—RoIt
 Epitaph ("Within this tomb a patriot lyes") A. Bradstreet.—ThI
 An epitaph and a reply. Unknown.—RoIt
 Epitaph for a lighthouse-keeper's horse. J. B. Morton.—CoPu
 Epitaph for a postal clerk. X. J. Kennedy.—LiWw
 Epitaph in Elgin cathedral. Unknown.—LiWw
 Epitaph intended for Sir Isaac Newton. A. Pope.—RoIt
  Intended for Sir Isaac Newton.—LiWw
 Epitaph on a dormouse, which some children were to bury. Unknown.—OpOx
 Epitaph on Charles II. J. Wilmot.—LiWw
 An epitaph on my dear and ever honoured mother Mrs Dorothy Dudley. A. Bradstreet.—ThI
 Epitaph to a Newfoundland dog. Lord Byron.—RoIt
 For a lady I know. C. Cullen.—AbM—LiWw
  Four epitaphs.—AdPb
 For John Keats, apostle of beauty. C. Cullen
  Four epitaphs.—AdPb
 For my grandmother. C. Cullen
  Four epitaphs.—AdPb
 For Paul Laurence Dunbar. C. Cullen
  Four epitaphs.—AdPb
 "Here lies old Jones." Unknown.—LiWw
 "Here lies the body of Jonathan Pound." Unknown.—TrG
 "Here lies the body of Robert Low." Unknown.—CoPu
 In memory of Colonel Charles Young. C. Cullen.—AdPb
 John Bun. Unknown.—LiWw
 A necessitarian's epitaph. T. Hardy.—PlP
 On Sir John Vanbrugh, architect. A. Evans.—LiWw
 Prig: Epitaph. C. Ellis.—LiWw
 Suffolk epitaph. Unknown.—RoIt
 "Wha lies here." Unknown.—CoPu
  Johnny Dow.—LiWw
Erasers
 Magical eraser. S. Silverstein.—SiW
"**Ere** on my bed my limbs I lay." See A child's evening prayer
Eremina, Svetlana
 An offering of joy.—MoM
Erevan is my city. Maya Nikogosian, tr. fr. the Russian by Miriam Morton.—MoM
"**Erevan,** my city Erevan." See Erevan is my city
"The **erl-king's** daughter. Johann Gottfried Herder, tr. fr. the German by Clarence Mangan.—CoPt
"**Esau** Wood sawed wood." Unknown.—EmN
Esbensen, Barbara Juster
 Hallowe'en.—HoH
Escape ("Shadows, shadows") Georgia Douglas Johnson.—AdPb
Escape ("When foxes eat the last gold grape") Elinor Wylie.—JoA-4
Escape at bedtime. Robert Louis Stevenson.—RoIt
Escapes
 Cross over the river. S. Cornish.—AdM
 Escape ("Shadows, shadows") G. D. Johnson.—AdPb
 Escape ("When foxes eat the last gold grape") E. Wylie.—JoA-4
 Escape at bedtime. R. L. Stevenson.—RoIt
 "I never hear the word *escape.*" E. Dickinson.—ThI
 Runagate runagate. R. Hayden.—AdPb
 "Running away." K. Kuskin.—KuN
Eskimos
 "Above the mist." Unknown.—LeIb
 Akjartoq's song of the olden days. Unknown.—LeIb
 "Beast of the sea." Unknown.—LeIb
 "Bring out your hair ornaments." Unknown.—LeIb
 Caribou hunting. Unknown.—LeIb
 "Come in kayaks." Unknown.—LeIb

The **exhortation** of a father to his children. Robert Smith.—OpOx
Exit Molloy. Derek Mahon.—CoPi
Exit x. David McCord.—McFm
Explanation, on coming home late. Richard Hughes.—CoPu
Exploding gravy. X. J. Kennedy.—KeO
Exploration. See Explorers and exploration
Explorers and exploration. See also names of explorers, as Columbus, Christopher
"Man flies through the universe." M. Goode.—JoV
An **expostulation.** Isaac Bickerstaffe.—CoPi—LiWw—RoIt
The **Express.** Stephen Spender.—ToM
"**Express** slams past the local stop." See Subway deaf
"**Extended** lies the city, lies Mexico, spreading circles of emerald light, radiating splendor like a quetzal plume." See Grandeur of Mexico
Extinction. See also names of extinct animals, as Auks; Dinosaurs; Dodoes
For a coming extinction. W. S. Merwin.—MoT
Exultation. Unknown.—LaS
"**Exultation** is the going." Emily Dickinson.—ThI
"**Eye-aya.**" See Ulivfak's song of the caribou
"The **eye** can hardly pick them out." See At grass
Eyes
Alexander's song. Mother Goose.—JoA-4
The man of Thessaly.—RoIt
"Awake, arise, pull out your eyes." Mother Goose.—AlC
Dawn. O. Paz.—MoT
The eyes or the heart. A.N.B.J. Bhalo.—AlPa
For Anne. L. Cohen.—PeS
Gypsy eyes. J. Hendrix.—MoG
Margaret. C. Sandburg.—SaT
My cat. A. Fisher.—FiM
The nose and the eyes. W. Cowper.—RoIt
On my short-sightedness. Prem Chaya.—MaFw
The powerful eyes o' Jeremy Tait. W. Irwin.—CoPt
"The snake fled." Takahama Kyoshi.—MaFw
A snowy day in school. D. H. Lawrence.—MaFw
Sweeping Wendy, study in fugue. C. Sandburg.—SaT
"There was a man of Newington." Mother Goose.—AlC
"There's a cross-eyed woman in our town." Unknown.—CoOh
To a woman loved. Unknown.—BiI
Woman. E. Loftin.—AdPb
Your cat and mine. A. Fisher.—FiM
Your eyes have their silence. G. W. Barrax.—AdPb
The **eyes** or the heart. Ahmad Nassir Bin Juma Bhalo, tr. by Lyndon Harries.—AlPa

F

FBI
Award. R. Durem.—AdPb
Fabio, Sarah Webster
Black man's feast.—AdPb
Evil is no black thing.—AdPb
A **fable.** Oliver Herford.—MaF
The **fable** of the piece of glass and the piece of ice. John Hookham Frere.—OpOx
Fable of the transcendent Tannenbaum. Scott Bates.—CoPt
Fables
The bee, the ant, and the sparrow. W. Cotton.—OpOx
The camel and the flotsam. J. De La Fontaine.—JoA-4
The dairymaid and her milk-pot. J. De La Fontaine.—JoA-4
The dove and the ant. J. De La Fontaine.—JoA-4
A fable. O. Herford.—MaF
The fable of the piece of glass and the piece of ice. J. H. Frere.—OpOx
The fox and the goat. J. De La Fontaine.—JoA-4
The horse and the mule. J. H. Wynne.—OpOx
"Please tell me just the fabuli." S. Silverstein.—CoPu
The sycophantic fox and the gullible raven. G. W. Carryl.—LiWw
Tit for tat: A tale. J. Aikin.—OpOx
"**Face** like a chocolate bar." See 125th street
The **face** of my mountains. Unknown, tr. fr. the Quiché by John Bierhorst.—BiI
"The **face** of the dragonfly." Chisoku, tr. fr. the Japanese by R. H. Blyth.—MaFw
Faces
Ancestral faces. K. Brew.—AlPa
Counter service. R. Froman.—FrSp
Looking into a face. R. Bly.—MoT
My face. A. Euwer.—LiWw
"O why was I born with a different face." W. Blake.—CoPu
"The opposite of *making faces.*" R. Wilbur.—WiO
Phizzog. C. Sandburg.—SaT
Questioning faces. R. Frost.—CoPu—HiN
Under a hat rim." C. Sandburg.—SaT
A valentine for a lady. Lucilius.—LiWw
Windows with faces. L. Lenski.—LeC
Facing up. James Scully.—HaWr
Factories
Factory. L. Lenski.—LeC
"Factory windows are always broken." V. Lindsay.—CoPu
Factory. Lois Lenski.—LeC
"**Factory** stands on a dingy street." See Factory
"**Factory** windows are always broken." Vachel Lindsay.—CoPu
"**Fade** in the sound of summer music." See Notes for a movie script

Fahy, Francis A.
The queen of Connemara.—CoPi
Failure
Big question. D. McCord.—McFm
Born without a star. Abraham ibn Ezra.—MeP
Dance song. Unknown.—LeIb
Dancing song. Unknown.—LeIb
Disillusionised. L. Carroll.—LiPc
"I return to my little song." Unknown.—LeIb
"Losers weepers." Unknown.—EmN
"My song was ready." Unknown.—LeIb
My stars. Abraham ibn Ezra.—MeP
"Nobody loses all the time." E. E. Cummings.—LiWw—MaFw
Paddler's song on bad hunting weather. Unknown.—LeIb
"Success is counted sweetest." E. Dickinson.—RoIt
"Those game animals, those long-haired caribou." Unknown.—LeIb
"**Fain** would I kiss my Julia's dainty leg." See Her legs
Fair, Anthony
"Christmas."—HoC
"Voices gay."—HoC
The **fair** Circassian. Richard Garnett.—CoPt
"A **fair** little girl sat under a tree." See Good night and good morning
"The **fair** maid who, the first of May." Mother Goose.—AlC
"**Faire** daffadills, we weep to see." See To daffadills
"**Fairest** flower, all flowers excelling." See To a child five years old
Fairies
April 30. N. Belting.—BeSc
"The best game the fairies play." R. Fyleman.—JaP
The birth of the poet. Q. Prettyman.—AdB
The brownies' year. Unknown.—JaP
The child and the fairies. Unknown.—JaP
City fairies. M. B. Armstrong.—JaP
Could it have been a shadow. M. Shannon.—JaP
The elf and the dormouse. O. Herford.—JaP—UnGb
The elfin plane. R. B. Bennett.—JaP
The elves' dance. Unknown.—JoA-4
Elves' song. B. J. Lee.—JaP
The erl-king's daughter. J. G. Herder.—CoPt
Escape. E. Wylie.—JoA-4
Fairies ("The fairies, it is said") Kikaku.—JaP
Fairies ("There are fairies at the bottom of our garden") R. Fyleman.—OpOx
The fairies ("Up the airy mountain") W. Allingham. JaP (sel.)—JoA-4—LiLc—OpOx
"The fairies have never a penny to spend." R. Fyleman.—OpOx
Fairy shoes. A. Wynne.—JaP
Fairy voyage. Unknown.—JaP
Fairy washing. R. B. Bennett.—JaP
"A fairy went a-marketing." R. Fyleman.—OpOx
"Faith, I wish I were a leprechaun." M. Ritter.—JaP
Fay folks. Unknown.—JaP
Finding fairies. M. Barrows.—JaP
Frost sprite. Unknown.—JaP
The gnome. H. Behn.—JaP
The goblin. Unknown.—JoA-4
A goblinade. F. P. Jaques.—JaP
The green fiddler. R. Field.—CoPt
The green gnome. R. Buchanan.—CoPt
The harvest elves. W. Thorley.—JaP
The house of the goblin. S. Brown.—HoH
I see the fairies. E. MacFarland.—JaP (sel.)
"If you see a fairy ring." Unknown.—JaP
Jamboree. L. Blair.—JaP
La belle dame sans merci. J. Keats.—JoA-4—RoIt
Lamia. J. Keats.—MaFw (sel.)
The land of heart's desire. W. B. Yeats.—MaFw (sel.)
The lepracaun; or, Fairy shoemaker. W. Allingham.—RoIt
The leprechaun. L. Blair.—JaP
Lester. S. Silverstein.—SiW
The light-hearted fairy. Unknown.—JaP
The little elf. J. K. Bangs.—JaP.—UnGb
Little Orphant Annie. J. W. Riley.—OpOx—RoIt
Lollocks. R. Graves.—MaFw
Magic. S. Silverstein.—SiW
Magic vine. Unknown.—JaP
Merrily float. T. Hood.—JaP
"Now the hungry lion roars." From A midsummer-night's dream. W. Shakespeare.—MaFw
"O, then, I see Queen Mab hath been with you." From Romeo and Juliet. W. Shakespeare.—MaFw
Queen Mab.—JoA-4
"One Saturday night." Unknown.—JaP
"Over hill, over dale." From A midsummer-night's dream. W. Shakespeare.—JoA-4
Overheard on a saltmarsh. H. Monro.—AdP—JoA-4—LiLc
The perils of invisibility. W. S. Gilbert.—CoPt
Pipes and drums. L. Holmes.—JaP (sel.)
Queen Mab. T. Hood.—JaP (sel.)
The seven ages of elf-hood. R. Field.—JaP
The sleeping beauty. E. Sitwell.—MaFw (sel.)
Ten nights before Christmas. D. McCord.—McFm
The treat. L. Blair.—JaP
The troll bridge. L. Moore.—MoSm
Troll trick. B. J. Lee.—JaP
True Thomas. Unknown.—CoPt
Thomas Rymer.—MaFw
What I think. L. Blair.—JaP
What they said. Unknown.—JaP
Where brownies are. Unknown.—JaP
Where the bee sucks. From The tempest. W. Shakespeare.—JoA-4—LiLc

"You spotted snakes." From A midsummer-night's dream. W. Shakespeare.—JoA-4
Fairies ("The fairies it is said") Kikaku.—JaP
Fairies ("There are fairies at the bottom of our garden") Rose Fyleman.—OpOx
The **fairies** ("Up the airy mountain") William Allingham.—JaP (sel.)—JoA-4—LiLc—OpOx
"The **fairies** all received an invitation." See The sleeping beauty
"The **fairies** have never a penny to spend." Rose Fyleman.—OpOx
"The **fairies** hung their washing out." See Fairy washing
"The **fairies,** it is said." See Fairies
"**Fairies** live in forests." See City fairies
Fairs
After the fair. T. Hardy.—PlP
"I went to the animal fair." Unknown.—EmN
Animal fair.—RoIt
May 8. N. Belting.—BeSc
"There were five fellows." C. Watson.—WaF
"A **fairy** seed I planted." See Magic vine
Fairy shoes. Annette Wynne.—JaP
Fairy voyage. Unknown.—JaP
Fairy washing. Rowena Bastin Bennett.—JaP
"A **fairy** went a-marketing." Rose Fyleman.—OpOx
Faith
Abraham and Isaac. From The Chester miracle play. Unknown.—MaFw
All the world moved. J. Jordan.—AdPb
Credo. G. D. Johnson.—AdPb
Do you want affidavits. C. Sandburg.—SaT
For the Lord's day evening. I. Watts.—OpOx
"I never saw a moor." E. Dickinson.—JoA-4—LiLc
Legend. Judith Wright.—MaFw
May 1. N. Belting.—BeSc
Mirth. C. Smart.—OpOx
Monument. F Holman.—HoI
Paddy O'Rafther. S. Lover.—CoPi
The right time. F. Holman.—HoI
Simon Soggs' Thanksgiving. W. A. Croffut.—CoPt
The tempest. J. T. Fields.—RoIt
The three hermits. W. B. Yeats.—MaFw
To my mother. G. Barker.—HiN—MaFw
Upon the swallow. J. Bunyan.—OpOx
Upon the weathercock. J. Bunyan.—OpOx
We have been believers. M. Walker.—AdPb
"**Faith,** I wish I were a leprechaun." Margaret Ritter.—JaP
Fake. Robert Froman.—FrSp
The **falcon.** Unknown.—MaFw
Falconry. See Falcons and falconry
Falcons and falconry
The falcon. Unknown.—MaFw
Fall. See Autumn
Fall down. Calvin C. Hernton.—AdPb
"**Fall** from a steamer's burning deck." Unknown.—MoBw
"**Fall** from an apple tree." Unknown.—EmN
Fall, leaves, fall. Emily Brontë.—PaF
"**Fall,** leaves, fall; die, flowers, away." See Fall, leaves fall
The **fall** of J. W. Beane. Oliver Herford.—CoPt
Falling. Bob Kaufman.—AdPb
Falling asleep. Siegfried Sassoon.—PaF
Falling in love. David Perkins.—HiN
The **fallow** deer at the lonely house. Thomas Hardy.—CoPu—PlP
Falsehood. See Truthfulness and falsehood
Fame
Fame. W. S. Landor—CoPu
"I often pause and wonder." Unknown.—BrM
"I think continually of those who were truly great." S. Spender.—RoIt
Irish-American dignitary. A. Clarke.—CoPi
On Homer's birthplace. T. Heyward.—PlM
Ozymandias. P. B. Shelley.—LiS—RoIt
Ozymandias revisited. M. Bishop.—LiS
Soup. C. Sandburg.—SaT
Fame. Walter Savage Landor.—CoPu
"The **famed** sword-swallower, looking bored." Jack Prelutsky.—PrC
"**Families,** when a child is born." See On the birth of his son
Family. See also Brothers and sisters; Children and childhood; Fathers and fatherhood; Home and family life; Married life; Mothers and motherhood; Relatives; also names of relatives, as Uncles
An addition to the family: for M. L. E. Morgan.—ToM
All of us a family. C. Meyer.—JoV
"The broad woods." Unknown.—JoT
"Daisy Deborah Delilah Dean." Unknown.—CoOr
Dunbarton. R. Lowell.—ToM
The family reunion. J. Ciardi.—CiFs
Gap. M. Horovitz.—CoPu
"Go to sleep." Mother Goose.—TucMg
"Godfrey Gordon Gustavus Gore." W. B. Rands.—CoOr
Housework. S. Harnick.—ThF
The idea of ancestry. E. Knight.—AdPb
In these dissenting times. A. Walker.—AdPb
"I've heard so much about other folks' folks." T. Hughes.—HuMf
Little brand new baby. T. Paxton.—PeS
Monument in black. V. Howard.—AdM—JoV
My Aunt Dora. T. Hughes.—HuMf
My Aunt Flo. T. Hughes.—HuMf
My brother Bert. T. Hughes.—HuMf
My dog is a plumber. D. Greenburg.—ThF
My family. M. Chute.—ChRu
My father. T. Hughes.—HuMf
My granny. T. Hughes.—HuMf
My mother. T. Hughes.—HuMf
My own true family. T. Hughes.—HuMf
My sister Jane. T. Hughes.—HuMf—MaFw
"My sweet old etcetera." E. E. Cummings.—PeS
My Uncle Mick. T. Hughes.—HuMf
The name. R. Creeley.—PeS
The old woman who lived in a shoe. J. Johnson.—ThF

Family.—*Continued*
The pain and the great one. J. Blume.—ThF
Parents are people. C. Hall.—ThF
Quoits M. E. L. Newsome.—RoIt
A social mixer. X. J. Kennedy.—KeO
Stark boughs on the family tree. M. Oliver.—PeS
"This is father, short and stout." Mother Goose.—TucMg
Uncle Bull-boy. J. Jordan.—AdPb
We are seven. W. Wordsworth.—LiS—OpOx—RoIt
The wholly family. E. Merriam.—MeF
The wild flower and the rose. D. Nikogosian.—MoM
William's doll. S. Harnick.—ThF
"A **family** business, not many of them left." See And son
Family life. See Home and family life.
The **family** reunion. John Ciardi.—CiFs
Famine
The famine year. Lady Wilde.—CoPi
The **famine** year. Lady Wilde.—CoPi
"The **famous** human cannonball." Jack Prelutsky.—PrC
Fans
The folding fan. G. Cohoe.—AlW
"When I think about why." Unknown.—BaSs
Fanshawe, Catherine Maria
A riddle.—RoIt
Fantasia ("I dream") Eve Merriam.—MeF
Fantasia ("I love my love with an M, said I") Winifred M. Letts.—CoPi
"**Far** enough down in China, somebody said." See Digging for China
"**Far** far from gusty waves, these children's faces." See An elementary school classroom in a slum
The **far** field. Theodore Roethke.—JoA-4 (sel.)
Far from Africa: Four poems. Margaret Danner.—AdPb
1. Garnishing the aviary
2. Dance of the Abakweta
3. The visit of the professor of aesthetics
4. Etta Moten's attic
"**Far** from far." See Bobadil
"**Far** from the jungle." See At the ocean
"**Far** in a western brookland." See A Shropshire lad
Far-off things. Lois Lenski.—LeC
"**Farewel** dear babe, my heart's too much content." See In memory of my dear grandchild Elizabeth Bradstreet
A **farewell** ("My fairest child, I have no song to give you") Charles Kingsley.—OpOx
Farewell ("O beloved farewell") Mazisi Kunene.—AlPa
Farewells. See also Parting
At the word *farewell.* T. Hardy.—PlP
A farewell ("My fairest child, I have no song to give you") C. Kingsley.—OpOx
Farewell ("O beloved farewell") M. Kunene.—AlPa
Goodbye and run. P. Irving.—AlW
Motswasele's farewell. L. D. Raditladi.—AlPa
"Shake hands, we shall never be friends, all's over." A. E. Housman.—CoPu
Farjeon, Eleanor
All schools have rules.—BrM
Blackfriars.—OpOx
Boys' names.—JoA-4
Girls' names.—JoA-4—NeA
Griselda.—UnGb
In the week when Christmas comes.—LiLc
Lewis Carroll.—OpOx
Minnie.—UnGb
"Mrs Malone."—OpOx
"The night will never stay."—JoA-4—OpOx
A prayer for little things.—JoA-4
"The sounds in the morning."—JoA-4
Tailor.—OpOx
The witch.—CoOr
— and Farjeon, Herbert
Henry VIII.—CoPt
Farjeon, Herbert. See Farjeon, Eleanor, jt. auth.
The **farm.** Vassar Miller.—HiN
Farm animals. See Animals; also names of farm animals, as Cows
Farm boy after summer. Robert Francis.—HiN
Farm child. R. S. Thomas.—CoPu—MaFw
Farm life. See also Country life; Fields; Harvests and harvesting; Plows and plowing; also names of farm products, as Wheat
Above Penmaenmawr. T. Connor.—ToM
After winter. S. A. Brown.—AdPb
A bummer. M. Casey.—MoT
The caboose who wouldn't come last. X. J. Kennedy.—KeO
Childhood. M. Walker.—AdB—AdPb
Country idyll. F. Cornford.—CoPu
Cynddylan on a tractor. R. S. Thomas.—ToM
A drover. P. Colum.—CoPi
The evacuee. R. S. Thomas.—ToM
The farm. V. Miller.—HiN
Farm boy after summer. R. Francis.—HiN
Farm child. R. S. Thomas.—CoPu—MaFw
The farmer and the queen. S. Silverstein.—SiW
Farmer Dunman's funeral. T. Hardy.—PlP
A farmer's boy. Unknown.—RoIt
Floodtide. A. M. Touré.—AdPb
Foreclosure. S. A. Brown.—AdPb
Good times. L. Clifton.—AdM—AdPb—HiN
Harvest sunset. C. Sandburg.—SaT
Haystacks. From Prairie. C. Sandburg.—SaT
The hill farmer speaks. R. S. Thomas.—ToM
"I went to my grandfather's farm." Unknown.—EmN
"If everyone were a chief." Kim Chang-up.—BaSs
Illinois farmer. C. Sandburg.—SaT
Improved farm land. C. Sandburg.—SaT
In the farmhouse. G. Kinnell.—HaWr
Laughing corn. C. Sandburg.—SaT
"Look at that strutting." Issa.—BeM
Morning. C. S. Calverley.—RoIt

"Nobody loses all the time." E. E. Cummings.—LiWw—MaFw
"Old Farmer Giles." Mother Goose.—TucMgl
The old man who lived in the woods. Unknown.—RoIt
"Only a bold man ploughs the Weald for corn." From The land. V. Sackville-West.—PaP
The ox-tamer. W. Whitman.—RoIt
Pome. D. McCord.—McAa
She opens the barn door every morning. C. Sandburg.—SaT
Sugarfields. B. Mahone.—AdPb
Summer morning. From Prairie. C. Sandburg.—SaT
Twerüre. Unknown.—SeS
Watching post. C. Day-Lewis.—ToM
The **farmer** and the queen. Shel Silverstein.—SiW
Farmer Dunman's funeral. Thomas Hardy.—PlP
"A **farmer** went trotting upon his grey mare." Mother Goose.—JoA-4
Farmers. See Farm life
A **farmer's** boy. Unknown.—RoIt
Farms and farming. See Farm life
Farrar, John (Chipman)
Bundles.—HoS
Farren, Robert
Rich morning.—CoPi
Fascination. John Banister Tabb.—CoOh
Fashions. See Clothing and dress
Fast and slow ("The old crow is getting slow") John Ciardi.—CiFs
Fast and slow ("The snail is slow. The swift gazelle") David McCord.—McFm—McS
Fast isn't far. John Ciardi.—CiFs
Faster. Lee Bennett Hopkins.—HoP
"**Faster** than fairies, faster than witches." See From a railway carriage
"**Fat.**" See Winter cardinal
"**Fat** torpedoes in bursting jackets." See Fourth of July
The **fat** white woman speaks. Gilbert Keith Chesterton.—LiS
Fate
Epitaph on a dormouse, which some children were to bury. Unknown.—OpOx
"The glories of our blood and state." From Contention of Ajax and Ulysses. J. Shirley.—RoIt
O thou seer, go, flee thee away. C. N. Bialik.—MeP
Of kings and things. L. Morrison.—HiN
The poet's fate. T. Hood.—CoPu
The road not taken. R. Frost.—RoIt
"**Father.**" See A small discovery
"**Father.**" Unknown, tr. fr. the Teton Sioux by Frances Densmore.—JoT
Father. Myra Cohn Livingston.—LiM
Father and child. William Butler Yeats.—CoPu
The **father** and his children. Unknown.—OpOx
Father and mother. X. J. Kennedy.—KeO
Father and son. F. R. Higgins.—CoPi
"A **father** deer." Issa, tr. fr. the Japanese by Hanako Fukuda.—HaW
Father Goose tells a story. Alexander Resnikoff.—CoOh
"**Father,** have pity on me." Unknown, tr. fr. the Arapaho.—ClFc
"**Father** Missouri takes his own." See Foreclosure
Father of night. Bob Dylan.—MoG
"**Father** of night, Father of day." See Father of night
Father O'Flynn. Alfred Perceval Graves.—CoPi
"**Father** said, Heh, heh, I'll fix her." See A social mixer
"A **father** sees a son nearing manhood." See What shall he tell that son
Father Son and Holy Ghost. Audre Lorde.—AdPb
"**Father** speaking: What is that awful noise." See Hot line to the nursery
"**Father,** the year is fallen." Audre Lorde.—AdPb
Father William. See Alice's adventures in wonderland—"You are old, Father William, the young man said"
Father William ("You are old, Father William, the young man said [and your nose has a look of surprise]") Unknown.—RoIt
Fathers and fatherhood
And son. E. Merriam.—MeF
Bringing him up. Lord Dunsany.—CoPu—LiWw
By the Exeter river. D. Hall.—ToM
The cataract at Lodore, July 31, 1936. H. Bevington.—LiS
"The child at winter sunset." M. Van Doren.—HiN
Daddy fell into the pond. A. Noyes.—BrM
Daedalus. A. Reid.—HiN
December 22: Window shopping. L. Clifton.—ClEa
Digging. S. Heaney.—ToM
"Each morning." From Hymn for Lanie Poo. LeRoi Jones.—AdPb
Efficiency apartment. G. W. Barrax.—AdPb
Epitaph. A. Bradstreet.—ThI
The exhortation of a father to his children. R. Smith.—OpOx
Father. M. C. Livingston.—LiM
Father and child. W. B. Yeats.—CoPu
Father and mother. X. J. Kennedy.—KeO
Father and son. F. R. Higgins.—CoPi
Father Son and Holy Ghost. A. Lorde.—AdPb
Find my father with freedom. L. Curry.—JoV
Follower. S. Heaney.—CoPi
For a fatherless son. S. Plath.—MoT
For de Lawd. L. Clifton.—AdM—AdPb
Fortunatus the R. A. Nikarchos.—LiWw
The geese. R. Peck.—PeS
Geographical knowledge. T. Hardy.—PlP
"Hail him." Unknown.—AlPa
Hat. S. Silverstein.—SiW
Having New England fathers. J. Holmes.—RoIt

Fathers and fatherhood—*Continued*
"If a man who turnips cries." S. Johnson.—MiMg
If I should ever by chance. E. Thomas.—OpOx
The lesson. E. Lucie-Smith.—HiN—ToM
Listening. W. Stafford.—MoT
Love from my father. C. G. Clemmons.—AdPb
The maple. E. J. Coatsworth.—LaM
May. L. Clifton.—ClE
"Mother, a dog is at the door." X. J. Kennedy.—KeO
Mousemeal. H. Nemerov.—HiN
My dad. L. Lenski.—LeC
My father. T. Hughes.—HuMf
My father paints the summer. R. Wilbur.—HiN
"My mother said." Mother Goose.—AlC
My papa's waltz. T. Roethke.—HiN—MaFw—PeS
"My son, let me grasp your hand." Unknown.—ClFc
Nails. X. J. Kennedy.—KeO
"Now the man has a child." Karai Senryū.—MaFw
"Old Caspar had six sons so fine." Mother Goose.—TucMg
On one who lived and died where he was born. T. Hardy.—PlP
On the birth of his son. Su Tung-p'o.—LiWw
One flesh. E. Jennings.—ToM
Our father. R. Mathew.—MaFw
The party. R. Whittemore.—HiN
Patience. H. Graham.—LiWw
Penguin chick. A. Fisher.—FiD
Questions, quistions & quoshtions. S. Milligan.—CoOr
"Rock, rock, sleep, my baby." C. Watson.—WaF
"Round about, round about." Unknown. Counting out rhyme.—LiS
Smart. S. Silverstein.—SiW
"Step on a nail." Unknown.—EmN
Sunday morning: Lonely. L. Clifton.—ClS
Tèma con variazíoni. L. Carroll.—LiS
That dark other mountain. R. Francis.—HiN—PeS
"There once was a king." Unknown.—BoI
"There was an old woman had three sons." Mother Goose.—JoA-4
"This is father, short and stout." Mother Goose.—TucMg
Those winter Sundays. R. Hayden.—AdPb
To Theon from his son Theon. C. A. Trypanis.—HiN
The tree is father to the man. L. Lipsitz.—HiN
Villikins and his Dinah. S. Cowell.—CoPt
What shall he tell that son. C. Sandburg.—PeS
When father carves the duck. E. V. Wright.—RoIt
"White mountains, seen also." Issa.—HaW
"William and Mary, George and Anne." Mother Goose.—AlC
"Fatty on a steamboat." Unknown.—EmN
"Fatty on the ocean." Unknown.—EmN
"Faucet's leaking." See Slum home
The **faun.** Ezra Pound.—MaFw
Fauset, Jessie Redmond
Oriflamme.—AdPb
Fawcett, Edgar
To an oriole.—RoIt
"The fawn." Issa.—AtM
Fay folks. Unknown.—JaP
Fear
Advice from an elderly mouse. E. J. Coatsworth.—BrM
Afraid of the dark. S. Silverstein.—SiW
"At the first sign of my horse's fright." Unknown.—BaSs
Brainstorm. H. Nemerov.—HiN
Carmen. V. H. Cruz.—AdPb
The city mouse and the country mouse. R. S. Sharpe.—OpOx
"Deep in a windless." Busōn.—BeM
Disturbances. A. Thwaite.—ToM
Efon (Buffalo). Unknown.—AlPa
"Evening swallows flying home." Issa.—HaW
"The exam." Unknown.—MoM
"Fear have I when it comes." L. Curry.—JoV
Frightened flower. W. J. Harris.—AdB
From riot rimes U.S.A. #79. R. R. Patterson.—AdM
Glimpse. P. C. Lomax.—AdPb
Here I am. M. C. Livingston.—LiM
Hunger. Unknown.—LeIb
"I am simply on the earth." Unknown.—ClFc
I think I understand. J. Mitchell.—MoG
"I walked on the ice of the sea." Unknown.—LeIb
Jitterbugging in the streets. C. C. Hernton.—AdPb
"Kicking your heels on the dusty road." P. Solomon.—JoV
"Little Miss Muffet." Mother Goose.—JoA-4
Mousemeal. H. Nemerov.—HiN
"One summer evening (led by her) I found." From The prelude. W. Wordsworth.—MaFw
The one who stayed. S. Silverstein.—SiW
The pay is good. R. Kell.—ToM
Phantoms of the steppe. A. Pushkin.—AbM
The pigeon hole. M. Segun.—AlPa
The sandhill crane. M. Austin.—AdP
Scare. R. Froman.—FrSp
Song ("And I think over again") Unknown.—BiI
Song ("Do not fear to put thy feet") From The river god's song. F. Beaumont and J. Fletcher.—RoIt
Song composed at the beginning of an autumn festival in honor of the ribbon seal. Unknown.—LeIb
A storm in childhood. T. H. Jones.—MaFw
Storm on the island. S. Heaney.—HiN

The tale of Custard the Dragon. O. Nash.—UnGb
Tears. A. Lopez.—AlW
"There's a cross-eyed woman in our town." Unknown.—CoOh
Thursday evening: Bedtime. L. Clifton.—ClS
"The tiger stalking in the night." E. N. Horn.—CoPu
"Tweedle-dum and Tweedle-dee." Mother Goose.—AlC
Very much afraid. Unknown.—BiS
War song. Unknown.—AlPa
Whooo. L. Moore.—MoSm
"A wolf." Unknown.—JoT
The worst. S. Silverstein.—SiW
"**Fear** have I when it comes." Linda Curry.—JoV
"**Fear** was about me." See Hunger
Fearing, Kenneth
Confession overheard in a subway.—PeS
Feathers
"A bantam rooster." Kikaku.—BeM
"An eagle feather I see." Unknown.—JoT
Feathers and moss. J. Ingelow.—LiS
"I like them feathery, too." A. Fisher.—FiFo
Looking for feathers. A. Fisher.—FiFo
"They are sailing on the breeze." Unknown.—JoT
Feathers and moss. Jean Ingelow.—LiS
February
February. L. Clifton.—ClE
February—It's an ill wind. F. Holman.—HoI
Ground hog day. M. Pomeroy.—CoPu
"In the month of February." Mother Goose.—TucMgl
February. Lucille Clifton.—ClE
February—It's an ill wind. Felice Holman.—HoI
"**February's** getting vicious." See February—It's an ill wind
The **feckless** dinner party. Walter De La Mare.—CoPt
Feeding the lions. Norman Jordan.—AdB—AdPb
"**Feedum,** fiddledum, fee." Mother Goose.—AlC
"**Feel** free." See To Bobby Seale
Feelings. See also specific emotions, as Fear; Happiness
Dawn is a feeling. M. Pinder.—MoG
No one else. E. Laron.—ThF
Feet
Feet. M. C. Livingston.—JoA-4
Montgomery. S. Cornish.—AdM—AdPb
"The opposite of *foot* is what." R. Wilbur.—WiO
Feet. Myra Cohn Livingston.—JoA-4
"**Feet** are very special things." See Feet
Feet o' Jesus. Langston Hughes.—HoD
Feigned courage. Charles and Mary Lamb.—OpOx
"**Fellows** is there anyone among you." See A week after the first Sputnik
Fence. Valerie Worth.—WoS
"The **fenceposts** wear marshmallow hats." See Snow
Fences
Fence. V. Worth.—WoS
The **feral** pioneers. Ishmael Reed.—AdPb
Ferguson, James
Auld Daddy Darkness.—OpOx
Ferguson, Samuel
Cashel of Munster. tr.—CoPi
Dear dark head. tr.—CoPi
Ferlinghetti, Lawrence
Number 7.—PeS
Number 20.—PeS
"Reading Yeats I do not think."—PlM
To paint the portrait of a bird. tr.—MaFw
Fern hill. Dylan Thomas.—JoA-4—PaF—PeS
Ferries
"Back and forth." L. S. Mitchell.—HoP
By ferry to the island. I. C. Smith.—ToM
"Ferry me across the water." C. G. Rossetti.—OpOx
Ferry, David
Dog and fox.—CoPu
Lines for a dead poet.—PlM
Ferry boats. See Ferries
"**Ferry** me across the water." Christina Georgina Rossetti.—OpOx
Fet, Afanasy
A magic landscape."—MoM
Fetching cows. Norman MacCaig.—MaFw
Fetters. Louis Ginsberg.—RoIt
"**Few** men in any age have second sight." See Pencil stubs—To a reviewer who admired my book
Fiacc, Padraic
The boy and the geese.—CoPi
Deranged.—CoPi
Fichman, Yaakov
Eve.—MeP
"**Fiddledy,** diddledy, dee." Unknown.—EmN
The **fiddler** of Dooney. William Butler Yeats.—JoA-4—RoIt
Fiddlers and fiddling
The fiddler of Dooney. W. B. Yeats.—JoA-4—RoIt
The green fiddler. R. Field.—CoPt
The mountain whippoorwill. S. V. Benét.—CoPt
"Old King Cole." Mother Goose.—JoA-4
"Terence McDiddler." Mother Goose.—HoMg
Field, Edward
Donkeys.—RoIt
Field, Eugene
The death of Robin Hood.—CoPt
The dinkey-bird.—RoIt
The fly-away horse.—UnGb
The sugar-plum tree.—OpOx
Wynken, Blynken, and Nod.—OpOx
Field, Rachel (Lyman)
Fourth of July.—LaM
Good green bus.—HoP (sel.)
The green fiddler.—CoPt
The hills.—LiLc

The flattered lightning bug. D. Marquis.—CoPt
Glowworm. D. McCord.—BrM
"I wonder, I wonder." Unknown.—EmN
Light my way to bed. Unknown.—BiS
Night travel. M. Chute.—ChRu
The nightingale and glow-worm. W. Cowper.—RoIt
"Please don't go, I called." Onitsura.—BeM
"What is life." Unknown.—ClFc
The **firefly** ("The firefly's flame") Ogden Nash.—LiWw
Firefly ("Like lamps between the trees") Kamimura Hajime, tr. fr. the Japanese by Harry and Lynn Guest and Kajima Shozo.—MoT
Firefly ("A little light is going by") Elizabeth Madox Roberts.—JoA-4—LiLc
"The **firefly** is a funny bug." Unknown.—BrM—CoOh
"The **firefly's** flame." See The firefly
Firehouses
Sliding. L. Moore.—MoSm
Firemen
A fine fat fireman. J. Ciardi.—CiFs
Number 7. L. Ferlinghetti.—PeS
"**Firemen,** firemen." See Help
"**Fireplug.**" See Waiting
Fireworks
"Fireworks." M. B. Timm.—HoC
Fireworks. J. Reeves.—JoA-4
Fourth of July. R. Field.—LaM
Gunpowder plot. V. Scannell.—MaFw—ToM
"**Fireworks.**" Mary Beth Timm.—HoC
Fireworks. James Reeves.—JoA-4
"**First.**" See The chestnuts are falling
The **1st.** Lucille Clifton.—MoT
First confession. X. J. Kennedy.—HiN
The **first** dandelion. Walt Whitman.—RoIt
"The **first** day of Christmas." See The twelve days of Christmas
First death in Nova Scotia. Elizabeth Bishop.—HiN
"**First** feel, then feel, then." See Young soul
"The **first** firefly." Issa, tr. fr. the Japanese by Hanako Fukuda.—HaW
First, goodbye. John Smith.—ToM
"**First** hear the story of Kaspar the rosy-cheeked." See Fräulein reads instructive rhymes
"**First** I saw the white bear, then I saw the black." See At the zoo
"**First,** I'll sing. Later, perhaps, I'll speak." See The condition
"The **first** joy of Mary was the joy of one." See The seven joys of Mary
"**First** man and first woman." Natalia Belting.—BeWi
First man was the first to emerge. Unknown, tr. fr. the Navajo by Harry Hoijer.—BiI
First Monday Scottsboro Alabama. Tom Weatherly.—AdPb
"The **first** of April, some do say." Unknown.—MaF
"**First** of God by whom all grace is spread." See Sources of good counsel
First or last. Thomas Hardy.—JoA-4
"**First** paint a cage." See To paint the portrait of a bird
First sight. Philip Larkin.—HiN—MoT
First sight of her and after. Thomas Hardy.—PlP
"The **first** sign was your hair." See I'm just a stranger here, Heaven is my home
The **first** snow of the year. Mark Van Doren.—HiN
First snowfall. Aileen Fisher.—FiFo
First song. Galway Kinnell.—HiN
First spring morning. Robert Bridges.—JoA-4
The **first** step. Constantine Cavafy, tr. by Rae Dalven.—PlM
First Thanksgiving of all. Nancy Byrd Turner.—RoIt
"**First,** the fish must be caught." See Through the looking-glass
"**First** the melody clean and hard." See How high the moon
"**First** the soul of our house left, up the chimney." See Tornado
"**First** they shot a female caribou." Unknown, fr. the Caribou Eskimo.—LeIb
The **first** tooth. Charles and Mary Lamb.—OpOx
"**First** we must have to build our own." See We can't always follow the white man's way
"The **first** whimper of the storm." See A local storm
"The **first** winter rain. Bashō.—AtM
"**First** you see me in the grass." Unknown.—EmN
"**First,** you think they are dead." See Lobsters in the window
"**First** you will say goodbye. You will turn." See First, goodbye
Fish. See also names of fish, as Starfish
Alas, alack. W. De La Mare.—OpOx
Allie. R. Graves.—JoA-4
Catchers. R. Froman.—FrSp
The caulker. M. A. Lewis.—CoPt
Do fishes go to school. R. Whitman.—RoIt
"First the fish must be caught." From Through the looking-glass. L. Carroll.—LiPc
Fish ("Fish have fins") J. Prelutsky,—PrT
Fish ("The little fish eats the tiny fish") S. Silverstein.—SiW
Fish crier. C. Sandburg.—SaT
Fish story. R. Armour.—FlH
"Fish swash." M. A. Hoberman.—HoN
The fishes of Kempenfelt bay. D. Lee.—LeA
Grunion. M. C. Livingston.—LiM
The guppy. O. Nash.—JoA-4
"A haddock, a haddock, a black-spotted haddock." Unknown.—EmN
The hen and the carp. I. Serraillier.—LiWw
"Hovering above." Onitsura.—BeM

Spring morning.—FiFo
Squirrel.—FiFo
Substitute.—FiM
The swans.—FiD
Tails.—FiFo
Tom.—FiM
Wags and purrs.—FiM
Waiting.—FiFo
Weasel.—FiFo
"What's for rabbits."—FiFo
Who.—FiFo
Winter birds.—FiFo—LaM
Winter nests.—FiFo
Winter surprise.—FiFo
The wrens.—FiFo
Your cat and mine.—FiM

"A **fisherman** discouraged by a storm." Chang Mann, tr. fr. the Korean by Chung Seuk Park and ad. by Virginia Olsen Baron.—BaSs

Fishermen and fishing
The angler's song. I. Walton.—FlH
Blackfriars. E. Farjeon.—OpOx
Fish story. R. Armour.—FlH
"A fisherman discouraged by a storm." Chang Mann.—BaSs
Fishing ("Grandfather and the oars are one body") A. T. Pratt.—AlW
Fishing ("Row to the fishing-ground, row away") Unknown.—JoA-4
"Fishing boats all drawn." H. L. Johnson.—HoP
Fishing harbour towards evening. R. Kell.—ToM
"Fishy, fishy, bite." Unknown.—EmN
The giant fisherman. W. King.—RoIt
The harpooning. T. Walker.—HaWr
Herring is king. A. P. Graves.—CoPi
How to catch tiddlers. B. Jones.—MaFw
"I return to my little song." Unknown.—LeIb
"Is that a cuckoo singing." Yun Sun-do.—BaSs
"Little Tommy Tittlemouse." Mother Goose.—AlC—MiMg
The nightfishing. W. S. Graham.—MaFw (sel.)
"Out fishing on the ocean." B. Pollack.—HoP
Pike. T. Hughes.—HiN—ToM
The right time. F. Holman.—HoI
"The river darkens on an autumn night." Yi Jung.—BaSs
"Row, row, row." Unknown.—BoI
Runover rhyme. D. McCord.—McFm—McS
A salmon trout to her children. Unknown.—LeIb
The silver fish. S. Silverstein.—BrM—SiW
Sunfish. D. McCord.—McAa
The taking of the salmon. T. T. Stoddart.—FlH
"Three big sailors had a tiny little boat." Mother Goose.—TucMg
To a fish of the brook. J. Wolcot.—RoIt
The trout. J. Montague.—CoPi
Uncle Roderick. N. MacCaig.—ToM
When a jolly young fisher. Unknown.—BrM
Wynken, Blynken, and Nod. Eugene Field.—OpOx

The **fishes** of Kempenfelt bay. Dennis Lee.—LeA

Fishing. See Fishermen and fishing

Fishing ("Grandfather and the oars are one body") Agnes T. Pratt.—AlW

Fishing ("Row to the fishing ground, row away") Unknown, tr. fr. the Danish by Rose Fyleman.—JoA-4

"**Fishing** boats all drawn." Hannah Lyons Johnson.—HoP

Fishing harbour towards evening. Richard Kell.—ToM

"**Fishy,** fishy, bite." Unknown.—EmN

Fitts, Dudley
Any author to any friend. tr.—PlM
Fortunatus the R.A. tr.—LiWw
The frugal host. tr.—LiWw
Meditation on beavers. tr.—LiWw
On a school-teacher. tr.—LiWw
On Apis the prizefighter. tr.—LiWw
On Mauros the rhetor. tr.—LiWw
On Torpid Marcus. tr.—LiWw
To a friend: constructive criticism.—LiWw
A valentine for a lady. tr.—LiWw

Fitzgerald, Robert
Birds. tr.—JoA-4
The boar hunt. See The Odyssey
The Odyssey, sels.
The boar hunt. tr.—MaFw
"Now this was the reply Odysseus made." tr.—PlM
The siren's song. tr.—MoG
"Now this was the reply Odysseus made." See The Odyssey
The siren's song. See The Odyssey

Fitzsimmons, Thomas
Invisible tree. tr.—MoT

"**Five** brave maids sitting on five broad beds." Unknown.—EmN

Five cent balloons. Carl Sandburg.—SaT

"**Five** ducks in the pond." See Railroad ducks

"**Five** gleaming crows." See In air

Five little chickens. See The chickens

"**Five** little monkeys." See The monkeys and the crocodile

"**Five** little owls in an old elm tree." Mother Goose.—TucMgl

Five little pussy cats. Unknown.—BlM

"**Five** little pussy cats sitting in a row." See Five little pussy cats

"**Five** little squirrels sat up in a tree." Unknown.—JoA-4

The **five** toes. Unknown, tr. fr. the Chinese by I. T. Headland.—JoA-4

Five vignettes. Jean Toomer.—AdPb

5 ways to kill a man. Edwin Brock.—MoT

"**Five** years have past; five summers, with the length." See Lines composed a few miles above Tintern abbey

Flag. Shel Silverstein.—SiW

Flags—United States
Flag. S. Silverstein.—SiW

Flamingo. Mary Ann Hoberman.—HoR
Flamingoes
Boy in the Roman zoo. A. MacLeish.—HiN
Flamingo. M. A. Hoberman.—HoR
Flanders
"Lady, Lady Landers." Unknown.—JoA-4
Flannan isle. W. W. Gibson.—CoPt
"Flapping into fog." Gyodai, tr. fr. the Japanese by Harry Behn.—BeM
"Flat on the bank I parted." See The trout
The **flattered** lightning bug. Don Marquis.—CoPt
Flattery
Sincere flattery of W. W. (Americanus). J. K. Stephen.—LiS
The spider and the fly. M. Howitt.—OpOx
A **flea** and a fly. Unknown.—BrM
"A fly and a flea in a flue."—EMN—RoIt
"A **flea** and a fly in a flue." See A flea and a fly
Fleas
The cannibal flea. T. Hood, Jr.—LiS
"Can't catch me." Unknown.—EmN
"Don't mind my small hut." Issa.—HaW
A flea and a fly. Unknown.—BrM
"A fly and a flea in a flue."—EmN—RoIt
The hockey game. D. Lee.—LeA
"A horse and a flea and three blind mice." Unknown.—TrG
"I went hunting in the wood." Unknown.—EmN
In the middle. D. McCord.—McS
"I've got a dog as thin as a rail." Unknown.—CoOr
"Oh dear me, Mother caught a flea." Mother Goose.—AlC
"Restless little flea." Issa.—BeM
Small talk. D. Marquis.—CoPt
"Some people say that fleas are black." Unknown.—BrM—CoOh
"There was a jolly miller." Mother Goose.—AlC
Flecker, James Elroy
Lord Arnaldos.—CoPt
"Flee thee away? A man like myself doesn't flee." See O thou seer, go, flee thee away
Fletcher, Alice
"Breathe on him." tr.—BiI
Fletcher, John. See also Beaumont, Francis, jt. auth.
The god of sheep.—RoIt
Fletcher, John Gould
Lincoln.—JoA-4
Rain in the desert.—HiN
Fliers and flight
"The blue wings." A. Karlov.—MoM
The canary's flight. J. R. Jiménez.—JoA-4
Children of the wind. From The people, yes. C. Sandburg.—SaT
Darius Green and his flying machine. J. T. Trowbridge.—OpOx
Eagle flight. A. Lopez.—AlW
Ego. P. Booth.—PeS
Flying crooked. R. Graves.—CoPu—MaFw
The Flying Festoon. S. Silverstein.—SiW
Flying out of holes. D. Lee.—LeA
From the shore. C. Sandburg.—SaT
"He bloomed among eagles." D. Ross.—RoIt
I, Icarus. A. Nowlan.—HiN
"I'm a pilot." M. C. Livingston.—HoP
An Irish airman foresees his death. W. B. Yeats.—PeS
Like a summer bird. A. Fisher.—FiFo
The long-haired boy. S. Silverstein.—SiW
Night travel. M. Chute.—ChRu
The old pilot's death. D. Hall.—ToM
Precision. P. Collenette.—MaFw
The story of Flying Robert. H. Hoffman.—LiS
To Beachey. C. Sandburg.—SaT
"What is the opposite of flying." R. Wilbur.—WiO
Flies
"Back in my home town." Issa.—BeM
A flea and a fly. Unknown.—BrM
"A fly and a flea in a flue."—EmN—RoIt
The fly in Rye. N. M. Bodecker.—BoL
"Flypaper, flypaper." Unknown.—EmN
"A horsefly mutters." Bokusui.—BeM
"How can a creature." Kikaku.—BeM
"I heard a fly buzz—when I died." E. Dickinson.—ThI
"If things were better." Issa.—HaW—LiWw
Math class. M. C. Livingston.—LiM
Mayday. E. Roberson.—AdPb
"Oh, do not swat the fly." Issa.—HaW
"Stop, don't swat the fly."—MaFw
On a fly drinking from his cup. W. Oldys.—RoIt
The spider and the fly. M. Howitt.—OpOx
"Then said the blowfly." Unknown.—LeIb
Flight. Lilian Moore.—MoSp
Flight of the roller coaster. Raymond Souster.—CoPt
Flint. Christina Georgina Rossetti.—OpOx
"Flint Boy tied his dog." Natalia Belting.—BeWi
Floccinaucinihilipilification. Eve Merriam.—MeO
"The **flock** of pigeons." See Pigeons
"A **flock** of sparrows, chattering." Unknown, tr. fr. the Korean by Chung Seuk Park and ad. by Virginia Olsen Baron.—BaSs
Floods
Floodtide. A. M. Touré.—AdPb
Foreclosure. S. A. Brown.—AdPb
The history of the flood. J. Heath-Stubbs.—MaFw
The Louisiana weekly #4. D. Henderson.—AdPb
Winter in the fens. J. Clare.—MaFw
Floodtide. Askia Muhammad Touré.—AdPb
Florida
Florida road workers. L. Hughes.—PeS
Florida road workers. Langston Hughes.—PeS
Flotsam
The camel and the flotsam. J. De La Fontaine.—JoA-4
"Flour of England, fruit from Spain." Unknown.—EmN

"**Flow** gently, sweet Afton, among thy green braes." See Afton water
Flower, Robin
The forest of Dean.—PaP
He that never read a line. tr.—CoPi
Pangur Bán. tr.—CoPi
The passage at night—the blaskets.—CoPi
"A **flower.**" See The poem of ten *ones.*
The **flower.** Volodga Lapin, tr. fr. the Russian by Miriam Morton.—MoM
The **flower-fed** buffaloes. Vachel Lindsay.—JoA-4
"The **flower-fed** buffaloes of the spring." See The flower-fed buffaloes
"**Flower** of the flock." See On sweet Killen hill
"**Flower** so red." Lois Lenski.—LeC
"A **flower** that no one ever saw." See Flowers
The **flower** trap. Felicia Holman.—HoI
Flower wagon. Lois Lenski.—LeC
"The **flowering** castor, abruptly at night grown dense." See Of bloom
"The **flowering** tree stands in Tamoanchan." See He wove the strands of our life
Flowers. See also Gardeners; Gardens and gardening; Plants; Trees; also names of flowers as Roses
Arabesque. F. Johnson.—AdPb
"As still as a flower." A. Atwood.—AtM
"Birds, do not blame the blossoms." Song Soon.—BaSs
Blossom themes. C. Sandburg.—MaFw—SaT
Butterflies. Chu Miao Tuan.—MaFw
"Butterflies playing happily." Unknown.—BaSs
By chance I walk. Yüan Mei.—MaFw
The city. D. Ignatow.—CoPu
"Come, come, you naughty scamp." Mother Goose.—TucMg
Comparisons. C. G. Rossetti.—OpOx
Crack in the wall holds flowers. A. D. Miller.—AdPb
Death songs. L. V. Mack.—AdPb
Do you know the man. S. Silverstein.—CoOh
A dream of wildflower names. M. Chute.—ChRu
Dream song. Unknown.—BiI
The field, revisited. F. Holman.—HoI
The flower. V. Lapin.—MoM
"Flower so red." L. Lenski.—LeC
The flower trap. F. Holman.—HoI
Flowers ("A flower that no one ever saw") J. Ciardi.—CiFs
Flowers ("From a golden step") J.-N.-A. Rimbaud.—MaFw
"Flowers, blooming in spring." T. Jastrzebski."—HoC
Flowers of darkness. F. M. Davis.—AdPb
Flowers tell months. C. Sandburg.—SaT
"The flowers that bloom in the spring." From The Mikado. W. S. Gilbert.—RoIt
Frightened flower. W. J. Harris.—AdB
A Gloria song (by Gloria). R. Hoban.—HoE
The idle flowers. R. Bridges.—JoA-4
If I should ever by chance. E. Thomas.—OpOx
The little girl. T. Iadchenko.—MoM
My Aunt Dora. T. Hughes.—HuMf
Of bloom. L. Goldberg.—MeP
Old florist. T. Roethke.—HiN
"One I love." Mother Goose.—EmN—HoMg
"The pampas flowers." Issa.—HaW
The question. P. B. Shelley.—PaF
September. M. Coleridge.—PaF
So, some tempestuous morn in early June." From Thyrsis. M. Arnold.—PaF
"Spring on the river." A. Atwood.—AtM
Thank you. L. Breek.—MoM
They shall not wither. Unknown.—BiI
To a child five years old. N. Cotton.—OpOx
To a nightingale. J. Keats.—PaF
To autumn. W. Blake.—PaF
"Violets, daffodils." E. J. Coatsworth.—CoPu
"Where have all the flowers gone." P. Seeger.—PeS
The wild flower and the rose. D. Nikogosian.—MoM
Winter poem. N. Giovanni.—AdM
"You buy some flowers for your table." From Poems in praise of practically nothing. S. Hoffenstein.—LiWw
Flowers ("A flower that no one ever saw") John Ciardi.—CiFs
Flowers ("From a golden step") Jean-Nicholas-Arthur Rimbaud, tr. fr. the French by Oliver Bernard.—MaFw
"The **flowers** are dead." See Scenery
"**Flowers,** blooming in spring." Teresa Jastrzebski.—HoC
Flowers of darkness. Frank Marshall Davis.—AdPb
"**Flowers** of the willow-herb are wool." See Seed-time
Flowers tell months. Carl Sandburg.—SaT
"The **flowers** that bloom in the spring." See The Mikado
Flummery. Eve Merriam.—MeO
Flute song. Unknown, ad. by John Bierhorst from the collections of Frances Densmore.—BiS
Flutes
The amateur flute. Unknown.—LiS
Flute song. Unknown.—BiS
"Neither spirit nor bird." M. Austin.—RoIt
"O moon, why must you." Koyo.—LiWw
Spring. W. Blake.—JoA-4—LiLc—PaF—RoIt—UnGb
The tooting tutor. Unknown.—BrM
"A tooter who tooted the flute."—EmN
Flux. Carl Sandburg.—SaT
"The **fly.**" See The fly in Rye
"A **fly** and a flea in a flue." See A flea and a fly
"**Fly** away, fly away, over the sea." See The swallow
The **fly-away** horse. Eugene Field.—UnGb
The **fly** in Rye. N. M. Bodecker.—BoL
"The **fly** is dying hard." See Mayday

Egg thoughts. R. Hoban.—HoE
Eighteen flavors. S. Silverstein.—SiW
Elephant. M. A. Hoberman.—HoR
"An epicure, dining at Crewe." Unknown.—RoIt—TrG
Exploding gravy. X. J. Kennedy.—KeO
Figgie hobbin. C. Causley.—CaF
Fish. S. Silverstein.—SiW
"Five little owls in an old elm tree." Mother Goose.—TucMgl
The fly in Rye. N. M. Bodecker.—BoL
From the kitchen, sels. D. McCord.—McA (Complete)
  1. Pie
  2. Macaroon
  3. Fudge
  4. Peanut butter
  5. Cake
  6. Pistachio ice cream.—McS
  7. Animal crackers.—McS
  8. People crackers.—McS
  9. Gingersnaps
  10. Cucumbers vs. pickles
The frugal host. Automedon.—LiWw
Get 'em here. L. B. Hopkins.—HoCs
Ginger bread mama. D. Long.—AdPb
The glutton. J. Oakman.—OpOx
"Great-great Grandma, don't sleep in your treehouse tonight." X. J. Kennedy.—KeO
Greedy Jane. Unknown.—NeA—OpOx
Greedy Richard. Jane Taylor.—OpOx
Gretchen. Unknown.—JoA-4
Griselda. E. Farjeon.—UnGb
The groaning board. Pink.—CoPu
"H-U huckle, B-U buckle, H-U huckle Y." Unknown.—EmN
"Half a pound of bacon." Mother Goose.—AlC
"Hannah Bantry in the pantry." Mother Goose.—AlC—CoOh—TrG
"Hello Mr Python." S. Milligan.—CoOh
The High Barbaree. L. E. Richards.—JoA-4
Homework. R. Hoban.—HoE
Hopper. R. Froman.—FrSp
"Hot boiled beans and very good butter." Unknown.—EmN
Hot cakes. S. Hsi.—MaFw
"Hot-cross buns." Mother Goose.—JoA-4—LaM
"Hot dog hot." L. Lenski.—LeC
The house mouse. J. Prelutsky.—PrP
Hungry. L. Lenski.—LeC
Hungry Mungry. S. Silverstein.—SiW
"I am the Grizzly Bear." Unknown.—ClFc
"I eat my peas with honey." Unknown.—BrM—TrG
"I must remember." S. Silverstein.—SiW
"I scream, you scream." Unknown.—EmN
I, too. L. Hughes.—RoIt
  "I, too, sing America."—AdPb
"Ice cream, ice cream." J. Price.—PeS
"Ice cream, is cold, soft, sweet." L. Mead.—HoC
"Ice cream slice." M. A. Hoberman.—HoN
I'd not be a robin. A. Fisher.—FiFo
"If all the food was paving-stone." Mother Goose.—AlC
If the world was crazy. S. Silverstein.—SiW
"I'm a navvy, you're a navvy." Mother Goose.—TucMgl
"I'm going to Lady Washington's." Unknown.—JoA-4
"In Kamloops." D. Lee.—LeA
"In stature the manlet was dwarfish." From Sylvie and Bruno concluded. L. Carroll.—LiPc
"In that case." P. Solomon.—JoV
"It's the nicht atween the saints and souls." Unknown.—MaF (sel.)
"Jack Sprat could eat no fat." Mother Goose.—AlC—JoA-4
"Jam." M. A. Hoberman.—HoN
Knoxville, Tennessee. N. Giovanni.—AdB—AdM—AdPb
"The lion and the unicorn." Mother Goose.—AlC—JoA-4
Listening. A. Fisher.—FiM
Little Billee. W. M. Thackeray.—RoIt
"Little General Monk." Mother Goose.—MiMg
"Little Jack Horner sat in the corner." Mother Goose.—AlC
  "Little Jack Horner."—JoA-4
"Little King Boggen he built a fine hall." Mother Goose.—AlC
"Little Miss Muffet." Mother Goose."—JoA-4
"Little Orphan Annie." Unknown.—EmN
"Little Tom Tucker." Mother Goose.—AlC
  "Little Tommy Tucker."—JoA-4
Lorna Doone: Last cookie song. R. Hoban.—HoE
Lost and found. L. Moore.—MoSm
"Maggie, Maggie, where is Jiggs." Unknown.—EmN
"The man in the moon (came tumbling down)." Mother Goose.—AlC—RoIt
"Maple sugar." Unknown.—ClFc
Melinda Mae. S. Silverstein.—SiW
Memories. R. Froman.—FrSp
Methuselah. Unknown.—RoIt
Millions of strawberries. G. Taggard.—UnGb
Miss T. W. De La Mare.—JoA-4
"Mr East gave a feast." Mother Goose.—JoA-4
Mr Weller. N. M. Bodecker.—BoL
"Ms Minnie McFinney, of Butte." Unknown.—NeA
"Mix a pancake." C. G. Rossetti.—LaM—LiLc
The monkeys and the crocodile. L. E. Richards.—JoA-4
The mouse. E. J. Coatsworth.—JoA-4
The mouse and the cake. E. Cook.—OpOx
My house. G. Burgess.—BrM
Natural history. W. T. Smith.—LiWw
The nightingale and glow-worm. W. Cowper—RoIt
The notorious glutton. A. Taylor.—OpOx
"Now this was the reply Odysseus made." From The Odyssey. Homer.—PlM

Wicked witch's kitchen. X. J. Kennedy.—KeO
"Wine and cakes for gentlemen." Mother Goose.—HoMg
Winter birds. A. Fisher.—FiFo—LaM
"Wish I was in Arkansas." Unknown.—EmN
Witch, witch. R. Fyleman.—JaP
With his mouth full of food. S. Silverstein.—SiW
The worm. R. Bergengren.—BrM
The youth and the northwind. J. G. Saxe.—CoPt
"A **fool** and his money soon part at the carnival." Unknown.—MoBw
"**Fool** be he who walks my track." See Ego swamp
The **fool** on the hill. John Lennon and Paul McCartney.—MoG
Fools
Epigram. A. Pope; also at. to S. T. Coleridge.—RoIt
The fool on the hill. J. Lennon and P. McCartney.—MoG
The fool's prayer. E. Sill.—RoIt
Lucy Lake. N. Macintosh.—LiS
Man is a fool. Unknown.—RoIt
"Simple Simon met a pieman." Mother Goose.—JoA-4
"Sir, I admit your general rule." S. T. Coleridge; also at. to A. Pope.—PlM
The song of wandering Aengus. W. B. Yeats.—JoA-4—RoIt
The stranger. Unknown.—OpOx
"Yes, every poet is a fool." M. Prior.—PlM
The **fool's** prayer. Edward Rowland Sill.—RoIt
Foot races. See Races and racing—Foot
Football
Dick Szymanski. O. Nash.—FlH
Rythm. I. C. Smith.—ToM
Street football. J. Gay.—FlH
Under the goal posts. A. Guiterman.—FlH
Foote, Samuel
The great panjandrum.—RoIt
The great panjandrum himself.—JoA-4
The great panjandrum himself. See The great panjandrum
Footprints ("In summertime") Aileen Fisher.—FiFo
Footprints ("It was snowing") Lilian Moore.—MoSm
For a blue page. Unknown.—MoBw
For a coming extinction. W. S. Merwin.—MoT
For a fatherless son. Sylvia Plath.—MoT
For a good and sweet New Year. Sadie Rose Weilerstein.—LaM
For a green page. Unknown.—MoBw
For a junior school poetry book. Christopher Middleton.—MaFw—ToM
For a lady I know. Countee Cullen.—AbM—LiWw
Four epitaphs.—AdPb
For a lamb. Richard Eberhart.—PeS
For a mouthy woman. Countee Cullen.—AbM—AdPb
For a poet. Countee Cullen.—AbM
For a white page. Unknown.—MoBw
For a wordfarer. Rolfe Humphries.—PlM
"**For** all this I considered in my heart." See Ecclesiastes—All things come alike to all
For Angela. Zack Gilbert.—AdPb
For Anne. Leonard Cohen.—PeS
For Anne Gregory. William Butler Yeats.—CoPi—LiWw
"**For**, behold, the day cometh, that shall burn as an oven." See Malachi—Judgment and sunrise
For Bill Hawkins, a black militant. William J. Harris.—AdPb
For black poets who think of suicide. Etheridge Knight.—AdPb
For children if they'll take them. X. J. Kennedy.—RoIt
"**For** days these curious cardboard buds have lain." See Gunpowder plot
For de Lawd. Lucille Clifton.—AdM—AdPb
For Eusi, Ayi Kwei & Gwen Brooks. Keorapetse Kgositsile.—AdPb
"**For** flowers that bloom about our feet." See We thank Thee
"**For** fun the schoolboys crack the ice." See Dog with schoolboys
"**For** he was a shrub among the poplars." Christopher Okigbo.—AlPa
For Hettie. LeRoi Jones.—PeS
"**For** I will consider my cat Jeoffry." See My cat Jeoffry
For John Keats, apostle of beauty. Countee Cullen
Four epitaphs.—AdPb
For K. R. on her sixtieth birthday. Richard Wilbur.—PlM
For Koras and Balafong. Léopold Sédar Senghor, tr. fr. the French by John Reed and Clive Wake.—AlPa (sel.)
"**For** lo! the new moon winter-bright." See Dejection: An ode—The new moon
For Mack C. Parker. Pauli Murray.—AdPb
For Malcolm: After Mecca. Gerald W. Barrax.—AdPb
For Malcolm who walks in the eyes of our children. Quincy Troupe.—AdPb
For Malcolm X ("All you violated ones with gentle hearts") Margaret Walker.—AdPb
For Malcolm X ("From my personal album") Nanina Alba.—AdPb
"**For** Malcolm's eyes, when they broke." See A poem for black hearts
"**For** me I shall buy an elderly one who will feed me." See In honor of a king who acquired several young wives
For my grandmother. Countee Cullen
Four epitaphs.—AdPb
For my people. Margaret Walker.—AdPb
"**For** my people everywhere singing their slave songs repeatedly: their dirges and." See For my people
For my unborn and wretched children. A. B. Spellman.—AdPb

For Nina Simone wherever you are. Linda Curry.—JoV
"**For** 120 years of happiness." Unknown.—MoBw
"**For** one shaft at Cleator Moor." See Cleator Moor
For Paul Laurence Dunbar. Countee Cullen
Four epitaphs.—AdPb
For poets. Al Young.—AdPb
For purple mountains' majesty. Myra Cohn Livingston.—LiM
For real. Jayne Cortez.—AdPb
For sale. Shel Silverstein.—CoOr—SiW
For Sammy Younge. Charlie Cobb.—AdPb
For scholars and pupils. George Wither.—OpOx
"**For** seven days it rained that June." See Wash
"**For** several days I have been under." See The prisoner
"**For** sixty years, the pine lumber barn." See The people, yes—Prairie barn
"**For** so long." See Us
For some poets. Mae Jackson.—AdB—AdPb
For Stephen Dixon. Zack Gilbert.—AdPb
"**For** the dim regions whence my fathers came." See Outcast
"**For** the first time." See A poem for positive thinkers
For the Lord's day evening. Isaac Watts.—OpOx
For the moment. Richard Weber.—CoPi
For the record. R. S. Thomas.—ToM
"**For** the sky, blue. But the six-year-old." See Drawing by Ronnie C., Grade One
For there is an upstart crow. Robert Greene.—PlM
"**For** there is an upstart crow, beautified with our." See For there is an upstart crow
"**For** this is not the road against which stand enemy lines, or foreign languages." See Piyyut for Rosh Hashana
For want of a nail. Unknown.—RoIt
"For want of a nail the shoe was lost."—TrG
"**For** want of a nail, the shoe was lost." See For want of a nail
For William Edward Burghardt Du Bois on his eightieth birthday. Bette Darcie Latimer.—AdPb
"**For** years, at least." See Revelation
Forbes, Calvin
Lullaby for Ann-Lucian.—AdPb
Reading Walt Whitman.—AdPb
The **force.** Peter Redgrove.—ToM
"**Forced** to the towns by rain on an August afternoon." See Homage to Arthur Waley
Foreclosure. Sterling A. Brown.—AdPb
The **forest** of Dean. Robin Flower.—PaP
Foresters. See Forests and forestry
Forests and forestry. See also Trees
Avenue in Savernake forest. W. L. Bowles.—PaP
The babes in the wood. Unknown.—OpOx
Beyond the hunting woods. D. Justice.—HiN
"The broad woods." Unknown.—JoT
"Deep in a windless." Busōn.—BeM
"Father." Unknown.—JoT
The forest of Dean. R. Flower.—PaP
"Into a forest." Otsuji.—BeM
Kilcash. Unknown.—CoPi
"My house is so deep in the woods." Unknown.—BaSs
Prologue to Evangeline. From Evangeline. H. W. Longfellow.—LiS
"Singing through the forests." J. G. Saxe.—RoIt
Sitting in the woods: A contemplation. W. R. Moses.—HiN
Stopping by woods on a snowy evening. R. Frost.—AdP—JoA-4—MaFw—PaF—RoIt
The thought-fox. T. Hughes.—HiN
Timber moon. C. Sandburg.—SaT
"Under the greenwood tree." From As you like it. W. Shakespeare.—RoIt
In Arden forest.—JoA-4
The **forge.** Seamus Heaney.—CoPi
Forgetfulness
The absent-minded man. G. H. MacPherson.—BrM
"I left my head." L. Moore.—MoSm
An odd fellow. L. Carroll.—BrM (sel.)
Forgiven. A. A. Milne.—BrM
Forgiveness. See Charity; Kindness
Forgotten language. Shel Silverstein.—SiW
"**Formed** long ago, yet made today." Unknown.—EmN
The **forsaken.** Duncan Campbell Scott.—CoPt
Fort of Rathangan
The Fort of Rathangan. Berchan.—CoPi
The **Fort** of Rathangan. Berchan, tr. fr. the Irish by Kuno Meyer.—CoPi
"The **fort** over against the oak-wood." See The Fort of Rathangan
Forts. See names of forts, as Fort of Rathangan
"**Fortunatus** the portrait-painter got twenty sons." See Fortunatus the R.A.
Fortunatus the R.A. Nikarchos, tr. fr. the Greek by Dudley Fitts.—LiWw
Fortune. See Success
"**Fortune.**" See Number 7
"A **fortune-teller** made the prophecy." Louise Labé, tr. fr. the French by Judith Thurman.—ThI
Fortune telling
"Bless you, bless you, burnie bee." Mother Goose.—JoA-4
"One I love." Mother Goose.—EmN—HoMg
"**Forty** viziers saw I go." See The fair Circassian
"**Forward** abrupt." See Night and a distant church
Foss, Sam Walter
The prayer of Cyrus Brown.—LiWw
Foul shot. Edwin A. Hoey.—FlH
"**Found** in the garden—dead in his beauty." See The burial of the linnet
"**Found.** One red starfish." See Low tide
The **fountains.** W. R. Rodgers.—CoPi
"**Fountains** that frisk and sprinkle." See Ballade

Four and twenty. Stephen Still.—MoG
"**Four** and twenty tailors." Mother Goose.—JoA-4
"**Four** and twenty years ago a-comin to this life." See Four and twenty
The **four** directions. Emerson Blackhorse ("Barney") Mitchell.—AlW
"**Four** ducks on a pond." See A memory
"**Four** furry seals, four funny fat seals." Jack Prelutsky.—PrC
Four glimpses of night. Frank Marshall Davis.—AdM (sel.)—AdPb
"**Four** horsemen rode out from the heart of the range." See The bushrangers
"**Four** legs up and four legs down." Unknown.—EmN
The **four** letters. James Reeves.—JoA-4
Four little foxes. Lew Sarett.—RoIt
The **four** seasons of the year, sel. Anne Bradstreet
Spring.—ThI
Four sheets to the wind. Conrad Kent Rivers.—AdPb
"**Four** walls to talk to me." Arlene Blackwell.—JoV
XIV ("I don't bother with rhymes. It is seldom") Alberto Caeiro, tr. fr. the Portugese by Jonathan Griffin.—MoT
"**14A.**" See December 25: Christmas night
Fourteen ways of touching the Peter. George MacBeth.—MaFw
"**Fourteen-year-old,** why must you giggle and dote." See The conventionalist
"The **Fourteenth** of May." See May 14
The **fourth.** Shel Silverstein.—SiW
Fourth dance poem. Gerald W. Barrax.—AdPb
Fourth graders, Springfield elementary school, Pleasant Valley
"Books make me feel like."—LaM
Fourth of July
Celebration of the day. F. Holman.—HoI
The 5th of July. F. Holman.—HoI
The Fourth. S. Silverstein.—SiW
Fourth of July ("Fat torpedoes in bursting jackets") R. Field.—LaM
Fourth of July ("Hold my hand, look away") E. Pennant.—RoIt
Fourth of July night. C. Sandburg.—SaT
Grandfather Watt's private Fourth.—H. C. Bunner.—CoPt
"I asked my mother for fifty cents." Unknown.—JoA-4
"I've got a rocket." Unknown.—JoA-4
July. L. Clifton.—ClE
Fourth of July ("Fat torpedoes in bursting jackets") Rachel Field.—LaM
Fourth of July ("Hold my hand, look away") Edmund Pennant.—RoIt
Fourth of July night. Carl Sandburg.—SaT
Fowler, Elsie Melchert
If you've never.—HoH
The **fox** ("Because the snow is deep") Kenneth Patchen.—ToM
The **fox** ("The fox went out on a chilly night") Unknown.—CoPt
The **fox** and the goat. Jean De La Fontaine, tr. fr. the French by Marianne Moore.—JoA-4
"A **fox** came into my garden." Charles Causley.—CaF
"The **fox** drags its wounded belly." See January
"The **fox** he came lolloping, lolloping." See Hunting song
Fox hunting. See Hunters and hunting
Fox Indians. See Indians of the Americas—Fox
"A **fox** went out in a hungry plight." See The ballad of the fox
"The **fox** went out on a chilly night." See The fox
Foxes
The ballad of red fox. M. W. LaFollette.—AdP
The ballad of the fox. Unknown.—RoIt
A call to the wild. Lord Dunsany.—CoPi
Dog and fox. D. Ferry.— CoPu
Early moon. C. Sandburg.—SaT
Four little foxes. L. Sarett.—RoIt
The fox ("Because the snow is deep") K. Patchen.—ToM
The fox ("The fox went out on a chilly night") Unknown.—CoPt
The fox and the goat. J. De La Fontaine.—JoA-4
"A fox came into my garden." C. Causley.—CaF
Foxes. M. A. Hoberman.—HoR
Hunting song. D. Finkel.—HiN
January. R. S. Thomas.—CoPu
Listening to foxhounds. J. Dickey.—HaWr
Little foxes. A. Fisher.—FiD
"Little Jock Sander of Dee." Unknown.—BoI
Orator. R. W. Emerson.—CoPu
"The sky is dark, there blows a storm." C. Watson.—WaF
Sleepyheads. C. Sandburg.—SaT
Story of the fowse or fox. D. McCord.—McFm
The sycophantic fox and the gullible raven. G. W. Carryl.—LiWw
The thought-fox. T. Hughes.—HiN
The three foxes. A. A. Milne.—OpOx
The trap. W. Beyer.—CoPt
"What is the opposite of *fox.*" R. Wilbur.—WiO
Foxes. Mary Ann Hoberman.—HoR
Foxton, Thomas
On a little boy's endeavouring to catch a snake.—OpOx
Upon boys diverting themselves in the river.—OpOx
"A **fragile** crystalline figurine." See The little girl
The **fragment.** Hilaire Belloc.—CoPu
Fragment of a Greek tragedy. Alfred Edward Housman.—LiS
Fragments of spring. Agnes T. Pratt.—AlW
"**Fraidy** calf, fool an a half." Unknown.—EmN

Framed in a first-story winder. Unknown.—CoOh
"**Framed** in a first-story winder of a burnin' buildin'." See Framed in a first-story winder
France—History. See also European war, 1914-1918; Naval battles; Warships; World war 1939-1945; also names of battles, as Waterloo, Battle of, 1815
A ballad for a boy. W. Cory.—OpOx
Four sheets to the wind. C. K. Rivers.—AdPb
Francis, Colin
Tony O.—CoPu
Francis of Assisi, Saint (about)
Saint Francis and the birds. S. Heaney.—MaFw
Francis, Robert
The base stealer.—FlH—HiN
Burial.—HiN
Catch.—HiN
Farm boy after summer.—HiN
"Sing a song of juniper."—HiN
Skier.—FlH—HiN
That dark other mountain.—HiN—PeS
Franklin, Aretha (about)
Poem for Aretha. N. Giovanni.—AdPb
Franklin, Benjamin
Epitaph.—RoIt
The **Franklin's** tale. See The Canterbury tales
Franz, G. H.
Song of praise to the Creator. tr.—AlPa (sel.)
Fraser, Kathleen
Mud pie.—HoCs
Fraser, Vanessa
"When the."—HoC
Fraülein reads instructive rhymes. Maxine W. Kumin.—LiS
Fred. Shel Silverstein.—SiW
Frederick Douglass ("A hush is over all the teeming lists") Paul Laurence Dunbar.—AdPb
Frederick Douglass ("My mother twice in her life on worn feet") Sam Cornish.—AdPb
Frederick Douglass ("When it is finally ours, this freedom, this liberty, this beautiful") Robert Hayden.—AdM—AdPb
"**Free** at last." Unknown.—BrW
Free to be you and me. Bruce Hart.—ThF
Free will. Walter Clark.—HiN
Freedom. See also Liberty
America. H. Dumas.—AdB—AdPb—CoPu
Bind my father with freedom. L. Curry.—JoV
"Don't dress your cat in an apron." D. Greenburg.—ThF
Drums of freedom. G. Thompson.—JoV
Everyone sang. S. Sassoon.—PaF
"Free at last." Unknown.—BrW
Free to be you and me. B. Hart.—ThF
Free will. W. Clark.—HiN
Freedom. L. Hughes.—AdPb
Go down, Moses. Unknown.—AbM—BrW
"The harp that once through Tara's halls." T. Moore.—RoIt
"How I'd like to live." Yang Ung-jeung.—BaSs
"It's a new kind of day." K. Grosvenor.—AdM
Monument in black. V. Howard.—AdM—JoB
"O freedom." Unknown.—BrW
Oh, freedom. Unknown.—AbM
Rudolph is tired of the city. G. Brooks.—UnGb
Runagate runagate. R. Hayden.—AdPb
A sense of property. A. Thwaite.—ToM
To my son Parker, asleep in the next room. B. Kaufman.—AdPb
The wolf and the dog. C. Rosario.—JoV
Freedom. Langston Hughes.—AdPb
"**Freedom** will not come." See Freedom
Freeman, Carol
"Christmas morning I."—AdPb
"Do not think."—AdM
Gift.—AbM
I saw them lynch.—AdPb
Freeman, Mary E. (Eleanor) Wilkins (Mary E. Wilkins)
"The ostrich is a silly bird."—BrM
Freeway. Myra Cohn Livingston.—LiM
French, Percy
Come back, Paddy Reilly.—CoPi
The mountains of Mourne.—CoPi
French nursery rhymes. See Nursery rhymes—French
French Persian cats having a ball. Edwin Morgan.—ToM
Frere, John Hookham
The boy and the parrot.—OpOx
The fable of the piece of glass and the piece of ice.—OpOx
"**Fresh** gingersnaps, bright brittle ones." See From the kitchen—Gingersnaps
Friars
Blackfriars. E. Farjeon.—OpOx
The prologue. From The Canterbury tales. G. Chaucer.—MaFw
"When a shadow appeared on the water." Unknown.—BaSs
Friday: Mom is home—Payday. Lucille Clifton.—ClS
Friday: Waiting for mom. Lucille Clifton.—ClS
Friend, Robert
Eve. tr.—MeP
His wife. tr.—MeP
Incense. tr.—MeP
The olive tree. tr.—MeP
Revolt. tr.—MeP
Song of the strange woman. tr.—MeP
Twilight piece. tr.—MeP
"**Friend.**" Unknown, tr. fr. the Teton Sioux by Frances Densmore.—JoT
"**Friend,** I have lost the way." See The way
"A **friend** in need." Unknown.—MoBw
A **friend** in the garden. Juliana Horatia Ewing.—OpOx
"**Friend** of Wakinyan." See I pass the pipe
Friendly. Robert Froman.—FrSp
The **friendly** beasts. Unknown.—RoIt

"The **friendly** cow, all red and white." See The cow
Friends. See Friendship
"Friends." Unknown, tr. fr. the Sioux.—ClFc
Friends ("Some of my best friends are white boys") Ray Durem.—AdPb
The **friends** ("When Egg and I sit down to tea") Dennis Lee.—LeA
"Friends, Romans, classmates." Unknown.—MoBw
Friendship
Bed-time story. M. Cane.—RoIt
The body politic. D. Hall.—PeS
The canary. E. Turner.—OpOx
Fascination. J. B. Tabb.—CoOh
Friday: Waiting for mom. L. Clifton.—ClS
"Friend." Unknown.—JoT
"A friend in need." Unknown.—MoBw
Friendly. R. Froman.—FrSp
"Friends." Unknown.—ClFc
Friends ("Some of my best friends are white boys") R. Durem.—AdPb
The friends ("When Egg and I sit down to tea") D. Lee.—LeA
Friendship. Unknown.—BiI
"Friendship is like china." Unknown.—MoBw
Glad to have a friend like you. C. Hall.—ThF
"The grapes hang green upon the vine." Unknown.—EmN
"I wish I was a head of cabbage." Unknown.—EmN
"I would like you for a comrade." E. A. Parry.—NeA—OpOx
"In the golden chain of friendship." Unknown.—EmN
Interlude. W. Smith.—AdPb
"I've tried to think of something." Unknown.—MoBw
"Judge not your friends from outward show." Unknown.—EmN
"Leaves may wither." Unknown.—EmN
Losing friends. A. Gutkina.—MoM
"May our friendship spread." Unknown.—EmN
Me and my giant. S. Silverstein.—SiW
My friend. L. Kirkman.—HoCs
My friend Thelma. R. Hoban.—HoE
My teddy bear. M. Chute.—ChRu
Na-na doll. R. Hoban.—HoE
"The only man that e'er I knew." W. Blake.—CoPu
Poem. L. Hughes.—HoD
"Remember me and bear in mind." Unknown.—EmN
"Sometimes a tie is round your neck." Unknown.—MoBw
The song of a dream. Unknown.—BiI
To a friend. V. Shlensky.—MoM
"True friends are like diamonds." Unknown.—EmN
Ttimba. Unknown.—SeS
Twelve articles. J. Swift.—LiWw
Us. S. Silverstein.—SiW
Vern. G. Brooks.—HoCs
Well met. A. H. Evans.—CoPu
What Johnny told me. J. Ciardi.—CiFs
"When all your friends have deserted you." Unknown.—EmN
"When in my lonely grave I sleep." Unknown.—EmN
"Would you like to know who my friends are." Yun Sun-do.—BaSs
Written in the album of a child. W. Wordsworth.—OpOx
"You are like a friend of mine." Unknown.—ClFc
Friendship. Unknown, tr. fr. the Aztec by Angel Garibay.—BiI
"Friendship is like china." Unknown.—MoBw
Frightened flower. William J. Harris.—AdB
Fripp, Robert and Sinfield, Peter
Pictures of a city.—MoG
The **frog** ("Be kind and tender to the frog") Hilaire Belloc.—BrM—JoA-4—LiLc—OpOx
The **frog** ("How nice to be") Conrad Aiken.—JoA-4
Frog ("Pollywiggle") Mary Ann Hoberman.—HoLb
The **frog** ("The spotted frog") Valerie Worth.—WoS
The **frog** ("What a wonderful bird the frog are") Unknown.—LiWw
"What a wonderful bird the frog are."—TrG
"A **frog** he would a-wooing go." Mother Goose.—JoA-4
Frog music. David McCord.—McFm
"The **frog** sits." Issa, tr. fr. the Japanese by Hanako Fukuda.—HaW
Frog songs. Carl Sandburg.—SaT
"A **froggie** sat on a lily pad." See Silly stanzas
Frogs. See also Toads; Tree toads
Bullfrog. T. Hughes.—MoT
"Croak, said the toad, I'm hungry, I think." Mother Goose.—TucMgl
Facing up. J. Scully.—HaWr
First song. G. Kinnell.—HiN
The frog ("Be kind and tender to the frog") H. Belloc.—BrM—JoA-4—LiLc—OpOx
The frog ("How nice to be") C. Aiken.—JoA-4
Frog ("Pollywiggle") M. A. Hoberman.—HoLb
Frog ("The spotted frog") V. Worth.—WoS
The frog ("What a wonderful bird the frog are") Unknown.—LiWw—RoIt
"What a wonderful bird the frog are."—TrG
"A frog he would a-wooing go." Mother Goose.—JoA-4
Frog music. D. McCord.—McFm
"The frog sits." Issa.—HaW
Frog songs. C. Sandburg.—SaT
"A froggie sat on a lily pad." From Silly stanzas. Unknown.—CoOh
A Gloria song (by Gloria). R. Hoban.—HoE
"Hands flat on the ground." Sokan.—BeM
Hospitality. J. B. Tabb.—BrM
"The old pond." Bashō.—HaW

Frogs.—*Continued*
The peepers in our meadow. A. MacLeish.—HiN
The pig tale. From Sylvie and Bruno. L. Carroll.—LiPc
"Riddlum, riddlum, raddy." Unknown.—EmN
"Skinny frog." Issa.—HaW
Song of the frog waiting for spring. Unknown.—BiS
The stone frog. G. Pritchard.—CoPu
The surprise. M. Chute.—ChRu
"What is the opposite of *prince.*" R. Wilbur.—WiO
"**From** a city window, 'way up high." See Motor cars
"**From** a distance, I watch." See Practical concerns
"**From** a golden step." See Flowers
From a railway carriage. Robert Louis Stevenson.—OpOx
From an airplane. Harry Behn.—HoP
"**From** Arranmore the weary miles I've come." See Mavrone, one of those sad Irish poems, with notes
From blackwoman poems. Don L. Lee.—AdM
"**From** Brooklyn, over the Brooklyn bridge, on this fine morning." See Invitation to Miss Marianne Moore
"**From** ghoulies and ghosties." See A prayer for Halloween
"**From** his shoulder Hiawatha." See Hiawatha's photographing
From jazz for five. John Smith.—ToM
From Mr Walter De La Mare makes the little ones dizzy. Samuel Hoffenstein.—LiS
"**From** my city bed in the dawn I." See SF
"**From** my mother's sleep I fell into the State." See The death of the turret gunner
"**From** my personal album." See For Malcolm X
"**From** out of the cold Caribbean." See Fred
"**From** out of the wood did a cuckoo fly." See The birds
"**From** Peapack to Hohokus." See On going to Hohokus (and why I live in New Jersey)
From riot rimes U.S.A. #78. Raymond Richard Patterson.—AdM
From riot rimes U.S.A. #79. Raymond Richard Patterson.—AdM
"**From** the bonny bells of heather." See Heather ale
"**From** the dark canoe." Ann Atwood.—AtM
From the dark tower. Countee Cullen—AdPb
"**From** the depth of the dreamy decline of the dawn through a notable nimbus of nebulous moonshine." See Nephelidia
From the kitchen, sels. David McCord.—McA (Complete)
1. Pie
2. Macaroon
3. Fudge
4. Peanut butter
5. Cake
6. Pistachio ice cream.—McS
7. Animal crackers.—McS
8. People crackers.—McS
9. Gingersnaps
10. Cucumbers vs. pickles
"**From** the middle." Unknown, tr. fr. the Chippewa.—ClFc
"**From** the place of the south." See War songs
From the prophecy against Egypt. See Isaiah
From the shore. Carl Sandburg.—SaT
"**From** the time of the early radishes." See Weeds
From the underworld. Howard Blaikley.—MoG
"**From** the wild fells I return to my lowland home." See Glaramara
"**From** too much love of living." See The garden of Proserpine
"**From** what great sleep." See Watts
"**From** whence arrived the praying mantis." See The praying mantis
"**From** whence cometh song." See Song
"**From** where I lingered in a lull in March." See Evening in a sugar orchard
"**From** where I stand now." See 12 October
"**From** you I have been absent in the spring." See Sonnets. William Shakespeare
Froman, Robert
Aimless.—FrSp
Appetizer.—FrSp
Awake and asleep.—FrSp
Blah-blah.—FrSp
Blow up.—FrSp
Catchers.—FrSp
The city question.—FrSp
City thunder.—FrSp
Counter service.—FrSp
Cover up.—FrSp
Dance.—FrSp
Easy diver.—FrSp
Fake.—FrSp
Friendly.—FrSp
Glider.—FrSp
The go-go goons.—FrSp
Greedy.—FrSp
Hail, polluters.—FrSp
Hardrock.—FrSp
Hopper.—FrSp
Humbleweeds.—FrSp
Ignored.—FrSp
Loud.—FrSp
Mad.—FrSp
Meanlight.—FrSp
Memories.—FrSp
No pretending.—FrSp
No sale.—FrSp
Nothingest.—FrSp
Off and away.—FrSp
On his way.—FrSp
On the avenue.—FrSp
On the job.—FrSp
Orders.—FrSp
Outside the window.—FrSp
Public library.—SrSp
Puzzle.—FrSp

Resting in peace.—FrSp
Roll, river, roll.—FrSp
Roofer.—FrSp
Scare.—FrSp
Secrets.—FrSp
Skyscratcher.—FrSp
Solid.—FrSp
SService SStation.—FrSp
Subway deaf.—FrSp
Sunday street, downtown.—FrSp
Superstink.—FrSp
Surgery.—FrSp
Table deportment.—FrSp
Undefeated.—FrSp
Upright.—FrSp
View.—FrSp
Waiting.—FrSp
Well, yes.—FrSp
Winter walk.—FrSp
Frontier and pioneer life. See also Cowboys; Indians of the Americas; United States—History
The feral pioneers. I. Reed.—AdPb
Frost, Frances M.
Railroad ducks.—HoP
Trains at night.—HoP
Frost, Robert
Brown's descent or The willy-nilly slide.—CoPt
A considerable speck.—AdP
Desert places.—HiN
Dust of snow. AdP—MoT—PaF
Evening in a sugar orchard.—HaWr
Haec fabula docet.—LiWw
Home burial.—PeS
An importer.—LiWw
The last word of a bluebird.—JoA-4—LiLc
The line-gang.—MaFw
A minor bird.—CoPu
Nothing gold can stay.—HiN—MoT
On being chosen poet of Vermont.—PlM
One guess.—CoPu
The pasture.—JoA-4—LiLc
A patch of old snow.—CoPu
Questioning faces.—CoPu—HiN
The road not taken.—RoIt
The span of life.—MaFw
Stopping by woods on a snowy evening.—AdP—JoA-4—MaFw—PaF—RoIt
A time to talk.—HiN
To E. T.—PlM
Frost, Robert (about)
On being chosen poet of Vermont. R. Frost.—PlM
On looking into Robert Frost in Kanji. W. T. Meredith.—PlM
Frost
Frost at midnight. S. T. Coleridge.—PaF (sel.)
The frost pane. D. McCord.—JoA-4
Frost sprite. Unknown.—JaP
Maroon with silver frost. C. Sandburg.—SaT
Splinter. C. Sandburg.—SaT
Winter. A. Tennyson.—PaF
Frost at midnight. Samuel Taylor Coleridge.—PaF
"The **frost** is here." See Winter
"The **frost** loosens cornhusks." See Prairie—Cornhuskers
The **frost** pane. David McCord.—JoA-4
Frost sprite. Unknown.—JaP
"The **frost** sprite always." See Frost sprite
"A **frosty** dawn, a waning moon." Unknown, tr. fr. the Korean by Chung Seuk Park and ad. by Virginia Olsen Baron.—BaSs
The **frugal** host. Automedon, tr. fr. the Greek by Dudley Fitts.—LiWw
"The **frugal** snail, with forecast of repose." See The housekeeper
Fruit. See also Orchards; also names of fruits, as Apples; also names of berries, as Raspberries
August weather. K. Tynan.—PaF
The garden. A. Marvell.—PaF (sel.)
Heat. H. D.—PaF
To autumn. W. Blake.—PaF
The tropics in New York. C. McKay.—AdPb—RoIt
Fudge. See From the kitchen
"**Fudge,** fudge, tell the judge." Unknown.—EmN
"**Fudge** is a kind of chocolate sludge." See From the kitchen—Fudge
"**Fueled.**" Marcie Hans.—HoP
"**Full** fathom five thy father lies." See The tempest—Ariel's song
The **full** heart. Robert Nicholson.—CoPu
Full moon. Walter De La Mare.—JoA-4
"A **full** moon comes up." Shiki, tr. fr. the Japanese by Harry Behn.—BeM
"The **full** moon half way up the sky." See Gulls
Full moonlight in spring. W. S. Merwin.—CoPu
Fuller, Hoyt W.
Lost moment.—AdPb
Seravezza.—AdPb
Fuller, Roy
Homage to Arthur Waley.—PlM
Fulton, Robin
Essentials.—CoPu
Funeral. Russell Hoban.—HoE
The **funeral** of Martin Luther King, Jr. Nikki Giovanni.—AdB
Funerals. See also Death; Grief; Laments
The ballad of the light-eyed little girl. G. Brooks.—PeS
Burial. R. Francis.—HiN
The burial of the linnet. J. H. Ewing.—OpOx
Cat's funeral. E. V. Rieu.—JoA-4
The choirmaster's burial. T. Hardy.—PlP
Farmer Dunman's funeral. T. Hardy.—PlP
Funeral. R. Hoban.—HoE
The funeral of Martin Luther King, Jr. N. Giovanni.—AdB
Home burial. R. Frost.—PeS
In these dissenting times. A. Walker.—AdPb
Last rites. C. G. Rossetti.—OpOx
Lingle, lingle. Unknown.—BlM
Little dead. M. C. Livingston.—LiM

G

"**George** Washington is tops with me." See George Washington
The **Georges.** Walter Savage Landor.—RoIt
Georgia
Georgia dusk. J. Toomer.—AdPb
Sun song. L. Hughes.—AdM—HoD
Georgia dusk. Jean Toomer.—AdPb
The **Georgics,** sels. Virgil
"Am I to tell you next of the storms and stars of autumn.—MaFw
"Next I came to the manna, the heavenly gift of honey."—MaFw
"Then are the trackless copses alive with the trilling of birds."—MaFw
"**Georgie** Porgie, pudding and pie." Mother Goose.—HoMg—JoA-4
The **geranium.** Theodore Roethke.—ToM
Geraniums
The geranium. T. Roethke.—ToM
German nursery rhymes. See Nursery rhymes—German
German shepherd. Myra Cohn Livingston.—LiM
Get 'em here. Lee Bennett Hopkins.—HoCs
Get lost. Myra Cohn Livingston.—LiM
"**Get** on a swing and swing up high." See The swing
"**Get** the ladder." Unknown.—MoBw
Get up and bar the door. Unknown.—CoPt—JoA-4
Get up, blues. James A. Emanuel.—AdB—AdPb
"**Get** up get up." See The clock ticks
Get up, get up. Unknown.—CoPu
"**Get** up, get up, for shame. The blooming morn." See Corinna's going a-Maying
"**Get** up, get up, you lazy-head." See Get up, get up
Getting about. Marchette Chute.—ChRu
Getting together. N. M. Bodecker.—BoL
Getting up early on a spring morning. Po Chüi-i, tr. fr. the Chinese by Arthur Waley.—MaFw
Ghana
Sebonwoma. C. A. A. Aidoo.—AlPa (sel.)
Ghetto. Vanessa Howard.—JoV
Ghettoes
An elementary school classroom in a slum. S. Spender.—ToM
Feeding the lions. N. Jordan.—AdPb
Ghetto. V. Howard.—JoV
Newark, for now. C. M. Rodgers.—AdPb
Two dedications. G. Brooks.—AdPb (sel.)
U name this one. C. M. Rodgers.—AdPb
Watts. A. Saxon.—AdPb
Ghose, Zulfikar
Geography lesson.—ToM
This landscape, these people.—ToM
Ghose, Zulfikar (about)
This landscape, these people. Z. Ghose.—ToM
Ghost dance
Songs of the ghost dance. Unknown.—BiI
The **ghost** in our apartment house. Lilian Moore.—MoSm
The **ghost** of Caupolicán. Unknown, tr. fr. the Araucanian by Tomás Guevara.—BiI
Ghost weather. Lee Blair.—JaP
Ghosts
The admiral's ghost. A. Noyes.—JoA-4
After a journey. T. Hardy.—PlP
"Amidst the mists and coldest frosts." Unknown.—EmN
Aunt Jemima of the ocean waves. R. Hayden.—AdPb
Autumn ghost sounds. Unknown.—JaP
Bedtime stories. L. Moore.—MoSm
Cape Horn gospel. J. Masefield.—CoPt
Cockles and mussels. Unknown.—RoIt
Colonel Fazackerley. C. Causley.—CaF
"Do ghouls." L. Moore.—MoSm
A dream. W. Allingham.—CoPi—CiPt
Empty house song. L. Moore.—MoSm
The fall of J. W. Beane. O. Herford.—CoPt
The ghost in our apartment house. L. Moore.—MoSm
The ghost of Caupolicán. Unknown.—BiI
Ghost weather. L. Blair.—JaP
The glory trail. B. Clark.—CoPt
The great auk's ghost. R. Hodgson.—LiWw
The haunter. T. Hardy.—PlP
The highwayman's ghost. R. Garnett.—CoPt
"House ghost." L. May.—HoC
"I never saw." L. Moore.—MoSm
"I travel as a phantom now." T. Hardy.—PlP
"The island of Yorrick." N. M. Bodecker.—BoL
"It's the nicht atween the saints and souls." Unknown.—MaF (sel.)
"Look at that." L. Moore.—MoSm
Lucy Gray; or, Solitude. W. Wordsworth.—OpOx
Magic words. Unknown.—LeIb
Mary's ghost. T. Hood.—CoPt—LiWw
Molly Means. M. Walker.—CoPt
My aunt's spectre. M. Collins.—CoPt
No one. L. Moore.—MoSm
No TV. L. Moore.—MoSm
Outside the window. R. Froman.—FrSp
Phantoms of the steppe. A. Pushkin.—AdM
A prayer for Halloween. Unknown.—LaM
Sea change. J. Masefield.—CoPt
Sliding. L. Moore.—MoSm
Songs of the ghost dance ("The sun's beams are running out") Unknown.—BiI
Songs of the ghost dance ("The wind stirs the willows") Unknown.—BiI
Southern mansion. A. Bontemps.—AdPb
The spirit will appear. Unknown.—BiS
Spirits. V. H. Cruz.—AdPb
"A teeny tiny ghost." L. Moore.—MoSm
Three ghostesses. Unknown.—HoH—JaP
We spirits dance. Unknown.—BiI
What they said. Unknown.—JaP
"Wind is a ghost." N. Belting.—BeWi
Ghosts. Lois Lenski.—LeC
Giant. Elizabeth Sawyer.—JaP
The **giant** fisherman. W. King.—RoIt
Giant snail. X. J. Kennedy.—KeO

The **giant** tortoise. Edward Lucie-Smith.—CoPu
"The **giant** tortoise had a look." See The giant tortoise
Giants
Giant. E. Sawyer.—JaP
"Lightning is a great giant." N. Belting.—BeWi
Like a giant in a towel. D. Lee.—LeA
Me and my giant. S. Silverstein.—SiW
The sleeping giant. D. Hall.—HiN
A small discovery. J. A. Emanuel.—LiLc
Thunder. B. J. Lee.—JaP
Gibbon, Monk
The discovery.—CoPi
I tell her she is lovely.—CoPi
Gibbons, Orlando
"The silver swan, who living had no note."—CoPu
Gibbs, Wolcott
Declaration of independence.—PeS
Gibson, W. W.
Flannan isle.—CoPt
Gibson, Walker
In memory of the circus ship Euzkera, wrecked in the Caribbean sea, 1 September 1948.—HiN
Thaw.—CoPu
The umpire.—FlH
Gift. Carol Freeman.—AbM
Gifts and giving. See also Charity; Thankfulness
Alice Fell: or, Poverty. W. Wordsworth.—LiS
Alligator pie. D. Lee.—LeA
"Apples for the little ones." C. Watson.—WaF
The blue gift. D. Perkins.—HiN
Bundles. J. Farrar.—HoS
Carol of the brown king. L. Hughes.—HoS—LiLc
A child's present. R. Herrick.—OpOx
The Christmas exchange. A. Guiterman.—BrM
The colour. T. Hardy.—PlP
December 25: Christmas morning. L. Clifton.—ClEa
"Eight o'clock is striking." Mother Goose.—AlC
Epigram engraved on the collar of a dog which I gave to his Royal Highness.—RoIt
"I am His Highness' dog at Kew."—TrG
The friendly beasts. Unknown.—RoIt
Gift. C. Freeman.—AbM
Handfuls of wind. Y. Mar.—MeP
"I saw a ship a-sailing." Mother Goose.—AlC—JoA-4—MiMg
I will make you brooches. R. L. Stevenson.—RoIt
Itinerant. E. Merriam.—MeO
Jane Smith. R. Kipling.—LiS
John Anderson, my jo. R. Burns.—RoIt
The keys of Canterbury. Unknown.—JoA-4
"Little girl, little girl, where have you been." Mother Goose.—AlC
My gift. N. Bukhteyeva.—MoM
Otto. G. Brooks.—HoS
The perils of invisibility. W. S. Gilbert.—CoPt
Presents ("I have counted every present with my name") M. C. Livingston.—HoS
Presents ("I wanted a rifle for Christmas") M. Chute.—BrM
Psalm 127. From Psalms, Bible, Old Testament.—MeP
The red cockatoo. Po Chü-i.—CoPu
"These few shoots cut from a mountain willow." Hong Nang.—BaSs
Three acres of land. Unknown.—RoIt
"Three little guinea pigs." Unknown.—BoI
We three kings. J. H. Hopkins.—LaS
"What can I give Him." From Carol. C. G. Rossetti.—HoS—LiLc
What shall I give. E. Thomas.—OpOx
"A young man going to war." Unknown.—JoT
Gilbert, Paul T.
Triolet.—CoPu
Gilbert, Sir William Schwenck
Bunthorne's song. See Patience
"The flowers that bloom in the spring." See The Mikado
Iolanthe, sel.
Lord Chancellor's song.—RoIt
Lord Chancellor's song. See Iolanthe
The Mikado, sels.
"The flowers that bloom in the spring."—RoIt
Titwillow.—RoIt
The modest couple.—CoPt
Pash Bailey Ben.—LiWw
Patience, sel.
Bunthorne's song.—LiWw
The perils of invisibility.—CoPt
There lived a king.—CoPt
"There was an old man of St Bees."—RoIt
Titwillow. See The Mikado
To Phoebe.—LiWw
To the terrestial globe.—LiWw
The yarn of the Nancy Bell.—RoIt
Gilbert, Zack
For Angela.—AdPb
For Stephen Dixon.—AdPb
My own hallelujahs.—AdPb
When I heard dat white man say.—AdPb
Gilboa, Amir
Birth.—MeP
Blue and red poem.—MeP
The circle of weeping.—MeP
"**Giles** Johnson." See Giles Johnson, Ph.D.
Giles Johnson, Ph.D. Frank Marshall Davis.—AdPb
Gill, Michael
The days of my people.—JoV
"The jazz world."—JoV
"**Gin** a body meet a body." See Rigid body sings
Ginger bread mama. Doughtry Long.—AdPb
Gingersnaps. See From the kitchen
The **gingham** umbrella. Laura E. Richards.—CoOr

Ginsberg, Louis
Fetters.—RoIt
Giovanni, Nikki
Dreams.—AdPb
The funeral of Martin Luther King, Jr.—AdB
Knoxville, Tennessee.—AdB—AdM—AdPb
My poem.—AdB—AdPb
Nikki-Rosa.—AdPb
Poem.—AdB
Poem for Aretha.—AdPb
Poem for Flora.—AdM—AdPb—NeA
Poem of Angela Yvonne Davis.—AdPb
Ten years old.—AdM
The true import of present dialogue, black vs. negro.—AdPb
12 gates to the city.—AdPb
Winter poem.—AdM
Word poem.—AdB—AdPb
Giovanni, Norman Thomas di
To a Saxon poet. tr.—PlM
Gipsies
The gypsies are coming. S. Silverstein.—SiW
Gypsy eyes. J. Hendrix.—MoG
"Gypsy, gypsy, lived in a tent." Unknown.—EmN
Meg Merrilies. J. Keats.—NeA—OpOx
Old Meg.—RoIt
"My mother said." Mother Goose.—AlC
The princess and the gypsies. F. Cornford.—CoPt
The sea gypsy. R. Hovey.—RoIt
The tale of the hermit told. A. Reid.—CoPt
"Time, you old gipsy man." R. Hodgson.—RoIt
A vagabond song. B. Carman.—RoIt
Giraffe ("At the zoo I saw: A long-necked, velvety giraffe") Carson McCullers.—HoCs
Giraffe ("You who descend river by river") Unknown, tr. by W. H. I. Bleek.—AbM
Giraffes
Baby giraffe. A. Fisher.—FiD
Conversation with a giraffe at dusk in the zoo. D. Livingstone.—ToM
Giraffe ("At the zoo I saw: A long-necked, velvety giraffe") C. McCullers.—HoCs
Giraffe ("You who descend river by river") Unknown.—AbM
Giraffes. H. A. Hoberman.—HoR
"Please." S. Silverstein.—SiW
Giraffes. Mary Ann Hoberman.—HoR
"A **girl** brought me into the house of love." See A secret kept
Girl held without bail. Margaret Walker.—AdPb
"The **girl** of my choice." Unknown.—MoBw
Girlhood. See Girls and girlhood
"**Girls** and boys, come out to play." Mother Goose.—AlC
Girls and girlhood
Girls' names. E. Farjeon.—JoA-4—NeA
Helga. C. Sandburg.—SaT
"Here am I, little jumping Joan." Mother Goose.—AlC
Hunchback girl: She thinks of heaven. G. Brooks.—PeS
I am rose. G. Stein.—NeA
Portrait of a girl with comic book. P. McGinley.—PeS
"See this pretty little girl of mine." Mother Goose.—AlC
What are little boys made of . . . (love and care). E. Laron.—ThF
"What are little boys made of, made of." Mother Goose.—AlC—EmN—JoA-4
"When I was a little girl." A. Milligan.—CoPi
"Where have all the flowers gone." P. Seeger.—PeS
"The **girl's** far treble, muted to the heat." See Milkmaid
Girls' names. Eleanor Farjeon.—JoA-4—NeA
Girls' secret love song. Unknown, tr. fr. the Kipsigi by J. G. Peristiany.—AlPa
Girl's song. Unknown, tr. fr. the Hlubi by A. C. Jordan.—AlPa
"**Girls** who chatter." Unknown.—MoBw
"**Girt** with a boyish garb for boyish task." Lewis Carroll.—LiPc
"**Give** him the darkest inch your shelf allows." See George Crabbe
"**Give** me a nickel." See Time
"**Give** me a race that is run in a breath." See The hundred yard dash
"**Give** me a sandwich." See Snack
"**Give** me my bow, said Robin Hood." See The death of Robin Hood
Give me the splendid silent sun. Walt Whitman.—JoA-4 (sel.)—RoIt
"**Give** me the splendid silent sun with all its beams full-dazzling." See Give me the splendid silent sun
"**Give** me three nickels and give me a dime." Unknown.—EmN
The **given** note. Seamus Heaney.—HiN
"The **Giver** of Life." See Song to the envious
Giving. See Gifts and giving
Glad to have a friend like you. Carol Hall.—ThF
Gladness of heart. Ecclesiasticus.—RoIt
"**Gladness** of heart is the life of man." See Gladness of heart
"**Glanced** down at Shannon from the sky-way." See Irish-American dignitary
Glaramara. R. C. Trevelyan.—PaP
Glass
The fable of the piece of glass and the piece of ice. J. H. Frere.—OpOx
Glass falling. Louis MacNeice.—CoPi
"The **glass** is going down, the sun." See Glass falling
A **glass** of beer. James Stephens.—HiN
Glass world. Dorothy Donnelly.—HiN
"**Gleaming** in silver are the hills." See Washed in silver
The **gleaner.** Jane Taylor.—OpOx
Glekiva, Nina
"Our garden is my world."—MoM
Glides. Robert Froman.—FrSp

Glimpse. Pearl Cleage Lomax.—AdPb
Glimpses #xii. Lawrence McGaugh.—AdB (sel.)
"**Glooscap's** wigwam." Natalia Belting.—BeWi
"**Gloria** and I have often." See Funeral
"**Gloria** is your name." Unknown.—MoBw
"**Gloria,** my little sister." Russell Hoban.—HoE
A **Gloria** song (by Gloria). Russell Hoban.—HoE
"The **glories** of our blood and state." See Contention of Ajax and Ulysses
"**Glorious** it is to see." Unknown, fr. the Copper Eskimo.—LeIb
"**Glory** be to God for dappled things." See Pied beauty
Glory, glory. . . . Raymond Richard Patterson.—AdM
"**Glory.** Hallelujah." See Prayer meeting
"The **glory** of the day was in her face." James Weldon Johnson.—AdPb
The **glory** trail. Badger Clark.—CoPt
Gloss. David McCord.—LiWw
Gloves
  "It's rotten." K. Kuskin.—KuA
  To a fat lady seen from the train. F. Cornford.—CoPu—LiS
Glowworm. David McCord.—BrM
Glow-worms. See Fireflies
Glue. Gelett Burgess.—CoOh
Gluk. N. M. Bodecker.—BoL
The **glutton.** John Oakman.—OpOx
The **gnat** and the gnu. Oliver Herford.—BrM
Gnats
  The gnat and the gnu. O. Herford.—BrM
The **gnome.** Harry Behn.—JaP
Gnomes. See Fairies
The **gnu** ("G stands for gnu, whose weapons of defense") Hilaire Belloc.—CoPu
The **gnu** ("There's this to remember about the gnu") Theodore Roethke.—BrM—LiWw
The **gnu** family. Ilo Orleans.—BrM
Gnus. See Antelopes
Go down death. James Weldon Johnson.—AdPb
Go down, Moses. Unknown.—AbM—BrW
The **go-go** goons. Robert Froman.—FrSp
"**Go** in the door." See Department store
"**Go,** little booklet, go." Bill Nye.—CoPu
"**Go,** my child." See Untitled
"**Go,** my son, and shut the shutter." See Shut the shutter
Go north, south, east and west, young man. Spike Milligan.—CoOr
"**Go** pet a kitten, pet a dog." See Who to pet and who not to
"**Go** pretty child, and bear this flower." See A child's present
"**Go** tell it on the mountain." Unknown.—AbM—BrW—HoS (sel.)—LaS
"**Go** through the gates with closed eyes." See Close your eyes
"**Go** to bed first, a golden purse." Mother Goose.—AlC
"**Go** to sleep." Mother Goose, tr. fr. the French.—TucMg
"**Go** way from my window." Unknown.—AbM
The **goat.** Unknown.—RoIt
The **goat** paths. James Stephens.—AdP—RoIt
Goats
  April. Y. Winters.—CoPu—JoA-4
  The fox and the goat. J. De La Fontaine.—JoA-4
  The goat. Unknown.—RoIt
  The goat paths. J. Stephens.—AdP—RoIt
  "The heart of the mountain goat is broken when it falls below." Unknown.—ClFc
  "I went to my grandfather's farm." Unknown.—EmN
  Meditation on beavers. Lucian of Samosata.—LiWw
  "Mother took me to the farm." Unknown.—EmN
  Old Hogan's goat. Unknown.—BrM
Goba, Ronald J.
  Compozishun—to James Herndon and others.—HiN
The **goblin.** Unknown, tr. fr. the French by Rose Fyleman.—JoA-4
"A **goblin** lives in our house, in our house, in our house." See The goblin
A **goblinade.** Florence Page Jaques.—JaP
Goblins. See Fairies
God. See also Faith; Hymns; Jesus Christ; Psalms
  Abou Ben Adhem. L. Hunt.—RoIt
  Above the bright blue sky. A. Midlane.—OpOx
  Akanyonyi. Unknown.—SeS
  All kinds of time. H. Behn.—JoA-4
  All things come alike to all. From Ecclesiastes, Bible, Old Testament.—MeP
  Alone. C. N. Bialik.—MeP
  And what shall you say. J. S. Cotter, Jr.—AdPb
  The Armada. J. Wilson.—OpOx
  At the scorpion's ascent. O. Hillel.—MeP
  Bahá'u'lláh in the garden of Ridwan. R. Hayden.—AdP
  Bessie Bobtail. J. Stephens.—CoPi
  Birth. A. Gilboa.—MeP
  The black cliffs, Ballybunion. B. Kennelly.—CoPi
  Black trumpeter. H. Dumas.—AdPb
  By the earth's corpse. T. Hardy.—PlP
  Caliban in the coal mines. L. Untermeyer.—PeS
  A child's present. R. Herrick.—OpOx
  The complaint to God. From Job, Bible, Old Testament.—MeP
  Composed on a May morning, 1838. W. Wordsworth.—PaF
  Covetousness. P. Idley.—OpOx
  The creation. J. W. Johnson.—AdPb—JoA-4
  The doctor's story. W. M. Carleton.—CoPt
  Evening. T. Miller.—OpOx
  Father of night. B. Dylan.—MoG
  God. Unknown.—AbM
  God-forgotten. T. Hardy.—PlP
  God to be first served. R. Herrick.—OpOx
  Gods in Vietnam. E. Redmond.—AdPb
  The great sad one. U. Z. Greenberg.—MeP

Goethe, Johann Wolfgang von
Mignon's song. See Wilhelm Meister
Wilhelm Meister, sel.
Mignon's song.—CoPu
Goetz, Delia and Morley, Sylvanus
Prayer. trs.—BiI
— and Recinos, Adrian
Plague. trs.—BiI
Gogarty, Oliver St John
"Back from the country."—CoPi
O boys, O boys.—CoPi
Goggins, Paul
Life.—JoV
Love.—JoV
Going. Lois Lenski.—LeC
Going into breeches. Charles and Mary Lamb.—OpOx
The **going** of the snow. Louise Townsend Nicholl.—RoIt
Going somewhere. Felice Holman.—HoI
Going to church. Lois Lenski.—LeC
Going where. Patricia Irving.—AlW
Gold, Ben Zion. See Mezey, Robert and Gold, Ben Zion
Gold (color)
Nothing gold can stay. R. Frost.—HiN—MoT
Gold (metal). See also Money
The search. S. Silverstein.—SiW
"Gold buttons in the garden today." See Flowers tell months
Gold-fish. See Goldfish
"Gold locks, and black locks." See The barber's
Goldberg, Leah
Of bloom.—MeP
Song of the strange woman.—MeP
Golden moonrise. William Stanley Braithwaite.—AdPb
"Golden slumbers kiss your eyes." See Lullaby
The **Golden** Vanity. Unknown.—RoIt
"The **goldenrod** is yellow." See September
Goldfinches. See Finches
Goldfish
Aquarium. V. Worth.—WoS
"Goldfish whisper." M. C. Livingston.—LiM
My fishes. M. Chute.—ChRu
"Goldfish." See Aquarium
"Goldfish whisper." Myra Cohn Livingston.—LiM
Goldman, Michael
The visitor.—HaWr
Goldsmith, Oliver
The deserted village, sel.
The village schoolmaster.—RoIt
An elegy on the death of a mad dog.—LiWw—RoIt
Parson Gray.—RoIt
The village schoolmaster. See The deserted village
Goldstein, David
An apple for Isaac. tr.—MeP
"In the morning I look for you." tr.—MeP
To Moses ibn Ezra, in Christian Spain. tr.—MeP
War. tr.—MeP
Goldwing moth. Carl Sandburg.—SaT
"A **goldwing** moth is between the scissors and the ink bottle on the desk." See Goldwing moth
Golf
Seaside golf. J. Betjeman.—FlH
Goliard poets
Carmina Burana, sel.
Roast swan song.—LiWw—MaFw
Roast swan song. See Carmina Burana
Goliath. See David and Goliath
Gone. David McCord.—McFm—McS
Gone away. Denise Levertov.—PeS
"Gone were but the winter." See Spring quiet
"Goneys and gullies an' all o' the birds o' the sea." See Sea change
Gonsui
"Resting from the noon."—BeM
Gonzales, Juan
"A tree with no leaves."—JoV
Goo-girl. Theodore Roethke.—LiWw
Good and bad children. Robert Louis Stevenson.—OpOx
"Good children, refuse not these lessons to learn." See A schoolmaster's admonition
"Good folks ever will have their way." See The doctor's story
"The **good** gray guardians of art." See Museum piece
Good green bus. Rachel Field.—HoP (sel.)
"Good guys, bad guys." Unknown.—MoBw
"Good heavens." Issa, tr. fr. the Japanese by Hanako Fukuda.—HaW
"Good little girls love their brothers." Unknown.—EmN
"Good morning." See Argument
Good morning ("Good morning, bright morning") Tanya Nichiporum, tr. fr. the Russian by Miriam Morton.—MoM
Good morning ("Good morning, daddy") Langston Hughes.—AdM
Good morning, America, sel. Carl Sandburg
Sky prayers.—SaT
"Good morning, bright morning." See Good morning
"Good morning, daddy." See Good morning
"Good morning; good morning, the general said." See The general
"Good morning, Mr Rabbit." Unknown.—EmN
Good-morning poems. See Wake-up poems
"Good morning when it's morning." Mary Ann Hoberman.—HoN
"Good morrow to you, Valentine." Mother Goose.—HoMg—LaM
Good night ("Here's a body—there's a bed") Thomas Hood.—JoA-4
Good night ("Many ways to spell good night") Carl Sandburg.—SaT
Good night and good morning. Richard Monckton Milnes, Lord Houghton.—OpOx
Good-night poems. See also Bed-time
Good night. C. Sandburg.—SaT
"Good night, sleep tight." Unknown.—EmN
The goodnight. L. Simpson.—ToM

"**Good** night, sleep tight." Unknown.—EmN
"**Good** or bad." Calvin O'John.—AlW
"**Good** people all, of every sort." See An elegy on the death of a mad dog
"**Good** reader, if you e'er have seen." See If you have seen
"**Good** Saint Benedict." Unknown.—AbM
"A **good** sword and a trusty hand." See Song of the Western men
Good times. Lucille Clifton.—AdM—AdPb—HiN
"**Good** women, don't reproach me if I have loved." Louise Labé, tr. fr. the French by Judith Thurman.—ThI
Goodbye. Alun Lewis.—ToM
Goodbye and run. Patricia Irving.—AlW
"**Goodbye,** goodbye to summer." See Robin Redbreast
Goode, Michael
  Addition problem.—JoV
  April 4, 1968.—JoV
  "Chesterfield cigarettes fill the light-colored room as I enter."—JoV
  "I am waiting."—JoV
  "Man flies through the universe."—JoV
  Sands.—JoV
  Talking.—JoV
  White man and black man are talking.—JoV
A **goodly** child. Unknown.—OpOx
Goodman, Paul
  "The engingines."—HoP
  Kent State, May 4, 1970.—MoT
Goodness. See Conduct of life
The **goodnight.** Louis Simpson.—ToM
"**Goody,** goody, gout." Unknown.—EmN
"**Goosey,** goosey, gander." Mother Goose.—AlC—JoA-4
"**Gopher** sees where the stone is." Unknown, tr. fr. the Navajo.—ClFc
Gophers
  "Gopher sees where the stone is." Unknown.—ClFc
"The **gorilla** lay on his back." See Au jardin des plantes
Gorillas. See also Monkeys
  Anthropoids. M. A. Hoberman.—HoR
  The armadillo. N. M. Bodecker.—BoL
  Best loved of Africa. M. Danner.—AdPb
  The family reunion. J. Ciardi.—CiFs
  Nsangi. Unknown.—SeS
  The orang utan. E. Lucie-Smith.—CoPu
  We must be polite. C. Sandburg.—SaT
"**Gosh,** look at all the food." See Delicatessen
Gosling. Aileen Fisher.—FiFo
"A **gosling** has a pleasant face." See Gosling
Gospel according to Luke
  Christ's nativity. See Gospel according to Luke
  Gospel according to Luke, sel. Bible, New Testament
    Christ's nativity.—RoIt
Gossip
  "Keep in dark." Unknown.—AlPa
  Rumor. E. Merriam.—MeF
"**Got** any boys, the Marshal said." See The puzzled census taker
"**Got** up this morning." See One thousand nine-hundred & sixty-eight winters"
Gould, Cornelia Brownell
  The dive.—FlH
Government
  The intellectuals. D. Randall.—AdPb
  An old story. H. Nemerov.—CoPu
A **grace** for children. Robert Herrick.—OpOx
Grace to be said at the supermarket. Howard Nemerov.—ToM
"**Graceful** and sure with youth, the skaters glide." See The skaters
Graces
  Another grace. R. Herrick.—OpOx
  A grace for children. R. Herrick.—OpOx
  Grace to be said at the supermarket. H. Nemerov.—ToM
Graduation
  Baccalaureate. D. McCord.—LiS
Graft, Joe de
  The avenue: N.Y. city.—AlPa
Graham, D. L.
  Soul.—AdPb
  Tony get the boys.—AdPb
  The west ridge is menthol cool.—AdPb
Graham, Harry
  Aunt Eliza.—LiWw
  Opportunity.—LiWw
  Patience.—LiWw
  Politeness.—CoOh
  Presence of mind.—LiWw
  Uncle.—CoOr
  Unselfishness.—CoOr
Graham, W. S.
  The nightfishing.—MaFw (sel.)
Grahame, Kenneth
  Ducks ditty. See The wind in the willows
  The wind in the willows, sel.
    Duck's ditty.—JoA-4—OpOx
Grain, Corney
  "Old Mr Parvenu gave a great ball."—CoPu
Grain. See names of grain, as Wheat
Grammar
  Grammar. M. H. Ets.—BrM
Grammar. Marie Hall Ets.—BrM
Grandeur of Mexico. Unknown, tr. fr. the Aztec by Angel Garibay.—BiI
"**Grandfather.**" See Prayer
"**Grandfather** and the oars are one body." See Fishing
"A **grandfather** poem." William J. Harris.—AdM—AdPb
"**Grandfather** Watt used to tell us boys." See Grandfather Watt's private Fourth
Grandfather Watt's private Fourth. H. C. Bunner.—CoPt
Grandfathers
  Adventures with my grandfather. A. Marx.—RoIt
  Digging. S. Heaney.—ToM
  Direction. A. Lopez.—AlW
  Dunbarton. R. Lowell.—ToM

Grandfathers—*Continued*
Fishing. A. T. Pratt.—AlW
"A grandfather poem." W. J. Harris.—AdM—AdPb
Grandfather Watt's private Fourth. H. C. Bunner.—CoPt
The grandfathers. D. Justice.—HiN
Grandpa dropped his glasses. L. F. Jackson.—BrM
"Grandpa Grig had a pig." Mother Goose.—AlC
Grandpa is ashamed. O. Nash.—CoPu
Manners. E. Bishop.—HiN
Mountain road. M. Oliver.—RoIt
Niño leading an old man to market. L. Nathan.—HiN
Once again. L. Sohappy.—AlW
"Our old family dog." Issa.—BeM
"Somebody saw a crow flying by and asked him where he was going." Unknown.—LeIb
The **grandfathers.** Donald Justice.—HiN
"**Grandma** snores." Nikita Tolstoy, tr. fr. the Russian by Miriam Morton.—MoM
Grandmothers
Advice to grandsons. Unknown.—CoOh
Child rest. P. George.—AlW
Glory, glory. . . . R. R. Patterson.—AdM
"Grandma snores." N. Tolstoy.—MoM
Granny. S. Milligan.—CoOr
"Great-great Grandma, don't sleep in your treehouse tonight." X. J. Kennedy.—KeO
"I am ashamed." Unknown.—LeIb
Lineage. M. Walker.—AdB—AdPb
Measles in the ark. S. Coolidge.—OpOx
Mountain road. M. Oliver.—RoIt
My grandmother. E. Jennings.—ToM
My granny. T. Hughes.—HuMf
#4. D. Long.—AdM—AdPb
One we knew. T. Hardy.—PlP
"Ride away, ride away." Mother Goose.—MiMg
Thanksgiving day. L. M. Child.—RoIt
Grandpa dropped his glasses. Leroy F. Jackson.—BrM
"**Grandpa** dropped his glasses once." See Grandpa dropped his glasses
"**Grandpa** Grig had a pig." Mother Goose.—AlC
Grandpa is ashamed. Ogden Nash.—CoPu
Granny. Spike Milligan.—CoOr
"**Granny** and I with dear Dadu." See A very odd fish
Grant, Richard E.
Broken heart, broken machine.—AdPb
Grantchester, England
"I only know that you may lie." From The old vicarage Grantchester. R. Brooke.—PaP
Grapes
Eating out in autumn. M. Chute.—ChRu
"The grapes hang green upon the vine." Unknown.—EmN
Judgment. T. Palmanteer.—AlW
"The **grapes** hang green upon the vine." Unknown.—EmN
Grass
At grass. P. Larkin.—HaWr
Grass. V. Worth.—WoS
Grassroots. C. Sandburg.—SaT
"Once upon a time." Issa.—BeM
Rabbit in the grass. A. Fisher.—FiFo
The rustling of grass. A. Noyes.—PaF
Secrets. R. Froman.—FrSp
Spring grass. C. Sandburg.—SaT
"Spring in the river." A. Atwood.—AtM
"Swinging, swaying grass." Issa.—BeM
What is the grass. From Song of myself. W. Whitman.—RoIt
"What's for rabbits." A. Fisher.—FiFo
Grass. Valerie Worth.—WoS
"**Grass** clutches at the dark dirt with finger holds." See Grassroots
"**Grass** grows low." Unknown.—MoBw
"**Grass** on the lawn." See Grass
"**Grasshopper.**" See The grasshopper
The **grasshopper.** Conrad Aiken.—JoA-4
"**Grasshopper,** grasshopper, grasshopper gray." Unknown.—EmN
"**Grasshopper,** take care." Issa, tr. fr. the Japanese by Hanako Fukuda.—HaW
Grasshoppers
"G-R-A double-S grass." Unknown.—EmN
The grasshopper. C. Aiken.—JoA-4
"Grasshopper, grasshopper, grasshopper gray." Unknown.—EmN
"Grasshopper, take care." Issa.—HaW
The hunter. A. Fisher.—FiM
On the grasshopper and cricket. J. Keats.—JoA-4—PaF
Grassroots. Carl Sandburg.—SaT
Gratitude. See Thankfulness
The **grave.** Saul Tchernichovsky, tr. fr. the Hebrew by Robert Mezey and Shula Starkman.—MeP
"The **grave** of Alexander Hamilton is in Trinity yard at the end of Wall street." See Trinity place
Graves, Alfred Perceval
Father O'Flynn.—CoPi
Herring is king.—CoPi
Graves, Robert
Allie.—JoA-4
Flying crooked.—CoPu—MaFw
"Henry was a young king."—AlC
In the wilderness.—JoA-4
Lollocks.—MaFw
Love without hope.—CoPu
Outlaws.—HaWr
The person from Porlock.—PlM
Star-talk.—PaF
Traveller's curse after misdirection.—HiN—LiWw
Warning to children.—MaFw
Wild strawberries.—PaF
Graves, Robert (about)
Poet with sea horse. A. Reid.—PlM
Graves. See Tombs

Graves. Moses ibn Ezra, tr. fr. the Hebrew by Robert Mezey.—MeP
Graveyards. See Cemeteries
Gray, Thomas
Elegy written in a country churchyard.—PaP (sel.)
On a distant prospect of Eton college.—PaP (sel.)
Gray (color)
"It is grey out." K. Kuskin.—KuN
"**Gray** goose and gander." See "Grey goose and gander"
"The **gray** sky." Linda Curry.—JoV
"**Gray** squirrel." See Squirrel
"**Gray** whale." See For a coming extinction
"The **great.**" See For Nina Simone wherever you are
"**Great** A, little a." Mother Goose.—EmN—JoA-4
The **great** auk's ghost. Ralph Hodgson.—LiWw
"The **great** auk's ghost rose on one leg." See The great auk's ghost
Great-aunts. Sean O'Críadáin.—CoPi
"The **Great** Bear has moved across the sky." Yi Jung-jin, tr. fr. the Korean by Chung Seuk Park and ad. by Virginia Olsen Baron.—BaSs
The **great** brown owl. Jane Euphemia Browne.—OpOx
"The **great** fire-eater, befitting his name." Jack Prelutsky.—PrC
"**Great-great** Grandma, don't sleep in your treehouse tonight." X. J. Kennedy.—KeO
"**Great** grief came over me." Unknown, fr. the Ammassalik Eskimo.—LeIb
"A **great** land and a wide land was the east land." See Who are they
The **great** merchant, Dives Pragmaticus, cries his wares. Thomas Newbery.—OpOx
The **great** panjandrum. Samuel Foote.—RoIt
The great panjandrum himself.—JoA-4
The **great** panjandrum himself. See The great panjandrum
The **great** sad one. Uri Zvi Greenberg, tr. fr. the Hebrew by Robert Mezey and Ben Zion Gold.—MeP
"The **great** sea." Unknown, tr. fr. the Eskimo by Knud Rasmussen.—BiI
"The **great** stone frog doorstop." See The stone frog
"**Great** swan, great swan." See Magic words to bring luck when hunting caribou
Great things. Thomas Hardy.—PlP
"**Great** was the stench of the dead." See Plague
"**Great,** wide, beautiful, wonderful world." See The world
"The **great** wrought-iron gates have been." See Twilight at the zoo
"**Greatly** shining." See Wind and silver
Greece
The geese in Greece. N. M. Bodecker.—BoL
Greed
Greedy. R. Froman.—FrSp
Greedy Jane. Unknown.—NeA—OpOx
Greedy Richard. Jane Taylor.—OpOx
Griselda. E. Farjeon.—UnGb
An old woman. C. H. Ross.—OpOx
"Sammy Smith would drink and eat." Mother Goose.—TucMgl
Sneaky Bill. W. Cole.—CoOr
Greedy. Robert Froman.—FrSp
Greedy Jane. Unknown.—NeA—OpOx
Greedy Richard. Jane Taylor.—OpOx
Greek mythology. See Mythology—Greek and Roman
Greek nursery rhymes. See Nursery rhymes—Greek
Green, Mary McB.
Aeroplane.—HoP
Green (color)
Green. L. Moore.—MoSp
Green with envy. E. Merriam.—MeO
Green. Lilian Moore.—MoSp
Green broom. Unknown.—CoPt
"The **green** bug sleeps in the white lily ear." See Small homes
"**Green** eye, greedy gut." Unknown.—EmN
The **green** fiddler. Rachel Field.—CoPt
The **green** gnome. Robert Buchanan.—CoPt
"**Green** head." Unknown.—EmN
"A **green** hobgoblin." See A goblinade
"**Green** is go." See Yellow
"**Green** is green." Unknown.—MoBw
"**Green** is the color I like best." See For a green page
"**Green** lawn." See Once
"**Green** rushes with red shoots." See Plucking the rushes
Green with envy. Eve Merriam.—MeO
Greenaway, Kate
Little wind.—JoA-4
Greenberg, Uri Zvi
The great sad one.—MeP
The hour.—MeP
How it is.—MeP
Like a woman.—MeP
On the pole.—MeP
There is a box.—MeP
To the mound of corpses in the snow.—MeP
The valley of men.—MeP
We were not like dogs.—MeP
With my God, the smith.—MeP
Greenburg, Dan
"Don't dress your cat in an apron."—ThF
My dog is a plumber.—ThF
Greene, Richard L.
Autolycus' song (in basic English).—LiS
Greene, Robert
Content.—RoIt
For there is an upstart crow.—PlM
Greenhouses
Big wind. T. Roethke.—HiN
Child on top of a greenhouse. T. Roethke.—HiN
Greenland
"Listen to my words." Unknown.—LeIb
The real slayer of the seal. Unknown.—LeIb

Greenland—*Continued*
A salmon trout to her children. Unknown.—LeIb
Taunt song against a clumsy kayak paddler. Unknown.—LeIb
"The wicked little Kukook." Unknown.—LeIb
"**Greeting,** Father's clansman." See Prayer
Greetings. See also Wake-up poems
"Good morning when it's morning." M. A. Hoberman.—HoN
"Hello's a handy word to say." M. A. Hoberman.—HoN
"One misty moisty morning." Mother Goose.—AlC—JoA-4—MiMg
Welcome here. Unknown.—LaS
Well, welcome, now that you're here. J. Ciardi.—CiFs
Greggs, Herbert D.
Multi-colored balloon.—AbM
Gregory, Lady (Isabella Augusta)
Donald Oge: Grief of a girl's heart. tr.—CoPi
Gretchen. Unknown, tr. fr. the Dutch by Alice Dalgliesh and Ernest Rhys.—JoA-4
"**Grey** as a mouse." See The adventures of Tom Bombadil—Oliphaunt
"**Grey** brick upon brick." See Dublin
"**Grey** crystal skies." See The bridges
"**Grey** goose and gander." Mother Goose.—AlC—CoPu—JoA-4
Grief. See also Laments; Melancholy
Autolycus' song. From The winter's tale. W. Shakespeare.—LiS
Autolycus' song (in basic English). R. L. Greene.—LiS
"Billy Batter." D. Lee.—LeA
The carousel. G. C. Oden.—AdPb
Crocodile. W. J. Smith.—BrM
Death of Dr King #1. S. Cornish.—AdM
Distance spills itself. Y. Bat-Miriam.—MeP
"Do not believe your Shakespeare's grief." From The argument. C. Aiken.—CoPu
Escape. G. D. Johnson.—AdPb
The eyes or the heart. A. N. B. J. Bhalo.—AlPa
First or last. T. Hardy.—JoA-4
"Great grief came over me." Unknown.—LeIb
"Grief streams down my chest." L. Jeffers.—AdPb
Had you wept. T. Hardy.—PlP
How it is. U. Z. Greenberg.—MeP
The husband's view. T. Hardy.—PlP
"I can wade grief." E. Dickinson.—ThI
"If teardrops were pearls." Unknown.—BaSs
If the stars should fall. S. Allen.—AdPb
In tenebris. T. Hardy.—PlP
Island. L. Hughes.—HoD
It never looks like summer. T. Hardy.—PlP
"It rained." Shin Heum.—BaSs
The lonely soul. R. E. G. Armattoe.—AlPa
Moon. N. Alterman.—MeP
The mourning dove. F. Holman.—HoI
"My heart moves as heavy as the horse that climbs the hill." Unknown, tr. fr. the Welsh by Menna Gallie.—CoPu
"My love is a thousand miles away." Wang Bang-yun.—BaSs
Nespelim man. Janet Campbell.—AlW
Quietly I shout. A. T. Pratt.—AlW
"Rain is falling on the paulownia." Kim Sang-yong.—BaSs
Sabbath stars. A. Shlonsky.—MeP
Sadness. Unknown.—LeIb
"The Sioux women." Unknown.—JoT
Songs of sorrow. K. Awoonor.—AlPa (sel.)
"Sorrow is the only faithful one." O. Dodson.—AdPb
Tears. A. Lopez.—AlW
There is a box. U. Z. Greenberg.—MeP
"This little man lived all alone." Mother Goose.—TucMgl
Troubled woman. L. Hughes.—HoD
"With rue my heart is laden." From A Shropshire lad. A. E. Housman.—RoIt
"**Grief** streams down my chest." Lance Jeffers.—AdPb
Griffin, Jonathan
XIV ("I don't bother with rhymes. It is seldom") tr.—MoT
Storm end.—MoT
Grimké, Angelina Weld
The black finger.—AdPb
Tenebris.—AdPb
A winter twilight.—AdPb
Your hands.—AdPb
Griselda. Eleanor Farjeon.—UnGb
"**Griselda** is greedy, I'm sorry to say." See Griselda
Grist mills. See Millers
Grizlov, Yuri
"To fling songs into the air."—MoM
Grizzly bear. Mary Austin.—RoIt
The **groaning** board. Pink.—CoPu
Grocery shops
Delicatessen. L. Lenski.—LeC
Mr Docer. N. M. Bodecker.—BoL
Supermarket. L. Lenski.—LeC
The unfortunate grocer. L. E. Richards.—CoOr
Grosser, Morton
Sand hill road.—PeS
Grosvenor, Kali
"It's a new kind of day."—AdM
Our black people.—AdM
"Where is my head going."—AdM
"**Grotesque,** jumping out." See Sky diver
Ground hog day
Ground hog day. M. Pomeroy.—CoPu
To the ground hog. K. Winters.—LaM
Ground hog day. Marnie Pomeroy.—CoPu
Ground hogs. See Woodchucks
Group, The
"Rain, shivering, wreaked the earth."—JoV
"**Grow** up, grow up." Unknown.—MoBw
Growing up
August. L. Clifton.—ClE

"Chesterfield cigarettes fill the light-colored room as I enter." M. Goode.—JoV
Elephant rock. Primus St John.—AdPb
El-Hajj Malik El-Shabazz. R. Hayden.—AdPb
Friday: Waiting for mom. L. Clifton.—ClS
"I cannot tell my future." A. Holmes.—JoV
"I remember how she sang." R. Penny.—AdPb
Interview. E. Merriam.—MeF
I've seen enough. C. Meyer.—JoV
Judeebug's country. J. Johnson.—AdPb
Letter to E. Franklin Frazier. L. Jones.—AdPb
Looking forward. R. L. Stevenson.—OpOx
Monday morning: Good morning. L. Clifton.—ClS
The old woman who lived in a shoe. J. Johnson.—ThF
Rites of passage. A. Lorde.—AdPb
Someone I know. Unknown.—MoM
Song of a boy growing up. Unknown.—BiS
Songs in the garden of the house god. Unknown.—BiI
Sophistication. V. Miller.—HiN
Swallow the lake. C. Major.—AdPb
Tim. D. McCord.—McAa
Timothy Winters. C. Causley.—ToM
"Way out there." F. Holman.—HoI
When I am me. F. Holman.—HoI
When we grow up. S. Miller.—ThF
Youth. L. Hughes.—HoD—JoA-4
A **growl.** Marchette Chute.—ChRu
"The **grown**-ups come." See December 23: Late
Grunion. Myra Cohn Livingston.—LiM
Gryll Grange, sel. Thomas Love Peacock
Love and age.—RoIt
Guadalupe, West Indies
Guadalupe, W. I. N. Guillén.—AbM
Guadalupe, W. I. Nicolás Guillén, tr. fr. the Spanish by Anselm Hollo.—AbM
A **guerilla** handbook. LeRoi Jones.—AdPb
"**Guess** a riddle now you must." Unknown.—EmN
"**Guess** what I have gone and done." See My invention
Guest, Harry and Lynn, and Kajima Shozo
Firefly. trs.—MoT
Guest, Lynn. See Guest, Harry and Lynn, and Kajima Shozo
Guests
"Don't bring out the straw mat." Han Hwak.—BaSs
House guest. E. Bishop.—HiN
"The lands around my dwelling." Unknown.—BiI—LaM
"Old Mr Parvenu gave a great ball." C. Grain.—CoPu
On Noman, a guest. H. Belloc.—CoPu
Thoughtless guest. V. Hobbs.—BrM
Guevara, Tomás
The ghost of Caupolicán. tr.—BiI
Guillén, Nicolás
Guadalupe, W. I.—AbM
"Last night somebody called me darky."—AbM
Little song for the children of the Antilles.—AbM
Proposition.—AbM
A **guinea-pig** song. Unknown.—OpOx
Guinea-pigs
A guinea-pig song. Unknown.—OpOx
"Three little guinea-pigs." Unknown.—BoI
Guineas
Life. A. Kreymborg.—CoPu
Guitars
The man with the blue guitar. W. Stevens.—PeS (sel.)
Guiterman, Arthur
The ambiguous dog.—BrM
The Christmas exchange.—BrM
The dog's cold nose.—CoPt
Dorlan's home walk.—CoPt
Eight oars and a coxswain.—FlH
Elegy.—LiWw
Local note.—CoPu
Mavrone, one of those sad Irish poems, with notes.—LiS
Motto for a dog.—CoPu
Ode to the amoeba.—LiWw
On the vanity of earthly greatness.—LiWw
Routine.—CoOh
Thanksgiving.—CoPu
Under the goal posts.—FlH
Gull. Felice Holman.—HoI
"**Gull,** ballast of its wings." See Stabilities
"The **gull,** it is said." Unknown, fr. the Netsilik Eskimo.—LeIb
Gulls
Afternoon: Amagansett beach. J. H. Wheelock.—HaWr
A broken gull. J. Moore.—HiN
Gull. F. Holman.—HoI
"The gull, it is said." Unknown.—LeIb
Gulls. E. A. Muir.—HiN
"Hey there, white seagull." Kim Kwang-wuk.—BaSs
"I close my book and open the window." Chung On.—BaSs
"The island of Mull." N. M. Bodecker.—BoL
"An ocean of clouds." A. Atwood.—AtM
"Only half-awakened from a nap on my pine-needle bed." Kim Sam-hyun.—BaSs
"Only white gull and I." Yi Hwang.—BaSs
Sails, gulls, sky, sea. F. Holman.—HoI
The seagull. M. Howitt.—OpOx
Torn down from glory daily. A. Sexton.—HaWr
"The waves are so cold." Bashō.—BeM
Gulls. E. A. Muir.—HiN
Gumballs. X. J. Kennedy.—KeO
"The **gun** explodes them." See The sprinters
Gunn, Thom
Blackie, the electric Rembrandt.—MaFw
Considering the snail.—HaWr—MaFw
Incident on a journey.—ToM
Jesus and his mother.—ToM
A mirror for poets.—PlM

Gunn, Thom—*Continued*
Touch.—ToM
Gunpowder plot. Vernon Scannell.—MaFw—ToM
The **gunpowder** plot, from the great speech of Sir Edward Philips, arranged by David Mackay.—David Mackay.—MaFw
Guns. See also Arms and armor; Hunters and hunting
A shooting song. W. B. Rands.—OpOx
Ultima ratio regum. S. Spender.—ToM
"The **guns** spell money's ultimate reason." See Ultimate ratio regum
The **guppy.** Ogden Nash.—JoA-4
Guri, Chaim
Odysseus.—MeP
Pictures of the Jews.—MeP
Piyyut for Rosh Hashana.—MeP
Gurvich, Mikhail
We, the young.—MoM
Gustafson, Ingemar
Locked in.—CoPt
Guthrie, A. B., Jr
Twin lakes hunter.—CoPt
Guthrie, Woody
I've got to know.—PeS
Pastures of plenty.—PeS
Gutkina, Asya
Losing friends.—MoM
Gutmann, Assia
"As for the world." tr.—MeP
I was the moon. tr.—MeP
In the middle of this century. tr.—MeP
Mayor. tr.—MeP
National thoughts. tr.—MeP
"The place where I have not been." tr.—MeP
They call me. tr.—MeP
To my mother. tr.—MeP
"**Guy** Fawkes and his companions." Unknown.—MaF
Guy Fawkes day
"Guy Fawkes and his companions." Unknown.—MaF
"Remember, remember." Unknown.—MaF
"**G'way** an' quit dat noise, Miss Lucy." See When Malindy sings
Gyodai
"Flapping into fog."—BeM
Gypsies. See Gipsies
The **gypsies** are coming. Shel Silverstein.—SiW
"The **gypsies** are coming, the old people say." See The gypsies are coming
Gypsy eyes. Jimi Hendrix.—MoG
"**Gypsy,** gypsy, lived in a tent." Unknown.—EmN
Gyre's galax. Norman Henry Pritchard II.—AdPb

H

"**H-U** huckle, B-U buckle, H-U huckle Y." Unknown.—EmN
"**Ha,** for the snow and hoar." See The dynasts—Mad soldier's song
"**Ha,** sir, I have seen you sniffing and snoozling about among my." See The faun
Habit
The elephant, or the force of habit. A. E. Housman.—LiWw
"Hello Mr Python." S. Milligan.—CoOh
Meditatio. E. Pound.—LiWw
Thumbs. S. Silverstein.—SiW
"What's for rabbits." A. Fisher.—FiFo
"**Had** a little chicky." Unknown.—EmN
"**Had** a little girl dressed in blue." Unknown.—EmN
"**Had** he and I but met." See The man he killed
Had I a golden pound. Francis Ledwidge.—CoPi
"**Had** I a golden pound to spend." See Had I a golden pound
"**Had** I the heavens' embroidered cloths." See He wishes for the cloths of Heaven
Had you wept. Thomas Hardy.—PlP
"**Had** you wept; had you but neared me with a hazed uncertain ray." See Had you wept
"A **haddock,** a haddock, a black-spotted haddock." Unknown.—EmN
Haec fabula docet. Robert Frost.—LiWw
Haida Indians. See Indians of the Americas—Haida
"**Haik,** the white bird of omen." Unknown, tr. fr. the Chippewa.—ClFc
Haiku poems (about)
Haiku. D. McCord.—McFm
Hokku/haikai/haiku. M. C. Livingston.—LiM
Haiku. David McCord.—McFm
"**Hail,** Bishop Valentine, whose day this is." John Donne.—MaF
"**Hail,** blessed morn." See Star in the East
"**Hail** him." Unknown, tr. fr. the Akan by J. H. Kwabena Nketia.—AlPa
"**Hail,** lofty." See Conversation with a giraffe at dusk in the zoo
"**Hail** O ye seven pupils." See On a school-teacher
"**Hail,** old October, bright and chill." See Old October
Hail, polluters. Robert Froman.—FrSp
"**Haily** paily." Unknown, tr. fr. the Scottish by Norah and William Montgomerie.—JoA-4
Haines, John
And when the green man comes.—HiN
If the owl calls again.—HiN
The mole.—HiN
Prayer to the snowy owl.—CoPu
Snowy night.—HiN
Hair
The bald cavalier. Unknown.—OpOx
The barber's. W. De La Mare.—JoA-4

Do you know the man. S. Silverstein.—CoOh
For Anne Gregory. W. B. Yeats.—CoPi—LiWw
"Haily paily." Unknown.—JoA-4
"Lambs are full of curly wool." M. A. Hoberman.—HoN
The long-haired boy. S. Silverstein.—SiW
My beard. S. Silverstein.—SiW
"Not to have any *hair* is called." R. Wilbur.—WiO
On getting a natural. D. Randall.—AdPb
"On Saturday night (shall be)." Mother Goose.—AlC
Ookpik. D. Lee.—LeA
"Riddle me, riddle me, What is that." Unknown.—EmN
Sam's world. S. Cornish.—AdM
"The skeeter lies a hairless man." Unknown.—CoOh
Téma con variazíoni. L. Carroll.—LiS
A tragic story. A. von Chamisso.—LiWw
Triolet against sisters. P. McGinley.—LiWw
Yak. W. J. Cole.—CoOr
The **hairy** dog. Herbert Asquith.—BrM
Haiti
Evening in Haiti. E. Roumer.—AbM
Hale, Horatio
At the wood's edge. tr.—BiI
Hale, Sarah Josepha (Buell)
Mary's lamb.—OpOx
"**Half** a league, half a league." See The charge of the Light Brigade
"**Half** a moon." Robert Rozhdestvensky, tr. fr. the Russian by Miriam Morton.—MoM
"**Half** a pound of bacon." Mother Goose.—AlC
Half asleep. Aileen Fisher.—FiM
Half black, half blacker. Sterling Plumpp.—AdPb
"**Half** close your eyelids, loosen your hair." See He thinks of those who have spoken evil of his beloved
"**Half-cracked** to Higginson, living." See I am in danger—Sir
"**Half** in the dim light from the hall." See To ——
"**Half** of his." See Spirits
"**Half** of my life." Calvin O'John.—AlW
Halfway down. A. A. Milne.—LiLc
"**Halfway** down the stairs." See Halfway down
Hall, Carol
Glad to have a friend like you.—ThF
"It's all right to cry."—ThF
Parents are people.—ThF
Hall, Donald
The body politic.—PeS
By the Exeter river.—ToM
The child.—HiN
Cold water.—HiN
"How God hath labored to produce the duck."—CoPu
In the kitchen of the old house.—ToM
The kill.—HaWr
The moon.—HiN
The old pilot's death.—ToM
The sleeping giant.—HiN
Hall, Keith, Jr
Creepy.—HoH
Hallelujah. Alfred Edward Housman.—CoOr
"Hallelujah, was the only observation."—CoPu—LiWw
"**Hallelujah,** was the only observation." See Hallelujah
"**Hallow** e'en will come, will come." Unknown.—MaF (sel.)
Hallowe'en
A-ha. D. Aldis.—LaM
"Cat." L. Moore.—MoSm
Cat. M. B. Miller.—HoH—LiLc
Creepy. K. Hall, Jr.—HoH
Dear country witch. L. Moore.—MoSm
Eight witches. B. J. Lee.—HoH
"Everyone is asleep." Seifu-Jo.—HoH
"Hallow e'en will come, will come." Unknown.—MaF (sel.)
Halloween ("Hooting") P. J. Perry.—HoH
Hallowe'en ("Leaf piles smoke in the whispering dark") B. J. Esbensen.—HoH
Hallowe'en ("Tonight is the night") H. Behn.—JoA-4
"Hey-how for Hallow e'en."—Unknown.—MaF (sel.)
"Hist whist." E. E. Cummings.—HoH
Hitchhiker. D. McCord.—McAa—McS
"The house at the corner." M. C. Livingston.—HoH
"House ghost." L. May.—HoC
The house of the goblin. S. Brown.—HoH
If you've never. E. M. Fowler.—HoH
"It's the nicht atween the saints and souls." Unknown.—MaF (sel.)
Little Ugh. L. Moore.—MoSm
"Look at that." L. Moore.—MoSm
Luck for Halloween. M. Justus.—HoH
Magic vine. Unknown.—JaP
Mr Macklin's visitor. D. McCord.—McAa
October ("Don't run when you see") L. Clifton.—ClE
October ("In October") M. Sendak.—HoH
October ("The month is amber") J. Updike.—JoA-4
October magic. M. C. Livingston.—HoH
Old Tim Toole. D. McCord.—McAa
On Halloween. N. W. Walter.—HoH
Pamela. D. McCord.—McFm
A prayer for Halloween. Unknown.—LaM
Pumpkin seed. D. McCord.—MaAa
Ready for Halloween. A. Fisher.—HoH
A riddle: What am I. D. Aldis.—HoH
"Spooky." K. Finnell.—HoC
Teeth. L. Moore.—MoSm
Theme in yellow. C. Sandburg.—HoH—LiLc—SaT
Trick or treat. C. McCullers.—HoH
"We three." L. Moore.—MoSm
What night would it be. J. Ciardi.—HoH
What witches do. L. B. Jacobs.—HoH
Witch's broom notes. D. McCord.—McAa
The witch's song. L. Moore.—HoH—MoSm

Halloween ("Hooting") Phyllis J. Perry.—HoH
Halloween ("Leaf piles smoke in the whispering dark") Barbara Juster Esbensen.—HoH
Hallowe'en ("Tonight is the night") Harry Behn.—JoA-4
"**Hambone,** jawbone, mulligatawney stew." See Bouncing song
"**Hamelin** Town's in Brunswick." See The Pied Piper of Hamelin
Hamilton, Bobb
"America."—AdB
Hamlet, sels. William Shakespeare
"Some say. . . . "—JoA-4
"Tomorrow is Saint Valentine's day."—LiLc
Hammock. David McCord.—McS
Han Hwak
"Don't bring out the straw mat."—BaSs
Hanako Fukuda
"Ah, cherry blossoms." tr.—HaW
"At his writing lesson." tr.—HaW
"Come and play with me." tr.—HaW
"Cricket, my boy." tr.—HaW
"Dear me, dear me." tr.—HaW
"Don't mind my small hut." tr.—HaW
"Even butterflies." tr.—HaW
"Evening swallows flying home." tr.—HaW
"A father deer." tr.—HaW
"The first firefly." tr.—HaW
"The frog sits." tr.—HaW
"Good heavens." tr.—HaW
"Grasshopper, take care." tr.—HaW
"Honorable Toad." tr.—HaW
"How cold it is." tr.—HaW
"I have nothing at all." tr.—HaW
"An icicle hangs." tr.—HaW
"If things were better." tr.—HaW—LiWw
"I'll try not to . . . but." tr.—HaW
"In the spring rain." tr.—HaW
"In this world, you see." tr.—HaW
"Keep looking at the prize." tr.—HaW
"Let's be off to the bamboo." tr.—HaW
"Little sparrows." tr.—HaW
"Moo, moo, moo." tr.—HaW
"A motherless child—see." tr.—HaW
"My first dream of the year." tr.—HaW
"The New Year's day." tr.—HaW
"No one could be. . . . " tr.—HaW
"Now, from today on." tr.—HaW
"Oh, do not swat the fly." tr.—HaW
"Oh, the Milky Way." tr.—HaW
"The old pond." tr.—HaW
"The pampas flowers." tr.—HaW
"The people, of course." tr.—HaW
"A poppy in his hand." tr.—HaW
"Rubbing my hands together." tr.—HaW
"Skinny frog." tr.—HaW
"A skylark circles." tr.—HaW
"The sleeping little fawn." tr.—HaW
"A step-child beats straw." tr.—HaW
"A sudden shower." tr.—HaW
"To owl, the dove says." tr.—HaW
"Whenever I see the ocean." tr.—HaW
"White mountains, seen also." tr.—HaW
"Wild goose, O wild goose." tr.—HaW
"The wind of autumn." tr.—HaW
"Yes, rain is leaking." tr.—HaW
Handfuls of wind. Yehiel Mar, tr. fr. the Hebrew by Ruth Finer Mintz.—MeP
Hands
"The first firefly." Issa.—HaW
Hands. G. Thompson.—JoV
I have seen black hands. R. Wright.—AdPb
A left-handed poem. E. Merriam.—MeO
On a hand. H. Belloc.—CoPu
Your hands. A. W. Grimké.—AdPb
Hands. Glen Thompson.—JoV
"**Hands** flat on the ground." Sokan, tr. fr. the Japanese by Harry Behn.—BeM
"**Hands** of all nations." See Hands
The **hands** of toil. James Russell Lowell.—RoIt
"**Hands** off the tablecloth." See Company manners
"**Handsome** boy." See Folk song from Fukushima
Handwriting
"At his writing lesson." Issa.—HaW
"Keep looking at the prize." Issa.—HaW
"**Hang** on." Unknown.—MoBw
"**Hanging** motionless in the sky." Unknown, tr. fr. the Papago.—ClFc
Hangings
"A Briton who swore at his king." D. Ross.—RoIt
The carpenter's son. From A Shropshire lad. A. E. Housman.—LiS
A dream of hanging. P. Beer.—ToM
The stranger's song. T. Hardy.—PlP
"What, still alive at twenty two." H. Kingsmill.—LiS
"When lads have done with labor." H. Wolfe.—LiS
Hanks, Nancy (about)
Nancy Hanks. S. V. Benét and R. Carr.—JoA-4
"**Hannah** Bantry in the pantry." Mother Goose.—AlC—CoOh—TrG
Hans, Marcie
"Fueled."—HoP
Hanson, Joan
"Fir tree tall."—HoS—LaM
Hanukkah
Chanukah poem. E-1 Class, Jewish Children's School of Philadelphia.—LaM
Dreidel song. E. Rosenzweig.—LaM
"Eight are the lights." I. Orleans.—LaM (sel.)
Hap. Thomas Hardy.—PlP
"**Happened** like this: it was hot as hell." See The death of a craneman
Happiness
"As New Year's day dawns." Ransetsu.—BeM
Autolycus' song. From The winter's tale. W. Shakespeare.—LiS
Autolycus' song (in basic English). R. L. Greene.—LiS
"Billy Batter." D. Lee.—LeA
Blessed is today. Kim Koo.—BaSs
The blind boy. C. Cibber.—OpOx

"A centipede was happy quite." Unknown.—RoIt
The character of a happy life. H. Wotton.—RoIt
Contentment. M. Chute.—ChRu
Crocodile. W. J. Smith.—BrM
Dance song. Unknown.—LeIb
Dinnertime. M. Chute.—ChRu
Dust of snow. R. Frost.—MoT—RoIt
The enchanted shirt. J. Hay.—CoPt
Everyone sang. S. Sassoon.—PaF
First or last. T. Hardy.—JoA-4
First song. G. Kinnell.—HiN
Glad to have a friend like you. C. Hall.—ThF
Good times. L. Clifton.—AdM—AdPb—HiN
Happiness. C. Sandburg.—SaT
The happy hedgehog. E. V. Rieu.—JoA-4
Happy thought. R. L. Stevenson.—OpOx
Heaven. L. Hughes.—HoD—JoA-4
Hoeing. J. Updike.—MoT
Hope and joy. C. G. Rossetti.—OpOx
How it is. U. Z. Greenberg.—MeP
How still, how happy. E. Brontë.—PaF
"How still, how happy! Those are words."—PaP
"I can wade grief." E. Dickinson.—ThI
"I hear you smiling." F. Holman.—HoI
Improvised song of joy. Unknown.—LeIb
"In a hermit's cottage, silent, still." Kim Soo-jang.—BaSs
"In the spring when the sun never sets." L. Evaloarjuak.—LeIb
Intimations of immortality. W. Wordsworth.—PaF (sel.)
January 3, 1970. M. Jackson.—AdPb
Joy. L. Hughes.—AbM
The kayak paddler's joy at the weather. Unknown.—LeIb
The Land of Happy. S. Silverstein.—SiW
Laughing song. W. Blake.—JoA-4—OpOx—RoIt
"Let us go to the Indian village, said all the rain gods." Unknown.—ClFc
Listening to music. M. Chute.—ChRu
Make merry. D. McCord.—McFm
"May your wing of happiness." Unknown.—EmN
Meditation. T. Traherne.—RoIt
Merry. S. Silverstein.—SiW
Merry are the bells. Unknown.—JoA-4—RoIt
Mirth. C. Smart.—OpOx
Monday morning: Good morning. L. Clifton.—ClS
The moon is up. Unknown.—RoIt
My Muse. S. Smith.—PlM
Nespelim man. Janet Campbell.—AlW
Nikki-Rosa. N. Giovanni.—AdPb
O boys, O boys. O. St J. Gogarty.—CoPi
Ode on solitude. A. Pope.—MaFw
Solitude.—RoIt
An offering of joy. S. Eremina.—MoM
Our joyful feast. G. Wither.—RoIt
A piper ("A piper in the street today") S. O'Sullivan.—CoPu
The piper ("Piping down the valleys wild") W. Blake.—LiLc—OpOx
Happy songs.—UnGb
Poems of solitary delights. Tachibama Akemi.—MaFw (sel.)
Prayer. Unknown.—BiI
The question. T. Kucherenko.—MoM
The seven joys of Mary. Unknown.—LaS
The sonnet-ballad. G. Brooks.—PeS
Spring. G. M. Hopkins.—PaF
The sun. J. Drinkwater.—LiLc
The tale of a dog. J. S. Lambert, Jr.—BrM
"There were five fellows." C. Watson.—WaF
"These are." J. Vitale.—HoC
"To cheer our minds." W. Ronksley.—OpOx
Utitiaq's song. Unknown.—LeIb
Wags and purrs. A. Fisher.—FiM
"The weather is gloomy." A. Tarasova.—MoM
"What is this I promise you." Unknown.—BiS
Why is happy. D. Whitewing.—AlW
"Happiness." Unknown.—MoBw
Happiness. Carl Sandburg.—SaT
"The **happiness** of hedgehogs." See The happy hedgehog
"Happy." Veronica Windley.—HoC
"Happy birthday, silly goose." Clyde Watson.—WaF
The **happy** cynic to his love. Eve Merriam.—MeF
The **happy** hedgehog. E. V. Rieu.—JoA-4
Happy new year. Eve Merriam.—MeO
The **happy** nightingale. Unknown.—OpOx
Happy songs. See The piper ("Piping down the valleys wild")
"Happy the man whose wish and care." See Ode on solitude
Happy thought. Robert Louis Stevenson.—OpOx
The **harbor.** Carl Sandburg.—HiN
Harbors
"Back and forth." L. S. Mitchell.—HoP
Fishing harbour towards evening. R. Kell.—ToM
Fog. C. Sandburg.—HoCs—JoA-4—MaFw—SaT—UnGb
The harbor. C. Sandburg.—HiN
In Falmouth harbour. L. Johnson.—PaP
In the dim city. A. Salmon.—PaP
"Only half-awakened from a nap on my pine-needle bed." Kim Sam-hyun.—BaSs
Upon an image from Dante. S. Sitwell.—PaP
"Whenever the stars are out of sight." R. Harnden.—HoP
Harder than granite. Robinson Jeffers.—CoPu
Harding, Robert
"Rain clouds."—HoC
Hardrock. Robert Froman.—FrSp
Hardships
The gleaner. Jane Taylor.—OpOx
The princess and the gypsies. F. Cornford.—CoPt
Hardy, Thomas
After a journey.—PlP

"Hark, the herald angels sing." Unknown.—TrG
Harlem
African China. M. B. Tolson.—AdPb
Good morning. L. Hughes.—AdM
Harlem freeze frame. L. Bethune.—AdPb
Harlem riot, 1943. P. Murray.—AdPb
Jitterbugging in the streets. C. C. Hernton.—AdPb
Juke box love song. L. Hughes.—AdPb
Keep on pushing. D. Henderson.—AdPb
Prime. L. Hughes.—AdPb
The still voice of Harlem. C. K. Rivers.—AdPb
The train runs late to Harlem. C. K. RIvers.—AdPb
Walk with de Mayor of Harlem. D. Henderson.—AdPb
Harlem freeze frame. Lebert Bethune.—AdPb
Harlem riot, 1943. Pauli Murray.—AdPb
Harnden, Ruth
"Whenever the stars are out of sight."—HoP
Harnick, Sheldon
Housework.—ThF
William's doll.—ThF
"The **harp** that once through Tara's halls." Thomas Moore.—RoIt
Harper, Michael S.
Barricades.—AdPb
Blue Ruth, America.—AdPb
Come back blues.—AdPb
Deathwatch.—AdPb
Effendi.—AdPb
Here where Coltrane is.—AdPb
Martin's blues.—AdPb
Newsletter from my mother.—AdPb
Photographs: A vision of massacre.—AdPb
The **harper.** Unknown, tr. fr. the Irish by Frank O'Connor.—CoPi
Harper's Ferry, Virginia
October 16: The raid. L. Hughes.—AdB—AdPb
The **harpooning**. Ted Walker.—HaWr
Harps
The ballad of the harp-weaver. E. St V. Millay.—CoPt—RoIt
"The harp that once through Tara's halls." T. Moore.—RoIt
The harper. Unknown.—CoPi
Harries, Lyndon
The eyes or the heart. tr.—AlPa
A male lion, I roar. tr.—AlPa
The poor man. tr.—FlH
"Harriet Hutch." Laura E. Richards.—NeA
"Harriet Tubman." See Cross over the river
Harrington, Edward
The bushrangers.—CoPt
Harris, Marguerite
"The little girl I used to be." RoIt
Harris, William J.
For Bill Hawkins, a black militant.—AdPb
Frightened flower.—AdB
"A grandfather poem."—AdM—AdPb
An historic moment.—AdB—CoPu
On wearing ears.—AdB
Practical concerns.—AdPb
The truth is quite messy.—AdB
"We live in a cage."—AdPb
"Why would I want."—AdPb
Hamson, De Leon
A collage for Richard Davis—two short forms.—AdPb
The room.—AdPb
"The seed of Nimrod."—AdPb
"Some days/out walking above."—AdPb
Yellow.—AdPb
Harrison, Jim
Cardinal.—HaWr
Horse.—HaWr
Morning.—HaWr
"Harry Docer." See Mr Docer
"Harry, Harry, ain't no good." Unknown.—EmN
"A **harsh** entry I had of it, Grasud." See Missionary
Hart, Bruce
Free to be you and me.—ThF
Sisters and brothers.—ThF
Hart, Elizabeth Anna
Mother Tabbyskins.—OpOx
Hart, Henry H.
Butterflies. tr.—MaFw
The hermit. tr.—MaFw
The poem of ten ones. tr.—MaFw
Riding at daybreak. tr.—MaFw
Harte, Bret
Dow's flat.—CoPt
The spelling bee at Angels.—CoPt
Harvest. Carl Sandburg.—HaWr
The **harvest** elves. Wilfrid Thorley.—JaP
Harvest sunset. Carl Sandburg.—SaT
"The **harvesters**—they say themselves." See The harvest elves
Harvestman. David McCord.—McFm—McS
Harvests and harvesting
A black man talks of reaping. A. Bontemps.—AdPb
"The boughs do shake and the bells do ring." Mother Goose.—JoA-4
Brown gold. C. Sandburg.—SaT
A celebration. V. Shepelev.—MoM
Cornhuskers. From Prairie. C. Sandburg.—SaT
The gleaner. Jane Taylor.—OpOx
Harvest. C. Sandburg.—HaWr
The harvest elves. W. Thorley.—JaP
Hay song. L. Moore.—MoSp
Hurrahing in harvest. G. M. Hopkins.—MaFw
Pastures of plenty. W. Guthrie.—PeS
Reapers. J. Toomer.—AdPb
Scythe song. A. Lang.—RoIt
The solitary reaper. W. Wordsworth.—RoIt
"Has a drift of snow." Bashō, tr. fr. the Japanese by Harry Behn.—BeM
"Hast thou given the horse strength." See Job—The horse
Hat. Shel Silverstein.—SiW

Hate
The angry man. P. McGinley.—PeS
The bishop orders his tomb at Saint Praxed's church. R. Browning.—MoG
Dog and fox. D. Ferry.—CoPu
The echo. P. Solomon.—JoV
Hatred. G. B. Bennett.—AdPb
Hit. T. Palmanteer.—AlW
"I am frightened that." V. Howard.—JoV
"Kicking your heels on the dusty road." P. Solomon.—JoV
Militant. L. Hughes.—AdPb
The new math. V. Howard.—JoV
The prophet's warning or shoot to kill. Ebon (Dooley).—AdPb
"Rain." C. Minor.—JoV
Tears. A. Lopez.—AlW
"You smiled." C. O'John.—AlW
Hatred. Gwendolyn B. Bennett.—AdPb
Hats
Hat. S. Silverstein.—SiW
Hats. C. Sandburg.—SaT
"I tried to tip my hat to Miss McCaffery." S. Silverstein.—CoOr
Tight hat.—SiW
May 14. N. Belting.—BeSc
A memory. L. A. G. Strong.—CoPi
Mr Slatter. N. M. Bodecker.—BoL
Patience. H. Graham.—LiWw
The quangle wangle's hat. E. Lear.—JoA-4
"Riddle me, riddle me, what is that." Unknown.—EmN
Sky pieces. C. Sandburg.—SaT
"There goes my best hat." Bashō.—BeM
"Trapped in a helmet." Bashō.—BeM
The trouble was simply that. D. McCord.—McFm
Upstairs. S. Silverstein.—SiW
"What is the opposite of *hat.*" R. Wilbur.—WiO
Hats. Carl Sandburg.—SaT
"**Hats,** where do you belong." See Hats
The **haunter.** Thomas Hardy.—PlP
Havasupai Indians. See Indians of the Americas—Havasupai
"**Have** thou no other gods but me." See The ten commandments
"**Have** you been to The Land of Happy." See The Land of Happy
"**Have** you ever heard of the sugar-plum tree." See The sugar-plum tree
"**Have** you ever heard the sun in the sky." See From Jazz for five
"**Have** you heard of the wonderful one-hoss shay." See The deacon's masterpiece; or, The wonderful one-hoss shay
"**Have** you heard of tiny Melinda Mae." See Melinda Mae
"**Have** you seen the sea roads." Joanne Oppenheim.—HoP
"**Having** attained success in business." See Robert Whitmore
Having New England fathers. John Holmes.—RoIt
"**Having** New England fathers in my blood." See Having New England fathers
The **hawk** ("Call down the hawk from the air") William Butler Yeats.—MaFw
The **hawk** ("Instead of using his wings to fly") Aileen Fisher.—FiFo
Hawk roosting. Ted Hughes.—ToM
Hawker, Robert Stephen
Song of the Western men.—RoIt
Hawkins, Walter Everette
The death of justice.—AdPb
A spade is just a spade.—AdPb
Hawks
"Hanging motionless in the sky." Unknown.—ClFc
The hawk ("Call down the hawk from the air") W. B. Yeats.—MaFw
The hawk ("Instead of using his wings to fly") A. Fisher.—FiFo
Hawk roosting. T. Hughes.—ToM
"Hidden by darkness." Bashō.—BeM
Hurt hawks. R. Jeffers.—PeS
"Little Jock Sander of Dee." Unknown.—BoI
Haworth (home of the Brontës)
Haworth in May. W. R. Childe.—PaP
Haworth in May. Wilfred Rowland Childe.—PaP
Hay, John
The enchanted shirt.—CoPt
Hay, Sara Henderson
The builders.—LiWw
Interview.—LiWw
Hay
Hay song. L. Moore.—MoSp
Haying before storm. M. Rukeyser.—HaWr
Haymaking. E. Thomas.—PaP
The haystack. A. Young.—CoPu
Haystacks. From Prairie. C. Sandburg.—SaT
Hay song. Lilian Moore.—MoSp
Hayden, Robert
Aunt Jemima of the ocean waves.—AdPb
Bahá'u'lláh in the garden of Ridwan.—AdPb
A ballad of remembrance.—AdPb
El-Hajj Malik El-Shabazz.—AdPb
Frederick Douglass.—AbM—AdPb
Homage to the Empress of the Blues.—AdPb
Kid.—HiN
Middle passage.—AdPb
Mourning poem for the Queen of Sunday.—AdPb
O Daedalus, fly away home.—AdPb—HiN
A road in Kentucky.—HiN
Runagate runagate.—AdPb
Summertime and the living.—AdPb—HiN
Those winter Sundays.—AdPb
Unidentified flying object.—HiN
The whipping.—AdPb—HiN
Hayes, Alfred
The death of the craneman.—HiN
Hayes, Donald Jeffrey
Appoggiatura.—AdPb
Haying before storm. Muriel Rukeyser.—HaWr
Haymaking. Edward Thomas.—PaP
The **haystack.** Andrew Young.—CoPu

"**He** who takes what isn't his'n." Unknown.—MoBw
"**He** will just do nothing at all." See Declaration of independence
He wishes for the cloths of Heaven. William Butler Yeats.—JoA-4
He wove the strands of our life. Unknown, tr. fr. the Aztec by Angel Garibay.—BiI
"**He's** bought a bed and a table too." See Mary Ann
"**He's** chasing me." See The chase
"**He's** got the whole world in His hands." See In His hands
"A **head** or tail—which does he lack." See The hippo
Headland, Isaac Taylor
Blind man's buff. tr.—JoA-4
The five toes. tr.—JoA-4
Lady bug. tr.—JoA-4
Old Chang the crab. tr.—JoA-4
Thistle-seed. tr.—JoA-4
The **headless** gardener. Ian Serraillier.—LiWw
"A **headlight** searches a snowstorm." See Prairie—Limited crossing Wisconsin
Heads
A boy's head. M. Holub.—MaFw
"I left my head." L. Moore.—MoSm
The loser. S. Silverstein.—SiW
Skulls and cups. J. P. Clark.—AlPa
That head. J. Bullmer.—CoOr
"There goes my best hat." Bashō.—BeM
"Were is my head going." K. Grosvenor.—AdM
You fancy wit. A. Pope.—RoIt
An empty house.—LiWw
Health
"Health and happiness." Unknown.—MoBw
"Health and long life to you." Unknown.—MoBw
A health to the birds. S. MacManus.—CoPi
Methuselah. Unknown.—RoIt
"**Health** and happiness." Unknown.—MoBw
"**Health** and long life to you." Unknown.—MoBw
A **health** to the birds. Seamus MacManus.—CoPi
Heaney, Seamus
An advancement of learning.—HiN
Death of a naturalist.—HiN
Digging.—ToM
The early purges.—HiN
Follower.—CoPi
The forge.—CoPi
The given note.—HiN
Mid-term break.—HiN
Saint Francis and the birds.—MaFw
Storm on the island.—HiN
Turkeys observed.—MaFw
Twice shy.—HiN
"**Heaps** of headlights." See Passing by the junkyard
"**Hear,** O my son, and receive my sayings." See Proverbs, Bible, Old Testament—The two paths
"**Hear** the fluter with his flute." See The amateur flute
"**Hear** the sledges with the bells." See The bells
Hear this. Myra Cohn Livingston.—LiM
Heard in a violent ward. Theodore Roethke.—PlM
Hearing
Hearing the wind at night. M. Swenson.—HaWr
Listening ("I can hear kittens and cows and dogs") H. Behn.—UnGb
Listening ("My father could hear a little animal step") W. Stafford.—MoT
"Old woman, old woman (shall we go)." Mother Goose.—HoMg
A robin. A. Fisher.—FiFo—LaM
The shell. D. McCord.—JoA-4—LiLc—McS
Hearing the wind at night. May Swenson.—HaWr
Heart
Can you can't. D. Whitewing.—AlW
The eyes or the heart. A. N. B. J. Bhalo.—AlPa
In the great night. Unknown.—BiI
"The **heart** of the mountain goat is broken when it falls below." Unknown, tr. fr. the Tsimshian.—ClFc
"The **heart,** that hideous bear." See Falling in love
Heart's content. Unknown.—RoIt
The **heart's** journey, sel. Siegfried Sassoon
"What is Stonehenge? It is the roofless past."—PaP
Heart's needle. W. D. Snodgrass.—HiN (sel.)
Heat
Heat. H. D.—PaF
Shiver my timbers. D. McCord.—McAa
Heat. H. D.—PaF
"**Heat** clamps down." See Shower bath
Heath-Stubbs, John
A charm against toothache.—MaFw
Epitaph.—ToM
The history of the flood.—MaFw
The poet of Bray.—PlM
The starling.—MaFw—ToM
Heath-Stubbs, John (about)
Epitaph. J. Heath-Stubbs.—ToM
Heather ale. Robert Louis Stevenson.—CoPt
Heaven
Above the bright blue sky. A. Midlane.—OpOx
"An awful tempest mashed the air." E. Dickinson.—ThI
The blessed damozel. D. G. Rossetti.—LiS (sel.)
"The dead who climb up to the sky." Unknown.—LeIb
The fiddler of Dooney. W. B. Yeats.—JoA-4—RoIt
For a lady I know. C. Cullen.—AbM—LiWw
Four epitaphs.—AdPb
For a mouthy woman. C. Cullen.—AbM—AdPb
Heaven. L. Hughes.—HoD—JoA-4

Heaven-haven. G. M. Hopkins.—JoA-4
The heaven of animals. J. Dickey.—HiN
The heavenly song. Unknown.—LeIb
Hunchback girl: She thinks of heaven. G. Brooks.—PeS
"I never saw a moor." E. Dickinson.—JoA-4—LiLc
"I wish you health." Unknown.—EmN
"If ever I go to Paradise." Unknown.—MoBw
"Mrs Malone." E. Farjeon.—OpOx
"My thoughts went constantly." Unknown.—LeIb
The night-wind. E. Brontë.—PaF
On slaughter. C. N. Bialik.—MeP
"The opposites of *earth* are two." R. Wilbur.—WiO
Sister Lou. S. A. Brown.—AdPb
"Small bird, forgive me." Unknown.—BeM
Song of a dead one. Unknown.—LeIb
"There's an autograph book in heaven." Unknown.—EmN
"Think of me early." Unknown.—EmN
To Theodora. Unknown.—OpOx
"Within this book so pure and white." Unknown.—EmN
Heaven. Langston Hughes.—HoD—JoA-4
"**Heaven,** ask pity for me." See On slaughter
Heaven-haven. Gerard Manley Hopkins.—JoA-4
"**Heaven** is." See Heaven
The **heaven** of animals. James Dickey.—HiN
The **heavenly** song. Unknown, fr. the Ammassalik Eskimo.—LeIb
"**Heavy** breathing fills all my chamber." See August 24, 1963—1:00 a.m.—Omaha
"A **heavy** cart rumbles." Kuroyanagi Shōha, tr. fr. the Japanese by Geoffrey Bownas and Alexander Thwaite.—MaFw
"**Heavy** with length of days, summer continues." See The visitor
Hebrides crofter's prayer. Unknown.—CoPu
Hecht, Anthony
It out-Herods Herod, pray you, avoid it.—HiN
Lizards and snakes.—HiN
"**Hector** Protector was dressed all in green." Mother Goose.—AlC
"**Hector** the collector." Shel Silverstein.—SiW
"A **hedgehog** lives in hedges." See Vice versa verse
Hedgehogs. See Porcupines
"The **heifer** eyed us both and chose." See Fur coat
"**Heigh-ho** Silver everywhere." Unknown.—EmN
The **height** of the ridiculous. Oliver Wendell Holmes.—RoIt
Helga. Carl Sandburg.—SaT
"A **helicopter** in the sky." See Street scene
Helicopters
Street scene. P. Suffolk.—CoPt
Hell
"Ah Faustus." From The tragical history of Doctor Faustus. C. Marlowe.—MaFw
For a mouthy woman. C. Cullen.—AbM—AdPb
Hell's pavement. J. Masefield.—CoPt
"Judging from the pictures." K. Senryū.—MaFw
No hiding place. Unknown.—BrW
"**Hello** Mr Python." Spike Milligan.—CoOh
"**Hello's** a handy word to say." Mary Ann Hoberman.—HoN
Hell's pavement. John Masefield.—CoPt
Help. X. J. Kennedy.—KeO
Helpers
Helping. S. Silverstein.—SiW—ThF
Helpfulness. See Service
Helping. Shel Silverstein.—SiW—ThF
"**Hemlock** and pine." See Evergreen
The **hen** and the carp. Ian Serraillier.—LiWw
Henderson, David
Do nothing till you hear from me.—AdPb
Keep on pushing.—AdPb
The Louisiana weekly #4.—AdPb
Number 5—December.—AdB
They are killing all the young men.—AdPb
Walk with de Mayor of Harlem.—AdPb
White people.—AdPb
Henderson, Harold G.
"A trout leaps high." tr.—MaFw
Hendrix, Jimi
Gypsy eyes.—MoG
Henley, William Ernest
Ballade.—PaF
Invictus.—RoIt
London voluntary.—PaP
Henri, Adrian
Adrian Henri's talking after Christmas blues.—ToM
"Tonight at noon."—ToM
Henry V, sels. William Shakespeare
The horse.—RoIt
King Henry's speech before Agincourt.—MaF
Henry VIII, King of England
Song.—MaFw
Henry VIII, King of England (about)
Henry VIII. E. and H. Farjeon.—CoPt
Henry VIII. Eleanor and Herbert Farjeon.—CoPt
Henry VIII, sel. William Shakespeare
"Orpheus with his lute made trees"
Music.—RoIt
Henry, John (about)
John Henry. Unknown.—AbM
Strange legacies. S. A. Brown.—AdPb
"**Henry** was a young king." Robert Graves.—AlC
"**Henry** was every morning fed." See The boy and the snake
"**Henry's** in the White House." Unknown.—MoBw
Henry's secret. Dorothy Kilner.—OpOx
Hens. See Chickens
The **hens.** Elizabeth Madox Roberts.—LiLc—UnGb
"**Her** eyes at night." See My cat

"Her eyes were gentle; her voice was for soft singing." See An old woman remembers
"Her face like a rain-beaten stone on the day she rolled off." See Elegy
"Her hand which touched my hand she moved away." See On a hand
Her legs. Robert Herrick.—LiS
"Her mama said, Don't eat with your fingers." See Ridiculous Rose
"Her scarf à la Bardot." See Twice shy
Her song. Thomas Hardy.—PlP
Her story. Naomi Long Madgett.—AdPb
Heraclitus (about)
Heraclitus. Callimachus.—CoPu—PlM
Heraclitus. Callimachus, tr. fr. the Greek by William Cory.—CoPu—PlM
Herbert, George
"By all means use sometimes to be alone."—CoPu
Herbs
Parsley for vice-president. O. Nash.—LiWw
"Rosemary green." Mother Goose.—AlC
The **herdboy.** Lu Yu, tr. fr. the Chinese by Arthur Waley.—MaFw
Herder, Johann Gottfried
The erl-king's daughter.—CoPt
Herdsmen
A drover. P. Colum.—CoPi
The herdboy. Lu Yu.—MaFw
Swineherd. E. N. Chuilleanáin.—CoPi
"Here a little child I stand." See Another grace
"Here am I." Unknown, tr. fr. the Teton Sioux by Frances Densmore.—JoT
"Here am I, a shape under a cedar." See Sitting in the woods: A contemplation
"Here am I, little jumping Joan." Mother Goose.—AlC
"Here and there in the searing beam." See Deer among cattle
"Here are sweet peas, on tiptoe for a flight." See "I stood tiptoe upon a little hill"—Sweet peas
"Here are the twins." Shel Silverstein.—CoOh
"Here come the elephants, ten feet high." Jack Prelutsky.—PrC
"Here come the line-gang pioneering by." See The line-gang
"Here comes a candle to light you to bed." Mother Goose.—AlC
"Here comes our noble." Issa, tr. fr. the Japanese by Harry Behn.—BeM
Here I am. Myra Cohn Livingston.—LiM
"Here I am, bully." See Here I am
"Here I come forth." See Song of the deer
"Here I go up, up, up." See Elevator boy
"Here I stand." See Ask the mountains
"Here I stand." See Religious hymn to be sung wearing a head decoration of the skin of the great northern diver
"Here I stand all nice and clean." Unknown.—MoBw
"Here I stand on two little chips." Unknown.—MoBw
"Here in the newspaper—the wreck of the East Bound." See It's here in the
"Here in the scuffled dust." See Heart's needle
"Here is a place that is no place." See The patient: Rockland County sanitarium
"Here is a thing my heart wishes the world had more of." See Poems done on a late night car—Home
"Here is cruel Frederick, see." See Cruel Frederick
"Here is the ancient floor." See The self-unseeing
"Here its like that." See Blue Tanganyika
"Here lie I. Martin Elginbrodde." See Epitaph in Elgin cathedral
"Here lies a man who always thought." See Prig: Epitaph
"Here lies a most beautiful lady." See An epitaph
"Here lies John Bun." See John Bun
"Here lies old Jones." Unknown.—LiWw
"Here lies our Sovereign Lord the King." See Epitaph on Charles II
"Here lies resting, out of breath." See Little elegy
"Here lies the body of Jonathan Pound." Unknown.—TrG
"Here lies the body of Robert Low." Unknown.—CoPu
"Here lies the lighthouse-keeper's horse." See Epitaph for a lighthouse-keeper's horse
"Here lies the poet, deaf and dumb." See Lines for a dead poet
"Here lies wrapped up tight in sod." See Epitaph for a postal clerk
"Here lieth one whose name was writ on water." See On Keats
"Here, little fawn." See Little deer
"Here lyes." See An epitaph on my dear and ever honoured mother Mrs Dorothy Dudley
"Here she comes." See Mom's mums
Here she is. Mary Britton Miller.—AdP
"Here something stubborn comes." See Seed leaves
"Here sparrows build upon the trees." See My early home
"Here stands a good apple tree." See An apple-tree rhyme
"Here the hangman stops his cart." See A Shropshire lad—The carpenter's Son
"Here they are. The soft eyes open." See The heaven of animals
"Here they lie fermenting." See Judgment
"Here we bring new water." See A new year carol
"Here we come a-piping." Unknown.—JoA-4
"Here we come a-wassailing." Unknown.—MaF
"Here we come a-whistling through the fields so green." See Twelfth night carol
"Here we stand." See Conflict
Here where Coltrane is. Michael S. Harper.—AdPb
"Here's A, B, and C." See A learned song

"Here's a baby. Here's another." See Twins
"Here's a body—there's a bed." See Good night
"Here's a health to the birds one and all." See A health to the birds
"Here's a nice advice." See Advice
"Here's a song of Tinker & Peter." C. Watson.—WaF
"Here's luck and hoping you sit on a tack." Unknown.—EmN
"Here's that little girl who wraps each gift." See A Christmas package
"Here's the place: stand still: how fearful." See King Lear
"Here's Tom Thumb." Mother Goose.—TucMgl
"Hereto I come to view a voiceless ghost." See After a journey
Herford, Oliver
The cantankerous 'gator.—BrM
The elf and the dormouse.—JaP—UnGb
A fable.—MaF
The fall of J. W. Beane.—CoPt
The gnat and the gnu.—BrM
"I heard a bird sing."—LiLc
A personal experience.—BrM
The platypus.—LiWw
The provident puffin.—BrM
The snail's dream.—BrM
Song.—LiS
Heritage
Ask the mountains. P. George.—AlW
Battle won is lost. P. George.—AlW
Beyond melody. N. Alterman.—MeP
Bottled: New York. H. Johnson.—AdPb
The four directions. E. B. Mitchell.—AlW
Heritage ("I want to see the slim palm trees") G. B. Bennett.—AdPb
Heritage ("What is Africa to me") C. Cullen.—AdPb
"I know everything in the bottom of my heart." Unknown.—ClFc
I was the moon. Y. Amichai.—MeP
If I should ever by chance. E. Thomas.—OpOx
O Daedalus, fly away home. R. Hayden.—AdPb—HiN
Of bloom. L. Goldberg.—MeP
The ploughboy in luck. Unknown.—RoIt
Rejoinder. J. Ekwere.—AlPa
The return. A. Bontemps.—AdPb
Sebonwoma. C. A. A. Aidoo.—AlPa (sel.)
A sense of property. A. Thwaite.—ToM
Song of the strange woman. L. Goldberg.—MeP
The Southern road. D. Randall.—AdPb
These days. C. Olsen.—MoT
Untitled. A. Lopez.—AlW
Heritage—Black
Black star line. H. Dumas.—AdPb
Bwagamoyo. L. Bethune.—AdPb
Effendi. M. S. Harper.—AdPb
For Eusi, Ayi Kwei & Gwen Brooks. K. Kgositsile.—AdPb
In Orangeburg my brothers did." A. B. Spellman.—AdPb
Ju Ju. A. M. Touré.—AdPb
The living truth. S. Plumpp.—AdPb
Now poem, for us. S. Sanchez.—AdPb
A poem for integration. A. Saxon.—AdPb
Tauhid. A. M. Touré.—AdPb
Heritage ("I want to see the slim palm trees") Gwendolyn B. Bennett.—AdPb
Heritage ("What is Africa to me") Countee Cullen.—AdPb
The **hermit.** Hsü Pên, tr. fr. the Chinese by Henry H. Hart.—MaFw
Hermits
The hermit. Hsü Pên.—MaFw
"In a hermit's cottage, silent, still." Kim Soo-jang.—BaSs
Mr Metter. N. M. Bodecker.—BoL
Riley. C. Causley.—CaF
The tale of the hermit told. A. Reid.—CoPt
The three hermits. W. B. Yeats.—MaFw
Hernton, Calvin C.
"D blues."—AdPb
The distant drum.—AdB
Fall down.—AdPb
Jitterbugging in the streets.—AdPb
The patient: Rockland County sanitarium.—AdPb
Herod, King of the Jews (about)
Innocent's song. C. Causley.—ToM
"It out-Herods Herod, pray you, avoid it. A. Hecht.—HiN
The **heroes.** Louis Simpson.—PeS
Heroes and heroines. See also names of heroes as, Douglass, Frederick
The Golden Vanity. Unknown.—RoIt
"He is more than a hero." Sappho.—ThI
The heroes. L. Simpson.—PeS
"I think continually of those who were truly great." S. Spender.—RoIt
A song of greatness. Unknown.—JoA-4
To some millions who survive Joseph E. Mander, Senior. S. E. Wright.—AdPb
Heroism. See Heroes and heroines
Herons
"Dragonflies and herons fly together." Kim Chun-taik.—BaSs
Egrets. Judith Wright.—AdP—HiN—JoA-4
"Hidden by darkness." Bashō.—BeM
Herrick, Robert
Another grace.—OpOx
Another on her.—LiS
A child's present.—OpOx
Corinna's going a-Maying.—MaF
God to be first served.—OpOx
A grace for children.—OpOx
Her legs.—LiS
His prayer to Ben Jonson.—PlM
"Now, now the mirth comes."—MaF
To daffadills.—PaF
To daffodils.—JoA-4
To daffodils. See To daffadills
To get thine ends.—RoIt
To music to becalme his fever.—RoIt
To the virgins, to make much of time.—LiS
Upon his Julia.—LiS

"**Higgledy-piggledy** (Ludwig van Beethoven)." E. William Seaman.—LiWw
"**Higgledy** piggledy (wiggledy wump)." Dennis Lee.—LeA
"**High** as a house." Unknown.—EmN
The **High** Barbaree. Laura E. Richards.—JoA-4
"**High** diddle ding." Mother Goose.—AlC
"The **high-diver** climbs to the ladder's top." Jack Prelutsky.—PrC
"**High** in the pine tree." Mother Goose.—TucMgl
"**High** in the sky I go." See Dream song
"The **high** majesty of Paul's." See London voluntary
"**High** on the thrilling strand he dances." See Tightrope walker
"**High-rise** project." Lois Lenski.—LeC
The **high** school band. Reed Whittemore.—HiN
"**High** upon highlands." See Bonnie George Campbell
Higheagle, Robert P. See Densmore, Frances and Higheagle, Robert P. jt. trs.
Higher. Unknown.—LiS
The **higher** pantheism. Alfred Tennyson.—LiS
The **higher** pantheism in a nutshell. Algernon Charles Swinburne.—LiS
"The **higher** the mountains." Unknown.—MoBw
"**Highway** turnpike thruway mall." See A charm for our time
The **highwayman's** ghost. Richard Garnett.—CoPt
Highwaymen. See Crime and criminals
Highways. See also Roads and trails
  Freeway. M. C. Livingston.—LiM
  Southbound on the freeway. M. Swenson.—PeS
  The toll taker. P. Hubbell.—HoCs
Higo, Aig
  Myself my slogan.—AlPa
Hiking. See Camping and hiking
Hill, Donald L.
  The buzzing doubt.—HiN
Hill, Leslie Pinckney
  So quietly.—AdPb
"**Hill** blue among the leaves in summer." See Cheap blue
The **hill** farmer speaks. R. S. Thomas.—ToM
"A **hill** flank overlooking the Axe valley." See Watching post
Hillel, Omer
  At the scorpions' ascent.—MeP
Hillert, Margaret
  A Christmas lullaby.—HoS
Hillery, Edmund
  "Summer."—HoC
Hills. See also Mountains
  "Clouds of morning mist." Busōn.—BeM
  "Has a drift of snow." Bashō.—BeM
  The hills. R. Field.—LiLc
  "Hills have disappeared." Joso.—BeM
  Miracle hill. E. B. Mitchell.—AlW
  On Holmburg hill. E. Shanks.—PaP
  On Sweet Killen hill. T. MacIntyre.—HiN
  Six-month song in the foothills. G. Snyder.—HaWr
  The sleeping giant. D. Hall.—HiN
  The Wrekin. From Adbaston. C. B. Ash.—PaP
The **hills.** Rachel Field.—LiLc
"**Hills** have disappeared." Joso, tr. fr. the Japanese by Harry Behn.—BeM
Hints on pronunciation for foreigners. T. S. W.—MaFw
"**Hinty,** minty, cuty, corn." Unknown
  Counting-out rhymes.—RoIt
"**Hippity** hop." Unknown.—EmN
The **hippo.** Theodore Roethke.—CoPu
"A **hippo** sandwich is easy to make." See Recipe for a hippopotamus sandwich
Hippopotami
  Grammar. M. H. Ets.—BrM
  The hippo. T. Roethke.—CoPu
  The hippopotamus ("The huge hippopotamus hasn't a hair") J. Prelutsky.—CoOr—PrT
  The hippopotamus ("I shoot the hippopotamus with bullets made of platinum") H. Belloc.—BrM
  Hippopotamus ("Pygmy hippopota—)" M. A. Hoberman.—HoR
  "Most people don't know it." Unknown.—EmN
  Recipe for a hippopotamus sandwich. S. Silverstein.—SiW
The **hippopotamus** ("The huge hippopotamus hasn't a hair") Jack Prelutsky.—CoOr—PrT
The **hippopotamus** ("I shoot the hippopotamus with bullets made of platinum") Hilaire Belloc.—BrM
Hippopotamus ("Pygmy hippopota—") Mary Ann Hoberman.—HoR
"**His** angle-rod made of a sturdy oak." See The giant fisherman
His answer to the critics. Solomon ibn Gabirol, tr. fr. the Hebrew by Robert Mezey.—MeP
His brother after dinner. See Uncle Bull-boy
"**His** desires, growing." See Black man's feast
"**His** drifter swung in the night." See Uncle Roderick
"**His** exclamation was *Chaste stars* not *Chase tars.*" Unknown.—EmN
"**His** gaze, going past those bars, has got so misted." See The panther
"**His** headstone said." See The funeral of Martin Luther King, Jr
"**His** lips move unceasingly." See Zebu
"**His** lordship's steed." See Riding
"**His** name is." See Rubin
His prayer to Ben Jonson. Robert Herrick.—PlM
"**His** shirt soon shrank in the suds." Unknown.—EmN
"**His** Spirit in smoke ascended to high heaven." See The lynching
His wife. Rachel, tr. fr. the Hebrew by Robert Friend.—MeP
"**Hist** whist." E. E. Cummings.—HoH

"Where in the world are the animals from."—HoR
Who am I (I).—HoLb
Who am I (II).—HoLb
"Windshield wipers wipe the windshield."—HoN
Wish.—HoR
Worm.—HoLb
"X."—HoN
"Yes."—HoN
"Zebra starts with Z—just look."—HoN
Zoogeography.—HoR
Hoboes
The big Rock Candy mountain. Unknown.—CoOh
The big Rock Candy mountains.—PeS
Hobsbaum, Philip
The place's fault.—ToM
Hockey. See Ice hockey
Hockey. Bob McLaughlin.—FlH
The **hockey** game. Dennis Lee.—LeA
Hockman, Sandra
Love song for a jellyfish.—CoPu
Hoddesdon. A. S. Wilson.—PaP
Hoddley, poddley. Unknown.—BlM
"**Hoddley,** poddley, puddle and fogs." See Hoddley, poddley
Hodgson, Ralph
After.—JoA-4
The bells of Heaven.—JoA-4
Eve.—CoPt
The great auk's ghost.—LiWw
"Time, you old gipsy man."—RoIt
Hoeing. John Updike.—MoT
Hoey, Edwin A.
Foul shot.—FlH
Hoffenstein, Samuel
From Mr Walter De La Mare makes the little ones dizzy.—LiS
Poems in praise of practically nothing, sels.
"You buy some flowers for your table."—LiWw
"You leap out of bed; you start to get ready."—LiWw
"You take a bath and sit there bathing."—LiWw
"You buy some flowers for your table." See Poems in praise of practically nothing
"You leap out of bed; you start to get ready." See Poems in praise of practically nothing
"You take a bath and sit there bathing." See Poems in praise of practically nothing
"Your little hands."—LiWw
Hoffman, Heinrich
Cruel Frederick.—LiS
The story of Augustus who would not have any soup.—LiS—OpOx
The story of Fidgety Philip.—OpOx
The story of Flying Robert.—LiS
The story of Johnny Head-in-Air.—OpOx
The story of little Suck-a-Thumb.—LiS
Hogg, James
A boy's song.—OpOx
Hogmanay
"Hogmanay." Unknown.—MaF
"**Hogmanay.**" Unknown.—MaF
Hogs. See Pigs
Hoh, Kafu
"A baby is a European." tr.—AlPa
The sky. tr.—AbM—AlPa
The sun. tr.—AlPa
Hoijer, Harry
First man was the first to emerge. tr.—BiI
"**Hokey,** pokey, whisky, thum." Mother Goose.—MiMg
Hokku/haikai/haiku. Myra Cohn Livingston.—LiM
Hokku poems. Richard Wright.—AdPb
"**Hold** fast to dreams." See Dreams
"**Hold** my hand, look away." See Fourth of July
"**Hold** on tight." See Baby monkey
Hole, Carol Combs
Sam at the library.—BrM
Holes
Flying out of holes. D. Lee.—LeA
For real. J. Cortez.—AdPb
My father. T. Hughes.—HuMf
"The opposite of a *hole's* a heap." R. Wilbur.—WiO
"There's a hole in my bucket, dear Conrad, dear Conrad." Mother Goose.—TucMg
"**Holes** in my arms." See For real
Holidays. See also names of holidays, as Christmas; Fourth of July
"I often pause and wonder." Unknown.—BrM
Monument in black. V. Howard.—AdM—JoV
Holland, Jerome
Ago love.—JoV
If everybody was black.—JoV
My intrigue.—JoV
Supernatural.—JoV
Tiny world.—JoV
Will I make it.—JoV
Holland
Such is Holland. P. A. De Genestet.—MaFw
Holland—Nursery rhymes. See Nursery rhymes—Dutch
"**Holland.**" Unknown.—MoBw
Hollander. John
Historical reflections.—LiWw
Wrath.—LiWw
Holliday, Billie (about)
Blues and bitterness. L. Bennett, Jr.—AdPb
Hollo, Anselm
Bimbo's pome. tr.—MaFw
Guadalupe, W. I. tr.—AbM
Hollyhocks
Hollyhocks. V. Worth.—WoS
Hollyhocks. V. Worth.—WoS
"**Hollyhocks** stand in clumps." See Hollyhocks
Holman, Felice
"Above the tree."—HoI
"An ant."—HoI
April snow.—HoI
Canada geese.—HoI
Celebrations of the day.—HoI
The child who cried.—HoI

"Now this was the reply Odysseus made." See The Odyssey
The Odyssey, sels.
The boar hunt.—MaFw
"Now this was the reply Odysseus made."—PlM
"The siren's song."—MoG
The siren's song. See The Odyssey
Homer (about)
On Homer's birthplace. T. Heyward.—PlM
Seven wealthy towns. Unknown.—CoPu
"**Homer** Beecher." See Mr Beecher
Homesick. Lois Lenski.—LeC
Homesickness
Aqalàni. Unknown.—BiI
The bear. L. Lenski.—LeC
The call of the fells. H. Palmer.—PaP
The County Mayo. A. Raftery, tr. by J. Stephens.—CoPi
Home no more. R. L. Stevenson.—RoIt
Home thoughts from abroad. R. Browning.—JoA-4—RoIt
Homesick. L. Lenski.—LeC
A husband's song. Unknown.—BiI
I've got a home in that rock. . . . R. R. Patterson.—AdM—AdPb
Message from a mouse, ascending in a rocket. P. Hubbell.—HoP
The mountains of Mourne. P. French.—CoPi
My heart is in the East. Judah Halevi.—MeP
Number 5—December. D. Henderson.—AdB
The oak and the ash. Unknown.—RoIt
That mountain far away. Unknown.—BiI
The tropics in New York. C. McKay.—AdPb—RoIt
The west wind. J. Masefield.—PaP—RoIt
Homework. Russell Hoban.—HoE
"**Homework** sits on top of Sunday, squashing Sunday flat." See Homework
Honesty. See Truthfulness and falsehood
Honey. See also Bees
Bees. R. Hoban.—HoE
"A dish full of all kinds of flowers." Unknown.—EmN
Sing a song of honey. B. E. Todd.—PaF
A taste of honey. K. D. Kuka.—AlW
"**Honey.**" See Sister Lou
"**Honey** from the white rose, honey from the red." See Sing a song of honey
"**Honey** people murder mercy U.S.A." See In memoriam, Martin Luther King, Jr
"**Honey,** pepper, leaf-green limes." See Jamaica market
"**Honeybees** are very tricky." See Bees
Hong Nang
"These few shoots cut from a mountain willow."—BaSs
"**Honk**—honk—honk." See City street
Honky. Charles Cooper.—AdPb
Honor
"I shall bring honour to my blood." I. Diaw.—AlPa
"**Honorable** Toad." Issa, tr. fr. the Japanese by Hanako Fukuda.—HaW
"**Honour** thy parents; but good manners call." See God to be first served
Hood, Thomas
Good night.—JoA-4
"I remember, I remember."—RoIt
Mary's ghost.—CoPt—LiWw
Merrily float.—JaP
November.—RoIt
Ode: Autumn.—PaF
The poet's fate.—CoPu
Queen Mab.—JaP (sel.)
The time of roses.—RoIt
To Henrietta, on her departure for Calais.—OpOx
Hood, Thomas (about)
Thomas Hood. E. A. Robinson.—PlM
Hood, Tom, Jr
The cannibal flea.—LiS
Hook, Theodore
Cautionary verses to youth of both sexes.—OpOx
"**Hooray.** Here comes the great parade." Jack Prelutsky.—PrC
"**Hooting.**" See Halloween
Hope
The darkling thrush. T. Hardy.—PaF—PlP—RoIt
"A frosty dawn, a waning moon." Unknown.—BaSs
Hope ("Jade charm of human life") Juana Inez De la Cruz.—ThI
Hope ("Sometimes when I'm lonely") L. Hughes.—HoD
Hope and joy. C. G. Rossetti.—OpOx
Love without hope. R. Graves.—CoPu
Pandora. M. C. Livingston.—LiM—NeA
Hope ("Jade charm of human life") Juana Inez De la Cruz, tr. fr. the Mexican by Judith Thurman.—ThI
Hope ("Sometimes when I'm lonely") Langston Hughes.—HoD
Hope and joy. Christina Georgina Rossetti.—OpOx
"**Hope** is like a harebell trembling from its birth." See Comparisons
Hope to keep. Agnes T. Pratt.—AlW
Hopi Indians. See Indians of the Americas—Hopi
Hopkins, Gerard Manley
Binsey poplars felled 1879.—MaFw
The candle indoors.—MaFw
Duns Scotus's Oxford, sel.
"Towery city and branchy between towers."—PaP
Heaven-haven.—JoA-4
Hurrahing in harvest.—MaFw
On a poetess.—CoPu
Pied beauty.—MaFw—RoIt
"Repeat that, repeat."—MaFw
Spring.—PaF
The starlight night.—JoA-4
To R. B.—PlM
"Towery city and branchy between towers." See Duns Scotus's Oxford

Upon the horse and his rider. J. Bunyan.—OpOx
Watering the horse. R. Bly.—HiN
"What horse is trying to catch me." Unknown.—ClFc
"Wilt thou lend me thy mare to go a mile." Unknown.—CoPu
Wind horses. C. Sandburg.—SaT
Ye carpette knyghte. L. Carroll.—LiPc
Horses ("And some are sulky, while some will plunge") Rudyard Kipling.—CoPu
The **horses** ("I climbed through woods in the hour-before-dawn dark") Ted Hughes.—HaWr
Horses ("Standing up for sleeping") Aileen Fisher.—FiFo
Horses aboard. Thomas Hardy.—PlP
"**Horses** in horseclothes stand in a row." See Horses aboard
"The **horses** of the sea." Christina Georgina Rossetti.—LiLc—RoIt
"The **horses** run around." Unknown.—CoH
Hosea
Hosea, sel. Bible, Old Testament
"Rejoice not, O Israel, for joy."—MeP
"Rejoice not, O Israel, for joy." See Hosea
Hoskyns, John
To his little son Benedict from the Tower of London.—OpOx
Hospital / poem. Sonia Sanchez.—AdPb
Hospitality
The frugal host. Automedon.—LiWw
Hospitality. J. B. Tabb.—BrM
"If things were better." Issa.—HaW—LiWw
October. M. Sendak.—HoH
"With my harp against my knee." Kim Chang-up.—BaSs
Hospitality. John Banister Tabb.—BrM
Hospitals
Heard in a violent ward. T. Roethke.—PlM
Hospital / poem. S. Sanchez.—AdPb
"**Hot** boiled beans and very good butter." Unknown.—EmN
Hot cake. Shu Hsi, tr. fr. the Chinese by Arthur Waley.—MaFw
"**Hot-cross** buns." Mother Goose.—JoA-4—LaM
The **hot** day. Marchette Chute.—ChRu
"**Hot** dog hot." Lois Lenski.—LeC
"**Hot** dogs with sauerkraut." See Get 'em here
Hot line to the nursery. David McCord.—McFm
"**Hot** time." Amelia Trias.—HoC
A **hot** weather song. Don Marquis.—CoPu
Hotels. See Inns and taverns
"**Hotness.**" Amelia Copeman.—HoC
"A **hound** sound." See Flight
The **hour.** Uri Zui Greenberg, tr. fr. the Hebrew by Robert Mezey and Ben Zion Gold.—MeP
"The **hour** is very weary, as before sleep." See The hour
"The **hour** of midnight met with a gathering of mothers." See Kariuki
"The **house** at the corner." Myra Cohn Livingston.—HoH
House blessing. Unknown, tr. fr. the Navajo by Cosmo Mindeleff.—BiI
"**House** ghost." Linda May.—HoC
House guest. Elizabeth Bishop.—HiN
"The **house** is in ruins." Irina Ivanova, tr. fr. the Russian by Miriam Morton.—MoM
"A **house** like a man all lean and coughing." See Even numbers
The **house** mouse. Jack Prelutsky.—PrP
"The **house** of snail upon his back." Karla Kuskin.—KuN
The **house** of the goblin. Susan Brown.—HoH
"The **house** on the hill." See Empty house song
The **house** on the hill. Edwin Arlington Robinson.—RoIt
The **house** that Jack built. See "This is the house that Jack built"
House to let." Mother Goose.—AlC
"The **house** was shaken by a rising wind." See Brainstorm
Household song. Unknown, tr. fr. the Amhara by Sylvia Pankhurst.—AlPa
The **housekeeper.** Charles Lamb.—RoIt
Housekeepers and housekeeping. See also Servants
Cleaning house. X. J. Kennedy.—KeO
Contemporary nursery rhyme. Unknown.—LiS
Home. E. Montgomery.—JoV
Housework. S. Harnick.—ThF
Washing windows. B. Spacks.—HiN
Housekeeping. See Housekeepers and housekeeping
Houses
"An ant." F. Holman.—HoI
Beautiful is our lodge. Unknown.—BiS
Beyond the hunting woods. D. Justice.—HiN
Bobadil. J. Reeves.—LiLc
The camel's complaint. From The admiral's caravan. C. E. Carryl.—JoA-4—OpOx
"The Chief of the world." N. Belting.—BeWi
"Cricket, my boy." Issa.—HaW
"Crow Indian." Unknown.—ClFc
"Don't mind my small hut." Issa.—HaW
Empty house song. L. Moore.—MoSm
Enter this deserted house. S. Silverstein.—SiW
Even numbers. C. Sandburg.—SaT
"Good heavens." Issa.—HaW
"The house at the corner." M. C. Livingston.—HoH
House blessing. Unknown.—BiI
The house of the goblin. S. Brown.—HoH
The house on the hill. E. A. Robinson.—RoIt
"House to let." Mother Goose.—AlC
The housekeeper. C. Lamb.—RoIt
"In my house this spring." Sodo.—BeM
In the kitchen of the old house. D. Hall.—ToM
"The lands around my dwelling." Unknown.—BiI—LaM
Little girl. Unknown.—JoA-4

"How do we tell if a window is open." See Stone telling
"How do you know that the pilgrim track." See The year's awakening
"How do you like to go up in a swing." See The swing
"How does the water." See The cataract of Lodore
How doth. See Alice's adventures in wonderland—"How doth the little crocodile"
"How doth the little busy bee." See Against idleness and mischief
"How doth the little crocodile." See Alice's adventures in wonderland
"How falls it oriole, thou hast come to fly." See To an oriole
"How fared you when you mortal were." See After
How foolish. Peter Wells.—BrM
"How God hath labored to produce the duck." Donald Hall.—CoPu
"How grand beneath the feet that company." See The Mendip hills over Wells
"How happy is he born and taught." See The character of a happy life.
"How hard is my fortune." See The convict of Clonmel
"How high the moon. Lance Jeffers.—AdPb
How I brought the good news from Aix to Ghent (or vice versa). R. J. Yeatman and W. C. Sellar.—LiS
"How I wish I could pigeon-hole myself." See The pigeon-hole
"How I'd like to live." Yang Ung-Jeung, tr. fr. the Korean by Chung Seuk Park and ad. by Virginia Olsen Baron.—BaSs
"How is it with him, your Alapa." See The real slayer of the seal
"How is it with you." See Complaint over bad hunting
How it is. Uri Zui Greenberg, tr. fr. the Hebrew by Robert Mezey and Ben Zion Gold.—MeP
"How limp they lie." See The kittens
"How long hast thou been a gravemaker." David Perkins.—HiN
"How long shall I pine for love." See Pining for love
"How lovely is the sound of oars at night." See Boats at night
How many ("How many seconds in a minute") Christina Georgina Rossetti.—RoIt
How many ("A mother skunk all black and white") Mary Ann Hoberman.—HoLb
"How many bullets does it take." See Death in Yorkville
"How many days to Christmas." See Counting the days
"How many islands in the bay." See Islands in Boston harbor
"How many miles to Babylon." Mother Goose.—AlC—JoA-4
"How many miles to Boston town." Unknown.—EmN
"How many miles to Old Norfolk." Clyde Watson.—WaF
"How many nights, oh, how many nights." See New Year's day
"How many seconds in a minute." See How many
"How much wood would a woodchuck chuck." Mother Goose.—EmN—JoA-4
"How nice to be." See The frog
"How perfect." See A piece of sky
"How pleasant it is." See Morning
"How pleasant to know Mr Lear." Edward Lear.—LiS—PlM
Lines to a young lady.—RoIt
"How pure, how beautiful, how fine." See Speaking of television—Reflections dental
"How rewarding to know Mr Smith." See Mr Smith (with nods to Mr Lear and Mr Eliot)
How Robin Hood rescued the widow's sons. Unknown.—CoPt
"How sad, they think, to see him homing nightly." See Academic
"How shall I be a poet." See Poeta fit, non nascitur
"How shall I begin my song." Unknown, tr. fr. the Papago.—ClFc
"How she has now become." See Young lady's song of retort
"How she held up the horses' heads." See A woman driving
How she resolved to act. Merrill Moore.—PeS
"How silent comes the water round that bend." See "I stood tip-toe upon a little hill"—Minnows
"How soothing sound the gentle airs that move." See Avenue in Savernake forest
"How still." See Sea calm
How still, how happy. Emily Brontë."—PaF
"How still, how happy. Those are words."—PaP
"How still, how happy. Those are words." See How still, how happy
"How straight it flew, how long it flew." See Seaside golf
"How strange to think of giving up all ambition." See Watering the horse
"How sweet is the shepherd's sweet lot." See The shepherd
"How swift along the winding way." See Upon boys diverting themselves in the river
"How the days went." See Now that I am forever with child
How the days will be. Unknown, tr. fr. the Zuñi by Ruth Bunzel.—BiI
How they brought the good news from Ghent to Aix. Robert Browning.—LiS
"How thin and sharp is the moon tonight." See Winter moon
How to catch tiddlers." Brian Jones.—MaFw
How to draw a monkey. David McCord.—McFm—McS

Sailor.—HoD
Sea calm.—HoD
Seascape.—HoD
Shepherd's song at Christmas.—AbM
Shout.—HoD
Snail.—AbM—HoD—JoA-4
Song for a dark girl.—AdPb
Special bulletin.—AdPb
Stars.—HoD
Suicide's note.—HoD
Sun song.—AdM—HoD
"Tambourines."—HoD
Troubled woman.—HoD
Verse written in the album of mademoiselle. tr.—AbM
Walkers with the dawn.—HoD
Water-front streets.—HoD
When Sue wears red.—JoA-4
Winter moon.—AbM—HoD
Wonder.—HoD
Youth.—HoD—JoA-4
Hughes, Langston (about)
Daybreak in Alabama. L. Hughes.—HoD
Do nothing till you hear from me. D. Henderson.—AdPb
Langston. M. Evans.—AdB
The Negro. L. Hughes.—HoD
Hughes, Richard
Explanation, on coming home late.—CoPu
Hughes, Ted
Bullfrog.—MoT
Hawk roosting.—ToM
The horses.—HaWr
"I've heard so much about older folks' folks."—HuMf
My Aunt Dora.—HuMf
My Aunt Flo.—HuMf
My brother Bert.—HuMf
My father.—HuMf
My granny.—HuMf
My mother.—HuMf
My own true family.—HuMf
My sister Jane.—HuMf—MaFw
My Uncle Dan.—CoOh—HuMf
My Uncle Mick.—HuMf
Pike.—HiN—ToM
Thistles.—ToM
The thought-fox.—HiN
View of a pig.—MaFw
Wind.—MaFw—ToM
Hugo, Victor (Marie, Vicomte)
Wings.—JoA-4
"Huh." See Awake and asleep
Human beings. David McCord.—McAa
Human body. See Body, human
The **human** heart. William Wordsworth.—RoIt
Human race
Abou Ben Adhem. L. Hunt.—RoIt
Anthropoids. M. A. Hoberman.—HoR
The avenue: N. Y. city. J. de Graft.—AlPa
Borders. S. Mosova.—MoM
Councils. M. Piercy.—MoT
Credo. G. D. Johnson.—AdPb
Fire, hair, meat and bone. F. Johnson.—AdPb
First man was the first to emerge. Unknown.—BiI
5 ways to kill a man. E. Brock.—RoI
Happy New year. E. Merriam.—MeO
Holey sonet V. J. Donne.—MaFw (sel.)
Human beings. D. McCord.—McAa
Life cycle of common man. H. Nemerov.—ToM
Lines written in early spring. W. Wordsworth.—RoIt
The man and the fish. L. Hunt.—RoIt
Man is a fool. Unknown.—RoIt
Man is nothing but. S. Tchernichovsky.—MeP
The measure of man. E. Merriam.—MeF
Meditatio. E. Pound.—LiWw
Of man and nature. H. Mungin.—AdB
On a spaniel called Beau killing a young bird. W. Cowper.—RoIt
The orang utan. E. Lucie-Smith.—CoPu
"Pity this busy monster, manunkind." E. E. Cummings.—PeS
Precision. P. Collenette.—MaFw
The riddle. G. D. Johnson.—AdPb
Telephone poles. J. Updike.—MaFw
The term. W. C. Williams.—MoT
Thoughts at midnight. T. Hardy.—PlP
To my son Parker, asleep in the next room. B. Kaufman.—AdPb
The **humble-bee.** Ralph Waldo Emerson.—PaF
Humbleweeds. Robert Froman.—FrSp
Humility
Humbleweeds. R. Froman.—FrSp
We are living humbly. Unknown.—BiI
The **hummingbird.** Jack Prelutsky.—PrT
Hummingbirds
The hummingbird. J. Prelutsky.—PrT
"A route of evanescence." E. Dickinson.—ThI
Ruby-throated hummingbird. E. Merriam.—MeO
The storm. E. J. Coatsworth.—CoPu
Humor (about)
The height of the ridiculous. O. W. Holmes.—RoIt
Korf's joke. C. Morgenstern.—CoPu
Humorous verse. Abu Dolama, tr. fr. the Arabian by Raoul Abdul.—AbM
The **hump.** See Just-so stories
Humphries, Rolfe
Aeneid, sels
The boat race. tr.—FlH
The boxing match. tr.—FlH
For a wordfarer.—PlM
Interval.—PlM
Metamorphoses, sel.
Orpheus and Eurydice. tr.—MoG
"Two hundred lines a day." tr.—PlM
"Why don't I send my books to you." tr.—PlM
"Humpty Dumpty sat on a wall." Mother Goose.—EmN—JoA-4
Humpty Dumpty's song. See Through the looking-glass

Hunchback girl: She thinks of heaven. Gwendolyn Brooks.—PeS
"A **hundred** mountains." Issa, tr. fr. the Japanese by Harry Behn.—BeM
The **hundred** yard dash. William Lindsey.—FlH
Hunger
Appetizer. R. Froman.—FrSp
Hunger ("Fear was about me") Unknown.—LeIb
Hunger ("Hunger makes a person climb up to the ceiling") Unknown.—AlPa
Hungry. L. Lenski.—LeC
The hungry black child. A. D. Miller.—AdPb
The hungry moths.—R. McCuaig.—CoPu
Hungry Mungry. S. Silverstein.—SiW
"I had a dream last night . . . of a thousand mothers." C. Meyer.—JoV
The little cart. Ch'ên Tzu-lung.—MaFw
No new music. S. Crouch.—AdPb
Poor Angus. S. Silverstein.—SiW
Street window. C. Sandburg.—SaT
"Though there is still quite a way to go." Unknown.—BaSs
Work song. Unknown.—AbM
Hunger ("Fear was about me") Unknown, fr. the Copper Eskimo.—LeIb
Hunger ("Hunger makes a person climb up to the ceiling") Unknown, tr. fr. the Yoruba by Ulli Beier and Bakare Ghadamosi.—AlPa
Hunger makes a person climb up to the ceiling." See Hunger
Hungry. Lois Lenski.—LeC
The **hungry** black child. Adam David Miller.—AdPb
The **hungry** moths. Ronald McCuaig.—CoPu
Hungry Mungry. Shel Silverstein.—SiW
"**Hungry** Mungry sat at supper." See Hungry Mungry
"A **hungry** wolf is in the street." Irina, tr. fr. the Russian by Miriam Morton.—MoM
Hunt, Evelyn Tooley
Taught me purple.—PeS
Hunt, John Dixon
The dune. tr.—MaFw
Hunt, (James Henry) Leigh
Abou Ben Adhem.—RoIt
Jenny kissed me.—RoIt
The man and the fish.—RoIt
Hunter, Robert
Casey Jones.—MoG
The **hunter.** Aileen Fisher.—FiM
Hunters and hunting. See also Falcons and falconry
"All in green went my love riding." E. E. Cummings.—JoA-4—MaFw
Alone. K. Raikin.—MoM
The ballad of Minepit Shaw. R. Kipling.—CoPt
The ballad of red fox. M. W. La Follette.—AdP
The bear hunt. A. Lincoln.—RoIt
"Beast of the sea." Unknown.—LeIb
Black-tailed deer song. Unknown.—BiI
The boar hunt. From The Odyssey. Homer.—MaFw
Buffalo. H. Dumas.—AdPb
"Bye, baby bunting." Mother Goose.—JoA-4—LiS
Caribou hunting. Unknown.—LeIb
Ceremonial hunt. E. J. Coatsworth.—JoA-4
"Comes the deer to my singing." Unknown.—ClFc
Complaint over bad hunting. Unknown.—LeIb
Crystal moment. R. P. T. Coffin.—PeS
Dance song ("Eastward I was idle") Unknown.—LeIb
Dance song ("I am quite unable") Unknown.—LeIb
"Digger Boy was hunting clams." N. Belting.—BeWi
Encounter. L. Moore.—MoSp
"First they shot a female caribou." Unknown.—LeIb
"Five little squirrels sat up in a tree." Unknown.—JoA-4
The fox. K. Patchen.—ToM
"The gull, it is said." Unknown.—LeIb
"He constantly bends it, he constantly sends it straight." Unknown.—LeIb
The hippopotamus. H. Belloc.—BrM
Humorous verse. Abu Dolama.—AbM
The hunter. A. Fisher.—FiM
The hunting of the Snark, sel. L. Carroll.—LiPc (Complete)
The beaver's lesson.—JoA-4
Hunting song ("The fox he came lolloping, lolloping") D. Finkel.—HiN
Hunting song ("Up, up, ye dames and lasses gay") S. T. Coleridge.—RoIt
"I am ashamed." Unknown.—LeIb
"I remember the white bear." Unknown.—LeIb
"I saw a jolly hunter." C. Causley.—CaF
"I wanted to use my weapon." Unknown.—LeIb
"In stature the Manlet was dwarfish." From Sylvie and Bruno concluded. L. Carroll.—LiPc
The kayak paddler's joy at the weather. Unknown.—LeIb
"Listen to my words." Unknown.—LeIb
Listening to foxhounds. J. Dickey.—HaWr
Lord Arnaldos. J. E. Flecker.—CoPt
Magic words to bring luck when hunting caribou. Unknown.—LeIb
A male lion, I roar. A. N. B. J. Bhalo.—AlPa
"My song was ready." Unknown.—LeIb
The night hunt. T. MacDonagh.—CoPi
"On a green, green hill." Unknown.—BoI
"On his very first hunt." Unknown.—LeIb
"Orphan." Unknown.—LeIb
"Over there I could think of nothing else." Unknown.—LeIb
Paddler's song on bad hunting weather. Unknown.—LeIb
Piano and drums. G. Okara.—AlPa

The real slayer of the seal. Unknown.—LeIb
Signal song on capture of polar bear. Unknown.—LeIb
Song of the deer. Unknown.—BiI
Song of the fallen deer. Unknown.—BiI
Song of the hunter. Unknown.—BiI
Song of the rain. Unknown.—AlPa
Sport. W. H. Davies.—CoPu
"There was a little man, and he had a little gun." Mother Goose.—JoA-4
"There were three jovial Welshmen." Mother Goose.—AlC—JoA-4
"Those game animals, those long-haired caribou." Unknown.—LeIb
The trap. W. Beyer.—CoPt
Ulivfak's song of the caribou. Unknown.—LeIb
"Wind thy horn, my hunter boy." T. Moore.—FlH
Winsor forest, sel.
"See from the brake the whining pheasant springs."—CoPu
Windsor forest.—MaFw
"Hunters, hunters." See Sport
Hunting. See Hunters and hunting
The **hunting** of the Snark, sel. Lewis Carroll.—LiPc (Complete)
The beaver's lesson.—JoA-4
Hunting song ("The fox he came lolloping, lolloping") Donald Finkel.—HiN
Hunting song ("Up, up, ye dames, and lasses gay") Samuel Taylor Coleridge.—RoIt
Huntley, Stanley
Annabel Lee.—LiS
The **Huron** Indian carol. Unknown.—LaS
Huron Indians. See Indians of the Americas—Huron
Hurrahing in harvest. Gerard Manley Hopkins.—MaFw
Hurricane. Archibald MacLeish.—HiN
A **hurricane** at sea. May Swenson.—HaWr
Hurricane Jackson. Alan Dugan.—HiN
Hurricanes. See Storms
Hurry. Eve Merriam.—MeO
"Hurry, say the voices." See Waiting
"Hurry, says the morning." See Hurry
Hurston, Zora Neale
The creation of man. ad.—AbM
"Hurt." See To all sisters
Hurt hawks. Robinson Jeffers.—PeS
Husbands. See Married life
A **husband's** song. Unknown, tr. fr. the Eskimo by Knud Rasmussen.—BiI
The **husband's** view. Thomas Hardy.—PlP
"Hush-a-bye, baby." Mother Goose.—BlM
"Hush-a-bye, baby, on the tree-top." Mother Goose.—JoA-4
"Hush-a-bye, hush-a-bye, lull Babirye to sleep." See Woowooto
"Hush, do you hear? Hear the loons singing up in the sky." See The loons are singing
"Hush, hush." See Now we are sick
"Hush hush hush the baby-sitter sighs." See The babysitter and the baby
"A **hush** is over all the teeming lists." See Frederick Douglass
"Hush, my babe." See Cradle hymn
"Hush, my babe, lie still and slumber." See Cradle hymn—Hush, my babe
"Hushaby, rockaby, softly to sleep." See A Christmas lullaby
Husky hi. Unknown, tr. fr. the Norwegian by Rose Fyleman.—JoA-4
"Husky hi, husky hi." See Husky hi
Hwang Chini
"Long and lonely December night."—BaSs
"You, blue stream, flowing around mountains."—BaSs
Hyde, Douglas
"Bruadar and Smith and Glinn." tr.—CoPi
"Ringleted youth of my love." tr.—CoPi
Were you on the mountain. tr.—CoPu
The **hyena.** Jack Prelutsky.—PrT
Hyenas
The hyena. J. Prelutsky.—PrT
Hymn. Unknown, tr. fr. the Aztec by D. G. Brinton.—BiI
Hymn for Lanie Poo, sel. LeRoi Jones
"Each morning."—AdPb
Hymn for Saturday. Christopher Smart.—OpOx
Hymn to the sun. Akhenaton, Pharaoh of Egypt, tr. fr. the Egyptian by J. E. Manchip White.—AbM
Hymns
All hail to the morning. S. Wakerfield.—LaS
The babe of Bethlehem. Unknown.—LaS
Battle-hymn of the Republic. J. W. Howe.—RoIt
A Christmas hymn. R. Wilbur.—ToM
Cradle hymn ("Away in a manger, no crib for a bed") M. Luther.—JoA-4
Away in a manger.—LaS
Cradle hymn ("Hush, my dear, lie still and slumber") I. Watts.—OpOx
Hush, my babe.—LaS
An evening hymn. T. Ken.—OpOx
Exultation. Unknown.—LaS
Hymn for Saturday. C. Smart.—OpOx
Hymn to the sun. Akhenaton, Pharaoh of Egypt.—AbM
A morning hymn. C. Smart.—OpOx
"Now the day is over." S. Baring-Gould.—OpOx
Religious hymn to be sung wearing a head decoration of the skin of the great northern diver. Unknown.—LeIb
The shepherds' hymn. R. Crashaw.—MaF
Shepherds in Judea. J. Ingalls.—LaS
The spirit will appear. Unknown.—BiS
Star in the East. Unknown.—LaS
A Virgin unspotted. W. Billings.—LaS
While shepherds watched. Unknown.—LaS
Wondrous love. Unknown.—LaS
"The **hypnotizing** neon light." See Wonderful New York

I

"I arise from rest with movements swift." See Magic prayer
"I arrive/Langston." See Do nothing till you hear from me
"I ask you this." See Prayer
"I asked if I got sick and died, would you." See A question
"I asked my mother for fifty cents." Unknown.—JoA-4
"I asked professors who teach the meaning of life to tell me what is happiness." See Happiness
"I bang, bang, bang." See My hammer
"I believe, I believe." See Praise to the end
"I believe in the ultimate justice of fate." See Credo
"I boiled hot water in an urn." Nicarchus.—JoA-4
I break the sky. Owen Dodson.—AdPb
"I bring accusations; let them reach every place." See The eyes or the heart
"I bring back a shell so I can always hear." See Souvenir
"I build again." See My succah
"I burn in fire, I drown, I live, I languish." Louise Labé, tr. fr. the French by Judith Thurman.—ThI
"I called to the wind." Kyorai, tr. fr. the Japanese by Harry Behn.—BeM
"I came as a shadow." See Nocturne varial
"I came from somewhere." See Poem of the future citizen
"I came upon a child of God." See Woodstock
"I can get through a doorway without any key." See The wind
"I can hear kittens and cows and dogs." See Listening
"I can look the sun in the face." See Song
"I can wade grief." Emily Dickinson.—ThI
"I cannot be hurt anymore." See Image
"I cannot forget you. Unknown, tr. fr. the Makah by Hazel Parker Butler.—BiI
"I cannot go to school today." See Sick
"I cannot see what flowers are at my feet." See To a nightingale
"I cannot tell my future." Anthony Holmes.—JoV
"I cannot tell why." See The rustling of leaves
"I can't go visit a snowbird." See Winter birds
"I can't hold you and I can't leave you." Juana Inez De la Cruz, tr. fr. the Mexican by Judith Thurman.—ThI (sel.)
"I can't wait." See New puppy
"I carry my keys like a weapon." See To nowhere
"I cast it away." See War songs
"I caught the American bull." See Buffalo
"I choose not to walk among ghosts." See Antigone VI
"I chopped down the house that you had been saving to live in next summer." See Variations on a theme by William Carlos Williams
"I circle around." Unknown, tr. fr. the Arapaho.—ClFc
"I climbed through woods in the hour-before-dawn dark." See The horses
"I close my book and open the window." Chung On, tr. fr. the Korean by Chung Seuk Park and ad. by Virginia Olsen Baron.—BaSs
"I come in the morn." See Born without a star.
"I come to work as well as play." See The wind
"I could eat it." Issa, tr. fr. the Japanese by R. H. Blyth.—MaFw
"I could not sleep for thinking of the sky." See The unending sky
"I could take the Harlem night." See Juke box love song.
"I count black-lipped." See Come back blues
"I cried because I didn't have." See Why is happy
"I cut from your middle the navel string." See Words spoken by a mother to her newborn son as she cuts the umbilical cord
"I danced in the morning when the world was begun." See The Lord of the Dance
"I deal in wisdom, not in dry desire." See Supper with Lindsay
"I determined to find out whose it was." See The rival
"I did not see a mermaid." Siddie Joe Johnson.—LiLc
"I dip my pen into the ink." Unknown.—MoBw
"I do confess, in many a sigh." See Lying
"I do not laugh or sing or smile or talk." Karla Kuskin.—KuA
"I do not like the way you slide." See Egg thoughts
"I do not like (love) thee, Doctor Fell." Martial, tr. fr. the Latin by Thomas Brown.—MiMg—TrG
"I do not sleep at night." See Night-piece
"I do not understand." Karla Kuskin.—KuA
"I do not want to stand." See My own hallelujahs
"I do not wish I were a cat." Karla Kuskin.—KuN
"I don't believe in Santa Claus, says Number One." See Ten nights before Christmas
"I don't bother with rhymes. It is seldom." See XIV
"I don't happen." See Making a home
"I don't know who tells me." Unknown.—MoBw
I don't like beetles. Rose Fyleman.—OpOx
"I don't like beetles, tho' I'm sure they're very good." See I don't like beetles
"I don't mind eels." See The eel
"I don't suppose you happen to know." See Why the sky is blue
"I don't think it important." See The beast section
"I don't want any money." Unknown.—MoBw
I doot, I doot. Unknown.—BlM

"I have awakened from the unknowing to the
knowing." See For William Edward
Burghardt Du Bois on his eightieth
birthday
"I have been a." See Homecoming
"I have been singing, singing." See Longing for
death
"I have but one story." See Summer is gone
"I have come to the borders of sleep." See
Lights out
"I have counted every present with my name."
See Presents
"I have desired to go." See Heaven-haven
"I have eaten." See This is just to say
I have folded my sorrows. Bob Kaufman.—
AdPb
"I have folded my sorrows into the mantle of
summer night." See I have folded my
sorrows
"I have found some little kittens." See Pussy
willows
"I have got a new-born sister." See Choosing a
name
"I have had not one word from her." Sappho,
tr. fr. the Greek by Mary Barnard.—ThI
"I have had playmates, I have had
companions." See The old familiar faces
"I have heard your voice floating, royal and
real." See To Dinah Washington
"I have just seen a most beautiful thing." See
The black finger
"I have listened for this and that." See Sioux
City: January—very late
"I have lived long enough to be rarely
mistaken." See Bacon and greens
"I have lived up half my life already." Yi
Myung-han, tr. fr. the Korean by Chung
Seuk Park and ad. by Virginia Olsen
Baron.—BaSs
"I have looked him round and looked him
through." See Nora Criona
"I have loved colours, and not flowers." See
Amends to nature
"I have made the sun." See Song of creation
"I have my own baton now." See Baton
"I have never been on the cloudy slopes of
Olympus." See The valley of men
"I have not ever seen my father's grave." See
Father Son and Holy Ghost
"I have nothing at all." Issa, tr. fr. the Japanese
by Hanako Fukuda.—HaW
"I have nothing to put in my stew, you see."
See Me-stew
"I have passed him." See A Negro labourer in
Liverpool
"I have seen black hands. Richard Wright.—
AdPb
"I have seen the smallest minds of my
generation." See Problem in social
geometry—the inverted square
"I have seen them at many hours." See Poems:
Birmingham 1962-1964
"I have sown beside all waters in my day." See
A black man talks of reaping

"I have sown upon the fields." See The idle
flowers
"I have stretched ropes from belfry to belfry."
See Phrases
"I have wished a bird would fly away." See A
minor bird
"I have wrapped my dreams in a silken cloth."
See For a poet
"I hear a sudden cry of pain." See The snare
"I hear a whistling." See Emmett Till
I hear America singing. Walt Whitman.—RoIt
"I hear America singing, the varied carols I
hear." See I hear America singing
"I hear leaves drinking rain." See The rain
"I hear the cooing music of doves." See
Lament of the exiles
"I hear the sound of affliction. They are
weeping." See How it is
"I hear you smiling." Felice Holman.—HoI
"I heard a bird at dawn." See The rivals
"I heard a bird sing." Oliver Herford.—LiLc
"I heard a fly buzz—when I died." Emily
Dickinson.—ThI
"I heard a mouse." See The mouse
"I heard a thousand blended notes." See Lines
written in early spring
"I heard him faintly, far away." See Corncrake
"I heard the bells on Christmas day." Henry
Wadsworth Longfellow.—RoIt
"I heard the dogs howl in the moonlight
night." See A dream
"I heard the weeping of the newly born in its
mother's bosom." See The circle of
weeping
"I heard the wind coming." See Hearing the
wind at night
"I hold a rod in one hand." Woo Tahk, tr. fr.
the Korean by Chung Seuk Park and ad.
by Virginia Olsen Baron.—BaSs
"I hung up a stocking." See A Christmas
package
"I hung you there, moccasins of worn
buckskin." See The moccasins of an old
man
I, Icarus. Alden Nowlan.—HiN
"I imagine this midnight moment's forest." See
The thought-fox
"I journeyed on a winter's day." See Jane
Smith
"I just once want to feel." See From riot rimes
U.S.A. #79
"I keep losing friends." See Losing friends
"I keep nothing." See Hope to keep
"I kneel at my mother's grave." See Mom
"I knew a Cappadocian." Alfred Edward
Housman.—LiWw
"I knew a man." Clyde Watson.—WaF
"I know." See Lenin
"I know." See October magic
"I know a funny little man." See Mr Nobody
"I know a Jew fish crier down on Maxwell
street with a voice like a north wind
blowing over corn stubble in January." See
Fish crier

"I know a little man both ept and ert." See Gloss
"I know a little red caboose." See The caboose who wouldn't come last
"I know an absent-minded man." See The absent-minded man
"I know everything in the bottom of my heart." Unknown, tr. fr. the Papago.—ClFc
"I know how, I know how, I know how to not-do things." See Not-things
"I know I'm not sufficiently obscure." Ray Durem.—AdPb
"I know kids who do not kick." See Some kids I know
"I know not whether you have been absent." See Love song
"I know not why my soul is rack'd." See Changed
"I know pines." Felice Holman.—HoI
"I know someone who is so slow." See Someone slow
"I know that I shall meet my fate." See An Irish airman foresees his death
"I know that I'm a runt." Unknown.—MoBw
"I know the serpent has unsheathed himself." See The brass serpent
"I know what the caged bird feels, alas." See Sympathy
"I know where I'm going." Unknown.—JoA-4
"I laugh that you should be so busy to pick up morsels." See Chopsticks
"I leant upon a coppice gate." See The darkling thrush
"I left home without my umbrella." Kim Jae, tr. fr. the Korean by Chung Seuk Park and ad. by Virginia Olsen Baron.—BaSs
"I left my head." Lilian Moore.—MoSm
"I left the little birds." See Adieu
"I like." See The furry ones
"I like." See To a friend
"I like best." See Of man and nature
"I like days." See December
"I like it here just fine." See Girl held without bail
"I like little pussy, her coat is so warm." See "I love (like) little pussy"
"I like the things that come at night." See Bedtime
"I like the whistle of trains at night." See Trains at night
"I like the zebra." See At the zoo
"I like them." See Giraffes
"I like them feathery, too." Aileen Fisher.—FiFo
"I like this book, said the King of Hearts." See The King of Hearts
"I like this book, said the King of Spain." See The King of Spain
"I like to go shopping with mama." See Shopping
"I like to help small things survive." See Worlds of different sizes
"I like to listen to the sound." See Words
"I like to look for feathers." See Looking for feathers
"I like to pick." See Picture people
"I like to remember airplane rides." See Sky's nice
"I like to rest on myself." See One for Novella Nelson
"I like to see it lap the miles." Emily Dickinson.—ThI
"I like to see the teetertails." See Sandpipers
"I like to walk." See Crows
"I like to watch the big bear walk." See Bear
"I like you, bamboo." Kim Kwang-wuk, tr. fr. the Korean by Chung Seuk Park and ad. by Virginia Olsen Baron.—BaSs
"I liked growing." Karla Kuskin.—KuA
"I live upstairs." Lois Lenski.—LeC
"I lived on a rooftop." See At first sight
"I longed to love a full-boughed beech." See The ivy-wife
"I look like you precisely." Karla Kuskin.—KuA
"I look out of my window." Olya, tr. fr. the Russian by Miriam Morton.—MoM
"I look out the window." See Look out the window
"I looked your album o'er and o'er." Unknown.—MoBw
"I lost a world, the other day." Emily Dickinson.—ThI
"I lost my mare in Lincoln lane." Mother Goose.—TucMgl
I love. Tanya Mitrofanova, tr. fr. the Russian by Miriam Morton.—MoM
"I love Adam. He has a good heart." See Eve
"I love cake, I love pie." Unknown.—EmN
"I love coffee, I love tea (I love the boys)." Unknown.—EmN
"I love coffee, I love tea (I want)." Unknown.—EmN
"I love cookies." Unknown.—MoBw
"I love (like) little pussy." Jane Taylor.—BlM—JoA-4
Pussy.—OpOx
"I love my house." See Two mothers
"I love my love with an M, said I." See Fantasia
"I love sixpence, jolly little sixpence." Mother Goose.—JoA-4
I love the city. Lois Lenski.—LeC
"I love the gentle dewdrop." See I love
"I love the life of the city." See I love the city
"I love the tinsel." See Christmas time
"I love thee, Mary, and thou lovest me." See The chemist to his love
"I love this little house because." See Motto for a dog house
"I love to go fishing." Unknown.—MoBw
"I love to rise in a summer morn." See The school boy
"I love you." See The people, yes—Mother and child
"I love you a little." Unknown.—EmN
"I love you for your brownness." See To a dark girl

"I love you ginger bread mama." See Ginger bread mama
"I love you in blue." Unknown.—MoBw
"I love you my child." See Cradlesong
"I love you, my Lord." See Triolet
"I love you on the hillside." Unknown.—MoBw
"I love you once." Unknown.—MoBw
"I love your hands." See Your hands
"I loved my friend." See Poem
"I made my song a coat." See A coat
"I made a pact with you, Walt Whitman." See A pact
"I marked when the weather changed." See A night in November
"I marvel at the ways of God." E. B. White.—LiWw
"I marvell'd why a simple child." See Only seven
"I may be silent, but." See Silent, but
"I may decide to leave this street." See On the sidewalk
I may, I might, I must. Marianne Moore.—JoA-4
"I may not know them all." Unknown, tr. fr. the Russian by Miriam Morton.—MoM
"I meant to do my work today." Richard LeGallienne.—JoA-4—UnGb
"I met a little elfman, once." See The little elf
I met a man. Unknown.—RoIt
"I met a man in an onion bed." See The man in the onion bed
"I met a squirrel the other day." See Politeness
"I met a traveler from an antique land." See Ozymandias
"I met a traveller from an antique land." See Ozymandias revisited
"I met an old lady." See The lonely soul
"I met four guinea hens today." See Life
"I met the love-talker one eve in the glen." See The love-talker
"I met your father yesterday. He asked me what I thought." See I am writing this at sea
"I might repeat in every line." Sasha Aleksandrovsky, tr. fr. the Russian by Miriam Morton.—MoM
"I move on feeling and have learned to distrust those who don't." See Poem of Angela Yvonne Davis
"I must go down to the sea again, to the lonely sea and the sky." See Sea-fever
"I must remember." Shel Silverstein.—SiW
"I must, Varus, tell you." Gaius Valerius Catullus, tr. fr. the Latin by Peter Whigham.—PlM
"I-N spells in." Mother Goose.—AlC
"I need not your needles, they're needless to me." See The baker's reply to the needle peddler
"I never cast a flower away." See Partings
"I never hear the word *escape.*" Emily Dickinson.—ThI
"I never loved a gay gazelle." See Tèma com variazíoni
"I never nursed a gay gazelle." See Lalla Rookh
"I never rear'd a young gazelle." See 'Twas ever thus
"I never saw." Lilian Moore.—MoSm
"I never saw a moor." Emily Dickinson.—JoA-4—LiLc
"I never smelled a smelt." Unknown.—EmN
"I often pause and wonder." Unknown.—BrM
"I often wonder whether." See Rhinoceros
"I once had a sweet little doll, dears." See The water babies—The little doll
"I once had a wolf and a bobcat." See Pets
"I only knew her as a spouse." See At flock Mass
"I only know that you may lie." See The old vicarage, Grantchester
"I opened my eyes." See Rain
"I paid my 30¢ and rode by the bus." See Ten years old
"I painted her a gushing thing." See Disillusionised
"I painted on the roof of a skyscraper." See People who must
I pass the pipe. Unknown, tr. fr. the Sioux by J. R. Walker.—BiI
"I passed by the house of the young man who loves me." See Love song
"I perceive the cows slightly." See Life in the country
"I pick frogs and I catch flowers." See A Gloria song
"I pitied one whose tattered dress." See The vesture of the soul
"I pity the river." Unknown.—EmN
"I plan to go a walk today." See Planning
"I play it cool." See Motto
"I play my sweet old airs." See Lost love
"I play'd with you 'mid cowslips growing." See Gryll Grange—Love and age
"I recollect a nurse call'd Ann." See A terrible infant
"I refused, of course I did." See Maiden's song
"I remember. . . . " Mae Jackson.—AdB—AdM—AdPb
"I remember black winter waters." See New Hampshire again
"I remember how she sang." Rob Penny.—AdPb
"I remember, I remember." Thomas Hood.—RoIt
"I remember the Chillicothe ball players." See Hits and runs
"I remember the neckcurls, limp and damp as tendrils." See Elegy for Jane
"I remember the white bear." Unknown, fr. the Netsilik Eskimo.—LeIb
"I remember Wednesday was the day." See Two lean cats
"I return to my little song." Unknown, fr. South Baffin island.—LeIb
"I ride through Queens." See An invitation to Madison county

"I sing for a moment and vaguely." See Signal song on capture of polar bear
I sing no new songs. Frank Marshall Davis.—AdPb
"I sing of a maiden." See Dew in Aprille
"I sit here so still in my secret place." See Refuge
"I sit in the top of the wood, my eyes closed." See Hawk roosting
"I sleep long and soundly." See Love songs
"I slumbered with your poems on my breast." See To E. T.
"I sometimes fear the younger generation will be deprived of the pleasure of hoeing." See Hoeing
I sometimes think. Thomas Hardy.—PlP
"I sometimes think as here I sit." See I sometimes think
"I sometimes think of Nan and the boys." See We saw days
"I speak of that great house." See Beyond the hunting woods
"I spied John Mouldy in his cellar." See John Mouldy
"I spoke to a gorilla who asked me about you." See The family reunion
"I spot the hills." See Theme in yellow
"I sprang to the stirrup, and Joris and he." See How they brought the good news from Ghent to Aix
"I stand here in the ditch, my feet on a rock in the water." See The blackberry thicket
"I stand in my door and look over the low field of Drynam." See The widow of Drynam
"I stand upon my miracle hill." See Miracle hill
"I step around a gate of bushes." See Cold water
"I stepped from plank to plank." Emily Dickinson.—ThI
"I stood at the back of the shop." See At the draper's
"I stood in the shelter of a great tree." See Tumbleweed
"I stood one day by the breezy bay." See A nautical extravaganza
"I stood tiptoe upon a little hill." sels. John Keats
Minnows.—JoA-4
On a summer's day.—PaF
Sweet peas.—JoA-4
"I stretched." See My friend
"I strolled across." See The waking
"I strolled beside the shining sea." See The cumberbunce
"I studied my tables over and over, and backward and forward, too." See A mortifying mistake
"I suppose I've passed." See The head
"I take it you already know." See Hints on pronunciation for foreigners
"I talked to old Lem." See Old Lem
"I tame the very fiercest beast." Jack Prelutsky.—PrC
I tell her she is lovely. Monk Gibbon.—CoPi
"I tell her she is lovely, and she laughs." See I tell her she is lovely
"I tell you a tale tonight." See The admiral's ghost
"I therefore will begin: Soule of the Age." See To the memory of my beloved, the author, Mr William Shakespeare: and what he hath left us
"I think about the elephant and flea." See In the middle
"I think children are slaves." See Children are slaves
"I think continually of those who were truly great." Stephen Spender.—RoIt
"I think I could turn and live with animals." See Song of myself
"I think I could turn and live with animals, they are so placid and self-contained." See Song of myself—"I think I could turn and live with animals"
"I think I see her sitting bowed and black." See Oriflamme
I think I understand. Joni Mitchell.—MoG
"I think I want some pies this morning." See Greedy Richard
"I think if I searched a thousand lands." See Truly my own
"I think it better that in times like these." See On being asked for a war poem
"I think of her where she lies there on her stone couch by the Thames." See Dreams of a summer night, part VI—The Cutty Sark
"I think that what he gave us most." See Kennedy
"I thought I was going to be a millionaire." See When I brought the news
"I thought of Chatterton, the marvelous boy." See Resolution and independence
"I thought that I knew all that there was to know." See Small, smaller
"I thought they'd be strangers aroun' me." See The curate's kindness
"I threw myself on the." See Endless sleep
"I told Jesus." Sterling Plumpp.—AdPb
"I told the sun that I was glad." See The sun
"I told them a thousand times if I told them once." See The builders
"I, too." Langston Hughes.—HoD—RoIt
"I, too, sing America."—AdPb
"I, too, dislike it." See Poetry
"I, too, dislike it: there are things that are important beyond all this fiddle." See Poetry
"I too have a garret of old playthings." See Upstairs
"I, too, sing America." See "I, too"
"I took a walk." Lois Lenski.—LeC
"I took away the ocean once." See The shell
"I took the embankment path." See An advancement of learning
"I took the pail for water when the sun was high." See The star in the pail
"I touched a tree." See Cry silent

"I towered far, and lo! I stood within." See God-forgotten
"I travel as a phantom now." Thomas Hardy.—PlP
"I travel'd thro' a Land of Men." See The Pickering manuscript—The mental traveller
"I traversed a dominion." See Mute opinion
"I tremble with each breath of air." Unknown.—EmN
"I tried to tip my hat to Miss McCaffery." Shel Silverstein.—CoOr
Tight hat.—SiW
"I tried to tip my hat to Miss McGaffry." See "I tried to tip my hat to Miss McCaffery"
"I used to wrap my white doll up in." Mae Jackson.—AdB—AdPb
"I vision God standing." See God
"I wait with a pencil in my hand." See Waiting
"I wake with morning yawning in my mouth." See Morning mood
"I walk all day through rain and snow." Unknown.—EmN
"I walk down the garden path." See Patterns
"I walk uphill through the snow." See Carrying food home in winter
"I walked abroad on a snowy day." See Soft snow
"I walked on the ice of the sea." Unknown, fr. South Baffin island.—LeIb
"I walked through the cave and shouted." See The echo
"I wander, alone." See Separation
"I wander thro' each charter'd street." See London
"I wandered angry as a cloud." Paul Dehn.—LiS
"I wandered lonely as a cloud." See Daffodils
"I want time to run, to race for me." Volodya Lapin, tr. fr. the Russian by Miriam Morton.—MoM
"I want to find the essence of." Boris Pasternak, tr. fr. the Russian by Miriam Morton.—MoM
"I want to laugh, I, because my sledge it is broken." Unknown, fr. the Copper Eskimo.—LeIb
"I want to see the slim palm trees." See Heritage
"I want you to live as long as you want." Unknown.—EmN
"I wanted a rifle for Christmas." See Presents
"I wanted to know my mother when she sat." See Leroy
"I wanted to use my weapon." Unknown, fr. the Copper Eskimo.—LeIb
"I was." See Love song
"I was a traveller then upon the moor." See Resolution and independence
"I was about to go, and said so." See Loneliness
"I was born about ten thousand years ago." See Ten thousand years ago
"I was born in a frying pan." Unknown.—EmN
"I was born in August, 1942—conceived on a Christmas leave." See Requiem of a war-baby
"I was born upon thy bank, river." Henry David Thoreau.—CoPu
"I was directed by my grandfather." See Direction
"I was in a hooker once, said Karlssen." See Cape Horn gospel
"I was jus." Bob O'Meally.—AdM
"I was sick." See Jesus was crucified or: It must be deep
"I was six when I first saw kittens drown." See The early purges
"I was startled by the knowledge. It was like the last punch." See Hit
I was the moon. Yehuda Amichai, tr. fr. the Hebrew by Assia Gutmann.—MeP
"I was the one they chose: See, he's the." See A riddle: What am I
"I washed my hands in water that never rained nor run." Unknown.—EmN
"I wasn't born here man." See Man I thought you was talking another language that day
"I wasn't late, the bell was early." Unknown.—MoBw
I watched a blackbird. Thomas Hardy.—PlP
"I watched a blackbird on a budding sycamore." See I watched a blackbird
"I went away last August." See Eat-it-all Elaine
"I went down to Malcolmland." See Half black half blacker
"I went downtown to see Mrs Brown." Unknown.—EmN
"I went hunting in the wood." Unknown.—EmN
"I went into the flea circus." See Small talk
"I went into the garden." Unknown.—MoBw
"I went out at the eastern gate." See The eastern gate
"I went out on." See Saying
"I went out to the hazel wood." See The song of wandering Aengus
"I went to find the pot of gold." See The search
"I went to look for joy." See Joy
"I went to my grandfather's farm." Unknown.—EmN
"I went to play in the park." See On Tuesdays I polish my uncle
"I went to play with Billy. He." See What Johnny told me
I went to the animal fair." Unknown.—EmN
Animal fair.—RoIt
"I went to the toad that lies under the wall." Mother Goose.—MiMg
"I went to your house for a piece of cheese." Unknown.—MoBw
"I went up one pair of stairs." Mother Goose.—JoA-4
"I went very quietly." See Rabbits
"I whispered, I am too young." See Brown penny

"**I** will always remember." See Basketball: A love song because it is
"**I** will arise and go now, and go to Innisfree." See The Lake Isle of Innisfree
"**I** will build you a house." See Little girl
"**I** will extol thee, O Lord." See Psalms—Psalm 30
"**I** will give my love an apple." See My valentine
"**I** will lift up mine eyes unto the hills." See Psalms—Psalm 121
I will make you brooches. Robert Louis Stevenson.—RoIt
"**I** will make you brooches and toys for your delight." See I will make you brooches
"**I** will not change my horse with any that treads." See Henry V—The horse
"**I** will not play at tug o' war." See Hug o' war
"**I** will tell my daddy when he comes home." Unknown.—TrG
"**I** will walk with leg muscles." Unknown, fr. the Iglulik Eskimo.—LeIb
"**I** wish." Lilian Moore.—MoSm
"**I** wish I could take a quiet corner in the heart of my." See Baby's world
"**I** wish I had a yellow cat." See Three wishes
"**I** wish I knew the reason for." See Natural history
"**I** wish I lived in a caravan." See The pedlar's caravan
"**I** wish I loved the human race." See Wishes of an elderly man
"**I** wish I was a head of cabbage." Unknown.—EmN
"**I** wish I were a china cup." Unknown.—EmN
"**I** wish I were a graham cracker." Unknown.—MoBw
"**I** wish I were a jelly fish." See Triolet
"**I** wish to buy a dog, she said." See On buying a dog
"**I** wish you a Merry Christmas." Mother Goose.—TucMgl
"**I** wish you health." Unknown.—EmN
"**I** wish you love." Unknown.—EmN
"**I** wish you luck, I wish you joy." Unknown.—EmN
"**I** wish you were a little mouse." Unknown.—MoBw
I wonder as I wander. Unknown.—JoA-4; also version by John Jacob Niles.—LaS
"**I** wonder as I wander out under the sky." See I wonder as I wander
"**I** wonder, Duddon, if you still remember." See To the river Duddon
"**I** wonder how." See A robin
"**I** wonder how many people in this city." Leonard Cohen.—CoPu
"**I** wonder, I wonder." Unknown.—EmN
"**I** wonder if everyone is up." Unknown, tr. fr. the Nez Percé.—JoT
"**I** wonder if you were able then to sing." See The heavenly song
"**I** wonder why." Tom Poole.—AdB
I won't hatch. Shel Silverstein.—SiW
"**I** would be ignorant as the dawn." See The dawn
"**I** would be wandering in distant fields." See In bondage
"**I** would change schools and the food in the school." See If I was president
"**I** would change the ways of living, it's not fair for." See If I were president
"**I** would if I could." Unknown.—EmN
"**I** would like to be that elderly Chinese gentleman." See Dreaming in the Shanghai restaurant
"**I** would like to be wise." See Contentment
"**I** would like to go." See Schonwoma
"**I** would like you for a comrade." Edward Abbott Parry.—NeA—OpOx
"**I** would that I were home again." See The call of the fells
"**I** write what I know on one side of the paper." See Paper II
"**I** wrote some lines once on a time." See The height of the ridiculous
Iadchenko, Tanya
The little girl.—MoM
Ibadan, Nigeria
"Ibadan." J. P. Clark.—AbM
"**Ibadan.**" John Pepper Clark.—AbM
"**Ibiddy,** bibiddy, sibiddy sab." Unknown.—EmN
"**Ibiddy,** bibiddy, sibiddy sail." Unknown.—EmN
Icarus. See also Daedalus
I, Icarus. A. Nowlan.—HiN
Musée des beaux arts.—W. H. Auden.—ToM
Ice
The fable of the piece of glass and the piece of ice. J. H. Frere.—OpOx
Ice. C. G. D. Roberts.—CoPu
"Icicles are the walking sticks of the winter winds." N. Belting.—BeWi
"Little Miss Price." Unknown.—BoI
Puzzle. R. Froman.—FrSp
"Under a spring mist." Teitoku.—BeM
Ice. Charles G. D. Roberts.—CoPu
"**Ice** cold." Deborah Adams.—HoC
Ice cream
Eighteen flavors. S. Silverstein.—SiW
"I scream, you scream." Unknown.—EmN
"Ice cream," L. Mead.—HoC
"Ice cream, i scream." J. Price.—PeS
Ice cream man. L. Lenski.—LeC
"Ice cream slice." M. A. Hoberman.—HoN
"Ice cream soda." Unknown.—EmN
"**Ice** cream." Lynn Mead.—HoC
"**Ice** cream, i scream." Jonathan Price.—PeS
Ice cream man. Lois Lenski.—LeC
"**Ice** cream slice." Mary Ann Hoberman.—HoN
"**Ice** cream soda." Unknown.—EmN
Ice hockey
Hockey. B. McLaughlin.—FlH
The hockey game. D. Lee.—LeA
"There's this that I like about hockey, my lad." J. Kieran.—FlH

Ice skating
Suddenly. D. McCord.—McFm
"**Ice** tinkled in glasses." See Blues and bitterness
Icebergs
The convergence of the twain. T. Hardy.—PlP
The **ichthyosaurus.** Isabel Frances Bellows.—CoOr
"**Icicle.**" See Aimless
"An **icicle** hangs." Issa, tr. fr. the Japanese by Hanako Fukuda.—HaW
Icicles
Aimless. R. Froman.—FrSp
"An icicle hangs." Issa.—HaW
"Icicles are the walking sticks of the winter winds." N. Belting.—BeWi
The thaw. J. Matthews.—HaWr
"**Icicles** are the walking sticks of the winter winds." Natalia Belting.—BeWi
"**Icicles,** which grow silently in the night." See The thaw
"**Ickle** me, pickle me, tickle me too." Shel Silverstein.—SiW
"**Ickle** ockle, blue bockle." Mother Goose.—HoMg
"The **icy** evil that struck his father down." See El-Hajj Malik El-Shabazz
"**I'd** been away a year, a year." See The ballad of Hagensack
"**I'd** fill up the house with guests this minute." See A revel
"**I'd** like." See A badger
"**I'd** like to be." See Wish
"**I'd** like to be able to say a good word for parsley, but I can't." See Parsley for vice-president
"**I'd** like to carve a moon." Chung Chul, tr. fr. the Korean by Chung Seuk Park and ad. by Virginia Olsen Baron.—BaSs
I'd not be a robin. Aileen Fisher.—FiFo
"**I'd** wed you without herds, without money, or rich array." See Cashel of Munster
Idandre. Wole Soyinka.—AlPa (sel.)
The **idea** of ancestry. Etheridge Knight.—AdPb
Ideals. See also Ambition; Conduct of life; Dreams
Eldorado. E. A. Poe.—RoIt
Idiosyncratic. Eve Merriam.—MeO
Idle chatter. Charles Cooper.—AdB
The **idle** flowers. Robert Bridges.—JoA-4
Idleness. See also Laziness
Against idleness and mischief. I. Watts.—LiS—OpOx
Au jardin des plantes. J. Wain.—MaFw
Dance song. Unknown.—LeIb
An immorality. E. Pound.—CoPu
"The island of Lundy." N. M. Bodecker.—BoL
"Lazy Lucy." N. M. Bodecker.—BoL
The lazy people. S. Silverstein.—CoOh
Midsummer melancholy. M. Fishback.—LiWw
"Moving through the silent crowd." S. Spender.—ToM
"On these summer days." Sung Hon.—BaSs
The sluggard. I. Watts.—LiS—OpOx
Idley, Peter
Covetousness.—OpOx
Sources of good counsel.—OpOx
If. See Rewards and fairies
"**If** a doctor is doctoring a doctor." Unknown.—BrM
"**If** a fellow tries to win your heart." Unknown.—MoBw
"**If** a Hottentot taught a Hottentot tot." Unknown.—EmN
"**If** a man who turnips cries." Samuel Johnson.—MiMg
"**If** a pig wore a wig." Christina Georgina Rossetti.—JoA-4
"**If** a place where they sell boots is called a bootery." See Booteries and fluteries and flatteries and things
"**If** all the food was paving-stones." Mother Goose.—AlC
"**If** all the land were apple pie." See "If all the world was apple pie"
"**If** all the seas were one sea." Mother Goose.—JoA-4
"**If** all the world and love were young." See Reply to the passionate shepherd
"**If** all the world was apple pie." Mother Goose.—EmN—JoA-4
"If all the land were apple pie."—RoIt
"**If** an eagle be imprisoned." See America
"**If** anybody asks you who I am." See The little cradle rocks tonight
"**If** apart we two must be." Unknown.—EmN
"**If** Bethlehem were here today." See Christmas morning
"**If** birds had gardens." See Bird gardens
If blood is black then spirit neglects my unborn son. Conrad Kent Rivers.—AdPb
"**If** but some vengeful god would call to me." See Hap
"**If** Cupid shoots." Unknown.—EmN
"**If** Daddy was here." See December 22: Window shopping
"**If** ever I go to Paradise." Unknown.—MoBw
"**If** ever I saw blessing in the air." See April rise
"**If** ever there lived a Yankee lad." See Darius Green and his flying machine
"**If** ever two were one, then surely we." See To my dear and loving husband
"**If** ever you go to Dublin town." Patrick Kavanagh.—ToM
If everybody was black. Jerome Holland.—JoV
"**If** everybody was black it would not be good." See If everybody was black
"**If** everyone were a chief." Kim Chang-up, tr. fr. the Korean by Chung Seuk Park and ad. by Virginia Olsen Baron.—BaSs
"**If** flowers want to grow." See The city
"**If** God had willed, He might have made me meeker." See Thanksgiving

"If grief comes early." See First or last
"If he folded me in an embrace." Louise Labé, tr. fr. the French by Judith Thurman.—ThI
"If hope grew on a bush." See Hope and joy
"If I bring back." See For my unborn and wretched children
"If I cud ever write a." See To P. J. (2 yrs old who sed write a poem for me in Portland, Oregon)
"If I had a brontosaurus." Shel Silverstein.—CoOr—SiW
"If I had a coat." See Cocoa skin coat
"If I had a donkey that wouldn't go." Mother Goose.—JoA-4
"If I had a kitchen." See Cookies
"If I lie down flat where the tall grass grows." See Neighbors
"If I, like Solomon." See O to be a dragon
"If I lived at the time." See To meet Mr Lincoln
"If I lived in Temagami." See Kahshe or Chicoutimi
"If I ride this train." Joe Johnson.—AdPb
If I should ever by chance. Edward Thomas.—OpOx
"If I should ever by chance grow rich." See If I should ever by chance
If I was president. Margaret Cowan.—JoV
"If I were an elephant." N. M. Bodecker.—BoL
"If I were butter I would melt." See The hot day
"If I were full of cheerfulness." See A growl
"If I were just a fairy small." See Fairy voyage
"If I were Lord of Tartary." See Tartary
If I were president. Isabel Velez.—JoV
"If I'd as much money as I could spend." Mother Goose.—AlC—JoA-4
"If *ifs* and *ands.*" Unknown.—EmN
"If, in the month of dark December." See Written after swimming from Sestos to Abydos
"If it comes." Philip Booth.—HiN
"If it had not been the Lord who was on our side." See Psalms—Psalm 124
"If it's ever spring again." Thomas Hardy.—PlP
"If my complaining." Issa, tr. fr. the Japanese.—BeM
"If Nancy Hanks." See Nancy Hanks
"If neither he sells sea shells." Unknown.—EmN
"If night nears your window." David Fogel, tr. fr. the Hebrew by Dom Moraes.—MeP
"If no one ever marries me." Laurence Alma-Tadema.—NeA—OpOx
"If not necessary, is essential." See Love
"If not today." See Snow in Jerusalem
"If one doctor doctors another doctor." Unknown.—EmN
"If only I were able." Borya Lapin, tr. fr. the Russian by Miriam Morton.—MoM
"If perchance this book should roam." Unknown.—EmN
"If Richard were king." Unknown.—MoBw
"If teardrops were pearls." Unknown, tr. fr. the Korean by Chung Seuk Park and ad. by Virginia Olsen Baron.—BaSs
"If the autumn would." See Winter is another country
"If the black frog will not ring." Ed Roberson.—AdPb
"If the butterfly courted the bee." See Topsyturvey-world
"If the cuckoo were." See The cuckoo
"If the moon shines." See What night would it be
"If the ocean was milk." Unknown.—MoBw
If the owl calls again. John Haines.—HiN
If the stars should fall. Samuel Allen.—AdPb
"If the streets were filled with glue." See Glue
If the world was crazy. Shel Silverstein.—SiW
"If the world was crazy, you know what I'd eat." See If the world was crazy
"If there were dreams to sell." See Dream-pedlary
"If things were better." Issa, tr. fr. the Japanese by Hanako Fukuda and by Harry Behn.—HaW—LiWw
"If this page were a pretty pink." See For a white page
"If thou survive my well-contented day." See Sonnets. William Shakespeare
"If to hoot and to toot, a Hottentot tot." Unknown.—EmN
If we cannot live as people. Charles Lynch.—AdPb
"If we meet a gorilla." See We must be polite
If we must die. Claude McKay.—AdPb
"If we must die, let it not be like dogs." See If we must die
"If wishes were horses." Mother Goose.—AlC—EmN
"If you." Karla Kuskin.—KuA
"If you are a dreamer, come in." See Invitation
"If you are a gentleman." Unknown.—TrG
"If you are merry sing away." See Mirth
"If you can keep your head when all about you." See Rewards and fairies—If
"If you could look into my heart." Unknown.—MoBw
"If you cross a cross across a cross." Unknown.—EmN
"If you don't know the kind of person I am." See A ritual to read to each other
"If you ever, ever, ever meet a grizzly bear." See Grizzly bear
"If you ever go to France." Unknown.—MoBw
"If you get a husband." Unknown.—EmN
"If you give a little whistle." See Procyonidae
"If you happen to meet." See Advice from an elderly mouse
"If you have a friend." Unknown, tr. fr. the Spanish.—MoBw
If you have seen. Thomas Moore.—LiWw
"If you love me as I love you." Unknown.—EmN
"If you see a fairy ring." Unknown.—JaP
"If you should ever choose." See Instructions

"**I'm** not going to Macy's any more, more, more." Unknown.—EmN
"**I'm** not much for lines." Unknown.—MoBw
I'm only going to tell you once. Agnes T. Pratt.—AlW
"**I'm** Reginald Clark, I'm afraid of the dark." See Afraid of the dark
"**I'm** rising five, he said." See Rising five
"**I'm** scratched and scuffed." Karla Kuskin.—KuA
"**I'm** sitting in the living room." See Sonic boom
I'm skeleton. Lilian Moore.—MoSm
"**I'm** Sneaky Bill, I'm terrible mean and vicious." See Sneaky Bill
"**I'm** swimming around in the sea, see." Karla Kuskin.—KuA
"**I'm** talking of a little train whose mother is a Diesel." See Whistle
"**I'm** thankful that the sun and moon." See Lines by an old fogy
"**I'm** the local skeleton." See I'm skeleton
"**I'm** the monster of Loch Ness." Unknown.—MoBw
"**I'm** thinking in bed." See Thinking in bed
"**I'm** tired of eating just beans, says I." See Sleeping sardines
"**I'm** trapped." See The flower trap
"**I'm** up here." Karla Kuskin.—KuA
Image. Henry Dumas.—AdB
Image from d'Orleans. Ezra Pound.—MaFw
Imagination
  Cold water. D. Hall.—HiN
  Follow the gleam. From Merlin and the gleam. A. Tennyson.—RoIt
"**Imagine** what Mrs Haessler would say." See Far from Africa: Four poems—Dance of the Abakweta
"The **immense** plain." See The ruined city
The **immigrant.** Okogbule Wonodi.—AlPa
Immigration and emigration
  The immigrant. O. Wonodi.—AlPa
"**Immobile.**" See Gull
An **immorality.** Ezra Pound.—CoPu
Immortality. See also Death and immortality
  Intimations of immortality. W. Wordsworth.—PaF (sel.)
  "A mountain." Yi Hwang.—BaSs
Impatience. See Patience
The **impercipient.** Thomas Hardy.—PlP
Imperial thumbprint. Tom Weatherly.—AdPb
Imperialists
  Imperialists in retirement. E. Lucie-Smith.—ToM
Imperialists in retirement. Edward Lucie-Smith.—ToM
The **importance** of being Western. See Speaking of television
An **importer.** Robert Frost.—LiWw
Improved farm land. Carl Sandburg.—SaT
Improvised song of joy. Unknown, fr. the Iglulik Eskimo.—LeIb
The **impulse** of October. W. R. Moses.—HiN
"**In** a boggy old bog." See Frog music
"**In** a bubble." See Elevator
"**In** a cavern, in a canyon." Paul Dehn.—CoPu
"**In** a fair imitation." See The robins
"**In** a far away northern county in the placid pastoral region." See The ox-tamer
In a grave-yard. William Stanley Braithwaite.—AdPb
"**In** a grey rectory a clergyman was reading." See Droit de Seigneur
"**In** a hermit's cottage, silent, still." Kim Soo-jang, tr. fr. the Korean by Chung Seuk Park and ad. by Virginia Olsen Baron.—BaSs
"**In** a little shanty town." See The twist
"**In** a milkweed cradle." See Baby seeds
"**In** a parlor containing a table." Galway Kinnell.—CoPu
"**In** a poor old village." Lida, tr. fr. the Russian by Miriam Morton.—MoM
"**In** a quiet water'd land, a land of roses." See The dead at Clonmacnoise
"**In** a shoe box stuffed in an old nylon stocking." See The meadow mouse
"**In** a snug little cot lived a fat little mouse." See The country mouse and the city mouse
"**In** a solitude of the sea." See The convergence of the twain
"**In** a stable lies a baby, little Jesus is his name." See En el portal de Belén (At the Crèche)
"**In** a stable of boats I lie still." See The lifeguard
"**In** a time like this time." See Witness
In a town garden. Donald Mattam.—CoPu
"**In** a valley where a stream flows." Unknown, tr. fr. the Korean by Chung Seuk Park and ad. by Virginia Olsen Baron.—BaSs
"**In** Africa." See What's their names
In air. Peter Clarke.—AbM
"**In** all the Eastern hemisphere." See The fall of J. W. Beane
"**In** America there is mourning." Andrei Karlov, tr. fr. the Russian by Miriam Morton.—MoM
"**In** an ocean, 'way out yonder." See The dinkey-bird
In and out. Aileen Fisher.—FiM
"**In** and out the bushes, up the ivy." See The chipmunk's day
"**In** another country, black poplars shake themselves over a pond." See The north country
In Arden forest. See As you like it—"Under the greenwood tree"
In autumn. Tanya Dinsburg, tr. fr. the Russian by Miriam Morton.—MoM
"**In** Baltimore there lived a boy." See The boy who laughed at Santa Claus
"**In** Barcelona city they dance the nights." See Barcelona
"**In** Bethlehem." See Christus natus est
"**In** black core of night, it explodes." See African dream

"**In** blowing your nose, you must expose your teeth." Unknown, tr. fr. the Yoruba by S. A. Babalola.—AlPa
In bondage. Claude McKay.—AdPb
"**In** Breughel's great picture, The Kermess." See The dance
"**In** calm fellowship they sleep." See In a grave-yard
In church. Thomas Hardy.—CoPt
"**In** corridors and caverns of my memory." See Twilight's feet
"**In** curve, out curve." Unknown.—MoBw
In defense of black poets. Conrad Kent Rivers.—AdB
"**In** Dublin's fair city." See Cockles and mussels
"**In** each of us you live on, the lodged seed." See To Wallace Stevens
In fall. Aileen Fisher.—FiFo
In Falmouth harbour. Lionel Johnson.—PaP
"**In** February when few gusty flakes." See Ground hog day
In fields of summer. Galway Kinnell.—HaWr
"**In** fir tar is." Unknown.—AlC
"**In** form and feature, face and limb." See The twins
"**In** 14 A." See December 21: Snow
"**In** 14 A, till mama comes home." See June
"**In** fragrant Dixie's arms." See Church burning: Mississippi
In freezing winter night. Robert Southwell.—MaFw
"**In** fury and terror." See The storm
In Glencullen. John M. Synge.—CoPi—CoPu
"**In** grimy winter dusk." See Stop
In Hardin county, 1809. Lulu E. Thompson.—CoPt
"**In** heaven, too." See Heard in a violent ward
In His hands. Unknown.—BrW
"**In** his sea lit." See The double-play
In honor of a king who acquired several young wives. Unknown, tr. fr. the Ganda by Leonard Doob and Apolo Kagwa.—AlPa
In honour of the city of London, sel. William Dunbar
  "Empresse of Townes, exalt in honour."—PaP
"**In** it there is a space-ship." See A boy's head
"**In** January the spirit dreams." See An almanac
"**In** jumping and tumbling." See Tumbling
"**In** just." See Chanson innocente
In just-spring. See Chanson innocente
"**In** Kamloops." Dennis Lee.—LeA
"**In** Little Rock the people bear." See The Chicago *Defender* sends a man to Little Rock
"**In** London was Young Beichan born." See Young Beichan
"**In** Madurai." See A river
"**In** marble halls as white as milk." Mother Goose.—EmN—JoA-4
  Riddle.—RoIt
"**In** May, when sea-winds pierced our solitudes." See The rhodora
In memoriam, sels. Alfred Tennyson
  "Now fades the last long streak of snow."—PaF
  Ring out, wild bells.—MaF—RoIt
  "Tonight the winds begin to rise."—PaF
In memoriam, Martin Luther King, Jr. June Jordan.—AdPb
In memory of Colonel Charles Young. Countee Cullen.—AdPb
In memory of my dear grandchild Anne Bradstreet. Anne Bradstreet.—ThI
In memory of my dear grandchild Elizabeth Bradstreet. Anne Bradstreet.—ThI
In memory of the Circus ship Euzkera, wrecked in the Caribbean sea, 1 September 1948. Walker Gibson.—HiN
In memory of the Spanish poet Federico García Lorca. Thomas Merton.—PlM
In memory of W. B. Yeats. W. H. Auden.—PlM
"**In** Mississippi." See No new music
"**In** moss-prankt dells which the sunbeams flatter." See Lovers, and a reflection
"**In** moving slow he has no peer." See The sloth
"**In** my childhood trees were green." See Autobiography
"**In** my distress I cried unto the Lord, and He heard me." See Psalms—Psalm 120
"**In** my dry cell." See The Riven quarry
"**In** my house this spring." Sodo, tr. fr. the Japanese by Harry Behn.—BeM
"**In** my kindergarten class." See Kindergarten
In my life. John Lennon and Paul McCartney.—MoG
In my mother's house, sel. Ann Nolan Clark
  "Yucca."—JoA-4
"**In** my younger years." See Dreams
"**In** November of Catherine wheels and rockets." See Dylan Thomas
"**In** October." See October
"**In** old age." Unknown, tr. fr. the Navajo.—ClFc
"**In** Orangeburg my brothers did." A. B. Spellman.—AdPb
"**In** our big maple tree." See The maple
"**In** our little village." See Life in our village
"**In** paper case." See Epitaph on a dormouse, which some children were to bury
"**In** pointed hat." See Witch ways
In praise of prairie. Theodore Roethke.—JoA-4
In reference to her children, 23 June, 1656. Anne Bradstreet.—ThI
In Romney marsh. John Davidson.—PaP
In school-days. John Greenleaf Whittier.—OpOx
"**In** se'enteen hunder an' forty-nine." See On Andrew Turner
"**In** silence I must take my seat." See Table rules for little folks
"**In** silent night when rest I took." See Upon the burning of our house, July 10, 1666
"**In** Sparkill buried lies that man of mark." See Local note
"**In** spring I am gay." Unknown.—EmN

"**In** the third-class seat sat the journeying boy." See Midnight on the Great Western
In the time of revolution. Julius Lester.—AdPb (sel.)
In the train. Vivian de Sola Pinto.—PaP
"**In** the tub we soak our skin." Edward Newman Horn.—CoPu
"**In** the undergrowth." See The bloath
In the valley. Unknown.—LaS
In the week when Christmas comes. Eleanor Farjeon.—LiLc
In the wilderness. Robert Graves.—JoA-4
"**In** the windy dark." See Outside the window
"**In** the witch's." See The witch's garden
"**In** the woodbox of memory." Unknown.—EmN
"**In** the zoo do view the zebu." See Zoo doings
"**In** their." See The educators
In these dissenting times. Alice Walker.—AdPb
"**In** this faraway village where the snow has melted." Yi Sek, tr. fr. the Korean by Chung Seuk Park and ad. by Virginia Olsen Baron.—BaSs
"**In** this green month when resurrected flowers." See Memorial wreath
"**In** this room." See No one
"**In** this stoned and." See Definition of nature
"**In** this world a tablecloth need not be laid." See Tea in a space-ship
"**In** this world, you can do as you please." Unknown.—MoBw
"**In** this world, you see." Issa, tr. fr. the Japanese by Hanako Fukuda.—HaW
In this year of grace. John Hewitt.—CoPi
"**In** tight pants, tight skirts." See The young ones, flip side
"**In** time of rain I come." See Songs of birds
"**In** time of silver rain." Langston Hughes.—AbM
In time of the breaking of nations. Thomas Hardy.—PlP
"**In** time the snowman always dies." See Thaw
"**In** town and temple I'm no longer seen." Louise Labé, tr. fr. the French by Graham Dunstan Martin.—ThI
"**In** us and into us and ours." See For Eusi, Ayi Kwei and Gwen Brooks
In Walpi. Elizabeth Jane Coatsworth.—JoA-4
In which are described rationally the irrational effects of love. Juana Inez De la Cruz, tr. fr. the Mexican by Samuel Beckett.—ThI (sel.)
In which she fears that much learning is useless for wisdom, and poisonous to real living. Juana Inez De la Cruz, tr. fr. the Mexican by Judith Thurman.—ThI (sel.)
"**In** winter I get up at night." See Bed in summer
In winter sky. David McCord.—McFm
"**In** winter, when the fields are white." See Through the looking-glass—Humpty Dumpty's song
"**In** wintertime I have such fun." See Quoits
"**In** words, in books." See Jewels
"**In** Xanadu did Kubla Khan." See Kubla Khan
"**In** your arithmetics." See Who hasn't played gazintas
Inca Indians. See Indians of the Americas—Inca
Incense
  Incense. S. Shalom.—MeP
Incense. Shin Shalom, tr. fr. the Hebrew by Robert Friend.—MeP
"**Incey** wincey spider." Mother Goose.—AlC
Incident. Countee Cullen.—AbM—AdPb—JoA-4
Incident in a rose garden. Donald Justice.—HiN
Incident on a journey. Thom Gunn.—ToM
Incidents in the life of my Uncle Arly. Edward Lear.—LiWw—RoIt
"**Income** taxes." See Taxes
An **inconvenience.** John Banister Tabb.—BrM
Indecision
  Conflict. M. Segun.—AlPa
"**Indeed,** the enemy." See How the days will be
Independence
  Declaration of independence. W. Gibbs.—PeS
  "If everyone were a chief." Kim Chang-up.—BaSs
  The limits of submission. F. Nuur.—AdM—AlPa (sel.)
  My own hallelujahs. Z. Gilbert.—AdPb
  No one else. E. Laron.—ThF
  The sun and the moon. E. Laron.—ThF
Independence day. See Fourth of July
India
  This landscape, these people. Z. Ghose.—ToM
The **Indian** market. Liz Sohappy.—AlW
Indian summer. See Autumn
Indian summer: Vermont. Anne Stevenson.—HiN
"The **Indians** come down from Mixco." Miguel Angel Asturias, tr. fr. the Spanish by Donald Devenish Walsh.—MoT
Indians of the Americas
  Brady's bend. M. Keller.—CoPt
  Ceremonial hunt. E. J. Coatsworth.—JoA-4
  Circles. From The people, yes. C. Sandburg.—MaFw—SaT
  Early moon. C. Sandburg.—SaT
  The gathering time. D. Whitewing.—AlW
  Going where. P. Irving.—AlW
  Goodbye and run. P. Irving.—AlW
  In Walpi. E. J. Coatsworth.—JoA-4
  "The Indians come down from Mixco." M. A. Asturias.—MoT
  Legend. P. Irving.—AlW
  Love song. D. Whitewing.—AlW
  Nespelim man. Janet Campbell.—AlW
  "One little, two little, three little Indians." Unknown.—EmN
  "Red Eagle." Janet Campbell.—AlW
  "A silver mist creeps along the shore." P. Irving.—AlW

The song of Hiawatha. H. W. Longfellow.—LiS (sel.)—RoIt (sel.)
Hiawatha's childhood.—JoA-4 (sel.)
Songs of the birds. Unknown.—BiI
"Sun dancers." P. Irving.—AlW
Sweet winds of love. P. Irving.—AlW
A vegetable, I will not be. D. Whitewing.—AlW
War songs, sels. Unknown.—BiI
"From the place of the south"
"I cast it away"
"On the front part of the earth"
Why. P. Irving.—AlW
You too. P. Irving.—AlW
Indians of the Americas—Acoma
"Butterfly, butterfly, butterfly, butterfly." Unknown.—JoT
Butterfly song.—BiI
"The mockingbird, the mockingbird." Unknown.—JoT
"Nicely, nicely, nicely, nicely, there away in the east." Unknown.—ClFc
"Nicely while it is raining." Unknown.—ClFc
Indians of the Americas—Apache. See also Indians of the Americas—Mescalero Apache
My breath became. Unknown.—BiI
Indians of the Americas—Arapaho
The dreamer rides the whirlwind. Unknown.—BiI
"Father, have pity on me." Unknown.—ClFc
"I circle around." Unknown.—ClFc
I gave them fruits. Unknown.—BiI
"My children." Unknown.—JoT
Indians of the Americas—Araucanian
The ghost of Caupolicán. Unknown.—BiI
Prayer. Unknown.—BiI
Indians of the Americas—Aztec
And yet the earth remains unchanged. Unknown.—BiI
Friendship. Unknown.—BiI
Grandeur of Mexico. Unknown.—BiI
He wove the strands of our life. Unknown.—BiI
Hymn. Unknown.—BiI
Not forever on earth. Unknown.—BiI
Omen ("By daylight a fire fell") Unknown.—BiI
Omen ("By night a voice was heard in the air") Unknown.—BiI
Prayer. Unknown.—BiI
Song. Unknown.—BiI
The song of a dream. Unknown.—BiI
Supplication to the rain god and the spirits of water. Unknown.—BiI
The surrender speech of Cuauhtémoc. Unknown.—BiI
They shall not wither. Unknown.—BiI
Thus it is told. Unknown.—BiI
"The weeping spreads." Unknown.—BiI
A woman's complaint. Unknown.—BiI
Words spoken by a mother to her newborn son as she cuts the umbilical cord. Unknown.—BiI
Indians of the Americas—Bella Bella
"Digger Boy was hunting clams." N. Belting.—BeWi
Indians of the Americas—Bella Coola
"The chief of the world." N. Belting.—BeWi
"Icicles are the walking sticks of the winter winds." N. Belting.—BeWi
"A man sits in the ice." N. Belting.—BeWi
"Not long after the earth was made." N. Belting.—BeWi
"Springs do not freeze in the cold of winter." N. Belting.—BeWi
"Sun rays shining through the dusty air." N. Belting.—BeWi
Indians of the Americas—Blackfeet
Ego swamp. K. D. Kuka.—AlW
A taste of honey. K. D. Kuka.—AlW
"What is life." Unknown.—ClFc
Indians of the Americas—Cakchiquel
Plague. Unknown.—BiI
Indians of the Americas—Cherokee
Beautiful is our lodge. Unknown.—BiS
Do not cry. Unknown.—BiS
Dream song. Unknown.—BiS
It is I, the little owl. Unknown.—BiS
Kindergarten. R. Rogers.—AlW
Light my way to bed. Unknown.—BiS
The loons are singing. Unknown.—BiS
Lullaby. Unknown.—BiS
Magic formula to destroy life. Unknown.—BiI
Magic formula to fix a bride's affection. Unknown.—BiI
Sioux City: January—very late. R. Rogers.—AlW
Sleep, little daughter. Unknown.—BiS
Song of a boy growing up. Unknown.—BiS
Song of the deer dancing. Unknown.—BiS
Song of the frog waiting for spring. Unknown.—BiS
Song to make a baby laugh. Unknown.—BiS
The spirit will appear. Unknown.—BiS
Taking off. R. Rogers.—AlW
Very much afraid. Unknown.—BiS
"What is this I promise you." Unknown.—BiS
"You are like a friend of mine." Unknown.—ClFc
Indians of the Americas—Cheyenne
Song of the ghost dance. Unknown.—BiI
"The stones are all that last long." Unknown.—ClFc
We are living humbly. Unknown.—BiI
"A young man going to war." Unknown.—JoT
Indians of the Americas—Chippewa
"And here, on my breast, have I bled." Unknown.—ClFc
Dream song ("As my eyes") Unknown.—BiI
"As my eyes."—JoT
Dream song ("Sometimes") Unknown.—BiI
"An eagle feather I see." Unknown.—JoT
The forsaken. D. C. Scott.—CoPt
"From the middle." Unknown.—ClFc
"Haik, the white bird of omen." Unknown.—ClFc

"Comes the deer to my singing." Unknown.—ClFc
First man was the first to emerge. Unknown.—BiI
The folding fan. G. Cohoe.—AlW
The four directions. E. B. Mitchell.—AlW
"Gopher sees where the stone is." Unknown.—ClFc
House blessing. Unknown. —BiI
"In old age." Unknown.—ClFc
It was the wind. Unknown.—BiI
Magic formula to make an enemy peaceful. Unknown.—BiI
Miracle hill. E. B. Mitchell.—AlW
Mom. G. Cohoe.—AlW
"My great corn plants." Unknown.—ClFc
The Navajo. E. J. Coatsworth.—JoA-4
Navajo children, Canyon de Chelly, Arizona. C. Middleton.—MaFw
The path I must travel. E. B. Mitchell.—AlW
Prayer. Unknown.—BiI
Snowflakes. G. Cohoe.—AlW
Songs in the garden of the House God. Unknown.—BiI
Talking to his drum. E. B. Mitchell.—AlW
Thirst. G. Cohoe.—AlW

Indians of the Americas—Nez Perce
Ambition. P. George.—AlW
Ask the mountains. P. George.—AlW
Battle won is lost. P. George.—AlW
Child rest. P. George.—AlW
Coyote's night. P. George.—AlW
"I wonder if everyone is up." Unknown.—JoT
Make me a man. P. George.—AlW
Monument in bone. P. George.—AlW
Morning beads. P. George.—AlW
Night blessing. P. George.—AlW
Old man, the sweat lodge. P. George.—AlW
Old man's plea. P. George.—AlW
Proviso. P. George.—AlW
Self. P. George.—AlW
Shadows and song. P. George.—AlW
Song of a new cradleboard. P. George.—AlW
The surrender speech of Chief Joseph. Unknown.—BiI
Through dawn's pink aurora. P. George.—AlW
Until then. P. George.—AlW

Indians of the Americas—Nootka
"Don't you ever." Unknown.—JoT
"You, whose day it is." Unknown.—JoT

Indians of the Americas—Omaha
"Death will come." Unknown.—ClFc

Indians of the Americas—Osage
Behold, this pipe. Unknown.—BiI

Indians of the Americas—Otomi
To a woman loved. Unknown.—BiI

Indians of the Americas—Paiute
Songs of the ghost dance. Unknown.—BiI

Indians of the Americas—Palouse
Behold: my world. L. Sohappy.—AlW
The Indian market. L. Sohappy.—AlW
Once again. L. Sohappy.—AlW
The parade. L. Sohappy.—AlW

Indians of the Americas—Papago
"At the edge of the world." Unknown.—JoT
"Brown owls come here in the blue evening." Unknown.—ClFc
Celebration. A. Lopez.—AlW
Come all. Unknown.—BiI
Direction. A. Lopez.—AlW
"Downy white feathers are moving beneath the sunset." Unknown.—ClFc
Dream song. Unknown.—BiI
"Dry and parched." A. Lopez.—AlW
Eagle flight. A. Lopez.—AlW
"The eagle speaks." Unknown.—JoT
Endless search. A. Lopez.—AlW
"Hanging motionless in the sky." Unknown.—ClFc
"How shall I begin my song." Unknown.—ClFc
"I am crying from thirst." A. Lopez.—AlW
"I go forth to move about the earth." A. Lopez.—AlW
"I know everything in the bottom of my heart." Unknown.—ClFc
"I see a star." A. Lopez.—AlW
In the great night. Unknown.—BiI
"In the night." Unknown.—BiI
The lavender kitten. A. Lopez.—AlW
"The little red spiders." Unknown.—JoT
"A little yellow cricket." Unknown.—JoT
"The morning star is up." Unknown.—ClFc
A question. A. Lopez.—AlW
"Raise your hands to the sky." A. Lopez.—AlW
Separation. A. Lopez.—AlW
Song of encouragement. Unknown.—BiI
Song of the deer. Unknown.—BiI
Song of the hunter. Unknown.—BiI
"To the medicine man's house they have led me." Unknown.—ClFc
Untitled. A. Lopez.—AlW
The wind blows from the sea. Unknown.—BiI

Indians of the Americas—Pawnee
"The bear stands." Unknown.—ClFc
"Breathe on him." Unknown.—BiI
Is this real. Unknown.—BiI

Indians of the Americas—Pima
"The Black Snake Wind came to me." Unknown.—JoT
Black-tailed deer song. Unknown.—BiI
Emergence song. Unknown.—BiI
"The evening glow yet lingers." Unknown.—ClFc
"The light glow of evening." Unknown.—ClFc
Song of creation. Unknown.—BiI
Song of the fallen deer. Unknown.—BiI
The taking of life brings serious thoughts. Unknown.—BiI
"What horse is trying to catch me." Unknown.—ClFc
Wind song. Unknown.—BiI

Indians of the Americas—Quechva
On the death of Atahualpa. Unknown.—BiI

Indians of the Americas—Quechva—*Continued*
Song. Unknown.—BiI
Indians of the Americas—Quiché
The face of my mountains. Unknown.—BiI
Prayer. Unknown.—BiI
Indians of the Americas—Salish
"My people are few." Unknown.—ClFc
Indians of the Americas—Seminole
"Sleep well." Unknown.—ClFc
Indians of the Americas—Shoshone
"The sky is a bowl of ice." N. Belting.—BeWi
Indians of the Americas—Sioux
"At night may I roam." Unknown.—BiI
"Crow Indian." Unknown.—ClFc
"Friends." Unknown.—ClFc
I pass the pipe. Unknown.—BiI
"A lone wolf I am." Unknown.—ClFc
"My son, let me grasp your hand." Unknown.—ClFc
Prayer. Unknown.—BiI
"A soldier." Unknown.—ClFc
Song of reproach. Unknown.—BiI
They will appear. Unknown.—BiI
War song. Unknown.—BiI
"The whole world is coming." Unknown.—ClFc
You shall live. Unknown.—BiI
Indians of the Americas—Skidi Pawnee
"Lightning is a great giant." N. Belting.—BeWi
Indians of the Americas—Suquamish
Bremerton, January 18, 1969. A. T. Pratt.—AlW
Death takes only a minute. A. T. Pratt.—AlW
Empathy. A. T. Pratt.—AlW
Fishing. A. T. Pratt.—AlW
Fragments of spring. A. T. Pratt.—AlW
Hope to keep. A. T. Pratt.—AlW
I'm only going to tell you once. A. T. Pratt.—AlW
Lamentation. A. T. Pratt.—AlW
Question. A. T. Pratt.—AlW
Quietly I shout. A. T. Pratt.—AlW
The sea is melancholy. A. T. Pratt.—AlW
So quickly came the summer. A. T. Pratt.—AlW
Sympathy. A. T. Pratt.—AlW
Twilight's feet. A. T. Pratt.—AlW
Untitled. A. T. Pratt.—AlW
Indians of the Americas—Taos Pueblo
"The stars are night birds with bright breasts." N. Belting.—BeWi
Indians of the Americas—Teton Sioux
"Brave Buffalo." Unknown.—JoT
"Father." Unknown.—JoT
"Friend." Unknown.—JoT
"Here am I." Unknown.—JoT
"The old men." Unknown.—JoT
"A voice." Unknown.—JoT
"A wolf." Unknown.—JoT
Indians of the Americas—Tewa
"Mad coyote." Unknown.—JoT
"My sun." Unknown.—JoT
Now we come southwards. Unknown.—BiI
Song of the sky loom. Unknown.—MoT
That mountain far away. Unknown.—BiI
Upward going. Unknown.—BiI
Indians of the Americas—Thompson River
"Moon sits smoking his pipe." N. Belting.—BeWi
Indians of the Americas—Tlingit
"North wind dresses her daughter winds." N. Belting.—BeWi
Indians of the Americas—Tsimshian
"The heart of the mountain goat is broken when it falls below." Unknown.—ClFc
"I am the Grizzly Bear." Unknown.—ClFc
Indians of the Americas—Tule
Love song. Unknown.—BiI
Indians of the Americas—Tupi
Long song. Unknown.—BiI
Indians of the Americas—Ute-Navajo
Afternoon and his unfinished poem. C. O'John.—AlW
"Dancing teepees." C. O'John.—AlW
Dirt road. C. O'John.—AlW
Doldrums. C. O'John.—AlW
"Good or bad." C. O'John.—AlW
"Half of my life." C. O'John.—AlW
Problems. C. O'John.—AlW
Speak to me. C. O'John.—AlW
"A tear rolled down my cheek." C. O'John.—AlW
That lonesome place. C. O'John.—AlW
This day is over. C. O'John.—AlW
Trees. C. O'John.—AlW
Water baby. C. O'John.—AlW
"You smiled." C. O'John.—AlW
Indians of the Americas—Wabanaki
"He is out of sight." Unknown.—ClFc
Indians of the Americas—Winnebago
Prayer. Unknown.—BiI
This newly created world. Unknown.—BiI
Indians of the Americas—Wintu
Dream song ("Above the place where the minnow maiden sleeps while her fins move gently in the water") Unknown.—BiI
Dream song ("Where will you and I sleep") Unknown.—BiI
Spirits. Unknown.—BiI
We spirits dance. Unknown.—BiI
You and I shall go. Unknown.—BiI
Indians of the Americas—Yana
Curse on people that wish one ill. Unknown.—BiI
"Flint Boy tied his dog." N. Belting.—BeWi
Indians of the Americas—Yaqui
"The quail in the bush is making his whirring." Unknown.—ClFc
Indians of the Americas—Yokut
"Do not touch me." Unknown.—ClFc
Indians of the Americas—Yuma
"The little blackbirds are singing this song." Unknown.—ClFc
"The owl hooted." Unknown.—LaM
"The water bug is dipping." Unknown.—ClFc

Intimations of immortality. William Wordsworth.—PaF (sel.)
"**Into** a closed mouth no flies will enter." Unknown, tr. fr. the Spanish.—MoBw
"**Into** a forest." Otsuji, tr. fr. the Japanese by Harry Behn.—BeM
"**Into** a golden chest." Unknown, tr. fr. the Spanish.—MoBw
"**Into** any little room." See Sleep song
Into blackness softly. Mari Evans.—AdPb
"**Into** drops of crystal dew." See Morning beads
"**Into** his pool of sorrow." See Sympathy
"**Into** love and out again." See Theory
Introduction ("This book you hold") William Cole.—CoOr
Introduction ("This skinny poem will introduce") William Cole.—CoOh
Invention. Shel Silverstein.—SiW
My invention.—CoPu
The **invention** of comics. LeRoi Jones.—AdPb
Inventions. See Inventors and inventions
Inventors and inventions
Darius Green and his flying machine. J. T. Trowbridge.—OpOx
The elf and the dormouse. O. Herford.—JaP—UnGb
Invention. S. Silverstein.—SiW
My invention.—CoPu
My Uncle Dan. T. Hughes.—CoOh—HuMf
Inversely, as the square of their distances apart. Kenneth Rexroth.—MoT
Invictus. William Ernest Henley.—RoIt
Invisible boy. Shel Silverstein.—SiW
Invisible tree. Ryuichi Tamura, tr. by Thomas Fitzsimmons.—MoT
Invisibility
Invisible boy. S. Silverstein.—SiW
Invisible tree. R. Tamura.—MoT
The perils of invisibility. W. S. Gilbert.—CoPt
The **invitation.** See Isaiah
Invitation. Shel Silverstein.—SiW
An **invitation** to Madison county. Jay Wright.—AdPb
Invitation to Miss Marianne Moore. Elizabeth Bishop.—PlM
Invitation to the bee. Charlotte Smith.—OpOx
Invitations
Invitation. S. Silverstein.—SiW
An invitation to Madison county. Jay Wright.—AdPb
Invitation to Miss Marianne Moore. E. Bishop.—PlM
Invitation to the bee. C. Smith.—OpOx
The pasture. R. Frost.—JoA-4—LiLc
S O S. LeRoi Jones.—AdM
Invocation. Vassar Miller.—HiN
Invocation of the Creator. Unknown, tr. fr. the Yoruba by Ulli Beier.—AlPa
Invocations
Invocation. V. Miller.—HiN
Invocation of the Creator. Unknown.—AlPa
Iolanthe, sel. William Schwenck Gilbert
Lord Chancellor's song.—RoIt
Ireland, Thelma
Marsupial transportation.—BrM
Ireland
Come back, Paddy Reilly. P. French.—CoPi
Deirdre. J. Stephens.—JoA-4
"The harp that once through Tara's halls." T. Moore.—RoIt
"I am of Ireland." W. B. Yeats.—CoPi
Irish-American dignitary. A. Clarke.—CoPi
The outlaw of Loch Lene. Unknown.—CoPi
The passage at night—the blaskets. R. Flower.—CoPi
Seascape. L. Hughes.—HoD
The Shandon bells. Father Prout.—CoPi
A song of winter. Unknown.—CoPi
The two travellers. C. J. Boland.—CoPi
Under Ben Bulben. W. B. Yeats.—PlM
Ireland—History
Brian Boy Magee. E. Carbery.—CoPi
The dead at Clonmacnoise. Unknown.—CoPi
Droit de Seigneur. R. Murphy.—CoPi
1867. J. M. Plunkett.—CoPi
Irish curse on the occupying English. Unknown.—CoPi
Lament for the death of Eoghan Ruadh O'Neill. T. Davis.—CoPi
Whack fol the diddle. P. Kearney.—CoPi
"When I was a little girl." A. Milligan.—CoPi
Iremonger, Valentin
Spring stops me suddenly.—CoPi
This houre her vigill.—CoPi
Irina
"A hungry wolf is in the street."—MoM
"The radish is blooming."—MoM
Irish
I'll wear a shamrock. M. C. Davies.—LaM
An Irish airman foresees his death. W. B. Yeats.—PeS
The Irish colonel. A. C. Doyle.—CoPu
Light dying. B. Kennelly.—CoPi
Mavrone, one of those sad Irish poems, with notes. A. Guiterman.—LiS
My Ulick. C. J. Kickham.—CoPi
Numerous Celts. J. C. Squire.—LiS
"Riggedy, higgedy, wiggedy, rig." Unknown.—LaM
"When Irish hearts are happy." Unknown.—LaM
An **Irish** airman foresees his death. William Butler Yeats.—PeS
Irish-American dignitary. Austin Clarke.—CoPi
The **Irish** colonel. A. Conan Doyle.—CoPu
Irish curse on the occupying English. Unknown, tr. fr. the Irish by Máire MacEntee.—CoPi
"**Irish** poets, learn your trade." See Under Ben Bulben
"The **iron** rails run into the sun." See Slow program
Iroquois Indians. See Indians of the Americas—Iroquois
Irving, Patricia
Going where.—AlW
Goodbye and run.—AlW

Legend.—AlW
"A silver mist creeps along the shore."—AlW
"Sun dancers."—AlW
Sweet winds of love.—AlW
Why.—AlW
You too.—AlW
Irwin, Wallace
The ballad of Hagensack.—CoPt
A nautical extravaganza.—CoPt
The powerful eyes o'Jeremy Tait.—CoPt
The sea serpant.—CoOh
"**Is.**" See Energy
"**Is** all our life, then, but a dream." Lewis Carroll.—LiPc
"**Is** black power a knife in your back." See What's black power
"**Is** Easter just a day of hats." See Easter morning
Is is like is. Adrien Stoutenberg.—MoT
"**Is** it a dream, or not. During my fever." See The blue gift
Is it a month. John M. Synge.—CoPi
"**Is** it a month since I and you." See Is it a month
"**Is** it for me to see you." See A question
"**Is** Mary in the dairy." See Where's Mary
"**Is** six times one a lot of fun." Karla Kuskin.—KuN
"**Is** that a cuckoo singing." Yun Sun-do, tr. fr. the Korean by Chung Seuk Park and ad. by Virginia Olsen Baron.—BaSs
"**Is** there a place where." See Shadows
Is there anybody here. Unknown.—BrW
"**Is** there anybody here that loves my Jesus." See Is there anybody here
"**Is** there anybody there, said the traveller." See The listeners
"**Is** there not an appointed time to man upon earth, are not his days also like the days of a hireling." See Job, Bible, Old Testament—The complaint to God
"**Is** this my country or is it mere soil." See Motswasele's farewell
Is this real. Unknown, tr. fr. the Pawnee.—BiI
Is this someone you know. John Ciardi.—UnGb
"**Is** yo eye so empty." See Signals
"**Isabel** met an enormous bear." See Adventures of Isabel
Isaiah
From the prophecy against Egypt. See Isaiah
The invitation. See Isaiah
Isaiah, sels. Bible, Old Testament
From the prophecy against Egypt.—MeP
The invitation.—MeP
The writing of Hezekiah King of Judah, when he had been sick, and was recovered of his sickness.—MeP
The writing of Hezekiah King of Judah, when he had been sick, and was recovered of his sickness. See Isaiah
Island. Langston Hughes.—HoD
"The **island** of Llince." N. M. Bodecker.—BoL
"The **island** of Lundy." N. M. Bodecker.—BoL
"The **island** of Mull." N. M. Bodecker.—BoL
"The **island** of Murray." N. M. Bodecker.—BoL
"The **island** of Rum." N. M. Bodecker.—BoL
"The **island** of Yarrow." N. M. Bodecker.—BoL
"The **island** of Yorrick." N. M. Bodecker.—BoL
The **island**: 1620-1942, sel. Francis Brett Young
Atlantic Charter.—JoA-4
Islands
By ferry to the island. I. C. Smith.—ToM
The castaways. E. V. Rieu.—CoPt
Flannan isle. W. W. Gibson.—CoPt
Isle of Arran. A. Reid.—HaWr
Island. L. Hughes.—HoD
"The island of Llince." N. M. Bodecker.—BoL
"The island of Lundy." N. M. Bodecker.—BoL
"The island of Mull." N. M. Bodecker.—BoL
"The island of Murray." N. M. Bodecker.—BoL
"The island of Rum." N. M. Bodecker.—BoL
"The island of Yarrow." N. M. Bodecker.—BoL
"The island of Yorrick." N. M. Bodecker.—BoL
Islands in Boston harbor. D. McCord.—McFm
The parting. A. Rich.—HaWr
Robinson Crusoe's island. From Davy and the goblin. C. E. Carryl.—RoIt
Sailing to an island. R. Murphy.—ToM
Storm on the island. S. Heaney.—HiN
The story of Samuel Jackson.—C. G. Leland.—CoPt
Verses. W. Cowper.—RoIt
Islands in Boston harbor. David McCord.—McFm
Isle of Arran. Alastair Reid.—HaWr
Isleta Indians. See Indians of the Americas—Isleta
Israel
A denunciation of the princes and prophets. From Micah.—MeP
Dress me, dear mother. A. Shlonsky.—MeP
Go down, Moses. Unknown.—AbM—BrW
In the middle of this century. Y. Amichai.—MeP
National thoughts. Y. Amichai.—MeP
"Rejoice not, O Israel, for joy." From Hosea.—MeP
Shepherds in Judea. J. Ingalls.—LaS
The silver tray. N. Alterman.—MeP
Issa.
"Ah, cherry blossoms."—HaW
"At his writing lesson."—HaW
"Back in my home town."—BeM
"Come and play with me."—HaW
"Cricket, my boy."—HaW
"Dear me, dear me."—HaW
"Don't mind my small hut."—HaW
"Even butterflies."—HaW
"Evening swallows flying home."—HaW
"A father deer."—HaW
"The fawn."—AtM
"The first firefly."—HaW

"It is not enough." See The prophet's warning or shoot to kill
"It is not growing like a tree." See To the immortal memory of that noble pair, Sir Lucius Cary and Sir Henry Morison.—The noble nature
"It is portentous, and a thing of state." See Abraham Lincoln walks at midnight
"It is the endless dance of the dead." See Dirge
"It is the first mild day of March." See To my sister
"It is the football season." See Autumn
"It is the picnic with Ruth in the spring." See The picnic
"It is to a goodly child well fitting." See A goodly child
"It is what he does not know." See On a squirrel crossing the road in autumn, in New England
"It is whatever day, whatever time it is." See Sunday morning
"It isn't proper, I guess you know." See Read this with gestures
"It lies ripe in the turnip patch." See The pumpkin
"It matters not what star I follow." See A time for singing
"It must have been a year." See Fire, hair, meat and bone
It never looks like summer. Thomas Hardy.—PlP
"It never looks like summer here." See It never looks like summer
It out-Herods Herod, pray you, avoid it. Anthony Hecht.—HiN
"It pleased her to step in front and sit." See The figure in the scene
"It rained." Shin Heum, tr. fr. the Korean by Chung Seuk Park and ad. by Virginia Olsen Baron.—BaSs
"It rely is ridikkelus." See Bobby's first poem
"It runs (or rather gallops) roughly as follows: we quote from memory (having no boots of reference at hand)." See How I brought the good news from Aix to Ghent (or vice versa)
"It runs up the hill." Unknown.—EmN
"It seems to me, said Booker T." See Booker T. and W. E. B.
"It seems wrong that out of this bird." See A blackbird singing
"It shouldn't start to rain today." See Spring Saturday
"It stands there under the open skies." See The little house
"It SUSHES." See Cynthia in the snow
"It takes a cool cool boy."—Unknown.—MoBw
"It tickles me." Unknown.—EmN
"It took place not long ago." See Ago love
"It walks east, west, north, and south." Unknown.—EmN
"It was a funky deal." Etheridge Knight.—AdB—AdPb
"It was a gentle sawbones and his name was Doctor Brown." See Gentle Doctor Brown
"It was a hungry pussy cat." See A fable
"It was a long time ago." See As I grew older
"It was a night in winter." See The witnesses
"It was a violent time, Wheels, racks, and fires." See A mirror for poets
"It was a wise old woman who gave this charm to me." See Luck for Halloween
"It was an old, old, old lady." See One, two, three
"It was as if Gaugin." See Far from Africa: Four poems—Etta Moten's attic
"It was bright day and all the trees were still." See Silence
"It was down by the dirty river." See And they lived happily ever after for a while
"It was in Juda's land by God's almighty hand." See In the valley
"It was laughing time, and the tall giraffe." See Laughing time
"It was Mabbie without the grammar school gates." See The ballad of Chocolate Mabbie
"It was many and many a year ago." See Annabel Lee
"It was many and many a year ago." See Cannibalee: A poem of passion
"It was many and many a year ago." See The cannibal flea
"It was my thirtieth year in heaven." See Poem in October
"It was nine o'clock at midnight and a quarter after three." See The bagpipe who didn't say no
"It was not I who began it." See Eve to her daughters
"It was not in the winter." See The time of roses
"It was one afternoon when I was young." See The tale of the hermit told
"It was six men of Indostan." See The blind men and the elephant
"It was snowing." See Footprints
"It was the schooner Hesperus." See The wreck of the Hesperus
"It was the time when lilies blow." See Lady Clare
It was the wind. Unknown, tr. fr. the Navajo by Washington Matthews.—BiI
"It was the wind that gave them life." See It was the wind
"It was upon a Maundy Thursday that Our Lord." See Judas
"It was water I was trying to think of all the time." See Appoggiatura
"It was what you bore with you, woman." See Without, not within her
"It was wild." See Assassination
"It was winter." See Christmas star
"It was you, Atthis, who said." Sappho, tr. fr. the Greek by Mary Barnard.—ThI
"It was your way, my dear." See Without ceremony

"It wasn't a sizable interruption." See The mole
"It wasn't intended that the cow should find the poppies." See Caprice
"It whistles, hisses, burbles and boils." See The teakettle
"It will not hurt me when I am old." See Moonlight
Italy
Tarantula. M. A. Hoberman.—HoR
Itinerant. Eve Merriam.—MeO
"It's a foggy day." David McCord
Two triolets.—McS
"It's a long way to Easy Street." Unknown.—MoBw
"It's a mighty hard row that my poor hands has hoed." See Pastures of plenty
"It's a new kind of day." Kali Grosvenor.—AdM
"It's a sun day." See Sun day
"It's a very odd thing." See Miss T
"It's a warm wind, the west wind, full of birds' cries." See The west wind
"It's all right to cry." Carol Hall.—ThF
"It's an old adage." See Rumor
"It's been a bad year for the moles." David McCord
Three limericks.—McS
"It's blowing, it's snowing." Mother Goose, tr. fr. the Dutch.—TucMg
"It's Christmas day. I did not get." See Otto
Its curtains. Ted Joans.—AdPb
It's dark in here. Shel Silverstein.—SiW
"It's fall." Myrna Campbell.—HoC
It's here in the. Russell Atkins.—AdPb—PeS
"It's hot." Andre Carrington.—HoC
"It's in the church." Unknown.—EmN
"It's little for glory I care." Charles Lever.—CoPi
"It's me." See Me, in Kulu Se and Karma
"It's me only me left in my world." See Tiny world
"It's nice to be natural." Unknown.—MoBw
"It's not all so simple in the yards of houses." See Not so simple
"It's not so easy." Unknown, tr. fr. the Japanese by Harry Behn.—BeM
"It's not the dead that shall praise you today, O Lord." See Those who go, not to return
"It's not the man who knows the most." Unknown.—MoBw
"It's once I courted as pretty a lass." Unknown.—TrG
"Its quick soft silver bell beating, beating." See Auto wreck
"It's raining, it's pouring." Unknown.—EmN
"It's raining, it's raining." Mother Goose.—TucMgl
"It's raining, said John Twaining." Unknown, tr. fr. the Danish by N. M. Bodecker.—BoI
"It's rotten." Karla Kuskin.—KuA
"It's sad." See Mayor
"It's sensible that icicles." See A song of thanks
"It's such a." See Ennui
"It's the nicht atween the saints and souls." Unknown.—MaF (sel.)
"It's true Mattie Lee." See Unidentified flying object
"It's very difficult for two shells to speak." See Quatrains—Shell to gentleman
"Its wicked little windows leer." See The witch's house
"Itty mitty tippity tab." Unknown.—EmN
Ivanova, Irina
"Hi there, friend or foe."—MoM
"The house is in ruins."—MoM
Ivanushkin, Anatoli
The nonconformist.—MoM
"I've an ingle, shady ingle, near a dusky bosky dingle." See Midsummer jingle
"I've been eating onions." Unknown.—MoBw
"I've been through Africa." See I've seen enough
"I've bought me a watermelon." See The watermelon
"I've built myself a stairway." See Untitled
"I've buried so many birds." See Little dead
"I've colored a picture with crayons." See Crayons
"I've done it, I've done it." See Invention
"I've got a dog as thin as a rail." Unknown.—CoOr
I've got a home in that rock. Raymond Richard Patterson.—AdM—AdPb
"I've got a rocket." Unknown.—JoA-4
"I've got a special person." See The special person
"I've got three hens. A rooster? No." See Plymouth rocks, of course
I've got to know. Woody Guthrie.—PeS
"I've heard so much about other folks' folks." Ted Hughes.—HuMf
"I've known rivers." See The Negro speaks of rivers
"I've looked behind the shed." See Gone
"I've never washed my shadow out." See Shadow wash
I've seen enough. Christopher Meyer.—JoV
"I've seen everything." Jōsō, tr. fr. the Japanese by Geoffrey Bownas and Anthony Thwaite.—MaFw
"I've stayed in the front yard all my life." See A song in the front yard
"I've tried to think of something." Unknown.—MoBw
I've watched you now. William Wordsworth.—RoIt
"I've watched you now a full half-hour." See I've watched you now
Ivory masks in orbit. Keorapetse Kgositsile.—AdPb
Ivy
Arson. L. Moore.—MoSp
The ivy-wife. T. Hardy.—PlP
The witch's garden. L. Moore.—MoSm
The **ivy-wife.** Thomas Hardy.—PlP

J

J. Prior, Esq. N. M. Bodecker.—BoL
Jabberwocky. See Through the looking-glass
Jack. Charles Henry Ross.—OpOx
"Jack and Jill went up the hill." Mother Goose.—AlC—JoA-4
"Jack be nimble." Mother Goose.—JoA-4
"Jack, Jack, the bread's a-burning." Mother Goose.—AlC
Jack, Jill, Spratts, and Horner. David McCord.—McAa
Jack-o'-lanterns. See Hallowe'en
"Jack Sprat could eat no fat." Mother Goose.—AlC—JoA-4
"The **jackals** prowl, the serpents hiss." See Elegy
"Jacko the Skunk, in black and white." See The skunk
Jackson, Barry
"You think you're smart."—MoBw
Jackson, Helen Hunt (H. H., pseud.; Helen Hunt; Saxe Holme, pseud.)
September.—RoIt
Jackson, Leroy F.
Grandpa dropped his glasses.—BrM
Off to Yakima.—BrM
Jackson, Mae
The blues today.—AdB—AdPb
For some poets.—AdB—AdPb
"I remember. . . . "—AdB—AdM—AdPb
"I used to wrap my white doll up in."—AdB—AdPb
January 3, 1970.—AdPb
Reincarnation.—AdPb
Jackson, Mahalia (about)
When Mahalia sings. Q. Prettyman.—AdPb
Jacob (about)
Jacob's ladder. Unknown.—BrW
Jacobs, A. C.
Alone. tr.—MeP
On the mound of corpses in the snow. tr.—MeP
Jacob's ladder. Unknown.—BrW
Jacobs, Leland B.
Bus stop.—HoP
Preferred vehicles.—HoP
What witches do.—HoH
When I'm an astronaut.—BrM
"Jade charm of human life." See Hope
"A **jagged** mountain." See From an airplane
Jaguars
"The night is black." K. Kuskin.—KuA
Jails. See also Prisons and prisoners
A surprise. M. Douglas.—CoOr
To Bobby Seale. L. Clifton.—AdM—AdPb
"Jake, Jake, open the gate." Unknown.—EmN
"Jam." Mary Ann Hoberman.—HoN
The **jam** fish. Edward Abbott Parry.—OpOx
"A **jam** fish sat on a hard-bake rock." See A jam fish
Jamaica
Jamaica market. A. Maxwell-Hall.—AbM
Jamaica market. Agnes Maxwell-Hall.—AbM
Jamboree. Lee Blair.—JaP
James II, King of England
Song of the Western men. R. S. Hawker.—RoIt
Jane Smith. Rudyard Kipling.—LiS
Janet waking. John Crowe Ransom.—HiN—PeS
"The **jangle** of the jeering crows." See Black humor
January
January ("The fox drags its wounded belly") R. S. Thomas.—CoPu
January ("Walk tall in the world") L. Clifton.—ClE
Odes of the months. Aneirin.—MaFw (sel.)
January ("The fox drags its wounded belly") R. S. Thomas.—CoPu
January ("Walk tall in the world") Lucille Clifton.—ClE
"January brings the snow." See The garden year
January 3, 1970. Mae Jackson.—AdPb
Japanese
Japanese children. J. Kirkup.—MaFw
Japanese lesson. D. McCord.—McAa
Japanese children. James Kirkup.—MaFw
Japanese lesson. David McCord.—McAa
Jaques, Florence Page
A goblinade.—JaP
Jarrell, Randall
Bats.—AdP—MoT—ToM
The bird of night.—AdP—HiN—MoT
The chipmunk's day.—HiN
The death of the ball turret gunner.—PeS
The elementary scene.—PeS
The lonely man.—ToM
"My aunt kept turnips in a flock."—LiW
Jars. See Pottery
Jastrzebski, Teresa
"Flowers."—HoC
Jaszi, Jean
Fight.—BrM
"Jay bird, jay bird." Unknown.—EmN
Jays
"Jay bird, jay bird." Unknown.—EmN
Jazz
Dance of the infidels. A. Young.—AdPb
From jazz for five. J. Smith.—ToM (sel.)
Here where Coltrane is. M. S. Harper.—AdPb
Jazz fantasia. C. Sandburg.—SaT
"The jazz world." M. Gill.—JoV
John Coltrane an impartial review. A. B. Spellman.—AdPb
Mingus. B. Kaufman.—AdPb
The move continuing. A. Young.—AdPb
Walking Parker home. B. Kaufman.—AdPb
Jazz fantasia. Carl Sandburg.—SaT
Jazz for five. John Smith.—ToM
"The **jazz** world." Michael Gill.—JoV
Jealousy
The bishop orders his tomb at Saint Praxed's church. R. Browning.—MoG
February—It's an ill wind. F. Holman.—HoI

Jealousy—*Continued*
The first tooth. C. and M. Lamb.—OpOx
The rival. T. Hardy.—PlP
"**Jean,** Jean, Jean." Unknown.—BlM
Jean Richepin's song. Herbert Trench.—CoPi—CoPt
"**Jean** said, No." See Secret
Jeffers, Lance
"Grief streams down my chest."—AdPb
How high the moon.—AdPb
"My blackness is the beauty of this land."—AdPb
On listening to the spirituals.—AdPb
Jeffers, Robinson
Eagle valor, chicken mind.—CoPu
Harder than granite.—CoPu
Hurt hawks.—PeS
Jeffries, Jim (about)
My Lord, what a morning. W. Cuney.—AbM
"**Jellicle** cats come out tonight." See The song of the Jellicles
Jellyfish
A jellyfish ("Visible, invisible") M. Moore.—JoA-4
The jellyfish ("Who wants my jellyfish") O. Nash.—CoOh
Love song for a jellyfish. S. Hockman.—CoPu
Triolet. G. K. Chesterton.—LiLc
A **jellyfish** ("Visible, invisible") Marianne Moore.—JoA-4
The **jellyfish** ("Who wants my jellyfish") Ogden Nash.—CoOh
Jenkins, Brooks
Loneliness.—PeS
Jennings, Elizabeth
My grandmother.—ToM
One flesh.—ToM
"**Jenny** kiss'd me in a dream." See Such stuff as dreams
"**Jenny** kiss'd me when we met." Paul Dehn.—LiS
Jenny kissed me. Leigh Hunt.—LiS—RoIt
"**Jenny** kissed me when we met." See Jenny kissed me
"**Jenny** Wren fell sick." Mother Goose.—JoA-4
"**Jerry** Hall." Unknown.—TrG
Jerusalem
Jerusalem. J. Halevi.—MeP
Mayor. Y. Amichai.—MeP
Rocking Jerusalem. Unknown.—BrW
Snow in Jerusalem. T. Carmi.—MeP
Jerusalem. Judah Halevi, tr. fr. the Hebrew by Robert Mezey.—MeP
"The **jester** walked in the garden." See The cap and bells
Jesus and his mother. Thom Gunn.—ToM
"**Jesus** born in Bethlea." Unknown.—LaS
Jesus Christ. See also Christmas; Easter; God
Ballad of the bread man. C. Causley.—ToM
Christ in Alabama. L. Hughes.—AdPb
Christ the Lord most glorious. J. Antes.—LaS
"Christmas." A. Fair.—HoC
A Christmas folk-song. L. W. Reese.—JoA-4
Christ's nativity. From Gospel according to Luke, Bible, New Testament.—RoIt
Christus natus est. C. Cullen.—AbM
Church burning: Mississippi. J. A. Emanuel.—AdPb
Conception. W. Cuney.—AbM
Confession stone. O. Dodson.—AbM
Cradle hymn. M. Luther.—JoA-4
Away in a manger.—LaS
En el portal de Belén (At the Crèche). Unknown.—LaS
Ex ore infantium. F. Thompson.—OpOx
"Gentle Jesus, meek and mild." C. Wesley.—OpOx
"Go tell it on the mountain." Unknown.—AbM—BrW—HoS (sel.)—LaS
God rest ye, merry gentlemen. D. M. Mulock.—JoA-4
"I told Jesus." S. Plumpp.—AdPb
I wonder as I wander. Unknown.—JoA-4; also version by J. J. Niles.—LaS
In freezing winter night. R. Southwell.—MaFw
In the wilderness. R. Graves.—JoA-4
Jesus and his mother. T. Gunn.—ToM
"Jesus born in Bethlea." Unknown.—LaS
Jesus was crucified or: It must be deep. C. M. Rodgers.—AdPb
King of kings. Unknown.—BrW
Long, long ago. Unknown.—HoS—RoIt
The Lord of the Dance. S. Carter.—LaS
Los royes oriente. Unknown.—LaS
Mary had a baby. Unknown.—BrW—LaS
"My song is love unknown." S. Crossman.—OpOx
"O little town of Bethlehem." P. Brooke.—JoA-4—LaS
"Once in royal David's city." C. F. Alexander.—OpOx
The second coming. W. B. Yeats.—MoG
Suzanne. L. Cohen.—MoG
There is a green hill. C. F. Alexander.—OpOx
To Christ our Lord. G. Kinnell.—HaWr
"Wake ev'ry breath." W. Billings.—LaS
When Jesus wept. W. Billings.—LaS
"While shepherds watched their flocks by night." N. Tate.—JoA-4
Who are you—who are you. D. Clarke, Jr.—JoV
The witnesses. C. Sansom.—MaFw (sel.)
"Woman, you'll never credit what." R. Ponchon.—CoPt
"**Jesus,** Estrella, Esperanza, Mercy." See Middle passage
"**Jesus,** Jesus, rest your head." John Jacob Niles.—LaS
"**Jesus'** mother never had no man." See Conception
"**Jesus** our brother, kind and good." See The friendly beasts
Jesus was crucified or: It must be deep. Carolyn M. Rodgers.—AdPb
Jewels. See Precious stones

Jewels. Valerie Worth.—WoS
Jews
Beyond melody. N. Alterman.—MeP
"Candles." A. Coors.—HoC
On the mound of corpses in the snow. U. Z. Greenberg.—MeP
Pictures of the Jews. C. Guri.—MeP
The silver tray. N. Alterman.—MeP
We were not like dogs. U. Z. Greenberg.—MeP
Jewsbury, Maria Jane
Partings.—OpOx
To a young brother.—OpOx
Jezrael (about)
Jezrael. A. Shlonsky.—MeP
Jezreel. T. Hardy.—PlP
Jezrael. Avraham Shlonsky, tr. fr. the Hebrew by Ruth Finer Mintz.—MeP (sel.)
Jezreel. Thomas Hardy.—PlP
"**Jg** mu qjl vgrv x ugemdt pupdeto? wxxl x ugmh vj f jji." Lewis Carroll.—LiPc
Jig. C. Day-Lewis.—CoPi
The **jigsaw** puzzle in the sky. Felice Holman.—HoI
"**Jill** told Bill." See Glad to have a friend like you
Jim, who ran away from his nurse, and was eaten by a lion. Hilaire Belloc.—OpOx
Jiménez, Juan Ramón
The canary's flight.—JoA-4
Peep show.—JoA-4
Platero.—JoA-4
Jimmy Jet and his TV set. Shel Silverstein.—SiW
"**Jimson** lives in a new." See A call to the wild
Jingle bells. James Pierpont.—RoIt
Jitterbugging in the streets. Calvin C. Hernton.—AdPb
Jo Myung-ri
"Since wild geese flew south."—BaSs
"**Joal.**" Léopold Sédar Senghor, tr. fr. the French by John Reed and Clive Wake.—AlPa
Joans, Ted
Black people.—AdM
Its curtains.—AdPb
My ace of spades.—AdB
"The protective grigri."—AdPb
Scenery.—AdPb
Souk.—AbM
The truth.—AdB
Job
The complaint to God. See Job
The horse. See Job
Job, sels. Bible, Old Testament
The complaint to God.—MeP
The horse.—RoIt
Job (about)
The complaint to God. From Job, Bible, Old Testament.—MeP
Joey. Shel Silverstein.—SiW
"**Joey** Joey took a stone." See Joey
Joey Kangaroo. Aileen Fisher.—FiD
"**Jog** on, jog on the footpath way." See The winter's tale—Autolycus' song
Jogging
Autolycus' song. From The winter's tale. W. Shakespeare.—LiS
Autolycus' song (in basic English). R. L. Greene.—LiS
Johannesburg, South Africa
Song of young men working in the gold mines of Johannesburg. Unknown.—AlPa
John. N. M. Bodecker.—BoL
"**John** and Mary." Unknown.—EmN
John Anderson, my jo. Robert Burns.—RoIt
"**John** Anderson, my jo, John." See John Anderson, my jo
John Bun. Unknown.—LiWw
"**John** Cabot, out of Wilma, once a Wycliffe." See Riot
John Coltrane an impartial review. A. B. Spellman.—AdPb
"**John** could take his clothes off." See John
John Henry. Unknown.—AbM
"**John** Henry said to his captain." See John Henry
John-John. Thomas MacDonagh.—CoPi—CoPt
"**John** Littlehouse the redhead was a large ruddy man." See The blacksmith's serenade
John Mouldy. Walter De La Mare.—HiN—OpOx
John Muir on Mt Ritter. See Burning
"**John** Oswald McGuffin he wanted to die." See But then
"**John** Smith's a very guid man." Unknown, tr. fr. the Scottish by Norah and William Montgomerie.—JoA-4
John, Tom, and James. Charles Henry Ross.—OpOx
"**John** was a bad boy, and beat a poor cat." See John, Tom, and James
"**John** Wesley Gaines." Unknown.—CoPu
"**Johnnie** Crack and Flossie Snail." See Under Milkwood
"**Johnny,** come home." Lois Lenski.—LeC
"**Johnny** Crow." See Johnny Crow's garden
Johnny Crow's garden. L. Leslie Brooke.—JoA-4
Johnny Dow. See "Wha lies here"
"**Johnny** drew a monster." Lilian Moore.—MoSm
Johnny has gone for a soldier. Unknown.—RoIt
"**Johnny,** Johnny, down by the sea." Unknown.—EmN
"**Johnny** made a custard." See Some cook
"**Johnny** over the ocean." Unknown.—EmN
"**Johnny** said to Tommy, How much are your geese." Unknown.—EmN
"**Johnny** shall have a new bonnet." Mother Goose.—JoA-4
"**Johnny** stole a penny once." Unknown.—CoOh
Johnson, Alicia Loy
A black poetry day.—AdB

The new pieta: For the mothers and children of Detroit.—AdPb
Uncle Bull-boy.—AdPb
Jordan, Norman
August 2.—AdPb
August 8.—AdM
Black warrior.—AdPb
Feeding the lions.—AdB—AdPb
July 31.—AdPb
Jordan river
"Deep river." Unknown.—BrW
One more river. Unknown.—RoIt
"Roll Jordan roll." Unknown.—BrW
"**Jorridge** and Porridge." Louise Ayres Garnett.—BrM
Joseph, Jenny
Warning.—ToM
Joseph Mica. Unknown.—MoG
"**Joseph** Mica was good engineer." See Joseph Mica
Joseph, Rosemary
Baking day.—ToM
Josephine. Alexander Resnikoff.—CoOr
"**Josephine,** Josephine." See Josephine
Jōsō
"Hills have disappeared."—BeM
"I've seen everything."—MaFw
"When cherry trees bloom."—BeM
Journey. Marchette Chute.—ChRu
Joy. See Happiness
Joy. Langston Hughes.—AbM
"**Joy** fills me." See Song of a dead one
"**Joy** of the springtime. How the sun." See Sisyphus
"**Joy** to Philip, he this day." See Going into breeches
Joyce, James
Chamber music, sels.
"Lean out of the window."—RoIt
The noise of waters.—RoIt
Chamber music (XXXV).—MaFw
"Strings in the earth and air"
Chamber music (I).—MaFw
"Lean out of the window." See Chamber music
The noise of waters. See Chamber music
"Strings in the earth and air." See Chamber music
"**J's** the jumping Jay-walker." See All around the town
Juan Chi
Fifteen poems of my heart.—MaFw (sel.)
Juba dance. Unknown.—AbM
"**Juba** jump and juba sing." See Juba dance
Judah al-Harizi
A secret kept.—MeP
Judah Halevi
The apple.—MeP
Cups without wine.—MeP
Jerusalem.—MeP
Mount Avarim.—MeP
My heart is in the East.—MeP
To Moses ibn Ezra, in Christian Spain.—MeP
Judas. Unknown.—MaFw
Judeebug's country. Joe Johnson.—AdPb
"**Judge** not your friends from outward show." Unknown.—EmN
"**Judging** from the pictures." Karai Senryū, tr. fr. the Japanese by Geoffrey Bownas and Anthony Thwaite.—MaFw
Judgment. Ted Palmanteer.—AlW
Judgment and sunrise. See Malachi
Judgment day
Holy sonnet VII. J. Donne.—MaFw
Judgment. T. Palmanteer.—AlW
Juggler. Richard Wilbur.—HiN
Juggler Doug. X. J. Kennedy.—KeO
Jugglers
Juggler. R. Wilbur.—HiN
Juggler Doug. X. J. Kennedy.—KeO
"The wiggling, wriggling, jiggling juggler." J. Prelutsky.—PrC
JuJu. Askia Muhammad Touré.—AdPb
A **Juju** of my own. Lebert Bethune.—AdPb
Juke box love song. Langston Hughes.—AdPb
"**Julia** loves her Rosalie." Karla Kuskin.—KuN
Julie-Jane. Thomas Hardy.—PlP
Juliet. Hilaire Belloc.—CoPu
Julius Caesar and the honey-bee. Charles Tennyson Turner.—RoIt
"**Julius** Caesar made a law." Mother Goose.—TucMgl
July
July. J. Clare.—PaF
July in Dutchess county. B. Deutsch.—HaWr
Snowman. S. Silverstein.—SiW
"What is the opposite of *July.*" R. Wilbur.—WiO
July ("Everett Anderson thinks he'll make") Lucille Clifton.—ClE
July ("Loud is the summer's busy song") John Clare.—PaF (sel.)
July in Dutchess county. Babette Deutsch.—HaWr
July 31. Norman Jordan.—AdPb
Jumble jingle. Laura E. Richards.—BrM
The **Jumblies.** Edward Lear.—JoA-4—OpOx—RoIt
"**Jump,** jump, jump." Unknown.—EmN
Jump-rope rhymes
"Apples, peaches, cream, and butter." Unknown.—EmN
"Apples, peaches, peanut butter." Unknown.—EmN
"Apples, peaches, pumpkin pie." Unknown.—EmN
"Barbara, Barbara." Unknown.—EmN
"Betty, Betty, Betty Jo." Unknown.—EmN
"Betty Boop." Unknown.—EmN
"Bluebells, cockle shells." Unknown.—EmN
"Charlie Chaplin sat on a pin." Unknown.—EmN
"Charlie Chaplin went to France." Unknown.—EmN
"Cinderella, dressed in black." Unknown.—EmN
"Cinderella, dressed in blue." Unknown.—EmN

The pig tale. From Sylvie and Bruno. L. Carroll.—LiPc
Jumping Joan. See "One-ery, two-ery, ziccary zan"
Jumping rope. Shel Silverstein.—SiW
June
June. L. Clifton.—ClE
June thunder. L. MacNeice.—ToM
The rose. J. Howell.—PaF
"So, some tempestuous morn in early June." From Thyrsis. M. Arnold.—PaF
The vision of Sir Launfal. J. R. Lowell, sel.
June.—RoIt
The vision of Sir Launfal.—PaF
June. See The vision of Sir Launfal
June. Lucille Clifton.—ClE
"The **June-bug's** got the golden wing." See Bedbug
June thunder. Louis MacNeice.—ToM
"**June's** here." Clifford Martindale.—HoC
"The **Junes** were free and full, driving through tiny." See June thunder
Jungle gym. Lois Lenski.—LeC
Jungle incident. Russell Gordon Carter.—BrM
"**Jungle** necklaces are hung." See Here she is
Junglegrave. S. E. Anderson.—AdPb
Jungles and jungle life
Magalu. H. Johnson.—AdPb
The nature of jungles. W. R. Moses.—HiN
The tropics in New York. C. McKay.—AdPb—RoIt
Junk and junkyards
"Hector the collector." S. Silverstein.—SiW
"The opposite of *junk* is *stuff*." R. Wilbur.—WiO
Passing by the junkyard. C. J. Egita.—HoP
Resting in peace. R. Froman.—FrSp
Rummage. E. Merriam.—MeO
"**Junked** car." See Resting in peace
Junod, Henri A.
Song of young men working in the gold mines of Johannesburg. tr.—AlPa
Jurin
"When nightingales burst."—BeM
"**Just** around the corner." David McCord.—McF
"**Just** as I'd sucked in wind to take." See A monstrous mouse
"**Just** as the moon was fading." See Kris Kringle
"**Just** because your head is shaped like an air conditioner." Unknown.—MoBw
Just before April came. Carl Sandburg.—SaT
Just born pig. Fred Lape.—CoPu
"**Just** for a handful of silver he left us." See The lost leader
"**Just** let old Stan swing by his." See Safety first
"**Just** like a puzzle, always mixed up." Unknown.—MoBw
Just me, just me. Shel Silverstein.—SiW
"**Just** off the highway to Rochester, Minnesota." See A blessing
"**Just** the place for a snark, the Bellman cried." See The hunting of the snark
Justice, Donald
Beyond the hunting woods.—HiN
The grandfathers.—HiN
Incident in a rose garden.—HiN
A local storm.—HiN
Memory of a porch.—HiN
On the death of friends in childhood.—HiN
Song.—HiN
Justice
The death of justice. W. E. Hawkins.—AdPb
The rain it raineth. Lord Bowen.—CoPu—LiWw
The rain.—RoIt
Sermonette. I. Reed.—AdPb
Wild strawberries. R. Graves.—PaF
Justus, May
Luck for Halloween.—HoH
Signs of Christmas.—HoS

K

Kagwa, Apolo. See Doob, Leonard and Kagwa, Apolo
"**Kah-ee-gwoo** nee-mah-jah." See Do not cry
Kahn, Sholom J.
At the scorpions' ascent. tr.—MeP
Kahshe or Chicoutime. Dennis Lee.—LeA
Kajima Shozo. See Guest, Harry and Lynn
Kaleeba. Unknown, tr. fr. the Luganda by W. Moses Serwadda.—SeS
Kamensky, Andrei
The young Cossack.—MoM
Kamimura Hajime
Firefly.—MoT
Kangaroo. D. H. Lawrence.—MaFw
Kangaroo and kiwi. X. J. Kennedy.—KeO
Kangaroos
The duck and the kangaroo. E. Lear.—JoA-4—OpOx
Joey Kangaroo. A. Fisher.—FiD
Kangaroo. D. H. Lawrence.—MaFw
Kangaroo and kiwi. X. J. Kennedy.—KeO
Marsupial transportation. T. Ireland.—BrM
Wish. M. A. Hoberman.—HoR
Kantner, Paul
"We can be together."—MoG
—See also Crosby, David; Kantner, Paul; and Stills, Stephen, jt. auths.
Karai Senryū
"The chicken wants."—MaFw
"Disturbed, the cat."—MaFw
"Judging from the pictures."—MaFw
"Now the man has a child."—MaFw
"Sheltering from the rain."—MaFw
"With his apology."—MaFw
Karener, Walta
Xmas time.—CoPu
Kariuki. Joseph Gatuira.—AlPa
Karlov, Andrei
"The blue wings."—MoM
"In America there is mourning."—MoM
"**Kate's** on for two, Elise is three." See Balloons

The caboose who wouldn't come last.—KeO
Caterpillar on a pillar.—KeO
Census nonsense.—KeO
Cleaning house.—KeO
Cocoa skin coat.—KeO
Constrictor restricter.—KeO
"A coughdrop lies in my doghouse."—KeO
Cows.—KeO
Epitaph for a postal clerk.—LiWw
Exploding gravy.—KeO
Father and mother.—KeO
First confession.—HiN
For children if they'll take them.—RoIt
Giant snail.—KeO
"Great-great Grandma, don't sleep in your treehouse tonight."—KeO
Gumballs.—KeO
Help.—KeO
Instant storm.—KeO
Juggler Doug.—KeO
Kangaroo and kiwi.—KeO
"King Tut."—KeO—LiWw
Little elegy.—CoPu—HiN
Lucky Sukey.—KeO
Mechanical menagerie.—KeO
Medusa.—KeO
Mingled yarns.—KeO
Mixed-up school.—KeO
A monstrous mouse.—KeO
"Mother, a dog is at the door."—KeO
Mother's nerves.—KeO
My birthday cake.—KeO
My yellow telephone.—KeO
Nails.—KeO
"A nervous sea captain from Cheesequake."—KeO
On the ocean floor.—KeO
"One winter night in August."—KeO
Overheard in the Louvre.—LiWw
Planets.—KeO
Sea horse and sawhorse.—KeO
"Sir Percival and the dragon."—KeO
The skeleton walks.—KeO
"Snowflake soufflé."—KeO
A social mixer.—KeO
Special delivery.—KeO
Spider Snyder.—KeO
Stan Stapler.—KeO
"The trouble with a dinosaur."—KeO
Unusual shoelaces.—KeO
Vulture.—KeO
Waking up uncle.—KeO
The whales off Wales.—KeO
Who to pet and who not to.—KeO
Wicked witch's kitchen.—KeO
Kennelly, Brendan
The black cliffs, Ballybunion.—CoPi
Light dying.—CoPi
Maloney remembers the resurrection of Kate Finucane.—CoPt
Kenneth Yasudo
The cuckoo. tr.—MaFw
Kent State, May 4, 1970
Kent State, May 4, 1970. P. Goodman.—MoT
Kent State, May 4, 1970. Paul Goodman.—MoT
Kentucky
The Kentucky wassail song. Unknown.—JoA-4
A road in Kentucky. R. Hayden.—HiN
Kentucky Belle. Constance Fenimore Woolson.—CoPt
The **Kentucky** wassail song. Unknown.—JoA-4
Keys
The keys of Canterbury. Unknown.—JoA-4
"Lock the dairy door." Mother Goose.—AlC
The **keys** of Canterbury. Unknown.—JoA-4
Keziah. Gwendolyn Brooks.—UnGb
Kgositsile, Keorapetse
For Eusi, Ayi Kwei, & Gwen Brooks.—AdPb
Ivory masks in orbit.—AdPb
My name is Afrika.—AdPb
Origins.—AdPb
Spirits unchained.—AdPb
Kickham, Charles J.
My Ulick.—CoPi
"**Kicking** your heels on the dusty road." Phillip Solomon.—JoV
Kid. Robert Hayden.—HiN
Kid stuff. Frank Horne.—AbM—AdPb
Kieran, John
"There's this that I like about hockey, my lad."—FlH
Kikaku
"A bantam rooster."—BeM
"The crickets are saying."—BeM
Fairies.—JaP
"How can a creature."—BeM
"There goes a beggar."—BeM
"Who can stay indoors."—BeM
Kilcash. Unknown, tr. fr. the Irish by Frank O'Connor.—CoPi
The **kill.** Donald Hall.—HaWr
Kilner, Dorothy
Henry's secret.—OpOx
Kim Chang-up
"If everyone were a chief."—BaSs
"With my harp against my knee."—BaSs
Kim Chun-taik
"Dragonflies and heron fly together."—BaSs
Kim Duk-ryung
"On the hill in spring."—BaSs
Kim In-hu
"The blue mountains are what they are."—BaSs
Kim Jae
"I left home without my umbrella."—BaSs
Kim Jong-su
"North wind blows hard through the trees."—BaSs
Kim Jung-hu
"Am I really old, as people say."—BaSs
Kim Koo
"Blessed is today."—BaSs
Kim Kwang-wuk
"Hey there, white seagull."—BaSs
"I like you, bamboo."—BaSs

Kim Sam-hyun
"Only half-awakened from a nap on my pine-needle bed."—BaSs
Kim Sang-yong
"If you talk too much, you are a swindler."—BaSs
"Rain is falling on the paulownia."—BaSs
Kim Soo-jang
"In a hermit's cottage, silent, still."—BaSs
Kim Yu-ki
"Peach and plum blossoms of spring."—BaSs
Kind of an ode to duty. Ogden Nash.—LiWw
Kindergarten. Ronald Rogers.—AlW
Kindness. See also Animals—Care; Service; Sympathy
The beggar man. L. Aikin.—OpOx
The curate's kindness. T. Hardy.—PlP
A curse on a closed gate. Unknown.—CoPi
Dives and Lazarus. Unknown.—MaFw
Forgiven. A. A. Milne.—BrM
The frog. H. Belloc.—BrM—JoA-4—LiLc—OpOx
Going somewhere. F. Holman.—HoI
Kentucky Belle. C. F. Woolson.—CoPt
Leave me alone. F. Holman.—UnGb
Speak gently. D. Bates.—LiS
Trees. H. Behn.—LaM—UnGb
"The warm of heart shall never lack a fire." E. J. Coatsworth.—CoPu
Worlds of different sizes. S. McPherson.—CoPu
You always have to pay. L. Lenski.—LeC
Kindness to animals. See Animals—Care
King Arthur. See Arthur, King (about)
"**King** Arthur and his knights." Ruth Williams.—CoOr
"The **king** asked." See The king's breakfast
King, Ben
But then.—CoPt
That cat.—RoIt
"**King** Dagobert, they say." Mother Goose, tr. fr. the French.—TucMg
"**King** Fisher courted Lady Bird." See Sylvie and Bruno
King Foo Foo. Charles Causley.—CaF
"**King** Foo Foo sat upon his royal throne." See King Foo Foo
"The **king** has married two wives." See The queens' rhyme
King Henry's speech before Agincourt. See King Henry V
King Hyo-jong
"What is so amusing about the rain falling."—BaSs
King Lear, sels. William Shakespeare
"Blow, winds, and crack your cheeks, rage, blow."—MaFw
"Here's the place: stand still: how fearful."—PaP
King, Martin Luther (about)
April 4, 1968. M. Goode.—JoV
Assassination. D. L. Lee.—AdPb—AlB
Death of Dr King. S. Cornish.—AdPb
Death of Dr King #1.—AdM (sel.)
The funeral of Martin Luther King, Jr. N. Giovanni.—AdB
In memoriam, Martin Luther King, Jr. J. Jordan.—AdPb
Martin Luther King, Jr. G. Brooks.—AdB—AdPb
Martin's blues. M. S. Harper.—AdPb
The **king** must die. Bernie Taupin.—MoG
"The **king** of China's daughter." Edith Sitwell.—JoA-4—MaFw
The **King** of Hearts. William Jay Smith.—BrM
King of kings. Unknown.—BrW
The **King** of Spain. William Jay Smith.—BrM
King Richard II, sel. William Shakespeare
The death of kings.—MoG
"The **king** said to Salome." Unknown.—CoOh
"The **king** sent for his wise men all." See Ragged Robin
"**King** Siegfried sat in his lofty hall." See The three songs
"The **king** sits in Dumferling town." See Sir Patrick Spens—The ballad of Sir Patrick Spens
"The **king** sits in Dunfermline town." See Sir Patrick Spens
"**King** Solomon and King David." Unknown.—RoIt
"**King** Tut." X. J. Kennedy.—KeO—LiWw
King, W.
The giant fisherman.—RoIt
"The **king** was on his throne." See The vision of Belshazzar
"The **king** was sick. His cheek was red." See The enchanted shirt
King wind. Mark Van Doren.—HiN
Kingfishers
One kingfisher and one yellow rose. E. Brennan.—CoPi
Kings. See Rulers; also names of kings and rulers, as David, King of Israel
"**Kings.**" See A history lesson
The **king's** breakfast. A. A. Milne.—OpOx
Kingsley, Charles
Alton Locke, sel.
The sands of Dee.—JoA-4—RoIt
A farewell.—OpOx
The knight's leap.—CoPt
The little doll. See The water babies
The old song. See The water babies—Young and old
The sands of Dee. See Alton Locke
The tide river. See The water babies
Young and old. See The water babies
The water babies, sels.
The little doll.—OpOx
The tide river.—OpOx—RoIt
Young and old.—OpOx
The old song.—RoIt
Kingsmill, Hugh
"What, still alive at twenty two."—LiS
Kinnell, Galway
First song.—HiN
"In a parlor containing a table."—CoPu

In fields of summer.—HaWr
In the farmhouse.—HaWr
Ruins under the stars.—HaWr (sel.)
Spring oak.—CoPu
To Christ our Lord.—HaWr
Vapor trail reflected in the frog pond.—PeS
Kinoshita Yūji
Late summer.—MaFw
Kinsella, Thomas
Thirty-three triads. tr.—CoPi
Kiowa Indians. See Indians of the Americas—Kiowa
Kipling, Rudyard
The ballad of Minepit Shaw.—CoPt
Horses.—CoPu
The hump. See Just-so stories
If. See Rewards and fairies
Jane Smith.—LiS
Just-so stories, sels.
The hump.—OpOx
Puck's song.—OpOx
Puck of Pook's hill, sel.
A smuggler's song.—CoPt—OpOx
Puck's song. See Just-so stories
Rewards and fairies, sels.
If.—OpOx
The way through the woods.—OpOx
Seal lullaby.—JoA-4
Seal mother's song.—CoPu
Seal mother's song. See Seal lullaby
A smuggler's song. See Puck of Pook's hill
Sussex.—PaP
"Twelve hundred million men are spread."—CoPu
The way through the woods. See Rewards and fairies
Kirkman, Larry
My friend.—HoCs
Kirkup, James
A correct compassion.—MaFw
Japanese children.—MaFw
Love in a space-suit.—ToM
The shepherd's tale. tr.—CoPt
Tea in a space-ship.—ToM
Waiting.—MaFw
Kiss. Al Young.—AdPb
Kissing
"Cinderella dressed in yellow." Unknown.—EmN
Comin' thro the rye. R. Burns.—LiS
"Down in the meadow." Unknown.—EmN
"Down in the valley." Unknown.—EmN
"Green is green." Unknown.—MoBw
"Health and happiness." Unknown.—MoBw
Her legs. R. Herrick.—LiS
"Here I stand all nice and clean." Unknown.—MoBw
"Here I stand on two little chips." Unknown.—MoBw
"Huckleberry, gooseberry, raspberry pie." C. Watson.—WaF
I saw Esau. Unknown.—BrM
"I saw Esau kissing Kate."—EmN
"Jenny kiss'd me when we met." P. Dehn.—LiS
Jenny kissed me. L. Hunt.—LiS—RoIt
"Johnny, Johnny, down by the sea." Unknown.—EmN
"May you kiss whom you please." Unknown.—MoBw
"Minny and a Minny and a ha, ha, ha." Unknown.—EmN
"Miss Quiss." C. Watson.—WaF
"Mister Lister sassed his sister." C. Watson.—WaF
Modern concert song. Unknown.—AlPa
"Roley Poley, pudding and pie." Mother Goose.—AlC
"Some kiss behind a lily." Unknown.—EmN
Such stuff as dreams. F. P. Adams.—LiS
"There is many a kiss to remember." Unknown.—MoBw
" 'Tis sweet to kiss." Unknown.—MoBw
"Willy, Willy Wilkin." Mother Goose.—HoMg
"Wine and cakes for gentlemen." Mother Goose.—HoMg
Kitahara Hakushū
Rain on Castle island.—MaFw
Kitchens
Early supper. B. Howes.—HiN
In the kitchen of the old house. D. Hall.—ToM
The **kite** ("How bright on the blue") Harry Behn.—JoA-4
The **kite** ("My kite is three feet broad, and six feet long") Adelaide O'Keefe.—OpOx
"**Kite** on the end of the twine." See Three signs of spring
Kites
"All day the kite pinned." A. Atwood.—AtM
I should never have trusted that bird. J. Ciardi.—CiFs
"I'm up here." K. Kuskin.—KuA
"King Arthur and his knights." R. Williams.—CoOr
The kite ("How bright on the blue") H. Behn.—JoA-4
The kite ("My kite is three feet broad, and six feet long") A. O'Keefe.—OpOx
"Kites in the sky." M. A. Hoberman.—HoN
Mr Skinner. N. M. Bodecker.—BoL
"The New Year's day." Issa.—HaW
String. R. Hoban.—HoE
Three signs of spring. D. McCord.—McS
"**Kites** in the sky." Mary Ann Hoberman.—HoN
A **kitten.** Aileen Fisher.—FiFo
"A **kitten,** a black one." See A kitten
"The **kitten** and the falling leaves." See The kitten playing with the falling leaves
Kitten capers. Aileen Fisher.—FiM
"**Kitten,** my kitten." See My kitten
The **kitten** playing with the falling leaves. William Wordsworth.—UnGb
The kitten and the falling leaves.—RoIt
Kitten talk. Aileen Fisher.—FiM
Kittens. See Cats
The **kittens.** Aileen Fisher.—FiM

Kitty cornered. Eve Merriam.—MeO
Kitty of Coleraine. Unknown.—CoPt
Kiwis
Kangaroo and kiwi. X. J. Kennedy.—KeO
Klauber, Edgar
On buying a dog.—CoPu
Klee, Paul
Bimbo's pome.—MaFw
"**Kneegrows** niggas." See Be cool, baby
"**Knickerbocker** knockabout." Clyde Watson.—WaF
"A **knife** and a fork." Unknown.—EmN
Knight, Etheridge
Cell song.—AdPb
For black poets who think of suicide.—AdPb
"He sees through stone."—AdPb
The idea of ancestry.—AdPb
"It was a funky deal."—AdB—AdPb
Portrait of Malcolm X.—AdPb
The sun came.—AdPb
To Dinah Washington.—AdPb
Knight, Max
Korf's joke. tr.—CoPu
"**Knighted** by the sun's." Ann Atwood.—AtM
Knighthood. See Knights and knighthood
Knights and knighthood. See also Arthur, King; Romance
Advice to a knight. T. Harri Jones.—MaFw
Eldorado. E. A. Poe.—RoIt
The falcon. Unknown.—MaFw
"King Arthur and his knights." R. Williams.—CoOr
"Knighted by the sun's." A. Atwood.—AtM
The knight's leap. C. Kingsley.—CoPt
The knight's tomb. S. T. Coleridge.—CoPu
La belle dame sans merci. J. Keats.—JoA-4—RoIt
Lochinvar. From Marmion. W. Scott.—CoPt—JoA-4
The prologue. From The Canterbury tales. G. Chaucer.—MaFw
The riddling knight. Unknown.—JoA-4—RoIt
"Sir Percival and the dragon." X. J. Kennedy.—KeO
View. R. Froman.—FrSp
Ye carpette knyghte. L. Carroll.—LiPc
Knights and ladies. See Knights and knighthood
The **knight's** leap. Charles Kingsley.—CoPt
Knights of the Round Table. See Arthur, King; Knights and knighthood
The **knight's** tomb. Samuel Taylor Coleridge.—CoPu
Knitted things. Karla Kuskin.—LaM (sel.)
Knitting
Knitted things. K. Kuskin.—LaM (sel.)
Knives
The bread-knife ballad. R. W. Service.—CoOr
"**Knock.** Knock. Anybody there." Clyde Watson.—WaF
Knock on wood. Henry Dumas.—AdPb
Knowledge
Circles. From The people, yes. C. Sandburg.—MaFw—SaT
The dawn. W. B. Yeats.—MoG
Fast and slow. J. Ciardi.—CiFs
For scholars and pupils. G. Wither.—OpOx
Giles Johnson, Ph.D. F. M. Davis.—AdPb
He that never read a line. Unknown.—CoPi
How. A. Fisher.—FiFo
The knowledgeable child. L. A. G. Strong.—CoPi
Lao-tzū. From The philosophers. Po Chüi-i.—LiWw
The odyssey of a snail. F. Garcia Lorca.—MaFw
September. L. Clifton.—ClE
Sophistication. V. Miller.—HiN
Tim. D. McCord.—McAa
The **knowledgeable** child. L. A. G. Strong.—CoPi
"**Know'st** thou the land where the pale citrons grow." See Wilhelm Meister—Mignon's song
Knoxville, Tennessee. Nikki Giovanni.—AdB—AdM—AdPb
"**Koala** means the world to her." Karla Kuskin.—KuN
Koch, Kenneth
Variations on a theme by William Carlos Williams.—LiS
Kodo
The cuckoo.—MaFw
Kolosova, Sveta
Before the summer downpour.—MoM
Koralova, Nastya
Nonsense.—MoM
"**Korf** invents a novel kind of joke." See Korf's joke
Korf's joke. Christian Morgenstern, tr. fr. the German by Max Knight.—CoPu
Kotewill and Smith
Chopsticks. trs.—MaFw
Kotul'sky, Alexander
The size of him.—MoM
Storm at sea.—MoM
Koyo
"O moon, why must you."—LiWw
Kreymborg, Alfred
Life.—CoPu
"Our window is stained."—RoIt
Race prejudice.—CoPu
Kriss Kringle. Thomas Bailey Aldrich.—RoIt
Ku Klux Klan
Lynching and burning. Primus St John.—AdPb
We can't always follow the white man's way. D. Clarke, Jr.—JoV
Kubik, Gerhard
"The train." tr.—AlPa
Kubla Khan. Samuel Taylor Coleridge.—RoIt
Kubutsu
"Watching a petal."—BeM
Kucherenko, Tanya
The question.—MoM
Kudus
Zoo doings. J. Prelutsky.—PrT

Kuka, King D.
Ego swamp.—AlW
A taste of honey.—AlW
Kulichkova, Lora
My bicycle and me.—MoM
Kumin, Maxine W.
Fräulein reads instructive rhymes.—LiS
The microscope.—CoPt—LiWw
The presence.—MoT
Song of weeds.—JoA-4
Kunene, Mazisi
As long as I live.—AlPa
Farewell.—AlPa
Kunitz, Stanley
The Muse. tr.—PlM
Spark of laurel.—PlM
Kuroyanagi Shōha
"A heavy cart rumbles."—MaFw
Kuskin, Karla
"All my legs were very tired."—KuA
"Bug."—KuN
"A bug sat in a silver flower."—KuN
"Buggity."—KuN
"Bugs never speak."—KuN
"Come out and ride around the block with me."—KuA
"Come picture this lonely and frightening scene."—KuA
"Cow sounds heavy."—KuN
"Days that the wind takes over."—KuN
"Examining the breeze."—KuN
"The house of snail upon his back."—KuN
"I am a snake."—KuA
"I am proud."—KuA
"I am softer."—KuA
"I do not laugh or sing or smile or talk."—KuA
"I do not understand."—KuA
"I do not wish I were a cat."—KuN
"I have a friend who keeps on standing on her hands."—KuN
"I liked growing."—KuA
"I look like you precisely."—KuA
"If you."—KuA
"If you stood with your feet in the earth."—KuA
"I'm scratched and scuffed."—KuA
"I'm swimming around in the sea, see."—KuA
"I'm up here."—KuA
"Is six times one a lot of fun."—KuN
"It is grey out."—KuN
"It's rotten."—KuA
"Julia loves her Rosalie."—KuN
Knitted things.—LaM (sel.)
"Koala means the world to her."—KuN
"Let me tell you all about me."—KuA
"Many people who are smart."—KuN
"Moon."—KuN
"My home is a white dome."—KuA
"My world is an enormous room."—KuA
"The night is black."—KuA
"Okay everybody, listen to this."—KuN
"One thing that you can say about roaring."—KuA
"Over a stone."—KuA
"Running away."—KuN
"Steel wheels."—KuA
"Stillness is my secret."—KuA
"The streets are filled with mustached men."—KuN
"Take a word like cat."—KuN
"The terrible cat of black velvet fur."—KuN
"That cat is crazy."—KuN
"This cat."—KuN
"Three wishes."—KuN
"Tick . . . tock."—KuA
"A tiny house."—KuN
"Tree birds."—KuN
"True."—KuA
"What there is of me to see."—KuA
"When a cat is asleep."—KuN
"When everything has drawn to a close."—KuA
"When it is dry."—KuA
"Where."—KuN
"Where do you get the idea for a poem."—KuN
"Who are you."—KuA
"Wordless words."—KuN
"Worm."—KuN
"Write about a radish."—KuN
Kwakiutl Indians. See Indians of the Americas—Kwakiutl
Kwaso
"Climbing a steel hill."—BeM
Kyorai
"Beyond stillness, a."—BeM
"Even a wise man."—BeM
"I called to the wind."—BeM
"There, where the skylark's."—BeM
Kyoroku
"A wintry blizzard."—BeM

L

La belle dame sans merci. John Keats.—JoA-4—RoIt
La marche des machines. A. S. J. Tessimond.—ToM
Labé, Louise
"Alas, what use to me if perfectly."—ThI
"A fortune-teller made the prophecy."—ThI
"Good women, don't reproach me if I have loved."—ThI
"I burn in fire, I drown, I live, I languish."—ThI
"If he folded me in an embrace."—ThI
"In town and temple I'm no longer seen."—ThI
"O sidelong glance, O dazzling dark eyes."—ThI
"What is the height of a great man? How large."—ThI
"When I catch sight of your fair head."—ThI

Labor. See Work
Labor day. See Work
Laborers. See Work
Lacrimas or there is a need to scream. K. Curtis Lyle.—AdPb
"A **ladder** sticking up at the open window." See Dog-days
Ladders
A fine fat fireman. J. Ciardi.—CiFs
"Up the ladder, down the ladder." Unknown.—EmN
"**Ladies** and gentlemen." See Manifesto
"**Ladies** and gentlemen (I'll tell you a fact)." Unknown.—EmN
"**Ladies** and gentlemen (take my advice)." Unknown.—MoBw
"**Ladies** and gentlemen, I come before you to." Unknown.—MoBw
The **lady** and the swine. See "There was a lady loved a swine"
Lady-bird. Caroline Southey.—UnGb
"**Lady-bird,** lady-bird, fly away home." See Lady-bird
Lady-birds. See Beetles
Lady bug. Unknown, tr. fr. the Chinese by I. T. Headland.—JoA-4
"**Lady-bug,** lady-bug." See Lady bug
"**Lady** bug, lady bug (fly away)." Unknown.—EmN
"**Lady** bug, lady bug (go home)." Unknown.—EmN
"**Lady** bug, lady bug (your house)." Unknown.—EmN
Lady bugs. See Beetles
Lady Clare. Alfred Tennyson.—CoPt
A **lady** comes to an inn. Elizabeth Jane Coatsworth.—CoPt
"The **lady** comes to the gate." See Albatross
Lady feeding the cats. Douglas Stewart.—MaFw (sel.)
Lady, lady. Anne Spencer.—AdPb
"**Lady,** lady, I saw your face." See Lady, lady
"**Lady,** Lady Landers." Unknown, tr. fr. the Scottish by Norah and William Montgomerie.—JoA-4
Lady Moon ("Lady Moon, Lady Moon, where are you roving") Richard Monckton Milnes, Lord Houghton.—OpOx
Lady Moon ("O Lady Moon, your horns point toward the east") Christina Georgina Rossetti.—OpOx
"**Lady** Moon, Lady Moon, where are you roving." See Lady Moon
The **lady** of the lake, sel. Walter Scott
Soldier rest.—RoIt
"**Lady** Queen Anne she sits in the sun." Mother Goose.—JoA-4
"**Ladybird,** ladybird, fly away home." Mother Goose.—AlC
Ladybirds. See Beetles
"**Ladybug,** ladybug, turn around." Unknown.—EmN
La Flesche, Frances
Behold, this pipe. tr.—BiI
La Follette, Melvin Walker
The ballad of red fox.—AdP
La Fontaine, Jean de
The camel and the flotsam.—JoA-4
The dairymaid and her milk-pot.—JoA-4
The dove and the ant.—JoA-4
The fox and the goat.—JoA-4
La Fontaine, Jean de (about)
Haec fabula docet. R. Frost.—LiWw
Laing, Dilys
Acknowledgement.—CoPu
The **laird** o' Cockpen. Lady Nairne.—CoPt
"The **laird** o' Cockpen, he's proud an' he's great." See The laird o' Cockpen
Lake, Richard
Atavism.—HiN
"A **lake** and a fairy boat." See Merrily float
Lake Chad
Chad. E. Brathwaite.—ToM
The **Lake** Isle of Innisfree. William Butler Yeats.—JoA-4
Lake Michigan
Swallow the lake. C. Major.—AdPb
Lake Tanganyika
Blue Tanganyika. L. Bethune.—AdPb
Lakes
The Lake Isle of Innisfree. W. B. Yeats.—JoA-4
"The old pond." Bashō.—HaW
Pier. J. Scully.—HaWr
Screaming tarn. R. Bridges.—CoPt
Vapor trail reflected in the frog pond. G. Kinnell.—PeS
"Whose is that face." B. Swann
Three riddles.—MoT
Lalla Rookh. Thomas Moore.—LiS (sel.)
Lamb, Charles
The housekeeper.—RoIt
The old familiar faces.—MoG
— and Lamb, Mary
The boy and the snake.—OpOx
Choosing a name.—OpOx
Cleanliness.—OpOx
Envy.—OpOx
Feigned courage.—OpOx
The first tooth.—OpOx
Going into breeches.—OpOx
The **lamb** ("The lamb just says, I am") Theodore Roethke.—LiLc
The **lamb** ("Little lamb, who made thee") William Blake.—JoA-4—LiLc—OpOx—RoIt
"The **lamb** just says, I am." See The lamb
Lambert, James H., Jr
The tale of a dog.—BrM
Lambs. See also Sheep
Composed on a May morning, 1838. W. Wordsworth.—PaF
Dame Wiggins of Lee. Unknown.—OpOx
First sight. P. Larkin.—HiN—MoT
For a lamb. R. Eberhart.—PeS
The lamb ("The lamb just says, I am") T. Roethke.—LiLc
The lamb ("Little lamb, who made thee") W. Blake.—JoA-4—LiLc—OpOx—RoIt

"Lambs are full of curly wool." M. A. Hoberman.—HoN
Mary's lamb. S. J. Hale.—OpOx
The pet lamb. W. Wordsworth.—OpOx
"Some people say that fleas are black." Unknown.—BrM—CoOh
Spring. W. Blake.—JoA-4—LiLc—PaF—RoIt—UnGb
"**Lambs** are full of curly wool." Mary Ann Hoberman.—HoN
"**Lambs** that learn to walk in snow." See First sight
A **lament.** See The Ozidi saga
Lament. Unknown, tr. fr. the Akan by J. H. Kwabena Nketia.—AlPa
Lament for lost lodgings. Phyllis McGinley.—LiS
Lament for the dead mother. Unknown, tr. fr. the Ewe by Geormbeeyi Adali-Mortty.—AlPa
Lament for the death of Eoghan Ruadh O'Neill. Thomas Davis.—CoPi
Lament for the makers. William Dunbar.—PlM (sel.)
Lament of the banana man. Evan Jones.—ToM
Lament of the drums. Christopher Obigbo.—AlPa (sel.)
Lament of the exiles. Okogbule Wonodi.—AlPa
Lament of the slave. Unknown, tr. fr. the Spanish by Raoul Abdul.—AbM
Lamentation. Agnes T. Pratt.—AlW
The **lamentation** of the old pensioner. William Butler Yeats.—CoPi
Laments. See also Death
Albert Ayler, eulogy for a decomposed saxophone player. S. Crouch.—AdPb
Anthem for doomed youth. W. Owen.—MaFw
At the grave of John Clare. C. Causley.—MaFw (sel.)
Autumn. P. B. Shelley.—PaF
David's lamentation. From The second book of Samuel, Bible, Old Testament.—MeP
Death of Dr King. S. Cornish.—AdPb
Dirge ("I see it") Unknown.—AlPa
Dirge ("It is the endless dance of the dead") Q. Troupe.—AdPb
A dirge ("Rough wind, that moanest loud") P. B. Shelley.—MoG
Dirge for the year. P. B. Shelley.—PaF
Do nothing till you hear from me. D. Henderson.—AdPb
Elegy ("Her face like a rain-beaten stone on the day she rolled off") T. Roethke.—HiN
Elegy ("The jackals prowl, the serpents hiss") A. Guiterman.—LiWw
Elegy for Alfred Hubbard. T. Connor.—ToM
Elegy for Jane. T. Roethke.—PeS
Elegy for J. F. K. W. H. Auden.—MaFw
Elegy for minor poets. L. MacNeice.—PlM
An elegy on the death of a mad dog. O. Goldsmith.—LiWw—RoIt
Elegy written in a country churchyard. T. Gray.—PaP (sel.)
Eve's lament. Unknown.—CoPi
Father and son. F. R. Higgins.—CoPi
For Stephen Dixon. Z. Gilbert.—AdPb
In memoriam, Martin Luther King, Jr. J. Jordan.—AdPb
In memory of my dear grandchild Anne Bradstreet. A. Bradstreet.—ThI
In memory of my dear grandchild Elizabeth Bradstreet. A. Bradstreet.—ThI
A lament ("Oh Ozidi my man, my man, my man, my man") From The Ozidi saga. Unknown.—AlPa
Lament ("Your death has taken me by surprise") Unknown.—AlPa
Lament for lost lodgings. P. McGinley.—LiS
Lament for the dead mother. Unknown.—AlPa
Lament for the death of Eoghan Ruadh O'Neill. T. Davis.—CoPi
Lament for the makers. W. Dunbar.—PlM (sel.)
Lament of the banana man. E. Jones.—ToM
Lament of the drums. C. Okigbo.—AlPa (sel.)
Lament of the exiles. O. Wonodi.—AlPa
Lament of the slave. Unknown.—AbM
Lamentation. A. T. Pratt.—AlW
The lamentation of the old pensioner. W. B. Yeats.—CoPi
Light dying. B. Kennelly.—CoPi
Little elegy. X. J. Kennedy.—CoPu—HiN
Lu Yün's lament. H. Read.—PlM
A lyke-wake dirge. Unknown.—MaFw
The mither's lament. S. G. Smith.—CoPu
O captain, my captain. W. Whitman.—RoIt
On the death of friends in childhood. D. Justice.—HiN
One sided shoot-out. D. L. Lee.—AdPb
Padraic O'Conaire, Gaelic storyteller. F. R. Higgins.—CoPi
The paper in the meadow. O. Williams.—RoIt
Requiem. R. L. Stevenson.—RoIt
Requiem for a black girl. Y. Ouologuem.—AlPa (sel.)
Requiem for a personal friend. E. Boland.—CoPi
A sea-dirge. L. Carroll.—LiPc
Song of Lawino: An African lament. O. P'Bitek.—AlPa (sel.)
Lamia. John Keats.—MaFw (sel.)
The **lamplighter.** Robert Louis Stevenson.—OpOx
Lamps
"Color yellow, color coral." F. Holman.—HoI
The lamplighter. R. L. Stevenson.—OpOx
Meanlight. R. Froman.—FrSp
"Who goes there, drifting." Etsujin.—BeM
The **land,** sel. V. Sackville-West
"Only a bold man ploughs the weald for corn."—PaP
"**Land** and sea." See Intimations of immortality
The **land** of counterpane. Robert Louis Stevenson.—OpOx

The **Land** of Happy. Shel Silverstein.—SiW
The **land** of heart's desire. William Butler Yeats.—MaFw (sel.)
The **land** of story-books. Robert Louis Stevenson.—RoIt—UnGb
Landlords
"Rent man." L. Lenski.—LeC
Landor, Walter Savage
Age.—CoPu
Before a saint's picture.—OpOx
Fame.—CoPu
The Georges.—RoIt
"The **lands** around my dwelling." Unknown, tr. fr. the Eskimo by Knud Rasmussen.—BiI—LaM
Landscape ("See the trees lean to the wind's way of learning") Carl Sandburg.—SaT
Landscape ("What will you find at the edge of the world") Eve Merriam.—MeF
"The **landscape** here is Africa." See Sand hill road
Landscape in concrete. Lois Lenski.—LeC
"The **landscape** sleeps in mist from morn till noon." See November
"The **landscape** was." See Canto 5
Landscapes
Landscape ("See the trees lean to the winds way of learning") C. Sandburg.—SaT
Landscape ("What will you find at the edge of the world") E. Merriam.—MeF
"A magic landscape." A. Fet.—MoM
View. R. Froman.—FrSp
"When next appeared a dam—so call the place." G. Crabbe.—PaP
"The **lanes** of England never end." See Hoddesdon
Lang, Andrew
Scythe song.—RoIt
Langdale: Nightfall, January 4th. Michael Roberts.—PaP
Langland, Joseph
Orioles.—HaWr
Langley, Timothy
The concrete mixer.—HoCs
Langston. Mari Evans.—AdB
Language. See also Words
The cumberbunce. P. West.—CoOh
Forgotten language. S. Silverstein.—SiW
Hints on pronunciation for foreigners. T. S. W.—MaFw
"If only I were able." B. Lapin.—MoM
Like you as it. D. McCord.—McAa
On looking into Robert Frost in Kanji. W. Meredith.—PlM
Perfect Arthur. N. M. Bodecker.—BoL
The purist. O. Nash.—LiWw
The tower of Babel. N. Crouch.—OpOx
"The **lanky** hank of a she in the inn over there." See A glass of beer
Lanterns
"About an excavation." C. Reznikoff.—CoPu
Lanty Leary. Samuel Lover.—CoPi
Lanusse, Armand
Epigram.—AbM
Lao-tzū (about)
Lao-tzū. From The philosophers. Po Chü-i.—LiWw
Lao-tzū. See The philosophers
Lape, Fred
Just born pig.—CoPu
Lapin, Borya
"If only I were able."—MoM
Lapin, Volodya
The flower.—MoM
"I want time to run, to race for me."—MoM
The lioness and her cub.—MoM
Making friends.—MoM
Our cat.—MoM
Spring mood.—MoM
The teakettle.—MoM
"To infinite heights will the roads of life."—MoM
"The **large,** calm harbour lies below." See In Falmouth harbour
"The **lark.**" See The lark in Sark
The **lark** in Sark. N. M. Bodecker.—BoL
Larkin, Philip
An Arundel tomb.—ToM
At grass.—HaWr
First sight.—HiN—MoT
The north ship.—MaFw
Places, loved ones.—PeS
Take one home for the kiddies.—CoPu
Larks
"Above the meadow." Chiyo.—BeM
The crow doth sing. From The merchant of Venice. W. Shakespeare.—RoIt
The lark in Sark. N. M. Bodecker.—BoL
Love without hope. R. Graves.—CoPu
The skylark. C. G. Rossetti.—RoIt
"A skylark circles." Issa.—HaW
"There, where the skylarks." Kyorai.—BeM
Laron, Elaine
No one else.—ThF
The sun and the moon.—ThF
"What are little boys made of . . . (love and care)."—ThF
"**Lars** Porsena of Clusium." See Lays of ancient Rome—Horatius at the bridge
Lasanta, Miriam
"My soul speaks Spanish."—JoV
What kind of world is this.—JoV
The **last** chrysanthemum. Thomas Hardy.—RoIt
Last laugh. Douglas Young.—CoPu
Last lines—1916. Padraic Pearse.—CoPi
"**Last** night a freezing cottontail." See Twin lakes hunter
"**Last** night and the night before (a lemon and a pickle)." Unknown.—EmN
"**Last** night and the night before (twenty four robbers)." Mother Goose.—AlC—EmN
"**Last** night somebody called me darky." Nicolás Guillén, tr. fr. the Spanish by Langston Hughes.—AbM
"**Last** night you were in a dream." See The dream
The **last** poem. Tom Meschery.—FlH

The **last** quatrain of the ballad of Emmett Till. Gwendolyn Brooks.—AdPb
The **last** riot. Vanessa Howard.—JoV
Last rites. Christina Georgina Rossetti.—OpOx
The **last** signal. Thomas Hardy.—PlM—PlP
The **last** soldier. Sergei Morozov, tr. fr. the Russian by Miriam Morton.—MoM
Last week in October. Thomas Hardy.—CoPu
The **last** word of a bluebird. Robert Frost.—JoA-4—LiLc
Last words before winter. Louis Untermeyer.—JoA-4
Late abed. Archibald MacLeish.—HiN
"**Late** afternoon: clouds made a hole." See In winter sky
"**Late** in the winter came one day." See Blossom themes
"**Late** lies the wintry sun a-bed." See Winter time
A **late** spring day in my life. Robert Bly.—HiN
Late summer. Kinoshita Yūji, tr. fr. the Japanese by Geoffrey Bownas and Anthony Thwaite.—MaFw
"**Late** summer evening." Shiki, tr. fr. the Japanese by Harry Behn.—BeM
"**Lately,** I've become accustomed to the way." See Preface to a twenty volume suicide note
Latimer, Bette Darcie
For William Edward Burghardt Du Bois on his eightieth birthday.—AdPb
Laughing child. See Three spring notations on bipeds
Laughing corn. Carl Sandburg.—SaT
"The **laughing** hyena's behavior is strange." See The hyena
Laughing song. William Blake.—JoA-4—OpOx—RoIt
Laughing time. William Jay Smith.—BrM
Laughter
Alligator/Crocodile. M. A. Hoberman.—HoR
Come all. Unknown.—BiI
Crocodile. W. J. Smith.—BrM
Early supper. B. Howes.—HiN
"I want to laugh, I, because my sledge it is broken." Unknown.—LeIb
Interlude. W. Smith.—AdPb
Laughing song. W. Blake.—JoA-4—OpOx—RoIt
Laughing time. W. J. Smith.—BrM
The lesser lynx. E. V. Rieu.—LiWw
Song to make a baby laugh. Unknown.—BiS
"What is so amusing about the rain falling." King Hyo-jong.—BaSs
"**Laughter** of children brings." See Early supper
"The **laughter** of the lesser lynx." See The lesser lynx
Laundresses and laundrymen. See Laundry
Laundry
Bendix. J. Updike.—PeS
Chocolate. R. Hoban.—HoE
Clothesline. L. Lenski.—LeC
Dance. R. Froman.—FrSp
The dolls' wash. J. H. Ewing.—OpOx
Fairy washing. R. B. Bennett.—JaP
"It chanced to be our washing day." O. W. Holmes.—RoIt
"Look at that." L. Moore.—MoSm
Shadow wash. S. Silverstein.—SiW
Wash. J. Updike.—MoT
"Wiggle to the laundromat." D. Lee.—LeA
Windy wash day. D. Aldis.—JoA-4
Laundrymen. See Laundry
Lavender (color)
"Lavender's blue, diddle, diddle." Mother Goose.—JoA-4
The **lavender** kitten. Alonzo Lopez.—AlW
"**Lavender's** blue, diddle, diddle." Mother Goose.—JoA-4
Law. See also Court trials; Lawyers
Tit for tat: A tale. J. Aikin.—OpOx
"A **law** there is of ancient fame." See Tit for tat: A tale
Lawrence, D. H.
Aware.—CoPu
Bare almond-trees.—MaFw
Intimates.—CoPt
Kangaroo.—MaFw
The North country.—PaP
The rainbow.—MaFw
A snowy day in school.—MaFw
Lawyers
"Tommy Trot, a man of law." Mother Goose.—AlC
Lay-away. Lois Lenski.—LeC
"**Lay** me on an anvil, O God." See Prayers of steel
The **lay** of the last minstrel, sel. Walter Scott
Patriotism.—RoIt
Laye, Camara
To my mother.—AlPa
Lays of ancient Rome, sel. Thomas Babington Macaulay
Horatius at the bridge.—RoIt
Lazarus
Dives and Lazarus. Unknown.—MaFw
Laziness. See also Idleness
Get up, get up. Unknown.—CoPu
Go north, south, east and west, young man. S. Milligan.—CoOr
A hot weather song. D. Marquis.—CoPu
Lazy Jane. S. Silverstein.—SiW
"Lazy Lucy." N. M. Bodecker.—BoL
The lazy man. Unknown.—AlPa
The lazy people. S. Silverstein.—CoOh
"Old Man Lazy." Unknown.—EmN
On torpid Marcus. Lucilius.—LiWw
"Rindle, randle." Unknown.—BlM
The slow starter. L. MacNeice.—ToM
"**Lazy.**" See Lazy Jane
Lazy Jane. Shel Silverstein.—SiW
"**Lazy** Lucy." N. M. Bodecker.—BoL
The **lazy** man. Unknown, tr. fr. the Yoruba by Ulli Beier and Bakare Gbadamosi.—AlPa
"**Lazy** Marcus once dreamed he was running a race." See On torpid Marcus
The **lazy** people. Shel Silverstein.—CoOh

"**Lazy** sheep, pray tell me why." See The sheep
Lead. Jayne Cortez.—AdPb
The **leaden-eyed.** Vachel Lindsay.—CoPu
"**Leaf** piles smoke in the whispering dark." See Halloween
"A **leaf** ran at my heels." See Companions
Leaflight. Dorothy Donnelly.—HiN
Leak. Eve Merriam.—MeO
"**Lean** and tall and stringy are the Navajo." See The Navajo
"The **lean** hands of wagon men." See The windy city—I am Chicago
"**Lean** out of the window." See Chamber music
"**Leaning** out over." See Symmetries and asymmetries
Lear, Edward
The Akond of Swat.—RoIt
An alphabet.—OpOx
Nonsense alphabet.—JoA-4
"The broom, the shovel, the poker and the tongs."—JoA-4
"Calico pie."—LiLc—UnGb
The courtship of the Yonghy-Bonghy-Bo.—JoA-4
The cummerbund.—LiWw
The duck and the kangaroo.—JoA-4—OpOx
"How pleasant to know Mr Lear."—LiS—PlM
Lines to a young lady.—RoIt
Incidents in the life of my Uncle Arly.—LiWw—RoIt
The Jumblies.—JoA-4—OpOx—RoIt
Lines to a young lady. See "How pleasant to know Mr Lear"
Mr and Mrs Discobbolos."—JoA-4
Mr and Mrs Spikky Sparrow.—OpOx
Nonsense alphabet. See An alphabet
The owl and the pussy-cat.—JoA-4—OpOx—UnGb
"The pobble who has no toes."—OpOx—UnGb
The quangle wangle's hat.—JoA-4
The table and the chair.—JoA-4—UnGb
"There is a young lady, whose nose (continually grows)"
Limericks.—JoA-4
"There is a young lady, whose nose (continually prospers)"
Limericks.—JoA-4
Nonsenses.—OpOx
"There was a young lady of Norway"
Limericks.—JoA-4
"There was a young lady, whose nose (was so long)"
Limericks.—JoA-4
"There was an old lady of Chertsey"
Nonsenses.—OpOx
"There was an old lady of France."—LiLc
"There was an old man in a tree (who was horribly bored)."—RoIt
Limericks.—JoA-4
Nonsenses.—OpOx
"There was an old man in a tree (whose whiskers were)"
Limericks.—JoA-4
"There was an old man of Dumbree"
Nonsenses.—OpOx
"There was an old man of the East"
Limericks.—JoA-4
"There was an old man on the Border."—LiLc
Limericks.—JoA-4
"There was an old man on whose nose"
Limericks.—JoA-4
"There was an old man who said, How"
Nonsenses.—OpOx
"There was an old man who said, Hush"
Limericks.—JoA-4
Nonsenses.—OpOx
"There was an old man, who when little"
Limericks.—JoA-4
"There was an old man with a beard."—RoIt
Nonsenses.—OpOx
"There was an old person of Gretna"
Nonsenses.—OpOx
"There was an old person of Ware."—LiLc
Limericks.—JoA-4
Lear, Edward (about)
Edward Lear. W. H. Auden.—PlM
"How pleasant to know Mr Lear." E. Lear.—LiS—PlM
Lines to a young lady.—RoIt
A **learned** song. Mother Goose.—JoA-4
Learner. Unknown.—CoOh
Learning to swim. Marchette Chute.—ChRu
Leave me alone. Felice Holman.—UnGb
Leaves
"Autumn." D. Dore.—HoC
The burning of the leaves. L. Binyon.—PaF
Companions. A. Stoutenburg.—HaWr
"Don't bring out the straw mat." Han Hwak.—BaSs
"A dry leaf drifting (down to an icy)." Bokusui.—BeM
"A dry leaf drifting (down to earth)." Bashō.—BeM
Fall, leaves, fall. E. Brontë.—PaF
Glider. R. Froman.—FrSp
"It's fall." M. Campbell.—HoC
The kitten playing with the falling leaves. W. Wordsworth.—UnGb
The kitten and the falling leaves.—RoIt
Last week in October. T. Hardy.—CoPu
"The leaves." O. Lermand.—HoC
"Leaves without trees." Y. Amichai.—MeP
"Let the fall leaves fall." C. Watson.—WaF
Little sketch. C. Sandburg.—SaT
Pussy willows. M. Chute.—ChRu
Secret intimations. J. H. Wheelock.—CoPu
Seed leaves. R. Wilbur.—HiN
Survivor. A. MacLeish.—HiN
"True." K. Kuskin.—KuA
The wave. D. McCord.—McFm
"The **leaves.**" Olivia Lermand.—HoC
"**Leaves** may wither." Unknown.—EmN
"The **leaves** shudder, the branch shakes." See Alone

The **lemming's** song. Unknown, fr. the Caribou Eskimo.—LeIb
Lenin (about)
Lenin. Y. Artiuschanko.—MoM
Lenin. Yura Artiuschanko, tr. fr. the Russian by Miriam Morton.—MoM
Leningrad, Russia
To Leningrad. N. Bugakova.—MoM
Lennon, John and McCartney, Paul
The continuing story of Bungalow Bill.—MoG
The fool on the hill.—MoG
In my life.—MoG
Strawberry fields forever.—MoG
"**Lenox** avenue is a big street." See Keep on pushing
Lenski, Lois
Accident.—LeC
"All the people on our street."—LeC
Ambulance.—LeC
Apartment house.—LeC
At the rink.—LeC
Bad boy.—LeC
Bakery shop.—LeC
Barber shop.—LeC
Baton.—LeC
The bear.—LeC
Bench in the park.—LeC
Birthday cake.—LeC
Boy down the hall.—LeC
The chase.—LeC
"Children of the city."—LeC
"Christmas in the city."—LeC
City child.—LeC
City city city.—LeC
City fire.—LeC
City lights.—LeC
City market.—LeC
City school.—LeC
City street.—LeC
Cleaning up the block.—LeC
Clothesline.—LeC
Delicatessen.—LeC
Department store.—LeC
Doctor.—LeC
"Don't cross the street."—LeC
Dream dog.—LeC
Elevator boy.—LeC
Factory.—LeC
Far-off things.—LeC
"Flower so red."—LeC
Flower wagon.—LeC
Gang.—LeC
Ghosts.—LeC
Going.—LeC
Going to church.—LeC
Hideout.—LeC
"High-rise project."—LeC
"Home in the basement."—LeC
Home in the sky.—LeC
Homesick.—LeC
"Hot dog hot."—LeC
Hungry.—LeC
"I live upstairs."—LeC
I love the city.—LeC
"I sat on the stoop."—LeC
"I took a walk."—LeC
Ice cream man.—LeC
In the city.—LeC
"Johnny, come home."—LeC
Jungle gym.—LeC
Landscape in concrete.—LeC
Lay-away.—LeC
Let's ride the bus.—LeC
Library.—LeC
Litter.—LeC
A little green thing.—LeC
Lonesome place.—LeC
A long life.—LeC
Look out the window.—LeC
The mailman.—LeC
Merry-go-round.—LeC
Milk-stand.—LeC
"Mom has a job."—LeC
My dad.—LeC
"My heart is in the city."—LeC
My nickel.—LeC
"My purse is full of money."—LeC
Neighbor.—LeC
Never a tree.—LeC
Newsboy.—LeC
No heat today.—LeC
Our block.—LeC
Our court.—LeC
"Our flat is hot."—LeC
Parade.—LeC
The park.—LeC
Penthouse.—LeC
People.—HoCs
People in the city.—LeC
People on the bus.—LeC
"Pigeons on the rooftop."—LeC
Play ball.—LeC
Playtime.—LeC
Pokey old mailman.—LeC
Policeman.—LeC
Rain in the city.—LeC
Rehabilitation.—LeC
"Rent man."—LeC
Riot.—LeC
Roses.—LeC
Shoeshine boy.—LeC
Shopping.—LeC
Shower bath.—LeC
"Sing a song of people."—LeC
The skyscraper.—LeC
Slippery slide.—LeC
Slum home.—LeC
Smells.—LeC
Snack.—LeC
Sparrows.—LeC
Spring in the city.—LeC
Stars in the sky.—LeC
"Street closed."—LeC
Subway.—LeC
Summer festival.—LeC
Sunday in the city.—LeC
Supermarket.—LeC
The swing.—LeC

Taxi driver.—LeC
Time.—LeC
Two-room flat.—LeC
Urban renewal.—LeC
A walk in the city.—LeC
"Walking on the sidewalk."—LeC
What is a city.—LeC
Whirlygig.—LeC
Windows with faces.—LeC
Winter cold.—LeC
You always have to pay.—LeC
Zoo-keeper.—LeC
The **Lent** lily. See A Shropshire lad
León-Portilla, Miguel
They shall not wither. tr.—BiI
Thus it is told. tr.—BiI
"The weeping spreads." tr.—BiI
A woman's complaint. tr.—BiI
Leopard. Edward Brathwaite.—AbM
Leopards
Enchantment. L. Alexander.—AdPb
Leopard. E. Brathwaite.—AbM
The **lepracaun;** or, Fairy shoemaker. William Allingham.—RoIt
The **leprechaun.** Lee Blair.—JaP
Lermand, Olivia
"Christmas (a season we)."—HoC
"The leaves."—HoC
Leroy. LeRoi Jones.—AdPb
Leslie, Shane
Muckish mountain (The pig's back).—CoPi
Prayer for fine weather.—CoPi
The **lesser** lynx. E. V. Rieu.—LiWw
Lessing, Gotthold Ephraim
To a slow walker and quick eater.—LiWw
The **lesson.** Edward Lucie-Smith.—HiN—ToM
A **lesson** for mamma. Sydney Dayre.—OpOx
"**Lest** it may more quarrels breed." See Twelve articles
Lester, Julius
In the time of revolution.—AdPb (sel.)
On the birth of my son, Malcolm Coltrane.—AdPb
Us.—AdPb
Lester. Shel Silverstein.—SiW
"**Lester** was given a magic wish." See Lester
"**Let** all the fish that swim the sea." See Herring is king
"**Let** all who will." See Militant
"**Let** dogs delight to bark and bite." See Against quarrelling and fighting
"**Let** earth give thanks, the deacon said." See Simon Soggs' Thanksgiving
"**Let** go of the present and death." See Once again
"**Let** it rock." See Storm at sea
"**Let** me ask you, Mind." Unknown, tr. fr. the Korean by Chung Seuk Park and ad. by Virginia Olsen Baron.—BaSs
"**Let** me be your baby, south wind." See Baby song of the four winds
"**Let** me dry you, says the desert." See Earth song
"**Let** me go where'er I will." See Music
"**Let** me see if Philip can." See The story of fidgety Philip
"**Let** me take you down." See Strawberry fields forever
"**Let** me tell you all about me." Karla Kuskin.—KuA
"**Let** not young souls be smothered out before." See The leaden-eyed
"**Let** the crows go by hawking their caw and caw." See River roads
"**Let** the fall leaves fall." Clyde Watson.—WaF
"**Let** the rain kiss you." See April rain song
"**Let** them keep it." See And was not improved
"**Let** there always be a sky." Kostya Barannikov, tr. fr. the Russian by Miriam Morton.—MoM
"**Let** uh revolution come, uh." See U name this one
Let us break bread together. Unknown.—BrW
"**Let** us break bread together on our knees." See Let us break bread together
"**Let** us go to the Indian village, said all the rain gods." Unknown, tr. fr. the Zuñi.—ClFc
"**Let** us leave this place, brother." See The Romanies in town
"**Let** us pretend I'm happy." See In which she fears that much learning is useless for wisdom, and poisonous to real living
"**Let** us see, is this real." See Is this real
"**Let** us walk in the white snow." See Velvet shoes
"**Let** x be this." See Exit x
"**Let's** be off to the bamboo." Issa, tr. fr. the Japanese by Hanako Fukuda.—HaW
"**Let's** count the bodies over again." See Counting small-boned bodies
"**Let's** go see old Abe." See Lincoln monument: Washington
"**Let's** go up to the hillside today." See Play song
"**Let's** hang up some suet for juncos and jays." See Country Christmas
"**Let's** marry, said the cherry." N. M. Bodecker.—BoL
Let's ride the bus. Lois Lenski.—LeC
"**Let's** talk of graves, of worms, and epitaphs." See King Richard II—The death of kings
"**Let's** think of eggs." See The poultries
"**Let's** write a poem about lazy people." See The lazy people
Letter from a death bed. John Ciardi.—HiN
Letter in winter. Raymond Richard Patterson.—AdPb
Letter to a friend. Lilian Moore.—MoSp
Letter to E. Franklin Frazier. LeRoi Jones.—AdPb
A **letter** to her husband, absent upon publick employment. Anne Bradstreet.—ThI
Letter to my sister. Anne Spencer.—AdPb
A **letter** to the child Lady Margaret Cavendish Holles-Harley. Matthew Prior.—OpOx
A **letter** to Yvor Winters. Kenneth Rexroth.—PlM

Letters and letter writing
Driving to town late to mail a letter. R. Bly.—MoT
How to write a letter. E. Turner.—OpOx
Letter from a death bed. J. Ciardi.—HiN
Pokey old mailman. L. Lenski.—LeC
"The way I read a letter's—this." E. Dickinson.—ThI
Letters of the alphabet. See Alphabet
Letts, Winifrid M.
The bold unbiddable child.—CoPi
The choice.—CoPi
Fantasia.—CoPi
Lettsom, John Coakley
On Dr Lettsom, by himself.—CoPu
The **levelled** churchyard. Thomas Hardy.—PlP
Lever, Charles
"It's little for glory I care."—CoPi
"The pope he leads a happy life."—CoPi
Leverett, Ernest
SF.—CoPu
Levertov, Denise
The breathing.—HaWr
The coming fall.—MoT (sel.)
Gone away.—PeS
The resolve.—HaWr
Sunday afternoon.—PeS
The willows of Massachusetts.—HaWr
Levi, Peter and Milner-Gulland, Robin
Schoolmaster. trs.—MaFw
"**Levinia** was a simple child, to whom words meant just what they said." See A word or two on Levinia
Levy, Newman
Midsummer jingle.—CoPu
Levy, Sara G.
Baking a hamantash.—LaM
Lewis, Alun
Goodbye.—ToM
"Must."—CoPu
Lewis, Angelo
America bleeds.—AdPb
Clear.—AdPb
Lewis, Bernard
The wall. tr.—MeP
Lewis, I. M. See Androzejewski, B. W. and Lewis, I. M.
Lewis, M. A.
The caulker.—CoPt
Lewis Carroll. Eleanor Farjeon.—OpOx
Li Po. See Li T'ai-po
Li T'ai-po (Li Po or Rihaku)
In the mountains on a summer day.—MaFw
"**Liar,** liar." Unknown.—EmN
Liberty. See also Freedom
The angry man. P. McGinley.—PeS
Choice. R. Mal'kova.—MoM
Fetters. L. Ginsberg.—RoIt
Frederick Douglass. R. Hayden.—AdM—AdPb
The mouse's petition. A. L. Barbauld.—OpOx
My Ulick. C. J. Kickham.—CoPi
The October anniversary. S. Slezsky.—MoM
The silkworms. D. Stewart.—MaFw
Sympathy. P. L. Dunbar.—AdPb
Libraries and librarians
"It aint no." B. O'Meally.—AdM
Library. L. Lenski.—LeC
Public library. R. Froman.—FrSp
"Quiet." M. C. Livingston.—LiM
Sam at the library. C. C. Hole.—BrM
Shut not your doors. W. Whitman.—PlM
Ten years old. N. Giovanni.—AdM
Library. Lois Lenski.—LeC
"The **library** is so full of books." See Library
The **licorice** fields at Pontefract. John Betjeman.—ToM
Lida
"In a poor old village."—MoM
"**Lie** low, grass blades." See Secrets
Lieberman, Elias
"Lincoln was a tall man."—RoIt
"**Liefer** would I turn and love." See Deranged
Lienhardt, Godfrey
War song. tr.—AlPa
Life
Addition problem. M. Goode.—JoV
After the visit. T. Hardy.—PlP
"The air is dirty." G. Thompson.—JoV
Albatross. J. Collins.—MoG
Amen. R. W. Thomas.—AdPb
Amends to nature. A. Symons.—PaF
"And the days are not full enough." E. Pound.—MaFw
As long as I live. M. Kunene.—AlPa
Beseeching the breath. Unknown.—BiI
Black jam for dr. negro. M. Evans.—AdPb
"The blue mountains are what they are." Kim In-hu.—BaSs
Bow harp. T. U Tam'si.—AlPa
"Breathe on him." Unknown.—BiI
"Change-up." D. L. Lee.—AdPb
A charm for our time. E. Merriam.—MeO
Cocoon. D. McCord.—JoA-4
Composed on a May morning, 1838. W. Wordsworth.—PaF
The condition. T. Carmi.—MeP
The counsels of O'Riordan, the rann maker. T. D. O'Bolger.—CoPi
Dark people. K. M. Cumbo.—AdB
"Death prosecuting life born." L. Curry.—JoV
The dream (Part I). Lord Byron.—MoG
Dreams. L. Hughes.—HoD
The eastern gate. Unknown.—MaFw
The elevator man adheres to form. M. Danner.—AdPb
Energy. V. H. Cruz.—AdPb
"Every day in your life." Unknown.—EmN
Five vignettes. J. Toomer.—AdPb
Four and twenty. S. Stills.—MoG
Four sheets to the wind. C. K. Rivers.—AdPb
"Four walls to talk to me." A. Blackwell.—JoV
The gangster's death. I. Reed.—AdPb
The garden. A. Marvell.—PaF (sel.)
"The gray sky." L. Curry.—JoV
"Half of my life." C. O'John.—AlW

Hap. T. Hardy.—PlP
Hear this. M. C. Livingston.—LiM
Her story. N. L. Madgett.—AdPb
The home of images. U. Okeke.—AlPa
How it is. U. Z. Greenberg.—MeP
I have folded my sorrows. B. Kaufman.—AdPb
"I have lived up half my life already." Yi Myung-han.—BaSs
I have seen black hands. R. Wright.—AdPb
I saw from the beach. T. Moore.—CoPi
I sing no new songs. F. M. Davis.—AdPb
"I stepped from plank to plank." E. Dickinson.—ThI
"If I ride this train." J. Johnson.—AdPb
"In a valley where a stream flows." Unknown.—BaSs
In fields of summer. G. Kinnell.—HaWr
In my life. J. Lennon and P. McCartney.—MoG
"In the storm of life you may need an umbrella." Unknown.—EmN
Is this real. Unknown.—BiI
It was the wind. Unknown.—BiI
"Leaves without trees." Y. Amichai.—MeP
Life ("I met four guinea hens today") A. Kreymborg.—CoPu
Life ("Life can be good") P. Goggins.—JoV
Life cycle of common man. H. Nemerov.—ToM
Lines. T. Hardy.—PlP
A long life. L. Lenski.—LeC
Lost moment. H. W. Fuller.—AdPb
The lyf so short. W. Stafford.—PlM
Magic song for him who wishes to live. Unknown.—LeIb
"May your life be like a piano." Unknown.—EmN
"May your life be like spaghetti." Unknown.—EmN—MoBw
"May your life have just enough clouds." Unknown.—EmN
The mood. Q. Prettyman.—AdPb
My life. J. Bryant.—JoV
My life has been the poem. D. Thoreau.—PlM
"My son, let me grasp your hand." Unknown.—ClFc
Myself when I am real. A. Young.—AdPb
The noble nature. From To the immortal memory of that noble pair, Sir Lucius Cary and Sir Henry Morison. B. Jonson.—RoIt
Notes found near a suicide. F. Horne.—AdPb
Ode to the west wind. P. B. Shelley.—PaF
On a fly drinking from his cup. W. Oldys.—RoIt
On my birthday. Y. Amichai.—MeP
On seeing two brown boys in a Catholic church. F. Horne.—AdPb
Once more, the pound. T. Roethke.—JoA-4
The paradox. P. L. Dunbar.—AdPb
The patient: Rockland county sanitarium. C. C. Hernton.—AdPb
Patterns. A. Lowell.—MoG
Phrases. Arthur Rimbaud.—MaF (sel.)
Picnic: The liberated. M. C. Holman.—AdPb
"The place where I have not been." Y. Amichai.—MeP
Poem for friends. Q. Troupe.—AdPb
Poem of Angela Yvonne Davis. N. Giovanni.—AdPb
Portrait. C. Rodgers.—AdM
Prayer. Unknown.—BiI
Prayer before birth. L. MacNeice.—CoPi—PeS—ToM
The question. T. Kucherenko.—MoM
A reflection on human life. W. Lloyd.—CoPu
Ripeness. R. Whitman.—MoT
The room. De Leon Harrison.—AdPb
Solace. C. S. Delany.—AdPb
Song to the envious. Unknown.—AlPa
Songs of sorrow. K. Awoonar.—AlPa (sel.)
Songs of the ghost dance. Unknown.—BiI
The spring will come. H. D. Lowry.—CoPu
Strange legacies. S. A. Brown.—AdPb
Supernatural. J. Holland.—JoV
Suzanne. L. Cohen.—MoG
Theme one: the variations. A. Wilson.—AdPb
They shall not wither. Unknown.—BiI
This is real. T. Palmanteer.—AlW
To the four courts, please. J. Stephens.—CoPi
To the reader. C. Baudelaire.—MoG
To the terrestial globe. W. S. Gilbert.—LiWw
Trio. E. Morgan.—ToM
Two lean cats. M. O'Higgins.—AdPb
Untitled. A. T. Pratt.—AlW
Untitled requiem for tomorrow. Conyus.—AdPb
Upon leaving the parole board hearing. Conyus.—AdPb
The valley of men. U. Z. Greenberg.—MeP
Way out West. LeRoi Jones.—AdPb
"We live in a cage." W. T. Harris.—AdPb
What are heavy. C. G. Rossetti.—OpOx
"What is life." Unknown.—ClFc
"What, still alive at twenty two." H. Kingsmill.—LiS
When thy king is a boy. E. Roberson.—AdPb (sel.)
With my God, the Smith. U. Z. Greenberg.—MeP
You shall live. Unknown.—BiI
A young man's epigram on existence. T. Hardy.—PlP
Youth. F. Cornford.—CoPu
Zapata and the landlord. A. B. Spellman.—AdPb
Life—Life and death
After many a summer. A. Tennyson.—RoIt
Autumn. H. W. Longfellow.—PaF
The bee, the ant, and the sparrow. N. Cotton.—OpOx
Black woman. L. A. Senghor.—AlPa
Blind angel. D. Rokeah.—MeP
The buck in the snow. E. St V. Millay.—AdP—RoIt
"Buggity." K. Kuskin.—KuN
The burning of the leaves. L. Binyon.—PaF

Life—Life and death—*Continued*
A chronicle. Unknown.—RoIt
Crystal moment. R. P. T. Coffin.—PeS
Death as history. Jay Wright.—AdPb
Elegy for J. F. K. W. H. Auden.—MaFw
An epitaph and a reply. Unknown.—RoIt
For the moment. R. Weber.—CoPi
The garden of Proserpine. A. C. Swinburne.—CoPu (sel.)
The grave. S. Tchernichovsky.—MeP
Heather ale. R. L. Stevenson.—CoPt
Hit. T. Palmanteer.—AlW
An Irish airman foresees his death. W. B. Yeats.—PeS
Last laugh. A. Young.—CoPu
Last lines—1916. P. Pearse.—CoPi
The leaden-eyed. V. Lindsay.—CoPu
Life after death. R. W. Thomas.—AdPb
Lines supposed to have been addressed to Fanny Brawne. J. Keats.—CoPu
Locked in. I. Gustafson.—CoPt
Meg Merrilies. J. Keats.—NeA—OpOx
Old Meg.—RoIt
Moloney remembers the resurrection of Kate Finucane. B. Kennelly.—CoPt
The observation. D. Leitch.—MoG
On Dr Lettsom, by himself. J. C. Lettsom.—CoPu
On one who lived and died where he was born. T. Hardy.—PlP
On the birth of my son, Malcolm Coltrane. J. Lester.—AdPb
On the pole. U. Z. Greenberg.—MeP
The pale blue casket. O. Pitcher.—AdPb
Paul Bunyan. S. Silverstein.—SiW
The poplar field. W. Cowper.—MaFw
Question. A. T. Pratt.—AlW
Requiem. R. L. Stevenson.—RoIt
The sea. B. Cornwall.—RoIt
Seed-time. G. Meredith.—PaF
Shrew. M. A. Hoberman.—HoLb
"Solomon Grundy." Mother Goose.—AlC—JoA-4
Spring dew. T. Palmanteer.—AlW
Stopping by woods on a snowy evening. R. Frost.—AdP—JoA-4—MaFw—PaF—RoIt
Those who go, not to return. B. Galai.—MeP
Time. J. H. Wynne.—OpOx
Time to die. R. G. Dandridge.—AdPb
To daffadills. R. Herrick.—PaF
To daffodils.—JoA-4
To Theodora. Unknown.—OpOx
Traveling through the dark. W. Stafford.—CoPt—HiN—MaFw—MoT—PeS
Travelling home. From In the fruitful flat land. F. Cornford.—PaP
Ultima ratio regum. S. Spender.—ToM
Life—Morality. See Conduct of life
"**Life.**" See Bow harp
Life ("I met four guinea hens today") Alfred Kreymborg.—CoPu
Life ("Life can be good") Paul Goggins.—JoV
Life after death. Richard W. Thomas.—AdPb
"**Life** can be good." See Life
Life cycle of common man. Howard Nemerov.—ToM
Life in our village. Matei Markwei.—AbM
Life in the country. Michael Silverton.—CoPu
"**Life** is ours like the real." See Theme one: The variations
"**The** life of an offensive center." See Dick Szymanski
"**Life** with yon lambs, like day, is just begun." See Composed on a May morning, 1838
The **lifeguard.** James Dickey.—PeS
"**Lift** sunward yr considerable nose." See To a friend: constructive criticism
Light dying. Brendan Kennelly.—CoPi
"A **light** exists in spring." Emily Dickinson.—PaF
"The **light** glow of evening." Unknown, tr. fr. the Pima.—ClFc
"The **light** glows bright." See The parade
The **light-hearted** fairy. Unknown.—JaP
The **light** is sweet. See Ecclesiastes
"A **light** little zephyr came flitting." See Morning compliments
Light my way to bed. Unknown, ad. by John Bierhorst from the collections of Henry Rowe Schoolcraft.—BiS
"The **light** on the leaves." See Never two songs the same
"**Light** sky, dark sky." Unknown.—EmN
Lighthouses
The Eddystone light. Unknown.—CoPt
Epitaph for a lighthouse-keeper's horse. J. B. Morton.—CoPu
Flannan isle. W. W. Gibson.—CoPt
Lightning
"Lightning is a great giant." N. Belting.—BeWi
Sycamore. M. C. Livingston.—LiM
"The **lightning** and thunder." See A baby-sermon
"A **lightning** bug." See The flattered lightning bug
Lightning bugs. See Fireflies
"**Lightning** is a great giant." Natalia Belting.—BeWi
Lights and lighting. See also Candles; Lamps; Lanterns; Lighthouses
City lights. L. Lenski.—LeC
"Eight are the lights." I. Orleans.—LaM (sel.)
"I wonder why." T. Poole.—AdB
Invitation. S. Silverstein.—SiW
"The light is sweet." From Ecclesiastes, Bible, Old Testament.—RoIt
My invention. S. Silverstein.—CoPu
No difference. S. Silverstein.—SiW
"A stairway of light." A. Atwood.—AtM
Traffic light. S. Silverstein.—SiW
"Vera had a little light." Unknown.—EmN
Wonder. L. Hughes.—HoD
"You've no need to light a night light." Unknown.—BrM
"The **lights** from the parlor and kitchen shone out." See Escape at bedtime
Lights out. Edward Thomas.—MaFw

"**Like** a bird in the butcher's palm you flutter in my hand." See Revolt
"**Like** a caricature, the scraggy arms, arthritic knuckles." See Der arme poet
"**Like** a gaunt, scraggly pine." See Lincoln
Like a giant in a towel. Dennis Lee.—LeA
"**Like** a queen enchanted who may not laugh or weep." See A ballad of Bath
"**Like** a quetzal plume, a fragrant flower." See Friendship
"**Like** a rushing wind." See Gang
"**Like** a sleeping swine upon the skyline." See Muckish mountain (The pig's back)
Like a sparkling bead. Ilya Bedniakov, tr. fr. the Russian by Miriam Morton.—MoM
Like a summer bird. Aileen Fisher.—FiFo
Like a woman. Uri Zui Greenberg, tr. fr. the Hebrew by Robert Mezey and Ben Zion Gold.—MeP
"**Like** a woman who knows that her body entices me." See Like a woman
"**Like** Achilles you had a goddess for mother." See On looking into E. V. Rieu's Homer
"**Like** an old windmill." See To my mother
"**Like** chapters of prophecy my days burn, in all the revelations." See With my God, the Smith
"**Like** hunch-backed old women the tents here hang out their tongues." See Jezrael
Like it should be. Myra Cohn Livingston.—LiM
"**Like** lamps between the trees." See Firefly
"**Like** London, always in a fog." Unknown.—MoBw
"**Like** night in broad daylight." See The black panther
"**Like** roundish letters—o c u." See The likes and looks of letters
"**Like** their looks." See Books
Like they say. Robert Creeley.—CoPu
Like you as it. David McCord.—McAa
Likes and dislikes
"Apples for the little ones." C. Watson.—WaF
At the zoo. A. Fisher.—FiFo
A badger. A. Fisher.—FiFo
The boy and the geese. P. Fiacc.—CoPi
Bunches of grapes. W. De La Mare.—LiLc—OpOx
Christmas time. L. B. Hopkins.—HoS
Circus. D. McCord.—McFm
Figgie hobbin. C. Causley.—CaF
The furry ones. A. Fisher.—FiFo
Getting together. N. M. Bodecker.—BoL
Giraffes. M. A. Hoberman.—HoR
Give me the splendid silent sun. W. Whitman.—JoA-4 (sel.)
Great things. T. Hardy.—PlP
A growl. M. Chute.—ChRu
Human beings. D. McCord.—McAa
I am writing this at sea. J. Ciardi.—CiFs
"I do not like (love) thee, Doctor Fell." Martial.—MiMg—TrG
I don't like beetles. R. Fyleman.—OpOx
"I like them feathery, too." A. Fisher.—FiFo
I love. T. Mitrofanova.—MoM
"I love coffee, I love tea." Unknown.—EmN
"Ice cream slice." M. A. Hoberman.—HoN
Idiosyncratic. E. Merriam.—MeO
"I'm a little Dutch girl." Unknown.—EmN
"Jam." M. A. Hoberman.—HoN
Kahshe or Chicoutimi.—D. Lee.—LeA
The King of Hearts. W. J. Smith.—BrM
Knoxville, Tennessee. N. Giovanni.—AdB—AdM—AdPb
Like it should be. M. C. Livingston.—LiM
The likes and looks of letters. D. McCord.—McAa
A little book of little beasts. M. A. Hoberman.—HoLb
Little things. J. A. Carney.—OpOx
Looking for feathers. A. Fisher.—FiFo
Loving and liking. D. Wordsworth.—OpOx
"Mother took me to the farm." Unknown.—EmN
No one else. E. Laron.—ThF
Of man and nature. H. Mungin.—AdB
On Noman, a guest. H. Belloc.—CoPu
Pease porridge poems. D. McCord.—McFm
Picture people. M. C. Livingston.—JoA-4
Preferred vehicles. L. B. Jacobs.—HoP
Prejudice. G. D. Johnson.—AdPb
Pruning trees. P. Chü-i.—MaFw
"Raspberry, strawberry." Unknown.—EmN
Sandpipers. A. Fisher.—FiFo
Shiver my timbers. D. McCord.—McAa
Simple song. M. Piercy.—MoT
Sometimes on my way back down to the block. V. H. Cruz.—AdB
"There's this that I like about hockey, my lad." J. Kieran.—FlH
Thirty-three triads. Unknown.—CoPi
Trains at night. F. M. Frost.—HoP
The trouble was simply that. D. McCord.—McFm
Us. S. Silverstein.—SiW
Waking up uncle. X. J. Kennedy.—KeO
Weathers. T. Hardy.—PlP
Which Washington. E. Merriam.—LaM
Wishes of an elderly man. W. Raleigh.—CoPu
"Yes." M. A. Hoberman.—HoN
The **likes** and looks of letters. David McCord.—McAa
Lilacs
Lilacs. A. Lowell.—PaF (sel.)
Lilacs. Amy Lowell.—PaF (sel.)
Lilies
The Lent lily. From A Shropshire lad. A. E. Housman.—PaF
Tiger lily. D. McCord.—AdP
"**Lily** ladled little Letty's lentil soup." Unknown.—EmN
Limericks. See also entries under Lear, Edward, beginning There was
About a monster-ous toothache. L. Moore.—MoSm
"As a little fat man of Bombay." Unknown
Anecdotes of four gentlemen.—OpOx

"There was an old person of Gretna." E. Lear
Nonsenses.—OpOx
"There was an old person of Ware." E. Lear.—LiLc
Limericks.—JoA-4
"There was an old soldier of Bicester." Unknown
Anecdotes of four gentlemen.—OpOx
"There was an old woman in Surrey." Mother Goose.—OpOx—TucMgl
"There was an old woman named Towl." Unknown
Three wonderful old women.—OpOx
The tooting tutor. Unknown.—BrM
"A tooter who tooted the flute."—EmN
Whale food. L. Moore.—MoSm
When a jolly young fisher. Unknown.—BrM
"A yak who was new to the zoo." D. Ross.—RoIt
Limited crossing Wisconsin. See Prairie
The **limits** of submission. Faarah Nuur, tr. fr. the Somalia by B. W. Andrzejewski and I. M. Lewis.—AdM—AlPa (sel.)
Lin Ho Ching
An enjoyable evening in the village near the lake.—MaFw
Lincoln, Abraham
The bear hunt.—RoIt
Lincoln, Abraham (about)
Abraham Lincoln walks at midnight. V. Lindsay.—JoA-4
Anne Rutledge. From The Spoon River antholgoy. E. L. Masters.—RoIt
In Hardin county, 1809. L. E. Thompson.—CoPt
Lincoln. J. G. Fletcher.—JoA-4
Lincoln monument: Washington. L. Hughes.—LaM
"Lincoln was a tall man." E. Lieberman.—RoIt
Nancy Hanks. S. V. Benét and R. Carr.—JoA-4
O captain, my captain. W. Whitman.—RoIt
To meet Mr Lincoln. E. Merriam.—LaM
"Two days." M. De Veaux.—HoC
Lincoln. John Gould Fletcher.—JoA-4
"**Lincoln,** Lincoln, I've been thinkin'." Unknown.—MoBw
Lincoln monument: Washington. Langston Hughes.—LaM
"**Lincoln** was a tall man." Elias Lieberman.—RoIt
Linden
Witches.—LaM
Lindsay, Norman
Puddin' song.—CoOr
Lindsay, Vachel (Nicholas)
Abraham Lincoln walks at midnight.—JoA-4
The blacksmith's serenade.—CoPt
"Factory windows are always broken."—CoPu
The flower-fed buffaloes.—JoA-4
The leaden-eyed.—CoPu
The little turtle.—LiLc—RoIt
"The moon's the north wind's cooky."—JoA-4—LiLc—UnGb
The mysterious cat.—JoA-4
What the moon saw.—LiWw
Lindsay, Vachel (Nicholas) (about)
Supper with Lindsay. T. Roethke.—PlM
Lindsay, William
The hundred yard dash.—FlH
The **line-gang.** Robert Frost.—MaFw
"A **line** in long array where they wind betwixt green islands." See Cavalry crossing a ford
Lineage. Margaret Walker.—AdB—AdPb
Lines. Herbert Martin.—AdPb
Lines by an old fogy. Unknown.—LiWw
Lines composed a few miles above Tintern Abbey, sel. William Wordsworth
"Five years have past; five summers, with the length."—PaP
Lines for a dead poet. David Ferry.—PlM
Lines for a night driver. Peter Kane Dufault.—HaWr
Lines for Cuscuscaraway and Mirza Murad Ali Beg. T. S. Eliot.—LiS—PlM
Lines from Snow-bound. See Snow-bound
Lines on the Mermaid tavern. John Keats.—PlM
"**Lines** parallel." See The room
Lines supposed to have been addressed to Fanny Brawne. John Keats.—CoPu
Lines to a movement in Mozart's E-flat symphony. Thomas Hardy.—PlP
Lines to a young lady. See "How pleasant to know Mr Lear"
Lines written for Gene Kelly to dance to. Carl Sandburg.—SaT
Lines written in early spring. William Wordsworth.—RoIt
Lingle, lingle. Unknown.—BlM
"**Lingle,** lingle, lang tang." See Lingle, lingle
Link rhymes. See Build-on rhymes
Linnets
The burial of the linnet. J. H. Ewing.—OpOx
Linton, Harold
"Sweating."—HoC
Lion ("The lion has a golden mane") Jack Prelutsky.—PrP
Lion ("Look") Mary Ann Hoberman.—HoR
"The **lion** and the unicorn." Mother Goose.—AlC—JoA-4
Lion cubs. Aileen Fisher.—FiD
"The **lion** has a golden mane." See Lion
The **lioness** and her cub. Volodya Lapin, tr. fr. the Russian by Miriam Morton.—MoM
Lions
Advice from an elderly mouse. E. J. Coatsworth.—BrM
"A bantam rooster." Kikaku.—BeM
Circus lion. C. Day-Lewis.—ToM
The glory trail. B. Clark.—CoPt
"I tame the very fiercest beast." J. Prelutsky.—PrC
It's dark in here. S. Silverstein.—SiW

"A **little** old man of the sea." See The ingenious little old man
"**Little** Orphan Annie." Unknown.—EmN
Little Orphant Annie. James Whitcomb Riley.—OpOx—RoIt
"**Little** Orphant Annie's come to our house to stay." See Little Orphant Annie
"**Little** piece of paper on the ground." See Off and away
"A **little** Pixie Piper went." See Pipes and drums
"**Little** Polly Flinders." Mother Goose.—AlC
"The **little** priest of Felton." Mother Goose.—MiMg
Little raindrops. Jane Euphemia Browne.—OpOx
"The **little** red spiders." Unknown, tr. fr. the Papago.—JoT
Little Rock, Arkansas
The Chicago *Defender* sends a man to Little Rock. G. Brooks.—AdPb
"The **little** shoes of fairies are." See Fairy shoes
"The **little** shrew is soricine." See Shrew
Little sketch. Carl Sandburg.—SaT
"**Little** snail." See Snail
Little snail. Hilda Conkling.—JoA-4
Little song for the children of the Antilles. Nicolás Guillén, tr. fr. the Spanish by Langston Hughes.—AbM
"**Little** sparrows." Issa, tr. fr. the Japanese by Hanaka Fukuda.—HaW
"A **little** square of earth." See Undefeated
The **little** star. Unknown.—LiS
Little things, Importance of
A considerable speck. R. Frost.—AdP
For want of a nail. Unknown.—RoIt
"For want of a nail the shoe was lost."—TrG
Little things ("Little drops of water") J. A. Carney.—OpOx
Little things ("Little things that run and quail") J. Stephens.—AdP—CoPu—JoA-4
The pin. A. Taylor.—OpOx
To a young brother. M. J. Jewsbury.—OpOx
Little things ("Little drops of water") Julia A. Carney.—OpOx
Little things ("Little things that run and quail") James Stephens.—AdP—CoPu—JoA-4
"**Little** things that run and quail." See Little things
"**Little** tiny puppy dog." Spike Milligan.—CoOh
"**Little** Tom Tucker." Mother Goose.—AlC
"Little Tommy Tucker."—JoA-4
"**Little** Tommy Tittlemouse." Mother Goose.—AlC—MiMg
"**Little** Tommy Tucker." See "Little Tom Tucker"
"**Little** Tradja of Norway." See Tradja of Norway
"**Little** tree." E. E. Cummings.—HoS—LiLc—MaFw
The **little** turtle. Vachel Lindsay.—LiLc—RoIt
Little Ugh. Lilian Moore.—MoSm
"A **little** white fence that's always wet." Unknown.—EmN
Little wind. Kate Greenaway.—JoA-4
"**Little** wind, blow on the hill-top." See Little wind
"**Little** wind, little sun." See Little
"**Little** winter cottontails." See The outdoor Christmas tree
"The **little** wren of tender mind." See The wren
"A **little** yellow cricket." Unknown, tr. fr. the Papago.—JoT
Liverpool, England
A Negro labourer in Liverpool. D. Rubadiri.—AlPa
"**Living** in an old house." See Great-aunts
Living tenderly. May Swenson.—AdP
The **living** truth. Sterling Plumpp.—AdPb
Livingston, Myra Cohn
August.—LiM
Beginnings.—LiM
A book.—LiM
Buildings.—JoA-4
Discovery.—LiLc
Driving.—HoP—LiM
Father.—LiM
Feet.—JoA-4
For purple mountains' majesty.—LiM
Freeway.—LiM
German shepherd.—LiM
Get lost.—LiM
"Goldfish whisper."—LiM
Grunion.—LiM
Hear this.—LiM
Here I am.—LiM
Hokku/haikai/haiku.—LiM
"The house at the corner."—HoH
"I'm a pilot."—HoP
It happened.—LiM
Like it should be.—LiM
Little dead.—LiM
Low tide.—LiM
The Malibu.—LiM
Math class.—LiM
The new one.—LiM
Not mine.—LiM
October magic.—HoH
On a bike.—LiM
One for Novella Nelson.—LiM
Only a little litter.—LiM
Pandora.—LiM—NeA
Picture people.—JoA-4
The pilgrimage.—LiM
Presents.—BrM—HoS
Punta De Los Lobos Marinos.—LiM
"Quiet."—LiM
Safety first.—LiM
74th street.—LiM
Sophie E. Schnitter.—LiM
Straight talk (from a surfer).—LiM
Sycamore.—LiM
Texas norther.—LiM
Theme with variation.—LiM
A time for building.—HoCs

Time to practice.—LiM
12 October.—LiM
The way that it's going.—LiM
"Whispers."—JoA-4—LiLc
"Who needs a poet."—LiM
Livingstone, Douglas
Conversation with a giraffe at dusk in the zoo.—ToM
Sunstrike.—ToM
Lizard. Agnes Maxwell-Hall.—AbM
Lizards
The chameleon. J. Prelutsky.—PrP
Lizard. A. Maxwell-Hall.—AbM
Lizards and snakes. A. Hecht.—HiN
Song for the sun that disappeared behind the rainclouds. Unknown.—AlPa
Ttimba. Unknown.—SeS
Lizards and snakes. Anthony Hecht.—HiN
Lizette. David McCord.—McAa
Llamas
A llyric of the llama. B. Johnson.—CoOh
Lloyd, A. L.
The smoked herring. tr.—CoPt
Lloyd, William
A reflection on human life.—CoPu
Llude sig kachoo. Eve Merriam.—MeF
A **llyric** of the llama. Burges Johnson.—CoOh
Lmntl. David McCord.—McFm
"**Lo,** I beheld Mauros." See On Mauros the rhetor
"**Lo,** in the middle of the wood." See The lotus eaters
The **lobster.** See Alice's adventures in wonderland—Alice's recitation
The **lobster** quadrille. See Alice's adventures in wonderland
Lobsters
Alice's recitation. From Alice's adventures in wonderland.—LiS
The lobster.—OpOx
'Tis the voice of the lobster.—JoA-4
'Tis the voice of the lobster, I heard him declare."—LiPc
The voice of the lobster.—RoIt
The lobster quadrille. From Alice's adventures in wonderland. L. Carroll.—OpOx
Lobsters in the window. W. D. Snodgrass.—HiN
Lobsters in the window. W. D. Snodgrass.—HiN
Local note. Arthur Guiterman.—CoPu
A **local** storm. Donald Justice.—HiN
"The **Loch** Achray was a clipper tall." See The yarn of the Loch Achray
Lochinvar. See Marmion
"**Lock** the dairy door." Mother Goose.—AlC
"**Locked** arm in arm they cross the way." See Tableau
Locked in. Ingemar Gustafson, tr. fr. the Swedish by May Swenson.—CoPt
Locker-Lampson, Frederick
A terrible infant.—CoPu
Locomotives. See Railroads
Locusts
Serenade. D. Donnelly.—HiN
Loftin, Elouise
Virginia.—AdPb
Weeksville women.—AdPb
Woman.—AdPb
Lofting, Hugh
Betwixt and Between.—BrM
Mister Beers.—BrM
"Scallywag and Gollywog."—BrM
Logan, John
The picnic.—HiN
Logic
The deacon's masterpiece; or, The wonderful one-hoss shay. O. W. Holmes.—RoIt
Logs of wood. Charles Causley.—CaF
Lollocks. Robert Graves.—MaFw
Lomax, Pearl Cleage
Glimpse.—AdPb
London, England
"As I was going o'er London bridge." Unknown.—TrG
Chelsea morning. J. Mitchell.—MoG
Composed upon Westminster bridge. W. Wordsworth.—PaP
"Empresse of townes, exalt in honour." From In honour of the city of London. W. Dunbar.—PaP
The fire of London. J. Dryden.—MaFw (sel.)
"Gay go up, and gay go down." Mother Goose.—AlC—JoA-4
In the Isle of Dogs. J. Davidson.—PaP
London. W. Blake.—MoG
London beautiful. R. Le Gallienne.—PaP
"London bridge is broken down." Mother Goose.—JoA-4
London, 1802. W. Wordsworth.—PlM
London snow. R. Bridges.—PaF
London voluntary. W. E. Henley.—PaP
"A mighty mass of brick, and smoke, and shipping." From Don Juan. Lord Byron.—PaP
November blue. A. Meynell.—PaP
Pete the parrot and Shakespeare. D. Marquis.—PlM
A refusal to mourn the death, by fire, of a child in London.—ToM
"See-saw sacradown." Mother Goose.—JoA-4
"Two n's, two o's, an l, and d." Unknown.—EmN
London. William Blake.—MoG
London beautiful. Richard Le Gallienne.—PaP
"**London** bridge is broken down." Mother Goose.—JoA-4
London, 1802. William Wordsworth.—PlM
"**London,** I heard one say, no more is fair." See London beautiful
London snow. Robert Bridges.—PaF
London voluntary. William Ernest Henley.—PaP
"A **lone** gray bird." See From the shore
Lone Ranger (about)
"Heigh-ho Silver everywhere." Unknown.—EmN

"A **lone** wolf I am." Unknown, tr. fr. the Sioux.—ClFc
Loneliness
Alone ("The leaves shudder, the branch shakes") K. Raikin.—MoM
Alone ("The wind took them, light swept them all away") C. N. Bialik.—MeP
Boy down the hall. L. Lenski.—LeC
The cave. G. W. Dresbach.—PeS
Chaka. L. S. Senghor.—AlPa (sel.)
"Do not blow in the garden, wind." Unknown.—BaSs
The empty woman. G. Brooks.—PeS
The fountains. W. R. Rodgers.—CoPi
Four and twenty. S. Stills.—MoG
The geranium. T. Roethke.—ToM
Gone away. D. Levertov.—PeS
Hope. L. Hughes.—HoD
"I sat on the stoop." L. Lenski.—LeC
I'm only going to tell you once. A. T. Pratt.—AlW
Keziah. G. Brooks.—UnGb
The land of heart's desire. W. B. Yeats.—MaFw (sel.)
Loneliness ("I was about to go, and said to") B. Jenkins.—PeS
Loneliness ("The poet is the dreamer") A. Young.—AdPb
The lonely man. R. Jarrell.—ToM
The lonely say. Avraham Ben Yitzhak.—MeP
The lonely soul. R. E. G. Armattoe.—AlPa
Lonesome place. L. Lenski.—LeC
My friend. L. Kirkman.—HoCs
Night-piece. R. R. Patterson.—AdPb
"No friends nor enemies." J. Bryant.—JoV
Oda oak oracle. T. Gabre-Medhin.—AlPa (sel.)
"Restless little flea." Issa.—BeM
Roofer. R. Froman.—FrSp
Separation. A. Lopez.—AlW
Sunday morning: Lonely. L. Clifton.—ClS
Tears. A. Lopez.—AlW
That lonesome place. C. O'John.—AlW
Tiny world. J. Holland.—JoV
"What is the opposite of *two.*" R. Wilbur.—WiO
Loneliness ("I was about to go, and said to") Brooks Jenkins.—PeS
Loneliness ("The poet is the dreamer") Al Young.—AdPb
The **lonely** man. Randall Jarrell.—ToM
The **lonely** say. Avraham Ben Yitzhak, tr. fr. the Hebrew by Robert Mezey.—MeP
"A **lonely,** sickly old man." See Casual lines
The **lonely** soul. R. E. G. Armattoe.—AlPa
Lonesome place. Lois Lenski.—LeC
Long, Doughtry
Ginger bread mama.—AdPb
"Negro dreams."—AdPb
#4.—AdM—AdPb
"One time Henry dreamed the number."—AdPb
"**Long** ago I learned how to sleep." See Wind song
"**Long** ago in the north." See Now we come southwards
"**Long** and lonely December night." Hwang Chini, tr. fr. the Korean by Chung Seuk Park and ad. by Virginia Olsen Baron.—BaSs
"**Long,** glossy caterpillar." See The word beautiful
The **long-haired** boy. Shel Silverstein.—SiW
"The **long-haired** yak has long black hair." See The yak
A **long** hard day. John Ciardi.—CiFs
"**Long** have I beat with timid hands upon life's leaden door." See The suppliant
"A **long,** lean, slim, slick sapling." See The saplings
"**Long** legs, crooked thighs." Mother Goose.—JoA-4
A **long** life. Lois Lenski.—LeC
Long, long ago. Unknown.—HoS—RoIt
"**Long** long ago when the world was a wild place." See Bedtime story
"**Long** long time ago there was a black man in the." See The lost black man
Long, long you have held between your hands. Léopold Sédar Senghor, tr. fr. the French by John Reed and Clive Wake.—AlPa
"**Long,** long you have held between your hands the black face of the warrior." See Long, long you have held between your hands
"A **long** time ago, when the earth was green." See The unicorn
Long trip. Langston Hughes.—HoD
"The **longest** nose." Shel Silverstein.—SiW
Longfellow, Henry Wadsworth
Autumn.—PaF
Chaucer.—PlM
The children's hour.—RoIt
The day is done.—RoIt
Evangeline, sel.
Prologue to Evangeline.—LiS
Excelsior.—LiS
Hiawatha's childhood. See The song of Hiawatha
"I heard the bells on Christmas day."—RoIt
The luck of Edenhall.—CoPt
My lost youth.—RoIt
Prelude.—PaF
Prologue to Evangeline. See Evangeline
Rain in summer.—PaF
The secret of the sea.—RoIt
Snow-flakes.—PaF—RoIt
The song of Hiawatha.—LiS (sel.)—RoIt (sel.)
Hiawatha's childhood.—JoA-4 (sel.)
"There was a little girl."—OpOx (sel.)—RoIt
"The tide rises, the tide falls."—RoIt
The wreck of the Hesperus.—RoIt
Longfellow, Henry Wadsworth (about)
The metre Columbian. Unknown.—LiS
The **Longford** legend. Unknown.—CoPt
Longing for death. Unknown, tr. fr. the Ewe by P. Wiegrabe.—AlPa
The **Longspur's** incantation. Unknown, fr. the Copper Eskimo.—LeIb

"Look." See Lion
The **look** and sound of words. David McCord.—McFm
"Look at Marcus and take warning." Lucilius.—JoA-4
"Look at me 8th." See Poem
"Look at me, friend." See To the cedar tree
"Look at six eggs." Carl Sandburg.—RoIt
"Look at that." Lilian Moore.—MoSm
"Look at that strutting." Issa, tr. fr. the Japanese by Harry Behn.—BeM
"Look at the stars, look, look up at the skies." See The starlight night
"Look at this village boy, his head is stuffed." See Farm child
"Look below you. The river is a thousand fathoms deep." Yi Hyun-bo, tr. fr. the Korean by Chung Seuk Park and ad. by Virginia Olsen Baron.—BaSs
"Look, Gregory, lay off." See Get lost
Look, Hart, that horse you ride is wood. Peter Viereck.—PlM
"Look, JP." See Skulls and cups
"Look, look, the spring is come." See First spring morning
"Look out, here comes Lucky Sukey." See Lucky Sukey
"Look out how you use proud words." See Primer lesson
"Look out the window." See Signs
Look out the window. Lois Lenski.—LeC
"Look, stranger, on this island now." See On this island
Look, the sea. William Zorach.—AdP
"Look, the sea—how it lifts me in its arms like a child." See Look, the sea
"Look there at the star." See Shepherd's song at Christmas
Look: What am I. David McCord.—McFm
Looking at the moon on putting out from the shore at Nagato. Unknown, tr. fr. the Japanese by Geoffrey Bownas and Anthony Thwaite.—MaFw
"Looking back at the dusty trail." See Will I make it
"Looking back in my mind I can see." See The elementary scene
Looking for feathers. Aileen Fisher.—FiFo
"Looking for my darling." See "Nnoonya mwana wange"
Looking forward. Robert Louis Stevenson.—OpOx
Looking into a face. Robert Bly.—MoT
Loomis, Charles Battell
Cruel Miss Newell.—BrM
Loons
The loons are singing. Unknown.—BiS
The **loons** are singing. Unknown, ad. by John Bierhorst from the collections of Frances Densmore.—BiS
Lopez, Alonzo
Celebration.—AlW
Direction.—AlW
"Dry and parched."—AlW
Eagle flight.—AlW
Endless search.—AlW
"I am crying from thirst."—AlW
"I go forth to move about the earth."—AlW
"I see a star."—AlW
The lavender kitten.—AlW
A question.—AlW
"Raise your hands to the sky."—AlW
Separation.—AlW
Tears.—AlW
Untitled.—AlW
Lorca, Federíco García. See García Lorca, Federíco
"Lord." See The hungry black child
Lord Arnaldos. James Elroy Flecker.—CoPt
"Lord, beloved." See Verses expressing the feelings of a lover
Lord Chancellor's song. See Iolanthe
The **Lord** hath done great things. See Psalms—Psalm 126
"Lord how delightful 'tis to see." See For the Lord's day evening
"The **Lord** is my shepherd." See Psalms—Psalm 23
"The **Lord** is my shepherd, I shall not want." See Psalms—Psalm 23
Lord most generous and compassionate, giver of all sustenance." See Supplication to the rain god and the spirits of water
"Lord most giving and resourceful." See Prayer
The **Lord** of the Dance. Sydney Carter.—LaS
Lord Thomas and fair Eleanor. Unknown.—MaFw
"Lord Thomas he was a bold forester." See Lord Thomas and fair Eleanor
"Lord, thou hast been our dwelling place." See Psalms—Psalm 90
Lorde, Audre
And what about the children.—AdPb
Coal.—AdPb
Father Son and Holy Ghost.—AdPb
"Father, the year is fallen."—AdPb
Now that I am forever with child.—AdPb
Rites of passage.—AdPb
Suffer the children.—AdPb
Summer oracle.—AdPb
"What my child learns of the sea."—AdPb
"Lord's lost Him His mockingbird." See Mourning poem for the Queen of Sunday
Lorna Doone: Last cookie song. Russell Hoban.—HoE
Los reyes oriente (Song of the wise men). Unknown, ad. fr. the Puerto Rican by Seymour Barab.—LaS
The **loser.** Shel Silverstein.—SiW
"Losers weepers." Unknown.—EmN
Losing friends. Asya Gutkina, tr. fr. the Russian by Miriam Morton.—MoM
Losing mittens. Marchette Chute.—ChRu
"Lost." See Lost and found
Lost. Carl Sandburg.—JoA-4—SaT
Lost and found. Lilian Moore.—MoSw
The **lost** black man. Loudel Baez.—JoV
The **lost** dancer. Jean Toomer.—AdPb

Gypsy eyes. J. Hendrix.—MoG
Had you wept. T. Hardy.—PlP
"Half a moon." R. Rozhdestvensky.—MoM
The happy cynic to his love. E. Merriam.—MeF
The haunter. T. Hardy.—PlP
"He stept so lightly to the land." From Sylvie and Bruno. L. Carroll.—LiPc
He wishes for the cloths of Heaven. W. B. Yeats.—JoA-4
Her song. T. Hardy.—PlP
Herrick's Julia. H. Bevington.—LiS
Home. From Poems done on a late night car. C. Sandburg.—SaT
Household song. Unknown.—AlPa
"Huckleberry, gooseberry, raspberry pie." C. Watson.—WaF
"I am seized with violent desire." Unknown.—LeIb
I cannot forget you. Unknown.—BiI
"I do not like (love) thee, Dr Fell." Martial.—MiMg—TrG
"I know where I'm going." Unknown.—JoA-4
"I love cake, I love pie." Unknown.—EmN
"I love coffee, I love tea." Unknown.—EmN
"I love you a little." Unknown.—EmN
"I love you in blue." Unknown.—MoBw
"I love you on the hillside." Unknown.—MoBw
"I love you once." Unknown.—MoBw
"I see your face." L. Issaluk.—LeIb
I will make you brooches. R. L. Stevenson.—RoIt
"Ickle ockle, blue bockle." Mother Goose.—HoMg
"I'd like to carve a moon." Chung Chul.—BaSs
"If it's ever spring again." T. Hardy.—PlP
"If night nears your window." D. Fogel.—MeP
"If teardrops were pearls." Unknown.—BaSs
"If the ocean was milk." Unknown.—MoBw
"If thou survive my well-contented day." W. Shakespeare
Sonnet.—PlM
"If you love me as I love you." Unknown.—EmN
"If you think you are in love." Unknown.—MoBw
"If you were coming in the fall." E. Dickinson.—ThI
An immorality. E. Pound.—CoPu
In my life. J. Lennon and P. McCartney.—MoG
In school-days. J. G. Whittier.—OpOx
"In the middle of this century." Y. Amichai.—MeP
In which are described rationally the irrational effects of love. Juana Inez De la Cruz.—ThI (sel.)
Is it a month. J. M. Synge.—CoPi
"It's a new kind of day." K. Grosvenor.—AdM
Ivory masks in orbit. K. Kgositsile.—AdPb
"Jenny Wren fell sick." Mother Goose.—JoA-4
Jig. C. Day-Lewis.—CoPi
John Anderson, my jo. R. Burns.—RoIt
Johnny has gone for a soldier. Unknown.—RoIt
"Johnny shall have a new bonnet." Mother Goose.—JoA-4
Joy. L. Hughes.—AbM
Juke box love song. L. Hughes.—AdPb
Juliet. H. Belloc.—CoPu
June thunder. L. MacNeice.—ToM
Just me, just me. S. Silverstein.—SiW
Kitty of Coleraine. Unknown.—CoPt
Lady Clare. A. Tennyson.—CoPt
The licorice fields at Pontefract. J. Betjeman.—ToM
Lines. T. Hardy.—PlP
"Listen children." L. Clifton.—AdM
Lochinvar. From Marmion. W. Scott.—CoPt—JoA-4
"Long and lonely December night." Hwang Chini.—BaSs
Love. N. H. Pritchard II.—AdPb
Love ("If not necessary, is essential") A. Stevenson.—HiN
Love ("Love is a funny thing") Unknown.—AbM
Love ("Love is beautiful") P. Goggins.—JoV
Love ("Ricky was L but he's home with the flu") S. Silverstein.—SiW
Love ("Slap down my brother") P. Solomon.—JoV
Love and age. From Gryll Grange. T. L. Peacock.—RoIt
Love apart. C. Okigbo.—AlPa
Love in a space-suit. J. Kirkup.—ToM
A love song ("Do I love you") R. R. Patterson.—AdB
Love song ("I go among the girls and see them all") Unknown.—BiI
Love song ("I know not whether you have been absent") Unknown.—BiI
Love song ("I passed by the house of the young man who loves me") Unknown.—AbM
Love song ("I was") A. Sexton.—HiN
Love song ("New moon, O new moon") Unknown.—BiI
Love song ("Your being has caused") D. Whitewing.—AlW
Love song for the future. V. Miller.—HiN
Love song of a young man. Unknown.—BiI
Love songs. Unknown.—AlPa
The love-talker. E. Carbery.—CoPt
Love without hope. R. Graves.—CoPu
The lover in winter plaineth for the spring. Unknown.—LiS
The lover tells of the rose in his heart. W. B. Yeats.—CoPi
Lovers, and a reflection. C. S. Calverley.—LiS
Loving and liking. D. Wordsworth.—OpOx
"The maidens came." Unknown.—MaFw
A man of experience. Unknown.—CoPi

Lu Yün's lament. Herbert Read.—PlM
Lucian of Samosata
Meditation on beavers.—LiWw
Luciano, Felipe
You're nothing but a Spanish colored kid.—AdPb
Lucie-Smith, Edward
The giant tortoise.—CoPu
Imperialists in retirement.—ToM
The lesson.—HiN—ToM
The orang utan.—CoPu
Lucilius
"Little Hermogenes is so small."—JoA-4
"Look at Marcus and take warning."—JoA-4
On Apis the prizefighter.—LiWw
On torpid Marcus.—LiWw
A valentine for a lady.—LiWw
Luck
Because I were shy. Unknown.—CoPt
The dam. P. Dickinson.—CoPt
Dow's flat. B. Harte.—CoPt
"Ducks are lucky." M. A. Hoberman.—HoN
"How God hath labored to produce the duck." D. Hall.—CoPu
Luck for Halloween. M. Justus.—HoH
The luck of Edenhall. H. W. Longfellow.—CoPt
Lucky Sukey. X. J. Kennedy.—KeO
Magic words to bring luck when hunting caribou. Unknown.—LeIb
The ploughboy in luck. Unknown.—RoIt
"See a pin and pick it up." Mother Goose.—EmN—JoA-4
Stupid old myself. R. Hoban.—HoE
Luck for Halloween. May Justus.—HoH
The **luck** of Edenhall. Henry Wadsworth Longfellow.—CoPt
Lucknow, Battle of, 1857
The relief of Lucknow. R. S. T. Lowell.—CoPt
"**Lucky** is the mushrooms' mother." See Mushrooms
Lucky Sukey. X. J. Kennedy.—KeO
Lucy Gray; or, Solitude. William Wordsworth.—OpOx
Lucy in the sky with diamonds. The Beatles.—PeS
Lucy Lake. Newton Mackintosh.—LiS
"**Lucy** Locket lost her pocket." Mother Goose.—JoA-4
Lukonin, Mikhail
"The dawn breaks over the mooring."—MoM
Lullabies
Better come quietly. From Six theological cradle songs. P. Viereck.—LiWw
"Bye, baby bunting." Mother Goose.—JoA-4—LiS
Ca, ca, ca. Unknown.—SeS
A Christmas lullaby. M. Hillert.—HoS
The cottager to her infant. D. Wordsworth.—OpOx
Cradle hymn ("Away in a [the] manger, no crib for a bed") M. Luther.—JoA-4
Away in a manger.—LaS
Cradle hymn ("Hush my dear, lie still and slumber") I. Watts.—OpOx
Hush, my babe.—LaS
A cradle song ("The angels are stooping") W. B. Yeats.—LiLc
Cradle song ("Sleep, sleep, beauty bright") W. Blake.—JoA-4
Cradle song. T. U Tam'ri.—AlPa (sel.)
The duchess's lullaby. From Alice's adventures in wonderland. L. Carroll.—LiS
"Speak roughly to your little boy."—LiPc
Dwarf's lullabye. B. J. Lee.—JaP
"Hush-a-bye, baby (pussy's a lady)." Mother Goose.—BlM
"Hush-a-bye, baby, on the tree top." Mother Goose.—JoA-4
Lullaby ("Golden slumbers kiss your eyes") at. to Thomas Dekker.—CoPu
A cradle song.—OpOx
Lullaby ("It is my big baby") Unknown.—LeIb
Lullaby ("My little dark baby") L. Hughes.—HoD
Lullaby ("Sh sh what do you wish") E. Merriam.—MeO
Lullaby ("Sleep, love, sleep") Q. Prettyman.—AdB
Lullaby ("Way way way way way") Unknown.—BiS
Lullaby for Ann-Lucian. C. Forbes.—AdPb
Lullaby of an infant chief. W. Scott.—JoA-4—OpOx
Menominee lullaby. Unknown.—BiS
"Puva, puva, puva." Unknown.—ClFc
Response. B. Kaufman.—AdB
"Rock-a-bye baby, thy cradle is green." Mother Goose.—AlC—JoA-4
"Rock, rock, sleep, my baby." C. Watson.—WaF
A rocking hymn. G. Wither.—OpOx
Seal lullaby. R. Kipling.—JoA-4
Seal mother's song.—CoPu
Sleep, little daughter. Unknown.—BiS
"Sleep well." Unknown.—ClFc
The sugar-plum tree. Eugene Field.—OpOx
Sung by a little girl to soothe a crying baby. Unknown.—LeIb
Sweet and low. From The princess. A. Tennyson.—JoA-4—RoIt
Two Spanish gypsy lullabies. Unknown.—MaFw
Wavvuuvuwmira. Unknown.—SeS
"What does little birdie say." From Sea dreams. A. Tennyson.—RoIt
Cradle song.—OpOx
Woowooto. Unknown.—SeS
Wynken, Blynken, and Nod. Eugene Field.—OpOx
Lullaby ("Golden slumbers kiss your eyes") at. to Thomas Dekker.—CoPu
A cradle song.—OpOx
Lullaby ("It is my big baby") Unknown, fr. the Thule Eskimo.—LeIb

Lullaby ("My little dark baby") Langston Hughes.—HoD
Lullaby ("Sh sh what do you wish") Eve Merriam.—MeO
Lullaby ("Sleep, love, sleep") Quandra Prettyman.—AdB
Lullaby ("Way way way way way") Unknown, ad. by John Bierhorst from the collections of Frances Densmore.—BiS
Lullaby for Ann-Lucian. Calvin Forbes.—AdPb
Lullaby of an infant chief. Walter Scott.—JoA-4—OpOx
Lullay my liking. Unknown.—MaF
"**Lullay** my liking, my dear Son, my sweeting." See Lullay my liking
"**Lully,** lullay, lully, lullay." See The falcon
Lumber yard pools at sunset. Carl Sandburg.—SaT
"**Lumbering** haunches, pussyfoot tread, a pride of lions." See Circus lion
"**Luminous** silence. . . . " Ann Atwood.—AtM
Lummis, Charles Fletcher
Cannibalee: A po'em of passion.—LiS
"**Luna,** la luna." Unknown, tr. fr. the Mexican by Patricia Fent Ross.—JoA-4
Luther, Martin
Cradle hymn.—JoA-4
Away in a manger.—LaS
Lydgate, John
The boy serving at table.—OpOx
The **lyf** so short. W. Stafford.—PlM
Lying. Thomas Moore.—CoPi
"**Lying** apart now, each in a separate bed." See One flesh
"**Lying** in bed in the dark, I hear the bray." See Weather ear
Lying on things. Dennis Lee.—LeA
A **lyke**-wake dirge. Unknown.—MaFw
Lyle, K. Curtis
Lacrimas or there is a need to scream.—AdPb
Sometimes I go to Camarillo and sit in the lounge.—AdPb
Songs for the Cisco Kid.—AdPb
Lynch, Charles
If we cannot live as people.—AdPb
Memo.—AdPb
The **lynching.** Claude McKay.—AdPb
Lynching and burning. Primus St John.—AdPb
Lynchings. See also Hangings
For Mack C. Parker. P. Murray.—AdPb
I saw them lynch. C. Freeman.—AdPb
The lynching. C. McKay.—AdPb
Lynching and burning. Primus St John.—AdPb
So quietly. L. P. Hill.—AdPb
Song for a dark girl. L. Hughes.—AdPb
Lynxes
The lesser lynx. E. V. Rieu.—LiWw
Lyon, Clara Odell
Winkelman Von Winkel.—CoOr
Lyres
"At noontime." Sappho.—ThI
"Squire McGuire." Unknown.—BoI
"**Lysander** talks extremely well." See The prater

M

M., D.
Standing at the foot of the steps at night. tr.—MaFw
"**M**—I, crooked letter, crooked letter, I." Unknown.—EmN
Ma and God. Shel Silverstein.—SiW
"**Mabel,** Mabel, set the table." Unknown.—EmN
Mabona, Mongameli
The sea.—AlPa
Macaroon. See From the kitchen
"The **macaroon** is quite a chewy cooky." See From the kitchen—Macaroon
Macaulay, Rose
The devourers.—PaP
Macaulay, Thomas Babington, Lord
Horatius at the bridge. See Lays of ancient Rome
Lays of ancient Rome, sel.
Horatius at the bridge.—RoIt
Macavity: The mystery cat. T. S. Eliot.—OpOx
"**Macavity's** a mystery cat: he's called the Hidden Paw." See Macavity: The mystery cat
MacBeth, George
Bedtime story.—CoPt—ToM
Fourteen ways of touching the Peter.—MaFw
Owl.—ToM
A riddle.—MoT
The wasps' nest.—MaFw
MacCaig, Norman
Aunt Julia.—ToM
Fetching cows.—MaFw
Power dive.—CoPu
Uncle Roderick.—ToM
McCarthy, Eugene
Silence.—CoPu
McCartney, Paul. See Lennon, John and McCartney, Paul
MacCathmhaoil, Seosamh. See Campbell, Joseph
McCord, David
The adventure of Chris.—McAa
Alarm.—McAa
"Alert live reindeer galloping on air." See A Christmas package
All about fireflies all about.—McS
Animal crackers. See From the kitchen
"Asked for another name for Santa Claus." See A Christmas package
"Away and ago."—McAa
Baccalaureate.—LiS
The ballade.—McFm
Ballade: An easy one.—McFm
Balloons.—McAa
Big question.—McFm

McCord, David—*Continued*
Pome.—McAa
The poultry show.—McAa
Pumpkin seeds.—McAa
Question.—McAa
"Question: What kind of rabbit can an Easter rabbit be." See Easter morning
Rain song.—McFm
"Rock candy: hard sweet crystals on a string." See A Christmas package
Runover rhyme.—McFm—McS
Secret.—McAa—McS
The shell.—JoA-4—LiLc—McS
Shiver my timbers.—McAa
Shrew.—McAa
Signs of the zodiac.—LiWw
Snowflakes.—McS
Sometimes.—McFm
Song of the train.—JoA-4
Spike spoke spook.—McAa
The star in the pail.—McS
The starfish.—McS
Story of the fowse or fox.—McFm
Suddenly.—McFm
Summer shower.—McFm
Sunfish.—McAa
"Take the curious case of Tom Pettigrew"
Three limericks.—McS
Ten nights before Christmas.—McFm
The tercet.—McFm
"That broken star." See A Christmas package
That's not.—McAa
"This is my rock."—JoA-4
"Though holly halos hang from many a nail." See A Christmas package
Three signs of spring.—McS
Tick-tock talk.—McAa—McS
Tiger lily.—AdP
Tim.—McAa
Tom and Joe.—McAa
Tooth trouble.—McS
Trinity place.—McAa
The trouble was simply that.—McFm
Turtle.—McFm
Under the white pine.—McFm
Up from down under.—JoA-4
The villanelle.—McFm
The wave.—McFm
"What are pockets for."—McAa
When I would travel.—McFm
Whistle.—McFm
Who hasn't played gazintas.—McFm
Witch's broom notes.—McAa
Wizzle.—McAa
A word or two on Levinia.—McAa
Yellow.—McAa—McS
Yellow jacket.—McAa
McCuaig, Ronald
The hungry moths.—CoPu
McCullers, Carson
Christmas eve rhyme.—HoS
Giraffe.—HoCs
Trick or treat.—HoH
MacDonagh, Donagh
Dublin made me.—CoPi
A revel.—CoPi
MacDonagh, Patrick
Dodona's oaks were still.—CoPi
She walked unaware.—CoPi
Song.—CoPi
The widow of Drynam.—CoPi
MacDonagh, Thomas
John-John.—CoPi—CoPt
The night hunt.—CoPi
MacDonald, George
A baby-sermon.—OpOx
"Where did you come from, baby dear."—OpOx
The wind and the moon.—LiL (sel.)
MacEntee, Máire
Irish curse on the occupying English. tr.—CoPi
MacFarland, Edrie
I see the fairies.—JaP (sel.)
McGaugh, Lawrence
Glimpses #xii.—AdB (sel.)
To children.—AdPb
Two mornings.—AdPb
Young training.—AdPb
McGinley, Phyllis
All around the town (sel.)
"J's the jumping Jay-walker."—BrM
The angry man.—PeS
The importance of being Western. See Speaking of television
"J's the jumping Jay-walker." See All around the town
Lament for lost lodgings.—LiS
Note to my neighbor.—LiWw
Portrait of a girl with comic book.—PeS
Reflections dental. See Speaking of television
Robin Hood. See Speaking of television
Speaking of television, sels.
The importance of being Western.—LiWw
Reflections dental.—LiWw
Robin Hood.—LiWw
To a lady in a phone booth.—LiWw
Triolet against sisters.—LiWw
Machinery. See also names of machines, as Steam shovels
"Gene, Gene made a machine." Unknown.—EmN
La marche des machines. A. S. J. Tessimond.—ToM
Mechanical menagerie. X. J. Kennedy.—KeO
"Red, white, and green." Unknown.—EmN
A time for building. M. C. Livingston.—HoCs
The worker. R. W. Thomas.—AdPb
MacIntyre, John
On sweet Killen hill.—HiN
Mack, L. V.
Biafra.—AdPb
Death songs.—AdPb
McKay, Claude
After the winter.—AdPb
America.—AdPb

Barcelona.—AbM
If we must die.—AdPb
In bondage.—AdPb
The lynching.—AdPb
Outcast.—AdPb
St Isaac's church, Petrograd.—AdPb
To the white fiends.—AdPb
The tropics in New York.—AdPb—RoIt
The white house.—AdPb
McKee, Lucie
Query.—CoPu
McKeesport, Pennsylvania
"All the smoke." E. Siegel.—CoPu
Mackenzie, Lewis
"Sleeping, waking." tr.—MaFw
"The snow thaws." tr.—MaFw
"Under the willow." tr.—MaFw
Mackintosh, Newton
Lucy Lake.—LiS
McLaughlin, Bob
Hockey.—FlH
McLean, G. R. D.
Childhood. tr.—MaFw
McLean, William Alfred, Jr
War.—AdB
MacLeish, Archibald
Black humor.—HiN
Boy in the Roman zoo.—HiN
Eleven.—HiN
The end of the world.—HiN
Hurricane.—HiN
Late abed.—HiN
Mother Goose's garland.—LiWw
The peepers in our meadow.—HiN
Spring in these hills.—HiN
Survivor.—HiN
Winter is another country.—HiN
MacManus, Seamus
A health to the birds.—CoPi
MacNeice, Louis
Autobiography.—MaFw
Dublin.—CoPi
Elegy for minor poets.—PlM
Glass falling.—CoPi
June thunder.—ToM
Museums.—PeS
Prayer before birth.—CoPi—PeS—ToM
The slow starter.—ToM
The streets of Laredo.—ToM
MacPherson, Georgia H.
The absent-minded man.—BrM
McPherson, Sandra
Worlds of different sizes.—CoPu
Mad. Robert Froman.—FrSp
"**Mad** coyote." Unknown, tr. fr. the Tewa.—JoT
The **mad** gardener's song. See Sylvie and Bruno
The **mad** hatter's song. See Alice's adventures in wonderland
Mad Judy. Thomas Hardy.—PlP
Mad soldier's song. See The dynasts
The **mad-woman.** L. A. G. Strong.—CoPi
"**Madame** Mouse trots." Edith Sitwell.—JoA-4
Madgett, Naomi Long
Black woman.—AdPb
Her story.—AdPb
Mortality.—AdPb
Simple.—AdPb
Mae Hwa
"The poor old plum tree."—BaSs
Magalu. Helene Johnson.—AdPb
"**Maggie,** Maggie." Unknown.—EmN
"**Maggie,** Maggie, where is Jiggs." Unknown.—EmN
Magic. See also Enchantment
Aladdin. J. R. Lowell.—RoIt
Magic. S. Silverstein.—SiW
Magic formula. Unknown.—BiI
Magic formula against disease. Unknown.—BiI
Magic formula to destroy life. Unknown.—BiI
Magic formula to fix a bride's affection. Unknown.—BiI
Magic formula to make an enemy peaceful. W. Matthews.—BiI
"A magic landscape." A. Fet.—MoM
Magic prayer. Unknown.—LeIb
Magic song for him who wishes to live. Unknown.—LeIb
Magic vine. Unknown.—JaP
Magic words. Unknown.—LeIb
Magic words to bring luck when hunting caribou. Unknown.—LeIb
Magical eraser. S. Silverstein.—SiW
Merlin. E. Muir.—MaFw
Purrrrr ce. Unknown.—SeS
The song of wandering Aengus. W. B. Yeats.—JoA-4—RoIt
The tale of the hermit told. A. Reid.—CoPt
"When I set out for Lyonnesse." T. Hardy.—PlP
The wife of Llew. F. Ledwidge.—CoPi
The youth and the northwind. J. G. Saxe.—CoPt
Magic. Shel Silverstein.—SiW
Magic formula. Unknown, tr. fr. the Iroquois by A. C. Parker.—BiI
Magic formula against disease. Unknown, tr. fr. the Maya by Ralph Roys.—BiI
Magic formula to destroy life. Unknown, tr. fr. the Cherokee by James Mooney.—BiI
Magic formula to fix a bride's affection. Unknown, tr. fr. the Cherokee by James Mooney.—BiI
Magic formula to make an enemy peaceful. Unknown, tr. fr. the Navajo by Washington Matthews.—BiI
"A **magic** landscape." Afanasy Fet, tr. fr. the Russian by Miriam Morton.—MoM
Magic prayer. Unknown, fr. the Iglulik Eskimo.—LeIb
Magic song for him who wishes to live. Unknown, fr. the Thule Eskimo.—LeIb
Magic vine. Unknown.—JaP
Magic words. Unknown, fr. the Iglulik Eskimo.—LeIb
Magic words to bring luck when hunting caribou. Unknown, fr. the Netsilik Eskimo.—LeIb

Magical eraser. Shel Silverstein.—SiW
Mahon, Derek
Exit Molloy.—CoPi
The prisoner.—CoPi
Mahone, Barbara
Colors for mama.—AdPb
Sugarfields.—AdPb
What color is black.—AdM
Mahoney, Francis Sylvester. See Prout, Father, pseud.
"A **maiden** at college, named Breeze." Unknown.—RoIt
The **maiden's** best adorning. Unknown.—OpOx
"The **maidens** came." Unknown.—MaFw
"**Maidens,** if you love the tale." Lewis Carroll.—LiPc
Maiden's song. Unknown, tr. fr. the Ziba by Leonard Doob and Hermann Rebse.—AlPa
Maidu Indians. See Indians of the Americas—Maidu
The **mailman.** Lois Lenski.—LeC
"The **mailman** brought our dog back home." See Special delivery
Mailmen
Epitaph for a postal clerk. X. J. Kennedy.—LiWw
The mailman. L. Lenski.—LeC
Pokey old mailman. L. Lenski.—LeC
"Postman, postman." Unknown.—EmN
Special delivery. X. J. Kennedy.—KeO
The traveling post office. A. B. Patterson.—CoPt
Major, Clarence
Blind old woman.—AdPb
The design.—AdPb
Swallow the lake.—AdPb
Vietnam.—AdPb
Vietnam #4.—AdB—AdPb
Makah Indians. See Indians of the Americas—Makah
Make-believe
The big Rock Candy mountain. Unknown.—CoOh
The big Rock Candy mountains.—PeS
Dream dog. L. Lenski.—LeC
I've seen enough. C. Meyer.—JoV
Pirate story. R. L. Stevenson.—JoA-4—UnGb
Safari. M. Ridlon.—HoCs
Saturday night: Late. L. Clifton.—ClS
Make me a man. Phil George.—AlW
Make merry. David McCord.—McFm
"**Make** merry, child, make merry." See Make merry
"**Make** up your mind, snail." Richard Wright Hokku poems.—AdPb
The **makers.** Richard Kell.—CoPi
Making a home. Marchette Chute.—ChRu
Making friends. Volodya Lapin, tr. fr. the Russian by Miriam Morton.—MoM
Malachi
Judgment and sunrise. See Malachi
Malachi, sel. Bible, Old Testament
Judgment and sunrise.—MeP
Malam, Charles
Steam shovel.—HoP
Malcolm. Kattie M. Cumbo.—AdB
Malcolm X. See Little, Malcolm
Malcolm X. Gwendolyn Brooks.—AbM—AdPb
"**Malcolm** X spoke to me and sounded you." See My ace of spades
A **male** lion, I roar. Ahmad Nassir Bin Juma Bhalo, tr. by Lyndon Harries.—AlPa
"The **male** raven sings." See The raven's song
The **Malibu.** Myra Cohn Livingston.—LiM
Malice at Buckingham palace. Spike Milligan.—CoOh
Mal'kova, Rita
Choice.—MoM
Malone, Pamela
"I saw."—HoC
"**Mama** said I'd lose my head." See The loser
"**Mama** spent pennies." See Portrait
Man. See Human race
"The **man.**" See For children if they'll take them
The **man** and the fish. Leigh Hunt.—RoIt
"The **man** bent over his guitar." See The man with the blue guitar
"**Man** building a brick wall." See Solid
"**Man** built." See Faster
"A **man,** encountering a camel." See The camel and the flotsam
"**Man** flies through the universe." Michael Goode.—JoV
The **man** he killed. Thomas Hardy.—PlP
"A **man** he lived by the sewer." See Silly stanzas
Man I thought you was talking another language that day. Victor Hernandez Cruz.—AdB
"A **man** in our town, Caleb Snyder." See Spider Snyder
"The **man** in the moon." Mother Goose.—AlC—RoIt
The **man** in the onion bed. John Ciardi.—BrM
"The **man** in the red Ferrari." See Freeway
"A **man** in the wilderness." See "The man in the wilderness asked of me"
"A **man** in the wilderness asked me." See "The man in the wilderness asked of me"
"The **man** in the wilderness asked of me." Mother Goose.—AlC
"A man in the wilderness."—RoIt
"A man in the wilderness asked me."—JoA-4
Man is a fool. Unknown.—RoIt
"The **man** is clothed." See And when the green man comes
"A **man** is driving." See Celebrations of the day
Man is nothing but. Saul Tchernichovsky, tr. fr. the Hebrew by Robert Mezey and Shula Starkman.—MeP
"**Man** is nothing but the soil of a small country." See Man is nothing but
A **man** of experience. Unknown, tr. fr. the Irish by Frank O'Connor.—CoPi
"A **man** of words and not of deeds." Mother Goose.—AlC

"**Man** on face on sidewalk." See The city question
The **man** on the flying trapeze. Unknown.—CoPt
"The **man** said." See An historic moment
"A **man** sits in the ice." Natalia Belting.—BeWi
"A **man** was drawing near to me." Thomas Hardy.—PlP
"A **man** went forth with gifts." See Martin Luther King, Jr
Man white, brown girl and all that jazz. Gloria C. Oden.—AdPb
"The **man** who cloaked his bitterness within." See Thomas Hood
The **man** who had shoes. John Ciardi.—CiFs
"The **man** who has plenty of good peanuts." Unknown.—MoBw
"A **man** who was fond of his skunk." David McCord
  Three limericks.—McS
"The **man** whose height his fear improved he." See Medgar Evers
The **man** with a past. Thomas Hardy.—PlP
The **man** with the blue guitar. Wallace Stevens.—PeS (sel.)
Manchester, England
  Murphy in Manchester. J. Montague.—CoPi
The **manciple's** tale. See The Canterbury tales
Mandan Indians. See Indians of the Americas—Mandan
"**Mandarin.**" See The yellow bird
Mangan, Charles
  The rune of Saint Patrick. tr.—MaF
Mangan, James Clarence
  Dark Rosaleen. tr.—CoPi
  The erl-king's daughter. tr.—CoPt
  Shapes and signs.—CoPi
  The woman of three cows. tr.—CoPi
Manhole covers. Karl Shapiro.—HiN—JoA-4
Manifesto. Nicanor Parra, tr. by Miller Williams.—MoT (sel.)
"**Mankind,** you dismay me." See Thoughts at midnight
Manners. See Etiquette
Manners. Elizabeth Bishop.—HiN
Manners at table when away from home. Unknown.—OpOx
Manual system. Carl Sandburg.—SaT
"**Many** a ship was lost at sea." Unknown.—EmN
"**Many** birds and the beating of wings." See Margaret
"A **many-colored** dome holds up the sky." See Cult
"**Many** eyes." Unknown.—EmN
"**Many**-maned scud-thumper, tub." See Winter ocean
"**Many,** many welcomes." See The snowdrop
"**Many** people who are smart." Karla Kuskin.—KuN
"**Many** ways to spell good night." See Good night
"**Many** winters ago." See Prophecy
"**Map** of a city with streets meeting at center." See Puzzle
The **maple.** Elizabeth Jane Coatsworth.—LaM
"**Maple** sugar." Unknown, tr. fr. the Chippewa.—ClFc
Maple trees
  The maple. E. J. Coatsworth.—LaM
Mar, Yehiel
  Handfuls of wind.—MeP
Marbles
  Marbles. V. Worth.—WoS
Marbles. Valerie Worth.—WoS
"**Marbles** picked up." See Marbles
March
  "Dear March, come in." E. Dickinson.—PaF
  Just before April came. C. Sandburg.—SaT
  March ("Blossom on the plum") N. Hopper.—PaF
  March ("What if a wind") L. Clifton.—ClE
  March ("Winter is long in this climate") W. C. Williams.—HiN
  March jewels. F. Holman.—HoI
  To my sister. W. Wordsworth.—PaF (sel.)
  Written in March. W. Wordsworth.—RoIt
    March.—JoA-4
March ("Blossom on the plum") Nora Hopper.—PaF
March ("The cock is crowing") See Written in March
March ("What if a wind") Lucille Clifton.—ClE
March ("Winter is long in this climate") William Carlos Williams.—HiN
March jewels. Felice Holman.—HoI
Marchant, John
  Little Miss and her parrot.—OpOx
  Young Master's account of a puppet show.—OpOx
Marching. See Parades
"**Marcia** and I went over the curve." See Millions of strawberries
Margaret. Carl Sandburg.—SaT
"**Margery** Mutton-pie and Johnny Bopeep." Mother Goose.—AlC
"**Maria** intended a letter to write." See How to write a letter
Marine nocturne. Tchicaya U Tam'si, tr. fr. the French by Gerald Moore.—AlPa
"The **market** place called the Souk." See Souk
Market square. A. A. Milne.—JoA-4
Market women's cries, sels. Jonathan Swift
  Apples.—CoPi
  Herrings.—CoPi
  Onions.—CoPi
Markets and marketing. See also Shops and shopkeepers
  "As I was going to Banbury." Mother Goose.—JoA-4—TucMgl
  "As I was going to sell my eggs." Mother Goose.—JoA-4
  City market. L. Lenski.—LeC
  "A fairy went a-marketing." R. Fyleman.—OpOx
  Grace to be said at the supermarket. H. Nemerov.—ToM

Markets and marketing.—*Continued*
"Hot-cross buns." Mother Goose.—JoA-4—LaM
"In the market on Monday morning." Unknown.—CoPu
The Indian market. L. Sohappy.—AlW
Jamaica market. A. Maxwell-Hall.—AbM
Market square. A. A. Milne.—JoA-4
Market women's cries, sels. J. Swift
Apples.—CoPi
Herrings.—CoPi
Onions.—CoPi
Mexican market woman. L. Hughes.—HoD
"My purse is full of money." L. Lenski.—LeC
Niño leading an old man to market. L. Nathan.—HiN
"Old Mother Hubbard." Mother Goose.—JoA-4
"Saw ye aught of my love a-coming from ye market." Mother Goose.—AlC
"Six silly sisters selling silk to six sickly seniors." Unknown.—EmN
Song of the banana man. E. Jones.—ToM
Souk. T. Joans.—AbM
"There was an old woman, as I've heard tell." Mother Goose.—JoA-4
"To market, to market, a gallop, a trot." Mother Goose.—AlC
"To market, to market, to buy a fat pig." Mother Goose.—AlC
"To market, to market."—JoA-4
To the shop. Unknown.—JoA-4
Who ever sausage a thing. Unknown.—CoOh
Witch goes shopping. L. Moore.—MoSm
"Your mother." S. Cornish.—AdM
Markham, Edwin
Outwitted.—CoPu
Markings: The comma. Eve Merriam.—MeF
Markings: The exclamation. Eve Merriam.—MeF
Markings: The period. Eve Merriam.—MeF
Markings: The question. Eve Merriam.—MeF
Markings: The semicolon. Eve Merriam.—MeF
Markwei, Matei
Life in our village.—AbM
Marlowe, Christopher
"Ah Faustus." See The tragical history of Doctor Faustus
The passionate shepherd to his love.—RoIt
The tragical history of Doctor Faustus, sel.
"Ah, Faustus."—MaFw
Marmion, sel. Walter Scott
Lochinvar.—CoPt—JoA-4
Maroon with silver frost. Carl Sandburg.—SaT
Marquis, Don (Donald Robert Perry Marquis)
The flattered lightning bug.—CoPt
A hot weather song.—CoPu
Pete the parrot and Shakespeare.—PlM
Small talk.—CoPt
Some natural history.—LiWw
"**Marquita** had blossom fists." See Portrait of a child settling down for an afternoon nap
Marriage. See also Brides and bridegrooms; Courtship; Married life
African China. M. B. Tolson.—AdPb
After ever happily; or, The princess and the woodcutter. I. Serraillier.—MaFw
"As sure as you get married." Unknown.—EmN
"Bobby Shaftoe's gone to sea." Mother Goose.—JoA-4
"Brave news is come to town." Mother Goose.—AlC
"A cat came fiddling out of a barn." Mother Goose.—AlC—JoA-4
"Don't be crooked." Unknown.—EmN
"Doodledy, doodledy, doodledy, dan." Mother Goose.—HoMg
Getting together. N. M. Bodecker.—BoL
Girl's song. Unknown.—AlPa
His wife. Rachel.—MeP
"I know where I'm going." Unknown.—JoA-4
"If no one ever marries me." L. Alma-Tadema.—NeA—OpOx
"If you get a husband." Unknown.—EmN
In the room of the bride-elect. T. Hardy.—PlP
"Let's marry, said the cherry." N. M. Bodecker.—BoL
"Little maiden, better tarry." Mother Goose.—TucMgl
"Little Tom Tucker." Mother Goose.—AlC
"Little Tommy Tucker."—JoA-4
Magic formula to fix a bride's affection. Unknown.—BiI
Maiden's song. Unknown.—AlPa
Mary Ann. J. Tabrar.—CoPu
"Mister Lister sassed his sister." C. Watson.—WaF
The modest couple. W. S. Gilbert.—CoPt
"Needles and pins, needles and pins." Mother Goose.—AlC—EmN
"Oh, mother, I shall be married to Mr Punchinello." Mother Goose.—AlC
Mr Punchinello.—JoA-4
"Oh, rare Harry Parry." Mother Goose.—HoMg
"On Saturday night." Mother Goose.—AlC
The queens' rhyme. I. Serraillier.—BrM
The Rachray man. M. O'Neill.—CoPi
"Scissors and string, scissors and string." Mother Goose.—HoMg
"She who could bind you." S. Teasdale.—CoPu
Song for unbound hair. G. Taggard.—RoIt
Song of a chief's daughter. Unknown.—BiI
Song to the wife of his youth. N. Alterman.—MeP
"There once was a king." Unknown.—BoI
To the virgins, to make much of time. R. Herrick.—LiS
The trouble-lover. Unknown.—AlPa
Villikins and his Dinah. S. Cowell.—CoPt
"What will I be married in." Unknown.—EmN

"What will I wear on my feet." Unknown.—EmN
"What will my house be." Unknown.—EmN
"What will my husband be." Unknown.—EmN
"When will I be married." Unknown.—EmN
"When you are married." Unknown.—EmN
"When you get married (and have a set of twins)." Unknown.—EmN
"When you get married (and your husband gets cross)." Unknown.—EmN
"When you get married (live at your ease)." Unknown.—EmN
"When you get married and live in a shanty." Unknown.—EmN
"When you get married."—MoBw
"Where are you going, my pretty maid." Mother Goose.—JoA-4
Married life
At flock Mass. F. R. Higgins.—CoPi
At the drapers. T. Hardy.—PlP
"A carrion crow sat on an oak." Mother Goose.—JoA-4
Chitterabob. Unknown.—BlM
"There was a man and his name was Dob."—TrG
"Cinderella, dressed in green (married)." Unknown.—EmN
The curate's kindness. T. Hardy.—PlP
The doctor's story. W. M. Carleton.—CoPt
"Eaper Weaper, chimbley sweeper." Mother Goose.—AlC
Early thoughts of marriage. N. Cotton.—OpOx
The first snow of the year. M. Van Doren.—HiN
For Hettie. LeRoi Jones.—PeS
Get up and bar the door. Unknown.—CoPt—JoA-4
Housework. S. Harnick.—ThF
A husband's song. Unknown.—BiI
The husband's view. T. Hardy.—PlP
Husky hi. Unknown.—JoA-4
"I had a little husband." Mother Goose.—AlC—JoA-4
"I love sixpence, jolly little sixpence." Mother Goose.—JoA-4
"I shall quit." Unknown.—AlPa
"If my complaining." Issa.—BeM
In honor of a king who acquired several young wives. Unknown.—AlPa
"In stature the manlet was dwarfish." From Sylvie and Bruno concluded. L. Carroll.—LiPc
"Jack Sprat could eat no fat." Mother Goose.—AlC—JoA-4
John-John. T. MacDonagh.—CoPi—CoPt
Kayak song in dialogue. Unknown.—LeIb
"Keep it dark." Unknown.—AlPa
Lady, lady. A. Spencer.—AdPb
Late abed. A. MacLeish.—HiN
A letter to her husband, absent upon publick employment. A. Bradstreet.—ThI
Man white, brown girl and all that jazz. G. C. Oden.—AdPb
"Master I have, and I am his man." Mother Goose.—AlC
"Mr and Mrs Discobbolos." E. Lear.—JoA-4
Mr and Mrs Spikky Sparrow. E. Lear.—OpOx
"My little old man and I fell out." Mother Goose.—JoA-4
My rules. S. Silverstein.—CoPu—SiW
"Nicholas Grouch." D. Lee.—LeA
"Now you're married and you must be good." Unknown.—EmN
The old man who lived in the woods. Unknown.—RoIt
The old-marrieds. G. Brooks.—AdPb
"On Saturday night I lost my wife." Mother Goose.—HoMg
"One time Henry dreamed the number." D. Long.—AdPb
The perils of invisibility. W. S. Gilbert.—CoPt
"Peter, Peter, pumpkin eater." Mother Goose.—HoMg—JoA-4
"The pope he leads a happy life." C. Lever.—CoPi
Purrrrr ce. Unknown.—SeS
The rival. T. Hardy.—PlP
"Saw ye aught of my love a-coming from ye market." Mother Goose.—AlC
Simple. N. L. Madgett.—AdPb
Song of a chief's daughter. Unknown.—BiI
Song of an old man about his wife. Unknown.—LeIb
Song of Lawino: An African lament. O. P'Bitek.—AlPa (sel.)
Sweet William, his wife, and the sheepskin. Unknown.—RoIt
"There was a man and he stayed within." Mother Goose.—TucMg
"There was an old woman in Surrey." Mother Goose.—OpOx—TucMgl
This is just to say. W. C. Williams.—LiS—MaFw
To my dear and loving husband. A. Bradstreet.—ThI
"Tommy Trot, a man of law." Mother Goose.—AlC
"Up and down Pie street." Mother Goose.—AlC
What Tottles meant. From Sylvie and Bruno concluded. L. Carroll.—LiPc
The workbox. T. Hardy.—PlP
Marryat, Frederick
The old navy.—CoPt
Mars (planet)
The planet of Mars. S. Silverstein.—SiW
SF. E. Leverett.—CoPu
The **marsh.** W. D. Snodgrass.—HaWr
Marshes
Dingman's marsh. J. Moore.—HiN
Facing up. J. Scully.—HaWr
Filling the marsh. F. Holman.—HoI
In Romney marsh. J. Davidson.—PaP
The marsh. W. D. Snodgrass.—HaWr

Marstiller, Diane
"At school."—HoC
Marsupial transportation. Thelma Ireland.—BrM
"**Martha.**" See Mary passed this morning
Martha. Walter De La Mare.—RoIt
Martial (Marcus Valerius Martialis)
Any author to any friend.—PlM
"I do not like (love) thee, Doctor Fell." Martial.—MiMg—TrG
"Two hundred lines a day."—PlM
"Why don't I send my books to you."—PlM
Martin, Graham Dunstan
"In town and temple I'm no longer seen." tr.—ThI
Martin, Herbert
Antigone I.—AdPb
Antigone VI.—AdPb
Lines.—AdPb
A Negro soldier's Viet Nam diary.—AdPb
Martin, Sarah Catherine
The comic adventures of Old Mother Hubbard and her dog.—OpOx
"The **martin** flew to the finch's nest." See Feathers and moss
Martin Luther King, Jr. Gwendolyn Brooks.—AdB—AdPb
Martindale, Clifford
"June's here."—HoC
Martins
Children of the wind. From The people, yes. C. Sandburg.—SaT
Feathers and moss. J. Ingelow.—LiS
Martin's blues. Michael S. Harper.—AdPb
Martyrdom. Richard W. Thomas.—AdPb
Martyrs
Martyrdom. R. W. Thomas.—AdPb
"**Marty's** party." David McCord.—McAa
Marvell, Andrew
The garden.—PaF (sel.)
The **marvellous** bear shepherd. Unknown.—MaFw
Marx, Anne
Adventures with my grandfather.—RoIt
Mary, Queen of Scots (about)
The crossing of Mary of Scotland. W. J. Smith.—CoOh
Mary, Virgin (about)
As dew in Aprille. Unknown.—MaFw
Ballad of the bread man. C. Causley.—ToM
The cherry tree carol. Unknown.—LaS
Confession stone. O. Dodson.—AbM
Jesus and his mother. T. Gunn.—ToM
Mary had a baby. Unknown.—BrW—LaS
Mary passed this morning. O. Dodson.—AdPb
The seven joys of Mary. Unknown.—LaS
"Sing me the Virgin Mary." Unknown.—LaS
Mary Ann. Joseph Tabrar.—CoPu
Mary had a baby. Unknown.—BrW—LaS
"**Mary** had a baby. Aye Lord." See Mary had a baby
"**Mary** had a baby, My Lord." See Mary had a baby
"**Mary** had a little bird." See The canary
"**Mary** had a little lamb." See Mary's lamb
"**Mary** had a little lamb (its fleece was white as snow, Mary passed a butcher shop)." Unknown.—MoBw
"**Mary** had a little lamb (whose fleece was white as snow; she took it down to Pittsburgh)." Unknown.—MoBw
"**Mary** has a thingamajig clamped on her ears." See Manual system
"**Mary** Mack, dressed in black." Unknown.—EmN
"**Mary,** Mary." Unknown.—EmN
"**Mary,** Mary, Queen of Scots." See The crossing of Mary of Scotland
"**Mary,** Mary, quite contrary." Mother Goose.—JoA-4
Mary passed this morning. Owen Dodson.—AdPb
"**Mary,** said Saint Joseph, can't we rest awhile." See Aguinaldo
"**Mary** stood in the kitchen." See Ballad of the bread man
Mary's ghost. Thomas Hood.—CoPt—LiWw
"**Mary's** it and has a fit." Unknown.—EmN
Mary's lamb. Sarah Josepha Hale.—OpOx
Masefield, John
Cape Horn gospel.—CoPt
Hell's pavement.—CoPt
On Eastnor knoll.—MaFw
Sea change.—CoPt
Sea-fever.—JoA-4
The tarry buccaneer.—CoPt
The unending sky.—MaFw
The west wind.—PaP—RoIt
The yarn of the Loch Achray.—CoPt
Masks
Prayer to masks. L. S. Senghor.—AlPa
"**Masks.** Masks." See Prayer to masks
Massachusetts
The willows of Massachusetts. D. Levertov.—HaWr
Massingham, Harold
Cow.—MaFw
"**Master** I have, and I am his man." Mother Goose.—AlC
"**Master** of discords John." See The harper
Masters, Edgar Lee
Anne Rutledge. See The Spoon River anthology
Percy Bysshe Shelley. See The Spoon River anthology
The Spoon River anthology, sels.
Anne Rutledge.—RoIt
Percy Bysshe Shelley.—PlM
Masters of war. Bob Dylan.—MoG
Matchett, William H.
Cedar waxwing.—HaWr
The mole.—HaWr
The moths.—HaWr
Math class. Myra Cohn Livingston.—LiM
"A **mathematician** named Lynch." Unknown.—BrM

Maya Indians. See Indians of the Americas—Maya
"**Mayakovsky** was right." See Kiss
Maybe the birds. June Jordan.—MoT
"**Maybe** the birds are worried." See Maybe the birds
Mayday. Ed Roberson.—AdPb
Mayo, E. L.
The mole.—JoA-4
Poem for Gerard.—PlM
Mayor. Yehuda Amichai, tr. fr. the Hebrew by Assia Gutmann.—MeP
Mayors
Mayor. Y. Amichai.—MeP
M'Baye, Annette
"Tomorrow belongs to God."—AlPa
Mbiti, John
The moon.—AlPa
New York skyscrapers.—AbM
"**Me** and him." See Us
"**Me** and I and you." Unknown, tr. fr. the Danish by N. M. Bodecker.—BoI
Me and my giant. Shel Silverstein.—SiW
Me, in Kulu Se and Karma. Carolyn M. Rodgers.—AdPb
"**Me,** ray, doh." Unknown, tr. fr. the German by Rose Fyleman.—JoA-4
Me-stew. Shel Silverstein.—SiW
Mead, Lynn
"Ice cream."—HoC
Meadow larks. See Larks
The **meadow** mouse. Theodore Roethke.—AdP—MoT
Meadows. See Fields
Meals. See Breakfast; Dinner; Supper
Meanlight. Robert Froman.—FrSp
Mearns, Hughes
"As I was falling down the stair."—BrM
The perfect reactionary.—LiWw
Measles in the ark. Susan Coolidge.—OpOx
"**Measure** me, sky." Leonora Speyer.—AdP—JoA-4
The **measure** of man. Eve Merriam.—MeF
Meat. See Food and eating
"**Mechanical.**" See Gods in Vietnam
Mechanical menagerie. X. J. Kennedy.—KeO
Meddlesome Matty. Ann Taylor.—OpOx
Medgar Evers. Gwendolyn Brooks.—AdPb
Medicine
"Hark, the herald angels sing." Unknown.—TrG
"I am going to be a great warrior." Unknown.—ClFc
"I wandered angry as a cloud." P. Dehn.—LiS
The remedy worse than the disease. M. Prior.—LiWw
Medicine men
"The evening glow yet lingers." Unknown.—ClFc
"I know everything in the bottom of my heart." Unknown.—ClFc
"To the medicine man's house they have led me." Unknown.—ClFc
Meditatio. Ezra Pound.—LiWw
Meditation. Thomas Traherne.—RoIt
Meditation on beavers. Lucian of Samosata, tr. fr. the Greek by Dudley Fitts.—LiWw
A **meditation** on Providence. See Psalms—Psalm 104
Meditations
Meditations divine and morall. A. Bradstreet.—ThI (sel.)
The poor girl's meditation. Unknown.—CoPi
Meditations divine and morall. Anne Bradstreet.—ThI (sel.)
Medusa
Medusa. X. J. Kennedy.—KeO
Medusa. X. J. Kennedy.—KeO
"**Medusa's** looks had what it takes." See Medusa
"**Meekly** the sea." See The even sea
"**Meet** me again as at that time." See To Louisa in the lane
Meetings
Councils. M. Piercy.—MoT
If the owl calls again. J. Haines.—HiN
If you should meet. D. Lee.—LeA
"If you should meet a crocodile." Unknown.—BrM
Jungle incident. R. G. Carter.—BrM
The man in the onion bed. J. Ciardi.—BrM
"Margery Mutton-pie and Johnny Bopeep." Mother Goose.—AlC
The skunk. A. Noyes.—BrM
Stanley meets Mutesa. D. Rubadiri.—AlPa (sel.)
Too polite. I. Serraillier.—BrM
Two boxes. S. Silverstein.—SiW
Meg Merrilies. John Keats.—NeA—OpOx
Old Meg.—RoIt
Melancholy
Blues. Q. Prettyman.—AdB
The day is done. H. W. Longfellow.—RoIt
Doldrums. C. O'John.—AlA
Leave me alone. F. Holman.—UnGb
Midsummer melancholy. M. Fishback.—LiWw
Ode: Autumn. T. Hood.—PaF
The sea is melancholy. A. T. Pratt.—AlW
The solitary reaper. W. Wordsworth.—RoIt
The tale of a dog. J. S. Lambert, Jr.—BrM
"There's a certain slant of light." E. Dickinson.—PaF—ThI
"We're all in the dumps." Mother Goose.—AlC
"We are all in the dumps."—MiMg
The wild swans at Coole. W. B. Yeats.—MaFw—PaF
Melinda Mae. Shel Silverstein.—SiW
"**Mellow** the moonlight to shine is beginning." See The spinning wheel
"The **mellow** year is hastening to its close." See November
"**Melvin** Martin Riley Smith." David McCord.—McFm
Memo. Charles Lynch.—AdPb
Memorabilia. Robert Browning.—PlM

Memorial day
The blue and the gray. F. M. Finch.—RoIt
Memorial wreath. Dudley Randall.—AdPb
Memories. See also Childhood recollections
After a journey. T. Hardy.—PlP
Annabel Lee. E. A. Poe.—JoA-4—LiS—RoIt
At Castle Boterel. T. Hardy.—PlP
Autumn. H. Wolfe.—PaF
The ballad of bouillabaisse. W. M. Thackeray.—RoIt
A ballad of remembrance. R. Hayden.—AdPb
Blue and red poem. A. Gilboa.—MeP
Captain Hook. S. Silverstein.—SiW
Chapter two. W. T. Scott.—RoIt
"Do you remember that night." Unknown.—CoPi
A dream or no. T. Hardy.—PlP
Fall down. C. C. Hernton.—AdPb
Falling asleep. S. Sassoon.—PaF
Forgotten language. S. Silverstein.—SiW
Four sheets to the wind. C. K. Rivers.—AdPb
The fragment. H. Belloc.—CoPu
Gunpowder plot. V. Scannell.—MaFw—ToM
"I must remember." S. Silverstein.—SiW
"I remember. . . . " M. Jackson.—AdB—AdM—AdPb
"I wish I were a china cup." Unknown.—EmN
"If apart we two must be." Unknown.—EmN
In my life. J. Lennon and P. McCartney.—MoG
"In the woodbox of memory." Unknown.—EmN
Ivory masks in orbit. K. Kgositsile.—AdPb
"Joal." L. S. Senghor.—AlPa
Maud Muller. J. G. Whittier.—RoIt
Memories. R. Froman.—FrSp
A memory ("Four ducks on a pond") W. Allingham.—PaF—RoIt
Memory ("My mind lets go a thousand things") T. B. Aldrich.—RoIt
A memory ("When I was as high as that") L. A. G. Strong.—CoPi
"My mama moved among the days." L. Clifton.—AdPb
New Hampshire again. C. Sandburg.— SaT
Now poem. For us. S. Sanchez.—AdPb
"Oft, in the stilly night." T. Moore.—CoPi
An old woman remembers. S. A. Brown.—AdPb
Once again. L. Sohappy.—AlW
"Please to remember." Mother Goose.—AlC
Poem at thirty. S. Sanchez.—AdPb
The profile on the pillow. D. Randall.—AdPb
"Remember Grant, remember Lee." Unknown.—EmN
"Remember me and bear in mind." Unknown.—EmN
"Remember me on the river." Unknown.—EmN
"Remember the boy from the country." Unknown.—EmN
"Remember the bride." Unknown.—EmN
"Remember the joy." Unknown.—EmN
Remembering Nat Turner. S. A. Brown.—AdPb
The rustling of grass. A. Noyes.—PaF
The sands of Dee. From Alton Locke. C. Kingsley.—JoA-4—RoIt
The secret of the sea. H. W. Longfellow.—RoIt
Seravezza. H. W. Fuller.—AdPb
"She turns the pages through and through." Unknown.—EmN
Song. A. Tennyson.—RoIt
Song of the strange woman. L. Goldberg.—MeP
Sonnet. A. A. Duckett.—AdPb
Stars, songs, faces. C. Sandburg.—MaFw
Tarantella. H. Belloc.—LiS
Tears. A. Lopez.—AlW
Tears, idle tears. From The princess. A. Tennyson.—RoIt
"There is a word in English spoken." Unknown.—EmN
Things to remember. J. Reeves.—JoA-4
"Think of me early." Unknown.—EmN
Tit for tat: A tale. J. Aikin.—OpOx
To Auden on his fiftieth. R. Eberhart.—PlM
The treehouse. J. A. Emanuel.—AdPb
The tropics in New York. C. McKay.—AdPb—RoIt
Twilight's feet. A. T. Pratt.—AlW
"U R 2 good." Unknown.—EmN
"When distant lands divide us." Unknown.—EmN
"When night folds its curtain." Unknown.—EmN
"When the golden sun is setting (and your mind)." Unknown.—EmN
When you are old. W. B. Yeats.—MaFw
"When you are old and cannot see." Unknown.—EmN
"When you get old and blind." Unknown.—EmN
"When you're in the country." Unknown.—EmN
"You asked me to write." Unknown.—EmN
Memories. Robert Froman.—FrSp
Memories of childhood. See Childhood recollections
A **memory** ("Four ducks on a pond") William Allingham.—PaF—RoIt
Memory ("My mind lets go a thousand things") Thomas Bailey Aldrich.—RoIt
A **memory** ("When I was as high as that") L. A. G. Strong.—CoPi
Memory of a porch. Donald Justice.—HiN
Men
His answer to the critics. Solomon ibn Gabirol.—MeP
Make me a man. P. George.—AlW
A satirical romance. Juana Inez De la Cruz.—ThI (sel.)
"The streets are filled with mustached men." K. Kuskin.—KuN
Men—Portraits. See People—Portraits—Men

Witness.—MeF
Word bird.—MeF
Merrily float. Thomas Hood.—JaP
Merry. Shel Silverstein.—SiW
Merry are the bells. Unknown.—JoA-4—RoIt
"**Merry** are the bells, and merry would they ring." See Merry are the bells
Merry Christmas. Aileen Fisher.—FiFo—HoS—LaM
Merry-go-round ("The tent is gay") Lois Lenski.—LeC
Merry-go-round ("Where is the Jim Crow section") Langston Hughes.—AbM—HoD
Merry-go-rounds
The carousel. G. C. Oden.—AdPb
Merry-go-round ("The tent is gay") L. Lenski.—LeC
Merry-go-round ("Where is the Jim Crow section") L. Hughes.—AbM—HoD
"The **merry** year is born." Hartley Coleridge.—MaF (sel.)
Merton, Thomas
In memory of the Spanish poet Federico Garcia Lorca.—PlM
Merwin, W. S.
Fog-horn.—MoT
For a coming extinction.—MoT
Full moonlight in spring.—CoPu
Mescalero Apache Indians. See Indians of the Americas—Mescalero Apache
Meschery, Tom
Basketball: A love song because it is.—FlH
The last poem.—FlH
The **mesh.** Kwesi Brew.—AlPa
Message from a mouse, ascending in a rocket. P. Hubbell.—HoP
The **messed** damozel. Charles Hanson Towne.—LiS
"The **messed** damozel looked out." See The messed damozel
"The **metaphor** man." See Metaphor man
Metaphor man. Eve Merriam.—MeO
Metaphors
Metaphor man. E. Merriam.—MeO
Metamorphoses, sel. Ovid
Orpheus and Eurydice, tr. fr. the Latin by Rolfe Humphries.—MoG
Meteors
"What is the opposite of *ball.*" R. Wilbur.—WiO
Methuselah (about)
Methuselah. Unknown.—RoIt
Methuselah. Unknown.—RoIt
"**Methuselah** ate what he found on his plate." See Methuselah
The **metre** Columbian. Unknown.—LiS
Metrical feet. Samuel Taylor Coleridge.—OpOx
Mew, Charlotte
Sea love.—CoPu
Mexican market woman. Langston Hughes.—HoD
Mexicans
Mexican market woman. L. Hughes.—HoD
Song. Unknown.—BiI
Mexico
Grandeur of Mexico. Unknown.—BiI
"The Indians come down from Mixco." M. A. Asturias.—MoT
Song. Unknown.—BiI
The surrender speech of Cuauhtémoc. Unknown.—BiI
"The weeping spreads." Unknown.—BiI
Meyer, Christopher
All of us a family.—JoV
"I had a dream last night . . . of a thousand mothers."—JoV
I've seen enough.—JoV
"Sitting on the dock."—JoV
Wonderful New York.—JoV
Meyer, Kuno
Eve's lament. tr.—CoPi
The Fort of Rathangan. tr.—CoPi
A song of winter. tr.—CoPi
The Viking terror. tr.—CoPi
The vision of Mac Conglinne. tr.—CoPi (sel.)
Meynell, Alice
November blue.—PaP
Mezey, Robert
The apple. tr.—MeP
Blessed are they that sow. tr.—MeP
Cups without wine. tr.—MeP
Dress me, dear mother. tr.—MeP
Graves. tr.—MeP
His answer to the critics. tr.—MeP
I have a garment. tr.—MeP
I saw. tr.—MeP
Jerusalem. tr.—MeP
The lonely say. tr.—MeP
Mount Avarim. tr.—MeP
My dead. tr.—MeP
My heart is in the East. tr.—MeP
My stars. tr.—MeP
Not so simple. tr.—MeP
A secret kept. tr.—MeP
Stop playing. tr.—MeP
There.—MoT
We were not like dogs. tr.—MeP
— and Bat-Miriam, Yocheved
Distance spills itself. trs.—MeP
— and Gold, Ben Zion
The great sad one. trs.—MeP
The hour. trs.—MeP
How it is. trs.—MeP
Like a woman. trs.—MeP
On the pole. trs.—MeP
There is a box. trs.—MeP
The valley of man. trs.—MeP
With my God, the Smith. trs.—MeP
— and Starkman, Shula
Beyond melody. trs.—MeP
Birth. trs.—MeP
Blind angel. trs.—MeP
Blue and red poem. trs.—MeP
The grave. trs.—MeP
"Leaves without trees." trs.—MeP
Man is nothing but. trs.—MeP
O thou seer, go, flee thee away. trs.—MeP
Odysseus. trs.—MeP

Migration—People
Good morning. L. Hughes.—AdM
Now we come southwards. Unknown.—BiI
Over the water. Unknown.—BiI
The **Mikado,** sel. William Schwenck Gilbert
"The flowers that bloom in the spring."—RoIt
Titwillow.—RoIt
"**Mike** says." See August
Mike 65. Lennox Raphael.—AdPb
Miles, Josephine
Reason.—HiN
Miles, Tammy
"Dreaming."—HoC
"**Miles** and miles of pasture." See The lavender kitten
"**Milford** Dupree, though he knew it was rude." See With his mouth full of food
Militant. Langston Hughes.—AdPb
Milk and milking
"Cinderella, dressed in silk." Unknown.—EmN
Cows. X. J. Kennedy.—KeO
Milk for the cat. H. Monro.—JoA-4
"Milk shake, milk shake." Unknown.—EmN
Milk-stand. L. Lenski.—LeC
A milking song. F. Macleod.—MaF
"Where are you going, my pretty maid." Mother Goose.—JoA-4
Winter milk. C. Sandburg.—SaT
"The **milk-drops** on your chin." See Winter milk
Milk for the cat. Harold Monro.—JoA-4
"**Milk** shake, milk shake." Unknown.—EmN
Milk-stand. Lois Lenski.—LeC
"The **milk-stand** at the corner." See Milk-stand
"**Milk-white** moon, put the cows to sleep." Carl Sandburg.—SaT
A **milking** song. Fiona Macleod.—MaF
Milkmaid ("The girl's far treble, muted to the heat") Laurie Lee.—ToM
The **milkmaid** ("A milkmaid, who poised a full pail on her head") Jeffreys Taylor.—RoIt
"A **milkmaid,** who poised a full pail on her head." See The milkmaid
Milkmaids
A milking song. F. Macleod.—MaF
Milkmaid ("The girl's far treble, muted to the heat") L. Lee.—ToM
The milkmaid ("A milkmaid, who poised a full pail on her head") Jeffreys Taylor.—RoIt
"Willy, Willy Wilkin." Mother Goose.—HoMg
"**Milkman,** milkman, where have you been." Unknown.—TrG
Milkmen
"Milkman, milkman, where have you been." Unknown.—TrG
Psalm of those who go forth before daylight. C. Sandburg.—MaFw—SaT
Milkweeds
Two voices in a meadow. R. Wilbur.—PeS
Milky Way
"Oh, the Milky Way." Issa.—HaW
Millay, Edna St Vincent
The ballad of the harp-weaver.—CoPt—RoIt
The buck in the snow.—AdP—RoIt
Portrait by a neighbor.—NeA
Miller, Adam David
Crack in the wall holds flowers.—AdPb
The hungry black child.—AdPb
Miller, Mary Britton
Cat.—HoH—LiLc
Here she is.—AdP
Miller, Shelley
When we grow up.—ThF
Miller, Thomas
Evening.—OpOx
The watercress seller.—OpOx
Miller, Vassar
The farm.—HiN
Invocation.—HiN
Love song for the future.—HiN
Sophistication.—HiN
Miller, William
Willie Winkie.—OpOx
Millers
The prologue. From The Canterbury tales. G. Chaucer.—MaFw
Song. From Love in a village. I. Bickerstaffe.—CoPi
"There was a jolly miller."—AlC
"There is a mill with seven corners." Unknown.—EmN
"There was a jolly miller." Mother Goose.—AlC
"There was an old woman (lived under a [the] hill)." Mother Goose.—JoA-4—MiMg
The unfortunate miller. A. E. Coppard.—CoPt
Milligan, Alice
"When I was a little girl."—CoPi
Milligan, Spike
The ABC.—CoOh
Ant and eleph-ant.—CoOr
"Down the stream the swans all glide."—CoOr
Eels.—CoOr
Go north, south, east and west, young man.—CoOr
Granny.—CoOr
"Hello Mr Python."—CoOh
"Little tiny puppy dog."—CoOh
Malice at Buckingham palace.—CoOh
Questions, quistions & quoshtions.—CoOr
"A thousand hairy savages."—CoPu
"A **millionaire's** money has two taints." Unknown.—MoBw
Millions of strawberries. Genevieve Taggard.—UnGb
Milne, A. (Alan) A. (Alexander)
Buckingham palace.—OpOx
"Diana Fitzpatrick Mauleverer James."—CoPu
Forgiven.—BrM
Halfway down.—LiLc
Howard.—CoOr
The king's breakfast.—OpOx

Mirrors. See also Reflections (mirrored)
Beware, do not read this poem. I. Reed.—AdPb—HiN
Was a man. P. Booth.—HiN
"What is the opposite of *mirror.*" R. Wilbur.—WiO
Mirth. Christopher Smart.—OpOx
Misfortune
"In a parlor containing a table." G. Kinnell.—CoPu
Monument in black. V. Howard.—AdM—JoV
Musée des beaux arts. W. H. Auden.—ToM
"Nobody loses all the time." E. E. Cummings.—LiWw—MaFw
"She wandered through the garden fence." K. Reid.—MoG
The unfortunate miller. A. E. Coppard.—CoPt
Miss Bitter. N. M. Bodecker.—BoL
"**Miss** Helen Slingsby was my maiden aunt." See Aunt Helen
Miss Hepzibah. Eve Merriam.—MeF
"**Miss** Hepzibah has a mania." See Miss Hepzibah
Miss Jane. Unknown.—BlM
"**Miss** Jane had a bag." See Miss Jane
"**Miss,** miss, little Miss, miss." Unknown.—EmN
"**Miss** M's a nightingale. 'Tis well." See On a poetess
"**Miss** Quiss." Clyde Watson.—WaF
Miss Rosie. Lucille Clifton.—AdPb
"**Miss** Seraphina Martha Newell." See Cruel Miss Newell
Miss T. Walter De La Mare.—JoA-4
"**Misshapen,** black, unlovely to the sight." See A bulb
Missionaries
The cassowary. Unknown.—CoOr
Missionary. D. M. Thomas.—ToM
Missionary. D. M. Thomas.—ToM
"**Mississauga** rattlesnakes." See Rattlesnake skipping song
Mississippi
Benign neglect/Mississippi. Primus St John.—AdPb
Church burning: Mississippi. J. A. Emanuel.—AdPb
An invitation to Madison county.—AdPb
"M-I, crooked letter, crooked letter, I." Unknown.—EmN
No new music. S. Crouch.—AdPb
Mississippi river
Brown river, smile. J. Toomer.—AdPb
"When it rains, the Mississippi river." Unknown.—EmN
Missouri river
Foreclosure. S. A. Brown.—AdPb
Mist. See also Fog
"Clouds of morning mist." Buson.—BeM
Mist. A. Young.—MaFw
"Moo, moo, moo." Issa.—HaW
Moon mist. C. Okigbo.—AlPa
November. J. Clare.—MaFw (sel.)
"A silver mist creeps along the shore." P. Irving.—AlW
"This unimportant." Bashō.—BeM
"Under a spring mist." Teitoku.—BeM
Mist. Andrew Young.—MaFw
"**Mr** and Mrs Discobbolos." Edward Lear.—JoA-4
Mr and Mrs Spikky Sparrow. Edward Lear.—OpOx
"**Mister** Bamboo Bug." See Wavvuuvuumira
Mister Banjo. Unknown.—AbM
Mr Beecher. N. M. Bodecker.—BoL
"**Mister** Beedle Baddlebug." See Tea party
Mister Beers. Hugh Lofting.—BrM
Mr Bidery's spidery garden. David McCord.—McFm
Mr Docer. N. M. Bodecker.—BoL
"**Mr** East gave a feast." Mother Goose.—JoA-4
Mr Flood's party. Edwin Arlington Robinson.—CoPt
Mr 'Gator. N. M. Bodecker.—BoL
"**Mr** Heath-Stubbs as you must understand." See Epitaph
Mr Kartoffel. James Reeves.—BrM
"**Mr** Kartoffel's a whimsical man." See Mr Kartoffel
"**Mister** Lister sassed his sister." Clyde Watson.—WaF
"**Mr** Maclin's back in town." See Mr Maclin's visitor
Mr Maclin's visitor. David McCord.—McAa
Mr Metter. N. M. Bodecker.—BoL
Mr Mixup tells a story. David McCord.—McS
"**Mr** Mole, Mr Mole, MR MOLE." See Flying out of holes
Mr Nobody. Unknown.—RoIt
Mr Pope. Allen Tate.—PlM
Mr Punchinello. See "Oh, mother, I shall be married to Mr Punchinello"
"**Mr** Rabbit, a basket on his arm." See Easter morning
Mr Roosevelt regrets. Pauli Murray.—AdPb
"**Mr** Scientist, is it too late." See Respectful request
Mr Skinner. N. M. Bodecker.—BoL
Mr Slatter. N. M. Bodecker.—BoL
Mr Smith (with nods to Mr Lear and Mr Eliot). William Jay Smith.—LiS
"**Mr** Squirrel, sitting under shelter." Mother Goose, tr. fr. the Swiss.—TucMg
"**Mister** Stone, all alone." See Stone-kicking song
"**Mister** Thomas Jones." See Bringing him up
Mr Walter De La Mare makes the little ones dizzy. Samuel Hoffenstein.—LiS
Mr Weller. N. M. Bodecker.—BoL
"**Mr** Zookeeper." Lee Bennett Hopkins.—HoCs
Mrs Brown. Rose Fyleman.—OpOx
"**Mrs** Malone." Eleanor Farjeon.—OpOx
"**Mrs** Mayer, Mrs Mayer." See The seasons on our block
"**Mrs** Noah in the Ark." See The ballad of Mrs Noah

Mrs Snipkin and Mrs Wobblechin. Laura E. Richards.—JoA-4—OpOx
"**Mrs** Someone's been to Asia." See An imposter
Mitchell, Emerson Blackhorse ("Barney")
The four directions.—AlW
Miracle hill.—AlW
The path I must travel.—AlW
Talking to his drum.—AlW
Mitchell, Joni
Cactus tree.—MoG
Chelsea morning.—MoG
I think I understand.—MoG
Woodstock.—MoG
Mitchell, Lucy Sprague
"Back and forth."—HoP
Mites
A considerable speck. R. Frost.—AdP
The **mither's** lament. Sydney Goodsir Smith.—CoPu
Mitrofanova, Tanya
I love.—MoM
Mittens. See also Gloves
Losing mittens. M. Chute.—ChRu
Mittens for kittens. Unknown.—BlM
The modern Hiawatha. G. A. Strong.—LiS
"Three little kittens." Mother Goose.—BlM
Mittens for kittens. Unknown.—BlM
"**Mix** a pancake." Christina Georgina Rossetti.—LaM—LiLc
Mixed-up school. X. J. Kennedy.—KeO
Mmenson. Edward Brathwaite.—ToM
The **moccasins** of an old man. Ramona Carden.—AlW
"The **mocking** bird." See Silence
Mockingbirds
"After yesterday." A. R. Ammons.—MoT
"Look at six eggs." C. Sandburg.—RoIt
"The mockingbird, the mockingbird." Unknown.—JoT
Silence. E. McCarthy.—CoPu
"**Mocking** is catching." Unknown.—EmN
"The **mockingbird,** the mockingbird." Unknown, tr. fr. the Acoma.—JoT
A **modern** ballad, The ups and downs of the elevator car. Caroline D. Emerson.—BrM
Modern concert song. Unknown, tr. fr. the Zulu by Hugh Tracey.—AlPa
The **modern** Hiawatha. George A. Strong.—LiS
Modern song. Unknown, tr. by B. W. Andrzejewski and I. M. Lewis.—AbM
The **modest** couple. William Schwenck Gilbert.—CoPt
Modesty
"She dwelt among the untrodden ways." W. Wordsworth.—LiS
Mojave Indians. See Indians of the Americas—Mojave
Mold
John Mouldy. W. De La Mare.—HiN—OpOx
Mole ("Follow the trail of the soft furry mole") Mary Ann Hoberman.—HoLb
The **mole** ("It wasn't a sizable interruption") William H. Matchett.—HaWr
The **mole** ("The mole's a solitary soul") Jack Prelutsky.—PrP
The **mole** ("Sometimes I envy those") John Haines.—HiN
The **mole** ("When the mole goes digging") E. L. Mayo.—JoA-4
Moles (animals)
The eagle and the mole. E. Wylie.—RoIt
Flying out of holes. D. Lee.—LeA
Funny old moles. A. Fisher.—FiFo
"It's been a bad year for the moles." D. McCord
Three limericks.—McS
Mole ("Follow the trail of the soft furry mole") M. A. Hoberman.—HoLb
The mole ("It wasn't a sizable interruption") W. H. Matchett.—HaWr
The mole ("The mole's a solitary soul") J. Prelutsky.—PrP
The mole ("Sometimes I envy those") J. Haines.—HiN
The mole ("When the mole goes digging") E. L. Mayo.—JoA-4
"The **mole's** a solitary soul." See The mole
Molière, pseud. (Jean Baptiste Poquelin)
Tartuffe.—LiWw (sel.)
Moll, Ernest G.
Robbing the tree hive.—CoPt
"**Moll-in-the-wad** and I fell out." Unknown.—TrG
Molly Means. Margaret Walker.—CoPt
"**Molly** O'Golly lived in Mount Holly." See I'll tell you if I find her
Moloney remembers the resurrection of Kate Finucane. Brendan Kennelly.—CoPt
Mom. Grey Cohoe.—AlW
"**Mom** has a job." Lois Lenski.—LeC
"**Mom** has roses." See Roses
Moment of visitation. Gustav Davidson.—RoIt
A **moment** please. Samuel Allen.—AdPb
"**Mommies** are people." See Parents are people
Mom's mums. David McCord.—McAa
Monday morning: Good morning. Lucille Clifton.—ClS
"**Monday** morning mother made mincemeat pie." Unknown.—EmN
"**Monday's** child is fair of face." Unknown.—JoA-4
Money. See also Wealth
America. H. Dumas.—AdB—AdPb—CoPu
Coins. V. Worth.—WoS
"Give me three nickels and give me a dime." Unknown.—EmN
Gumballs. X. J. Kennedy.—KeO
"Gypsy, gypsy, lived in a tent." Unknown.—EmN
"Here we come a-wassailing." Unknown.—MaF
"How many seconds in a minute." C. G. Rossetti.—RoIt
"I love sixpence, jolly little sixpence." Mother Goose.—JoA-4
"If I'd as much money as I could spend." Mother Goose.—AlC—JoA-4

"A **moon**, brimful of light." See Passover night
"The **moon** cannot fight." See The moon
"The **moon** comes every night to peep." See The white window
"The **moon** has a face like the clock in the hall." See The moon
"The **moon** has ascended between us." See Love apart
"The **moon** holds nothing in her arms." R. P. Lister.—PeS
The **moon** is up. Unknown.—RoIt
"The **moon** is up, the moon is up." See The moon is up
"The **moon** lights the earth." See The moon
"The **moon** mentions." See Grunion
Moon mist. Christopher Okigbo.—AlPa
"The **moon** moved over last night." See The 5th of July
"**Moon** moves down the sky." Buson, tr. fr. the Japanese by Harry Behn.—BeM
Moon poem. Saundra Sharp.—AbM
"**Moon** sits smoking his pipe." Natalia Belting.—BeWi
"The **moon** this night is like a silver sickle." See The path on the sea
Mooney, James
The dreamer rides the whirlwind. tr.—BiI
I gave them fruits. tr.—BiI
Magic formula to destroy life. tr.—BiI
Magic formula to fix a bride's affection. tr.—BiI
Song of the ghost dance. tr.—BiI
That wind. tr.—BiI
"The **moonlight**." See Enchantment
Moonlight. Sara Teasdale.—CoPu
Moonlight night: Carmel. Langston Hughes.—HoD
Moonlit apples. John Drinkwater.—PaF
"The **moon's** the north wind's cooky." Vachel Lindsay.—JoA-4—LiLc—UnGb
Moore, Clement C.
A visit from St Nicholas.—JoA-4—OpOx
Moore, Gerald
Bow harp. tr.—AlPa
Cradlesong. tr.—AlPa (sel.)
Marine nocturne. tr.—AlPa
Obolus. tr.—AlPa (sel.)
Moore, John
A broken gull.—HiN
Dingman's marsh.—HiN
Squall.—HiN
Moore, Lilian
About a monster-ous toothache.—MoSm
Arson.—MoSp
Bedtime stories.—MoSm
"Bellowed the ogre."—MoSm
"Cat."—MoSm
The chestnuts are falling.—MoSp
Dear country witch.—MoSm
"Do ghouls."—MoSm
Dry spell.—MoSp
Ecology.—MoSp
Empty house song.—MoSm
Encounter.—MoSp
Flight.—MoSp
Fog.—MoSm
Footprints.—MoSm
The ghost in our apartment house.—MoSm
Green.—MoSp
Hay song.—MoSp
"I left my head."—MoSm
"I never saw."—MoSm
"I wish."—MoSm
I'm skeleton.—MoSm
"Johnny drew a monster."—MoSm
Letter to a friend.—MoSp
Little Ugh.—MoSm
"Look at that."—MoSm
Lost and found.—MoSm
No one.—MoSm
No TV.—MoSm
Patriarchs.—MoSp
Recycled.—MoSp
Said a long crocodile.—MoSm
Said the monster.—MoSm
September.—MoSp
Shadows.—MoSm
The Shawangunks—early April.—MoSp
Sliding.—MoSm
Snowy morning.—UnGb
"Something is there."—MoSm
Squirrel.—MoSp
Sun day.—MoSp
Sunset.—MoSp
Teeny tiny ghost.—MoSm
Teeth.—MoSm
The troll bridge.—MoSm
"We three."—MoSm
Weather report.—MoSp
Wet.—MoSp
Whale food.—MoSm
Whooo.—MoSm
Why.—MoSm
Willow yellow.—MoSp
Wind song.—UnGb
Winter cardinal.—MoSp
Witch goes shopping.—MoSm
The witch's garden.—MoSm
The witch's song.—HoH—MoSm
Moore, Marianne
The camel and the flotsam. tr.—JoA-4
The dairymaid and her milk-pot. tr.—JoA-4
The dove and the ant. tr.—JoA-4
The fox and the goat. tr.—JoA-4
A jellyfish.—JoA-4
I may, I might, I must.—JoA-4
O to be a dragon.—JoA-4
Poetry.—MoT—PlM (sel.)
Silence.—MaFw
A talisman.—HiN
Moore, Marianne (about)
Invitation to Miss Marianne Moore. E. Bishop.—PlM
Moore, Merrill
How she resolved to act.—PeS
The noise that time makes.—RoIt

Moore, Thomas
"The harp that once through Tara's halls."—RoIt
I saw from the beach.—CoPi
If you have seen.—LiWw
Lalla Rookh.—LiS (sel.)
Lying.—CoPi
"Oft, in the stilly night."—CoPi
"The time I've lost in wooing."—CoPi
What's my thought like.—LiWw
"Wind thy horn, my hunter boy."—FlH
Moore, Thomas (about)
To Thomas Moore. Lord Byron.—PlM—RoIt
Moraes, Dom
Bells for William Wordsworth.—PlM
The brass serpent. tr.—MeP (sel.)
"If night nears your window." tr.—MeP
Of bloom. tr.—MeP
Parting. tr.—MeP
Quatrains, sels.
Gentleman to lady. tr.—MeP
Shell to gentleman. tr.—MeP
Sabbath stars. tr.—MeP
Snow in Jerusalem. tr.—MeP
A **moral** tetrastitch. Unknown, tr. fr. the Persian by William Jones.—CoPu
"The **more** I think of you." Unknown.—MoBw
More or less. David McCord.—McFm
Moreland, Wayne
Sunday morning.—AdPb
Morgan, Edwin
An addition to the family: for M. L.—ToM
The computer's first Christmas card.—ToM
French Persian cats having a ball.—ToM
Trio.—ToM
Morgan, R. S.
And other poems.—MaFw
Morgenstern, Christian
Korf's joke.—CoPu
Night song of the fish.—MaFw
Morley, Christopher
Unearned increment.—LiWw
Morley, Sylvanus. See Goetz, Delia and Morley, Sylvanus
Morning. See also Wake-up poems
"An awful tempest mashed the air." E. Dickinson.—ThI
"Brother John, Brother John." Mother Goose.—TucMg
Chelsea morning. J. Mitchell.—MoG
Christmas morning. E. M. Roberts.—JoA-4
Composed on a May morning, 1830. W. Wordsworth.—PaF
Corinna's going a-Maying. R. Herrick.—MaF
The dawn. W. B. Yeats.—MoG
Daybreak. C. Sandburg.—SaT
"Each morning." From Hymn to Lanie Poo. LeRoi Jones.—AdPb
Early astir. H. Read.—CoPu
Getting up early on a spring morning. Po Chü-i.—MaFw
Good morning. T. Nichiporum.—MoM
"I wonder if everyone is up." Unknown.—JoT
"In the morning the city." From City. L. Hughes.—HoCs—LiLc
Magic prayer. Unknown.—LeIb
"The mockingbird, the mockingbird." Unknown.—JoT
Morning ("How pleasant it is") M. Chute.—ChRu
Morning ("The mirror tastes him") J. Harrison.—HaWr
Morning ("'Tis the hour when white-horsed day") C. S. Calverley.—RoIt
Morning beads. P. George.—AlW
Morning compliments. S. Dayre.—OpOx
Morning light (the dew-drier). E. L. Newsome.—AdPb
Morning mood. M. Panegoosho.—LeIb
Morning prayer. O. Nash.—OpOx
A morning song. From Cymbeline. W. Shakespeare.—JoA-4
"The morning star is up." Unknown.—ClFc
The morning watch. From The Silex Scintillans. H. Vaughan.—MoG
"The morns are meeker than they were." E. Dickinson.—JoA-4—PaF
Autumn.—RoIt
"My Lord, what a morning." Unknown.—LaS
New morning. B. Dylan.—MoG
One morning, oh, so early. J. Ingelow.—OpOx
"The owl hooted." Unknown.—LaM
Psalm of those who go forth before daylight. C. Sandburg.—MaFw—SaT
"A reckless morning. . . . " A. Atwood.—AtM
Reveille. From A Shropshire lad. A. E. Housman.—RoIt
Rich morning. R. Farren.—CoPi
Riding at daybreak. Sun Yün Fêng.—MaFw
Song. D. Justice.—HiN
Song on May morning. J. Milton.—PaF
On May morning.—RoIt
Song: The owl. A. Tennyson.—RoIt
The owl.—UnGb
"The sounds in the morning." E. Farjeon.—JoA-4
Spring morning. A. Fisher.—FiFo
Summer song. W. C. Williams.—HaWr
This morning. Jay Wright.—AbM
Those winter Sundays. R. Hayden.—AdPb
Time to rise. R. L. Stevenson.—OpOx
Two mornings. L. McGaugh.—AdPb
When I awoke. R. R. Patterson.—AdPb
"Will there really be a morning." E. Dickinson
Morning.—RoIt
Winter morning. W. J. Smith.—HiN
Winter time. R. L. Stevenson.—OpOx
The wrong start. M. Chute.—ChRu
Morning. See "Will there really be a morning"
Morning ("How pleasant it is") Marchette Chute.—ChRu
Morning ("The mirror tastes him") Jim Harrison.—HaWr
Morning ("'Tis the hour when white-horsed day") Charles Stuart Calverley.—RoIt

"The **morning** after." Walter Clark.—HiN
Morning beads. Phil George.—AlW
Morning compliments. Sydney Dayre.—OpOx
A **morning** hymn. Christopher Smart.—OpOx
Morning light (the dew-drier). Effie Lee Newsome.—AdPb
Morning mood. M. Panegoosho.—LeIb
"**Morning.** Morning will produce." See Breakfast
"**Morning** opened." See Song
Morning prayer. Ogden Nash.—OpOx
A **morning** song. See Cymbeline
The **morning** star. Primus St John.—AdPb
"The **morning** star is up." Unknown, tr. fr. the Papago.—ClFc
The **morning** watch. See The Silex Scintillans
Morning workout. Babette Deutsch.—FlH
"The **morns** are meeker than they were." Emily Dickinson.—JoA-4—PaF
  Autumn.—RoIt
Morozov, Sergei
  The last soldier.—MoM
Morris, J. W.
  What I think of Hiawatha.—LiS
Morrison, Lillian
  At first sight.—JoA-4
  Of kings and things.—HiN
  The sprinters.—JoA-4
Mortality
  After. R. Hodgson.—JoA-4
  Mortality. N. L. Madgett.—AdPb
  Oh the vanity of earthly greatness. A. Guiterman.—LiWw
  The selfsame song. T. Hardy.—PlP
  "The stones are all that last long." Unknown.—ClFc
Mortality. Naomi Long Madgett.—AdPb
A **mortifying** mistake. Anna Maria Pratt.—BrM
Morton, J. B.
  Epitaph for a lighthouse-keeper's horse.—CoPu
  Now we are sick.—CoPu—LiS
Morton, Miriam
  Alone. tr.—MoM
  At home. tr.—MoM
  The baby tigers. tr.—MoM
  Before the summer downpour. tr.—MoM
  A bit of cobweb. tr.—MoM
  The black panther. tr.—MoM
  "The blue wings." tr.—MoM
  Borders. tr.—MoM
  The brook. tr.—MoM
  "A caressing breeze touched." tr.—MoM
  A celebration. tr.—MoM
  The children of Vietnam. tr.—MoM
  Choice. tr.—MoM
  "The dawn breaks over the mooring." tr.—MoM
  "Do the Russians want war." tr.—MoM
  Erevan is my city. tr.—MoM
  "The exam." tr.—MoM
  The flower. tr.—MoM
  Good morning. tr.—MoM
  "Grandma snores." tr.—MoM
  "Half a moon." tr.—MoM
  "Hi there, friend or foe." tr.—MoM
  "The house is in ruins." tr.—MoM
  "A hungry wolf is in the street." tr.—MoM
  "I am in the all, the all in me." tr.—MoM
  "I look out of my window." tr.—MoM
  I love. tr.—MoM
  "I may not know them all by name." tr.—MoM
  "I might repeat in every line." tr.—MoM
  "I saw an apple." tr.—MoM
  "I want time to run, to race for me." tr.—MoM
  "I want to find the essence of." tr.—MoM
  "If only I were able." tr.—MoM
  "In a poor old village." tr.—MoM
  "In America there is mourning." tr.—MoM
  In autumn. tr.—MoM
  The last soldier. tr.—MoM
  Lenin. tr.—MoM
  "Let there always be a sky." tr.—MoM
  Like a sparkling bead. tr.—MoM
  The lioness and her cub. tr.—MoM
  The little girl. tr.—MoM
  The little house. tr.—MoM
  Losing friends. tr.—MoM
  "A magic landscape." tr.—MoM
  Making friends. tr.—MoM
  My bicycle and me. tr.—MoM
  My gift. tr.—MoM
  My hammer. tr.—MoM
  "My mama has been clever." tr.—MoM
  "My mother and me." tr.—MoM
  "My teddy stands in the nook." tr.—MoM
  "No matter how he ties." tr.—MoM
  The nonconformist. tr.—MoM
  The October anniversary. tr.—MoM
  An offering of joy. tr.—MoM
  "Open, open the gates." tr.—MoM
  Our cat. tr.—MoM
  "Our garden is my world." tr.—MoM
  Out skiing. tr.—MoM
  The path on the sea. tr.—MoM
  Perfection. tr.—MoM
  "A pretty boat." tr.—MoM
  The pumpkin. tr.—MoM
  The question. tr.—MoM
  The radiance of creativity. tr.—MoM
  "The radish is blooming." tr.—MoM
  The refrigerator. tr.—MoM
  A riddle. tr.—MoM
  Russian snow. tr.—MoM
  A schoolboy's lament. tr.—MoM
  The shore of the universe. tr.—MoM
  The size of him. tr.—MoM
  Small change. tr.—MoM
  Someone I know. tr.—MoM
  Something peaceful. tr.—MoM
  The sorceress. tr.—MoM
  Spring mood. tr.—MoM
  Storm at sea. tr.—MoM
  "The sun is today so enchanting." tr.—MoM
  The teakettle. tr.—MoM
  Thank you. tr.—MoM

Mother Goose—*Continued*
"If all the world was apple pie."—EmN—JoA-4
"If all the land were apple pie."—RoIt
"If I had a donkey that wouldn't go."—JoA-4
"If I'd as much money as I could spend."—AlC—JoA-4
"If wishes were horses."—AlC—EmN
"If you sneeze on Monday, you sneeze for danger."—AlC
"I'll tell you a story."—AlC—JoA-4
"I'm a navvy, you're a navvy."—TucMgl
"I-N spells in."—AlC
"In marble halls as white as milk."—EmN—JoA-4
Riddle.—RoIt
In the dumps. See "We're all in the dumps"
"In the month of February."—TucMgl
"Incey wincey spider."—AlC
"Intery, mintery, cutery, corn."—EmN—JoA-4
"It's blowing, it's snowing."—TucMg
"It's raining, it's raining."—TucMgl
"Jack and Jill went up the hill."—AlC—JoA-4
"Jack be nimble."—JoA-4
"Jack, Jack, the bread's a-burning."—AlC
"Jack Sprat could eat no fat."—AlC—JoA-4
"Jenny Wren fell sick."—JoA-4
"Johnny shall have a new bonnet."—JoA-4
"Julius Caesar made a law."—TucMgl
Jumping Joan. See "One-ery, two-ery, ziccary zan"
"King Dagobert, they say."—TucMg
"Lady Queen Anne she sets in the sun."—JoA-4
"Ladybird, ladybird, fly away home."—AlC
"Last night and the night before."—AlC—EmN
"Lavender's blue, diddle, diddle."—JoA-4
A learned song.—JoA-4
"The lion and the unicorn."—AlC—JoA-4
"Little Bo-peep has lost her sheep."—JoA-4—LiS
Little Boy Blue.—JoA-4
"Little General Monk."—MiMg
"Little girl, little girl, where have you been."—AlC
"Little Jack Horner." See "Little Jack Horner sat in the corner"
"Little Jack Horner sat in the corner."—AlC
"Little Jack Horner."—JoA-4
"Little King Boggen he built a fine hall."—AlC
"Little maiden, better tarry."—TucMgl
"Little Miss Muffet."—JoA-4
"Little Nancy Etticoat."—EmN—JoA-4
"Little Polly Flinders."—AlC
"The little priest of Felton."—MiMg
"Little Tom Tucker."—AlC
"Little Tommy Tucker."—JoA-4
"Little Tommy Tittlemouse."—AlC—MiMg
"Little Tommy Tucker." See "Little Tom Tucker"
"Lock the dairy door."—AlC
"London Bridge is broken down."—JoA-4
"Long legs, crooked thighs."—JoA-4
"Lucy Locket lost her pocket."—JoA-4
"The man in the moon (came tumbling down)."—AlC—RoIt
"A man in the wilderness." See "The man in the wilderness asked of me"
"A man in the wilderness asked me." See "The man in the wilderness asked of me"
"The man in the wilderness asked of me."—AlC
"A man in the wilderness."—RoIt
"A man in the wilderness asked me."—JoA-4
"A man of words and not of deeds."—AlC
"Margery Mutton-pie and Johnny Bopeep."—AlC
"Mary, Mary, quite contrary."—JoA-4
"Master I have, and I am his man."—AlC
"Matthew, Mark, Luke and John."—MiMg
"Mr East gave a feast."—JoA-4
Mr Punchinello. See "Oh, mother I shall be married to Mr Punchinello"
"Mr Squirrel, sitting under shelter."—TucMg
"My little old man and I fell out."—JoA-4
"My mother said."—AlC
"Needles and pins, needles and pins."—AlC—EmN
"The north wind doth blow."—AlC—JoA-4
"Oh dear me, mother caught a flea."—AlC
"Oh, mother, I shall be married to Mr Punchinello."—AlC
Mr Puncinello.—JoA-4
"Oh my dear, what a cold you've got."—TucMgl
"Oh, rare Harry Parry."—HoMg
"Oh, the brave old Duke of York."—JoA-4
"O the cuckoo she's a pretty bird."—AlC
"Old Abram Brown is dead and gone."—AlC
"Old Caspar had six sons so fine."—TucMg
"Old Farmer Giles."—TucMgl
"Old King Cole."—JoA-4
"Old Mother Goose."—JoA-4
"Old Mother Hubbard."—JoA-4
"Old Mother Roundabout."—AlC
"Old Mother Shuttle."—MiMg
"Old Sir Simon the king."—AlC
"Old woman, old woman (shall we go)."—HoMg
"On Saturday night (shall be)."—AlC
"On Saturday night I lost my wife."—HoMg
"On the bridge of Avignon."—TucMg
"One-eyed Jack, the pirate chief."—TucMgl
"One I love."—EmN—HoMg
"One misty moisty morning."—AlC—JoA-4—MiMg
"1, 2 (buckle my shoe)." See "One, two (buckle my shoe)"
"One, two (buckle my shoe)."—AlC—EmN
"1, 2 (buckle my shoe)."—JoA-4
"1, 2, 3, 4, 5."—AlC
"One-ery, two-ery." See "One-ery, two-ery, ziccary zan"

"One-ery, two-ery, ziccary zan"
Jumping Joan.—NeA
"One-ery, two-ery."—AlC
"Our saucy boy, Dick."—TucMgl
"Pat-a-cake, pat-a-cake, baker's man."—JoA-4
"Pease porridge hot." See "Pease-pudding hot"
"Pease-pudding hot."—AlC
"Pease porridge hot."—EmN—JoA-4
"Penny on the water."—AlC—EmN
"Peter, Peter, pumpkin eater."—HoMg—JoA-4
"Peter Piper pick'd a peck of pepper."—EmN—HoMg—JoA-4
"Peter White will ne'er go right."—AlC
"Piggy on the railway."—AlC
"Please to remember."—AlC
"Policeman, policeman, don't take me."—AlC—EmN
"Poor old Robinson Crusoe."—AlC
Pop goes the weasel.—JoA-4
"Pussy cat, pussy cat." See "Pussy-cat, pussy-cat, where have you been"
"Pussy-cat, pussy-cat, where have you been."—AlC
"Pussy cat, pussy cat."—BlM—JoA-4
"The Queen of Hearts."—JoA-4
"Rain, rain, go away."—EmN—JoA-4
"Ride a cock-horse to Banbury cross."—AlC—JoA-4
"Ride away, ride away."—MiMg
"Robin the Bobbin, the big-bellied Ben."—AlC
"Rock-a-bye baby, thy cradle is green."—AlC—JoA-4
"Roley Poley, pudding and pie."—AlC
"The rose is red, the grass is green."—AlC
"Rosemary green."—AlC
"Rub-a-dub dub."—JoA-4
"St Dunstan, as the story goes."—MiMg—TrG
"Sally go round the sun."—AlC
"Sammy Smith would drink and eat."—TucMgl
"Saw ye aught of my love a-coming from ye market."—AlC
"Scissors and string, scissors and string."—HoMg
"See a pin and pick it up."—EmN—JoA-4
"See saw, Margery Daw."—JoA-4
"See-saw sacradown."—JoA-4
"See this pretty little girl of mine."—AlC
"Simple Simon met a pieman."—JoA-4
"Sing a song of sixpence."—AlC—EmN—JoA-4—LiS
"Six little mice sat down to spin."—BlM—JoA-4—TrG
"Snail, snail."—JoA-4
"Solomon Grundy."—AlC—JoA-4
"Sukey, you shall be my wife."—TucMgl
"A swarm of bees in May."—AlC
"Taffy was a Welshman, Taffy was a thief."—AlC
"Tell tale, tit."—AlC—EmN
"Terence McDiddler."—HoMg
"There was a crooked man."—AlC—BlM
"There was a crooked man, and he went a crooked mile."—JoA-4
"There was a crooked man, and he went a crooked mile." See "There was a crooked man"
"There was a lady loved a swine."—MiMg
The lady and the swine.—CoOh
"There was a little man, and he had a little gun."—JoA-4
"There was a man, and he had nought."—AlC
"There was a man and he stayed within."—TucMg
"There was a man of Newington."—AlC
"There was a monkey climb'd up a tree."—AlC
"There was a piper, he'd a cow."—AlC
"There was a rat, for want of stairs."—MiMg—TrG
"There was an old man (and he had a calf)."—JoA-4
"There was an old woman (lived under a [the] hill)."—JoA-4—MiMg
"There was an old woman and what do you think."—JoA-4—TrG
"There was an old woman, as I've heard tell."—JoA-4
"There was an old woman called Nothing-at-all."—AlC
"There was an old woman had three sons."—JoA-4
"There was an old woman, her name it was Peg."—AlC
"There was an old woman in Surrey."—OpOx—TucMgl
"There was an old woman sat spinning."—AlC
"There was an old woman toss'd (tossed) up in a basket."—AlC—JoA-4—MiMg
"There was an old woman who lived in a shoe."—AlC—JoA-4
"There were three jovial Welshmen."—AlC—JoA-4
"There's a hole in my bucket, dear Conrad, dear Conrad."—TucMg
"Thirty days hath September."—JoA-4
"Thirty white horses."—EmN—JoA-4
"This is father, short and stout."—TucMg
"This is the house that Jack built."—JoA-4
The house that Jack built.—LiS
"This little man lived all alone."—TucMgl
"This little pig went to market."—JoA-4
"Three big sailors had a tiny little boat."—TucMg
"Three blind mice, see how they run."—AlC
"Three children sliding on the ice."—AlC—JoA-4
"Three little kittens."—BlM
"Three wise men of Gotham."—AlC—JoA-4
"Three young rats with black felt hats."—BlM—JoA-4
"Tiny man."—TucMg

Motswasele's farewell. L. D. Raditladi, tr. fr. the Botswana by D. T. Cole and ad. by Peggy Rutherfoord.—AlPa
Motto. Langston Hughes.—AdPb—CoPu
Motto for a dog house. Arthur Guiterman.—CoPu
Mount Avarim
Mount Avarim. Judah Halevi.—MeP
Mount Avarim. Judah Halevi, tr. fr. the Hebrew by Robert Mezey.—MeP
"**Mount** Taishan is high and steep." Sa Eun Yang, tr. fr. the Korean by Chung Seuk Park and ad. by Virginia Olsen Baron.—BaSs
"A **mountain.**" Yi Hwang, tr. fr. the Korean by Chung Seuk Park and ad. by Virginia Olsen Baron.—BaSs
Mountain road. Mary Oliver.—RoIt
"The **mountain** sheep are sweeter." See The war song of Dinas Vawr
The **mountain** whippoorwill. Stephen Vincent Benét.—CoPt
Mountains
Ask the mountains. P. George.—AlW
"At the first sign of my horse's fright." Unknown.—BaSs
"The bear went over the mountain." Unknown.—EmN—JoA-4
The big Rock Candy mountain. Unknown.—CoOh
The big Rock Candy mountains.—PeS
"The blue mountains are what they are." Kim In-hu.—BaSs
"Butterfly, let's fly to the green mountains." Unknown.—BaSs
Dream song. Unknown.—BiI
"A dromedary standing still." J. Prelutsky.—PrT
The face of my mountains. Unknown.—BiI
"First man and first woman." N. Belting.—BeWi
For purple mountains' majesty. M. C. Livingston.—LiM
"A hundred mountains." Issa.—BeM
In the mountains on a summer day. Li T'ai-po.—MaFw
"Look below you. The river is a thousand fathoms deep." Yi Hyun-bo.—BaSs
"Low clouds are shattered." Bashō.—BeM
"Mount Taishan is high and steep." Sa Eun Yang.—BaSs
"A mountain." Yi Hwang.—BaSs
The mountain whippoorwill. S. V. Benét.—CoPt
Muckish mountain (The pig's back). S. Leslie.—CoPi
"One summer evening (led by her) I found." From The prelude. W. Wordsworth.—MaFw
"Only white gull and I." Yi Hwang.—BaSs
Pier. J. Scully.—HaWr
The poem that took the place of a mountain. W. Stevens.—PlM
"Ten years it took." Song Soon.—BaSs
That dark other mountain. R. Francis.—HiN—PeS
That mountain far away. Unknown.—BiI
"This unimportant." Bashō.—BeM
Were you on the mountain. Unknown.—CoPu
"White and wise and old." Buson.—BeM
"White mountains, seen also." Issa.—HaW
"**Mountains** are moving, rivers." See The redwoods
"**Mountains** may rise." Unknown.—MoBw
The **mountains** of Mourne. Percy French.—CoPi
The **mourning** dove. Felice Holman.—HoI
"The **mourning-dove,** that sang all evening." See Dismal observation
Mourning poem for the Queen of Sunday. Robert Hayden.—AdPb
Mouse ("Dear little") Mary Ann Hoberman.—HoLb
The **mouse** ("I heard a mouse") Elizabeth Jane Coatsworth.—JoA-4
The **mouse** and the cake. Eliza Cook.—OpOx
"A **mouse** found a beautiful piece of plum cake." See The mouse and the cake
"A **mouse** in her room woke Miss Dowd." Unknown.—TrG
Mouse night: One of our games. William Stafford.—HiN
Mousemeal. Howard Nemerov.—HiN
The **mouse's** petition. Anna Laetitia Barbauld.—OpOx
Mouths
"There was an old woman called Nothing-at-all." Mother Goose.—AlC
The **move** continuing. Al Young.—AdPb
Moving
The 1st. L. Clifton.—MoT
The move continuing. A. Young.—AdPb
"**Moving** into the project." See Watching the wrecking crane
"**Moving** through the silent crowd." Stephen Spender.—ToM
"The **mower's** in the meadow." See Hay song
"**Mowers,** weary and brown, and blithe." See Scythe song
Mowing. See Farm life; Harvests and harvesting
"**Ms** Minnie McFinney, of Butte." Unknown.—NeA
"**Much** have I travell'd in the realms of gold." See On first looking into Chapman's Homer
Much nicer people. Elizabeth Jane Coatsworth.—CoPu
Muckish mountain (The pig's back). Shane Leslie.—CoPi
Mud pie. Kathleen Fraser.—HoCs
The **muddle.** Marchette Chute.—ChRu
"**Muffled** in my muffler." See The new muffler
Muir, Edwin
Gulls.—HiN
Merlin.—MaFw
The way.—JoA-4

Mules
The horse and the mule. T. H. Wynne.—OpOx
New farm tractor. C. Sandburg.—SaT
Two legs behind and two before. Unknown.—CoOh
Mulikita, F. M.
Shaka Zulu.—AlPa (sel.)
Muller, Inna
The path on the sea.—MoM
"The sun is today so enchanting."—MoM
Mulock, Dinah Maria
God rest ye, merry gentlemen.—JoA-4
The new year.—RoIt
Multi-colored balloon. Herbert D. Greggs.—AbM
"**Mumbo** Jumbo." Dennis Lee.—LeA
"The **mummers** go out." See May day
Mumps
"Higgledy piggledy (wiggledy wump)." D. Lee.—LeA
Mumps. E. M. Roberts.—BrM
Mumps. Elizabeth Madox Roberts.—BrM
Mungin, Horace
Blues.—AdB
Of man and nature.—AdB
Munkittrick, Richard Kendall
A bulb.—CoPu
Murder. See also Crime and criminals
At that moment. R. R. Patterson.—AdPb
Between the world and me. R. Wright.—AdPb
Birmingham 1963. R. R. Patterson.—AdPb
The bread-knife ballad. R. W. Service.—CoOr
The continuing story of Bungalow Bill. J. Lennon and P. McCartney.—MoG
5 ways to kill a man. E. Brock.—MoT
"In America there is mourning." A. Karlov.—MoM
Kent State, May 4, 1970. P. Goodman.—MoT
The last quatrain of the ballad of Emmett Till. G. Brooks.—AdPb
Nora Criona. J. Stephens.—CoPi
Old Lem. S. A. Brown.—AdPb
On slaughter. C. N. Bialik.—MeP
One eyed black man in Nebraska. S. Cornish.—AdPb
Panther. S. Cornish.—AdPb
Prelude. C. K. Rivers.—AdPb
They are killing all the young men. D. Henderson.—AdPb
"Willie built a guillotine." W. E. Engel.—CoOh
"**Murderers.**" See Salute
Murphy, Richard
Droit de Seigneur.—CoPi
Sailing to an island.—ToM
Murphy in Manchester. John Montague.—CoPi
Murray, Pauli
Death of a friend.—AdPb
For Mack C. Parker.—AdPb
Harlem riot, 1943.—AdPb
Mr Roosevelt regrets.—AdPb
Without name.—AdPb

The **Muse.** Anna Akhmatova, tr. by Stanley Kunitz.—PlM
Musée des beaux arts. W. H. Auden.—ToM
Muses
The Muse. A. Akhmatova.—PlM
Museum piece. Richard Wilbur.—LiWw
Museums
The dodo. H. Belloc.—CoOh
Museums. L. MacNeice.—PeS
The story of the zeros. V. H. Cruz.—AdPb
Museums. Louis MacNeice.—PeS
"**Museums** offer us, running from among the 'buses." See Museums
Mushrooms
"A dry leaf drifting." Bashō.—BeM
Mushrooms. Unknown.—JoA-4
Mushrooms. Unknown, tr. fr. the Russian by Rose Fyleman.—JoA-4
Music and musicians. See also Singing; also names of musical instruments, as Pianos; also names of types of musicians, as Pipers; also names of musicians, as Haydn, Franz Joseph; also Orchestras
Albert Ayler, eulogy for a decomposed saxophone player. S. Crouch.—AdPb
At the railway station, Upway. T. Hardy.—MaFw—PlP
Baton. L. Lenski.—LeC
Beyond melody. N. Alterman.—MeP
Chamber music, sels. J. Joyce
"Lean out of the window."—RoIt
The noise of waters.—RoIt
Chamber music (XXXV).—MaFw
"Strings in the earth and air"
Chamber music (I).—MaFw
Charles. L. Clark.—MaFw
The choirmaster's burial. T. Hardy.—PlP
Choric song. From The lotus-eaters. A. Tennyson.—RoIt
Concert. Ibn Sharaf.—AbM
Dance of the infidels. A. Young.—AdPb
December music. W. T. Scott.—RoIt
The design. C. Major.—AdPb
Effendi. M. S. Harper.—AdPb
Frog music. D. McCord.—McFm
The given note. S. Heaney.—HiN
The green fiddler. R. Field.—CoPt
Here where Coltrane is. M. S. Harper.—AdPb
"Higgledy-piggledy." E. W. Seaman.—LiWw
The high school band. R. Whittemore.—HiN
John Coltrane an impartial review. A. B. Spellman.—AdPb
Lead. J. Cortez.—AdPb
"Listen to the music, listen to the din." J. Prelutsky.—PrC
Listening to music. M. Chute.—ChR
The man with the blue guitar. W. Stevens.—PeS (sel.)
Me, in Kulu Se and Karma. C. M. Rodgers.—AdPb
Music. R. W. Emerson.—RoIt
Music I heard with you. From Discordants. C. Aiken.—RoIt

Music and musicians.—*Continued*
O black and unknown bards. J. W. Johnson.—AdPb
Ode. A. Shaughnessy.—CoPi—RoIt
"Orpheus with his lute made trees." From Henry VIII. W. Shakespeare
Music.—RoIt
Ourchestra. S. Silverstein.—SiW
A piper. S. O'Sullivan.—CoPi
Poems: Birmingham 1962-1964. J. Fields.—AdPb
Psalm 150. From Psalms, Bible, Old Testament
"Praise ye the Lord (praise God)."—RoIt
"Ride a cock-horse to Banbury cross." Mother Goose.—AlC—JoA-4
Rythm. I. C. Smith.—ToM
Serenade. D. Donnelly.—HiN
Soul. D. L. Graham.—AdPb
The sound of Afroamerican history chapt II. S. E. Anderson.—AdPb
Souvenir. E. Merriam.—MeO
Spanish music in winter. D. Avidan.—MeP (sel.)
Summer music. M. Sarton.—HiN
"Tambourines." L. Hughes.—HoD
"Terence McDiddler." Mother Goose.—HoMg
Theme with variation. M. C. Livingston.—LiM
"There was an old lady of Steen." Unknown.—RoIt
"There's music in a hammer." Unknown.—RoIt
Time to practice. M. C. Livingston.—LiM
To——. W. S. Braithwaite.—AdPb
To Jane. P. B. Shelley.—RoIt
To music to becalme his fever. R. Herrick.—RoIt
The tooting tutor. Unknown.—BrM
Trio. E. Morgan.—ToM
Tuning up. F. Holman.—HoI
"Waterfall, only." Issa.—BeM
Woodstock. J. Mitchell.—MoG
You are alms. J. W. Thompson.—AdPb
Music. See Henry VIII—"Orpheus with his lute made trees"
Music. Ralph Waldo Emerson.—RoIt
"The **music** and its harmony." See The design
Music I heard with you. See Discordants
"**Music** I heard with you was more than music." See Discordants—Music I heard with you
Musical instruments. See names of musical instruments, as Pianos
"A **musical** poet, collector of basset-horns." See An addition to the family: for M. L.
Musicians. See Music and musicians
"**Musing** on roses and revolutions." See Roses and revolutions
Muskrat. Mary Ann Hoberman.—HoLb
Muskrats
Muskrat. M. A. Hoberman.—HoLb
"**Must.**" Alun Lewis.—CoPu
"**Must** I lay down and die to feel the Earth." See The question
"**Must** I shoot the." See Watts
"**Mustard** when it's hot." See Pease porridge poems
Mute opinion. Thomas Hardy.—PlP
My ace of spades. Ted Joans.—AdB
"**My** ancestors can't see me." Yi Hwang, tr. fr. the Korean by Chung Seuk Park and ad. by Virginia Olsen Baron.—BaSs
"**My** aspens dear, whose airy cages quelled." See Binsey poplars felled 1879
My Aunt Dora. Ted Hughes.—HuMf
My Aunt Flo. Ted Hughes.—HuMf
"**My** aunt kept turnips in a flock." Randall Jarrell.—LiWw
My aunt's spectre. Mortimer Collins.—CoPt
"**My** background is working class." See Myself my slogan
My beard. Shel Silverstein.—SiW
"**My** beard grows to my toes." See My beard
My bed is a boat. Robert Louis Stevenson.—RoIt
"**My** bed is like a little boat." See My bed is a boat
"**My** best friend is Jimmy." See Christmas Eve rhyme
My bicycle and me. Lora Kulichkova, tr. fr. the Russian by Miriam Morton.—MoM
My birthday cake. X. J. Kennedy.—KeO
"**My** birthday cake's so full of eggs." See My birthday cake
"**My** black mothers I hear them singing." See Black star line
"**My** blackness is the beauty of this land." Lance Jeffers.—AdPb
"**My** blessing on the patient cows." See A blessing on the cows
"**My** boat is on the shore." See To Thomas Moore
"**My** body a rounded stone." See Living tenderly
"**My** body in the walls captived." Sir Walter Raleigh.—MaFw
"**My** breath." See Cold morning
My breath became. Unknown, tr. fr. the Apache by Pliny Earle Goddard.—BiI
"**My** brother Ben's face, thought Eugene." See Ben
My brother Bert. Ted Hughes.—HuMf
"**My** brother is homemade." Sam Cornish.—AdM
"**My** brother you flash your teeth in response to every hypocrisy." See The renegade
"**My** brother's a pain." See The pain and the great one
My cat. Aileen Fisher.—FiM
"**My** cat has eyes." See Your cat and mine
"**My** cat is fond." See Boxes
My cat Jeoffrey. Christopher Smart.—RoIt
"**My** cat, washing her tail's tip, is a whorl." See Cat on couch
"**My** child is very sad." See I was the moon

"**My** child, the duck-billed platypus." See The platypus
"**My** children." Unknown, tr. fr. the Arapaho-Comanche.—JoT
"**My** children, when at first I liked the whites." See I give them fruits
"**My** clumsy poem on the inn-wall none cared to see." See The poem on the wall
"**My** cousin John was most polite." See Politeness
My dad. Lois Lenski.—LeC
"**My** dad gave me one dollar bill." See Smart
"**My** dad is a big strong man." See My dad
"**My** daddy has paid the rent." See Good times
"**My** daddy is dead, but I can't tell you how." See The ploughboy in luck
"**My** dame had a tame lame crane." Unknown.—EmN
My dead. Rachel, tr. fr. the Hebrew by Robert Mezey.—MeP
"**My** dear child, first thyself enable." See The boy serving at table
"**My** dear, do you know." See The babes in the wood
"**My** dear, let me tell you about the shark." See The shark
"**My** dears, 'tis said in days of old." See The bee, the ant, and the sparrow
"**My** dinner yesterday was the skin of an elderly goat." See The frugal host
My dog is a plumber. Dan Greenburg.—ThF
"**My** dog is a plumber, he must be a boy." See My dog is a plumber
"**My** dog is big and his name is Rocky." See Dream dog
"**My** dog's so furry I've not seen." See The hairy dog
My early home. John Clare.—RoIt
"**My** eighth spring in England I walk among." See This landscape, these people
My face. Anthony Euwer.—LiWw
"**My** fairest child, I have no song to give you." See A farewell
My family. Marchette Chute.—ChRu
"**My** family was the very proudest." See School concert
"**My** fang aches, cried monster. Oh dear." See About a monster-ous toothache
My father. Ted Hughes.—HuMf
"**My** father could go down a mountain faster than I." See That dark other mountain
"**My** father could hear a little animal step." See Listening
"**My** father, he was a mountaineer." See The ballad of William Sycamore
"**My** Father, it is surely a blue place." See Hunchback girl: She thinks of heaven
"**My** father left me three acres of land." See Three acres of land
"**My** father lies black and hushed." See The worker
My father paints the summer. Richard Wilbur.—HiN
"**My** father says he's hard as nails." See Nails
"**My** father used to say." See Silence
"**My** father was the first to hear." See The geese
"**My** father was the keeper of the Eddystone light." See The Eddystone light
"**My** father who owned the wagon-shop." See The Spoon River anthology—Percy Bysshe Shelley
"**My** father worked with a horse plough." See Follower
"**My** father's friend came once to tea." See A recollection
"**My** father's name is Frankenstein." See Father and mother
"**My** feet have felt the sands." See Determination
My first cigar. Robert J. Burdette.—CoPt
"**My** first dream of the year." Issa, tr. fr. the Japanese by Hanako Fukuda.—HaW
"**My** first English fog." See Nature's gentleman
"**My** first is in pork." See What flower is this
My fishes. Marchette Chute.—ChRu
My friend. Larry Kirkman.—HoCs
"**My** friend Stan Stapler, he's the most." See Stan Stapler
My friend Thelma. Russell Hoban.—HoE
My gift. Natasha Bukhteyeva, tr. fr. the Russian by Miriam Morton.—MoM
"**My** goldfish swim like bits of light." See My fishes
My good Lord's done been here. Unknown.—BrW
"**My** grandfather kept no." See Mountain road
"**My** grandfather said to me." See Manners
My grandmother. Elizabeth Jennings.—ToM
"**My** grandmother sent me a new-fashioned." Unknown.—EmN
"**My** grandmothers were strong." See Lineage
My granny. Ted Hughes.—HuMf
"**My** granny is an octopus." See My granny
"**My** great corn plants." Unknown, tr. fr. the Navajo.—ClFc
"**My** gumballs come from a machine." See Gumballs
"**My** hair is springy like the forest grasses." See Black woman
My hammer. Alesha, tr. fr. the Russian by Miriam Morton.—MoM
"**My** head, my heart, mine eyes, my life, nay more." See A letter to her husband, absent upon publick employment
"**My** head spins and my feet tingle." Unknown.—MoBw
"**My** heart aches, and a drowsy numbness pains." See Ode to a nightingale
"**My** heart is in the city." Lois Lenski.—LeC
My heart is in the East. Judah Halevi, tr. fr. the Hebrew by Robert Mezey.—MeP
"**My** heart is in the East, and I in the uttermost West." See My heart is in the East
My heart leaps up. William Wordsworth.—JoA-4—RoIt
"**My** heart leaps up when I behold." See My heart leaps up

"**My** opinion of Sands is it's not one of the best." See Sands
My own hallelujahs. Zack Gilbert.—AdPb
"**My** own little newly hatched one." See To our babies
My own true family. Ted Hughes.—HuMf
My papa's waltz. Theodore Roethke.—HiN—MaFw—PeS
My parents. See "My parents kept me from children who were rough"
"**My** parents kept me from children who were rough." Stephen Spender.—PeS
My parents.—MaFw
"**My** parents when they left me behind." See The Longspur's incantation
"**My** pen is poor." Unknown.—EmN
My people ("My people are gray") Carl Sandburg.—SaT
My people ("The night is beautiful") Langston Hughes.—AdM—HoD
"**My** people are few." Unknown, tr. fr. the Salish.—ClFc
"**My** people are gray." See My people
My poem. Nikki Giovanni.—AdB—AdPb
"**My** puppy can't speak English." See Off for a hike
"**My** puppy needs a brushing." See After school
"**My** purse is full of money." Lois Lenski.—LeC
"**My** quiet prison guards, much tried. My lovers." See Pictures of the Jews
My rules. Shel Silverstein.—CoPu—SiW
"**My** serious son, I see thee look." See Before a saint's picture
My shadow. Robert Louis Stevenson.—OpOx
My sister Jane. Ted Hughes.—HuMf—MaFw
"**My** skin is kind of sort of brownish." See Colors
"**My** son has birds in his head." See Daedalus
"**My** son invites me to witness with him." See Mousemeal
"**My** son, let me grasp your hand." Unknown, tr. fr. the Sioux.—ClFc
"**My** son, keep well thy tongue, and keep thy friend." See The Canterbury tales—The manciple's tale—Controlling the tongue
"**My** son, listen once more to the words of your mother." See Death of a son
"**My** song is love unknown." Samuel Crossman.—OpOx
"**My** song, that one, it begins to want to come out." See Dance song
"**My** song was ready." Unknown, fr. the Ammassalik.—LeIb
"**My** sons." See Efficiency apartment
"**My** sorrow cannot travel." See Lamentation
"**My** soul is an enchanted boat." See Asia's song
"**My** soul speaks Spanish." Miriam Lasanta.—JoV
"**My** soul was an old horse." See Pegasus
My spoon was lifted. Naomi Replansky.—CoPu
"**My** spoon was lifted when the bomb came down." See My spoon was lifted
My stars. Abraham ibn Ezra, tr. fr. the Hebrew by Robert Mezey.—MeP
"**My** stocking's where." See Christmas eve
"**My** stocking's where." See A Christmas package
My succah. Edna Bockstein.—LaM (sel.)
"**My** sun." Unknown, tr. fr. the Tewa by Herbert J. Spinden.—JoT
"**My** sweet old etcetera." E. E. Cummings.—PeS
"**My** tail rattles." Unknown, tr. fr. the Mandan.—ClFc
My tang's tungled. Unknown.—BrM
"**My** tea is nearly ready and the sun has left the sky." See The lamplighter
"**My** teacher is mad; he wants to know." See Dumbbell
My teddy bear. Marchette Chute.—ChRu
"**My** teddy stands in the nook." Olga, tr. fr. the Russian by Miriam Morton.—MoM
"**My** thoughts went constantly." Unknown, fr. the Copper Eskimo.—LeIb
"**My** tired old nag shakes." Issa, tr. fr. the Japanese by Harry Behn.—BeM
"**My** trainer steps into the ring." Jack Prelutsky.—PrC
My Ulick. Charles J. Kickham.—CoPi
"**My** Ulick is sturdy and strong." See My Ulick
"**My** Uncle Artemus McPhail." See Giant snail
My Uncle Dan. Ted Hughes.—HuMf—CoOh
"**My** Uncle Dan's an inventor, you may think that's very fine." See My Uncle Dan
"**My** uncle, General Doug MacDougal." See Waking up uncle
"**My** Uncle Ike's an engineer." See Mechanical menagerie
My Uncle Jehoshaphat. Laura E. Richards.—OpOx
"**My** Uncle Jehoshaphat had a pig." See My Uncle Jehoshaphat
My Uncle Mick. Ted Hughes.—HuMf
"**My** Uncle Mick the portrait artist painted nature's creatures." See My Uncle Mick
My valentine. Unknown.—LaM
"**My** voice speaks out." See The face of my mountains
"**My** wife is left-handed." See For Hettie
"**My** wife, not all is vanity." See Song to the wife of his youth
"**My** window opens out into the trees." See Solace
My wings are plucked. Unknown, tr. fr. the Ewe by Geormbeeyi Adali-Mortty.—AlPa
"**My** wings are plucked;—woe's the day." See My wings are plucked
"**My** world is an enormous room." Karla Kuskin.—KuA
My yellow telephone. X. J. Kennedy.—KeO
"**My** younger years I did employ." See A reflection on the course of human life
"**My** zipper is stuck." See A problem
Myself my slogan. Aig Higo.—AlPa
Myself when I am real. Al Young.—AdPb
Mysterious biography. Carl Sandburg.—SaT
The **mysterious** cat. Vachel Lindsay.—JoA-4

Mythology—Greek and Roman. See also names of mythical characters, as Ulysses
Orpheus and Eurydice. From Metamorphoses. Ovid.—MoG
Pandora. M. C. Livingston.—LiM—NeA
"You know the place then." Sappho.—ThI

N

"**N.**" See The four letters
Na-na doll. Russell Hoban.—HoE
Nahuatl Indians. See Indians of the Americas—Nahuatl
Nails
"I walk all day through rain and snow." Unknown.—EmN
Nails. X. J. Kennedy.—KeO
"Step on a nail." Unknown.—EmN
"There is a lady in this land." Unknown.—EmN
Nails. X. J. Kennedy.—KeO
Nairne, Lady
The laird o' Cockpen.—CoPt
Naitō Jōsō. See Jōsō
Naitō Meisetsu
"The wind blows grey."—MaFw
"A **naked** sun, a yellow sun." See Omen
"**Naked** woman, black woman." See Black woman
The **name.** Robert Creeley.—PeS
Names. See also Christenings
"Apples, peaches, cream, and butter." Unknown.—EmN
"Apples, peaches, peanut butter." Unknown.—EmN
"Big A, little a, ron." Unknown.—EmN
Boys' names. E. Farjeon.—JoA-4
Choosing a name. C. and M. Lamb.—OpOx
"Diana Fitzpatrick Mauleverer James." A. A. Milne.—CoPu
"Down in the meadow." Unknown.—EmN
A dream of wildflower names. M. Chute.—ChRu
"Elizabeth, Elspeth, Betsy, and Bess." Mother Goose.—JoA-4
Fred. S. Silverstein.—SiW
Girls' names. E. Farjeon.—JoA-4—NeA
"I am nobody." A. Wright
Hokku poems.—AdPb
I am rose. G. Stein.—NeA
"Ice cream soda." Unknown.—EmN
"If I had a brontosaurus." S. Silverstein.—CoOr—SiW
"I'm Cliff." Unknown.—MoBw
"I'm the monster of Loch Ness." Unknown.—MoBw
Kariuki. J. Gatuira.—AlPa
"Light sky, dark sky." Unknown.—EmN
Louinda. D. McCord.—McFm
"Ministers sign their names to texts." Unknown.—MoBw
"My name is Anna." Unknown.—EmN
"My name is Barbara." Unknown.—EmN
"My name is Connie." Unknown.—EmN
"My name is Diana." Unknown.—EmN
"My name is Esther." Unknown.—EmN
"My name's Jimmy." Unknown.—MoBw
"My sun." Unknown.—JoT
The name. R. Creeley.—PeS
Names. From Prologue to the family of man. C. Sandburg.—SaT
The naming of cats. T. S. Eliot.—LiWw
Naming of parts. H. Reed.—PeS—ToM
"1, 2, 3, O'Leary (my first name)." Unknown.—EmN
Ozymandias revisited. M. Bishop.—LiS
Pat-cat. A. Fisher.—FiFo
The platypus. O. Herford.—LiWw
"Quail." Unknown.—BoI
"Raspberry, raspberry." Unknown.—EmN
"Red, white, and blue (stars shining over you)." Unknown.—EmN
Slippery. C. Sandburg.—SaT
Sophie E. Schnitter. M. C. Livingston.—LiM
"Star thistle, Jim Hill Mustard, white tops." R. Sund.—CoPu
"Strawberry shortcake." Unknown.—EmN
"There once was a king." Unknown.—BoI
"This is page one." Unknown.—MoBw
To his grandson, Gerald C. A. Jackson. A. E. Housman.—CoPu
"What is it that belongs to you." Unknown.—EmN
What's their names. M. A. Hoberman.—HoR
"What's your name (John Brown)." Unknown.—EmN
"What's your name (Pudding-and-Tame)." Unknown.—EmN
"Worm." K. Kuskin.—KuN
Names. See Prologue to the family of man
The **naming** of cats. T. S. Eliot.—LiWw
"The **naming** of cats is a difficult matter." See The naming of cats
Naming of parts. Henry Reed.—PeS—ToM
Nancy Hanks. Rosemary Carr and Stephen Vincent Benét.—JoA-4
"**Nancy,** Nancy." Unknown.—EmN
"**Nanny** banny bumblebee." Clyde Watson.—WaF
Napoleon I, Emperor of France (about)
"Napoleon with his sword." Unknown.—MoBw
The sergeant's song. T. Hardy.—PlP
"**Napoleon** with his sword." Unknown, tr. fr. the Spanish.—MoBw
Narrative. Russell Atkins.—AdPb
"A **narrow** fellow in the grass." Emily Dickinson.—AdP—MaFw—ThI
The snake.—UnGb
"The **narrow** paths branch every way up here." See On Holmbury hill
Nash, Ogden
The adventures of Isabel.—NeA
The boy who laughed at Santa Claus.—CoPt
Brief lines in not so brief.—PlM
Dick Szymanski.—FlH

Neighbors
Neighbor. L. Lenski.—LeC
Neighbors. M. Chute.—ChRu
The new little boy. H. Behn.—LiLc
Note to my neighbor. P. McGinley.—LiWw
Our court. L. Lenski.—LeC
Portrait by a neighbor. E. St V. Millay.—NeA
Neighbors. Marchette Chute.—ChRu
"**Neither** on horseback nor seated." See Walt Whitman at Bear mountain
"**Neither** spirit nor bird." Mary Austin.—RoIt
Nelson, Alice Dunbar
Sonnet.—AdPb
Nelson, Lord Horatio (about)
The admiral's ghost. A. Noyes.—JoA-4
Nemerov, Howard
Brainstorm.—HiN
Grace to be said at the supermarket.—ToM
Life cycle of common man.—ToM
Mousemeal.—HiN
An old story.—CoPu
Presidential address to a party of exiles leaving for the moon.—PlM
The remorse for time.—HiN
A spell before winter.—HaWr
Nephelidia. Algernon Charles Swinburne.—LiS
"A **nervous** sea captain from Cheesequake." X. J. Kennedy.—KeO
Nesbit, Edith (Edith Nesbit Bland)
Child's song in spring.—OpOx
Nespelim man. Janet Campbell.—AlW
Neuteronomy. Eve Merriam.—MeF
Neutral tones. Thomas Hardy.—PlP
Never a tree. Lois Lenski.—LeC
"**Never** a tree to climb." See Never a tree
"**Never** shall a young man." See For Anne Gregory
"**Never** talk down to a glowworm." See Glowworm
"**Never** trust to luck." Unknown, tr. fr. the Spanish.—MoBw
Never two songs the same. Carl Sandburg.—SaT
"**Never** until the mankind making." See A refusal to mourn the death, by fire, of a child in London
Neville, Mary
Social studies.—CoPu
New England
Having New England fathers. J. Holmes.—RoIt
Lilacs. A. Lowell.—PaF
New farm tractor. Carl Sandburg.—SaT
New Hampshire
New Hampshire again. C. Sandburg.—SaT
Pier. J. Scully.—HaWr
New Hampshire again. Carl Sandburg.—SaT
The **new** integrationist. Don L. Lee.—AdB
New Kittens. Aileen Fisher.—FiM
The **new** little boy. Harry Behn.—LiLc
"A **new** little boy moved in next door." See A new little boy
The **new** math. Vanessa Howard.—JoV
The **new** moon. See Dejection: An ode
"**New** moon, O new moon." See Love song
New morning. Bob Dylan.—MoG
The **new** muffler. Marchette Chute.—ChRu
The **new** one. Myra Cohn Livingston.—LiM
The **new** pieta: For the mothers and children of Detroit. June Jordan.—AdPb
New puppy. Aileen Fisher.—FiFo
"**New** shoes, new shoes." See Choosing shoes
New year. See also Rosh Hashana
Happy New year. E. Merriam.—MeO
"I wish you a merry Christmas." Mother Goose.—TucMgl
January. L. Clifton.—ClE
The new year. D. M. Mulock.—RoIt
A new year carol. Unknown.—JoA-4—MaFw
"The old year now is fled." Unknown.—MaF
Ring out, wild bells. From In memoriam. A. Tennyson.—MaF—RoIt
Sonnet. E. Spenser.—PaF
Spring. W. Blake.—JoA-4—LiLc—PaF—RoIt—UnGb
Twelfth night carol. Unknown.—RoIt
"We wish you a merry Christmas." Unknown.—RoIt
The **new** year. Dinah Maria Mulock.—RoIt
A **new** year carol. Unknown.—JoA-4—MaFw
New year's day
An apple tree rhyme. Unknown.—JoA-4
"As New year's day dawns." Ransetsu.—BeM
"Here we come a-wassailing." Unknown.—MaF
"Hogmanay." Unknown.—MaF
"I saw three ships come sailing by." Mother Goose.—JoA-4
"Keep looking at the prize." Issa.—HaW
"The merry year is born." H. Coleridge.—MaF (sel.)
"The New year's day." Issa.—HaW
New year's day. Unknown.—JoA-4
"The old year now is fled." Unknown.—MaF
The snowman's resolution. A. Fisher.—LaM
"The **New** year's day." Issa, tr. fr. the Japanese by Hanako Fukuda.—HaW
New year's day. Unknown, tr. fr. the Japanese by Rose Fyleman.—JoA-4
New York. Léopold Sédar Senghor, tr. fr. the French by John Reed and Clive Wake.—AlPa
"**New** York. At first your beauty confused me, and your great long-legged golden girls." See New York
New York city
All around the town, sel. P. McGinley
"J's the jumping Jay-walker."—BrM
The avenue: N. Y. city. J. De Graft.—AlPa
Bottled: New York. H. Johnson.—AdPb
Chapter two. W. T. Scott.—RoIt
Invitation to Miss Marianne Moore. E. Bishop.—PlM
"A knife and a fork." Unknown.—EmN
New York. L. S. Senghor.—AlPa
New York skyscrapers. J. Mbiti.—AbM
125th street. L. Hughes.—HoCs
"Reading Yeats I do not think." L. Ferlinghetti.—PlM

Review from Staten island. G. C. Oden.—AdPb
Saturday in New York. A. Beresford.—ToM
Summer: West Side. J. Updike.—PeS
The tropics in New York. C. McKay.—AdPb—RoIt
Wonderful New York. C. Meyer.—JoV
New York skyscrapers. John Mbiti.—AbM
Newark, New Jersey
Newark, for now. C. M. Rodgers.—AdPb
Newark, for now. Carolyn M. Rodgers.—AdPb
Newberry, Thomas
The great merchant, Dives Pragmaticus, cries his wares.—OpOx
Newman, Joseph S.
Baby Kate.—BrM
News
"Brave news is come to town." Mother Goose.—AlC
How I brought the good news from Aix to Ghent (or vice versa). R. J. Yeatman and W. C. Sellar.—LiS
How they brought the good news from Ghent to Aix. R. Browning.—LiS
In Hardin county, 1809. L. E. Thompson.—CoPt
"What's the news of the day." Mother Goose.—AlC—MiMg
When I brought the news. J. P. Donleavy.—CoPt
"The **news** is yellowing in the rain." See The paper in the meadow
Newsboy. Lois Lenski.—LeC
Newsletter from my mother. Michael S. Harper.—AdPb
Newsome, Mary Effie Lee
Morning light (the dew-drier).—AdPb
Quoits.—RoIt
Newspapers
For children if they'll take them. X. J. Kennedy.—RoIt
The morning star. Primus St John.—AdPb
Newsboy. L. Lenski.—LeC
Outside the window. R. Froman.—FrSp
They are killing all the young men. D. Henderson.—AdPb
Newton, Sir Isaac (about)
Epitaph intended for Sir Isaac Newton.—RoIt
Intended for Sir Isaac Newton.—LiWw
Newts. See Salamanders
"**Next** I came to the manna, the heavenly gift of honey." See The Georgics
"The **next** time you go to the zoo." See Anthropoids
"**Next** to of course god America i." E. E. Cummings.—HiN—PeS
Nez Perce Indians. See Indians of the Americas—Nez Perce
"**NHTPOMY.**" Unknown.—MoBw
Niagara. See The people, yes
Nicarchus. See also Nikarchos
"I boiled hot water in an urn."—JoA-4
"**Nicely,** nicely, nicely, nicely, there away in the east." Unknown, tr. fr. the Acoma.—ClFc
"**Nicely** while it is raining." Unknown, tr. fr. the Acoma.—ClFc
Nichiporum, Tanya
Good morning.—MoM
Nicholas, Saint. See Santa Claus
"**Nicholas** Grouch." Dennis Lee.—LeA
Nicholl, Louise Townsend
The going of the snow.—RoIt
Nichols, Robert
The full heart.—CoPu
Nicholson, Norman
Cleator Moor.—ToM
Cowper.—PlM
Rising five.—ToM
To the river Duddon.—PaP
Wales.—PaP
Weather ear.—ToM
"**Niddy,** niddy, noddy." Unknown.—EmN
Nigeria—History
Night song. J. P. Clark.—AlPa (sel.)
Skulls and cups. J. P. Clark.—AlPa
Song. J. P. Clark.—AlPa
"**Nigger.**" See The true import of present dialogue, black vs. Negro
Night
Afraid of the dark. S. Silverstein.—SiW
All about fireflies all about. D. McCord.—McS
Amen. R. W. Thomas.—AdPb
Auld Daddy Darkness. J. Ferguson.—OpOx
The black panther. K. Raikin.—MoM
Boats at night. E. Shanks.—MaFw
The clock ticks. E. Merriam.—MeO
Coyote's night. P. George.—AlW
The day is done. H. W. Longfellow.—RoIt
Dream variation. L. Hughes.—AdM—AdPb—HoD
"Everyone is asleep." Seifu-Jo.—HoH
For Bill Hawkins, a black militant. W. J. Harris.—AdPb
Four glimpses of night. F. M. Davis.—AdM (sel.)—AdPb
Frost at midnight. S. T. Coleridge.—PaF
The full heart. R. Nichols.—CoPu
Full moonlight in spring. W. S. Merwin.—CoPu
Hearing the wind at night. M. Swenson.—HaWr
The hens. E. M. Roberts.—LiLc—UnGb
Hidden treasure. B. Katz.—HoCs
In the great night. Unknown.—BiI
In the night. M. Chute.—ChRu
Into blackness softly. M. Evans.—AdPb
Inversely. K. Rexroth.—MoT
Kiss. A. Young.—AdPb
Lines for a night driver. R. K. Dufault.—HaWr
"Long and lonely December night." Hwang Chini.—BaSs
"Luminous silence. . . . " A. Atwood.—AtM
"Moon." K. Kuskin.—KuN
Moonlight night: Carmel. L. Hughes.—HoD

"The **night** will never stay." Eleanor Farjeon.—JoA-4—OpOx
The **night-wind.** Emily Brontë.—PaF
Night wind in fall. W. R. Moses.—HiN
The **nightfishing.** W. S. Graham.—MaFw (sel.)
The **nightingale** and glow-worm. William Cowper.—RoIt
"The **nightingale,** in dead of night." See The happy nightingale
"A **nightingale,** that all day long." See The nightingale and glow-worm
Nightingales
The happy nightingale. Unknown.—OpOx
The nightingale and glow-worm. W. Cowper.—RoIt
Ode to a nightingale. J. Keats.—LiS
On a poetess. G. M. Hopkins.—CoPu
To a nightingale. J. Keats.—PaF
"When nightingales burst." Jurin.—BeM
"**Nightingales'** tongues, your majesty." See Figgie hobbin
"The **nightly** drinking, why should I oppose it." See Hymn
Nightsong. Carl Sandburg.—SaT
Nightsong city. Dennis Brutus.—AlPa
Nikarchos. See also Nicarchus
Fortunatus the R.A.—LiWw
Nikki-Rosa. Nikki Giovanni.—AdPb
Nikogosian, David
The wild flower and the rose.—MoM
Nikogosian, Maya
Erevan is my city.—MoM
A riddle.—MoM
"Three little birches."—MoM
Niles, John Jacob
The carol of the birds.—LaS
I wonder as I wander. Unknown.—JoA-4; also version by John Jacob Niles.—LaS
"Jesus, Jesus, rest your head."—LaS
Nimrod (about)
The seed of Nimrod. De Leon Harrison.—AdPb
"**Nine** grenadiers, with bayonets in their guns." See The dream of a boy who lived at Nine Elms
"**Nine** out of ten times." See Ghetto
"**Nine** swallows sat on a telephone wire." See The swallows
"**Nine** white chickens come." See A black November turkey
"**Ninety-nine** apes with their tales on fire." See A fog full of apes
Niño leading an old man to market. Leonard Nathan.—HiN
"The **ninth,** last half; the score was tied." See Dorlan's home walk
"**Nipper** and the Nanny-Goat." See Off to Yakima
Nketia, J. H. Kwabena
Drum chant. tr.—AlPa
"Hail him." tr.—AlPa
Lament. tr.—AlPa
Love songs. tr.—AlPa
Song for an absent chief. tr.—AlPa
"**Nnoonya** mwana wange." Unknown, tr. fr. the Luganda by W. Moses Serwadda.—SeS
Nnyonyi. Unknown, tr. fr. the Luganda by W. Moses Serwadda.—SeS
"**No.**" See War
"**No** chains." See Find my father with freedom
"**No** closer the glove clings to the sweaty hand." See Little-league baseball fan
No dawns. Julianne Perry.—AdPb
No difference. Shel Silverstein.—SiW
"**No** dust have I to cover me." See An inscription by the sea
"**No** friends nor enemies." Juanita Bryant.—JoV
No heat today. Lois Lenski.—LeC
No hiding place. Unknown.—BrW
"**No,** I have never found." See Places, loved ones
"**No** lovelier hills than thine have laid." See England
"**No** man is born into the world whose work." See The hands of toil
"**No** man's a jester playing Shakespeare." See The king must die
"**No** matter how hard I try to forget you, you always came back to my thoughts." See I cannot forget you
"**No** matter how he ties." Sasha Aleksandrovsky, tr. fr. the Russian by Miriam Morton.—MoM
"**No** matter what anyone says." Unknown.—MoBw
"**No** matter what we are and who." See Routine
"**No** matter where I travel." See Who am I (II)
No moon, no star. Babette Deutsch.—HaWr
No new music. Stanley Crouch.—AdPb
"**No** new poems his brush will trace." See On hearing someone sing a poem by Yüan Chēn
No one. Lilian Moore.—MoSm
"**No** one at Sam's place." See Patriarchs
"**No** one could be. . . . " Issa, tr. fr. the Japanese by Hanako Fukuda.—HaW
"**No** one could have a blacker tail." See Othello Jones dresses for dinner
No one else. Elaine Laron.—ThF
"**No** one for spelling at a loss is." See Rhinoceroses
"**No** one's going to read." See A dance for militant dilettantes
"**No** one's hangin' stockin's up." See Merry
No present like the time. David McCord.—McFm
No pretending. Robert Froman.—FrSp
No sale. Robert Froman.—FrSp
"**No** sun—no moon." See November
"**No** thing." See Cathexis
"**No** time like the present, they used to say." See No present like the time
No TV. Lilian Moore.—MoSm
No way out. Linda Curry.—JoV
Noah
The dog's cold nose. A. Guiterman.—CoPt

"A horse and a flea and three blind mice." Unknown.—TrG
"The horses run around." Unknown.—CoOh
"I am a pretty wench." Unknown.—TrG
"I boiled hot water in an urn." Nicarchus.—JoA-4
"I eat my peas with honey." Unknown.—BrM—TrG
"I found a silver dollar." D. Lee.—LeA
"I had a little pig." Unknown.—EmN
I met a man. Unknown.—RoIt
I saw a peacock. Unknown.—RoIt
"I saw a peacock with a fiery tail."—EmN
"I went to my grandfather's farm." Unknown.—EmN
"I went to the animal fair." Unknown.—EmN
"I will tell my daddy when he comes home." Unknown.—TrG
The ichthyosaurus. I. F. Bellows.—CoOr
"Ickle me, pickle me, tickle me too." S. Silverstein.—SiW
"If a pig wore a wig." C. G. Rossetti.—JoA-4
"If I were an elephant." N. M. Bodecker.—BoL
If you should meet. D. Lee.—LeA
"In fir tar is." Unknown.—AlC
The ingenious little old man. J. Bennett.—BrM—CoOr
"The island of Llince." N. M. Bodecker.—BoL
"The island of Yarrow." N. M. Bodecker.—BoL
"It's once I courted as pretty a lass." Unknown.—TrG
"It's raining, it's pouring." Unknown.—EmN
A jam fish. E. A. Parry.—OpOx
"Jay bird, jay bird." Unknown.—EmN
The jellyfish. O. Nash.—CoOh
"Jerry Hall." Unknown.—TrG
Jimmy Jet and his TV Set. S. Silverstein.—SiW
Joey. S. Silverstein.—SiW
Jolly red nose. F. Beaumont and J. Fletcher.—RoIt
Nose, nose, jolly red nose.—TrG
"Jolly Roger lived up a tree." Unknown.—TrG
Josephine. A. Resnikoff.—CoOr
"King Arthur and his knights." R. Williams.—CoOr
"King Tut." X. J. Kennedy.—KeO—LiWw
"Let's marry, said the cherry." N. M. Bodecker.—BoL
"Little Hermogenes is so small." Lucilius.—JoA-4
A long hard day. J. Ciardi.—CiFs
"Look at Marcus and take warning." Lucilius.—JoA-4
The loser. S. Silverstein.—SiW
Malice at Buckingham palace. S. Milligan.—CoOh
"The man in the wilderness asked of me." Mother Goose.—AlC
"A man in the wilderness."—RoIt
"A man in the wilderness asked me."—JoA-4
The man of Thessaly. Unknown.—RoIt
"Milkman, milkman, where have you been." Unknown.—TrG
Miss Bitter. N. M. Bodecker.—BoL
Mr Beecher. N. M. Bodecker.—BoL
Mister Beers. H. Lofting.—BrM
Mr Docer. N. M. Bodecker.—BoL
Mr Kartoffel. J. Reeves.—BrM
Mr Mixup tells a story. D. McCord.—McS
Mr Slatter. N. M. Bodecker.—BoL
"Moll-in-the-wad and I fell out." Unknown.—TrG
The monotony song. T. Roethke.—CoOr
The moon is up. Unknown.—RoIt
"Most people don't know it." Unknown.—EmN
"Mother, may I go and swim." Unknown.—TrG
"Mumbo Jumbo." D. Lee.—LeA
"Nicholas Grouch." D. Lee.—LeA
Nonsense. N. Koralova.—MoM
A norrible tale. Unknown.—CoOr
An odd fellow. L. Carroll.—BrM (sel.)
Off to Yakima. L. F. Jackson.—BrM
"Oh, mother, I shall be married to Mr Punchinello." Mother Goose.—AlC
Mr Punchinello.—JoA-4
"An old grey horse stood on the wall." Unknown.—TrG
Old Joe Clarke. Unknown.—CoOh
"Old Mrs Thing-um-e-bob." C. Causley.—CaF
"Old Quin Queeribus." N. B. Turner.—BrM
On Tuesdays I polish my uncle. D. Lee.—LeA
"Once I had a rooster." Unknown.—EmN
"Once upon a time." Unknown.—EmN
"One winter night in August." X. J. Kennedy.—KeO
"The ostrich is a silly bird." M. E. W. Freeman.—BrM
"Out in the garden pickin' peas." Unknown.—EmN
Parson Gray. O. Goldsmith.—RoIt
Pasha Bailey Ben. W. S. Gilbert.—LiWw
"Psychapoo." D. Lee.—LeA
The puffin. R. W. Wood.—CoOh
"Quack, said the billy goat." C. Causley.—CaF
"Quail." Unknown.—BoI
Questions, quistions & quoshtions. S. Milligan.—CoOr
Rain. S. Silverstein.—CoOr—SiW
"Rain or hail." E. E. Cummings.—LiWw
Rhyme for a simpleton. Unknown.—RoIt
The roof. G. Burgess.—CoOr
"Said the monkey to the donkey." Unknown.—TrG
"Scallywag and Gollywog." H. Lofting.—BrM

"The longest nose." S. Silverstein.—SiW
The nose and the eyes. W. Cowper.—RoIt
"Noses are red." Unknown.—EmN
"Peter White will ne'er go right." Mother Goose.—AlC
"The razor-tailed wren." S. Silverstein.—SiW
"St Dunstan, as the story goes." Mother Goose.—MiMg—TrG
The song of Quoodle. G. K. Chesterton.—JoA-4
"There is a young lady, whose nose (continually prospers)." E. Lear
Limericks.—JoA-4
Nonsenses.—OpOx
"There lived an old woman at Lynn." Unknown
Three wonderful old women.—OpOx
"There was a young lady, whose nose (was so long)." E. Lear
Limericks.—JoA-4
"There was an old man on whose nose." E. Lear
Limericks.—JoA-4
Warning. S. Silverstein.—SiW
A winter scene. R. Whittemore.—HiN
"**Noses** are red." Unknown.—EmN
"The **noses** are running at our house." See A winter scene
"**Not** a line of her writing have I." See Thoughts of Phena
"**Not** a man is stirring." See Riding at daybreak
Not again. Pete Brown.—CoPu
"**Not** all the nests are empty." See Winter nests
"**Not** by hammering the furious word." See Harlem riot, 1943
Not forever on earth. Unknown, tr. fr. the Aztec by Angel Garibay.—BiI
"**Not** long after the earth was made." Natalia Belting.—BeWi
Not mine. Myra Cohn Livingston.—LiM
"**Not** of the sunlight." See Merlin and the gleam—Follow the gleam
"**Not** quite." See At breakfast
Not so simple. Shin Shalom, tr. fr. the Hebrew by Robert Mezey.—MeP
Not-things. Russell Hoban.—HoE
"**Not** to have any *hair* is called." Richard Wilbur.—WiO
"**Not** writ in water nor in mist." See For John Keats, apostle of beauty
Not yet enough. Unknown, tr. fr. the Yoruba by S. A. Babalola.—AlPa
"**Not** yet half drest." See To a late poplar
Note to my neighbor. Phyllis McGinley.—LiWw
Note to Wang Wei. John Berryman.—PlM
Notes for a movie script. M. Carl Holman.—AdPb
Notes found near a suicide. Frank Horne.—AdPb
Nothing gold can stay. Robert Frost.—HiN—MoT
"**Nothing** in the voice of the cicada." Bashō, tr. fr. the Japanese by R. H. Blyth.—MaFw
Nothing is. Sun Ra.—AdPb
"**Nothing** is so beautiful as spring." See Spring
Nothingest. Robert Froman.—FrSp
The **notorious** glutton. Ann Taylor.—OpOx
Nova Scotia
First death in Nova Scotia. E. Bishop.—HiN
November
"The fields of November." M. Van Doren.—HaWr
A night in November. T. Hardy.—PlP
November ("The landscape sleeps in mist from morn till noon") J. Clare.—MaFw (sel.)
November ("The mellow year is hastening to its close") H. Coleridge.—PaF
November ("No sun—no moon") T. Hood.—RoIt
November ("Sybil of months, and worshipper of winds") J. Clare.—PaF
November ("Thank you for the things we have") L. Clifton.—ClE
The willows of Massachusetts. D. Levertov.—HaWr
November ("The landscape sleeps in mist from morn till noon") John Clare.—MaFw
November ("The mellow year is hastening to its close") Hartley Coleridge.—PaF
November ("No sun—no moon") Thomas Hood.—RoIt
November ("Sybil of months, and worshipper of winds") John Clare.—PaF
November ("Thank you for the things we have") Lucille Clifton.—ClE
November blue. Alice Meynell.—PaP
"**Now** a spring rain falls." Chiyo, tr. fr. the Japanese by Harry Behn.—BeM
"**Now** all aloud the wind and rain." See The watercress seller
"**Now** another day is breaking." See Morning prayer
"**Now** as I was young and easy under the apple boughs." See Fern hill
"**Now** at the end I smell the smells of spring." See Exit Molloy
"**Now** children may." See May
"**Now** do we pass our hands through your tears in sympathy." See Requickening
"**Now** do you suppose that bee." See The buzzing doubt
"**Now** every day the bracken browner grows." See September
"**Now** fades the last long streak of snow." See In memoriam
"**Now**, from today on." Issa, tr. fr. the Japanese by Hanako Fukuda.—HaW
"**Now** goes the plow-man to his merry toyle." See The four seasons of the year—Spring
"**Now** here it is straight." See Straight talk (from a surfer)
"**Now** his nose's bridge is broken, one eye." See On Hurricane Jackson
"**Now** I am dead you sing to me." See An upbraiding
"**Now** I am seven mama can stay." See August

"**Now** I go down here and bring up a moon." See Auctioneer
"**Now** is the newborn time of year." See Spring dew
"**Now** is the time for the burning of the leaves." See The burning of the leaves
"**Now,** my friends, please hear." See The song of a dream
"**Now** my legs begin to walk." See Thaw in the city
"**Now** no more the paleface strangers." See Rejoinder
"**Now,** not a tear begun." See A woman mourned by daughters
"**Now,** now the mirth comes." Robert Herrick.—MaF
"**Now** over the path." See The odyssey of a snail
"**Now,** please sing the chorus of this song with me." See Not yet enough
Now poem. For us. Sonia Sanchez.—AdPb
"**Now** rock the boat to a fare-thee-well." See Rites of passage
"**Now,** someone else can tell you how." See No one else
"**Now** tell me, tell me what you think of this world." See What kind of world is this
Now that I am forever with child. Audre Lorde.—AdPb
"**Now** that night is gone." Buson, tr. fr. the Japanese by Harry Behn.—BeM
"**Now** the bright morning star, day's harbinger." See Song on May morning
"**Now** the day is over." Sabine Baring-Gould.—OpOx
"**Now** the drowsy sunshine." See Evening
"**Now** the hungry lion roars." See A midsummer-night's dream
"**Now** the man has a child." Karai Senryū, tr. fr. the Japanese by Geoffrey Bownas and Alexander Thwaite.—MaFw
"**Now** the snow." See Winter
"**Now** this is the day." See Presenting an infant to the sun
"**Now** this was the reply Odysseus made." See The odyssey
"**Now** today I have been greatly startled by your voice coming through the forest to this opening." See At the wood's edge
Now we are sick. J. B. Morton.—CoPu—LiS
Now we come southwards. Unknown, tr. fr. the Tewa by Herbert J. Spinden.—BiI
"**Now** we've made a child." See And what about the children
"**Now** what is he after below in the street." See The bold unbiddable child
"**Now** winter as a shrivelled scroll." See Winter
"**Now** winter nights enlarge." Thomas Campion.—MaFw—RoIt
"**Now** with the coming in of the spring the days will stretch a bit." See The County Mayo
"**Now** you're married and you must be good." Unknown.—EmN
"**Nowhere** in the world." See Perfect Arthur
Nowlan, Alden
I, Icarus.—HiN
"**Now's** the time for mirth and play." See Hymn for Saturday
Noyes, Alfred
The admiral's ghost.—JoA-4
Daddy fell into the pond.—BrM
The rustling of grass.—PaF
The skunk.—BrM
A song of Sherwood.—JoA-4
Nsangi. Unknown, tr. fr. the Luganda by W. Moses Serwadda.—SeS
"**Nsangi** my own baby." See Nsangi
Number 5—December. David Henderson.—AdB
#4. Doughtry Long.—AdM—AdPb
A **number** of words. Eve Merriam.—MeF
Number 7. Lawrence Ferlinghetti.—PeS
Number 20. Lawrence Ferlinghetti.—PeS
Numbers. Elizabeth Madox Roberts.—LiLc
Numerous Celts. J. C. Squire.—LiS
Nuns
The convent. S. O'Sullivan.—CoPi
Heaven-haven. G. M. Hopkins.—JoA-4
House guest. E. Bishop.—HiN
Nursery play
"Adam and Eve and Pinch-me-tight." Mother Goose.—AlC
The baby's dance. A. Taylor.—OpOx
"Bimbo, bombo, tomkin pie." C. Watson.—WaF
Blind man's buff. Unknown.—JoA-4
Bouncing song. D. Lee.—LeA
"A farmer went trotting upon his grey mare." Mother Goose.—JoA-4
The five toes. Unknown.—JoA-4
"Here comes a candle to light you to bed." Mother Goose.—AlC
"Here's Tom Thumb." Mother Goose.—TucMgl
Hide and seek. Unknown.—EmN
"I am a gold lock." Mother Goose.—JoA-4
"I went up one pair of stairs." Mother Goose.—JoA-4
"If you are a gentleman." Unknown.—TrG
"Jack be nimble." Mother Goose.—JoA-4
"Lady Queen Anne she sits in the sun." Mother Goose.—JoA-4
"London Bridge is broken down." Mother Goose.—JoA-4
"Nanny banny bumblebee." C. Watson.—WaF
"Nnoonya mwana wange." Unknown.—SeS
"Oh, the brave old Duke of York." Mother Goose.—JoA-4
"Pat-a-cake, pat-a-cake, baker's man." Mother Goose.—JoA-4
Pop goes the weasel. Mother Goose.—JoA-4
Queen Nefertiti. Unknown.—NeA
"Ride away, ride away." Mother Goose.—MiMg
"See-saw sacradown." Mother Goose.—JoA-4
Singa songa. D. Lee.—LeA

O

"**O** 'Melia, my dear, this does everything crown." See The ruined maid
"**O** merciful God, hear this our request." See A prayer to be said when thou goest to bed
"**O** Merlin in your crystal cave." See Merlin
"**O** Mistress mine, where are you roaming." See Twelfth night—Sweet-and-twenty
"**O** moon, why must you." Koyo, tr. fr. the Japanese by Harry Behn.—LiWw
"**Oh,** mother, I shall be married to Mr Punchinello." Mother Goose.—AlC
Mr Punchinello.—JoA-4
"**O** mother, mother, what is happiness." See The sonnet-ballad
"**O** my agèd Uncle Arly." See Incidents in the life of my Uncle Arly
"**Oh,** my boat can swiftly float." See The queen of Connemara
"**Oh** my boy: Jesus." See Confession stone
"**O,** my dark Rosaleen." See Dark Rosaleen
"**Oh** my dear, what a cold you've got." Mother Goose.—TucMgl
"**O,** my good Lord's done been here." See My good Lord's done been here
"**Oh** my goodness, oh my dear." Clyde Watson.—WaF
"**Oh** my Lord." See My Lord, what a morning
"**O** my trade it is the rarest one." See The stranger's song
"**Oh,** never marry Ishmael." See Song for unbound hair
"**O** nuclear wind, when wilt thou blow." Paul Dehn.—LiS
"**Oh** our Mother the Earth oh our Father the Sky." See Song of the sky loom
"**Oh** Ozidi my man, my man, my man, my man." See The Ozidi saga—A lament
"**O** passenger, pray list and catch." See The levelled churchyard
"**O** penguin, do you ever try." See Penguin
"**O** possum, I followed." See Opossum
"**O** quick quick quick, quick hear the song-sparrow." See Cape Ann
"**Oh,** rare Harry Parry." Mother Goose.—HoMg
"**O** say, what is that thing called light." See The blind boy
"**O,** she walked unaware of her own increasing beauty." See She walked unaware
"**O** she was the handsome corpse, he said." See Moloney remembers the resurrection of Kate Finucane
"**O** sidelong glance, O dazzling dark eyes." Louise Labé, tr. fr. the French by Judith Thurman.—ThI
"**Oh,** sing a song of phosphates." See Boston nursery rhymes—Rhyme for a chemical baby
"**O** small bird wakening." See Bring the day
"**O** soft embalmer of the still midnight." See Sonnet to sleep
"**Oh,** somewhere there are people who." See Midsummer melancholy
"**O** suitably-attired-in-leather-boots." See Fragment of a Greek tragedy
"**O,** sweep of stars over Harlem streets." See Stars
"**O** sweet Saint Bride of the." See A milking song
"**Oh,** that last day in Lucknow fort." See The relief of Lucknow
"**O** that moon last night." Teitoku, tr. fr. the Japanese by Harry Behn.—BeM
"**O** that the peats would cut themselves." See Hebrides crofter's prayer
"**O** that thou wert as my brother." See The song of Solomon—The fire of love
"**Oh,** the brave old Duke of York." Mother Goose.—JoA-4
"**O** the cuckoo she's a pretty bird." Mother Goose.—AlC
"**Oh,** the Milky Way." Issa, tr. fr. the Japanese by Hanako Fukuda.—HaW
"**O** the opal and the sapphire of that wandering western sea." See Beeny cliff
"**O** the raggedy man, he works fer Pa." See The raggedy man
"**O** the spring will come." See The spring will come
"**Oh,** the swift plunge into the cool, green dark." See Swimmers
"**Oh** the thumb-sucker's thumb." See Thumb
"**Oh** the white seagull, the wild seagull." See The seagull
"**Oh,** the wind is brisk and biting." See Christmas shoppers
"**O,** then, I see Queen Mab hath been with you." See Romeo and Juliet
"**Oh,** they found her now." See Hokku/haikai/haiku
"**Oh** this is." See Fog
O thou seer, go, flee thee away. Chaim Nachman Bialik, tr. fr. the Hebrew by Robert Mezey and Shula Starkman.—MeP
"**Oh** thou, Tzacol, Bitol." See Prayer
"**O** thou, who lately closed my eyes." See A morning hymn
"**Oh,** 'tis of a bold major a tale I'll relate." See The Longford legend
O to be a dragon. Marianne Moore.—JoA-4
"**Oh** to be in England." See Home thoughts from abroad
"**O,** to have a little house." See An old woman of the roads
"**Oh** trees, say something." See Speak to me
"**O,** walk together children." See Walk together children
"**O** warmth of summer sweeping over the land." Unknown, fr. the Thule Eskimo.—LeIb
"**O,** were you on the mountain, or saw you my love." See Were you on the mountain
"**O** what a beautiful city." Unknown.—BrW
"**O** what a tangled web we weave." See A word of encouragement
"**O,** what can ail thee, knight-at-arms." See La belle dame sans merci
"**Oh** what do you do, poor Angus." See Poor Angus

O what is that sound. W. H. Auden.—MaFw—ToM
"**O** what is that sound which so thrills the ear." See O what is that sound
"**O**, what would people say if you." See Lizard
"**O** what's the weather in a beard." See Dinky
"**Oh**, where do you come from." See Little raindrops
" '**O** where have you been, my long, long love.' " See The daemon lover
"**Oh**, who is so merry, so merry, heigh ho." See The light-hearted fairy
"**Oh**, who would be a puddin'." See Puddin' song
"**O** why do you walk through the fields in gloves." See To a fat lady seen from the train
"**O** why was I born with a different face." William Blake.—CoPu
"**O** wild west wind thou breath of autumn's being." See Ode to the west wind
"**O** wind, rend open the heat." See Heat
"**O** woman of three cows, agra, don't let your tongue thus rattle." See The woman of three cows
"**O** woman passing by." See Kaleeba
"**O** year, grow slowly. Exquisite, holy." See Slow spring
"**O**, young Lochinvar is come out of the west." See Marmion—Lochinvar
The **oak** and the ash. Unknown.—RoIt
"The **oak** is called the king of trees." See Trees
Oak trees
"Deep in earth's opaque mirror." From Symmetries and asymmetries. W. H. Auden.—MaFw
Dodona's oaks were still. P. MacDonogh.—CoPi
"Don't worry if your job is small." Unknown.—BrM
Lu Yün's lament. H. Read.—PlM
My own true family. T. Hughes.—HuMf
Oda oak oracle. T. Gabre-Melkin.—AlPa (sel.)
Single majesty. M. Van Doren.—RoIt
Spring oak. G. Kinnell.—CoPu
Survivor. A. MacLeish.—HiN
Oakman, John
The glutton.—OpOx
O'Bolger, T. D.
The counsels of O'Riordan, the rann maker.—CoPi
Obolus. Tchicaya U Tam'si, tr. fr. the French by Gerald Moore.—AlPa (sel.)
The **observation.** Donovan Leitch.—MoG
"**Occasions** drew me early to this city." See Samson Agonistes
Occupations. See also names of occupations, as Carpenters and carpentry
Green broom. Unknown.—CoPt
I hear America singing. W. Whitman.—RoIt
"Moving through the silent crowd." S. Spender.—ToM
Parents are people. C. Hall.—ThF
The ploughboy in luck. Unknown.—RoIt
Preoccupation. Unknown.—AlPa
Street window. C. Sandburg.—SaT
"What will my husband be." Unknown.—EmN
Ocean
Albatross. J. Collins.—MoG
At sea. E. Merriam.—MeO
At the ocean. E. Merriam.—MeO
"Beast of the sea." Unknown.—LeIb
"Bobby Shaftoe's gone to sea." Mother Goose.—JoA-4
Christmas at sea. R. L. Stevenson.—CoPt—RoIt
"The dead man dragged from the sea." C. Gardner.—AdPb
Descent. E. Merriam.—MeO
The Eddystone light. Unknown.—CoPt
The even sea. M. Swenson.—HaWr
German shepherd. M. C. Livingston.—LiM
"The great sea." Unknown.—BiI
The harpooning. T. Walker.—HaWr
"Have you seen the sea roads." J. Oppenheim.—HoP
"Here lies the body of Jonathan Pound." Unknown.—TrG
"The horses of the sea." C. G. Rossetti.—LiLc—RoIt
A hurricane at sea. M. Swenson.—HaWr
I am writing this at sea. J. Ciardi.—CiFs
"I walked on the ice of the sea." Unknown.—LeIb
An inscription by the sea. E. A. Robinson.—CoPu
Long trip. L. Hughes.—HoD
Look, the sea. W. Zorach.—AdP
Marine nocturne. T. U. Tam'si.—AlPa
"The moon almost full." A. Atwood.—AtM
My granny. T. Hughes.—HuMf
"O billows bounding far." A. E. Housman.—LiWw
Ocean. A. Stoutenburg.—HaWr
Old deep sing-song. C. Sandburg.—MaFw—SaT
On the ocean floor. X. J. Kennedy.—KeO
On this island. W. H. Auden.—MaFw—ToM
"Out fishing on the ocean." B. Pollack.—HoP
The owl critic. J. T. Fields.—CoPt
The parting. A. Rich.—HaWr
The path on the sea. I. Muller.—MoM
"A pretty boat." N. Tolstoy.—MoM
Sails, gulls, sky, sea. F. Holman.—HoI
Sandpipers. A. Fisher.—FiFo
"Scallywag and Gollywog." H. Lofting.—BrM
The sea ("And I have loved thee, Ocean, and my joy") Lord Byron.—RoIt
The sea ("Behold the wonders of the mighty deep") Unknown.—LiWw
The sea ("Ocean") M. Mongameli.—AlPa
The sea ("The sea, the sea, the open sea") B. Cornwall.—RoIt
Sea calm. L. Hughes.—HoD
A sea-dirge. L. Carroll.—LiPc
" . . . the sea fanning out." A. Atwood.—AtM
Sea-fever. J. Masefield.—JoA-4

Odors—*Continued*
Roll, river, roll. R. Froman.—FrSp
The skunk ("Jacko the Skunk, in black and white") A. Noyes.—BrM
The skunk ("Whenever you may meet a skunk") J. Prelutsky.—PrP
"A skunk sat on a stump." Unknown.—BrM—EmN
Smells. L. Lenski.—LeC
Sniffing. A. Fisher.—FiFo
The song of Quoodle. G. K. Chesterton.—JoA-4
SService SStation. R. Froman.—FrSp
Superstink. R. Froman.—FrSp
"That bottle of perfume that Willie sent." Unknown.—RoIt
This newly created world. Unknown.—BiI
"Violets, daffodils." E. J. Coatsworth.—CoPu
The wind blows from the sea. Unknown.—BiI
Yellow. D. McCord.—McAa—McS
Odysseus. See Ulysses
Odysseus. Chaim Guri, tr. fr. the Hebrew by Robert Mezey and Shula Starkman.—MeP
The **Odyssey,** sels. Homer, tr. fr. the Greek by Robert Fitzgerald
The boar hunt.—MaFw
"Now this was the reply Odysseus made."—PlM
The siren's song.—MoG
The **odyssey** of a snail. Federico García Lorca, tr. fr. the Spanish by Roy Campbell.—MaFw
Oeharu
"Snow, softly, slowly."—BeM
"**O'er** the wild gannet's bath." See Runilda's chant
"**Of** all the beasts." See The gnu family
"**Of** all the forms of life that still dwell in man as in a living ark." See Birds
"**Of** all the rides since the birth of time." See Skipper Ireson's ride
"**Of** all the saws I ever saw saw." Unknown.—EmN
"**Of** all the souls that stand create." Emily Dickinson.—ThI
"**Of** all the weathers wind is king." See King wind
Of bloom. Leah Goldberg, tr. fr. the Hebrew by Dom Moraes.—MeP
Of bombs and boys. Richard Corbin.—PeS
"**Of** course I find it fun to write." See Ballade: An easy one
"**Of** course the belly remains pure." See The belly remains
"**Of** Edenhall, the youthful Lord." See The luck of Edenhall
Of kings and things. Lillian Morrison.—HiN
"**Of** life and its ceasing to be, with changes of sea wind." See Blind angel
Of man and nature. Horace Mungin.—AdB
"**Of** priests we can offer a charmin' variety." See Father O'Flynn
Of the boy and butterfly. John Bunyan.—OpOx
Of the child with the bird on the bush. John Bunyan.—OpOx
"**Of** the islands, Puerto Rico." Unknown, tr. fr. the Spanish.—MoBw
"**Of** the three Wise Men." See Carol of the brown king
"**Of** white and tawny, black as ink." See Variation on a sentence
O'Faolain, Sean
Summer is gone. tr.—CoPi
Off and away. Robert Froman.—FrSp
Off for a hike. Aileen Fisher.—FiFo
"**Off** the coast of Ireland." See Seascape
Off the ground. Walter De La Mare.—CoPt
Off they flew. Aileen Fisher.—FiFo
Off to Yakima. Leroy F. Jackson.—BrM
Offering. Unknown, tr. fr. the Zuñi by Ruth Bunzel.—BiI
An **offering** of joy. Svetlana Eremina, tr. fr. the Russian by Miriam Morton.—MoM
"**Oft** I had heard of Lucy Gray." See Lucy Gray; or, Solitude
"**Oft,** in the stilly night." Thomas Moore.—CoPi
"**Often** I think of the beautiful town." See My lost youth
Ogden Nash gets all the cash. David McCord.—PlM
Ogilvie, Will H.
The death of Ben Hall.—CoPt
O'Grady, Desmond
Afternoon.—CoPi
O'Higgins, Myron
Two lean cats.—AdPb
Vaticide.—AdPb
Young poet.—AdPb
Ojenke. See Saxon, Alvin
"**Ojo** is his name, Ojo the trouble-lover." See The trouble-lover
O'John, Calvin
Afternoon and his unfinished poem.—AlW
"Dancing teepees."—AlW
Dirt road.—AlW
Doldrums.—AlW
"Good or bad."—AlW
"Half of my life."—AlW
Problems.—AlW
Speak to me.—AlW
"A tear rolled down my cheek."—AlW
That lonesome place.—AlW
This day is over.—AlW
Trees.—AlW
Water baby.—AlW
"You smiled."—AlW
"The **okapi** is shy and high-strung." See Can you copy
Okapis
Can you copy. M. A. Hoberman.—HoR
Okara, Gabriel
One night at Victoria beach.—AlPa
Piano and drums.—AlPa
"The snow flakes sail gently."—AlPa
Spirit of the wind.—AlPa
"**Okay** everybody, listen to this." Karla Kuskin.—KuN

"**Okay,** my starsick beauty." See Unknown shores
O'Keefe, Adelaide
Beasts and birds.—OpOx
The kite.—OpOx
Okeke, Uche
The home of images.—AlPa
Okigbo, Christopher
"For he was a shrub among the poplars."—AlPa
Lament of the drums.—AlPa (sel.)
Love apart.—AlPa
Moon mist.—AlPa
"The stars have departed."—AbM
Watermaid.—AlPa
"**Ol'** man Simon, planted a diamond." See The garden
"**Old** Abram Brown is dead and gone." Mother Goose.—AlC
Old age. See also Birthdays; Childhood recollections; Youth and age
Age. W. S. Landor.—CoPu
The aged aged man. From Through the looking-glass. L. Carroll.—LiPc—LiS—OpOx
Ways and means.—RoIt
Akjartoq's song of the olden days. Unknown.—LeIb
"Am I really old, as people say." Kim Jung-ku.—BaSs
Ambition. P. George.—AlW
Angry old men. B. Payne.—CoPi
At grass. P. Larkin.—HaWr
"Autographs are finger kisses." Unknown.—EmN
Blind old woman. C. Major.—AdPb
Casual lines. Su Shih.—MaFw
First or last. T. Hardy.—JoA-4
The forsaken. D. C. Scott.—CoPt
Ghosts. L. Lenski.—LeC
The grandfathers. D. Justice.—HiN
"He sees through stone." E. Knight.—AdPb
"I hold a rod in one hand." Woo Tahk.—BaSs
I'm just a stranger here, Heaven is my home. C. G. Clemmons.—AdPb
Imperialists in retirment. E. Lucie-Smith.—ToM
"In a poor old village." Lida.—MoM
"In old age." Unknown.—ClFc
"In the old man's eyes." Takahama Kyoshi.—MaFw
Jenny kissed me. L. Hunt.—LiS—RoIt
"King Solomon and King David." Unknown.—RoIt
A long life. L. Lenski.—LeC
"Loveliest of trees, the cherry now." From A Shropshire lad. A. E. Housman.—MaFw
Loveliest of trees.—JoA-4—PaF
Methuselah. Unknown.—RoIt
Mr Flood's party. E. A. Robinson.—CoPt
The moccasins of an old man. J. Carden.—AlW
Moonlight. S. Teasdale.—CoPu
"My body in the walls captived." W. Raleigh.—MaFw
Old Dan'l. L. A. G. Strong.—CoPu
Old man, the sweat lodge. P. George.—AlW
Old man's plea. P. George.—AlW
One flesh. E. Jennings.—ToM
"Remember, dear, when you grow old." Unknown.—EmN
Sandwriting. E. Merriam.—MeF
Schoolmaster. Y. Yevtushenko.—MaFw
Sebonwoma. C. A. A. Aidoo.—AlPa (sel.)
The song of the old mother. W. B. Yeats.—CoPi
Song of the old woman. Unknown.—LeIb
The span of life. R. Frost.—MaFw
Swineherd. E. N. Chuilleanáin.—CoPi
Talking to his drum. E. B. Mitchell.—AlW
Three old brothers. F. O'Connor.—CoPi
"Tonight I've watched." Sappho.—ThI
Warning. J. Joseph.—ToM
Weeksville women. E. Loftin.—AdPb
When you are old. W. B. Yeats.—MaFw
"When you are old and cannot see." Unknown.—EmN
"When you get old and blind." Unknown.—EmN
Wishes of an elderly man. W. Raleigh.—CoPu
"**Old** black ladies." See Weeksville women
Old black men. Georgia Douglas Johnson.—AdPb
Old black men say. James Emanuel.—AdM—AdPb
The **old** brown horse goes plodding." See Flower wagon
"**Old** Caspar had six sons so fine." Mother Goose, tr. fr. the German.—TucMg
Old Chang the crab. Unknown, tr. fr. the Chinese by I. T. Headland.—JoA-4
"The **old,** cold scold stole." Unknown.—EmN
"The **old** crow is getting slow." See Fast and slow
"**Old** Daddy Longlegs, harvestman." See Harvestman
Old Dan'l. L. A. G. Strong.—CoPu
Old deep sing-song. Carl Sandburg.—MaFw—SaT
"The **old** dog barks backward without getting up." See The span of life
"**Old** Eben Flood, climbing alone one night." See Mr Flood's party
The **old** familiar faces. Charles Lamb.—MoG
"**Old** Farmer Giles." Mother Goose.—TucMgl
"The **old** fence." See Fence
Old florist. Theodore Roethke.—HiN
"**Old** friend of man, and made." See Look: What am I
"**Old** Grandpa Fishkein." See A long life
"An **old** grey horse stood on the wall." Unknown.—TrG
Old Hogan's goat. Unknown.—BrM
"**Old** Hogan's goat was feeling fine." See Old Hogan's goat
Old Ironsides. Oliver Wendell Holmes.—RoIt
Old Joe Clarke. Unknown.—CoOh

"**Old** Joe Clarke, he had a house." See Old Joe Clarke
"**Old** King Cole." Mother Goose.—JoA-4
"**Old** lady, old lady." Unknown.—EmN
Old Lem. Sterling A. Brown.—AdPb
"An **old,** mad, blind, despised, and dying king." See England in 1819
The **old** man and Jim. James Whitcomb Riley.—CoPt
"**Old** man Chang, I've oft heard it said." See Old Chang the crab
"An **old** man in a lodge within a park." See Chaucer
"**Old** man Lazy." Unknown.—EmN
"The **old** man, listening to the careful." See The first snow of the year
"**Old** man/man black man." See Tony get the boys
"**Old** man never had much to say." See The old man and Jim
Old man, the sweat lodge. Phil George.—AlW
"**The** old man walks to me." See Glimpses #xii
"**Old** man weighed down with a bundle on your head." Chung Chui, tr. fr. the Korean by Chung Seuk Park and ad. by Virginia Olsen Baron.—BaSs
The **old** man who lived in the woods. Unknown.—RoIt
"**Old** man Woolworth put up a building." See Again
"The **old** mandarin." See Unearned increment
The **old** man's comforts and how he gained them. Robert Southey.—LiS—OpOx
An **old** man's herd—On the Friday before Christmas. Felice Holman.—HoI
Old man's plea. Phil George.—AlW
The **old-marrieds.** Gwendolyn Brooks.—AdPb
Old Meg. See Meg Merrilies
"**Old** Meg she was a gipsy." See Meg Merrilies
"The **old** men." Unknown, tr. fr. the Teton Sioux by Frances Densmore.—JoT
"**Old** Mr Parvenu gave a great ball." Corney Grain.—CoPu
"**Old** Mrs Thing-um-e-bob." Charles Causley.—CaF
"**Old** Molly Means was a hag and a witch." See Molly Means
"**Old** Mother Goose." Mother Goose.—JoA-4
"**Old** Mother Hubbard." See The comic adventures of Old Mother Hubbard and her dog
"**Old** Mother Hubbard." Mother Goose.—JoA-4
"**Old** Mother Roundabout." Mother Goose.—AlC
"**Old** Mother Shuttle." Mother Goose.—MiMg
"**Old** Mother Twitchett had but one eye." Unknown.—EmN
"**Old** Mother Witch fell in a ditch." Unknown.—EmN
The **old** navy. Frederick Marryat.—CoPt
"**Old** Noah once he built the ark." See One more river
Old October. Thomas Constable.—RoIt
"**Old** old lady." See Much nicer people
"**Old** Peter led a wretched life." See The perils of invisibility
The **old** pilot's death. Donald Hall.—ToM
"The **old** pond." Bashō, tr. fr. the Japanese by Hanako Fukuda.—HaW
"**Old** Quin Queeribus." Nancy Byrd Turner.—BrM
"**Old** rusty-belly thing will soon be gone." See The Sappa creek
The **old** school scold. Unknown.—BrM
"The **old** school scold sold." See The old school scold
"An **old** sea dog on a sailor's log." See The powerful eyes o' Jeremy Tait
Old Shellover. Walter De La Mare.—LiLc—OpOx
"**Old** Sir Simon the king." Mother Goose.—AlC
The **old** song. See Water babies—Young and old
"The **old** sow whistles." Unknown.—MoBw
An **old** story. Howard Nemerov.—CoPu
Old Tim Toole. David McCord.—McAa
"The **old** timer on the desert was gray." See The people, yes—Children of the desert
The **old** vicarage, Grantchester, sel. Rupert Brooke
  "I only know that you may lie."—PaP
Old Walt. Langston Hughes.—PlM
"**Old** Walt Whitman." See Old Walt
"The **old** watch: their." See Vapor trail reflected in the frog pond
Old winter. Thomas Noël.—RoIt
"**Old** winter sad, in snowy clad." See Old winter
An **old** woman. Charles Henry Ross.—OpOx
"The **old** woman across the way." See The whipping
An **old** woman of the roads. Padraic Colum.—RoIt
"**Old** woman, old woman (shall we go)." Mother Goose.—HoMg
An **old** woman remembers. Sterling A. Brown.—AdPb
The **old** woman who lived in a shoe. Joyce Johnson.—ThF
The **old** year. John Clare.—RoIt
"The **old** year now is fled." Unknown.—MaF
"The **old** year's gone away." See The old year
"**Oldsmobile,** Chevrolet, Studebaker, Ford." Unknown.—EmN
Oldys, William
  On a fly drinking from his cup.—RoIt
"**Olé.** All yea. All no. No. He who is getting old and slow." See Spanish music in winter
Olga
  "I look out of my window."—MoM
  "My teddy stands in the nook."—MoM
Oliphaunt. See The adventures of Tom Bombadil
The **olive** tree. Natan Alterman, tr. fr. the Hebrew by Robert Friend.—MeP
Olive trees
  The olive tree. N. Alterman.—MeP

Oliver, Mary
Mountain road.—RoIt
Stark boughs on the family tree.—PeS
"**Oliver** Oglethorpe ogled an owl and oyster." Unknown.—EmN
"**Olley,** olley outs in free." Unknown.—EmN
Olsen, Charles
These days.—MoT
Omaha Indians. See Indians of the Americas—Omaha
Omaha, Nebraska
August 24, 1963—1:00 A.M.—Omaha. D. Whitewing.—AlW
O'Meally, Bob
"I was jus."—AdM
"It aint no."—AdM
Omen ("By daylight a fire fell") Unknown, tr. fr. the Aztec by Bernardino de Sahagún.—BiI
Omen ("By night a voice was heard in the air") Unknown, tr. fr. the Aztec by Bernardino de Sahagún.—BiI
Omen ("A naked sun, a yellow sun") Birago Diop.—MaFw
Omens. See also Prophecies
"Haik, the white bird of omen." Unknown.—ClFc
The loons are singing. Unknown.—BiS
Omen ("By daylight a fire fell") Unknown.—BiI
Omen ("By night a voice was heard in the air") Unknown.—BiI
Omen ("A naked sun, a yellow sun") B. Diop.—MaFw
"Presentiment—is that long shadow—on the lawn." E. Dickinson.—ThI
Song. Unknown.—BiI
"To the medicine man's house they have led me." Unknown.—ClFc
On a bad singer. Samuel Taylor Coleridge.—LiWw
"**On** a bare branch." Bashō, tr. fr. the Japanese by Geoffrey Bownas and Anthony Thwaite.—MaFw
On a bike. Myra Cohn Livingston.—LiM
"**On** a cold sand dune in the desert." See Caterpillar on a pillar
On a distant prospect of Eton college. Thomas Gray.—PaP (sel.)
"**On** a flat road runs the well-trained runner." See The runner
On a fly drinking from his cup. William Oldys.—RoIt
On a friend's escape from drowning off the Norfolk coast. George Barker.—ToM
"**On** a green, green hill." Unknown, tr. fr. the Danish by N. M. Bodecker.—BoI
On a hand. Hilaire Belloc.—CoPu
"**On** a hot July day." See Lay-away
"**On** a ladder, in an old checkered skirt." See Washing windows
On a little boy's endeavouring to catch a snake. Thomas Foxton.—OpOx
"**On** a little piece of wood." See Mr and Mrs Spikky Sparrow
On a poetess. Gerard Manley Hopkins.—CoPu
On a railroad right of way. Carl Sandburg.—SaT
On a school-teacher. Unknown, tr. fr. the Greek by Dudley Fitts.—LiWw
On a spaniel called Beau killing a young bird. William Cowper.—RoIt
On a squirrel crossing the road in autumn, in New England. Richard Eberhart.—JoA-4—RoIt
On a summer's day. See "I stood tiptoe upon a little hill"
"**On** a summer's day in the month of May." See The big Rock Candy mountain
On a sundial. Hilaire Belloc.—CoPu—LiWw
"**On** a tree by a river a little tom-tit." See The Mikado—Titwillow
On a waiter. David McCord.—LiWw
"**On** a winter night." See Christmas eve
"**On** an oak in autumn." See Survivor
On Andrew Turner. Robert Burns.—CoPu
On Apis the prizefighter. Lucilius, tr. fr. the Latin by Dudley Fitts.—LiWw
On being asked for a war poem. William Butler Yeats.—CoPi
On being chosen poet of Vermont. Robert Frost.—PlM
On being too right to be polite. John Ciardi.—CiFs
On buying a dog. Edgar Klauber.—CoPu
On Dr Lettsom by himself. John Coakley Lettsom.—CoPu
On Eastner knoll. John Masefield.—MaFw
"**On** far hills." Takahama Kyoshi, tr. fr. the Japanese by Geoffrey Bownas and Anthony Thwaite.—MaFw
On first looking into Chapman's Homer. John Keats.—PlM
On getting a natural. Dudley Randall.—AdPb
On going to Hohokus (and why I live in New Jersey). John Ciardi.—CiFs
On guard. Aileen Fisher.—FiM
On Halloween. Nina Willis Walter.—HoH
"**On** Halloween, what bothers some." See Witch's broom notes
On hearing someone sing a poem by Yüan Chēn. Po Chü-i, tr. fr. the Chinese by Arthur Waley.—PlM
On her portrait. Juana Inez De la Cruz, tr. fr. the Mexican by Judith Thurman.—ThI
On himself. Jonathan Swift.—CoPi
On his blindness. John Milton.—MaFw
"**On** his very first hunt." Unknown, fr. the Aivilik Eskimo.—LeIb
On his way. Robert Froman.—FrSp
On Holmbury hill. Edward Shanks.—PaP
On Homer's birthplace. Thomas Heywood.—PlM
On Hurricane Jackson. Alan Dugan.—HiN
On Keats. Percy Bysshe Shelley.—PlM
On learning to adjust to things. John Ciardi.—CiFs

On listening to the spirituals. Lance Jeffers.—AdPb
On looking into E. V. Rieu's Homer. Patrick Kavanagh.—PlM
On looking into Robert Frost in Kanji. William Meredith.—PlM
On Mauros the rhetor. Palladas, tr. fr. the Greek by Dudley Fitts.—LiWw
On May morning. See Song on May morning
"**On** mules we find two legs behind." See Two legs behind and two before
On my birthday. Yehuda Amichai, tr. fr. the Hebrew by Ruth Finer Mintz.—MeP
On my short-sightedness. Prem Chaya.—MaFw
On Noman, a guest. Hilaire Belloc.—CoPu
"**On** ochre walls in ice-formed caves shaggy Neanderthals." See To my son Parker, asleep in the next room
On one who lived and died where he was born. Thomas Hardy.—PlP
"**On** parents' knees, a naked new-born child." See A moral tetrastitch
"**On** rainy days alone I dine." See On himself
On re-reading the complete works of an elder poet. W. T. Scott.—PlM
"**On** sale everywhere: Spicer's instant poetry." See Spicer's instant poetry
"**On** Saturday night (shall be)." Mother Goose.—AlC
"**On** Saturday night I lost my wife." Mother Goose.—HoMg
"**On** Saturday on Saturday." See Saturday in New York
On seeing two brown boys in a Catholic church. Frank Horne.—AdPb
"**On** shallow straw, in shadeless grass." See Take one home to the kiddies
On Sir John Vanbrugh, architect. Abel Evans.—LiWw
On slaughter. Chaim Nachman Bialik, tr. fr. the Hebrew by Robert Mezey and Shula Starkman.—MeP
On sweet Killen hill. Tom MacIntyre.—HiN
"**On** that gray night of mournful drone." See A man was drawing near to me
"**On** the avenue. Robert Froman.—FrSp
On the birth of his son. Su Tung-p'o, tr. fr. the Chinese by Arthur Waley.—LiWw
On the birth of my son, Malcolm Coltrane. Julius Lester.—AdPb
"**On** the bridge of Avignon." Mother Goose, tr. fr. the French.—TucMg
On the burning of our house, July 10, 1666. Anne Bradstreet.—ThI
"**On** the coast of Coromandel." See The courtship of the Yonghy-Bonghy-Bo
"**On** the corner, 116th and Lenox." See Harlem freeze frame
"**On** the day I was born." See My stars
On the death-bed. Thomas Hardy.—PlP
On the death of Atahualpa. Unknown, tr. fr. the Quechua by D. Alomías Robles.—BiI
On the death of friends in childhood. Donald Justice.—HiN
On the death of William Edward Burghardt Du Bois by African moonlight and forgotten shores. Conrad Kent Rivers.—AdPb
"**On** the dunes." See Star night
On the fine arts garden, Cleveland. Russell Atkins.—AdPb
"**On** the fine wire of her whine she walked." See Mosquito
"**On** the first day." See The Easter bunny blues or all I want for Christmas is the Loop
"**On** the front part of the earth." See War songs
"**On** the front porch." See Porches
On the gifts of God. See Psalms—Psalm 127
On the grasshopper and cricket. John Keats.—JoA-4—PaF
"**On** the hill in spring." Kim Duk-ryung, tr. fr. the Korean by Chung Seuk Park and ad. by Virginia Olsen Baron.—BaSs
"**On** the hill there is a green house." Unknown.—EmN
On the job. Robert Froman.—FrSp
"**On** the lips of the child Janet float changing dreams." See Sixteen months
"**On** the most westerly Blasket." See The given note
On the ocean floor. X. J. Kennedy.—KeO
"**On** the planet of Mars." See The planet of Mars
On the pole. Uri Zvi Greenberg, tr. fr. the Hebrew by Robert Mezey and Ben Zion Gold.—MeP
"**On** the road." See Driving to the beach
"**On** the sea of the Antilles." See Little song for the children of the Antilles
"**On** the shores of Lake Michigan." See The people, yes—Children of the wind
On the sidewalk. Marchette Chute.—ChRu
"**On** the sidewalk the people are bustling." See The observation
"**On** the small table, the early mellowed." Park In-ro, tr. fr. the Korean by Chung Seuk Park and ad. by Virginia Olsen Baron.—BaSs
"**On** the snow I found prints." See Invisible tree
"**On** the subway I can read the ads." See Subway ride
"**On** the summer road that ran by our front porch." See Lizards and snakes
"**On** the top of the Crumpetty tree." See The Quangle Wangle's hat
On the vanity of earthly greatness. Arthur Guiterman.—LiWw
"**On** the wind-beaten plains." See Ancestors
"**On** these summer days." Sung Hon, tr. fr. the Korean by Chung Seuk Park and ad. by Virginia Olsen Baron.—BaSs
On this island. W. H. Auden.—MaFw—ToM
"**On** this page of pinky pink." See For a blue page
On torpid Marcus. Lucilius, tr. fr. the Latin by Dudley Fitts.—LiWw

On Tuesdays I polish my uncle. Dennis Lee.—LeA
"**On** up the sea slant." See Sea slant
"**On** wan dark night on Lac St Pierre." See The wreck of the Julie Plante
"**On** warm days in September the high school band." See The high school band
On wearing ears. William J. Harris.—AdB
"**On** Wednesday night." See Wednesday night prayer meeting
"**On** Wenlock Edge the wood's in trouble." See A Shropshire lad
"**On** Willy's birthday, as you see." See A party
"**On** windy days the mill." See The unfortunate miller
"**On** yellow days in summer when the early heat." See The cicadas
Once. Alice Walker.—AdPb (sel.)
"**Once** a farmer had a dog." Unknown.—EmN
"**Once** a jolly swagman camped by a billabong." See Waltzing Matilda
"**Once** a snowflake fell." See Winter poem
"**Once,** after a rotten day at school." See The place's fault
Once again. Liz Sohappy.—AlW
"**Once** around is enough, my grandfather said." See Adventures with my grandfather
"**Once** as I travelled through a quiet evening." See Egrets
"**Once** at midday, at the zoo." See Making friends
"**Once,** at the Agriculture Show." See The pat of butter
"**Once**—but no matter when——." See A chronicle
"**Once** I crept in an oak wood—I was looking for a stag." See My own true family
"**Once** I cried for new songs to sing, a black rose, a brown sky, the." See I sing no new songs
"**Once** I dressed up." See Fifteen poems of my heart
"**Once** I had a nickel." See My nickel
"**Once** I had a rooster." Unknown.—EmN
"**Once** I spoke the language of the flowers." See Forgotten language
"**Once** I was good like the Virgin Mary and the minister's wife." See The scarlet woman
"**Once** I was happy, but now I'm forlorn." See The man on the flying trapeze
"**Once** in a dream." See Three birds flying
"**Once,** in a roostery." See The hen and the carp
"**Once** in a saintly passion." James Thomson.—RoIt
"**Once** in royal David's city." Cecil Frances Alexander.—OpOx
"**Once** in the winter." See The forsaken
"**Once** more around should do it, the man confided." See Flight of the roller coaster
"**Once** more, listening to the wind and rain." See The return
"**Once** more the rising sun has lit a." See The nonconformist
Once more, the round. Theodore Roethke.—JoA-4
"**Once** on a time, it came to pass." See The fable of the piece of glass and the piece of ice
"**Once** on a time—'twas long ago." See The youth and the northwind
"**Once** . . . once upon a time. . . . " See Martha
"**Once** or twice this side of death." See Crystal moment
"**Once** riding in old Baltimore." See Incident
"**Once** there was a cassowary." See The cassowary
"**Once** there was a spaniel." See Bed-time story
"**Once** there was a wolf who was very skinny." See The wolf and the dog
"**Once** there was an elephant." See Eletelephony
"**Once** up u hurl a stone." See Mike 65
"**Once** upon a midnight dreary, while I pondered, weak and weary." See The raven
"**Once** upon a time (a chicken)." Unknown.—EmN
"**Once** upon a time (there was)." Issa, tr. fr. the Japanese by Harry Behn.—BeM
"**Once** upon a time there were three little foxes." See The three foxes
"**Once** we saw a weasel." See Weasel
One big rain. Russell Hoban.—HoE
"**One** big rain, one big rain." See One big rain
"**One** cricket said to another." See Crickets
"**One** day." See Dream voyage to the center of the subway
"**One** day." Wilford Horne, Jr.—HoC
"**One** day a boy went walking." See Who ever sausage a thing
"**One** day in Thrift-Rite Supermart." See Instant storm
"**One** day mamma said Conrad dear." See The story of little Suck-a-Thumb
One day only. Marchette Chute.—ChRu
"**One** day the green canary." See The canary's flight
"**One-ery,** two-ery." See "One-ery, two-ery, ziccary zan"
"**One-ery,** two-ery, ziccary zan." Mother Goose
Jumping Joan.—NeA
"One-ery, two-ery."—AlC
"**One** evenin' as the sun went down." See The big Rock Candy mountain
One eyed black man in Nebraska. Sam Cornish.—AdPb
"**One-eyed** Jack, the pirate chief." Mother Goose.—TucMgl
"**One** fine day in the middle of the night." Unknown.—MoBw
One flesh. Elizabeth Jennings.—ToM
"**One** foot in the river." See Giant
One for Novella Nelson. Myra Cohn Livingston.—LiM
"**One** for the money." Unknown.—EmN
One guess. Robert Frost.—CoPu

"Our bugles sang truce,—for the night-cloud had lowered." See The soldier's dream
Our cat ("The cat goes out") Marchette Chute.—ChRu
Our cat ("Though it is New Year's eve") Volodya Lapin, tr. fr. the Russian by Miriam Morton.—MoM
Our court. Lois Lenski.—LeC
Our father. Ray Mathew.—MaFw
"Our father, the whirlwind." See The dreamer rides the whirlwind
"Our flat is hot." Lois Lenski.—LeC
"Our garden is my world." Nina Glekiva, tr. fr. the Russian by Miriam Morton.—MoM
"Our glances spin silver threads." See Empathy
"Our grandfathers, now long dead." See The being without a face
"Our great fathers talked together." See They stooped over and came out
"Our hammock swings between two trees." See Hammock
Our history. M'bella Sonne Dipoko.—AlPa
"Our journey had advanced." Emily Dickinson.—MoG
Our joyful feast. George Wither.—RoIt
"Our life is two-fold: Sleep hath its own world." See The dream (Part I)
"Our little fleet in July first." See The Armada, 1588
"Our Mr Toad." David McCord.—JoA-4—McS
"Our moulting days are in their twilight stage." See Far from Africa: Four poems—Garnishing the aviary
"Our old family dog." Issa, tr. fr. the Japanese by Harry Behn.—BeM
"Our roads are ridden." See For Sammy Younge
"Our saucy boy, Dick." Mother Goose.—TucMgl
Our saviour's golden rule. Isaac Watts.—OpOx
"Our window is stained." Alfred Kreymborg.—RoIt
Ourchestra. Shel Silverstein.—SiW
"Out fishing on the ocean." Bretton Pollack.—HoP
"Out goes the cat." Unknown.—EmN
"Out in the garden pickin' peas." Unknown.—EmN
"Out in the marsh the sumac sighs." See Filling the marsh
Out into Essex. John Betjeman.—PaP
"Out of his cottage to the sun." See Old Dan'l
"Out of me unworthy and unknown." See The Spoon River anthology—Anne Rutledge
"Out of the bosom of the air." See Snow-flakes
"Out of the dark raw earth." See Alabama
"Out of the land of shadows and darkness." See From the underworld
"Out of the night that covers me." See Invictus
"Out of the shadow, I am come in to you whole a black holy man." See Study peace
"Out of their slumber Europeans spun." See Snow in Europe
"Out on the fire escape." See Clothesline
Out skiing. Larissa Shakhovich, tr. fr. the Russian by Miriam Morton.—MoM
Outcast. Claude McKey.—AdPb
The **outdoor** Christmas tree ("Little winter cottontails") Aileen Fisher.—FiFo
The **outdoor** Christmas tree ("Suet chunks and popcorn strings") Marchette Chute.—ChRu
Outdoor life. See Adventure and adventurers; Country life; Gipsies; Nature; Roads and trails; also names of outdoor sports, as Hunters and hunting
Outer space. See Space and space travel
The **outlaw** of Loch Lene. Unknown, tr. fr. the Irish by J. J. Callanan.—CoPi
Outlaws. See Crime and criminals
Outlaws. Robert Graves.—HaWr
"Outside Buckingham palace." See Malice at Buckingham palace
"Outside my window." See A proper place
"Outside my window." See Squirrel
Outside the window. Robert Froman.—FrSp
Outwitted. Edwin Markham.—CoPu
"Ouu." See Moon poem
"Over a stone." Karla Kuskin.—KuA
"Over and over again to people." See The limits of submission
"Over and over the tumblers tumble." Jack Prelutsky.—PrC
"Over hill, over dale." See A midsummer night's dream
"Over hills, over hollows." Unknown.—EmN
"Over latch." Unknown.—MoBw
"Over the bleak and barren snow." See Tony O
"Over the hill there is a school." Unknown.—MoBw
"Over the land freckled with snow half-thawed." See Thaw
"Over the mythical earthlodge above." See Spirits
"Over the ocean." Unknown.—MoBw
"Over the river and through the wood." See Thanksgiving day
"Over the warts on the bumpy." See Sadie's playhouse
Over the water. Unknown, tr. fr. the Delaware by D. G. Brinton.—BiI
"Over there, far off, he runs." See Song of the hunter
"Over there I could think of nothing else." Unknown, fr. the Copper Eskimo.—LeIb
Overheard in the Louvre. X. J. Kennedy.—LiWw
Overheard on a saltmarsh. Harold Monro.—AdP—JoA-4—LiLc
Overlooking the river Stour. Thomas Hardy.—PaP—PlP
Ovid
  Metamorphoses, sel.
    Orpheus and Eurydice.—MoG
  Orpheus and Eurydice. See Metamorphoses
Owen, Wilfred
  Anthem for doomed youth.—MaFw
  Disabled.—CoPt

Owen, Wilfred—*Continued*
The parable of the old man and the young.—MaFw—MoG
"**Owl.**" See Prayer
The **owl** ("In the hollow tree, in the old gray tower") Barry Cornwall.—RoIt
Owl ("Owl is my favourite. Who flies") George MacBeth.—ToM
The **owl** ("When cats run home and light is come") See Song: The owl
"The **owl** and the eel and the warming-pan." Laura E. Richards.—JoA-4
The **owl** and the pussy-cat. Edward Lear.—JoA-4—OpOx—UnGb
"The **owl** and the pussy-cat went to sea." See The owl and the pussy-cat
The **owl** critic. James Thomas Fields.—CoPt
"The **owl** hooted." Unknown.—LaM
"**Owl** is my favourite. Who flies." See Owl
Owls
Alabama. J. Fields.—AdPb
The bird of night. R. Jarrell.—AdP—HiN—MoT
"Brown owls come here in the blue evening." Unknown.—ClFc
"Five little owls in an old elm tree." Mother Goose.—TucMgl
The great brown owl. J. E. Browne.—OpOx
Hitchhiker. D. McCord.—McAa—McS
"I went to the toad that lies under the wall." Mother Goose.—MiMg
If the owl calls again. J. Haines.—HiN
It is I, the little owl. Unknown.—BiS
"Oliver Oglethorpe ogled an owl and oyster." Unknown.—EmN
Outlaws. R. Graves.—HaWr
The owl ("In the hollow tree, in the old gray tower") B. Cornwall.—RoIt
Owl ("Owl is my favourite. Who flies") G. MacBeth.—ToM
The owl and the pussy-cat. E. Lear.—JoA-4—OpOx—UnGb
The owl critic. J. T. Fields.—CoPt
"The owl hooted." Unknown.—LaM
Prayer to the snowy owl. J. Haines.—CoPu
Questioning faces. R. Frost.—CoPu—HiN
Song: The owl. A. Tennyson.—RoIt
The owl.—UnGb
"There was an old woman named Towl." Unknown
Three wonderful old women.—OpOx
"To owl, the dove says." Issa.—HaW
"To the medicine man's house they have led me." Unknown.—ClFc
Very much afraid. Unknown.—BiS
The visitor. M. Chute.—ChRu
"When icicles hang by the wall." W. Shakespeare.—JoA-4—RoIt
Winter.—PaF
"Who is this." Unknown.—JoT
Whooo. L. Moore.—MoSm
"A wolf." Unknown.—JoT
The woods at night. M. Swenson.—JoA-4
"**Owls**—they whinny down the night." See Outlaws
The **ox-tamer.** Walt Whitman.—RoIt
Oxen. See Cattle
The **oxen.** Thomas Hardy.—PlP
Oxford, England
"How changed is here each spot man makes or fills." From Thyrsis. M. Arnold.—PaP
Oxford. X. Johnson.—PaP
"Towery city and branchy between towers." From Duns Scotus's Oxford. G. M. Hopkins.—PaP
Oxford. Lionel Johnson.—PaP
Oysters
"First, the fish must be caught." From Through the looking-glass. L. Carroll.—LiPc
"If teardrops were pearls." Unknown.—BaSs
"A noisy noise annoys an oyster." Unknown.—EmN
"Oliver Oglethorpe ogled an owl and oyster." Unknown.—EmN
"Oysters." J. Prelutsky.—PrT
"Row, row, row (to Oyster bay") Unknown.—BoI
"**Oysters.**" Jack Prelutsky.—PrT
The **Ozidi** saga, sel. Unknown
A lament. tr. fr. the Ijaw by J. P. Clark.—AlPa
Ozymandias. Percy Bysshe Shelley.—LiS—RoIt
Ozymandias revisited. Morris Bishop.—LiS

P

"**P** U double unkin." Unknown.—EmN
"**P-U** ennekin ennekin Y." Unknown.—EmN
"**P-U-N** Punkin'." Unknown.—EmN
The **pack** rat. Jack Prelutsky.—PrP
"The **pack** rat's day is spent at play." See The pack rat
A **pact.** Ezra Pound.—PlM
Paddler's song on bad hunting weather. Unknown, fr. Ammassalik.—LeIb
"**Paddy,** in want of a dinner one day." See Paddy O'Rafther
Paddy O'Rafther. Samuel Lover.—CoPi—CoPt
Padraic O'Conaire, Gaelic storyteller. F. R. Higgins.—CoPi
Paige, Satchell (about)
To Satch. S. Allen.—AbM—AdPb
Pain
About a monster-ous toothache. L. Moore.—MoSm
Hurt hawks. R. Jeffers.—PeS
"Must." A. Lewis.—CoPu
Pain. M. S. Dipoko.—AlPa
The pain and the great one. J. Blume.—ThF
Quietly I shout. A. T. Pratt.—AlW
Surgical ward. W. H. Auden.—PeS
Sweet winds of love. P. Irving.—AlW
"There was a faith-healer of Deal." Unknown.—LiWw—RoIt

Pain. M'bella Sonne Dipoko.—AlPa
The **pain** and the great one. Judy Blume.—ThF
Paintings and pictures
My father paints the summer. R. Wilbur.—HiN
Picture people. M. C. Livingston.—JoA-4
"Primitive paintings. . . . " A. Atwood.—AtM
To paint the portrait of a bird. J. Prévert.—MaFw
Paiute Indians. See Indians of the Americas—Paiute
"**Pal** of my cradle days." Unknown.—MoBw
The **pale** blue casket. Oliver Pitcher.—AdPb
Palladas
On Mauros the rhetor.—LiWw
Palmanteer, Ted
Hit.—AlW
Judgment.—AlW
Spring dew.—AlW
The strings of time.—AlW
This is real.—AlW
We saw days.—AlW
Palmer, Herbert
The call of the fells.—PaP
Palouse Indians. See Indians of the Americas—Palouse
Pamela. David McCord.—McFm
"**Pamela**—you may call her that." See Pamela
"The **pampas** flowers." Issa, tr. fr. the Japanese by Hanako Fukuda.—HaW
"The **pampered** steed, of swiftness proud." See The horse and the mule
Pan
The god of sheep. J. Fletcher.—RoIt
Pancake. Shel Silverstein.—SiW
Pancho Villa. Lou Lipsitz.—HiN
"A **panda.**" See Panda
Panda. Mary Ann Hoberman.—HoR
Pandas
Panda. M. A. Hoberman.—HoR
Procyonidae. M. A. Hoberman.—HoR
Pandora
Pandora. M. C. Livingston.—LiM—NeA
Pandora. Myra Cohn Livingston.—LiM—NeA
Panegoosho, M.
Morning mood.—LeIb
Pangur Ban. Unknown, tr. fr. the Irish by Robin Flower.—CoPi
Pankhurst, Sylvia
Household song. tr.—AlPa
The worthless lover. tr.—AlPa
"A **pant** hunter, pantless, is panting for pants." Unknown.—EmN
Pantheism
The higher pantheism. A. Tennyson.—LiS
The higher pantheism in a nutshell. A. C. Swinburne.—LiS
The **panther** ("His gaze, going past those bars, has got so misted") Rainer Maria Rilke, tr. fr. the German by J. B. Leishman.—MaFw
The **panther** ("The panther is like a leopard") Ogden Nash.—BrM—CoOh
Panther ("Three black boys") Sam Cornish.—AdPb
"The **panther** is like a leopard." See The panther
Panthers
The black panther. K. Raikin.—MoM
The panther ("His gaze, going past those bars, has got so misted") R. M. Rilke.—MaFw
The panther ("The panther is like a leopard") O. Nash.—BrM—CoOh
Pao Chao
The ruined city.—MaFw
Papago Indians. See Indians of the Americas—Papago
Paper
Off and away. R. Froman.—FrSp
Paper I. C. Sandburg.—SaT
Paper II. C. Sandburg.—SaT
The term. W. C. Williams.—MoT
Paper I. Carl Sandburg.—SaT
Paper II. Carl Sandburg.—SaT
Paper boats. Rabindranath Tagore.—MaFw (sel.)
The **paper** in the meadow. Oscar Williams.—RoIt
"**Paper** is two kinds, to write on, to wrap with." See Paper I
"**Paper,** paper." See Newsboy
The **parable** of the old man and the young. Wilfred Owen.—MaFw—MoG
Parade ("A band is playing") Lois Lenski.—LeC
The **parade** ("The light glows bright") Liz Sohappy.—AlW
Parades
April 23. N. Belting.—BeSc
"Hooray. Here comes the great parade." J. Prelutsky.—PrC
Parade ("A band is playing") L. Lenski.—LeC
The parade ("The light glows bright") L. Sohappy.—AlW
Paradise. See Heaven
The **paradox.** Paul Laurence Dunbar.—AdPb
"**Parched** by the shrill song." Soseki, tr. fr. the Japanese by Harry Behn.—BeM
Parents and parenthood. See Family; Fathers and fatherhood; Home and family life; Mothers and motherhood
Parents are people. Carol Hall.—ThF
Paris, France
The ballad of bouillabaisse. W. M. Thackeray.—RoIt
Park In-ro
"On the small table, the early mellowed."—BaSs
"The **park.**" Mary Claire Wolfe.—HoC
The **park.** Lois Lenski.—LeC
Parker, A. C.
Magic formula. tr.—BiI
Parker, Dorothy
Theory.—LiWw
Parker, Ely S.
Death of a son. tr.—BiI
Prayer. tr.—BiI
Prophecy. tr.—BiI

Parks, Rosa (about)
Montgomery. S. Cornish.—AdM—AdPb
Parks
Bench in the park. L. Lenski.—LeC
Glimpses #xii. L. McGaugh.—AdB (sel.)
My friend. L. Kirkman.—HoCs
On the fine arts garden, Cleveland. R. Atkins.—AdPb
"The park." M. C. Wolfe.—HoC
The park. L. Lenski.—LeC
"The **park's** beautiful." See On the fine arts garden, Cleveland
Parodies
The aged aged man. From Through the looking-glass. L. Carroll.—LiPc—LiS—OpOx
Ways and means.—RoIt
The amateur flute. Unknown.—LiS
Ancient music. E. Pound.—LiS—MaFw
Annabel Lee. S. Huntley.—LiS
Autolycus' song (in basic English). R. L. Greene.—LiS
Baccalaureate. D. McCord.—LiS
Ballad. C. S. Calverley.—LiS
The cannibal flea. T. Hood, Jr—LiS
Cannibelee: A poem of passion. C. F. Lummis.—LiS
The cataract at Lodore, July 31, 1936. H. Bevington.—LiS
A classic waits for me. E. B. White.—LiS
"Come unto these yellow sands." P. Dehn.—LiS
Contemporary nursery rhyme. Unknown.—LiS
Disaster. C. S. Calverley.—LiS
The Duchess's lullaby. From Alice's adventures in wonderland. L. Carroll.—LiS
"Speak roughly to your little boy."—LiPc
The fat white woman speaks. G. K. Chesterton.—LiS
Father William. Unknown.—RoIt
Fragment of a Greek tragedy. A. E. Housman.—LiS
From Mr Walter De La Mare makes the little ones dizzy. S. Hoffenstein.—LiS
"Geiger, geiger, ticking slow." P. Dehn.—LiS
Herrick's Julia. H. Bevington.—LiS
Hiawatha's photographing. L. Carroll.—LiPc—LiS
Higher. Unknown.—LiS
The higher pantheism in a nutshell. A. C. Swinburne.—LiC
"How doth the little crocodile." From Alice's adventures in wonderland. L. Carroll.—LiLc—LiPc
The crocodile.—JoA-4
How doth.—LiS
How I brought the good news from Aix to Ghent (or vice versa). R. J. Yeatman and W. C. Sellar.—LiS
"I wandered angry as a cloud." P. Dehn.—LiS
Jane Smith. R. Kipling.—LiS
"Jenny kiss'd me when we met." P. Dehn.—LiS
Lament for lost lodgings. P. McGinley.—LiS
Lewis Carroll. E. Farjeon.—OpOx
Lines for Cuscuscaraway and Mirza Murad Ali Beg. T. S. Eliot.—LiS—PlM
The little star. Unknown.—LiS
Lovers, and a reflection. C. S. Calverley.—LiS
Lucy Lake. N. Mackintosh.—LiS
The mad hatter's song. From Alice's adventures in wonderland. L. Carroll.—LiS
"Twinkle, twinkle, little bat."—LiPc
Mavrone, one of those sad Irish poems, with notes. A. Guiterman.—LiS
The messed damozel. C. H. Towne.—LiS
The metre Columbian. Unknown.—LiS
Miniver Cheevy, Jr. D. F. Parry.—LiS
Mr Smith (with nods to Mr Lear and Mr Eliot). W. J. Smith.—LiS
The modern Hiawatha. L. A. G. Strong.—LiS
Nephelidia. A. C. Swinburne.—LiS
Now we are sick. J. B. Morton.—LiS
Numerous Celts. J. C. Squire.—LiS
Nursery song in pidgin English. Unknown.—LiS
"O have you caught the tiger." A. E. Housman.—LiS
"O nuclear wind, when wilt thou blow." P. Dehn.—LiS
Ode on a jar of pickles. B. Taylor.—LiS
Only seven. H. S. Leigh.—LiS
Pentagonia. G. E. Bates.—LiS
Plane geometry. E. Rounds.—LiS
The promissory note. B. Taylor.—LiS
Rigid body sings. J. Clerk-Maxwell.—LiS
"Ring-a-ring o' neutrons." P. Dehn.—LiS
"The shades of night were falling fast." A. E. Housman.—LiS
Sincere flattery of W. W. (Americanus). J. K. Stephen.—LiS
Song. O. Herford.—LiS
A sonnet on Wordsworth. J. K. Stephen.—PlM
A sonnet.—LiS
Such stuff as dreams. F. P. Adams.—LiS
Tèma con variazioni. L. Carroll.—LiS
"There lived among the untrodden ways." H. Coleridge.—LiS
Turtle soup. From Alice's adventures in wonderland. L. Carroll.—LiPc—LiS
'Twas ever thus. H. S. Leigh.—LiS
Variations on a theme by William Carlos Williams. K. Koch.—LiS
"What, still alive at twenty two." H. Kingsmill.—LiS
Parra, Nicanor
Manifesto.—MoT (sel.)
"**Parrot,** if I had your wings." See The boy and the parrot
Parrots
The boy and the parrot. J. H. Frere.—OpOx
"I am proud." K. Kuskin.—KuA
Little Miss and her parrot. J. Marchant.—OpOx

"My little parrot seemed to live." W. Wood.—CoPu
Pete the parrot and Shakespeare. D. Marquis.—PlM
Parry, David Fisher
Miniver Cheevy, Jr—LiS
Parry, Edward Abbott
"I would like you for a comrade."—NeA—OpOx
The jam fish.—OpOx
Pater's bathe.—OpOx
Parsley for vice-president. Ogden Nash.—LiWw
Parson Gray. Oliver Goldsmith.—RoIt
"Part of my family is grown-up and tall." See My family
Parties
August. M. C. Livingston.—LiM
The butterfly's ball. W. Roscoe.—OpOx
Celebration. A. Lopez.—AlW
"Come to my party." Unknown.—EmN
December 23: Late. L. Clifton.—ClEa
The feckless dinner party. W. De La Mare.—CoPt
Jamboree. L. Blair.—JaP
Juliet. H. Belloc.—CoPu
'Keenene. Unknown.—SeS
"Marty's party." D. McCord.—McAa
"Now, now the mirth comes." R. Herrick.—MaF
"Old Mr Parvenu gave a great ball." C. Grain.—CoPu
A party ("On Willy's birthday, as you see") L. E. Richards.—BrM
The party ("They served tea in the sandpile, together with") R. Whittemore.—HiN
The peacock at home. C. A. Dorset.—OpOx
A revel. D. MacDonagh.—CoPi
Spaghetti. S. Silverstein.—SiW
Thoughts while driving home. J. Updike.—PeS
Two sad tales. Unknown.—CoOh
Wishes of an elderly man. W. Raleigh.—CoPu
Parting. See also Farewells
"A caressing breeze touched." Unknown.—MoM
Chaka. L. S. Senghor.—AlPa (sel.)
Goodbye. A. Lewis.—ToM
"My love is a thousand miles away." Wang Bang-Yun.—BaSs
"Oh, do not pull yourself away." Yi Myung-han.—BaSs
Parting ("And dawn shall trail after me to the shore") Y. Bat-Miriam.—MeP
The parting ("The ocean twanging away there") A. Rich.—HaWr
Partings. M. J. Jewsbury.—OpOx
The time has come. S. Voronov.—MoM
Parting ("And dawn shall trail after me to the shore") Yocheved Bat-Miriam, tr. fr. the Hebrew by Dom Moraes.—MeP
The **parting** ("The ocean twanging away there") Adrienne Rich.—HaWr
Partings. Maria Jane Jewsbury.—OpOx
Partridges and quails
"The light glow of evening." Unknown.—ClFc
"The quail in the bush is making his whirring." Unknown.—ClFc
A **party** ("On Willy's birthday, as you see") Laura E. Richards.—BrM
The **party** ("They served tea in the sandpile, together with") Reed Whittemore.—HiN
Pasha Bailey Ben. William Schwenck Gilbert.—LiWw
Pass, Cynthia
"This boy think he bad to get."—JoV
The **passage** at night—the blaskets. Robin Flower.—CoPi
Passing by the junkyard. Charles J. Egita.—HoP
"Passing through huddled and ugly walls." See The harbor
"Passing through the strings of time." See The strings of time
The **passionate** shepherd to his love. Christopher Marlowe.—RoIt
Passover
Passover night. E. Bockstein.—LaM
Passover night. Edna Bockstein.—LaM
Past. See Time—Past
Pasternak, Boris
Christmas star.—MaFw
"I want to find the essence of."—MoM
The zoo.—MaFw
Pasternak, Lydia
Christmas star. tr.—MaFw
The zoo. tr.—MaFw
"The **pastimes** of people." See Idiosyncratic
Pastoral. William Carlos Williams.—PeS
The **pasture.** Robert Frost.—JoA-4—LiLc
Pastures of plenty. Woody Guthrie.—PeS
"Pat-a-cake (pat-a-cake, what shall we bake)." Unknown, tr. fr. the Danish by N. M. Bodecker.—BoI
"Pat-a-cake, pat-a-cake." See Baking a hamantash
"Pat-a-cake, pat-a-cake, baker's man." Mother Goose.—JoA-4
"The **patagonian."** See Some natural history
Pat-cat. Aileen Fisher.—FiFo
The **pat** of butter. Thomas Hardy.—PlP
A **patch** of old snow. Robert Frost.—CoPu
Patch-Shaneen. John M. Synge.—CoPi
Patchen, Kenneth
The fox.—ToM
Who walks there.—HaWr
Pater's bathe. Edward Abbott Parry.—OpOx
The **path** I must travel. Emerson Blackhorse ("Barney") Mitchell.—AlW
The **path** on the sea. Inna Muller, tr. fr. the Russian by Miriam Morton.—MoM
Patience. See also Perseverance
The breathing. D. Levertov.—HaWr
"The ghost in our apartment house." L. Moore.—MoSm
Patience. H. Graham.—LiWw
Patience, sel. William Schwenck Gilbert
Bunthorne's song.—LiWw

Patience ("When ski-ing in the Engadine") Harry Graham.—LiWw
The **patient:** Rockland County sanitarium. Calvin C. Hernton.—AdPb
"**Patiently,** how patiently." See The hunter
Patmore, Coventry
The year.—RoIt
Patriarchs. Lilian Moore.—MoSp
Patrick, Saint (about)
The rune of Saint Patrick. Unknown.—MaF
Patriotic ode on the fourteenth anniversary of the persecution of Charlie Chaplin. Bob Kaufman.—AdPb
Patriotism. See Fourth of July; Heroes and heroines; Memorial day; Veteran's day; also names of countries, as England; United States
Patriotism. See The lay of the last minstrel
"**Pat's** pa, Pete, poked to the pea patch." Unknown.—EmN
Patterns. Amy Lowell.—MoG
Patterson, A. B.
The traveling post office.—CoPt
Patterson, Raymond Richard
At that moment.—AdPb
Birmingham 1963.—AdPb
Black all day.—AdB—AdPb
From riot rimes U.S.A. #78.—AdM
From riot rimes U.S.A. #79.—AdM
Glory, glory. . . . —AdM
I've got a home in that rock.—AdM—AdPb
Letter in winter.—AdPb
A love song.—AdB
Night-piece.—AdPb
When I awoke.—AdPb
You are the brave.—AdPb
Paul Bunyan. Shel Silverstein.—SiW
Paul Robeson. Gwendolyn Brooks.—AdPb
"The **pawn-shop** man knows hunger." See Street window
Pawnee Indians. See Indians of the Americas—Pawnee
Paxton, Tom
"Bishop Cody's last request."—MoG
Little brand new baby.—PeS
The **pay** is good. Richard Kell.—ToM
"**Pay** me a visit." Unknown, tr. fr. the Yoruba by S. A. Babalola.—AlPa
Payne, Basil
Angry old men.—CoPi
Paz, Octavio
Dawn.—MoT
Pazharskaya, Liuda
The sorceress.—MoM
P'Bitek, Okot
Song of Lawino: An African lament.—AlPa (sel.)
"**Pea** pods cling to stems." See Pods
Peace. See also Memorial day; Veteran's day
Behold, this pipe. Unknown.—BiI
Christmas: 1924. T. Hardy.—PlP
The echo. P. Solomon.—JoV
"How I'd like to live." Yang Ung-jeung.—BaSs
"I go forth to move about the earth." A. Lopez.—AlW
"I have nothing at all." Issa.—HaW
I pass the pipe. Unknown.—BiI
Magic formula to make an enemy peaceful. Unknown.—BiI
On wearing ears. W. J. Harris.—AdB
Sheep. J. Prelutsky.—PrP
Strategies. W. Smith.—AdPb
Who are they. Unknown.—BiI
"**Peace** and mercy and Jonathan." See First Thanksgiving of all
"**Peace** upon earth, was said. We sing it." See Christmas: 1924
"**Peach** and plum blossoms of spring." Kim Yu-ki, tr. fr. the Korean by Chung Seuk Park and ad. by Virginia Olsen Baron.—BaSs
Peaches and peach trees
"Keep straight down this block." R. Wright Hokku poems.—AdPb
Monument. F. Holman.—HoI
"Only white gulls and I." Yi Hwang.—BaSs
"Peach and plum blossoms of spring." Kim Yu-ki.—BaSs
"Standing here with my hand on the jade rail." Unknown.—BaSs
"Wind last night blew down." Unknown.—BaSs
"**Peaches** in the parlor." Unknown.—MoBw
Peacock, Thomas Love
Dream pedlary.—LiLc (sel.)
Gryll Grange, sel.
Love and age.—RoIt
Love and age. See Gryll Grange
The priest and the mulberry tree.—CoPt
The war song of Dinas Vawr.—CoPt
The world.—CoPu
The **peacock** at home. Catherine Ann Dorset.—OpOx
"A **peacock** feather." See Blind man's buff
Peacocks
"The child at winter sunset." M. Van Doren.—HiN
The peacock at home. C. A. Dorset.—OpOx
Peanut butter. See From the kitchen
"**Peanut** butter, considered as a spread." See From the kitchen—Peanut butter
Peanut-butter sandwich. Shel Silverstein.—SiW
"A **peanut** sat on a railroad track." See Silly stanzas
Pearl cobwebs. See Smoke and steel
"**Pearl** cobwebs in the windy rain." See Smoke and steel—Pearl cobwebs
Pears and pear trees
"Hickle them, pickle them." Mother Goose.—TucMgl
"Peter Prangle." Unknown.—BrM
"Peter Prangle, the prickly prangly pear picker." Unknown.—EmN
Pearse, Padraic
Last lines—1916.—CoPi
Peasants
Death of a peasant. R. S. Thomas.—MaFw

"**Pease** porridge hot." See Pease-pudding hot"
Pease porridge poems. David McCord.—McFm
"**Pease-pudding** hot." Mother Goose.—AlC
  "Pease porridge hot."—EmN—JoA-4
Pebbles. Valerie Worth.—WoS
"**Pebbles** belong to no one." See Pebbles
Peck, Richard
  The geese.—PeS
Peddlers and venders
  The baker's reply to the needle peddler. Unknown.—BrM
  Cockles and mussels. Unknown.—RoIt
  Dream pedlary. T. L. Peacock.—LiLc (sel.)
  Fish crier. C. Sandburg.—SaT
  Flower wagon. L. Lenski.—LeC
  For children if they'll take them. X. J. Kennedy.—RoIt
  Get 'em here. L. B. Hopkins.—HoCs
  The great merchant, Dives Pragmaticus, cries his wares. T. Newbery.—OpOx
  "Hot-cross buns." Mother Goose.—JoA-4—LaM
  Ice cream man. L. Lenski.—LeC
  "If I'd as much money as I could spend." Mother Goose.—AlC—JoA-4
  "Knock. Knock. Anybody there." C. Watson.—WaF
  Logs of wood. C. Causley.—CaF
  Mexican market woman. L. Hughes.—HoD
  Mom's mums. D. McCord.—McAa
  Newsboy. L. Lenski.—LeC
  The pedlar's caravan. W. B. Rands.—OpOx
  Shoeshine boy. L. Lenski.—LeC
  "Simple Simon met a pieman." Mother Goose.—JoA-4
  "There was an old woman, as I've heard tell." Mother Goose.—JoA-4
  The watercress seller. T. Miller.—OpOx
"**Peddling.**" See Four glimpses of night
Pedigrees. See Ancestry
Pedlars. See Peddlers and venders
The **pedlar's** caravan. William Brighty Rand.—OpOx
Peep show. Juan Ramón Jiménez, tr. fr. the Spanish by Eloise Roach.—JoA-4
The **peepers** in our meadow. Archibald MacLeish.—HiN
Pegasus
  Pegasus. P. Kavanagh.—CoPi
Pegasus. Patrick Kavanagh.—CoPi
The **pelican.** Aileen Fisher.—FiFo
Pelicans
  The pelican. A. Fisher.—FiFo
  Questions, quistions & quostions. S. Milligan.—CoOr
Pencil stubs, sels. John Ciardi
  After a fire.—LiWw
  To a reviewer who admired my book.—LiWw
Penguin. Mary Ann Hoberman.—HoR
Penguin chick. Aileen Fisher.—FiD
Penguins
  Penguin. M. A. Hoberman.—HoR
  Penguin chick. A. Fisher.—FiD
  Penguins. V. Hobbs.—BrM
Penguins. Valine Hobbs.—BrM
"**Penguins** with their chests puffed out." See Penguins
Penkethman, John
  A schoolmaster's precepts.—OpOx
  Some boys.—OpOx
Penn, William (about)
  "William Penn." W. J. Smith.—LiWw
Pennant, Edmund
  Fourth of July.—RoIt
Pennell, Isabel (about)
  To Mistress Isabel Pennell. J. Skelton.—MaFw
Pennington, Anne
  Donkey. tr.—MoT
Pennsylvania
  "William Penn." W. J. Smith.—LiWw
Penny, Rob
  "And we conquered."—AdPb
  Be cool, baby.—AdPb
  "I remember how she sang."—AdPb
  "The real people loves one another."—AdM—AdPb
"**Penny** candy." Clyde Watson.—WaF
"**Penny** on the water." Mother Goose.—AlC—EmN
"The **pennycandystore** beyond the El." See Number 20
Pentagonia. G. E. Bates.—LiS
Penthouse. Lois Lenski.—LeC
Peonies
  "Dear me, dear me." Issa.—HaW
  "What flower is this." Unknown.—EmN
People
  The adventure of Chris. D. McCord.—McAa
  City street. F. Holman.—HoI
  "The folk who live in Backward Town." M. A. Hoberman.—BrM
  Going. L. Lenski.—LeC
  "I do not understand." K. Kuskin.—KuA
  "I wonder how many people in this city." L. Cohen.—CoPu
  Idiosyncratic. E. Merriam.—MeO
  Much nicer people. E. J. Coatsworth.—CoPu
  My people. C. Sandburg.—SaT
  "My people are few." Unknown.—ClFc
  O country people. J. Hewitt.—CoPi
  Parents are people. C. Hall.—ThF
  People. L. Lenski.—HoCs
  People in the city. L. Lenski.—LeC
  "The people, of course." Issa.—HaW
  The puzzled census taker. J. G. Saxe.—CoPt
  "The real people loves one another." R. Penny.—AdM—AdPb
  Silence. M. Moore.—MaFw
  "Sing a song of people." L. Lenski.—LeC
  Small talk. D. Marquis.—CoPt
  The story of the zeros. V. H. Cruz.—AdPb
  "Subways are people." L. B. Hopkins.—HoP
  "Twelve hundred million men are spread." R. Kipling.—CoPu
  "The winds are people dwelling." N. Belting.—BeW
People. Lois Lenski.—HoCs

People crackers. See From the kitchen
"**People** crackers. Or don't you know." See From the kitchen—People crackers
People in the city. Lois Lenski.—LeC
"**People** pass me in the street." See Someone I know
People—Portraits. See also Boys and boyhood; Girls and girlhood
Kid. R. Hayden.—HiN
My Uncle Mick. T. Hughes.—HuMf
On her portrait. Juana Inez De la Cruz.—ThI
A thought. S. Ukachev.—MoM
People—Portraits—Men
"At nine of the night I opened my door." C. Causley.—CaF
Henry VIII. E. and H. Farjeon.—CoPt
"If ever you go to Dublin town." P. Kavanagh.—ToM
My Lord Tomnoddy. R. B. Brough.—CoPu
Old Dan'l. L. A. G. Strong.—CoPu
On Andrew Turner. R. Burns.—CoPu
"One winter afternoon." E. E. Cummings.—HiN
Riley. C. Causley.—CaF
People—Portraits—Women
After snow. W. Clark.—HiN
Aunt Helen. T. S. Eliot.—PeS
Awo. Unknown.—SeS
Bells for John Whiteside's daughter. J. C. Ransom.—PeS
Carmen. V. H. Cruz.—AdPb
Councils. M. Piercy.—MoT
The empty woman. G. Brooks.—PeS
Eve to her daughters. Judith Wright.—ToM
"The girl of my choice." Unknown.—MoBw
Martha. W. De La Mare.—RoIt
Maud Muller. J. G. Whittier.—RoIt
Miss Rosie. L. Clifton.—AdPb
Negro woman. L. Alexander.—AdPb
Portrait by a neighbor. E. St V. Millay.—NeA
The ruined maid. T. Hardy.—PlP
A satirical romance. Juana Inez De la Cruz.—ThI (sel.)
To a dark girl. G. B. Bennett.—AdPb
To a fat lady seen from the train. F. Cornford.—CoPu—LiS
Upon his Julia. R. Herrick.—LiS
Weeksville women. E. Loftin.—AdPb
Wise nature. Unknown.—CoPu
A woman driving. T. Hardy.—PlP
Woman with girdle. A. Sexton.—HiN
W. W. LeRoi Jones.—AdPb
People—Size
Adelaide. J. Prelutsky.—CoOh
Alice. S. Silverstein.—SiW
City blockades. L. B. Hopkins.—HoCs
"Here are the twins." S. Silverstein.—CoOh
"Jerry Hall." Unknown.—TrG
"Little Hermogenes is so small." Lucilius.—JoA-4
The measure of man. E. Merriam.—MeF
Mrs Snipkin and Mrs Wobblechin. L. E. Richards.—JoA-4—OpOx
My family. M. Chute.—ChRu
"Okay everybody, listen to this." K. Kuskin.—KuN
On the sidewalk. M. Chute.—ChRu
One inch tall. S. Silverstein.—SiW
The size of him. A. Kotul'sky.—MoM
Skinny. S. Silverstein.—SiW
"There was an old man, who when little." E. Lear
Limericks.—JoA-4
"The **people,** of course." Issa, tr. fr. the Japanese by Hanako Fukuda.—HaW
People of the eaves, I wish you good morning. Carl Sandburg.—SaT
People on the bus. Lois Lenski.—LeC
"**People** say they have a hard time." See For de Lawd
People who must. Carl Sandburg.—SaT
The **people,** yes, sels. Carl Sandburg
Children of the desert.—SaT
Children of the wind.—SaT
Circles.—MaFw
Mother and child.—SaT
Niagara.—SaT
Night too has numbers.—SaT
Prairie barn.—SaT
Proverbs.—SaT
Pepper, Lisa
"Always."—HoC
"**Pepper** and salt." See Disgrace
Perambulator poems, sel. David McCord
"When I was christened."—LiWw
"**Perch** in my plum tree." Onitsura, tr. fr. the Japanese by Harry Behn.—BeM
"**Perchance** do we truly live on earth." See Not forever on earth
Percy Bysshe Shelley. See The Spoon River anthology
Perfect. Glyn Jones.—MaFw
Perfect Arthur. N. M. Bodecker.—BoL
The **perfect** reactionary. Hughes Mearns.—LiWw
Perfection
Perfect Arthur. N. M. Bodecker.—BoL
Perfection ("It is enough for spring to be itself") G. Ost'or.—MoM
Perfection ("Surely the turkey") F. Holman.—HoI
Perfection ("It is enough for spring to be itself") Grigory Ost'or, tr. fr. the Russian by Miriam Morton.—MoM
Perfection ("Surely the turkey") Felice Holman.—HoI
"**Perfection** ever rising to perfection." See Song of praise to the Creator
"**Perhaps.**" See Antigone I
"**Perhaps.**" See October 16: The raid
"**Perhaps** in some succeeding year." Unknown.—MoBw
The **perils** of invisibility. William Schwenck Gilbert.—CoPt
Peristiany, J. G.
Girls' secret love song. tr.—AlPa
"**Periwinkle,** periwinkle." Unknown.—EmN

Perkins, David
The blue gift.—HiN
Falling in love.—HiN
"How long hast thou been a gravemaker."—HiN
Perkins, Lucy Fitch
Twins.—CoOr
Perlberg, Mark
The cry.—CoPu
Perleberg, Max
An enjoyable evening in the village near the lake. tr.—MaFw
Permanence
Harder than granite. R. Jeffers.—CoPu
Stabilities. A. Stevenson.—HiN
"**Perrette's** milk-pot fitted her head-mat just right." See The dairymaid and her milk-pot
Perry, Julianne
No dawns.—AdPb
To L.—AdPb
Perry, Phyllis J.
Halloween.—HoH
Perse, St John
Birds.—JoA-4
Perseverance
Before a saint's picture. W. S. Landor.—OpOx
For de Lawd. L. Clifton.—AdM—AdPb
For Hettie. LeRoi Jones.—PeS
A letter to Yvor Winters. K. Rexroth.—PlM
On his way. R. Froman.—FrSp
Strange legacies. S. A. Brown.—AdPb
Strong men. S. A. Brown.—AdPb
Upon a snail. J. Bunyan.—OpOx
"What can't be cured." Unknown.—RoIt
Persimmons
"At twilight a bell." Shiki.—BeM
"On the small table, the early mellowed." Park In-ro.—BaSs
"A **person**." See Monument
The **person** from Porlock. Robert Graves.—PlM
Personal beauty. See Beauty, Personal
A **personal** experience. Oliver Herford.—BrM
"**Peruse** these simple rhymes." Unknown.—MoBw
Pessimism. See Failure; Optimism; Misfortune
Pessoa, Fernando. See Caeiro, Alberto
The **pet** lamb. William Wordsworth.—OpOx
Pete the parrot and Shakespeare. Don Marquis.—PlM
Peter Bell, sel. William Wordsworth
The crescent boat.—RoIt
"**Peter,** Peter, pumpkin eater." Mother Goose.—HoMg—JoA-4
"**Peter** Piper pick'd a peck of pepper." Mother Goose.—EmN—HoMg—JoA-4
"**Peter** Prangle." Unknown.—BrM
"**Peter** Prangle, the prickly prangly pear picker."—EmN
"**Peter** Prangle, the prickly prangly pear picker." See "Peter Prangle"
Peter Rabbit. Dennis Lee.—LeA
"**Peter** Rabbit's." See Peter Rabbit
Peter Tatter. Rodney Bennett.—BrM
"**Peter** Tatter popped his batter." See Peter Tatter
"**Peter** White will ne'er go right." Mother Goose.—AlC
Petrie, Phil W.
It happened in Montgomery.—AbM
Pets
The canary's flight. J. R. Jiménez.—JoA-4
Drats. S. Silverstein.—SiW
"I wish." L. Moore.—MoSm
Janet waking. J. C. Ransom.—HiN—PeS
"Julia loves her Rosalie." K. Kuskin.—KuN
A kitten. A. Fisher.—FiFo
The lady and the swine. Unknown.—CoOh
Little Miss and her parrot. J. Marchant.—OpOx
Lost and found. L. Moore.—MoSm
"A man who was fond of his skunk." D. McCord
Three limericks.—McS
Milk for the cat. H. Monro.—JoA-4
My brother Bert. T. Hughes.—HuMf
My kitten. M. Chute.—ChRu
"Our Mr Toad." D. McCord.—JoA-4—McS
The pet lamb. W. Wordsworth.—OpOx
Pets. J. Ciardi.—CiFs
Platero. J. R. Jiménez.—JoA-4
The python. H. Belloc.—OpOx
To a young brother. M. J. Jewsbury.—OpOx
Who to pet and who not to. X. J. Kennedy.—KeO
The yak. H. Belloc.—JoA-4—OpOx
Pets. John Ciardi.—CiFs
"**Pets** are the hobby of my brother Bert." See My brother Bert
Phantoms. See Ghosts
Phantoms of the steppe. Alexander Pushkin, tr. fr. the Russian by Edna Worthley Underwood.—AbM
The **pheasant.** From Windsor forest. Alexander Pope.—RoIt (sel.)
Windsor forest.—CoPu (sel.)—MaFw (sel.)
Pheasants
The pheasant. From Windsor forest. A. Pope.—RoIt (sel.)
Windsor forest.—CoPu (sel.)—MaFw (sel.)
Philips, Edward
The gunpowder plot, from the great speech of Sir Edward Philips, arranged by David Mackay.—MaFw
Phillips, Hubert
Story of Reginald.—CoOr
The **philosophers,** sel. Po Chü-i, tr. fr. the Chinese by Arthur Waley
Lao-tzŭ.—LiWw
Phizzog. Carl Sandburg.—SaT
"A **phone** duet over the radio." See The Louisiana Weekly #4
Photograph. Quandra Prettyman.—AdPb
Photographers and photography
Hiawatha's photographing. L. Carroll.—LiPc—LiS
"I look like you precisely." K. Kuskin.—KuA
It's here in the. R. Atkins.—AdPb—PeS

Photographers and photography—*Continued*
Photograph. Q. Prettyman.—AdPb
Photographs: A vision of massacre. Michael S. Harper.—AdPb
Phrases. Jean-Nicolas-Arthur Rimbaud, tr. fr. the French by Oliver Bernard.—MaFw (sel.)
Physicians. See Doctors
Pi Ssu Yao (about)
To Pi Ssu Yao. Tu Fu.—PlM
Piano and drums. Gabriel Okara.—AlPa
"The **piano** hums." See Effendi
Pianos
Piano and drums. G. Okara.—AlPa
"**Pick** up a stick up." See Jumble jingle
The **Pickering** manuscript, sel. William Blake
The mental traveller.—MoG
The **picnic.** John Logan.—HiN
Picnic: the liberated. M. Carl Holman.—AdPb
Picnics
Happiness. C. Sandburg.—SaT
The picnic. J. Logan.—HiN
Picture people. Myra Cohn Livingston.—JoA-4
"**Picture** yourself in a boat on a river." See Lucy in the sky with diamonds
Pictures. See Paintings and pictures
Pictures of a city. Robert Fripp and Peter Sinfield.—MoG
Pictures of the Jews. Chaim Guri, tr. fr. the Hebrew by Ruth Finer Mintz.—MeP
Pie. See From the kitchen
Pie. Valerie Worth.—WoS
"A **piece** of sky." See Sky seasoning
A **piece** of sky. Felice Holman.—HoI
"**Piecemeal** the summer dies." See Exeunt
Pied beauty. Gerard Manley Hopkins.—MaFw—RoIt
The **Pied** Piper of Hamelin. Robert Browning.—OpOx
Pier. James Scully.—HaWr
Piercy, Marge
Councils.—MoT
Simple song.—MoT
Pierpont, James
Jingle bells.—RoIt
Pies
Alligator pie. D. Lee.—LeA
Kangaroo and kiwi. X. J. Kennedy.—KeO
"Monday morning mother made mincemeat pies." Unknown.—EmN
"Mother, a dog is at the door." X. J. Kennedy.—KeO
Mud pie. K. Fraser.—HoCs
Pie. V. Worth.—WoS
"P U double unkin." Unknown.—EmN
"P-U ennekin ennekin Y." Unknown.—EmN
"Rindle, randle." Unknown.—BlM
Yellow jacket. D. McCord.—McAa
"**Pietro** has twenty red and blue balloons on a string." See Five cent balloons
Pig. Valerie Worth.—WoS
"The **pig** is bigger." See Pig
"The **pig** lay on a barrow dead." See View of a pig
The **pig** tale. See Sylvie and Bruno
The **pigeon-hole.** Mabel Segun.—AlPa
"**Pigeon** on the roof." See Easy diver
Pigeons
The ballad of the light-eyed little girl. G. Brooks.—PeS
The dove and the ant. J. De La Fontaine.—JoA-4
Easy diver. R. Froman.—FrSp
"High in the pine tree." Mother Goose.—TucMgl
The mourning dove. F. Holman.—HoI
Perfect. G. Jones.—MaFw
Pigeons. W. H. Smith.—CoPu
"Pigeons on the rooftop." L. Lenski.—LeC
Song. J. Keats.—RoIt
"To owl, the dove says." Issa.—HaW
Pigeons. W. Hart Smith.—CoPu
"**Pigeons** on the rooftop." Lois Lenski.—LeC
"**Piggy** on the railway." Mother Goose.—AlC
Pigs
"Barber, barber, shave a pig." Mother Goose.—AlC—JoA-4
"Dickery, dickery, dare." Mother Goose.—AlC—TrG
"Grandpa Grig had a pig." Mother Goose.—AlC
"I had a little pig." Unknown.—EmN
"If a pig wore a wig." C. G. Rossetti.—JoA-4
Just born pig. F. Lape.—CoPu
"Little Martha piggy-wig." C. Watson.—WaF
"My little dad had five little piggies." Unknown.—BoI
My uncle Jehoshaphat. L. E. Richards.—OpOx
Perfection. F. Holman.—HoI
Pig. V. Worth.—WoS
The pig tale. From Sylvie and Bruno. L. Carroll.—LiPc
"Piggy on the railway." Mother Goose.—AlC
Pigs. J. Prelutsky.—CoOh
Song to make a baby laugh. Unknown.—BiS
Table talk. E. Moody.—BrM
"There was a lady loved a swine." Mother Goose.—MiMg
The lady and the swine.—CoOh
"This little pig went to market." Mother Goose.—JoA-4
The three little pigs. A. S. Gatty.—OpOx
"To market, to market, to buy a fat pig." Mother Goose.—AlC
"To market, to market."—JoA-4
"Tom, Tom, the piper's son (stole a pig)." Mother Goose.—AlC—JoA-4
View of a pig. T. Hughes.—MaFw
Pigs. Jack Prelutsky.—CoOh
"**Pigs** are stout." See Pigs
Pike. Ted Hughes.—HiN—ToM
"**Pike,** three inches long, perfect." See Pike
Pilgrim Fathers. See Thanksgiving day
The **pilgrimage.** Myra Cohn Livingston.—LiM
Pilgrims
Atlantic Charter: 1620-1942. From The island. F. B. Young.—JoA-4

The pilgrimage. M. C. Livingston.—LiM
"Pilgrims plod slowly." Ransetsu.—BeM
The prologue. From The Canterbury tales. G. Chaucer.—MaFw
"**Pilgrims** plod slowly." Ransetsu, tr. fr. the Japanese by Harry Behn.—BeM
Pilots and piloting. See Fliers and flight
Pima Indians. See Indians of the Americas—Pima
The **pin.** Ann Taylor.—OpOx
Pinder, Mike
Dawn is a feeling.—MoG
"**Pine** tree in the green mountain." Unknown, tr. fr. the Korean by Chung Seuk Park and ad. by Virginia Olsen Baron.—BaSs
Pine trees
"Butterflies, beware." Shosen.—BeM
"A drowsy breeze sighs." Onitsura.—BeM
"I know pines." F. Holman.—HoI
In autumn. T. Dinsburg.—MoM
"Peach and plum blossoms of spring." Kim Yu-ki.—BaSs
"Pine tree in the green mountain." Unknown.—BaSs
Pines. A. Fisher.—FiFo
Under the white pine. D. McCord.—McFm
"What shall I be." Sung Sam Mun.—BaSs
"When I see the pine trees." Unknown.—LaM
Pines. Aileen Fisher.—FiFo
"**Pines** on the hill." See Pines
Ping pong
Dr Ping and Mr Pong. D. McCord.—McAa
Ping-pong. E. Merriam.—MeF
Ping-pong. Eve Merriam.—MeF
"**Pinging** rain." See Weather report
Pining for love. Francis Beaumont.—CoPu
Pink
The groaning board.—CoPu
"**Pinky** Pauper picked my pocket." Clyde Watson.—WaF
Pins
"Charlie Chaplin sat on a pin." Unknown.—EmN
"Needles and pins, needles and pins." Mother Goose.—AlC—EmN
The pin. A. Taylor.—OpOx
"There is one that has a head without an eye." C. G. Rossetti
A riddle.—OpOx
Pioneer life. See Frontier and pioneer life
A **piper** ("A piper in the street today") Seumas O'Sullivan.—CoPi—CoPu
The **piper** ("Piping down the valleys wild") William Blake.—LiLc—OpOx
Happy songs.—UnGb
"A **piper** in the street today." See A piper
Pipers
"As I was going up the hill." Mother Goose.—AlC
"Doodledy, doodledy, doodledy, dan." Mother Goose.—HoMg
"On a green, green hill." Unknown.—BoI
The one who stayed. S. Silverstein.—SiW
The Pied Piper of Hamelin. R. Browning.—OpOx
A piper ("A piper in the street today") S. O'Sullivan.—CoPi—CoPu
The piper ("Piping down the valleys wild") W. Blake.—LiLc—OpOx
Happy songs.—UnGb
The piper's progress. Father Prout.—CoPi
Pipes and drums. L. Holmes.—JaP (sel.)
The seven ages of elf-hood. R. Field.—JaP
"There was a piper, he'd a cow." Mother Goose.—AlC
"Tom he was a piper's son." Mother Goose.—AlC
The **piper's** progress. Father Prout.—CoPi
Pipes and drums. Lilian Holmes.—JaP (sel.)
"**Piping** down the valleys wild." See The piper
Pippa passes, sels. Robert Browning
Pippa's song.—LiLc—MoG—RoIt
Song ("The year's at the spring")—MoG
Pippa's song. See Pippa passes
Pirate Captain Jim. Shel Silverstein.—SiW
Pirate story. Robert Louis Stevenson.—JoA-4—UnGb
Pirates
Captain Hook. S. Silverstein.—SiW
"One-eyed Jack, the pirate chief." Mother Goose.—TucMgl
Pirate captain Jim. S. Silverstein.—SiW
Pirate story. R. L. Stevenson.—JoA-4—UnGb
The tale of Custard the Dragon. O. Nash.—UnGb
The tarry buccaneer. J. Masefield.—CoPt
Pistachio ice cream. See From the kitchen
"**Pistachio** ice cream, all green." See From the kitchen—Pistachio ice cream
Pitcher, Oliver
The pale blue casket.—AdPb
Salute.—AdPb
Pitt, Valerie
The city.—HoCs
"**Pitter** patter, falls the rain." See The umbrella brigade
"**Pity** for him who suffers from his waste." See Suffer the children
"**Pity** this busy monster, manunkind." E. E. Cummings.—PeS
"**Pity** without relief." Unknown.—MoBw
Piyyut for Rosh Hashana. Chaim Guri, tr. fr. the Hebrew by Ruth Finer Mintz.—MeP
"The **place** where I have not been." Yehuda Amichai, tr. fr. the Hebrew by Assia Gutmann.—MeP
Places. See also names of places, as San Francisco
A dream or no. T. Hardy.—PlP
Geographical knowledge. T. Hardy.—PlP
Gluk. N. M. Bodecker.—BoL
The place's fault. P. Hobsbaum.—ToM
Places, loved ones. P. Larkin.—PeS
Where. W. De La Mare.—CoPu
The **place's** fault. Philip Hobsbaum.—ToM
Places, loved ones. Philip Larkin.—PeS

Plague. Unknown, tr. fr. the Cakchiquel by Adrián Recinos (with Delia Goetz).—BiI
Plain talk for a pachyderm. Peggy Bennett.—LiWw
The **plane.** Celia Urhman.—HoP
The **plane:** earth. Sun Ra.—AdPb
Plane geometry. Emma Rounds.—LiS
"The **plane** tilts in to Nashville." See The homecoming singer
"The **plane** up in the sky." See The plane
The **planet** of Mars. Shel Silverstein.—SiW
The **planet** on the table. Wallace Stevens.—PlM
Planets. See also Moon; Stars; World
Missionary. D. M. Thomas.—ToM
The planet on the table. W. Stevens.—PlM
Planets. X. J. Kennedy.—KeO
Unknown shores. D. M. Thomas.—ToM
Planets. X. J. Kennedy.—KeO
"Plank." See Recycled
Planning. Marchette Chute.—ChRu
"A **plant** without moisture sweet." See Rising in the morning
Plantation life. See Slavery
The **planter's** daughter. Austin Clarke.—CoPi
Plants and planting. See also names of plants, as Dandelions
"For he was a shrub among the poplars." C. Okigbo.—AlPa
Little bush. E. M. Roberts.—LiLc
A little green thing. L. Lenski.—LeC
Planets. X. J. Kennedy.—KeO
The right time. F. Holman.—HoI
The round. P. Booth.—HiN
Seed-time. G. Meredith.—PaF
Transplanting. T. Roethke.—HaWr
"Won't you plant your seeds with care." Mother Goose.—TucMg
Plastics
The wholly family. E. Merriam.—MeF
Platero. Juan Ramón Jiménez, tr. fr. the Spanish by Eloise Roach.—JoA-4
"Platero is a small donkey." See Platero
Plath, Sylvia
Balloons.—HiN—ToM
Blackberrying.—ToM
Child.—MaFw
For a fatherless son.—MoT
The moon and the yew tree.—ToM
You're.—HiN
The **platypus** ("My child, the duck-billed platypus") Oliver Herford.—LiWw
The **platypus** ("The platypus thought, but his thinking was stuck") Jack Prelutsky.—PrP
"The **platypus** thought, but his thinking was stuck." See The platypus
Platypuses
The platypus ("My child, the duck-billed platypus") O. Herford.—LiWw
The platypus ("The platypus thought, but his thinking was stuck") J. Prelutsky.—PrP
Play. See also Counting-out rhymes; Games; Nursery play
After dinner. M. Chute.—ChRu
August. L. Clifton.—ClE
Autumn. E. M. Roberts.—CoPt
Baby. L. Hughes.—HoD
A badger. A. Fisher.—FiFo
Balloons. D. McCord.—McAa
Bed in summer. R. L. Stevenson.—OpOx
Bobby's first poem. N. Gale.—CoPu
"Boys and girls come out to play." Mother Goose.—JoA-4
A boy's song. J. Hogg.—OpOx
Castles. M. Ridlon.—HoCs
Cat play. A. Fisher.—FiM
The chase. L. Lenski.—LeC
"Come and play with me." Issa.—HaW
Discovery. M. C. Livingston.—LiLc
"Dolphin daughter." A. Fisher.—FiD
The dumb soldier. R. L. Stevenson.—OpOx
The echoing green. W. Blake.—JoA-4—PaF
Fascination. J. B. Tabb.—CoOh
The 1st. L. Clifton.—MoT
George. H. Belloc.—CoOh
"Girls and boys, come out to play." Mother Goose.—AlC
Heart's needle. W. D. Snodgrass.—HiN (sel.)
Hideout. L. Lenski.—LeC
The hot day. M. Chute.—ChRu
"The house is in ruins." I. Ivanova.—MoM
Hug o' war. S. Silverstein.—SiW
"Is six times one a lot of fun." K. Kuskin.—KuN
Is this someone you know. J. Ciardi.—UnGb
Jumping rope. S. Silverstein.—SiW
Jungle gym. L. Lenski.—LeC
Kitten capers. A. Fisher.—FiM
Kitty cornered. E. Merriam.—MeO
Knock on wood. H. Dumas.—AdPb
The land of counterpane. R. L. Stevenson.—OpOx
The land of story-books. R. L. Stevenson.—RoIt—UnGb
Leisure. W. H. Davies.—RoIt
Little foxes. A. Fisher.—FiD
Little raindrops. J. E. Browne.—OpOx
Merry-go-round. L. Lenski.—LeC
Mrs Brown. R. Fyleman.—OpOx
My bed is a boat. R. L. Stevenson.—RoIt
My friend Thelma. R. Hoban.—HoE
Mud pies. K. Fraser.—HoCs
Muse's song. W. Blake.—JoA-4—OpOx
One, two, three. H. C. Bunner.—RoIt
"Our garden is my world." N. Glekiva.—MoM
Paper boats. R. Tagore.—MaFw (sel.)
The party. R. Whittemore.—HiN
Pirate story. R. L. Stevenson.—JoA-4—UnGb
Play ball. L. Lenski.—LeC
Play song. P. Clarke.—AbM
Playtime. L. Lenski.—LeC
Romping. J. Ciardi.—HiN
Sea horse and sawhorse. X. J. Kennedy.—KeO
Shower bath. L. Lenski.—LeC
Slippery slide. L. Lenski.—LeC
Something peaceful. T. Tsyganok.—MoM
Spring Saturday. M. Chute.—ChRu

For K. R. on her sixtieth birthday. R. Wilbur.—PlM
For poets. A. Young.—AdPb
For some poets. M. Jackson.—AdB—AdPb
For there is an upstart crow. R. Greene.—PlM
XIV. Alberto Caeiro.—MoT
The fragment. H. Belloc.—CoPu
The general public. S. V. Benét.—PlM
Genesis. E. Sewell.—PlM
George Crabbe. E. A. Robinson.—PlM
Haiku. D. McCord.—McFm
"Hands flat on the ground." Sokan.—BeM
Harder than granite. R. Jeffers.—CoPu
Heard in a violent ward. T. Roethke.—PlM
The height of the ridiculous. O. W. Holmes.—RoIt
Higher. Unknown.—LiS
His answer to the critics. Solomon ibn Gabirol.—MeP
An historic moment. W. J. Harris.—AdB—CoPu
Homage to Arthur Waley. R. Fuller.—PlM
"How pleasant to know Mr Lear." E. Lear.—LiS—PlM
Lines to a young lady.—RoIt
I am in danger—Sir. A. Rich.—PlM
I am Raftery. A. Raftery.—CoPi
I have folded my sorrows. B. Kaufman.—AdPb
"I know I'm not sufficiently obscure." R. Durem.—AdPb
"I must, Varus, tell you." Catullus.—PlM
I sing no new songs. F. M. Davis.—AdPb
"If I were an elephant." N. M. Bodecker.—BoL
"If thou survive my well-contented day." From Sonnets. W. Shakespeare.—PlM
In defense of black poets. C. K. Rivers.—AdB
In memory of the Spanish poet Federico García Lorca. T. Merton.—PlM
In memory of W. B. Yeats. W. H. Auden.—PlM
In the backs. F. Cornford.—PaP
In the time of revolution. J. Lester.—AdPb (sel.)
Inniskeen road, July evening. P. Kavanagh.—CoPi
Interval. R. Humphries.—PlM
Introduction ("This book you hold") W. Cole.—CoOr
Introduction ("This skinny poem will introduce") W. Cole.—CoOh
Invitation to Miss Marianne Moore. E. Bishop.—PlM
It's dark in here. S. Silverstein.—SiW
John Bun. Unknown.—LiWw
Keats at Teignmouth. C. Causley.—PlM
"The king sent for his wise men all." From Ragged Robin. J. Reeves.—AlC
Kiss. A. Young.—AdPb
The last signal. T. Hardy.—PlM—PlP
The lazy people. S. Silverstein.—CoOh
A letter to Yvor Winters. K. Rexroth.—PlM
Light dying. B. Kennelly.—CoPi
Lines for a dead poet. D. Ferry.—PlM
Lines for Cuscuscaraway and Mirza Murad Ali Beg. T. S. Eliot.—LiS—PlM
Lines on the Mermaid Tavern. J. Keats.—PlM
London, 1802. W. Wordsworth.—PlM
Loneliness. A. Young.—AdPb
Look, Hart, that horse you ride is wood. P. Viereck.—PlM
The lost leader. R. Browning.—PlM
Love to Stephen. E. Wylie.—PlM
Lu Yun's lament. H. Read.—PlM
Man is nothing but. S. Tchernichovsky.—MeP
Manifesto. Nicanor Parra.—MoT (sel.)
Mavrone, one of those sad Irish poems, with notes. A. Guiterman.—LiS
Memorabilia. R. Browning.—PlM
The metre Columbian. Unknown.—LiS
Metrical feet. S. T. Coleridge.—OpOx
A mirror for poets. T. Gunn.—PlM
Mr Pope. A. Tate.—PlM
Mr Smith (with nods to Mr Lear and Mr Eliot). W. J. Smith.—LiS
Motionless swaying. J. Ritsos.—MoT
The Muse. A. Akhmatova.—PlM
Music. R. W. Emerson.—RoIt
My life has been the poem. D. Thoreau.—PlM
My Muse. S. Smith.—PlM
My poem. N. Giovanni.—AdB—AdPb
Nephelidia. A. C. Swinburne.—LiS
Note to Wang Wei. J. Berryman.—PlM
O black and unknown bards. J. W. Johnson.—AdPb
Ode. A. Shaughnessy.—CoPi—RoIt
Ode on a jar of pickles. B. Taylor.—LiS
Old Walt. L. Hughes.—PlM
On a poetess. G. M. Hopkins.—CoPu
On being chosen poet of Vermont. R. Frost.—PlM
On first looking into Chapman's Homer. J. Keats.—PlM
On hearing someone sing a poem by Yüan Chēn. Po Chü-i.—PlM
On Homer's birthplace. T. Heywood.—PlM
On Keats. P. B. Shelley.—PlM
On looking into E. V. Rieu's Homer. P. Kavanagh.—PlM
On looking into Robert Frost in Kanji. W. Meredith.—PlM
On re-reading the complete works of an elder poet. W. T. Scott.—PlM
On the grasshopper and cricket. J. Keats.—JoA-4—PaF
Only seven. H. S. Leigh.—LiS
A pact. E. Pound.—PlM
Paddler's song on bad hunting weather. Unknown.—LeIb
Percy Bysshe Shelley. From The Spoon River anthology. E. L. Masters.—PlM
The person from Porlock. R. Graves.—PlM
Pete the parrot and Shakespeare. D. Marquis.—PlM
The planet on the table. W. Stevens.—PlM

Points of view
The blind men and the elephant. J. G. Saxe.—JoA-4—RoIt
Point of view ("The little bat hangs upside down") D. McCord.—BrM
Point of view ("Thanksgiving dinner's sad and thankless") S. Silverstein.—SiW
Points of view. A. Lowell.—CoPu
Points of view. Amy Lowell.—CoPu
"**Poised** between going on and back, pulled." See The base stealer
Poison ivy
Poison ivy. K. Gallagher.—JaP
Poison ivy. Katherine Gallagher.—JaP
"The **pokey** old mailman." See Pokey old mailman
Pokey old mailman. Lois Lenski.—LeC
The **polar** bear. Jack Prelutsky.—PrT
"The **polar** bear by being white." See The polar bear
"A **pole** stands at the corner." See Barber shop
The **pole-vaulter.** Unknown.—FlH
Police
Bear with me and you may learn. J. Ciardi.—CiFs
Definition for blk/children. S. Sanchez.—AdPb
The electric cop. V. H. Cruz.—AdPb
"I'm not going to Macy's any more, more, more." Unknown.—EmN
Keep on pushing. D. Henderson.—AdPb
Love. P. Solomon.—JoV
Policeman. L. Lenski.—LeC
"Policeman, policeman, don't take me." Mother Goose.—AlC—EmN
Psalm of those who go forth before daylight. C. Sandburg.—MaFw—SaT
"A **policeman.**" See Definition for blk/children
Policeman. Lois Lenski.—LeC
"The **policeman** buys shoes slow and careful, the teamster." See Psalm of those who go forth before daylight
"**Policeman,** policeman, don't take me." Mother Goose.—AlC—EmN
"**Policeman** wears a uniform." See Policeman
Politeness. See Etiquette
Politeness ("I met a squirrel the other day") Marchette Chute.—ChRu
Politeness ("My cousin John was most polite") Harry Graham.—CoOh
Politics
Politics. W. B. Yeats.—CoPi
Poll. E. Roberson.—AdPb
What the moon saw. V. Lindsay.—LiWw
Politics. William Butler Yeats.—CoPi
Poll. Ed Roberson.—AdPb
Pollack, Bretton
"Out fishing on the ocean."—HoP
Pollution
And they lived happily ever after for a while. J. Ciardi.—CiFs
Hail, polluters. R. Froman.—FrSp
Like it should be. M. C. Livingston.—LiM
Roll, river, roll. R. Froman.—FrSp
The tide river. From The water babies. C. Kingsley.—OpOx—RoIt
"**Polly** Vole." See Shiver my timbers
"**Pollywiggle.**" See Frog
Pome. David McCord.—McAa
Pomeroy, Marnie
Ground hog day.—CoPu
Ponchon, Raoul
The shepherd's tale.—CoPt
Ponds. See Lakes
Ponies. See Horses
A **pony.** Aileen Fisher.—FiFo
"The **pool** players." See We real cool
Poole, Tom
"I wonder why."—AdB
Poor. See Poverty
Poor Angus. Shel Silverstein.—SiW
"**Poor** Benjamin Bunnn." See Benjamin Bunnn
"**Poor** bird." Walter De La Mare.—MaFw
The **poor** girl's meditation. Unknown, tr. fr. the Irish by Padraic Colum.—CoPi
"**Poor** hungry white moths." See The hungry moths
"**Poor** it is: this land." Unknown, fr. the Ammassalik Eskimo.—LeIb
"A **poor** lad once and a lad so trim." See Jean Richepin's song
"**Poor** little Jesus." Unknown, ad. by Seymour Barab.—LaS
"**Poor** Lucy Lake was overgrown." See Lucy Lake
The **poor** man. Unknown, tr. fr. the Swahili by Lyndon Harries.—FlH
"The **poor** man knows not how to eat with the rich man." See The poor man
"**Poor** Myrtle would sigh, Sweet my Coz." See Goo-girl
"**Poor** old Mr Bidery." See Mr Bidery's spidery garden
"The **poor** old plum tree." Mae Hwa, tr. fr. the Korean by Chung Seuk Park and ad. by Virginia Olsen Baron.—BaSs
"**Poor** old Robinson Crusoe." Mother Goose.—AlC
"**Poor** tired Tim. It's sad for him." See Tired Tim
"**Pop-bottles** pop-bottles." See Song of the pop-bottlers
Pop goes the weasel. Mother Goose.—JoA-4
Pope, Alexander
Epigram; also at. to S. T. Coleridge.—RoIt
Epigram engraved on the collar of a dog which I gave to his Royal Highness.—RoIt
"I am His Highness' dog at Kew."—TrG
Epitaph intended for Sir Isaac Newton.—RoIt
Intended for Sir Isaac Newton.—LiWw
"I am His Highness' dog at Kew." See Epigram engraved on the collar of a dog which I gave to his Royal Highness
Intended for Sir Isaac Newton. See Epitaph intended for Sir Isaac Newton
Ode on solitude.—MaFw
Solitude.—RoIt

Pope, Alexander—*Continued*
The pheasant. From Windsor forest.—RoIt (sel.)
Windsor forest.—CoPu (sel.)—MaFw (sel.)
Solitude. See Ode on solitude
Windsor forest. See The pheasant
You fancy wit.—RoIt
An empty house.—LiWw
Pope, Alexander (about)
Mr Pope. A. Tate.—PlM
"The **Pope** he leads a happy life." Charles Lever.—CoPi
Pope, Jessie
A word of encouragement.—CoPu
Pope, The
"The Pope he leads a happy life." C. Lever.—CoPi
The **poplar** field. William Cowper.—MaFw
Poplar trees
Binsey poplars felled 1879. G. M. Hopkins.—MaFw
"For he was a shrub among the poplars." C. Okigbo.—AlPa
The poplar field. W. Cowper.—MaFw
Southern mansion. A. Bontemps.—AdPb
To a late poplar. P. Kavanagh.—CoPi
"The **poplars** are felled, farewell to the shade." See The poplar field
"**Poplars** are standing there still as death." See Southern mansion
Poppies
Caprice. D. S. Shaw.—CoPt
"A poppy in his hand." Issa.—HaW
"A **poppy** in his hand." Issa, tr. fr. the Japanese by Hanako Fukuda.—HaW
Porches. Valerie Worth.—WoS
The **porcupine** ("Rebecca Jane") N. M. Bodecker.—BoL
The **porcupine** ("The porcupine is puzzled") Jack Prelutsky.—PrT
"The **porcupine** is puzzled." See The porcupine
Porcupines
"As I went over Lincoln bridge." Unknown.—TrG
"Backward running porcupines." M. A. Hoberman.—HoR
Courtship. A. Resnikoff.—CoOh
The porcupine ("Rebecca Jane") N. M. Bodecker.—BoL
The porcupine ("The porcupine is puzzled") J. Prelutsky.—PrT
"The sun is a yellow-tipped porcupine." N. Belting.—BeWi
Vice versa verse. M. A. Hoberman.—HoLb
"**Poring** on Caesar's death with earnest eye." See Julius Caesar and the honey-bee
Porpoises. See Dolphins
Portland, Maine
My lost youth. H. W. Longfellow.—RoIt
Portrait. Carolyn Rodgers.—AdM
Portrait by a neighbor. Edna St Vincent Millay.—NeA
Portrait of a child settling down for an afternoon nap. Carl Sandburg.—SaT
Portrait of a girl with comic book. Phyllis McGinley.—PeS
Portrait of Malcolm X. Etheridge Knight.—AdPb
Portraits. See Paintings and pictures; also People—Portraits
Positives. Johari Amini.—AdPb
Positives: For Sterling Plumpp. Don L. Lee.—AdPb
"**Positives,** positives, ain u sumthin." See Positives
Possessions. See Wealth
Possums. See Opossums
"**Possums** have a pocket." See Lion cubs
Post, Laurens van der
Song of the rain. tr.—AlPa
The **post-boy** drove with fierce career. See Alice Fell: or, Poverty
"**Postman,** postman." Unknown.—EmN
Postmen. See Mailmen
Postscript. W. H. Auden.—MaFw
Potatoes
Dearly beloved brethren. J. Tabrar.—CoPu
"Hokey, pokey, whisky, thum." Mother Goose.—MiMg
"Many eyes." Unknown.—EmN
"Put 10, put 20, put 30, put 40, put 50." Unknown.—EmN
"A riddle, a riddle, as I suppose." Unknown.—EmN
Potomac river
Potomac town in February. C. Sandburg.—LiLc—SaT
Potomac town in February. Carl Sandburg.—LiLc—SaT
Pottery
Auctioneer. E. Merriam.—MeO
"Cinderella, dressed in pink." Unknown.—EmN
Cups without wine. Judah Halevi.—MeP
"First, the fish must be caught." From Through the looking-glass. L. Carroll.—LiPc
Kaleeba. Unknown.—SeS
"Round as an apple (Black)." Unknown.—EmN
The **poultries.** Ogden Nash.—CoOr
Poultry. See names of kinds of poultry, as Chickens
The **poultry** show. David McCord.—McAa
Pound, Ezra
Ancient music.—LiS—MaFw
"And the days are not full enough."—MaFw
Doria.—MaFw
The faun.—MaFw
Image from d'Orleans.—MaFw
An immorality.—CoPu
Meditatio.—LiWw
A pact.—PlM
Pound, Ezra (about)
A pact. E. Pound.—PlM
"**Pour,** O pour that parting soul in song." See Song of the son

Poverty
Alice Fell: or, Poverty. W. Wordsworth.—LiS
The ballad of the harp-weaver. E. St V. Millay.—CoPt—RoIt
Baudelaire. D. Schwartz.—PlM
Der arme poet. M. Roberts.—PlM
Ennui. L. Hughes.—HoD
Four and twenty. S. Stills.—MoG
"Here we come a-wassailing." Unknown.—MaF
"How cold it is." Issa.—HaW
I have seen black hands. R. Wright.—AdPb
"If you talk too much, you are a swindler." Kim Sang-yong.—BaSs
An invitation to Madison county. Jay Wright.—AdPb
Letter in winter. R. R. Patterson.—AdPb
"Moving through the silent crowd." S. Spender.—ToM
Nikki-Rosa. N. Giovanni.—AdPb
No heat today. L. Lenski.—LeC
No new music. S. Crouch.—AdPb
Pastoral. W. C. Williams.—PeS
Poor Angus. S. Silverstein.—SiW
"Poor it is: this land." Unknown.—LeIb
The poor man. Unknown.—FlH
The ruined maid. T. Hardy.—PlP
Saturday's child. C. Cullen.—AdPb
Scenery. T. Joans.—AdPb
Slum home. L. Lenski.—LeC
Snapshots of the cotton South. F. M. Davis.—AdPb
Time. L. Lenski.—LeC
Timothy Winters. C. Causley.—ToM
The watercress seller. T. Miller.—OpOx
"The **power** digger." See The power shovel
Power dive. Norman MacCaig.—CoPu
The **power** shovel. Rowena Bastin Bennett.—HoP
The **powerful** eyes o' Jeremy Tait. Wallace Irwin.—CoPt
Practical concerns. William J. Harris.—AdPb
Prairie, sels. Carl Sandburg
Cornhuskers.—SaT
Haystacks.—SaT
Limited crossing Wisconsin.—SaT
Songs.—SaT
Summer morning.—SaT
Prairie barn. See The people, yes
Prairie waters by night. Carl Sandburg.—SaT
Prairies
"As my eyes." Unknown.—JoT
In praise of prairie. T. Roethke.—JoA-4
Praise. Christopher Smart.—OpOx
Praise of a child. Unknown, tr. fr. the Yoruba by Ulli Beier and Bakare Gbadamosi.—AlPa
Praise to the end. Theodore Roethke.—JoA-4 (sel.)
"**Praise** ye the Lord (praise God)." See Psalms—Psalm 150
The **prater.** Matthew Prior.—LiWw
Pratt, Agnes T.
Bremerton, January 18, 1969.—AlW
Death takes only a minute.—AlW
Empathy.—AlW
Fishing.—AlW
Fragments of spring.—AlW
Hope to keep.—AlW
I'm only going to tell you once.—AlW
Lamentation.—AlW
Question.—AlW
Quietly I shout.—AlW
The sea is melancholy.—AlW
So quickly came the summer.—AlW
Sympathy.—AlW
Twilight's feet.—AlW
Untitled.—AlW
Pratt, Anna M. (Maria)
A mortifying mistake.—BrM
Prayer ("Creator, you who dwell at the ends of the earth") Unknown, tr. fr. the Inca by Christóbal de Molina.—BiI
Prayer ("Earthmaker, our Father, listen to me") Unknown, tr. fr. the Winnebago by Paul Radin.—BiI
Prayer ("Grandfather") Unknown, tr. fr. the Sioux by Benjamin Black Elk.—BiI
Prayer ("Greeting, Father's clansman") Unknown, tr. fr. the Crow by Robert Lowie.—BiI
Prayer ("I ask you this") Langston Hughes.—HoD
Prayer ("Lord most giving and resourceful") Unknown, tr. fr. the Aztec by Bernardino de Sahagún.—BiI
Prayer ("Oh thou, Tzacol, Bitol") Unknown, tr. fr. the Quiché by Delia Goetz and Sylvanus Morley.—BiI
Prayer ("Owl") Unknown, tr. fr. the Navajo by Washington Matthews.—BiI
Prayer ("We kneel before you today, Father") Unknown, tr. fr. the Araucanian.—BiI
Prayer ("We return thanks to our mother, the earth, which sustains us") Unknown, tr. fr. the Iroquois by Ely S. Parker.—BiI
Prayer before birth. Louis MacNeice.—CoPi—PeS—ToM
Prayer before the dead body. Unknown, tr. fr. the Hottentot by P. Trilles.—AlPa
Prayer for fine weather. Shane Leslie.—CoPi
A **prayer** for Halloween. Unknown.—LaM
A **prayer** for little things. Eleanor Farjeon.—JoA-4
Prayer for reptiles. Patricia Hubbell.—AdP
Prayer meeting. Langston Hughes.—HoD
The **prayer** of Cyrus Brown. Sam Walter Foss.—LiWw
The **prayer** of the little ducks. Carmen Bernos de Gasztold.—AdP
Prayer of warriors. Unknown, tr. fr. the Virgusu by Günter Wagner.—AlPa
A **prayer** to be delivered from liars and warmongers. See Psalms—Psalm 120
A **prayer** to be restored to the sanctuary. See Psalms—Psalm 84
A **prayer** to be said when thou goest to bed. Francis Seager.—OpOx

Prayer to masks. Léopold Sédar Senghor, tr. fr. the French by John Reed and Clive Wake.—AlPa
"**Prayer** to my lady of Paphos." Sappho, tr. fr. the Greek by Mary Barnard.—ThI
Prayer to the snowy owl. John Haines.—CoPu
Prayers. See also Grace; Hymns
"Breathe on him." Unknown.—BiI
Call to prayer. Unknown.—AbM
A child's evening prayer. S. T. Coleridge.—OpOx
The convent. S. O'Sullivan.—CoPi
Cover my earth mother. Unknown.—BiI
"Don't you ever." Unknown.—JoT
Ex ore infantium. F. Thompson.—OpOx
"Father." Unknown.—JoT
"Father, have pity on me." Unknown.—ClFc
Father of night. B. Dylan.—MoG
Feet o' Jesus. L. Hughes.—HoD
The fool's prayer. E. Sill.—RoIt
"Gentle Jesus, meek and mild." C. Wesley.—OpOx
"Goosey, goosey, gander." Mother Goose.—AlC—JoA-4
Hebrides crofter's prayer. Unknown.—CoPu
His prayer to Ben Jonson. R. Herrick.—PlM
I gave them fruits. Unknown.—BiI
Little things. J. Stephens.—AdP—CoPu—JoA-4
Magic prayer. Unknown.—LeIb
Morning prayer. O. Nash.—OpOx
"My children." Unknown.—JoT
"My sun." Unknown.—JoT
"Now the day is over." S. Baring-Gould.—OpOx
"O Lord, save we beseech Thee." Unknown.—MeP
Offering. Unknown.—BiI
One morning, oh, so early. J. Ingelow.—OpOx
One night at Victoria beach. G. Okara.—AlPa
Prayer ("Creator, you who dwell at the ends of the earth") Unknown.—BiI
Prayer ("Earthmaker, our Father, listen to me") Unknown.—BiI
Prayer ("Grandfather") Unknown.—BiI
Prayer ("Greeting, Father's clansman") Unknown.—BiI
Prayer ("I ask you this") L. Hughes.—HoD
Prayer ("Lord most giving and resourceful") Unknown.—BiI
Prayer ("Oh thou, Tzacol, Bitol") Unknown.—BiI
Prayer ("Owl") Unknown.—BiI
Prayer ("We kneel before you today, Father") Unknown.—BiI
Prayer ("We return thanks to our mother, the earth, which sustains us") Unknown.—BiI
Prayer before birth. L. MacNeice.—CoPi—PeS—ToM
Prayer before the dead body. Unknown.—AlPa
Prayer for fine weather. S. Leslie.—CoPi
A prayer for Halloween. Unknown.—LaM
A prayer for little things. E. Farjeon.—JoA-4
Prayer for reptiles. P. Hubbell.—AdP
Prayer meeting. L. Hughes.—HoD
The prayer of Cyrus Brown. S. W. Foss.—LiWw
Prayers of steel. C. Sandburg.—SaT
The prayer of the little ducks. C. B. de Gasztold.—AdP
Prayer of warriors. Unknown.—AlPa
A prayer to be said when thou goest to bed. F. Seager.—OpOx
Prayer to masks. L. S. Senghor.—AlPa
"Prayer to my lady of Paphos." Sappho.—ThI
Prayer to the snowy owl. J. Haines.—CoPu
Presenting an infant to the sun. Unknown.—BiI
"Rudy Felsh." S. Silverstein.—SiW
Shout. L. Hughes.—HoD
The suppliant. G. D. Johnson.—AdPb
Supplication to the rain god and the spirits of water. Unknown.—BiI
"There was a rat, for want of stairs." Mother Goose.—MiMg—TrG
"Three little mice ran up the stairs." Unknown.—TrG
Vespers. A. A. Milne.—LiS—OpOx
"A voice." Unknown.—JoT
We are living humbly. Unknown.—BiI
We thank Thee. R. W. Emerson.—LaM
"With rejoicing mouth." Unknown.—BiI
"You, whose day it is." Unknown.—JoT
Prayers of steel. Carl Sandburg.—SaT
The **praying** mantis ("From whence arrived the praying mantis") Ogden Nash.—CoPu
The **praying** mantis ("The praying mantis may not rate") Felice Holman.—HoI
"The **praying** mantis may not rate." See The praying mantis
Praying mantises
The praying mantis ("From whence arrived the praying mantis") O. Nash.—CoPu
The praying mantis ("The praying mantis may not rate") F. Holman.—HoI
Preachers. See Ministers of the gospel; Sermons
Precious stones
Flint. C. G. Rossetti.—OpOx
Jewels. V. Worth.—WoS
March jewels. F. Holman.—HoI
Precision
Precision. P. Collenette.—MaFw
Precision. Peter Collenette.—MaFw
Preface to a twenty volume suicide note. LeRoi Jones.—AdPb—PeS
Prefatory poems
"All in the golden afternoon." From Alice's adventures in wonderland. L. Carroll.—LiPc
"Child of the pure unclouded brow." From Through the looking-glass. L. Carroll.—LiPc
Prologue to Evangeline. From Evangeline. H. W. Longfellow.—LiS
Preferred vehicles. Leland B. Jacobs.—HoP

Prejudice. Georgia Douglas Johnson.—AdPb
Prejudices
Note to my neighbor. P. McGinley.—LiWw
Prejudice. G. D. Johnson.—AdPb
The **prelude,** sels. William Wordsworth
"And in the frosty season, when the sun."—PaF
"Bright was the summer's moon when quickening steps."—PaP
"One summer evening (led by her) I found."—MaFw
Prelude ("Night and the hood") Conrad Kent Rivers.—AdPb
Prelude ("Pleasant it was, when woods were green") Henry Wadsworth Longfellow.—PaF
Prelutsky, Jack
The aardvark.—PrT
Adelaide.—CoOh
The armadillo.—PrT
The beaver.—PrT
Bees.—BrM—PrT
The black bear.—PrP
"Bring on the clowns."—PrC
The chameleon.—PrP
The cheetah.—PrP
The cow.—PrP
Don't ever seize a weasel by the tail.—BrM
"A dromedary standing still."—PrT
"Eight big black bears six feet tall."—PrC
Electric eels.—PrP
"The famed sword-swallower, looking bored."—PrC
"The famous human cannonball."—PrC
Fish.—PrT
"Four furry seals, four funny fat seals."—PrC
The gallivanting gecko.—PrP
"The great fire-eater, befitting his name."—PrC
"Here come the elephants, ten feet high."—PrC
"The high-diver climbs to the ladder's top."—PrC
The hippopotamus.—CoOr—PrT
"Hooray. Here comes the great parade."—PrC
The house mouse.—PrP
The hummingbird.—PrT
The hyena.—PrT
"I tame the very fiercest beast."—PrC
The lion.—PrP
"Listen to the music, listen to the din."—PrC
"The mightiest strong man on all of the planet."—PrC
The mole.—PrP
"My trainer steps into the ring."—PrC
"Over and over the tumblers tumble."—PrC
"Oysters."—PrT
The pack rat.—PrP
Pigs.—CoOh
The platypus.—PrP
The polar bear.—PrT
The porcupine.—PrT
Sheep.—PrP
The skunk.—PrP
The snail.—PrT
Toucans two.—BrM—PrT
The turtle.—PrT
"The two-horned black rhinoceros."—PrP
"Two horses race into the ring."—PrC
The walrus.—PrP
"The wiggling, wriggling, jiggling juggler."—PrC
The zebra.—PrT
Zoo doings.—PrT
Prem Chaya
On my short-sightedness.—MaFw
Premonitions. See Omens; Prophecies
Preoccupation. Unknown, tr. fr. the Mbundu by Merlin Ennis.—AlPa
Preparedness
"Let the fall leaves fall." C. Watson.—WaF
Youth. F. Cornford.—CoPu
The **presence.** Maxine W. Kumin.—MoT
Presence of mind. Harry Graham.—LiWw
"**Presentiment**—is that long shadow—on the lawn." Emily Dickinson.—ThI
Presenting an infant to the sun. Unknown, tr. fr. the Zuñi by Ruth Bunzel.—BiI
Presents ("I have counted every present with my name") Myra Cohn Livingston.—BrM—HoS
Presents ("I wanted a rifle for Christmas") Marchette Chute.—BrM
Presidential address to a party of exiles leaving for the moon. Howard Nemerov.—PlM
Presidents. See also names of presidents, as Lincoln, Abraham
Historical reflections. J. Hollander.—LiWw
"I am waiting to hear from the president, to ask." V. Bryant.—JoV
If I was president. M. Cowan.—JoV
If I were president. I. Velez.—JoV
"**Pretend** you are a dragon." See Things to do if you are a subway
"A **pretty** boat." Nikita Tolstoy, tr. fr. the Russian by Miriam Morton.—MoM
"**Pretty** prating poll." See Little Miss and her parrot
Prettyman, Quandra
The birth of the poet.—AdB
Blues.—AdB
"Crawl into bed."—AdB
Lullaby.—AdB
The mood.—AdPb
Photograph.—AdPb
Still life: Lady with birds.—AdPb
When Mahalia sings.—AdPb
Prévert, Jacques
The dunce.—MaFw
To paint the portrait of a bird.—MaFw
Price, Jonathan
"Ice cream."—PeS
"The **price** seemed reasonable, location." See Telephone conversation
Pride and vanity. See also Conceit
Black people. T. Joans.—AdM
Color. L. Hughes.—AdB—HoD

Prologue to The family of man, sel. Carl Sandburg
Names.—SaT
The **promissory** note. Bayard Taylor.—LiS
A **proper** place. Robert Nye.—CoPu
"The **proper** way for a man to pray." See The prayer of Cyrus Brown
Prophecies. See also Omens
Amos, sels. Bible, Old Testament
The basket of summer fruit.—MeP
The prophecies against Moab, Judah, and Israel.—MeP
Bad moon rising. J. Fogerty.—MoG
The belly remains. T. U Tam'si.—AlPa (sel.)
A denunciation of the princes and prophets. From Micah, Bible, Old Testament.—MeP
From the prophecy against Egypt. From Isaiah, Bible, Old Testament.—MeP
Judgment and sunrise. From Malachi, Bible, Old Testament.—MeP
Prophecy ("Eat, eat, thou hast bread") Unknown.—BiI
Prophecy ("Many winters ago") Unknown.—BiI
The **prophecies** against Moab, Judah, and Israel. See Amos
Prophecy ("Eat, eat, thou hast bread") Unknown, tr. fr. the Maya by D. G. Brinton.—BiI
Prophecy ("Many winters ago") Unknown, tr. fr. the Iroquois by Ely S. Parker.—BiI
The **prophet's** warning or shoot to kill. Ebon (Dooley).—AdPb
Proposition. Nicolás Guillén, tr. fr. the Spanish by Langston Hughes.—AbM
Proprietor. A. M. Sullivan.—RoIt
"The **protective** grigri." Ted Joans.—AdPb
Protests
England in 1819. P. B. Shelley.—MoG
"I was jus." B. O'Meally.—AdM
Kent State, May 4, 1970. P. Goodman.—MoT
Masters of war. B. Dylan.—MoG
Old black men say. J. A. Emanuel.—AdM—AdPb
"A **proud** Pasha was Bailey Ben." See Pasha Bailey Ben
Proud songsters. Thomas Hardy.—MaFw
"**Proudly** the fedoras march on the heads of the somewhat careless men." See Sky pieces
"**Proudly** the moon rides, crest." See Lines for a night driver
Prout, Father, pseud. (Francis Sylvester Mahoney)
The Shandon bells.—CoPi
Proverbs. See also Superstitions
"Love and a cough cannot be hid." Unknown.—MoBw
Meditations divine and morall. A. Bradstreet.—ThI (sel.)
Proverbs. From The people, yes. C. Sandburg.—SaT
A spade is just a spade. W. E. Hawkins.—AdPb
The two paths. From Proverbs, Bible, Old Testament.—JoA-4
"What can't be cured." Unknown.—RoIt
Proverbs—Bible—Old Testament
The two paths
Proverbs. See The people, yes
The **provident** puffin. Oliver Herford.—BrM
Proviso. Phil George.—AlW
Pruning trees. Po Chü-i, tr. fr. the Chinese by Arthur Waley.—MaFw
Psalm 1. See Psalms
Psalm 23. See Psalms
Psalm 24. See Psalms
Psalm 30. See Psalms
Psalm 46. See Psalms
Psalm 84. See Psalms
Psalm 90. See Psalms
Psalm 91. See Psalms
Psalm 104. See Psalms
Psalm 107. See Psalms
Psalm 120. See Psalms
Psalm 121. See Psalms
Psalm 124. See Psalms
Psalm 126. See Psalms
Psalm 127. See Psalms
Psalm 137. See Psalms
Psalm 150. See Psalms
A **psalm** of thanksgiving. See Psalms—Psalm 124
Psalm of those who go forth before daylight. Carl Sandburg.—MaFw—SaT
Psalms, sels. Bible—Old Testament
Psalm 1
The tree and the chaff.—JoA-4
Psalm 23
"The Lord is my shepherd."—JoA-4
Psalm 24
The earth is the Lord's.—JoA-4
Psalm 30
"I will extol thee, O Lord."—MeP
Psalm 46
God is our refuge and strength.—JoA-4
Psalm 84
A prayer to be restored to the sanctuary.—MeP
Psalm 90
"Lord, thou hast been our dwelling place."—MeP
Psalm 91
"Abiding in the shadow of the Almighty."—JoA-4
Psalm 104
A meditation on Providence.—MeP
Psalm 107
They that go down.—RoIt
Psalm 120
A prayer to be delivered from liars and warmongers.—MeP
Psalm 121
"I will lift up mine eyes unto the hills."—JoA-4
Psalm 124
A psalm of thanksgiving.—MeP

Pussy willows. See Willow trees
Pussy willows. Marchette Chute.—ChRu
"Put my black father on the penny." See Monument in black
"Put 10, put 20, put 30, put 40, put 50." Unknown.—EmN
"Put your brains in a jaybird's head." Unknown.—MoBw
"Put your feet down with pollen." See Magic formula to make an enemy peaceful
"Put your head, darling, darling, darling." See Dear dark head
"Puva, puva, puva." Unknown, tr. fr. the Hopi.—ClFc
Puzzle. Robert Froman.—FrSp
The **puzzled** census taker. John Godfrey Saxe.—CoPt
The **puzzled** centipede. Unknown.—BrM
"A centipede was happy quite."—RoIt
The **puzzled** game-birds. Thomas Hardy.—PlP
Puzzles
Puzzle. R. Froman.—FrSp
Puzzles from wonderland. L. Carroll.—LiPc
"There was a girl in our town." Unknown.—EmN
"When .a.y and I. a told .a..ie they'd seen a." L. Carroll.—LiPc
Puzzles from wonderland. Lewis Carroll.—LiPc
Pygmalion
To poor Pygmalion. E. J. Coatsworth.—CoPu
"Pygmy hippopota—." See Hippopotamus
The **python.** Hilaire Belloc.—OpOx
"A **python** I should not advise." See The python
"Python, python, python." See Ttimba
Pythons
"Hello Mr Python." S. Milligan.—CoOh
The python. H. Belloc.—OpOx
Pythons. M. A. Hoberman.—HoR
Ttimba. Unknown.—SeS
Pythons. Mary Ann Hoberman.—HoR

Q

" '**Quack.**' said the billy goat." Charles Causley.—CaF
"Quadroon mermaids, afro angels, black saints." See A ballad of remembrance
The **quagga.** D. J. Enright.—ToM
Quaggas
The quagga. D. J. Enright.—ToM
"Quail." Unknown, tr. fr. the Danish by N. M. Bodecker.—BoI
"The **quail** in the bush is making his whirring." Unknown, tr. fr. the Yaqui.—ClFc
Quails. See Partridges and quails
The **quangle** wangle's hat. Edward Lear.—JoA-4
Quarrels and quarreling. See also Fights
"Belly & Tubs went out in a boat." C. Watson.—WaF
Captain Spud and his First Mate, Spade. J. Ciardi.—CiFs
Crickets. C. Aiken.—RoIt
"The cuckoo and the donkey." Mother Goose.—TucMg
"Moll-in-the-wad and I fell out." Unknown.—TrG
"Tweedle-dum and Tweedle-dee." Mother Goose.—AlC
"A **quarter** horse, no rider." See Horse
Quasimodo, Salvatore
Alleyway.—MaFw
Quatrains, sels. T. Carmi, tr. fr. the Hebrew by Dom Moraes
Gentleman to lady.—MeP
Shell to gentleman.—MeP
Quechua Indians. See Indians of the Americas—Quechua
"Queen Anne." See The field, revisited
Queen Mab. See Romeo and Juliet—"O, then, I see Queen Mab hath been with you"
Queen Mab. Thomas Hood.—JaP (sel.)
Queen Nefertiti. Unknown.—NeA
The **queen** of Connemara. Francis A. Fahy.—CoPi
"The **Queen** of Hearts." Mother Goose.—JoA-4
"The **queen** was in the parlour." See Contemporary nursery rhyme
Queens. See Rulers
The **queens'** rhyme. Ian Serraillier.—BrM
Query ("And when") Ebon (Dooley).—AdPb
Query ("What would it be") Lucie McKee.—CoPu
Question ("Angled sunbeam lowered") Chinua Achebe.—AlPa
Question ("Body my house") May Swenson.—JoA-4
Question ("Did you ever ever ever think") Mary Ann Hoberman.—HoLb
A **question** ("I asked if I got sick and died, would you") John M. Synge.—CoPi
The **question** ("I dream'd that, as I wander'd by the way") Percy Bysshe Shelley.—PaF
A **question** ("Is it for me to see you") Alonzo Lopez.—AlW
The **question** ("Must I lay down and die to feel the Earth") Vanessa Howard.—JoV
The **question** ("Something follows everything") Tanya Kucherenko, tr. fr. the Russian by Miriam Morton.—MoM
Question ("Whence the beginning") Agnes T. Pratt.—AlW
Question ("Who says, But one month more") David McCord.—McAa
"Question: What kind of rabbit can an Easter rabbit be." See Easter morning
Questioning faces. Robert Frost.—CoPu—HiN
Questions
Question ("Angled sunbeam lowered") C. Achebe.—AlPa
Question ("Body my house") M. Swenson.—JoA-4
Question ("Did you ever ever ever think") M. A. Hoberman.—HoLb

R

Broken heart, broken machine. R. E. Grant.—AdPb
Brothers. L. Hughes.—HoD
The Chicago *Defender* sends a man to Little Rock. G. Brooks.—AdPb
Children's rhymes. L. Hughes.—AdB
Colors for mama. B. Mahone.—AdPb
Cross. L. Hughes.—AdPb
Cultural exchange. L. Hughes.—AdPb
A dance for militant dilettantes. A. Young.—AdPb
The dancer. A. Young.—AdPb
The day-breakers. A. Bontemps.—AdPb
Daybreak in Alabama. L. Hughes.—HoD
Death in Yorkville. L. Hughes.—AdPb
Deathwatch. M. S. Harper.—AdPb
Determination. D. Randall.—AdPb
Feeding the lions. N. Jordan.—AdB
First Monday Scottsboro Alabama. T. Weatherly.—AdPb
For my people. M. Walker.—AdPb
For Nina Simone wherever you are. L. Curry.—JoV
For Stephen Dixon. Z. Gilbert.—AdPb
Fourth dance poem. G. W. Barrax.—AdPb
Friends. R. Durem.—AdPb
A guerilla handbook. LeRoi Jones.—AdPb
Hands. G. Thompson.—JoV
He rather die. K. Jones.—JoV
He's doing natural life. Conyus.—AdPb
I gave them fruits. Unknown.—BiI
I have seen black hands. R. Wright.—AdPb
I, too. L. Hughes.—HoD—RoIt
"I, too, sing America."—AdPb
"I used to wrap my white doll up in." M. Jackson.—AdB—AdPb
Idle chatter. H. Dumas.—AdB
If everybody was black. J. Holland.—JoV
If we cannot live as people. C. Lynch.—AdPb
Image. H. Dumas.—AdB
In the time of revolution. J. Lester.—AdPb (sel.)
It happened in Montgomery. P. W. Petrie.—AbM
Jitterbugging in the streets. C. C. Hernton.—AdPb
Keep on pushing. D. Henderson.—AdPb
The lost black man. L. Baez.—JoV
The Louisiana *Weekly* #4. D. Henderson.—AdPb
Lynching and burning. Primus St John.—AdPb
Man white, brown girl and all that jazz. G. C. Oden.—AdPb
Merry-go-round. L. Hughes.—AbM—HoD
Militant. L. Hughes.—AdPb
Montgomery. S. Cornish.—AdM—AdPb
Monument in black. V. Howard.—AdM—JoV
"My children." Unknown.—JoT
My name is Afrika. K. Kgositsile.—AdPb
My poem. N. Giovanni.—AdB—AdPb
"My soul speaks Spanish." M. Lasanta.—JoV
The new integrationist. D. L. Lee.—AdB
The new math. V. Howard.—JoV
Newsletter from my mother. M. S. Harper.—AdPb
No difference. S. Silverstein.—SiW
No way out. L. Curry.—JoV
Old Lem. S. A. Brown.—AdPb
An old woman remembers. S. A. Brown.—AdPb
Once. A. Walker.—AdPb (sel.)
One eyed black man in Nebraska. S. Cornish.—AdPb
One sided shoot-out. D. L. Lee.—AdPb
Panther. S. Cornish.—AdPb
Poem (No name No. 2). N. Giovanni.—AdB
Poem of Angela Yvonne Davis. N. Giovanni.—AdPb
Prelude. C. K. Rivers.—AdPb
Primary lesson: The second class citizens. Sun Ra.—AdPb
The prophets warning or shoot to kill. Ebon (Dooley).—AdPb
PSI. M. B. Tolson.—AdPb
A question. A. Lopez.—AlW
Race prejudice. A. Kreymborg.—CoPu
Rejoinder. J. Ekwere.—AlPa
Remembering Nat Turner. S. A. Brown.—AdPb
Respectful request. R. Durem.—AbM
Right on, white America. S. Sanchez.—AdPb
Riot. G. Brooks.—AdPb
Salute. O. Pitcher.—AdPb
Sands. M. Goode.—JoV
Snapshots of the cotton South. F. M. Davis.—AdPb
So quietly. L. P. Hill.—AdPb
Song for a dark girl. L. Hughes.—AdPb
Strong men. S. A. Brown.—AdPb
Tableau. C. Cullen.—AdPb
Tenebris. A. W. Grimké.—AdPb
"There's a certain illness within you." A. Blackwell.—JoV
They are killing all the young men. D. Henderson.—AdPb
They came from the east. Unknown.—BiI
To the white fiends. C. McKay.—AdPb
"Tomorrow the heroes." A. B. Spellman.—AdPb
The true import of present dialogue, black vs. Negro. N. Giovanni.—AdPb
12 gates to the city. N. Giovanni.—AdPb
Until they have stopped. S. E. Wright.—AdPb
Vet's rehabilitation. R. Durem.—AdPb
Vietnam #4. C. Major.—AdB—AdPb
Vive noir. M. Evans.—AdB—AdPb
Walk with de Mayor of Harlem. D. Henderson.—AdPb
War chant. Unknown.—AlPa
Watts. C. K. Rivers.—AdB—AdPb
We can't always follow the white man's way. D. Clarke, Jr.—JoV
We have been believers. M. Walker.—AdPb
What kind of world is this. M. Lasanta.—JoV
What's black power. L. Baez.—JoV

Race relations—*Continued*
"When black people are." A. B. Spellman.—AdPb
"Where the rainbow ends." R. Rive.—AbM
The white house. C. McKay.—AdPb
White man and black man are talking. M. Goode.—JoV
White people. D. Henderson.—AdPb
Who are they. Unknown.—BiI
Will I make it. J. Holland.—JoV
"You know, Joe." R. Durem.—AdB
Young Africa's plea. D. Osadebay.—AlPa
"A **race** with the sun as he downed." See Cynic's epitaph
Races and racing
The cheetah. J. Prelutsky.—PrP
The horse and the mule. J. H. Wynne.—OpOx
Races and racing—Boat
The boat race. From Aeneid. Virgil.—FlH
Eight oars and a coxswain. A. Guiterman.—FlH
The yachts. W. C. Williams.—FlH—MaFw—PeS
Races and racing—Foot
The hundred yard dash. W. Lindsey.—FlH
"Look at Marcus and take warning." Lucilius.—JoA-4
On torpid Marcus. Lucilius.—LiWw
The runner. W. Whitman.—FlH
The sprinters. L. Morrison.—JoA-4
Races and racing—Horse
The horse and the mule. J. H. Wynne.—OpOx
Morning workout. B. Deutsch.—FlH
"Two horses race into the ring." J. Prelutsky.—PrC
Rachel
His wife.—MeP
My dead.—MeP
Revolt.—MeP
The **Rachray** man. Moira O'Neill.—CoPi
Racing. See Races and racing
"The **racing** flag whips up." See Markings: The exclamation
The **radiance** of creativity. Olya Beshenkovskaya, tr. fr. the Russian by Miriam Morton.—MoM
"**Radiator's** cold." See No heat today
Radin, Paul
Prayer. Unknown.—BiI
This newly created world. tr.—BiI
Radio
Umbilical. E. Merriam.—MeF
The **radish.** Ibn Quzman, tr. fr. the Spanish by A. J. Arberry.—AbM
"The **radish** is a good." See The radish
"The **radish** is blooming." Irina, tr. fr. the Russian by Miriam Morton.—MoM
Radishes
The radish. Ibn Quzman.—AbM
"The radish is blooming." Irina.—MoM
"Write about a radish." K. Kuskin.—KuN
Raditladi, L. D.
Motswasele's farewell.—AlPa
Raftery, Anthony
The County Mayo.—CoPi
I am Raftery.—CoPi
Raftery, Anthony (about)
I am Raftery. A. Raftery.—CoPi
"The **ragged** phantom." Boncho, tr. fr. the Japanese by Harry Behn.—BeM
Ragged Robin, sel. James Reeves
"The king sent for his wise men."—AlC
The **raggedy** man. James Whitcomb Riley.—OpOx
Raikin, Kostya
Alone.—MoM
The baby tigers.—MoM
The black panther.—MoM
"A **railroad** crossing." Unknown.—EmN
Railroad ducks. Frances Frost.—HoP
Railroadmen. See Railroads
Railroads
Adlestrop. E. Thomas.—MaFw—PaP
At the railway station, Upway. T. Hardy.—MaFw—PlP
Bang-klang. S. Silverstein.—SiW
The caboose who wouldn't come last. X. J. Kennedy.—KeO
Casey Jones. R. Hunter.—MoG
"Engine, engine, Number Nine." Unknown.—EmN
The Express. S. Spender.—ToM
The fat white woman speaks. G. K. Chesterton.—LiS
Firefly. Kamimura Hajime.—MoT
From a railway carriage. R. L. Stevenson.—OpOx
The goat. Unknown.—RoIt
Hallelujah. A. E. Housman.—CoOr
"Hallelujah, was the only observation."—CoPu—LiWw
"I like to see it lap the miles." E. Dickinson.—ThI
"I'm a navvy, you're a navvy." Mother Goose.—TucMgl
In Texas grass. Q. Troupe.—AdPb
In the train. V. de Sola Pinto.—PaP
Joseph Mica. Unknown.—MoG
Late summer. Kinoshita Yūji.—MaFw
Limited crossing Wisconsin. From Prairie. C. Sandburg.—SaT
The little blue engine. S. Silverstein.—SiW
"The little dog ran around the engine." Unknown.—EmN
Midnight on the Great Western. T. Hardy.—PlP
Old Hogan's goat. Unknown.—BrM
On a railroad right of way. C. Sandburg.—SaT
The pay is good. R. Kell.—ToM
"A peanut sat on a railroad track." From Silly stanzas. Unknown.—CoOh
"Piggy on the railway." Mother Goose.—AlC
Pods. C. Sandburg—SaT
"A railroad crossing." Unknown.—EmN

Railroad ducks. F. Frost.—HoP
"Singing through the forests." J. G. Saxe.—RoIt
Slow program. C. Sandburg.—SaT
The snail's dream. O. Herford.—BrM
Song of the train. D. McCord.—JoA-4
Stop. R. Wilbur.—HaWr
To a fat lady seen from the train. F. Cornford.—CoPu—LiS
"The train." Unknown.—AlPa
Train ride. D. Aldis.—HoP
The trains. R. Spencer.—HoP
Trains at night. F. Frost.—HoP
Whistle. D. McCord.—McFm
Railways. See Railroads
Rain
After rain. E. Thomas.—HiN
After the rain. Y. Ritsos.—MoT
"Ah, lovely Devon." Unknown.—TrG
April. L. Clifton.—ClE
April rain song. L. Hughes.—HoD—LiLc
Atavism. R. Lake.—HiN
Before the summer downpour. S. Kolosova.—MoM
Birds in the rain. D. McCord.—McFm
Birth. A. Gilboa.—MeP
Cover my earth mother. Unknown.—BiI
Darkling summer, ominous dusk, rumerous rain. D. Schwartz.—HaWr
"Do ghouls." L. Moore.—MoSm
"Doctor Foster went to Gloucester." Mother Goose.—JoA-4
A dog and a cat. Mother Goose.—BlM
 "A dog and a cat went out together."—TucMgl
Drippy weather. A. Fisher.—FiFo
"Dry and parched." A. Lopez.—AlW
"Eentsie weentsie spider." Unknown.—EmN
The elf and the dormouse. O. Herford.—JaP—UnGb
"The first winter rain." Bashō.—AtM
Glass falling. L. MacNeice.—CoPi
"I am crying from thirst." A. Lopez.—AlW
"I left home without my umbrella." Kim Jae.—BaSs
"In the night." Unknown.—BiI
"In the spring rain." Issa.—HaW
"In time of silver rain." L. Hughes.—AbM
"It rained." Shin Heum.—BaSs
"It's raining, it's pouring." Unknown.—EmN
"It's raining, it's raining." Mother Goose.—TucMgl
"It's raining said John Twining." Unknown.—BoI
Lazy Jane. S. Silverstein.—SiW
"Let us go to the Indian village, said all the rain gods." Unknown.—ClFc
Like a giant in a towel. D. Lee.—LeA
Little raindrops. J. E. Browne.—OpOx
"The little red spiders." Unknown.—JoT
March. W. Wordsworth.—JoA-4
"Moon sits smoking his pipe. N. Belting.—BeWi

Mouse night: One of our games. W. Stafford.—HiN
My father paints the summer. R. Wilbur.—HiN
"Nicely, nicely, nicely, nicely, there away in the east." Unknown.—ClFc
"Nicely while it is raining." Unknown.—ClFc
Night rain. J. P. Clark.—AlPa
"Now a spring rain falls." Chiyo.—BeM
One big rain. R. Hoban.—HoE
"Rain." C. Minor.—JoV
Rain ("All day long") S. O'Sullivan.—CoPi
The rain ("I hear leaves drinking rain") W. H. Davies.—PaF
Rain ("I opened my eyes") S. Silverstein.—CoOr—SiW
Rain ("The rain is raining all around") R. L. Stevenson.—JoA-4
The rain ("The rain it raineth every day") Unknown.—RoIt
"Rain clouds." R. Harding.—HoC
Rain in summer. H. W. Longfellow.—PaF
Rain in the city. L. Lenski.—LeC
Rain in the desert. J. G. Fletcher.—HiN
"Rain is falling on the paulownia." Kim Sang-yong.—BaSs
The rain it raineth. Lord Bowen.—CoPu
Rain on a grave. T. Hardy.—PlP
Rain on Castle island. Kitahara Hakushū.—MaFw
"Rain on the green grass." Unknown.—TrG
"Rain, rain, go away." Mother Goose.—EmN—JoA-4
Rain song. D. McCord.—McFm
The rainy day. R. Tagore.—MaFw
"Sheltering from the rain." Karai Senryū.—MaFw
The shower. H. Vaughan.—CoPu—MaFw
Showers. M. Chute.—ChRu
"The sky is a bowl of ice." N. Belting.—BeWi
"Slanting, windy rain. . . ." Buson.—BeM
Song. Unknown.—BiI
Song of the rain. Unknown.—AlPa
Sophistication. V. Miller.—HiN
"Spring rain." Chiyo-Ni.—MaFw
Spring Saturday. M. Chute.—ChRu
"A sudden shower." Issa.—HaW
Summer shower. D. McCord.—McFm
Supplication to the rain god and the spirits of water. Unknown.—BiI
Thank you. L. Breek.—MoM
Theme with variation. M. C. Livingston.—LiM
"There goes my best hat." Bashō.—BeM
Thirst. G. Cohoe.—AlW
"Three young rats with black felt hats." Mother Goose.—BlM—JoA-4
"To owl, the dove says." Issa.—HaW
Tuesday all day: Rain. L. Clifton.—ClS
Wash. J. Updike.—MoT
"What is so amusing about the rain falling." King Hyo-jong.—BaSs
"When it rains, the Mississippi river." Unknown.—EmN

Topsy-turvey-world.—OpOx
Winifred Waters.—OpOx
The world.—OpOx
"**Randy** Raccoon." Aileen Fisher.—FiFo
Ransetsu
"As New Year's day dawns."—BeM
"Pilgrims plod slowly."—BeM
"Under a small, cold."—BeM
Ransom, John Crowe
Bells for John Whiteside's daughter.—PeS
Blue girls.—RoIt
Janet waking.—HiN—PeS
Raphael, Lennox
Mike 65.—AdPb
Rasmussen, Knud
"The great sea." tr.—BiI
A husband's song. tr.—BiI
"The lands around my dwelling." tr.—BiI—LaM
Song. tr.—BiI
Raspberries
'Keenene. Unknown.—SeS
"**Raspberry,** raspberry." Unknown.—EmN
"**Raspberry,** strawberry." Unknown.—EmN
Rat a tat tat. Unknown.—BlM
"**Rat** a tat tat, who is that." See Rat a tat tat
Rat riddles. Carl Sandburg.—SaT
Rats
An advancement of learning. S. Heaney.—HiN
Bishop Hatto. R. Southey.—CoPt
Dame Trot. Mother Goose.—BlM
Drats. S. Silverstein.—SiW
Hoddley, poddley. Unknown.—BlM
An inconvenience. J. B. Tabb.—BrM
"Jerry Hall." Unknown.—TrG
The pack rat. J. Prelutsky.—PrP
The Pied Piper of Hamelin. R. Browning.—OpOx
Race prejudice. A. Kreymborg.—CoPu
Rat riddles. C. Sandburg.—SaT
"Scampering over saucers." Buson.—MaFw
"There was a rat, for want of stairs." Mother Goose.—MiMg—TrG
"Three young rats with black felt hats." Mother Goose.—BlM—JoA-4
What became of them. Unknown.—OpOx
"Your house is so classy." Unknown.—MoBw
Rattlesnake skipping song. Dennis Lee.—LeA
"The **raucous** auk must squawk to talk." See Auk talk
"**Raven.**" Unknown, tr. fr. the Mandan.—ClFc
The **raven.** Edgar Allan Poe.—RoIt
"A **raven** sat upon a tree." See The sycophantic fox and the gullible raven
Ravens
"A farmer went trotting upon his grey mare." Mother Goose.—JoA-4
"Raven." Unknown.—ClFc
The raven. E. A. Poe.—RoIt
The raven's song. Unknown.—LeIb
The sycophantic fox and the gullible raven. G. W. Carryl.—LiWw
Twa corbies. Unknown.—CoPt—MaFw
The **raven's** song. Unknown.—LeIb
"**Ravished** arms." See Boy in the Roman zoo
Raw carrots. Valerie Worth.—WoS
"**Raw** carrots taste." See Raw carrots
Ray, Melanie
Bus noises.—HoP
"**Ray** Charles is the black wind of Kilimanjaro." See Blues note
"**Ray** John." See Honky
"The **razor-tailed** wren." Shel Silverstein.—SiW
"**Reach** like you never reached before past night's somber robes." See Tauhid
Read, Herbert
Early astir.—CoPu
Lu Yün's lament.—PlM
Read this with gestures. John Ciardi.—CiFs
"**Read** up and down." Unknown.—EmN
"**Read** yr/exile." See A poem for a poet
Reading. See Books and reading
Reading. Marchette Chute.—ChRu
Reading Walt Whitman. Calvin Forbes.—AdPb
"**Reading** Yeats I do not think." Lawrence Ferlinghetti.—PlM
Ready for Halloween. Aileen Fisher.—HoH
"The **real** people loves another." Rob Penny.—AdM—AdPb
The **real** slayer of the seal. Unknown, fr. North Greenland.—LeIb
"**Really,** what a shocking scene." See A man of experience
Reapers. Jean Toomer.—AdPb
Reason. Josephine Miles.—HiN
"The **reason** for a lawn." See Reasons
Reasons. Marchette Chute.—ChRu
Reavey, George
Envy. tr.—MaFw
"**Rebecca** Jane." See The porcupine
Rebecca, who slammed doors for fun and perished miserably. Hilaire Belloc.—NeA
The **rebel.** Mari Evans.—AdPb—PeS
Rebse, Hermann. See Doob, Leonard and Rebse, Hermann
"**Recall** from Time's abysmal chasm." See Ode to the amoeba
Recinos, Adrián
Plague. tr.—BiI
—See also Goetz, Delia, jt. auth.
Recipe for a hippopotamus sandwich. Shel Silverstein.—SiW
"The **recipe** for mud pie." See Mud pie
"A **reckless** morning . . . " Ann Atwood.—AtM
A **recollection** ("My father's friend came once to tea") Frances Cornford.—CoPu
Recollection ("Softly the crane's foot crumples a star") Dorothy Donnelly.—HiN
Recycled. Lilian Moore.—MoSp
Recycling
Recycled. L. Moore.—MoSp
Red (color)
When Sue wears red. L. Hughes.—JoA-4
Red birds
Cardinal. J. Harrison.—HaWr
Revelation. F. Holman.—HoI
Winter cardinal. L. Moore.—MoSp

Magalu. H. Johnson.—AdPb
Mourning poem for the Queen of Sunday. R. Hayden.—AdPb
Resurrection. F. Horne.—AdPb
Sermonette. I. Reed.—AdPb
Verses. W. Cowper.—RoIt
Wednesday night prayer meeting. Jay Wright.—AdPb
The winged worshippers. C. Sprague.—RoIt
Religious hymn to be sung wearing a head decoration of the skin of the great northern diver. Unknown, fr. the Copper Eskimo.—LeIb
"**Remarkable,** truly, is art." Gelett Burgess.—CoOr
The **remedy** worse than the disease. Matthew Prior.—LiWw
"**Remember.**" See The discoveries of fire
"**Remember,** dear, when you grow old." Unknown.—EmN
"**Remember** Grant, remember Lee." Unknown.—EmN
"**Remember** man that passeth by." See An epitaph and a reply
"**Remember** me." Unknown.—MoBw
"**Remember** me and bear in mind." Unknown.—EmN
"**Remember** me on the river." Unknown.—EmN
"**Remember** now thy Creator." See Ecclesiastes
"**Remember,** remember." Unknown.—MaF
"**Remember** the beer." Unknown.—MoBw
"**Remember** the bottle." Unknown.—MoBw
"**Remember** the boy from the country." Unknown.—EmN
"**Remember** the bride." Unknown.—EmN
"**Remember** the joy." Unknown.—EmN
"**Remember** the M." Unknown.—MoBw
"**Remember** the pen." Unknown.—MoBw
"**Remember** the pen (remember the book)." Unknown.—MoBw
"**Remember** the river." Unknown.—MoBw
"**Remember** the row." Unknown.—MoBw
"**Remember** the school." Unknown.—MoBw
"**Remember** the time we took a ride." See May
Remembering Nat Turner. Sterling A. Brown.—AdPb
The **reminder.** Thomas Hardy.—PlP
Remonstrance with the snails. Unknown.—RoIt
The **remorse** for time. Howard Nemerov.—HiN
"**Remove** no object." See Punta De Los Lobos Marinos
The **renegade.** David Diop, tr. fr. the French by Sangodare Akanji.—AlPa
"**Rent** man." Lois Lenski.—LeC
"**Repeat** that, repeat." Gerard Manley Hopkins.—MaFw
Repentance
Greedy Richard. Jane Taylor.—OpOx
Holy sonnet VII. J. Donne.—MaFw
Replansky, Naomi
My spoon was lifted.—CoPu
Reply to the passionate shepherd. Walter Raleigh (1552-1618).—RoIt
Reptiles. See also Crocodiles; Lizards; Snakes
Prayer for reptiles. P. Hubbell.—AdP
Requickening. Unknown, tr. fr. the Iroquois by J.N.B. Hewitt.—BiI
Requiem. Robert Louis Stevenson.—RoIt
Requiem for a black girl. Yambo Ouologuem, tr. fr. the French by Samuel Allen.—AlPa (sel.)
Requiem for a personal friend. Eavan Boland.—CoPi
Requiem of a war-baby. Joan Watton.—CoPi
Requiems. See Laments
The **rescue.** Hal Summers.—CoPt
Resnikoff, Alexander
Advice.—CoOh
Courtship.—CoOh
Father Goose tells a story.—CoOh
Josephine.—CoOr
Two witches.—BrM—CoOh
Resolution and independence. William Wordsworth.—LiS (sel.)—MaFw (sel.)—PlM (sel.)
The **resolve.** Denise Levertov.—HaWr
Respectful request. Ray Durem.—AbM
Response. Bob Kaufman.—AdB
Restaurants
Dreaming in the Shanghai restaurant. D. J. Enright.—ToM
Eating at the restaurant of How Chow Now. D. McCord.—McFm
On a waiter. D. McCord.—LiWw
"**Resting** from the noon." Gonsui, tr. fr. the Japanese by Harry Behn.—BeM
Resting in peace. Robert Froman.—FrSp
"**Restless** little flea." Issa, tr. fr. the Japanese by Harry Behn.—BeM
Resurrection. Frank Horne.—AdPb
Resurrection day. See Judgment day
Retribution. See also Punishment
"Bruadar and Smith and Glinn." Unknown.—CoPi
Cruel Frederick. H. Hoffman.—LiS
Fräulein reads instructive rhymes. M. W. Kumin.—LiS
The story of little Suck-a-Thumb. H. Hoffman.—LiS
The **return.** Arna Bontemps.—AdPb
Reveille. See A Shropshire lad
Reveilles. See Wake-up poems
A **revel.** Donagh MacDonagh.—CoPi
Revelation. Felice Holman.—HoI
Revenge
Brian Boy Magee. E. Carbery.—CoPi
On slaughter. C. N. Bialik.—MeP
"The **Reverend** Henry Ward Beecher." Oliver Wendell Holmes.—RoIt
Review from Staten island. Gloria C. Oden.—AdPb
Revolt. Rachel, tr. fr. the Hebrew by Robert Friend.—MeP
Revolution. See United States—History—Revolution
Rewards and fairies, sels. Rudyard Kipling
If.—OpOx

Rewards—*Continued*
The way through the woods.—OpOx
Rexroth, Kenneth
Inversely.—MoT
A letter to Yvor Winters.—PlM
South wind. tr.—MaFw
To Pi Ssu Yao. tr.—PlM
Reynolds, Malvina
Little boxes.—PeS
Reynolds, Sir Joshua (about)
Sir Joshua Reynolds. W. Blake.—CoPu
Reznikoff, Charles
"About an excavation."—CoPu
Rhinoceros. Mary Ann Hoberman.—HoR
Rhinoceroses
"Most people don't know it." Unknown.—EmN
Rhinoceros. M. A. Hoberman.—HoR
Rhinoceroses. Unknown.—CoOh
"The two-horned black rhinoceros." J. Prelutsky.—PrP
Rhinoceroses. Unknown.—CoOh
Rhodes, Hugh
Rising in the morning.—OpOx
The **rhodora.** Ralph Waldo Emerson.—RoIt
Rhodoras
The rhodora. R. W. Emerson.—RoIt
Rhyme for a chemical baby. See Boston nursery rhymes
Rhyme for a geological baby. See Boston nursery rhymes
Rhyme for a simpleton. Unknown.—RoIt
Rhyme for astronomical baby. See Boston nursery rhymes
Rhyme for botanical baby. See Boston nursery rhymes
Rhymes (about)
Bennington. N. M. Bodecker.—BoL
Local note. A. Guiterman.—CoPu
Rhys, Ernest
An autobiography.—CoPu
—See also Dalgliesh, Alice, jt. auth.
Rhys, Ernest (about)
An autobiography. E. Rhys.—CoPu
"**Rhythm** and blues." See The blues today
"**Rhythm** runs." See Theme with variations
Rich, Adrienne (Cecile)
Bears.—HiN
I am in danger—Sir.—PlM
The parting.—HaWr
Snapshots of a daughter-in-law (Part I).—HiN
The trees.—HaWr
A woman mourned by daughters.—HiN
Rich days. William Henry Davies.—PaF
"**Rich** men spoil the city." Unknown.—MoBw
Rich morning. Robert Farren.—CoPi
Richard Cory. Edwin Arlington Robinson.—CoPt
Richards, Laure E. (Elizabeth)
Bobbily Boo and Wollypotump.—LiLc
Eletelephony.—BrM—JoA-4—OpOx
The gingham umbrella.—CoOr
"Harriet Hutch."—NeA
The High Barbaree.—JoA-4
Jumble jingle.—BrM
Mrs Snipkin and Mrs Wobblechin.—JoA-4—OpOx
The monkeys and the crocodile.—JoA-4
My Uncle Jehoshaphat.—OpOx
"The owl and the eel and the warming-pan."—JoA-4
A party.—BrM
The umbrella brigade.—JoA-4
The unfortunate grocer.—CoOr
Riches. See Wealth
"**Ricky** was L but he's home with the flu." See Love
Riddle. See "In marble halls as white as milk"
A **riddle.** See "There is one that has a head without an eye"
Riddle. See "What shoemaker makes shoes without leather"
A **riddle** ("The beginning of eternity") Unknown.—RoIt
A **riddle** ("It is always handled") George MacBeth.—MoT
A **riddle** ("She glows brighter than the sun") Maya Nikogosian, tr. fr. the Russian by Miriam Morton.—MoM
A **riddle** ("'Twas in heaven pronounced, and 'twas muttered in hell") Catherine Maria Fanshawe.—RoIt
Riddle ("What do you do when you're up in a tree") John Ciardi.—CiFs
The **riddle** ("White men's children spread over the earth") George Douglas Johnson.—AdPb
"A **riddle,** a riddle, as I suppose." Unknown.—EmN
"**Riddle** cum riddle cum rawley." Unknown.—EmN
Riddle-go-round. Eve Merriam.—MeO
"**Riddle** go round and roundabout." See Riddle-go-round
"**Riddle** me, riddle me, riddle me." Unknown.—EmN
"**Riddle** me, riddle me, what is that." Unknown.—EmN
The **riddle** song. Unknown.—EmN
A **riddle:** What am I. Dorothy Aldis.—HoH
Riddles
"All saddled, all bridled, all ready to go." Unknown.—EmN
"As I walked down the lane." Unknown.—EmN
"As I was crossing London bridge." Unknown.—EmN
"As I was going to St Ives." Mother Goose.—BlM—EmN—JoA-4
"As I went down the country road." Unknown.—EmN
"As I went through a field of wheat." Unknown.—EmN
"As round as an apple, as deep as a cup." Mother Goose.—JoA-4
At breakfast. M. Swenson.—PeS
"Behind the bush, behind the thorn." Unknown.—EmN

"Between the earth." Unknown.—EmN
"Big at the bottom." Unknown.—EmN
"Black we are and much admired." Unknown.—EmN
"Black within and red without." Mother Goose.—EmN—JoA-4
"Brothers and sisters have I none." Unknown.—EmN
"Brown I am and much admired." Unknown.—EmN
"Chip, chip, cherry." Unknown.—EmN
"A dish full of all kinds of flowers." Unknown.—EmN
"Elizabeth, Elspeth, Betsy, and Bess." Mother Goose.—JoA-4
"First, the fish must be caught." From Through the looking-glass. L. Carroll.—LiPc
"First you see me in the grass." Unknown.—EmN
"Flour of England, fruit from Spain." Unknown.—EmN
"Formed long ago, yet made today." Unknown.—EmN
"Four legs up and four legs down." Unknown.—EmN
"The garden is framed." B. Swann
Three riddles.—MoT
Green head. Unknown.—EmN
"Guess a riddle now you must." Unknown.—EmN
"Hick-a-more, hack-a-more." Mother Goose.—EmN—JoA-4
"High as a house." Unknown.—EmN
"Humpty Dumpty sat on a wall." Mother Goose.—EmN—JoA-4
"I am not found on the ground." Unknown.—EmN
"I have a little sister, they call her Peep, Peep." Mother Goose.—EmN—JoA-4
"I like to see it lap the miles." E. Dickinson.—ThI
"I tremble with each breath of air." Unknown.—EmN
"I walk all day through rain and snow." Unknown.—EmN
"I washed my hands in water that never rained nor run." Unknown.—EmN
"I went hunting in the wood." Unknown.—EmN
"In marble halls as white as milk." Mother Goose.—EmN—JoA-4
Riddle.—RoIt
"In spring I am gay." Unknown.—EmN
"It can run and it can walk." Unknown.—EmN
"It has four legs and a foot." Unknown.—EmN
"It runs up the hill." Unknown.—EmN
"It walks east, west, north, and south." Unknown.—EmN
"It's in the church." Unknown.—EmN
The little girl. T. Iadchenko.—MoM
"A little house full of meat." Unknown.—EmN
"Little Jock Sander of Dee." Unknown.—BoI
"Little Nancy Etticoat." Mother Goose.—EmN—JoA-4
"A little white fence that's always wet." Unknown.—EmN
"Long legs, crooked thighs." Mother Goose.—JoA-4
Look: What am I. D. McCord.—McFm
"Many eyes." Unknown.—EmN
Mingled yarns. X. J. Kennedy.—KeO
My valentine. Unknown.—LaM
The new one. M. C. Livingston.—LiM
"Niddy, niddy, noddy." Unknown.—EmN
"Old Mother Twitchett had but one eye." Unknown.—EmN
"On the hill there is a green house." Unknown.—EmN
One guess. R. Frost.—CoPu
"Over hills, over hollows." Unknown.—EmN
"A railroad crossing." Unknown.—EmN
Rat riddles. C. Sandburg.—SaT
"Red within and red without." Unknown.—EmN
A riddle ("The beginning of eternity") Unknown.—RoIt
A riddle ("Is it always handled") G. MacBeth.—MoT
A riddle ("She glows brighter than the sun") M. Nikogosian.—MoM
A riddle ("'Twas in heaven pronounced, and 'twas muttered in hell") C. M. Fanshawe.—RoIt
Riddle ("What do you do when you're up in a tree") J. Ciardi.—CiFs
The riddle ("White men's children spread over the earth") G. D. Johnson.—AdPb
"A riddle, a riddle, as I suppose." Unknown.—EmN
"Riddle cum riddle cum rawley." Unknown.—EmN
Riddle-go-round. E. Merriam.—MeO
"Riddle me, riddle me, riddle me." Unknown.—EmN
"Riddle me, riddle me, what is that." Unknown.—EmN
The riddle song. Unknown.—EmN
A riddle: What am I. D. Aldis.—HoH
The riddling knight. Unknown.—JoA-4—RoIt
"Riddlum, riddlum, raddy." Unknown.—EmN
"Round as a biscuit (busy as a bee)." Unknown.—EmN
"Round as a biscuit (deep as a cup)." Unknown.—EmN
"Round as an apple (black)." Unknown.—EmN
"Round as an apple (flat as a)." Unknown.—EmN
"Round as an apple (yellow as gold)." Unknown.—EmN
"Round as an apple and thin as a knife." Unknown.—EmN

Riding. W. Allingham.—OpOx
Riding across John Lee's finger. Stanley Crouch.—AdPb
"**Riding** against the east." See To Beachey, 1912
Riding at daybreak. Sun Yün Fêng, tr. fr. the Chinese by Henry H. Hart.—MaFw
Ridlon, Marci
Castles.—HoCs
Safari.—HoCs
Rieu, E. V.
The castaways.—CoPt
Cat's funeral.—JoA-4
The happy hedgehog.—JoA-4
The lesser lynx.—LiWw
Tony the turtle.—BrM
Rieu, E. V. (about)
On looking into E. V. Rieu's *Homer.* P. Kavanagh.—PlM
"**Riggedy,** higgedy, wiggedy, rig." Unknown.—LaM
"**Right** after our Thanksgiving feast." See The skeleton walks
"**Right** down the shocked street with a siren-blast." See A fire-truck
Right on: white America. Sonia Sanchez.—AdB—AdPb
The **right** time. Felice Holman.—HoI
"**Right** under their noses, the green." See The dusk of horses
Rigid body sings. James Clerk Maxwell.—LiS
Riley, James Whitcomb
Little Orphant Annie.—OpOx—RoIt
The old man and Jim.—CoPt
The raggedy man.—OpOx
Riley. Charles Causley.—CaF
Rilke, Rainer Maria
The panther.—MaFw
Rimbaud, Jean-Nicolas-Arthur
The bridges.—MaFw
Flowers.—MaFw
Phrases.—MaFw (sel.)
"**Rime** Intrinsica, Fontwell Magna, Sturminster." See Dorset
"**Rin** Tin Tin." Unknown.—EmN
"**Rindle,** randle." Unknown.—BlM
"**Ring-a-ring** o' neutrons." Paul Dehn.—LiS
"A **ring** is round." Unknown.—MoBw
"**Ring** out the old." See Happy new year
Ring out, wild bells. See In memoriam
"**Ring** out, wild bells, to the wild sky." See In memoriam—Ring out, wild bells
"**Ring,** sing, ring, sing, pleasant Sabbath bells." See The green gnome
"**Ring-ting.** I wish I were a primrose." See Wishing
"**Ringleted** youth of my love." Unknown, tr. fr. the Irish by Douglas Hyde.—CoPi
Rings (jewelry)
Birthday verses written in a child's album. J. R. Lowell.—OpOx
The riddle song. Unknown.—EmN
Riot ("John Cabot, out of Wilma, once a Wycliffe") Gwendolyn Brooks.—AdPb
Riot ("Keep off the streets") Lois Lenski.—LeC
Riot rimes U.S.A. #78. Raymond Richard Patterson.—AdM
Riot rimes U.S.A. #79. Raymond Richard Patterson.—AdM
Riots
Death of Dr King. S. Cornish.—AdPb
From riot rimes U.S.A. #78. R. R. Patterson.—AdM
From riot rimes U.S.A. #79. R. R. Patterson.—AdM
Harlem riot, 1943. P. Murray.—AdPb
"In Orangeburg my brothers did." A. B. Spellman.—AdPb
In this year of grace. J. Hewitt.—CoPi
Jitterbugging in the streets. C. Hernton.—AdPb
Keep on pushing. D. Henderson.—AdPb
The last riot. V. Howard.—JoV
Mr Roosevelt regrets. P. Murray.—AdPb
The new pieta: For the mothers and children of Detroit. J. Jordan.—AdPb
Newsletter from my mother. M. S. Harper.—AdPb
On the birth of my son, Malcolm Coltrane. J. Lester.—AdPb
Riot ("John Cabot, out of Wilma, once a Wycliffe") G. Brooks.—AdPb
Riot ("Keep off the streets") L. Lenski.—LeC
Riots and rituals. R. W. Thomas.—AdPb
Tony get the boys. D. L. Graham.—AdPb
Watts. C. K. Rivers.—AdPb
"What is the opposite of *riot.*" R. Wilbur.—WiO
You are the brave. R. R. Patterson.—AdPb
Riots and rituals. Richard W. Thomas.—AdPb
Ripe corn. Carl Sandburg.—SaT
Ripeness. Ruth Whitman.—MoT
Rise up shepherd, and follow. Unknown.—LaS
Rising five. Norman Nicholson.—ToM
Rising in the morning. Hugh Rhodes.—OpOx
Rites of passage. Audre Lorde.—AdPb
Ritsos, Yannis
After the rain.—MoT
Motionless swaying.—MoT
Ritter, Margaret
"Faith, I wish I were a leprechaun."—JaP
A **ritual** to read to each other. William Stafford.—PeS
The **rival.** Thomas Hardy.—PlP
The **rivals.** James Stephens.—RoIt
Rive, Richard
"Where the rainbow ends."—AbM
The **Riven** quarry. Gloria C. Oden.—AdPb
A **river** ("In Madurai") A. K. Ramanujan.—ToM
The **river** ("We move from one") Sam Cornish.—AdPb
"**River** bird, river bird." See Streamside exchange
"The **river** darkens on an autumn night." Yi Jung, tr. fr. the Korean by Chung Seuk Park and ad. by Virginia Olsen Baron.—BaSs

The **river-god**'s song. Francis Beaumont and John Fletcher
Song.—RoIt
River-mates. Padraic Colum.—CoPi
River moons. Carl Sandburg.—MaFw—SaT
River roads. Carl Sandburg.—SaT
Rivers, Conrad Kent
Four sheets to the wind.—AdPb
If blood is black then spirit neglects my unborn song.—AdPb
In defense of black poets.—AdB
On the death of William Edward Burghardt Du Bois by African moonlight and forgotten shores.—AdPb
Prelude.—AdPb
The still voice of Harlem.—AdPb
To Richard Wright.—AdPb
The train runs late to Harlem.—AdPb
Watts.—AdB—AdPb
Rivers. See also names of rivers, as Mississippi river
Afton water. R. Burns.—RoIt
"The blue mountains are what they are." Kim In-hu.—BaSs
By the Exeter river. D. Hall.—ToM
The cataract of Lodore. R. Southey.—OpOx
Cavalry crossing a ford. W. Whitman.—CoPu
"The chiming river." Rokwa.—BeM
Divided. J. Ingelow.—LiS
Explanation, on coming home late. R. Hughes.—CoPu
Fetters. L. Ginsberg.—RoIt
"Grey goose and gander." Mother Goose.—AlC—CoPu—JoA-4
"I was born upon thy bank, river." H. D. Thoreau.—CoPu
"A mountain." Yi Hwang.—BaSs
"My love is a thousand miles away." Wang Bang-yun.—BaSs
The Negro speaks of rivers. L. Hughes.—AdPb—HoD—MoT—PeS
No moon, no star. B. Deutsch.—HaWr
On a railroad right of way. C. Sandburg.—SaT
Overlooking the river Stour. T. Hardy.—PaP—PlP
A river ("In Maduri") A. K. Ramanujan.—ToM
The river ("We move from one") S. Cornish.—AdPb
"River bird, river bird." J. P. Clark.—AlPa
The river-god's song. F. Beaumont and J. Fletcher
Song.—RoIt
River-mates. P. Colum.—CoPi
Rivers. J. C. Squire.—PaP
"Roll Jordan roll." Unknown.—BrW
Roll, river, roll. R. Froman.—FrSp
"Spring in the river." A. Atwood.—AtM
"Spring on the river." A. Atwood.—AtM
Suicide's note. L. Hughes.—HoD
"Ten years it took." Song Soon.—BaSs
The tide river. From The water babies. C. Kingsley.—OpOx—RoIt
To the river Duddon. N. Nicholson.—PaP
Where go the boats. R. L. Stevenson.—LiLc—OpOx
"You, blue stream, flowing around mountains." Hwang Chini.—BaSs
Rivers. J. C. Squire.—PaP
Roach, Eloise
The canary's flight. tr.—JoA-4
Peep show. tr.—JoA-4
Platero. tr.—JoA-4
A **road** in Kentucky. Robert Hayden.—HiN
The **road** not taken. Robert Frost.—RoIt
Roads and trails. See also Streets
Baby. L. Hughes.—HoD
Blast off. J. Oppenheim.—HoP
Dirt road. C. O'John.—AlW
Florida road workers. L. Hughes.—PeS
"In old age." Unknown.—ClFc
"It runs up the hill." Unknown.—EmN
"It's not so easy." Unknown.—BeM
Mountain road. M. Oliver.—RoIt
The path I must travel. E. B. Mitchell.—AlW
River roads. C. Sandburg.—SaT
A road in Kentucky. R. Hayden.—HiN
The road not taken. R. Frost.—RoIt
The Roman road. T. Hardy.—PlP
The way. E. Muir.—JoA-4
The way through the woods. From Rewards and fairies. R. Kipling.—OpOx
Roast swan song. See Carmina Burana
Robbing the tree hive. Ernest G. Moll.—CoPt
Roberson, Ed
Blue horses.—AdPb
"If the black frog will not ring."—AdPb
Mayday.—AdPb
Othello Jones dresses for dinner.—AdPb
Poll.—AdPb
Seventh son.—AdPb
When thy king is a boy.—AdPb (sel.)
"**Robert** Rowley rolled a round roll 'round." Unknown.—EmN
"**Robert** Rutter dreamt a dream." Unknown.—EmN
Robert Whitmore. Frank Marshall Davis.—AdPb
Roberts, Charles G. D.
Ice.—CoPu
Roberts, Elizabeth Madox
Autumn.—CoPt
The branch.—JoA-4
Christmas morning.—JoA-4
Firefly.—JoA-4—LiLc
The hens.—LiLc—UnGb
Little bush.—LiLc
Mumps.—BrM
Numbers.—LiLc
Roberts, Michael
Der arme poet.—PlM
Langdale: Nightfall, January 4th.—PaP
Robeson, Paul (about)
Paul Robeson. G. Brooks.—AdPb
Until they have stopped. S. E. Wright.—AdPb
A **robin.** Aileen Fisher.—FiFo—LaM

Robin Hood
The death of Robin Hood ("Give me my bow, said Robin Hood") Eugene Field.—CoPt
The death of Robin Hood ("When Robin Hood and Little John") Unknown.—MaFw
How Robin Hood rescued the widow's sons. Unknown.—CoPt
May 8. N. Belting.—BeSc
"Robin Hood." G. Burr.—HiN
Robin Hood. From Speaking of television. P. McGinley.—LiWw
Robin Hood and Little John. Unknown.—JoA-4
A song of Sherwood. A. Noyes.—JoA-4
Robin Hood. See Speaking of television
"**Robin** Hood." Gray Burr.—HiN
Robin Hood and Little John. Unknown.—JoA-4
Robin Redbreast ("Goodbye, goodbye to summer") William Allingham.—OpOx
Robin Redbreast ("Welcome Robin with thy greeting") Unknown.—RoIt
"**Robin** the Bobbin, the big-bellied Ben." Mother Goose.—AlC
Robins
I'd not be a robin. A. Fisher.—FiFo
"Jenny Wren fell sick." Mother Goose.—JoA-4
"The north wind doth blow." Mother Goose.—AlC—JoA-4
A robin. A. Fisher.—FiFo—LaM
Robin Redbreast ("Goodbye, goodbye to summer") W. Allingham.—OpOx
Robin Redbreast ("Welcome Robin with thy greeting") Unknown.—RoIt
The robins. F. Holman.—HoI
"Who killed Cock Robin." Mother Goose.—JoA-4
Winter. C. G. Rossetti.—RoIt
The **robins.** Felice Holmes.—HoI
Robinson, Alfred
Love song. tr.—BiI
Robinson, Edwin Arlington
George Crabbe.—PlM
The house on the hill.—RoIt
An inscription by the sea.—CoPu
A mighty runner.—FlH
Miniver Cheevy.—LiS
Mr Flood's party.—CoPt
Richard Cory.—CoPt
Thomas Hood.—PlM
Two men.—LiWw
Robinson Crusoe
"Poor old Robinson Crusoe." Mother Goose.—AlC
Robinson Crusoe's island. From Davy and the goblin. C. E. Carryl.—RoIt
Robinson Crusoe's island. See Davy and the goblin
Rochester, Earl of. See Wilmot, John, Earl of Rochester
"**Rock-a-bye** baby, thy cradle is green." Mother Goose.—AlC—JoA-4
"**Rock** candy: hard sweet crystals on a string." See A Christmas package
"**Rock,** rock, sleep, my baby." Clyde Watson.—WaF
Rockets
"Fueled." M. Hans.—HoP
"I've got a rocket." Unknown.—JoA-4
Message from a mouse, ascending in a rocket. P. Hubbell.—HoP
A **rocking** hymn. Goerge Wither.—OpOx
Rocking Jerusalem. Unknown.—BrW
Rocks
Hardrock. R. Froman.—FrSp
I've got a home in that rock. R. R. Patterson.—AdM—AdPb
"Step on a rock." Unknown.—EmN
"This is my rock." D. McCord.—JoA-4
Rodger, Alex
Twilight at the zoo.—HiN
Rodgers, Carolyn M.
Jesus was crucified or: It must be deep.—AdPb
Me, in Julu Se and Karma.—AdPb
Newark, for now.—AdPb
Portrait.—AdM
U name this one.—AdPb
We dance like Ella riffs.—AdPb
Rodgers, W. R.
Armagh.—CoPi
Carol.—MaFw
The fountains.—CoPi
White Christmas.—CoPi
Roethke, Theodore
The bat.—JoA-4—MaFw—PeS
Big wind.—HiN
Bring the day, sel.
"O small bird wakening."—JoA-4
The ceiling.—LiLc
The chair.—RoIt
Child on top of a greenhouse.—HiN
Dinky.—LiWw
Elegy.—HiN
Elegy for Jane.—PeS
The far field.—JoA-4 (sel.)
The geranium.—ToM
The gnu.—BrM—LiWw
Goo-girl.—LiWw
Heard in a violent ward.—PlM
The hippo.—CoPu
In praise of prairie.—JoA-4
The lamb.—LiLc
The meadow mouse.—AdP—MoT
Mid-country blow.—CoPu
The monotony song.—CoOr
My papa's waltz.—HiN—MaFw—PeS
Night crow.—HiN
"O small bird wakening." See Bring the day
Old florist.—HiN
Once more, the round.—JoA-4
Praise to the end.—JoA-4 (sel.)
The sloth.—RoIt
Song.—HiN
The storm.—HiN
Supper with Lindsay.—PlM

The time of roses. T. Hood.—RoIt
The wind is round. H. Moss.—HaWr
Roses. Lois Lenski.—LeC
Roses and revolutions. Dudley Randall.—AdPb
"**Roses** are red (coal is black)." Unknown.—MoBw
"**Roses** are red (green grow)." Unknown.—MoBw
"**Roses** are red (lilies are white)." Unknown.—MoBw
"**Roses** are red (the sea is deep)." Unknown.—MoBw
"**Roses** are red (stems are green)." Unknown.—MoBw
"**Roses** are red (violets are black)." Unknown.—EmN
"**Roses** are red (violets are blue, how the heck)." Unknown.—MoBw
"**Roses** are red (violets are blue, I love me)." Unknown.—MoBw
"**Roses** are red (violets are blue, I'd spell)." Unknown.—MoBw
"**Roses** are red (violets are blue, if I)." Unknown.—EmN
"**Roses** are red (violets are blue, if you forget me)." Unknown.—MoBw
"**Roses** are red (violets are blue, I'm the mad Russian)." Unknown.—MoBw
"**Roses** are red (violets are blue, let's hope the teachers)." Unknown.—MoBw
"**Roses** are red (violets are blue, please shut the door)." Unknown.—MoBw
"**Roses** are red (violets are blue, St Joseph's is glad)." Unknown.—MoBw
"**Roses** are red (violets are blue, skunks)." Unknown.—EmN
"**Roses** are red (violets are blue, sugar)." Unknown.—EmN
"**Roses** are red (violets are blue, sugar is sweet, and good in your coffee)." Unknown.—MoBw
"**Roses** are red (violets are blue, umbrellas get lost)." Unknown.—MoBw
"**Roses** are red (violets are blue, unless you have a garden)." Unknown.—MoBw
"**Roses** are red (violets are blue, what you need)." Unknown.—MoBw
"**Roses** are red (violets are blue, you vote for me)." Unknown.—MoBw
"**Roses** are red (violets are blue, your nose)." Unknown.—EmN
"**Roses** are red (violets are green, I think you're in love)." Unknown.—MoBw
"**Roses** are red (violets are green, take my advice)." Unknown.—MoBw
"**Roses** are red (violets are green, you have a shape)." Unknown.—MoBw
"**Roses** are red (Washington's dead)." Unknown.—MoBw
"**Roses** are red . . . when I choose." Unknown.—EmN
"**Roses** on my shoulders." Unknown.—MoBw
Rosh Hashana (Jewish New Year)
For a good and sweet New Year. S. R. Weilerstein.—LaM
Piyyut for Rosh Hashana. C. Guri.—MeP
Rosh Hashanah. B. Aronin.—LaM
Rosh Hashanah. Ben Aronin.—LaM
Ross, Charles Henry
An old woman.—OpOx
Jack.—OpOx
John, Tom, and James.—OpOx
Ross, David
As I float.—RoIt
"A Briton who swore at his king."—RoIt
"He bloomed among eagles."—RoIt
"A yak who was new to the zoo."—RoIt
Ross, Patricia Fent
"Luna, la luna." tr.—JoA-4
Rossetti, Christina Georgina
"All the bells were ringing."—LiLc
"Brown and furry."—RoIt
Caterpillar.—OpOx
The caterpillar.—JoA-4—UnGb
Carol, sel.
"What can I give Him.—HoS—LiLc
Caterpillar. See "Brown and furry"
The caterpillar. See "Brown and furry"
The city mouse. See The city mouse and the garden mouse
The city mouse and the garden mouse.—UnGb
The city mouse.—JoA-4—RoIt
Clouds.—RoIt
Comparisons.—OpOx
A crown of windflowers.—OpOx
"Ferry me across the water."—OpOx
Flint.—OpOx
Hope and joy.—OpOx
The horses of the sea.—LiLc—RoIt
How many.—RoIt
"If a pig wore a wig."—JoA-4
Lady Moon.—OpOx
Last rites.—OpOx
"Mix a pancake."—LaM—LiLc
The rainbow.—OpOx
A riddle. See "There is one that has a head without an eye"
The skylark.—RoIt
Spring quiet.—PaF—RoIt
Summer.—PaF
The swallow.—UnGb
"There is one that has a head without an eye"
A riddle.—OpOx
What are heavy.—OpOx
"What can I give Him." See Carol
"What does the bee do."—OpOx
What is pink.—OpOx
"Who has seen the wind."—JoA-4—LiLc—RoIt
The wind.—OpOx
The wind. See "Who has seen the wind"
Winter.—RoIt
Rossetti, Dante Gabriel
The blessed damozel.—LiS (sel.)

"**Rosy** apple, lemon or pear." Unknown
Counting-out rhymes.—RoIt
"**Rough** wind, that moanest loud." See Dirge
"**Roughly** figured, this man of modern habits." See Life cycle of common man
Roumer, Emile
Evening in Haiti.—AbM
The **round** ("Skunk cabbage, bloodroot") Philip Booth.—HiN
A **round** ("Spaghetti") Eve Merriam.—MeF
"**Round** about, round about." See The elves' dance
"**Round** about, round about." Unknown
Counting out rhyme.—LiS
"**Round** and round and round I spin." See Discovery
"**Round** as a biscuit (busy as a bee)." Unknown.—EmN
"**Round** as a biscuit (deep as a cup)." Unknown.—EmN
"**Round** as an apple (black)." Unknown.—EmN
"**Round** as an apple (flat as a)." Unknown.—EmN
"**Round** as an apple (yellow)." Unknown.—EmN
"**Round** as an apple and thin as a knife." Unknown.—EmN
"The **round**, calm faces rosy with the cold." See Japanese children
Rounds, Emma
Plane geometry.—LiS
"A **route** of evanescence." Emily Dickinson.—ThI
Routine. Arthur Guiterman.—CoOh
"The **roving** breezes come and go, the reed beds sweep and sway." See The traveling post office
"**Row,** row, row (to Oyster bay)." Unknown, tr. fr. the Danish by N. M. Bodecker.—BoI
"**Row** to the fishing-ground, row away." See Fishing
Rowse, A. L.
April landscape.—PaP
"The **royal** feast was done; the king." See The fool's prayer
Roys, Ralph
The beginning of sickness. Unknown. tr.—BiI
Magic formula against disease. tr.—BiI
"Then he descended." tr.—BiI
They came from the east. Unknown.—BiI
Rozhdestvensky, Robert
"Half a moon."—MoM
"**Rub-a-dub** dub." Mother Goose.—JoA-4
Rubadiri, David
A Negro labourer in Liverpool.—AlPa
Stanley meets Mutesa.—AlPa (sel.)
"**Rubber** baby-buggy bumpers." Unknown.—EmN
"**Rubbing** my hands together." Issa, tr. fr. the Japanese by Hanako Fukuda.—HaW
Rubin. Charles Cooper.—AdPb
"The **ruby-throated** hummingbird." See The hummingbird
Ruby-throated hummingbird. Eve Merriam.—MeO
Rudolph is tired of the city. Gwendolyn Brooks.—UnGb
"**Rudy** Felsh." Shel Silverstein.—SiW
A **ruffian.** Thomas Lovell Beddoes.—CoPu
Rugs
The flower trap. F. Holman.—HoI
"Rugs go over floors." M. A. Hoberman.—HoN
"**Rugs** go over floors." Mary Ann Hoberman.—HoN
The **ruined** city. Pao Chao, tr. fr. the Chinese by Ch'ên and Bullock.—MaFw
The **ruined** maid. Thomas Hardy.—PlP
Ruins under the stars. Galway Kinnell.—HaWr (sel.)
Rukeyser, Muriel
Haying before storm.—HaWr
Salamander.—HaWr
Rulers. See also Princes and princesses; also names of rulers, as David, King of Israel
The Akond of Swat. E. Lear.—RoIt
And in the hanging gardens. C. Aiken.—CoPt
April 23. N. Belting.—BeSc
Birthday verses written in a child's album. J. R. Lowell.—OpOx
Black majesty. C. Cullen.—AdPb
Bobbily Boo and Wollypotump. L. E. Richards.—LiLc
Buckingham palace. A. A. Milne.—OpOx
Bump on your thumb. D. Lee.—LeA
Contemporary nursery rhyme. Unknown.—LiS
The death of kings. From King Richard II. W. Shakespeare.—MoG
Deirdre. J. Stephens.—JoA-4
England in 1819. P. B. Shelley.—MoG
The English succession. Unknown.—OpOx
Epitaph on Charles II. J. Wilmot.—LiWw
The farmer and the queen. S. Silverstein.—SiW
The Georges. W. S. Landor.—RoIt
"Grey goose and gander." Mother Goose.—AlC—CoPu—JoA-4
"Hector Protector was dressed all in green." Mother Goose.—AlC
"Henry was a young king." R. Graves.—AlC
"Hokey, pokey, whisky, thum." Mother Goose.—MiMg
If the world was crazy. S. Silverstein.—SiW
In honor of a king who acquired several young wives. Unknown.—AlPa
The Irish colonel. A. C. Doyle.—CoPu
"King Dagobert, they say." Mother Goose.—TucMg
King Foo Foo. C. Causley.—CaF
The king must die. B. Taupin.—MoG
King of kings. Unknown.—BrW
The King of Spain. W. J. Smith.—BrM
"The king said to Salome." Unknown.—CoOh
"The king sent for his wise men all." From Ragged Robin. J. Reeves.—AlC
The king's breakfast. A. A. Milne.—OpOx

"Lavender's blue, diddle, diddle." Mother Goose.—JoA-4
"Little girl, little girl, where have you been." Mother Goose.—AlC
"Little King Boggen he built a fine hall." Mother Goose.—AlC
"Old King Cole." Mother Goose.—JoA-4
"Old Sir Simon the king." Mother Goose.—AlC
An old story. H. Nemerov.—CoPu
"The opposite of a *king,* I'm sure." R. Wilbur.—WiO
Ozymandias. P. B. Shelley.—LiS—RoIt
Peanut-butter sandwich. S. Silverstein.—SiW
"The pope he leads a happy life." C. Lever.—CoPi
The princess and the gypsies. F. Cornford.—CoPt
The queens' rhyme. I. Serraillier.—BrM
Question. M. A. Hoberman.—HoLb
"Sing a song of sixpence." Mother Goose.—AlC—EmN—JoA-4—LiS
The song of the smoke. W. E. B. Du Bois.—AdPb
Tartary. W. De La Mare.—OpOx
There lived a king. W. S. Gilbert.—CoPt
"There once was a king." Unknown.—BoI
"Thomas Thomas Tinkertoes." C. Watson.—WaF
The three kings. R. Dario.—AbM
"Three little guinea pigs." Unknown.—BoI
Ultima ratio regum. S. Spender.—ToM
We three kings. J. H. Hopkins.—LaS
"When good King Arthur ruled this land." Mother Goose.—AlC—JoA-4
Zachary Zed. J. Reeves.—CoOh
Rules
My ruler. S. Silverstein.—CoPu—SiW
The **Rum** Tum Tugger. T. S. Eliot.—BrM—RoIt
"The **Rum** Tum Tugger is a curious cat." See The Rum Tum Tugger
A **rumble.** Virginia Schonborg.—HoP
"**Rumbling** and ratty good green bus." See Good green bus
Rummage. Eve Merriam.—MeO
Rumor. Eve Merriam.—MeF
"**Rumors** open up." See The morning star
"A **rumpled** sheet." See The term
Rumsey, Philippa
Poem of the future citizen. tr.—AbM
"**Run** on, run on, in a way causing shaking motion of the sidewalk." See Autolycus' song
Runagate runagate. Robert Hayden.—AdPb
The **rune** of Saint Patrick. Unknown, tr. fr. the Gaelic by Charles Mangan.—MaF
Runilda's chant. George Darley.—CoPi
The **runner.** Walt Whitman.—FlH
Runners and running. See also Races and racing—Foot
Getting about. M. Chute.—ChRu
A mighty runner. E. A. Robinson.—FlH
The runner. W. Whitman.—FlH
Running. R. Wilbur.—HiN
Running. Richard Wilbur.—HiN
"**Running** away." Karla Kuskin.—KuN
Runover rhyme. David McCord.—McFm—McS
"**Runs** and jumps." Unknown.—EmN
"**Runs** as smooth as any rhyme." Unknown.—EmN
"**Runs** falls rises stumbles on from darkness into darkness." See Runagate runagate
Rural scenery. John Scott.—PaP
"**Rush** the washing, Russell." Unknown.—EmN
Russell, Frank
"The Black Snake Wind came to me." tr.—JoT
Black-tailed deer song. Unknown.—BiI
Emergence song. tr.—BiI
Song of creation. tr.—BiI
Song of the fallen deer. tr.—BiI
The taking of life brings serious thoughts. tr.—BiI
Wind song. Unknown.—BiI
Russell, George William (A. E., pseud.)
The vesture of the soul.—CoPi
Russia
Abdul Abulbul Amir. Unknown.—RoIt
"Do the Russians want war." Y. Yevtushenko.—MoM
Russian snow. Olga Teitelman.—MoM
The young Cossack. A. Kamensky.—MoM
Russian nursery rhymes. See Nursery rhymes—Russian
Russian snow. Olga Teitelman, tr. fr. the Russian by Miriam Morton.—MoM
Rust
"Over hills, over hollows." Unknown.—EmN
Season. W. Soyinka.—AlPa—MaFw
"**Rust** is ripeness, rust." See Season
The **rustling** of grass. Alfred Noyes.—PaF
Rutledge, Anne (about)
Anne Rutledge. From The Spoon River anthology. E. L. Masters.—RoIt
Ryan, Richard
The thrush's nest.—CoPi
Rye
Comin thro the rye. R. Burns.—LiS
Ryojirô Yamanaka
Wind poem.—MoT
Rythm. Iain Crichton Smith.—ToM
"**Rythm** it is we." See Spirits unchained
Ryuichi Tamuira
Invisible tree.—MoT

S

Sa Eun Yang
"Mount Taishan is high and steep."—BaSs
Sabbath stars. Avraham Shlonsky, tr. fr. the Hebrew by Dom Moraes.—MeP
"The **Sabbath** stars have climbed high, more peaceful than you." See Sabbath stars
Sach, Natan
I saw.—MeP

Sackville-West, V.
Beechwoods at Knole.—PaP
The land, sel.
"Only a bold man ploughs the Weald for corn."—PaP
"Only a bold man ploughs the Weald for corn." See The land
"The **sacred** blue corn-seed I am planting." See Songs in the garden of the House God
Sacrifices
Offering. Unknown.—BiI
Story of Isaac. L. Cohen.—MoG
"**Sad** I sit on Butternut hill." See Johnny has gone for a soldier
"The **sad** seamstress." See House guest
The **sad** tale of Mr Mears. Unknown.—CoPt
"The **saddest** place that e'er I saw." See Screaming tarn
Sadie's playhouse. Margaret Danner.—AdPb
Sadness. Unknown, fr. Ammassalik Eskimo.—LeIb
Safari. Marci Ridlon.—HoCs
"**Safari** to Bwagamoyo." See Bwagamoyo
Safety
Baby. L. Hughes.—HoD
"Cross crossings cautiously." Unknown.—EmN
"Don't cross the street." L. Lenski.—LeC
"Hidden by darkness." Bashō.—BeM
Little foxes. A. Fisher.—FiD
Orders. R. Froman.—FrSp
Safety first. M. C. Livingston.—LiM
Safety first. Myra Cohn Livingston.—LiM
"**Said** a census taker to a centaur." See Census nonsense
Said a long crocodile. Lilian Moore.—MoSm
"**Said** a porcupine." See Courtship
"**Said** a snake to a frog with a wrinkled skin." See Hospitality
"**Said** a tiny ant." See Ant and eleph-ant
"**Said** a very l - o - n - g crocodile." See Said a long crocodile
"**Said** Dr Ping to Mr Pong." See Dr Ping and Mr Pong
"**Said** General Clay to General Gore." See The generals
"**Said** Madam Goose to Mr Pig." See Table talk
"**Said** the duck to the kangaroo." See The duck and the kangaroo
"**Said** the first little chicken." See The chickens
"**Said** the king to the colonel." See The Irish colonel
"**Said** the monkey to the donkey." Unknown.—TrG
Said the monster. Lilian Moore.—MoSm
"**Said** the monster, You all think that I." See Said the monster
"**Said** the table to the chair." See The table and the chair
"**Said** the Victory of Samothrace." See Overheard in the Louvre
"**Said** the wind to the moon, I will blow you out." See The wind and the moon
"A **sail** a sail. Oh, whence away." See Heart's content
Sailing. See Boats and boating; Ships
Sailing to an island. Richard Murphy.—ToM
Sailor. Langston Hughes.—HoD
"**Sailor,** sailor, over the sea." Unknown.—EmN
"A **sailor** went to sea." Unknown.—EmN
Sailors. See Seamen
The **sailor's** consolation. Charles Dibdin.—RoIt
"**Sails.**" See Sails, gulls, sky, sea
Sails, gulls, sky, sea. Felice Holman.—HoI
Saint Benedict
Good Saint Benedict. Unknown.—AbM
Saint Bride's day
A milking song. F. Macleod.—MaF
Saint Crispin's day
King Henry's speech before Agincourt. From King Henry V. W. Shakespeare.—MaF
"**St** Dunstan, as the story goes." Mother Goose.—MiMg—TrG
Saint Francis and the birds. Seamus Heaney.—MaFw
Saint George's day
April 23. N. Belting.—BeSc
"**St** George's day." See April 23
St Isaac's church, Petrograd. Claude McKay.—AdPb
St John, Primus
Benign neglect/Mississippi, 1970.—AdPb
Elephant rock.—AdPb
Lynching and burning.—AdPb
The morning star.—AdPb
Tyson's corner.—AdPb
"**Saint** Joseph, let you send me a comrade true and kind." See The choice
"**Saint** Joseph, Saint Peter, Saint Paul." See Prayer for fine weather
Saint Mark's eve
April 24. N. Belting.—BeSc
"**St** Mark's eve." See April 24
Saint Nicholas. See Santa Claus
Saint Patrick's day. See also Patrick, Saint
I'll wear a shamrock. M. C. Davies.—LaM
"**St** Patrick's day is with us." See I'll wear a shamrock
Saint Valentine's day
Courtship. A. Resnikoff.—CoOh
"Good morrow to you, Valentine." Mother Goose.—HoMg—LaM
"Hail, Bishop Valentine, whose day this is." J. Donne.—MaF
My valentine. Unknown.—LaM
"Tomorrow is Saint Valentine's day." From Hamlet. W. Shakespeare.—LiLc
Valentine ("I got a valentine from Timmy") S. Silverstein.—LaM
Valentine ("I'll make a card for my valentine") M. Chute.—ChRu
"Valentines, I like them fine." M. A. Hoberman.—HoN
Won't you. S. Silverstein.—SiW
Saints. See names of saints, as Francis of Assisi, Saint
Salamander. Muriel Rukeyser.—HaWr

Salamanders
Salamander. M. Rukeyser.—HaWr
Salish Indians. See Indians of the Americas—Salish
"**Sally** ate some marmalade." Unknown.—EmN
"**Sally** go round the sun." Mother Goose.—AlC
"**Sally** is the laundress, and every Saturday." See The dolls' wash
"**Sally** over the water." Unknown.—EmN
Salmon, Arthur
In the dim city.—PaP
A **salmon** trout to her children. Unknown, fr. North Greenland.—LeIb
Salomé (about)
"The king said to Salomé." Unknown.—CoOh
Salute. Oliver Pitcher.—AdPb
Salvation army
"There is Hallelujah Hannah." A. E. Housman.—LiWw
Sam at the library. Carol Combs Hole.—BrM
"The **same** gold of summer was on the winter hills." See Winter gold
"**Sammy** Smith would drink and eat." Mother Goose.—TucMgl
"**Sam's** mother has." See Sam's world
Sam's world. Sam Cornish.—AdM
Samson (about)
"Occasions drew me early to this city." From Samson Agonistes. J. Milton.—MaFw
Samson Agonistes, sel. John Milton
"Occasions drew me early to this city."—MaFw
Samuel II
David's lamentation.—MeP
Samuel the Prince
War.—MeP
San Francisco county jail cell b-6. Conyus.—AdPb
Sanchez, Sonia
Definition for blk/children.—AdPb
Homecoming.—AdPb
Hospital/poem.—AdPb
Now poem. For us.—AdPb
Poem.—AdPb
Poem at thirty.—AdPb
Right on: white America.—AdB—AdPb
To all sisters.—AdPb
To P. J. (2 yrs old who sed write a poem for me in Portland, Oregon).—AdM
Sand
Sand scribblings. C. Sandburg.—SaT
Sand hill road. Morton Grosser.—PeS
"**Sand** of the sea runs red." See Flux
Sand scribblings. Carl Sandburg.—SaT
"**Sand** Sh: Sea shells." Unknown.—EmN
"**Sand,** shovel and shingle." See The concrete mixer
Sandburg, Carl
Again.—SaT
"Alice Corbin is gone."—SaT
Arithmetic.—MaFw—SaT
Auctioneer.—SaT
Baby face.—SaT
Baby song of the four winds.—SaT
Baby toes.—LiLc—SaT
Basket.—SaT
Be ready.—SaT
Bee song.—SaT
"Between two hills."—SaT
Bitter summer thoughts.—SaT
Blossom themes.—MaFw—SaT
"Bluebird, what do you feed on."—SaT
Boxes and bags.—SaT
Broken sky.—SaT
Brown gold.—SaT
Bubbles.—SaT
Buffalo Bill.—SaT
Buffalo dusk.—AdP—SaT
Bug spots.—SaT
Cheap blue.—SaT
Chicago poet.—SaT
Child Margaret.—MaFw—SaT
Child moon.—SaT
Children of the desert. See The people, yes
Children of the wind. See The people, yes
Circles. See The people, yes
Cornfield ridge and stream.—SaT
Cornhuskers. See Prairie
Crabapples.—SaT
Cricket march.—SaT
Crisscross.—SaT
Dan.—SaT
Daybreak.—SaT
Do you want affidavits.—SaT
Docks.—SaT
Drowsy.—SaT
Early moon.—SaT
Even numbers.—SaT
Evening waterfall.—SaT
Fish crier.—SaT
Five cent balloons.—SaT
Flowers tell months.—SaT
Flux.—SaT
Fog.—HoCs—JoA-4—MaFw—SaT—UnGb
Fourth of July night.—SaT
Frog songs.—SaT
From the shore.—SaT
Goldwing moth.—SaT
Good morning, America, sel.
Sky prayers.—SaT
Good night.—SaT
Grassroots.—SaT
Happiness.—SaT
The harbor.—HiN
Harvest.—HaWr
Harvest sunset.—SaT
Hats.—SaT
Haystacks. See Prairie
Haze gold.—SaT
Helga.—SaT
Hits and runs.—FlH—SaT
I am Chicago. See The windy city
Illinois farmer.—SaT
Improved farm land.—SaT
Jazz fantasia.—SaT
Just before April came.—SaT
Landscape.—SaT

Wind song.—SaT
Window.—SaT
Winds of the windy city. See The windy city
The windy city, sels.
I am Chicago.—SaT
Night.—SaT
Winds of the windy city.—SaT
Winter gold.—SaT
Winter milk.—SaT
Winter weather.—SaT
Young sea.—SaT
The **sandhill** crane. Mary Austin.—AdP
The **sandpiper.** Celia Thaxter.—OpOx—RoIt
Sandpipers
The sandpiper. C. Thaxter.—OpOx—RoIt
Sandpipers ("I like to see the teetertails") A. Fisher.—FiFo
Sandpipers ("Ten miles of flat land along the sea") C. Sandburg.—SaT
Sandpipers ("I like to see the teetertails") Aileen Fisher.—FiFo
Sandpipers ("Ten miles of flat land along the sea") Carl Sandburg.—SaT
"**Sandra** and that boy that's going to get her in trouble." See Cora punctuated with strawberries
"**Sandra's** seen a leprechaun." See Magic
Sands. Michael Goode.—JoV
Sands junior high school. Arlene Blackwell.—JoV
The **sands** of Dee. See Alton Locke
Sandwriting. Eve Merriam.—MeF
"**Sandy** Candy." Unknown, tr. fr. the Scottish by Norah and William Montgomerie.—JoA-4
Sansom, Clive
The Dorset nose.—ToM
Schoolmistress.—ToM
The witnesses.—MaFw (sel.)
Santa and the reindeer. Shel Silverstein.—SiW
Santa Claus
The boy who laughed at Santa Claus. O. Nash.—CoPt
Christmas eve rhyme. C. McCullers.—HoS
Kriss Kringle. T. B. Aldrich.—RoIt
Santa and the reindeer. S. Silverstein.—SiW
Ten nights before Christmas. D. McCord.—McFm
A visit from St Nicholas. C. C. Moore.—JoA-4—OpOx
Santa Fe, New Mexico
Santa Fe sketch. C. Sandburg.—SaT
Sapir, Edward
Curse on people that wish one ill. tr.—BiI
The **saplings.** Unknown.—EmN
The **Sappa** creek. Gary Snyder.—HiN
Sappho
"At noontime."—ThI
"But you, monkey face."—ThI
"Don't ask me what to wear."—ThI
"He is more than a hero."—ThI
"I have had not one word from her."—ThI
"It was you, Atthis, who said."—ThI
"Prayer to my lady of Paphos."—ThI
"Sleep darling."—ThI
"Tonight I've watched."—ThI
"We know this much."—ThI
"Without warning."—ThI
"You know the place, then."—ThI
Sappho (about)
"It was you, Atthis, who said." Sappho.—ThI
"**Sarah** Cynthia Sylvia Stout." See Sarah Cynthia Sylvia Stout would not take the garbage out
Sarah Cynthia Sylvia Stout would not take the garbage out. Shel Silverstein.—SiW
"**Sarah** saw a shot-silk sash shop." Unknown.—EmN
Sarchuk, Lena
A bit of cobweb.—MoM
Sarett, Lew
Four little foxes.—RoIt
Sarton, May
Summer music.—HiN
Sassoon, Siegfried
The dug-out.—MaFw
Everyone sang.—PaF
Falling asleep.—PaF
The general.—CoPu
The heart's journey, sel.
"What is Stonehenge? It is the roofless past."—PaP
"What is Stonehenge? It is the roofless past." See The heart's journey
"**Sat** in the sun." See Virginia
Satan. See Devil
A **satirical** romance. Juana Inez De la Cruz, tr. fr. the Mexican by Judith Thurman.—ThI (sel.)
Saturday. See Days of the week—Saturday
Saturday in New York. Anne Beresford.—ToM
Saturday night: Late. Lucille Clifton.—ClS
"**Saturday,** Saturday." See At home
Saturday's child. Countee Cullen.—AdPb
Satyrs
The crackling twig. J. Stephens.—CoPu
"**Save** your money." Unknown.—MoBw
"**Saw,** saw." See Twelfth night
"**Saw** ye aught of my love a-coming from ye market." Mother Goose.—AlC
Saws
"Esau Wood sawed wood." Unknown.—EmN
"Of all the saws I ever saw saw." Unknown.—EmN
Sawyer, Elizabeth
Giant.—JaP
Saxe, John Godfrey
The blind men and the elephant.—CoPt—JoA-4—RoIt
The puzzled census taker.—CoPt
"Singing through the forests."—RoIt
Solomon and the bees.—RoIt
The youth and the northwind.—CoPt
Saxon, Alvin
Black power.—AdPb
A poem for integration.—AdPb
Watts.—AdPb

"The **saxophone** turned into a dolphin." See Albert Ayler, eulogy for a decomposed saxophone player
Say, did you say. Unknown.—BrM
"**Say,** did you say, or did you not say." See Say, did you say
"**Say** it." Unknown.—MoBw
Sayers, Frances Clarke
Who calls.—LiLc
Saying. A. R. Ammons.—MoT
Sayings. See Proverbs
Sayles, James M.
Star of the evening.—LiS
"**Says** William to Henry, I cannot conceive." See Henry's secret
"A **scallop** met a polyp." See On the ocean floor
"**Scallywag** and Gollywog." Hugh Lofting.—BrM
"**Scampering** over saucers." Buson, tr. fr. the Japanese by Geoffrey Bownas and Anthony Thwaite.—MaFw
Scandinavia. See Denmark; Norsemen; Norway
Scannell, Vernon
Autobiographical note.—ToM
Autumn.—MaFw—ToM
Gunpowder plot.—MaFw—ToM
Tightrope walker.—HiN
Scannell, Vernon (about)
Autobiographical note. V. Scannell.—ToM
Scare. Robert Froman.—FrSp
Scarecrows
"Even before His Majesty." Dansui.—MaFw
"The people, of course." Issa.—HaW
"A wintry blizzard." Kyoroku.—BeM
"With a whispering." Boncho.—BeM
The **scarlet** woman. Fenton Johnson.—AdPb
"**Scattered** on the sand." Bashō, tr. fr. the Japanese by Harry Behn.—BeM
"**Scccrrrrubbb** it, scccrrrrubbb it, scccrrrrubbb it." See No sale
Scenery. Ted Joans.—AdPb
The **scholars.** William Butler Yeats.—PlM
Schonborg, Virginia
A rumble.—HoP
Song of ships.—HoP
Subway swinger (going).—HoP
School. See also Teachers and teaching
The ABC. S. Milligan.—CoOh
An advancement of learning. S. Heaney.—HiN
After school. A. Fisher.—FiFo
All schools have rules. E. Farjeon.—BrM
"At his writing lesson." Issa.—HaW
"At school." D. Marstiller.—HoC
The ballad of Chocolate Mabbie. G. Brooks.—PeS
Booker T. and W. E. B. D. Randall.—AbM
Cathexis. F. J. Bryant, Jr.—AdPb
City school. L. Lenski.—LeC
"Cleopatra ruled the Nile." Unknown.—MoBw
The collegiate angels. R. Alberti.—MaFw
"Confucius say." Unknown.—MoBw
The description of a good boy. H. Dixon.—OpOx
"A diller, a dollar." Mother Goose.—AlC—JoA-4
Do fishes go to school. R. Whitman.—RoIt
Dog with schoolboys. J. Follain.—CoPu
The dunce. J. Prévert.—MaFw
An elementary school classroom in a slum. S. Spender.—ToM
"The exam." Unknown.—MoM
For a junior school poetry book. C. Middleton.—ToM
For scholars and pupils. G. Wither.—OpOx
"Friends, Romans, classmates." Unknown.—MoBw
Grammar. M. H. Ets.—BrM
The high school band. R. Whittemore.—HiN
A history lesson. M. Holub.—MaFw
"Hit 'em in the head." Unknown.—MoBw
Homework. R. Hoban.—HoE
"I was jus." B. O'Meally.—AdM
"I wasn't late, the bell was early." Unknown.—MoBw
I'm no animal. C. Minor.—JoV
"I'm not a genius." Unknown.—MoBw
In school-days. J. G. Whittier.—OpOx
Inspection. Unknown.—AlPa
"Jake, Jake, open the gate." Unknown.—EmN
"Keep looking at the prize." Issa.—HaW
Kindergarten. R. Rogers.—AlW
A learned song. Mother Goose.—JoA-4
Love. S. Silverstein.—SiW
"A maiden at college, named Breeze." Unknown.—RoIt
Math class. M. C. Livingston.—LiM
Mid-term break. S. Heaney.—HiN
Mixed-up school. X. J. Kennedy.—KeO
A mortifying mistake. A. M. Pratt.—BrM
New puppy. A. Fisher.—FiFo
"The old, cold scold stole." Unknown.—EmN
The old school scold. Unknown.—BrM
"Over the hill there is a school." Unknown.—MoBw
The pay is good. R. Kell.—ToM
The place's fault. P. Hobsbaum.—ToM
Poem. S. Sanchez.—AdPb
Portrait. C. Rodgers.—AdM
"Remember the bottle." Unknown.—MoBw
"Remember the bride." Unknown.—EmN
"Remember the pen (remember the book)." Unknown.—MoBw
"Remember the row." Unknown.—MoBw
"Remember the school." Unknown.—MoBw
"Roses are red (coal is black)." Unknown.—MoBw
Sands. M. Goode.—JoV
The school boy. W. Blake.—MaFw
School concert. M. Chute.—ChRu
A schoolboy's lament. Unknown.—MoM
Schoolmistress. C. Sansom.—ToM
September. L. Clifton.—ClE
Sick. S. Silverstein.—SiW

Sea horses—*Continued*
Sea horse and sawhorse. X. J. Kennedy.—KeO
"The **sea** is a wilderness of waves." See Long trip
"The **sea** is calm tonight." See Dover Beach
The **sea** is melancholy. Agnes T. Pratt.—AlW
"The **sea** is never still." See Young sea
Sea life. See Ocean; Seamen
Sea love. Charlotte Mew.—CoPu
"**Sea** of stretch'd ground-swells." See Song of myself
"**Sea** risen sunbird." See Flamingo
The **sea** serpant. Wallace Irwin.—CoOh
Sea serpents
"I'm the monster of Loch Ness." Unknown.—MoBw
The sea serpant. W. Irwin.—CoOh
Sea shell. Amy Lowell.—LiLc
"**Sea** shell, sea shell." See Sea shell
Sea shells. See Shells
Sea slant. Carl Sandburg.—SaT
"**Sea** sunsets, give us keepsakes." See Good morning, America—Sky prayers
"The **sea,** the sea, the open sea." See The sea
The **sea** turtle and the shark. Melvin B. Tolson.—AdP—AdPb
"The **sea** was always the sea." See Sea wisdom
"The **sea** was calm." Carlton Minor.—JoV
Sea-wash. Carl Sandburg.—SaT
"The **sea-wash** never ends." See Sea-wash
"**Sea** way." Sylvia Briody.—HoC—HoP
Sea wisdom. Carl Sandburg.—SaT
Seafaring life. See Ocean; Seamen
Seager, Francis
A prayer to be said when thou goest to bed.—OpOx
The **seagull.** Mary Howitt.—OpOx
Seal lullaby. Rudyard Kipling.—JoA-4
Seal mother's song.—CoPu
Seal mother's song. See Seal lullaby
Seale, Bobby (about)
To Bobby Seale. L. Clifton.—AdM—AdPb
Seals (animals)
"Four furry seals, four funny fat seals." J. Prelutsky.—PrC
"I wanted to use my weapon." Unknown.—LeIb
"Listen to my words." Unknown.—LeIb
"On his very first hunt." Unknown.—LeIb
"Orphan." Unknown.—LeIb
The real slayer of the seal. Unknown.—LeIb
Seal lullaby. R. Kipling.—JoA-4
Seal mother's song.—CoPu
"Six sleek, slippery seals slipped silently ashore." Unknown.—EmN
Song composed at the beginning of an autumn festival in honor of the ribbon seal. Unknown.—LeIb
Seaman, E. William
"Higgledy-piggledy."—LiWw
Seamen. See also Naval battles; Ocean; Ships
The admiral's ghost. A. Noyes.—JoA-4
A ballad for a boy. W. Cory.—OpOx
The ballad of Hagensack. W. Irwin.—CoPt
The ballad of Sir Patrick Spens. Unknown.—RoIt
Beowulf's voyage to Denmark. Unknown.—MaFw (sel.)
Captain Spud and his First Mate, Spade. J. Ciardi.—CiFs
Christmas at sea. R. L. Stevenson.—RoIt
Follow the gleam. From Merlin and the gleam. A. Tennyson.—RoIt
Geographical knowledge. T. Hardy.—PlP
"He stept so lightly to the land." From Sylvie and Bruno. L. Carroll.—LiPc
Heart's content. Unknown.—RoIt
Hell's pavement. J. Masefield.—CoPt
How's my boy. S. Dobell.—RoIt
The Jumblies. E. Lear.—JoA-4—OpOx—RoIt
Little Billee. W. M. Thackeray.—RoIt
Lord Arnaldos. J. E. Flecker.—CoPt
"Me and I and you." Unknown.—BoI
The mermaid. Unknown.—RoIt
A nautical extravaganza. W. Irwin.—CoPt
"A nervous sea captain from Cheesequake." X. J. Kennedy.—KeO
The powerful eyes o' Jeremy Tait. W. Irwin.—CoPt
The prologue. From The Canterbury tales. G. Chaucer.—MaFw
Psalm 107. From Psalms, Bible, Old Testament
They that go down.—RoIt
Sailing to an island. R. Murphy.—ToM
Sailor. L. Hughes.—HoD
"Sailor, sailor, over the sea." Unknown.—EmN
"A sailor went to sea." Unknown.—EmN
The sailor's consolation. C. Dibdin.—RoIt
Sails, gulls, sky, sea. F. Holman.—HoI
The sea. B. Cornwall.—RoIt
Sea change. J. Masefield.—CoPt
The secret of the sea. H. W. Longfellow.—RoIt
Sheep. W. H. Davies.—CoPt
The story of Samuel Jackson. C. G. Leland.—CoPt
"Three big sailors had a tiny little boat." Mother Goose.—TucMg
To sea. T. L. Beddoes.—RoIt
The walloping window-blind. From Davy and the goblin. C. E. Carryl.—RoIt
"A wet sheet and a flowing sea." A. Cunningham.—RoIt
The yarn of the Loch Ackray. J. Masefield.—CoPt
The yarn of the Nancy Bell. W. S. Gilbert.—RoIt
The **search.** S. Silverstein.—SiW
"**Searching.**" See Endless search
"A **searching** pain." See Quietly I shout
Sears, Edmund Hamilton
"It came upon a midnight clear."—LaS
Seascape. Langston Hughes.—HoD
Seashore. See also Ocean
At the ocean. E. Merriam.—MeO

At the seaside. R. L. Stevenson.—LiLc—OpOx
At the sea-side.—JoA-4
The black cliffs, Ballybunion. B. Kennelly.—CoPi
Celia. Unknown.—BrM
Dover Beach. M. Arnold.—MaFw (sel.)—MoG—PaP (sel.)—RoIt
Driving to the beach. J. Cole.—HoP
Flux. C. Sandburg.—SaT
Grunion. M. C. Livingston.—LiM
"I had a little castle upon the sea sand." Mother Goose.—TucMgl
The Malibu. M. C. Livingston.—LiM
Punta De Los Lobos Marinos. M. C. Livingston.—LiM
Sand scribblings. C. Sandburg.—SaT
The sandpiper. C. Thaxter.—OpOx—RoIt
"Scattered on the sand." Bashō.—BeM
She sells seashells. Unknown.—BrM
Sketch. C. Sandburg.—SaT
A very odd fish. D'Arcy W. Thompson
Seaside. See Seashore
Seaside golf. John Betjeman.—FlH
Season. Wole Soyinka.—AlPa—MaFw
The **season** for singing. Seymour Barab.—LaS
"The **season** for singing a joyous refrain." See The season for singing
"**Season** into season, as the weathers go." See The wind is round
"**Season** of mists and mellow fruitfulness." See To autumn
Seasons. See also Autumn; Spring; Summer; Winter; also names of months, as January
The black bear. J. Prelutsky.—PrP
The brownies' year. Unknown.—JaP
Darkling summer, ominous dusk, rumerous rain. D. Schwartz.—HaWr
"Deep in the mountains we have no calendar." Unknown.—BaSs
Dream song. Unknown.—BiI
Dry season. K. Brew.—AlPa
First spring morning. R. Bridges.—JoA-4
Footprints. A. Fisher.—FiFo
Frost at midnight. S. T. Coleridge.—PaF (sel.)
Humpty Dumpty's song. From Through the looking-glass. L. Carroll.—OpOx
"In winter, when the fields are white."—LiPc
"I saw." P. Malone.—HoC
"The leaves." O. Lermand.—HoC
The lover in winter plaineth for the spring. Unknown.—LiS
May day. N. Belting.—BeSc
"The most." S. Suggs.—HoC
One big rain. R. Hoban.—HoE
Pleasant changes. J. E. Browne.—OpOx
Season. W. Soyinka.—AlPa—MaFw
The season for singing. S. Barab.—LaS
Seasons. M. Chute.—ChRu
The seasons on our block. E. Merriam.—MeF
September. H. H. Jackson.—RoIt
The Shawangunks—early April. L. Moore.—MoSp
Six-month song in the foothills. G. Snyder.—HaWr
So quickly came the summer. A. T. Pratt.—AlW
Solace. C. S. Delany.—AdPb
"Summer." E. Hillery.—HoC
Summer. C. G. Rossetti.—PaF
The swallow. C. G. Rossetti.—UnGb
The thaw. J. Matthews.—HaWr
"These are the days when birds come back." E. Dickinson.—PaF
Things to remember. J. Reeves.—JoA-4
Two songs. E. Sitwell.—JoA-4
"Voices gay." A. Fair.—HoC
Waiting. H. Behn.—JoA-4
The wind is round. H. Moss.—HaWr
The year. C. Patmore.—RoIt
Seasons. Marchette Chute.—ChRu
The **seasons** on our block. E. Merriam.—MeF
"A **seated** statue of himself he seems." See Farm boy after summer
Sebonwoma. Christina Ama Ata Aidoo.—AlPa (sel.)
The **Second Book of Samuel**
David's lamentation. See The second book of Samuel
The second book of Samuel, sel. Bible—Old Testament
David's lamentation.—MeP
"The **second** class is the second grade." See Primary lesson: The second class citizens
The **second** coming. William Butler Yeats.—MoG
"**Second-hand** sights, like crumpled." See Newark, for now
"The **second** man I love." See Spring
The **second** sermon on the warpland. Gwendolyn Brooks.—AdPb
Secret ("Jean said, No") David McCord.—McAa—McS
The **secret** ("A secret is a secret, any size") Robert P. Tristram Coffin.—PaF
Secret intimations. John Hall Wheelock.—CoPu
"A **secret** is a secret, any size." See The secret
A **secret** kept. Judah al-Harizi, tr. fr. the Hebrew by Robert Mezey.—MeP
The **secret** of the sea. Henry Wadsworth Longfellow.—RoIt
Secrets
"Ears like a mule." Unknown.—EmN
Henry's secret. D. Kilmer.—OpOx
It happened. M. C. Livingston.—LiM
"Keep it dark." Unknown.—AlPa
Keyiah. G. Brooks.—UnGb
"Only white gull and I." Yi Hwang.—BaSs
Secret ("Jean said, No") D. McCord.—McAa—McS
The secret ("A secret is a secret, any size") R. P. T. Coffin.—PaF
Secret intimations. J. H. Wheelock.—CoPu
A secret kept. Judah al-Harizi.—MeP
The secret of the sea. H. W. Longfellow.—RoIt
Secrets. R. Froman.—FrSp

"A **shadow** is floating through the moonlight." See The bird of night
Shadow wash. Shel Silverstein.—SiW
Shadows
Could it have been a shadow. M. Shannon.—JaP
"Digger Boy was hunting clams." N. Belting.—BeWi
Escape. G. D. Johnson.—AdPb
My shadow. R. L. Stevenson.—OpOx
Nocturne varial. L. Alexander.—AdPb
Shadow wash. S. Silverstein.—SiW
Shadows. L. Moore.—MoSm
Shadows and song. P. George.—AlW
Tenebris. A. W. Grimké.—AdPb
"There is a thing that nothing is." Unknown.—EmN
"We three." L. Moore.—MoSm
"What is life." Unknown.—ClFc
"When a shadow appeared on the water." Unknown.—BaSs
Zebra. I. Dinesen.—AdP
Shadows. Lilian Moore.—MoSm
Shadows and song. Phil George.—AlW
"The **shadows** of night were a-comin' down swift." See Higher
"The **shadows** of the ships." See Sketch
"**Shadows,** shadows." See Escape
"**Shaggy,** and lean, and shrewd, with pointed ears." See The woodman's dog
"**Shaka** was the Great Elephant who stamped his enemies." See Shaka Zulu
Shaka, Chief of the Zulus (about)
Shaka Zulu. F. M. Mulikita.—AlPa (sel.)
Shaka Zulu. F. M. Mulikita.—AlPa (sel.)
"**Shake** hands, we shall never be friends, all's over." Alfred Edward Housman.—CoPu
Shakespeare, William
Ariel's song. See The tempest
As you like it, sels.
"Blow, blow, thou winter wind."—PaF—RoIt
"Under the greenwood tree."—RoIt
In Arden forest.—JoA-4
Autolycus' song. See The winter's tale
"Be not afeared, the isle is full of noises." See The tempest
"Blow, blow, thou winter wind." See As you like it
"Blow, winds, and crack your cheeks, rage, blow." See King Lear
"Come into these yellow sands." See The tempest
The crow doth sing. See The merchant of Venice
Cymbeline, sel.
A morning song.—JoA-4
The death of kings. See King Richard II
"From you I have been absent in the spring." See Sonnets
Hamlet, sels.
"Some say. . . . "—JoA-4
"Tomorrow is Saint Valentine's day."—LiLc
Henry V, sels.
The horse.—RoIt
King Henry's speech before Agincourt.—MaF
Henry VIII, sel.
"Orpheus with his lute made trees"
Music.—RoIt
"Here's the place: stand still: how fearful." See King Lear
The horse. See Henry V
"If thou survive my well-contented day." See Sonnets
In Arden forest. See As you like it—"Under the greenwood tree"
King Henry's speech before Agincourt. See King Henry V
King Lear, sels.
"Blow, winds, and crack your cheeks, rage, blow."—MaFw
"Here's the place: stand still: how fearful."—PaP
King Richard II, sel.
The death of kings.—MoG
Love's labour's lost, sels.
Spring ("When daisies pied and violets blue").—PaF
"When icicles hang by the wall."—JoA-4—RoIt
Winter.—PaF
The merchant of Venice, sels.
The crow doth sing.—RoIt
Song ("Tell me where is fancy bred").—RoIt
A midsummer night's dream, sels.
"Now the hungry lion roars."—MaFw
"Over hill, over dale."—JoA-4
"You spotted snakes."—JoA-4
A morning song. See Cymbeline
Music. See Henry VIII—"Orpheus with his lute made trees"
"Now the hungry lion roars." See A midsummer night's dream
"O, then, I see Queen Mab hath been with you." See Romeo and Juliet
"Orpheus with his lute made trees." See Henry VIII
"Over hill, over dale." See A midsummer night's dream
Queen Mab. See Romeo and Juliet—"O, then, I see Queen Mab hath been with you"
Romeo and Juliet, sels.
"O, then, I see Queen Mab hath been with you."—MaFw
Queen Mab.—JoA-4
"Some say. . . . " See Hamlet
Song. See The merchant of Venice
Sonnet IV. Unthrifty loveliness. See Sonnets
Sonnets, sels.
"From you I have been absent in the spring"
Sonnet.—PrF
"If thou survive my well-contented day."—PlM

Sonnet IV. Unthrifty loveliness.—MoG
"That time of year thou may'st in me behold"
Sonnet.—PaF
"Was it the proud full sail of his great verse."—PlM
Spring. See Love's labour's lost
Sweet-and-twenty. See Twelfth night
The tempest, sels.
Ariel's song.—MaFw—RoIt
"Be not afeared, the isle is full of noises."—MaFw
"Come into these yellow sands."—LiS
Where the bee sucks.—JoA-4—LiLc
"That time of year thou may'st in me behold." See Sonnets
"Tomorrow is Saint Valentine's day." See Hamlet
Twelfth night, sel.
Sweet-and-twenty.—MoG
"Under the greenwood tree." See As you like it
"Was it the proud full sail of his great verse." See Sonnets
"When icicles hang by the wall." See Love's labour's lost
Where the bee sucks. See The tempest
Winter. See Love's labour's lost—"When icicles hang by the wall"
The winter's tale, sel.
Autolycus' song.—LiS
"You spotted snakes." See A midsummer night's dream
Shakespeare, William (about)
Pete the parrot and Shakespeare. D. Marquis.—PlM
To the memory of my beloved, the author, Mr William Shakespeare: and what he hath left us. B. Jonson.—PlM (sel.)
"**Shakespeare** would have savored his coarse, irate." See "How long hast thou been a gravemaker"
Shakhovich, Larissa
Out skiing.—MoM
"**Shall** I compare thee." See Spring blossom
Shalom, Shin
Incense.—MeP
Not so simple.—MeP
"**Shalom,** Mount Avarim. Blessed be your slopes." See Mount Avarim
"**Shame** on you." Unknown.—MoBw
The **Shandon** bells. Father Prout.—CoPi
"**Shaneen** and Maurya Prendergast." See Patch-Shaneen
Shanghai, China
Dreaming in the Shanghai restaurant. D. J. Enright.—ToM
"**Shango,** I prostrate to you every morning." Unknown, tr. fr. the Yoruba by Bakare Gbadamosi and Ulli Beier.—AlPa
Shanks, Edward
Boats at night.—MaFw
On Holmbury hill.—PaP
Shannon, Monica
Could it have been a shadow.—JaP
Country trucks.—HoP
Shapes and signs. James Clarence Mangan.—CoPi
"**Shapes** of men." See The avenue: N. Y. city
Shapiro, Karl
Auto wreck.—MaFw—PeS
The conscientious objector.—PeS
Manhole covers.—HiN—JoA-4
Shapiro, Norman R.
To my mother. tr.—AlPa
Sharaf, Ibn
Concert.—AbM
The **shark.** John Ciardi.—CiFs
Sharks
The powerful eyes o' Jeremy Tait. W. Irwin.—CoPt
The sea turtle and the shark. M. B. Tolson.—AdP—AdPb
The shark. J. Ciardi.—CiFs
Sharp, Martin. See Clapton, Eric and Sharp, Martin
Sharp, Saundra
Moon poem.—AbM
Sharp, William (Fiona Macleod, pseud.)
An almanac.—JoA-4
A milking song.—MaF
The wasp.—JoA-4
Sharpe, Richard Scrafton
The country mouse and the city mouse.—OpOx
Shaw, Dorothy Stott
Caprice.—CoPt
The **Shawangunks**—early April. Lilian Moore.—MoSp
She. Thomas Hardy.—PlP
"**She** always tries." See Cat bath
"**She** danced, near nude, to tom-tom beat." See Zalka Peetruza
"**She** didn't know she was beautiful." See On getting a natural
"**She** drank from a bottle called DRINK ME." See Alice
"**She** dwelt among the untrodden ways." William Wordsworth.—LiS
"**She** even thinks that up in heaven." See For a lady I know
"**She** glows brighter than the sun." See A riddle
"**She** goes but softly, but she goeth sure." See Upon a snail
"**She** had on sandals." See Abandoned
"**She** has the immaculate look of the new." See Chinese baby asleep
"**She** hears me strike the board and say." See Father and child
"**She,** in dowdy dress and dumpy." See Still life: Lady with birds
"**She** kept an antique shop—or it kept her." See My grandmother
"**She** looked like a bird from a cloud." See At the word *farewell*
She opened the door. Thomas Hardy.—JoA-4—PlP

"If neither he sells sea shells." Unknown.—EmN
"Minnie and Winnie." A. Tennyson.—OpOx
"Periwinkle, periwinkle." Unknown.—EmN
"Primitive paintings. . . . " A. Atwood.—AtM
"Sand Sh: Sea shells." Unknown.—EmN
Sea shell. A. Lowell.—LiLc
"She sells sea shells at the sea shore." Unknown.—EmN
"She sells sea shells on the sea shell shore." Unknown.—BrM—EmN
She sells seashells. Unknown.—BrM
The shell ("And then I pressed the shell") J. Stephens.—MaFw
The shell ("I took away the ocean once") D. McCord.—JoA-4—LiLc—McS
Shell to gentleman. From Quatrains. T. Carmi.—MeP
Souvenir. E. Merriam.—MeO
"**Sheltering** from the rain." Karai Senryū, tr. fr. the Japanese by Geoffrey Bownas and Anthony Thwaite.—MaFw
Shepelev, Volodimir
A celebration.—MoM
The **shepherd.** William Blake.—RoIt
Shepherdesses. See Shepherds and shepherdesses
Shepherds and shepherdesses. See also Sheep
"Castles and candlelight." J. Reeves.—CoPt
John Anderson, my jo. R. Burns.—RoIt
"Little Boy Blue." Mother Goose.—JoA-4
The marvellous bear shepherd. Unknown.—MaFw
Nod. W. De La Mare.—JoA-4
"Oh my dear, what a cold you've got." Mother Goose.—TucMgl
The passionate shepherd to his love. C. Marlowe.—RoIt
Psalm 23. From Psalms, Bible, Old Testament.—RoIt
Reply to the passionate shepherd. Walter Raleigh (1552-1618).—RoIt
Rise up shepherd, and follow.—Unknown.—LaS
The shepherd. W. Blake.—RoIt
The shepherds' hymn. R. Crashaw.—MaF
Shepherds in Judea. J. Ingalls.—LaS
Shepherd's song at Christmas. L. Hughes.—AbM
The stranger's song. T. Hardy.—PlP
Weathers. T. Hardy.—PlP
While shepherds watched. N. Tate.—LaS
"While shepherds watched their flocks by night."—JoA-4
The **shepherds'** hymn. Richard Crashaw.—MaF
Shepherds in Judea. Jeremiah Ingalls.—LaS
Shepherd's song at Christmas. Langston Hughes.—AbM
The **shepherd's** tale. Raoul Ponchon, tr. fr. the French by James Kirkup.—CoPt
Sherwood forest, England
A song of Sherwood. A. Noyes.—JoA-4
"**Sherwood** in the twilight, is Robin Hood awake." See A song of Sherwood
"**She's** coming, the farmer said to the owl." See The farmer and the queen
Sheyanova, Ira
Two mothers.—MoM
Shiki
"After thunder goes."—BeM
"At twilight a bell."—BeM
"Drifting, feathery."—BeM
"Eleven horsemen."—BeM
"A full moon comes up."—BeM
"Late summer evening."—BeM
Shin Heum
"It rained."—BaSs
"What if a rafter is too short or too long."—BaSs
"**Shine,** mister, shine." See Shoeshine boy
Shine out fair sun. Unknown.—MaFw
"**Shine** out fair sun, with all your heat." See Shine out fair sun
"**Shining** soldiers." Unknown.—EmN
"A **shiny** stone by a dirt road." See Dirt road
The **ship** of Rio. Walter De La Mare.—BrM
Ships. See also Boats and boating; Ocean; Seamen; Shipwrecks; Warships
The caulker. M. A. Lewis.—CoPt
The clipper Dunbar to the clipper Cutty Sark. E. Anderson.—CoPt
The convergence of the twain. T. Hardy.—PlP
Docks. C. Sandburg.—SaT
The figurehead. C. Garstin.—CoPt
The Golden Vanity. Unknown.—RoIt
Horses aboard. T. Hardy.—PlP
"I saw a ship a-sailing." Mother Goose.—AlC—JoA-4—MiMg
I saw three ships. Unknown.—LaS
Lord Arnaldos. J. E. Flecker.—CoPt
Middle passage. R. Hayden.—AdPb
The north ship. P. Larkin.—MaFw
Sea slant. C. Sandburg.—SaT
Seascape. L. Hughes.—HoD
The ship of Rio. W. De La Mare.—BrM
"Sitting on the dock." C. Meyer.—JoV
Six ten sixty-nine. Conyus.—AdPb
Sketch. C. Sandburg.—SaT
Song of ships. V. Schonborg.—HoP
Tugs. J. S. Tippett.—HoP
Wooden ships. D. Crosby, P. Kantner and S. Stills.—MoG
Shipwrecks
The caulker. M. A. Lewis.—CoPt
The Cutty Sark. From Dreams of a summer night, part VI. G. Barker.—MaFw
In memory of the circus ship Euzkera, wrecked in the Caribbean sea, 1 September 1948. W. Gibson.—HiN
The mermaid. Unknown.—RoIt
Sir Patrick Spens. Unknown.—JoA-4—MaFw
The ballad of Sir Patrick Spens. Unknown.—RoIt
Skipper Ireson's ride. J. G. Whittier.—RoIt
The story of Samuel Jackson. C. G. Leland.—CoPt

Shipwrecks—*Continued*
The wreck of the Hesperus. H. W. Longfellow.—RoIt
The wreck of the Julie Plante. W. H. Drummond.—CoPt
The yarn of the Loch Achray. J. Masefield.—CoPt
Shirley, James
Contention of Ajax and Ulysses, sel.
"The glories of our blood and state."—RoIt
"The glories of our blood and state." See Contention of Ajax and Ulysses
Shiver my timbers. David McCord.—McAa
Shlensky, Vitaly
To a friend.—MoM
Shlonsky, Avraham
Dress me, dear mother.—MeP
Jezrael.—MeP (sel.)
Sabbath stars.—MeP
Shneour, Zalman
Stop playing.—MeP
Shoemakers. See also Boots and shoes
The lepracaun; or, Fairy shoemaker. W. Allingham.—RoIt
The leprechaun. L. Blair.—JaP
Shoes. See Boots and shoes
Shoeshine boy. Lois Lenski.—LeC
A **shooting** song. William Brighty Rands.—OpOx
Shopkeepers. See Shops and shopkeepers
Shopping. See Markets and marketing; Peddlers and venders; Shops and shopkeepers
Shopping. Lois Lenski.—LeC
Shops and shopkeepers. See also names of shops and shopkeepers, as Barbers and barbershops
Again. C. Sandburg.—SaT
Department store. L. Lenski.—LeC
The great merchant, Dives Pragmaticus, cries his wares. T. Newbery.—OpOx
My grandmother. E. Jennings.—ToM
Nothingest. R. Froman.—FrSp
Number 20. L. Ferlinghetti.—PeS
"Sarah saw a shot-silk sash shop." Unknown.—EmN
"She stood at the door." Unknown.—EmN
Shopping. L. Lenski.—LeC
Shore. See Seashore
The **shore** of the universe. Kolya Zinoviev, tr. fr. the Russian by Miriam Morton.—MoM
Short, John
Carol.—ToM
"A **short** pause." See Markings: The comma
Shosen
"Butterflies, beware."—BeM
Shoshone Indians. See Indians of the Americas—Shoshone
"**Should** old acquaintance be forgot." Unknown.—MoBw
"**Should** you ask me, whence these stories." See The song of Hiawatha
Shout. Langston Hughes.—HoD
"**Shouts** and squeaks." See The house of the goblin
"**Show** me again the time." See Lines
The **shower.** Henry Vaughan.—CoPu—MaFw
Shower bath. Lois Lenski.—LeC
Showers. Marchette Chute.—ChRu
Showers, clearing later in the day. Eve Merriam.—MeF
Shrew ("The little shrew is soricine") David McCord.—McAa
Shrew ("The shrew is so busy she makes me quite dizzy") Mary Ann Hoberman.—HoLb
"The **shrew** is so busy she makes me quite dizzy." See Shrew
Shrews
Shrew ("The little shrew is soricine") D. McCord.—McAa
Shrew ("The shrew is so busy she makes me quite dizzy") M. A. Hoberman.—HoLb
Small, smaller. R. Hoban.—CoPu
A **Shropshire** lad, sels. Alfred Edward Housman
The carpenter's son.—LiS
"Far is a western brookland."—PaP
The Lent lily.—PaF
"Loveliest of trees, the cherry now."—MaFw
Loveliest of trees.—JoA-4—PaF
"On Wenlock Edge the wood's in trouble."—PaP
Reveille.—RoIt
" 'Tis time, I think, by Wenlock town."—PaP
"With rue my heart is laden."—RoIt
Shu Hsi
Hot cake.—MaFw
"**Shuffling** along in her broken shoes from the slums." See Lady feeding the cats
Shultze, Leonhard. See Doob, Leonard and Shultze, Leonhard
Shut not your doors. Walt Whitman.—PlM
"**Shut** not your doors to me, proud libraries." See Shut not your doors
Shut the shutter. Unknown.—BrM
"**Shut** up, and leave me be." See I'm only going to tell you once
Siberia
Song. Unknown.—LeIb
Sick. Shel Silverstein.—SiW
Sick in winter. Russell Hoban.—HoE
Sickness. See also names of diseases, as Mumps
Angina pectoris. W. R. Moses.—HiN
The beginning of sickness. Unknown.—BiI
Breakfast. D. McCord.—McFm
A child that has a cold. T. Dibdin.—CoPu
The confession. T. Ingoldsby.—RoIt
The crossing of Mary of Scotland. W. T. Smith.—CoOh
"Jenny kiss'd me when we met." P. Dehn.—LiS
"Jenny Wren fell sick." Mother Goose.—JoA-4
The land of counterpane. R. L. Stevenson.—OpOx
Magic formula against disease. Unknown.—BiI
Measles in the ark. S. Coolidge.—OpOx

Modern song. Unknown.—AbM
"Mother, mother, I am sick, sick, sick." Unknown.—EmN
Mumps. E. M. Roberts.—BrM
"Oh my dear, what a cold you've got." Mother Goose.—TucMgl
Old Tim Toole. D. McCord.—McAa
On Dr Lettsome, by himself. J. C. Lettsom.—CoPu
The remedy worse than the disease. M. Prior.—LiWw
Sick. S. Silverstein.—SiW
Sick in winter. R. Hoban.—HoE
"There was a young lady of Spain." Unknown
A young lady of Spain.—CoOr
"There was an old man on the Border." E. Lear.—LiLc
Limericks.—JoA-4
"There's a certain illness within you." A. Blackwell.—JoV
To a poet who has had a heart attack. R. Eberhart.—PlM
To music to becalme his sleep. R. Herrick.—RoIt
"Who's that ringing." Unknown.—BlM
The writing of Hezekiah King of Judah, when he had been sick, and was recovered of his sickness. From Isaiah.—MeP
"**Side** by side, their faces blurred." See An Arundel tomb
"**Sidewalk.**" See Street song
"The **sidewalk** is my yard." See City child
Siegel, Eli
"All the smoke."—CoPu
Siegfried, King (about)
The three songs. B. Taylor.—CoPt
Sight
"In the old man's eyes." Takahama Kyoshi.—MaFw
On my short-sightedness. P. Chaya.—MaFw
Signal song on capture of polar bear. Unknown, fr. the Ammassalik Eskimo.—LeIb
Signals. Johari Amini.—AdPb
Signs
"Always." L. Pepper.—HoC
"East is east and west is west." Unknown.—CoOh
Loud. R. Froman.—FrSp
Orders. R. Froman.—FrSp
Signal song on capture of polar bear. Unknown.—LeIb
Signs. L. B. Hopkins.—HoP
Staying alive. D. Wagoner.—MoT
"There are." D. J. Taylor.—HoC
Trucks. J. S. Tippett.—HoP—JoA-4
Signs. Lee Bennett Hopkins.—HoP
Signs of Christmas. May Justus.—HoS
Signs of the Zodiac. See Zodiac, Signs of
Signs of the zodiac. David McCord.—LiWw
Silence
Acknowledgement. D. Laing.—CoPu
Cry silent. D. Whitewing.—AlW
"Eleven horsemen." Shiki.—BeM
How still, how happy. E. Brontë.—PaF
"How still, how happy! Those are words."—PaP
"Luminous silence. . . . " A. Atwood.—AtM
Mute opinion. T. Hardy.—PlP
On wearing ears. W. J. Harris.—AdB
"Quiet." M. C. Livingston.—LiM
The quiet child. R. Field.—NeA
Refuge. M. Chute.—ChRu
Silence ("It was bright day and all the trees were still") W. J. Turner.—PaF
Silence ("The mocking bird") E. McCarthy.—CoPu
Silence ("My father used to say") M. Moore.—MaFw
Silent, but. . . . Tsuboi Shigeji.—MaFw
Snowy morning. L. Moore.—UnGb
Spring quiet. C. G. Rossetti.—PaF—RoIt
Stephen's green revisited. R. Weber.—CoPi
Your eyes have their silence. G. W. Barrax.—AdPb
Silence ("It was bright day and all the trees were still") W. J. Turner.—PaF
Silence ("The mocking bird") Eugene McCarthy.—CoPu
Silence ("My father used to say") Marianne Moore.—MaFw
"A **silence** hovers over the earth." See A late spring day in my life
"A **silence** slipping around like death." See A winter twilight
"**Silent** alone, where none or saw, or heard." See Contemplations
"**Silent** are the woods, and the dim green boughs are." See On Eastnor knoll
Silent, but. . . . Tsuboi Shigeji, tr. fr. the Japanese by Geoffrey Bownas and Anthony Thwaite.—MaFw
"**Silent** silhouettes." See Sunday sculpture
"**Silently** I footed by an uphill road " See The last signal
The **Silex** Scintillans, sel. H. Vaughan
The morning watch.—MoG
Silkworms
The silkworms. D. Stewart.—MaFw
Sill, Edward Rowland
The fool's prayer.—RoIt
"**Silly.** All giggles and ringlets and never." See Romping
"**Silly** Sally swiftly shooed seven silly sheep." Unknown.—EmN
Silly stanzas. Unknown.—CoOh
"A froggie sat on a lily pad"
"A man he lived by the sewer"
"A peanut sat on a railroad track"
"A rabbit raced a turtle"
Silver, Philip
Walnut. tr.—CoPu
Silver (color)
Silver. W. De La Mare.—JoA-4—UnGb
Washed in silver. J. Stephens.—RoIt
Silver. Walter De La Mare.—UnGb
"The **silver** birch is a dainty lady." See Child's song in spring

Skinny.—SiW
Sky seasoning.—SiW
Sleeping sardines.—SiW
"The Slithergadee has crawled out of the sea."—TrG
Smart.—SiW
Snowman.—SiW
Spaghetti.—SiW
Standing.—SiW
Stone telling.—SiW
Thumbs.—SiW
Tight hat. See "I tried to tip my hat to Miss McCaffery"
The toucan.—SiW
Traffic light.—SiW
Tree house.—SiW
True story.—SiW
Two boxes.—SiW
The unicorn.—SiW
Upstairs.—SiW
Us.—SiW
Valentine.—LaM
Vegetables.—CoOr
Warning.—SiW
"What a day."—SiW
What's in the sack.—SiW
Where the sidewalk ends.—SiW
Who.—SiW
Wild boar.—SiW
With his mouth full of food.—SiW
Won't you.—SiW
The worst.—SiW
The yipiyuk.—SiW

Silverton, Michael
Life in the country.—CoPu

Simon Soggs' Thanksgiving. W. A. Croffut.—CoPt

Simone, Nina (about)
For Nina Simone wherever you are. L. Curry.—JoV

Simple. Naomi Long Madgett.—AdPb

"**Simple** and fresh and fair from winter's close emerging." See The first dandelion

"A **simple** child." See We are seven

"**Simple** Simon met a pieman." Mother Goose.—JoA-4

Simple song. Marge Piercy.—MoT

Simpson, Louis
Carentan O Carentan.—ToM
Columbus.—ToM
The goodnight.—ToM
The heroes.—PeS
The redwoods.—MaFw
Walt Whitman at Bear mountain.—PlM

Simultaneously. David Ignatow.—HiN

"**Simultaneously,** five thousand miles apart." See Simultaneously

Sin
Dearly beloved brethren. J. Tabrar.—CoPu
"Once in a saintly passion." J. Thomson.—RoIt
"You asked me to write in your album." Unknown.—EmN

"**Since** Christmas they have lived with us." See Balloons

"**Since** he weighs nothing." See Postscript

"**Since** Malcolm died." See Aardvark

"**Since** money talks." See Flummery

"**Since** wild geese flew south." Jo Myung-ri, tr. fr. the Korean by Chung Seuk Park and ad. by Virginia Olsen Baron.—BaSs

Sincere flattery of W. W. (Americanus). James Kenneth Stephen.—LiS

Sincerity. See Conduct of life

Sinfield, Peter. See Fripp, Robert and Sinfield, Peter

Sing a song of honey. Barbara Euphan Todd.—PaF

"**Sing** a song of juniper." Robert Francis.—HiN

"**Sing** a song of monkeys." See The monkeys

"**Sing** a song of people." Lois Lenski.—LeC

"**Sing** a song of sixpence." Mother Goose.—AlC—EmN—JoA-4—LiS

"**Sing;** how 'a would sing." See Julie-Jane

Sing me a new song. John Henrik Clarke.—AdPb

"**Sing** me a new song, young black singer." See Sing me a new song

Sing me a song. Robert Louis Stevenson.—RoIt

"**Sing** me a song of a lad that is gone." See Sing me a song

"**Sing** we for love and idleness." See An immorality

"**Sing** we the Virgin Mary." Unknown, ad. by John Jacob Niles.—LaS

Singa songa. Dennis Lee.—LeA

"**Singa** songa sea." See Singa songa

"**Singee** a songee sick a pence." See Nursery song in pidgin English

"The **singers** are gone from the Cornmarket-place." See After the fair

Singing
"After yesterday." A. R. Ammons.—MoT
"And the old women gathered." M. Evans.—AdPb
Answer to a child's question. S. T. Coleridge.—OpOx—RoIt
A blackbird singing. R. S. Thomas.—MaFw
The crazy woman. G. Brooks.—AbM
Cross over the river. S. Cornish.—AdM
The crow doth sing. From The merchant of Venice. W. Shakespeare.—RoIt
"The cuckoo and the donkey." Mother Goose.—TucMg
The cumberbunce. P. West.—CoOh
The darkling thrush. T. Hardy.—PaF—PlP—RoIt
"Ding, dong." C. Watson.—WaF
The dinkey-bird. Eugene Field.—RoIt
Dreams. N. Giovanni.—AdPb
"Dry and parched." A. Lopez.—AlW
Everyone sang. S. Sassoon.—PaF
First song. G. Kinnell.—HiN
For Nina Simone wherever you are. L. Curry.—JoV
Homage to the Empress of the Blues. R. Hayden.—AdPb

"The king of China's daughter."—JoA-4—MaFw
"Madame Mouse trots."—JoA-4
The sleeping beauty.—MaFw (sel.)
Two songs, sels.—JoA-4
"The clouds are bunchèd roses"
"In summer when the rose-bushes"
Sitwell, Sacheverell
Upon an image from Dante.—PaP
"**Six** brave maids sat on six broad beds." Unknown.—EmN
"The **six-foot** nest of the sea-hawk." See Sea-hawk
"**Six** gray geese sat on the grass." Unknown.—EmN
"**Six** little mice sat down to spin." Mother Goose.—BlM—JoA-4—TrG
"The **six** month child." See Slippery
Six-month song in the foothills. Gary Snyder.—HaWr
"**Six** seven minutes after death." See The staircase
"**Six** silly sisters selling silk to six sickly seniors." Unknown.—EmN
"**Six** sleek, slippery seals slipped silently ashore." Unknown.—EmN
Six ten sixty-nine. Conyus.—AdPb
Six theological cradle songs, sel. Peter Viereck
Better come quietly.—LiWw
"**Sixpence** a week, says the girl to her lover." See By her aunt's grave
Sixteen months. Carl Sandburg.—SaT
"**Sixty** sticky thumbs." Unknown.—EmN
Size. See also People—Size
Fish. S. Silverstein.—SiW
The hummingbird. J. Prelutsky.—PrT
In the middle. D. McCord.—McS
Little. D. McCord.—McFm—McS
The little elf. J. K. Bangs.—JaP—UnGb
"The longest nose." S. Silverstein.—SiW
One inch tall. S. Silverstein.—SiW
The ram. Unknown.—RoIt
Small, smaller. R. Hoban.—CoPu
Susie's new dog. J. Ciardi.—CiFs
"Take the curious case of Tom Pettigrew." D. McCord
Three limericks.—McS
"Tiny man." Mother Goose.—TucMg
Worlds of different sizes. S. McPherson.—CoPu
"Your little hands." S. Hoffenstein.—LiWw
The **size** of him. Alexander Kotul'sky, tr. fr. the Russian by Miriam Morton.—MoM
The **skaters.** John Williams.—FlH
Skating
At the rink. L. Lenski.—LeC
74 street. M. C. Livingston.—LiM
The skaters. J. Williams.—FlH
"The **skeeter** likes a hairless man." Unknown.—CoOh
The **skeleton** walks. X. J. Kennedy.—KeO
Skeletons
Bedtime stories. L. Moore.—MoSm
I'm skeleton. L. Moore.—MoSm
The skeleton walks. X. J. Kennedy.—KeO
Skelton, John
To Mistress Isabel Pennell.—MaFw
Sketch. Carl Sandburg.—SaT
Skidi Pawnee Indians. See Indians of the Americas—Skidi Pawnee
Skier. Robert Francis.—FlH—HiN
Skiing
"I want time to run, to race for me." V. Lapin.—MoM
Out skiing. L. Shakhovich.—MoM
Patience. H. Graham.—LiWw
Skier. R. Francis.—FlH—HiN
Skill
"How God hath labored to produce the duck." D. Hall.—CoPu
Juggler. R. Wilbur.—HiN
Of kings and things. L. Morrison.—HiN
Tightrope walker. V. Scannell.—HiN
"The **skin** quickens to noises." See One eyed black man in Nebraska
"**Skin** that is a closed curtain." See Poll
Skinny. Shel Silverstein.—SiW
"**Skinny** frog." Issa, tr. fr. the Japanese by Hanako Fukuda.—HaW
"**Skinny** McGuinn." See Skinny
"**Skinny** Mrs Snipkin." See Mrs Snipkin and Mrs Wobblechin
Skipper Ireson's ride. John Greenleaf Whittier.—RoIt
Skipping
Rattlesnake skipping song. D. Lee.—LeA
Street song. D. Lee.—LeA
"Wiggle to the laundromat." D. Lee.—LeA
"**Skirting** the river road (my forenoon walk, my rest)." See The dalliance of the eagles
Skulls and cups. J. P. Clark.—AlPa
The **skunk** ("Jacko the Skunk, in black and white") Alfred Noyes.—BrM
The **skunk** ("Whenever you may meet a skunk") Jack Prelutsky.—PrP
"**Skunk** cabbage, bloodroot." See The round
"A **skunk** sat on a stump." Unknown.—BrM—EmN
Skunks
How many. M. A. Hoberman.—HoLb
"A man who was fond of his skunk." D. McCord
Three limericks.—McS
"My tail rattles." Unknown.—ClFc
The skunk ("Jacko the Skunk, in black and white") A. Noyes.—BrM
The skunk ("Whenever you may meet a skunk") J. Prelutsky.—PrP
"A skunk sat on a stump." Unknown.—BrM—EmN
Sky
"After thunder goes." Shiki.—BeM
"All day the kite pinned." A. Atwood.—AtM
Dream song. Unknown.—BiI
I break the sky. O. Dodson.—AdPb
In winter sky. D. McCord.—McFm
The jigsaw puzzle in the sky. F. Holman.—HoI

Falling asleep. S. Sassoon.—PaF
"Go to sleep." Mother Goose.—TucMg
"Great-great Grandma, don't sleep in your treehouse tonight." X. J. Kennedy.—KeO
Half asleep. A. Fisher.—FiM
"Hey there, white seagull." Kim Kwang-wuk.—BaSs
Horses. A. Fisher.—FiFo
"The island of Murray." N. M. Bodecker.—BoL
"It's raining, it's pouring." Unknown.—EmN
Lights out. E. Thomas.—MaFw
Like a summer bird. A. Fisher.—FiFo
"Little Boy Blue." Mother Goose.—JoA-4
Lord Chancellor's song. From Iolanthe. W. S. Gilbert.—RoIt
"Minnie and Winnie." A. Tennyson.—OpOx
The moon. Unknown.—RoIt
Nightsong city. D. Brutus.—AlPa
"O that moon last night." Teitoku.—BeM
"On these summer days." Sung Hon.—BaSs
"Parched by the shrill song." Soseki.—BeM
Poems for my brother Kenneth. O. Dodson.—AdPb (sel.)
Portrait of a child settling down for an afternoon nap. C. Sandburg.—SaT
Response. B. Kaufman.—AdB
Sheep. C. Sandburg.—SaT
Sleep and poetry. J. Keats.—PaF (sel.)
Sleep impression. C. Sandburg.—SaT
Sleep song. C. Sandburg.—SaT
"Sleep well." Unknown.—ClFc
The sleeping beauty. E. Sitwell.—MaFw
"The sleeping little fawn." Issa.—HaW
Sleeping outdoors. M. Chute.—ChRu
The sleepyheads ("I feel sorry") A. Fisher.—FiFo
Sleepyheads ("Sleep is a maker of makers. Birds sleep. Feet cling to a perch") C. Sandburg.—SaT
The sluggard. I. Watts.—LiS—OpOx
"Softly, drowsily." From A child's day. W. De La Mare.—JoA-4
Sonnet to sleep. J. Keats.—MaFw
Sweet and low. From The princess. A. Tennyson.—JoA-4—OpOx—RoIt
The sweetest thing. Unknown.—AbM
Waking. A. Higgins.—CoPu
"The waves are so cold." Bashō.—BeM
"When a cat is asleep." K. Kuskin.—KuN
"When the day is cloudy." Unknown.—JoT
Wind song. C. Sandburg.—SaT
"With my harp against my knee." Kim Chang-up.—BaSs

Sleep and poetry. John Keats.—PaF (sel.)
"**Sleep** at noon. Window blind." See Hurricane
"**Sleep** darling." Sappho, tr. fr. the Greek by Mary Barnard.—ThI
Sleep impression. Carl Sandburg.—SaT
"**Sleep** is a maker of makers. Birds sleep. Feet cling to a perch." See Sleepyheads
"**Sleep** is the gift of many spiders." See Drowsy
"**Sleep** late with your dream." See Poems for my brother Kenneth
"**Sleep,** legend, but call me when you wake." See Legend
Sleep, little daughter. Unknown, ad. by John Bierhorst from the collection of Henry Rowe Schoolcraft.—BiS
"**Sleep,** little one, sleep for me." See Response
"**Sleep,** love, sleep." See Lullaby
"**Sleep,** my child." See Dwarf's lullabye
"**Sleep** plays hide-and-seek with darkness." See Night blessing
"**Sleep,** sleep, beauty bright." See Cradle song
Sleep song. Carl Sandburg.—SaT
"**Sleep** well." Unknown, tr. fr. the Seminole.—ClFc
"**Sleep** well, my love, sleep well." See Nightsong city
The **sleeping** beauty. Edith Sitwell.—MaFw (sel.)
The **sleeping** giant. Donald Hall.—HiN
"The **sleeping** little fawn." Issa, tr. fr. the Japanese by Hanako Fukuda.—HaW
Sleeping outdoors. Marchette Chute.—ChRu
Sleeping sardines. Shel Silverstein.—SiW
"**Sleeping,** waking." Issa, tr. fr. the Japanese by Lewis Mackenzie.—MaFw
The **sleepyheads** ("I feel sorry") Aileen Fisher.—FiFo
Sleepyheads ("Sleep is a maker of makers. Birds sleep. Feet cling to a perch") C. Sandburg.—SaT
Sleighs. See Sleds and sleighs
Slezsky, Seriozha
The October anniversary.—MoM
Sliding. Lilian Moore.—MoSm
"**Sliding** over stones." See Serpent
Slippery. Carl Sandburg.—SaT
Slippery slide. Lois Lenski.—LeC
"The **slippery** slide is very steep." See Slippery slide
"The **Slithergadee** has crawled out of the sea." Shel Silverstein.—TrG
The **sloth** ("In moving slow he has no peer") Theodore Roethke.—RoIt
Sloth ("A tree's a trapeze for a sloth") Mary Ann Hoberman.—HoR
Sloths
The sloth ("In moving slow he has no peer") T. Roethke.—RoIt
Sloth ("A tree's a trapeze for a sloth") M. A. Hoberman.—HoR
"**Slow,** horses, slow." See Spring night
"**Slow** May." See Spring in these hills
"**Slow** moves the acid breath of noon." See Field of autumn
Slow program. Carl Sandburg.—SaT
Slow spring. Katherine Tynan.—PaF
The **slow** starter. Louis MacNeice.—ToM
Slowly. James Reeves.—JoA-4
"**Slowly** (in the long hot days)." See Arson
"**Slowly** a floor rises, almost becomes a wall." See A hurricane at sea
"**Slowly,** silently, now the moon." See Silver
"**Slowly** the moon is rising out of the ruddy haze." See Aware

"**Slowly** the night blooms, unfurling." See Flowers of darkness
"**Slowly** the tide creeps up the sand." See Slowly
The **sluggard.** Isaac Watts.—LiS—OpOx
Slum home. Lois Lenski.—LeC
"A **slumber** did my spirit seal." William Wordsworth.—MaFw
"**Small** as a peanut." See No difference
"**Small** bird, forgive me." Unknown, tr. fr. the Japanese by Harry Behn.—BeM
Small change. Tatiana Ostrovskaya, tr. fr. the Russian by Miriam Morton.—MoM
A **small** discovery. James A. Emanuel.—LiLc
Small homes. Carl Sandburg.—SaT
"A **small** red-painted helicopter." See Precision
"**Small** service is true service while it lasts." See Written in the album of a child
Small, smaller. Russell Hoban.—CoPu
Small song. A. R. Ammons.—CoPu
Small talk. Don Marquis.—CoPt
Smart, Christopher
  Consideration for others.—OpOx
  Hymn for Saturday.—OpOx
  Mirth.—OpOx
  A morning hymn.—OpOx
  My cat Jeoffry.—RoIt
  Praise.—OpOx
Smart. Shel Silverstein.—SiW
"**Smarty,** smarty." See Two sad tales
Smedley, Menella Bute
  A North Pole story.—OpOx
"The **smell** of burned-out candles." See Chanukah poem
Smells. Lois Lenski.—LeC
Smith, Captain John (about)
  Pocahontas. W. M. Thackeray.—RoIt
Smith, Charlotte
  Invitation to the bee.—OpOx
Smith, Iain Crichton
  By ferry to the island.—ToM
  Rythm.—ToM
Smith, John
  First, goodbye.—ToM
  From jazz for five.—ToM (sel.)
  Somewhere around Christmas.—MaFw
Smith, Robert
  The exhortation of a father to his children.—OpOx
Smith, Stevie
  The conventionalist.—CoPu
  My Muse.—PlM
Smith, Sydney Goodsir
  The mither's lament.—CoPu
Smith, Welton
  The beast section.—AdPb
  Interlude.—AdPb
  Strategies.—AdPb
Smith, W. Hart
  Pigeons.—CoPu
Smith, William Jay
  Crocodile.—BrM
  The crossing of Mary of Scotland.—CoOh
  The King of Hearts.—BrM
  The King of Spain.—BrM
  Laughing time.—BrM
  Mr Smith (with nods to Mr Lear and Mr Eliot).—LiS
  Natural history.—LiWw
  The toaster.—BrM
  "William Penn."—LiWw
  Winter morning.—HiN
  Yak.—CoOr
Smith, William Jay (about)
  Mr Smith (with nods to Mr Lear and Mr Eliot). W. J. Smith.—LiS
"**Smith** at the organ is like an anvil being." See Sound of Afroamerican history chapt II
Smoke and smoking
  "All the smoke." E. Siegel.—CoPu
  "Chip, chip, cherry." Unknown.—EmN
  First man was the first to emerge. Unknown.—BiI
  I pass the pipe. Unknown.—BiI
  "Moon sits smoking his pipe." N. Belting.—BeWi
  My first cigar. R. J. Burdette.—CoPt
  "The northern lights are the flames and smoke." N. Belting.—BeWi
  The song of the smoke. W. E. B. Du Bois.—AdPb
Smoke and steel, sel. Carl Sandburg
  Pearl cobwebs.—SaT
A **smoke** of birds. Malcolm Cowley.—MoT
Smoke rose gold. Carl Sandburg.—SaT
The **smoked** herring. Charles Cros, tr. fr. the French by A. L. Lloyd.—CoPt
"A **smoky** rain riddles the ocean plains." See My father paints the summer
"**Smooth** it feels." See Driving
"The **smooth** smell of Manhattan taxis." See Dance of the infidels
"**Smooth** the edges of jagged glass." See Sandwriting
Smugglers
  A smuggler's song. From Puck of Pook's hill. R. Kipling.—CoPt—OpOx
A **smuggler's** song. See Puck of Pook's hill
Snack. Lois Lenski.—LeC
"The **snail.**" See The snail at Yale
The **snail** ("At sunset, when the night-dews fall") James Reeves.—JoA-4
Snail ("Little snail") Langston Hughes.—AbM—HoD—JoA-4
The **snail** ("The snail doesn't know where he's going") Jack Prelutsky.—PrT
The **snail** ("The snail he lives in his hard round house") Unknown.—RoIt
Snail ("Snail upon the wall") John Drinkwater.—LiLc
The **snail** ("To grass, or leaf, or fruit, or wall") William Cowper.—RoIt
The **snail** at Yale. N. M. Bodecker.—BoL
"The **snail** doesn't know where he's going." See The snail
"The **snail** he lives in his hard round house." See The snail

"The **snail** is slow. The swift gazelle." See Fast and slow
"The **snail** pushes through a green." See Considering the snail
"**Snail,** snail." Mother Goose.—JoA-4
"**Snail** upon the wall." See Snail
"A **snail,** who had a way, it seems." See The snail's dream
Snails
Aquarium. V. Worth.—WoS
Considering the snail. T. Gunn.—HaWr—MaFw
"Even a wise man." Kyorai.—BeM
Fast and slow. D. McCord.—McFm—McS
"Four and twenty tailors." Mother Goose.—JoA-4
Giant snail. X. J. Kennedy.—KeO
"The house of snail upon his back." K. Kuskin.—KuN
The housekeeper. C. Lamb.—RoIt
Little snail. H. Conkling.—JoA-4
Make up your mind, snail. R. Wright
Hokku poems.—AdPb
Nursery snail. R. Herschberger.—AdP—RoIt
The odyssey of a snail. F. Garcia Lorca.—MaFw
Old Shellover. W. De La Mare.—LiLc—OpOx
"Red sky in the morning." Issa.—MaFw
Remonstrance with the snails. Unknown.—RoIt
The snail ("At sunset when the night-dews fall") J. Reeves.—JoA-4
Snail ("Little snail") L. Hughes.—AbM—HoD—JoA-4
The snail ("The snail doesn't know where he's going") J. Prelutsky.—PrT
The snail ("The snail he lives in his hard round house") Unknown.—RoIt
Snail ("Snail upon the wall") J. Drinkwater.—LiLc
The snail ("To grass, or leaf, or fruit, or wall") W. Cowper.—RoIt
The snail at Yale. N. M. Bodecker.—BoL
"Snail, snail." Mother Goose.—JoA-4
The snail's dream. O. Herford.—BrM
"So slowly, you come." A. Atwood.—AtM
"A sudden shower." Issa.—HaW
Upon a snail. J. Bunyan.—OpOx
"When C. J. G. Arden goes out in the garden." A. E. Housman.—CoPu
"Where can he be going." Issa.—MaFw
Who am I (II). M. A. Hoberman.—HoLb
The **snail's** dream. Oliver Herford.—BrM
The **snake.** See "The narrow fellow in the grass"
Snake. Mary Ann Hoberman.—HoLb
"The **snake** fled." Takahama Kyoshi, tr. fr. the Japanese by Geoffrey Bownas and Anthony Thwaite.—MaFw
"**Snake,** snake, run in the grass." Unknown.—EmN
"A **snake** will sometimes slither by." See Snake
Snakes
Boa constrictor. S. Silverstein.—SiW
The boy and the snake. C. and M. Lamb.—OpOx
The brass serpent. T. Carmi.—MeP (sel.)
"Do not touch me." Unknown.—ClFc
Hospitality. J. B. Tabb.—BrM
"I am a snake." K. Kuskin.—KuA
"In the back back garden, Thomasina." A. E. Housman.—LiWw
Lizards and snakes. A. Hecht.—HiN
Medusa. X. J. Kennedy.—KeO
"A narrow fellow in the grass." E. Dickinson.—AdP—MaFw—ThI
The snake.—UnGb
On a little boy's endeavouring to catch a snake. T. Foxton.—OpOx
Rattlesnake skipping song. D. Lee.—LeA
Snake. M. A. Hoberman.—HoLb
"The snake fled." Takahama Kyoshi.—MaFw
"Snake, snake, run in the grass." Unknown.—EmN
Serpent. E. Merriam.—AdM
"You spotted snakes." From A midsummer night's dream. W. Shakespeare.—JoA-4
Snapshots of a daughter-in-law (Part I). Adrienne Rich.—HiN
Snapshots of the cotton South. Frank Marshall Davis.—AdPb
The **snare.** James Stephens.—AdP
Sneaky Bill. William Cole.—CoOr
"**Snee** A-P snap." Unknown.—EmN
Sneezing
And they lived happily ever after for a while. J. Ciardi.—CiFs
"If you sneeze on Monday, you sneeze for danger." Mother Goose.—AlC
"Julius Caesar made a law." Mother Goose.—TucMgl
Llude sig kachoo. E. Merriam.—MeF
"**Sniff,** sniff, sniff." See Sniffing
Sniffing. Aileen Fisher.—FiFo
Snodgrass, W. (William) D. (DeWitt)
Heart's needle.—HiN (sel.)
Lobsters in the window.—HiN
The marsh.—HaWr
Snoring
"Grandma snores." N. Tolstoy.—MoM
Snow. See also Winter
After snow. W. Clark.—HiN
April snow. F. Holman.—HoI
"At nine of the night I opened my door." C. Causley.—CaF
Cardinal. J. Harrison.—HaWr
Cat & weather. M. Swenson.—HaWr
Cat in the snow. A. Fisher.—FiM
Cynthia in the snow. G. Brooks.—LiLc
December. A. Fisher.—HoS
December 21: Snow. L. Clifton.—ClEa
Desert places. R. Frost.—HiN
"Drifting, feathery." Shiki.—BeM
Driving to town late to mail a letter. R. Bly.—MoT
Dust of snow. R. Frost.—AdP—MoT—PaF

"**Snow** melting." Katō Gyōdai, tr. fr. the Japanese by Geoffrey Bownas and Anthony Thwaite.—MaFw
"The **snow-piles** in dark places are gone." See Just before April came
"**Snow,** softly, slowly." Oeharu, tr. fr. the Japanese by Harry Behn.—BeM
The **snow-storm** ("Announced by all the trumpets of the sky") Ralph Waldo Emerson.—PaF—RoIt
Snow storm ("What a night, the wind howls, hisses, and but stops") John Clare.—MaFw (sel.)
"The **snow** thaws." Issa, tr. fr. the Japanese by Lewis Mackenzie.—MaFw
"**Snow** White gave a party." Unknown.—MoBw
The **snowdrop.** Alfred Tennyson.—PaF
Snowdrops (flowers)
  The snowdrop. A. Tennyson.—PaF
The **snowflake.** See The snow-flake
"**Snowflake** soufflé." X. J. Kennedy.—KeO
Snowflakes ("Snowflakes are falling amidst") Grey Cohoe.—AlW
Snowflakes ("Sometime this winter if you go") David McCord.—McS
"**Snowflakes** are falling amidst." See Snowflakes
Snowman. Shel Silverstein.—SiW
"The **snowman's** hat was crooked." See The snowman's resolution
The **snowman's** resolution. Aileen Fisher.—LaM
Snowmen
  Boy at the window. R. Wilbur.—PeS
  Snowman. S. Silverstein.—SiW
  Thaw. W. Gibson.—CoPu
A **snowy** day in school. D. H. Lawrence.—MaFw
Snowy morning. Lilian Moore.—UnGb
Snowy night. John Haines.—HiN
"**Snub** nose, the guts of twenty mules are in your cylinders and transmission." See New farm tractor
Snuff
  The snuffboxes. Unknown.—CoPt
  "Some snuff shop snuff." Unknown.—EmN
The **snuffboxes.** Unknown.—CoPt
Snyder, Gary
  Burning, sel.
    John Muir on Mt Ritter.—MaFw
  John Muir on Mt Ritter. See Burning
  Mid-August at Sourdough mountain lookout.—HiN
  The Sappa creek.—HiN
  Six-month song in the foothills.—HaWr
"**So** Abram rose, and clave the wood, and went." See The parable of the old man and the young
"**So** have I seen a silver swan." See Song
"**So** moping flat and low over valleys lie." See Winter in the fens
"**So** much depends." See The red wheelbarrow
"**So,** now is come our joyful feast." See Our joyful feast
So quickly came the summer. Agnes T. Pratt.—AlW
So quietly. Leslie Pinckney Hill.—AdPb
"**So** quietly they stole upon their prey." See So quietly
"**So** she went into the garden." See The great Panjandrum
"**So** slowly you come." Ann Atwood.—AtM
"**So** slowly you walk, and so quickly you eat." See To a slow walker and quick eater
"**So,** some tempestuous morn in early June." See Thyrsis
"**So** soon, so soon, so soon, said Sam." Unknown.—EmN
"**So** the foeman have fired the gate, men of mine." See The knight's leap
"**So** they came riding." See The warrior bards
So to speak. Carl Sandburg.—SaT
"**So** we must say goodbye, my darling." See Goodbye
"**So** you haven't got a drum, just beat your belly." See Ourchestra
Soap
  No sale. R. Froman.—FrSp
  A riddle. G. MacBeth.—MoT
  Social studies. M. Neville.—CoPu
  "You use it between your head and your toes." Unknown.—EmN
A **social** mixer. X. J. Kennedy.—KeO
Social studies. Mary Neville.—CoPu
Social workers
  Feeding the lions. N. Jordan.—AdB—AdPb
Sodo
  "In my house this spring."—BeM
"**Soft** falls the snow." Clyde Watson.—WaF
Soft snow. William Blake.—PaF
"**Soft:** the way her eyes view her children." See From blackwoman poems
"**Softly.**" See Snow
"**Softly** along the road of evening." See Nod
"**Softly,** drowsily." See A child's day
"**Softly** the crane's foot crumples a star." See Recollection
Sohappy, Liz
  Behold: My world.—AlW
  The Indian market.—AlW
  Once again.—AlW
  The parade.—AlW
Sokan
  "Hands flat on the ground."—BeM
Sola Pinto, Vivian de
  In the train.—PaP
Solace. Clarissa Scott Delany.—AdPb
"A **soldier.**" Unknown, tr. fr. the Sioux.—ClFc
Soldier rest. See The lady of the lake
"**Soldier,** rest, thy warfare o'er." See The lady of the lake—Soldier rest
"A **soldier** that to Black-heath-field went." Unknown.—EmN
Soldiers. See also Memorial day; War; also names of wars, as European war, 1914-1918; also names of battles, as Waterloo, Battle of, 1815
  Abdul Abulbul Amir. Unknown.—RoIt
  Bedtime story. G. MacBeth.—CoPt—ToM
  Bonny George Campbell. Unknown.—RoIt

Soldiers.—*Continued*
Carentan O Carentan. L. Simpson.—ToM
Cavalry crossing a ford. W. Whitman.—CoPu
Conquerors. H. Treece.—ToM
The conscientious objector. K. Shapiro.—PeS
The dead at Clonmacnoise. Unknown.—CoPi
The dug-out. S. Sassoon.—MaFw
The dumb soldier. R. L. Stevenson.—OpOx
Ego. P. Booth.—PeS
The fox. K. Patchen.—ToM
The general. S. Sassoon.—CoPu
The generals. S. Silverstein.—CoOr—SiW
The grave. S. Tchernichovsky.—MeP
"High diddle ding." Mother Goose.—AlC
Incident on a journey. T. Gunn.—ToM
The Irish colonel. A. C. Doyle.—CoPu
Johnny has gone for a soldier. Unknown.—RoIt
Kariuki. J. Gatuira.—AlPa
The lady of the lake. sel. W. Scott
Soldier rest.—RoIt
The last soldier. S. Morozov.—MoM
Long, long you have held between your hands. L. S. Senghor.—AlPa
Memorial wreath. D. Randall.—AdPb
Naming of parts. H. Reed.—PeS—ToM
Night encounter. K. Tsaro-Wiwa.—AlPa
"North wind blows hard through the trees." Kim Jong-su.—BaSs
Notes for a movie script. M. C. Holman.—AdPb
O what is that sound. W. H. Auden.—MaFw—ToM
The old man and Jim. J. W. Riley.—CoPt
Patterns. A. Lowell.—MoG
Pentagonia. G. E. Bates.—LiS
"Shining soldiers." Unknown.—EmN
"A soldier." Unknown.—ClFc
The soldier's dream. T. Campbell.—RoIt
Sonnet to Negro soldiers. J. S. Cotter, Jr.—AdPb
Ultima ratio regum. S. Spender.—PeS—ToM
Vet's rehabilitation. R. Durem.—AdPb
When I peruse the conquer'd fame. W. Whitman.—CoPu
"Where have all the flowers gone." P. Seeger.—PeS
"Who comes here." Mother Goose.—AlC
The **soldier's** dream. Thomas Campbell.—RoIt
Solid. Robert Froman.—FrSp
"A **solitary** prospector." See Sunstrike
The **solitary** reaper. William Wordsworth.—RoIt
Solitude. See also Loneliness; Silence
Dodona's oaks were still. P. MacDonogh.—CoPi
Get lost. M. C. Livingston.—LiM
Lucy Gray; or, Solitude. W. Wordsworth.—OpOx
The mole. J. Prelutsky.—PrP
Ode on solitude. A. Pope.—MaFw
Solitude.—RoIt
One for Novella Nelson. M. C. Livingston.—LiM
The solitary reaper. W. Wordsworth.—RoIt
Solitude. A. A. Milne.—LiLc
Verses. W. Cowper.—RoIt
Solitude. See Ode on solitude
Solitude. A. A. Milne.—LiLc
Soloman, Phillip
"Black child."—JoV
The echo.—JoV
"In that case."—JoV
"Kicking your heels on the dusty road."—JoV
Love.—JoV
"Touch me not, for I am fragile."—JoV
Soloman ibn Gabirol
An apple for Isaac.—MeP
His answer to the critics.—MeP
"In the morning I look for you."—MeP
Solomon, King of Israel (about)
"King Solomon and King David." Unknown.—RoIt
Solomon and the bees. J. G. Saxe.—RoIt
Solomon and the bees. John Godfrey Saxe.—RoIt
"**Solomon** Grundy." Mother Goose.—AlC—JoA-4
Solutions to puzzles from wonderland. Lewis Carroll.—LiPc
"**Some** are teethed on a silver spoon." See Saturday's child
"**Some** at beaches." See Summer doings
Some boys. John Penkethman.—OpOx
"**Some** boys (their minds denying virtue room)." See Some boys
"**Some** candle clear burns somewhere I come by." See The candle indoors
"**Some** clouds are rainclouds." See On the pole
Some cook. John Ciardi.—BrM
"**Some** corn for this baby." See Ca, ca, ca
"**Some** day, when trees have shed their leaves." See After the winter
"**Some** days/out walking above." De Leon Harrison.—AdPb
"**Some** fathers work at the office, others work at the store." See My father
"**Some** for a little while do love, and some for long." See Sonnet
"**Some** friend must now, perforce." Unknown.—TrG
"**Some** have a dog." See Human beings
Some kids I know. Russell Hoban.—HoE
"**Some** kiss behind a lily." Unknown.—EmN
Some little poems without the word love. Eve Merriam.—MeF
Some natural history. Don Marquis.—LiWw
"**Some** of my best friends are white boys." See Friends
"**Some** of my books were burned. I must." See Pencil stubs—After a fire
"**Some** of us." See Resurrection
"**Some** of us will die." See Drums of freedom
Some one. Walter De La Mare.—JoA-4—LiLc
"**Some** one came knocking." See Some one
"**Some** people say that fleas are black." Unknown.—BrM—CoOh
"**Some** people talk in the hall." See Talking

"**Some** say." See Hamlet
"**Some** shun sunshine." Unknown.—EmN
Some sights sometimes seen and seldom seen. William Cole.—CoOh
"**Some** snuff shop snuff." Unknown.—EmN
Some sound advice from Singapore. John Ciardi.—CiFs
"**Some** things are very dear to me." See Sonnet II. Gwendolyn B. Bennett
"**Some** think that in the Christian scheme." See Consideration for others
"**Some** write for pleasure." Unknown.—EmN
"**Somebody.**" See Young poet
"**Somebody** said that it couldn't be done." Unknown.—CoPu—LiWw
"**Somebody** saw a crow flying by and asked him where he was going." Unknown, from Point Barrow, Alaska.—LeIb
"**Someday** I'll go to Winnipeg." See Tongue twister
"**Someday** wooed a peacock." See Calendar
"**Somehow** we survive." See Poem
"**Someone** about as big as a bump." See Sit up when you sit down
"**Someone** ate the baby." See Dreadful
"**Someone** came to see me when I was not at home." See I hate to wait
Someone I know. Unknown, tr. fr. the Russian by Miriam Morton.—MoM
Someone slow. John Ciardi.—UnGb
"**Somersault** & pepper-upper." Clyde Watson.—WaF
"**Something** follows everything." See The question
"**Something** has happened to me." See Songs of sorrow
"**Something** is bleeding." See September
"**Something** is there." Lilian Moore.—MoSm
Something peaceful. Tanya Tsyganok, tr. fr. the Russian by Miriam Morton.—MoM
"**Something** told the wild geese." Rachel Field.—JoA-4
"**Something** went crabwise." See The presence
"**Something's** happened very fine." See An event
"**Sometime** this winter if you go." See Snowflakes
"**Sometimes.**" See Dream song
Sometimes. David McCord.—McFm
"**Sometimes** a horse." See A horse to ride.
"**Sometimes** a tie is round your neck." Unknown.—MoBw
"**Sometimes** he brays." See Donkey
"**Sometimes** I envy others, fear them." See The cure
"**Sometimes** I envy those." See The mole
"**Sometimes** I feel like I will never stop." See To Satch
"**Sometimes** I get the feeling that I have been here before." See Reincarnation
Sometimes I go to Camarillo and sit in the lounge. K. Curtis Lyle.—AdPb
"**Sometimes** I see them." See Ruins under the stars
"**Sometimes** I stare into an awning of spirit." See Sometimes I go to Camarillo and sit in the lounge
"**Sometimes** I think the hills." See The hills
Sometimes on my way back down to the block. Victor Hernandez Cruz.—AdB
"**Sometimes** there seems." See All kinds of time
"**Sometimes** when I'm lonely." See Hope
"**Sometimes** when the boy was troubled he would go." See The cave
"**Sometimes** your voices call me back." See Alleyways
Somewhere around Christmas. John Smith.—MaFw
"**Somewhere** I have lost my shoe." See Opportunity
Somewhere I have never travelled. E. E. Cummings.—PeS
"**Somewhere** I have never travelled, gladly beyond." See Somewhere I have never travelled
"**Somewhere** nowhere in Utah, a boy by the roadside." See Utah
"**Somewhere** outside your window." See A sense of coolness
"**Son,** said my mother." See The ballad of the harp-weaver
Song ("And I think over again") Unknown, tr. fr. the Eskimo by Knud Rasmussen.—BiI
Song ("April, April") William Watson.—JoA-4
Song ("As the holly groweth green") Henry VIII, King of England.—MaFw
Song ("Do not fear to put thy feet") See The river god's song
Song ("From whence cometh song") Theodore Roethke.—HiN
Song ("Gather kittens while you may") Oliver Herford.—LiS
Song ("I almost went to bed") Leonard Cohen.—PeS
Song ("I can look the sun in the face") J. P. Clark.—AlPa
Song ("I found here for myself a woman. She walks much in an overcoat of calico") fr. Northern Siberia. Unknown.—LeIb
Song ("I had a dove, and the sweet dove died") John Keats.—RoIt
Song ("Mine is a proud village, such as it is") Unknown, tr. fr. the Makah by Frances Densmore.—BiI
Song ("Morning opened") Donald Justice.—HiN
Song ("My mother bore one") Unknown, tr. fr. the Quechua by R. and M. d'Harcourt.—BiI
A **song** ("My name is sweet Jenny, my age is sixteen") Unknown.—CoPu
Song ("She spoke to me gently with words of sweet meaning") Patrick MacDonogh.—CoPi
Song ("So have I seen a silver swan") Unknown.—CoPu

Sounds—*Continued*
Bus noises. M. Ray.—HoP
City thunder. R. Froman.—FrSp
The crackling twig. J. Stephens.—CoPu
Dance. R. Froman.—FrSp
December 20: 5 more days. L. Clifton.—ClEa
"Do not blow in the garden, wind." Unknown.—BaSs
The Fourth. S. Silverstein.—SiW
"From the dark canoe." A. Atwood.—AtM
Funny the way different cars start. D. W. Baruch.—HoP
The go-go-goons. R. Froman.—FrSp
The grasshopper. C. Aiken.—JoA-4
Gyre's galax. N. H. Pritchard II.—AdPb
Hearing the wind at night. M. Swenson.—HaWr
"I hear you smiling." F. Holman.—HoI
"In this world, you see." Issa.—HaW
Listening ("I can hear kittens and cows and dogs") H. Behn.—UnGb
Listening ("When it's time") A. Fisher.—FiM
The look and sound of words. D. McCord.—McFm
Loud. R. Froman.—FrSp
"Mingled with the wild." A. Atwood.—AtM
Nightsong city. D. Brutus.—AlPa
The noise of waters. From Chamber music. J. Joyce.—RoIt
Chamber music (XXXV).—MaFw
The noise that time makes. M. Moore.—RoIt
"The old pond." Bashō.—HaW
Pipes and drums. L. Holmes.—JaP (sel.)
The power shovel. R. B. Bennett.—HoP
"The quail in the bush is making his whirring." Unknown.—ClFc
The rain. W. H. Davies.—PaF
A rumble. V. Schonborg.—HoP
Saturday night: Late. L. Clifton.—ClS
"Scampering over saucers." Buson.—MaFw
Scare. R. Froman.—FrSp
The shell. J. Stephens.—MaFw
Snowy morning. L. Moore.—UnGb
So to speak. C. Sandburg.—SaT
Song of the train. D. McCord.—JoA-4
"The sounds in the morning." E. Farjeon.—JoA-4
Subway deaf. R. Froman.—FrSp
Trains at night. F. M. Frost.—HoP
Underground rumbling. J. S. Tippett.—HoP
Watching the wrecking crane. B. Katz.—HoP
Wing song. L. Moore.—UnGb
Winter night. M. Chute.—ChRu
"The winter storm." Buson.—AtM
Words. M. Chute.—ChRu
"Worm." K. Kuskin.—KuN
"You will always find me." Unknown.—ClFc
"The **sounds** in the morning." Eleanor Farjeon.—JoA-4
Soup
Baby Kate. J. S. Newman.—BrS
"Betty Boop." Unknown.—EmN
"Lilly ladled little Letty's lentil soup." Unknown.—EmN
Soup. C. Sandburg.—SaT
"There was a young lady from Cork." O. Nash.—BrM
Turtle soup. From Alice's adventures in wonderland. L. Carroll.—LiPc—LiS
"What is the opposite of *nuts.*" R. Wilbur.—WiO
Soup. Carl Sandburg.—SaT
Sources of good counsel. Peter Idley.—OpOx
Sourdough mountain
Mid-August at Sourdough mountain lookout. G. Snyder.—HiN
Souster, Raymond
Flight of the roller coaster.—CoPt
The South
Legacy: My South. D. Randall.—AdPb
October journey. M. Walker.—AdPb
Picnic: The liberated. M. C. Holman.—AdPb
Snapshots of the cotton South. F. M. Davis.—AdPb
Southern road ("Swing dat hammer—hunh") S. A. Brown.—AdPb
The Southern road ("There the black river, boundary to hell") D. Randall.—AdPb
South Africa, Republic of
Poem. D. Brutus.—AlPa (sel.)
A Zulu lyric. Unknown.—AlPa
The **South** country. Hilaire Belloc.—PaP
"**South** of the bridge on Seventeenth." See Fifteen
South wind. Tu Fu, tr. fr. the Chinese by Kenneth Rexroth.—MaFw
Southbound on the freeway. May Swenson.—PeS
Southern mansion. Arna Bontemps.—AdPb
Southern road ("Swing dat hammer—hunh") Sterling A. Brown.—AdPb
The **Southern** road ("There the black river, boundary to hell") Dudley Randall.—AdPb
Southey, Caroline. See Bowles, Caroline Anne
Southey, Robert
Bishop Hatto.—CoPt
The cataract of Lodore.—LiS—OpOx
The old man's comforts and how he gained them.—LiS—OpOx
Winter portrait.—CoPu
Southwell, Robert
The burning babe.—MaFw
In freezing winter night.—MaFw
Souvenir. E. Merriam.—MeO
Soyinka, Wole
Idandre.—AlPa (sel.)
Season.—AlPa—MaFw
Telephone conversation.—MaFw
Space and space travel. See also Outer space
Blast off. J. Oppenheim.—HoP
The crescent boat. From Peter Bell. W. Wordsworth.—RoIt
Faster. L. B. Hopkins.—HoP
"Fueled." M. Hans.—HoP
Love. A. Stevenson.—HiN
Love in a space-suit. J. Kirkup.—ToM
"Man flies through the universe." M. Goode.—JoV

Message from a mouse, ascending in a rocket. P. Hubbell.—HoP
The moon. J. Mbiti.—AlPa
Moon poem. S. Sharp.—AbM
Only a little litter. M. C. Livingston.—LiM
Presidential address to a party of exiles leaving for the moon. H. Nemerov.—PlM
SF. S. Leverett.—CoPu
The shore of the universe. K. Zinoviev.—MoM
Southbound on the freeway. M. Swenson.—PeS
Tea in a space-ship. J. Kirkup.—ToM
Unidentified flying object. R. Hayden.—HiN
Unknown shores. D. M. Thomas.—ToM
A week after the first Sputnik. Unknown.—MoM
Spacks, Barry
Washing windows.—HiN
A **spade** is just a spade. Walter Everette Hawkins.—AdPb
"**Spaghetti.**" See A round
Spaghetti. Shel Silverstein.—SiW
"**Spaghetti,** spaghetti, all over the place." See Spaghetti
Spain
The Golden Vanity. Unknown.—RoIt
The King of Spain. W. J. Smith.—BrM
"Me and I and you." Unknown.—BoI
My heart is in the East. Judah Halevi.—MeP
Spanish music in winter. D. Avidan.—MeP (sel.)
"Three big sailors had a tiny little boat." Mother Goose.—TucMg
Spain—History
The Armada, 1588. J. Wilson.—OpOx
The **span** of life. Robert Frost.—MaFw
"The **spangled** pandemonium." Palmer Brown.—CoOr
"A **spaniel,** Beau, that fares like you." See On a spaniel called Beau killing a young bird
"**Spanish** dancer, do the split." Unknown.—EmN
Spanish music in winter. David Avidan, tr. fr. the Hebrew by David Avidan.—MeP (sel.)
Spanish nursery rhymes. See Nursery rhymes—Spanish
Spark of laurel. Stanley Kunitz.—PlM
The **sparrow.** Aileen Fisher.—FiFo
"**Sparrow** on the walk." See Hopper
Sparrows
"As New Year's day dawns." Ransetsu.—BeM
The bee, the ant, and the sparrow. N. Cotton.—OpOx
"Come and play with me." Issa.—HaW
"A flock of sparrows, chattering." Unknown.—BaSs
"Here comes our noble." Issa.—BeM
Hopper. R. Froman.—FrSp
"Let's be off to the bamboo." Issa.—HaW
"Little sparrows." Issa.—HaW
Mr and Mrs Spikky Sparrow. E. Lear.—OpOx
The song of the reed sparrow. Unknown.—OpOx
The sparrow. A. Fisher.—FiFo
Sparrows. L. Lenski.—LeC
"When nightingales burst." Jurin.—BeM
Sparrows. Lois Lenski.—LeC
"**Spatial** depths of being survive." See The lost dancer
Speak gently. David Bates.—LiS
"**Speak** gently. It is better far." See Speak gently
"**Speak** gently, spring, and make no sudden sound." See Four little foxes
"**Speak** roughly to your little boy." See Alice's adventures in wonderland—The duchess's lullaby
"**Speak,** sir, and be wise." See Basket
"**Speak** them slowly, space them so." See For a wordfarer
Speak to me. Calvin O'John.—AlW
Speaking of television, sels. Phyllis McGinley
The importance of being Western.—LiWw
Reflections dental.—LiWw
Robin Hood.—LiWw
Special bulletin. Langston Hughes.—AdPb
Special delivery. X. J. Kennedy.—KeO
The **special** person. Dennis Lee.—LeA
"A **speck** that would have been beneath my sight." See A considerable speck
"**Speckled** with glints of star and moonshine." See From Mr Walter De La Mare makes the little ones dizzy
Spectacles (eye glasses)
Grandpa dropped his glasses. L. F. Jackson.—BrM
Speech
Cautionary verses to youth of both sexes. T. Hook.—OpOx
Councils. M. Piercy.—MoT
Say, did you say. Unknown.—BrM
Saying. A. R. Ammons.—MoT
Spike spoke spook. D. McCord.—McAa
These days. C. Olsen.—MoT
Speed
Casey Jones. R. Hunter.—MoG
The cheetah. J. Prelutsky.—PrP
Fast and slow ("The old crow is getting slow") J. Ciardi.—CiFs
Fast and slow ("The snail is slow: The swift gazelle") D. McCord.—McFm—McS
Faster. L. B. Hopkins.—HoP
Freeway. M. C. Livingston.—LiM
Giant snail. X. J. Kennedy.—KeO
Hurry. E. Merriam.—MeO
Joseph Mica. Unknown.—MoG
"One day." W. Horne, Jr.—HoC
"The opposite of *fast* is *loose.*" R. Wilbur.—WiO
Slowly. J. Reeves.—JoA-4
The snail. J. Prelutsky.—PrT
"So slowly, you come." A. Atwood.—AtM
Someone slow. J. Ciardi.—UnGb
"There was a young lady named Bright." Unknown.—LiWw—RoIt
"There was an old woman in Surrey." Mother Goose.—OpOx—TucMgl

Rivers.—PaP
"**Squirm.**" See The hockey game
Squirrel ("Gray squirrel") Mary Ann Hoberman.—HoLb
Squirrel ("Outside my window") Aileen Fisher.—FiFo
Squirrel ("The squirrel in the hickory tree's a") Lilian Moore.—MoSp
The **squirrel** ("Whisky, frisky") Unknown.—RoIt
"The **squirrel** has a bush tail." Unknown.—EmN
Squirrel in sunshine. William Cowper.—CoPu
"The **squirrel** in the hickory tree's a." See Squirrel
Squirrels
Epitaph. B. Franklin.—RoIt
"Five little squirrels sat up in a tree." Unknown.—JoA-4
The migration of the grey squirrels. W. Howitt.—OpOx
"Mr Squirrel, sitting under shelter." Mother Goose.—TucMg
On a squirrel crossing the road in autumn, in New England. R. Eberhart.—JoA-4—RoIt
Politeness. M. Chute.—ChRu
Squirrel ("Gray squirrel") M. A. Hoberman.—HoLb
Squirrel ("Outside my window") A. Fisher.—FiFo
Squirrel ("The squirrel in the hickory tree's a") L. Moore.—MoSp
The squirrel ("Whisky, frisky") Unknown.—RoIt
Squirrel in sunshine. W. Cowper.—CoPu
Tails. A. Fisher.—FiFo
To a squirrel at Kyle-na-no. W. B. Yeats.—AdP—CoPu—LiLc—RoIt
Winter surprise. A. Fisher.—FiFo
"**Squirrels** are lucky that they wear." See Tails
SService SStation. Robert Froman.—FrSp
Stabilities. Anne Stevenson.—HiN
"A **stable-lamp** is lighted." See A Christmas hymn
"The **stacks,** like blunt impassive temples, rise." See Cambridgeshire
Stafford, William
Fifteen.—PaS
Listening.—MoT
The lyf so short.—PlM
Mouse night: One of our games.—HiN
A ritual to read to each other.—PeS
A story.—CoPt
Tornado.—HaWr
Traveling through the dark.—CoPt—HiN—MaFw—MoT—PeS
The **staircase** ("Six seven minutes after death") Unknown, David Avidan, tr. fr. the Hebrew by David Avidan.—MeP
The **staircase** ("The stairs mount to his eternity") Samuel Allen.—AdPb
Stairs
"Cinderella, dressed in brown." Unknown.—EmN
Halfway down. A. A. Milne.—LiLc
"Something is there." L. Moore.—MoSm
"There was a rat, for want of stairs." Mother Goose.—MiMg—TrG
"Three little mice ran up the stairs." Unknown.—TrG
"The **stairs** mount to his eternity." See The staircase
"A **stairway** of light." Ann Atwood.—AtM
Stan Stapler. X. J. Kennedy.—KeO
Stancher, Mark
"April."—HoC
"**Stand** straight, tree." See Upright
Standing. Shel Silverstein.—SiW
Standing at the foot of the steps at night. Yüan Mei, tr. fr. the Chinese by D. M.—MaFw
"**Standing** here with my hand on the jade rail." Unknown, tr. fr. the Korean by Chung Seuk Park and ad. by Virginia Olsen Baron.—BaSs
"**Standing** on my elbow." See Standing
"**Standing** on 127th the." See Langston
"**Standing** up for sleeping." See Horses
"**Stand** still, table." See Table deportment
Stanford, Ann
The blackberry thicket.—HaWr
Stangos, Nikos
After the rain. tr.—MoT
Motionless swaying. tr.—MoT
Stanley meets Mutesa. David Rubadiri.—AlPa (sel.)
Stanley, Sir Henry Morton (about)
Stanley meets Mutesa. D. Rubadiri.—AlPa (sel.)
The **star.** Jane Taylor.—LiS—OpOx
Star in the East. Unknown.—LaS
The **star** in the pail. David McCord.—McS
"A **star** looks down at me." See Waiting both
Star night. Felice Holman.—HoI
Star of the evening. James M. Sayles.—LiS
Star-talk. Robert Graves.—PaF
"**Star** thistle, Jim Hill Mustard, white tops." Robert Sund.—CoPu
"A **star-white** sky." See Witches
Starbird, Kaye
Abigail.—NeA
Eat-it-all Elaine.—NeA
The toad.—BrM
Starbuck, Georgie
Cora punctuated with strawberries.—HiN
Starfish
The starfish. D. McCord.—McS
The **starfish.** David McCord.—McS
The **stargazer.** Unknown.—OpOx
"A **stargazer** out late at night." See The stargazer
"**Staring** at the field." Ann Atwood.—AtM
Stark boughs on the family tree. Mary Oliver.—PeS
Starkman, Shula. See Mezey, Robert and Starkman, Shula; also Everwine, Peter and Starkman, Shula, jt. auths.
The **starlight** night. Gerard Manley Hopkins.—JoA-4
The **starling.** John Heath-Stubbs.—MaFw—ToM

Stones—*Continued*
Stone telling. S. Silverstein.—SiW
"The stones are all that last long." Unknown.—ClFc
Telephone pole stone-throwing song. R. Hoban.—HoE
Two voices in a meadow. R. Wilbur.—PeS
"The **stones** are all that last long." Unknown, tr. fr. the Cheyenne.—ClFc
"**Stones** are very hard to break." See Song of young men working in the gold mines of Johannesburg
"**Stools** straight in a row." See Counter service
Stop. Richard Wilbur.—HaWr
"**Stop,** don't swat the fly." See "Oh, do not swat the fly"
Stop playing. Zalman Shneour, tr. fr. the Hebrew by Robert Mezey.—MeP
"**Stop** playing with words, you wastrels." See Stop playing
Stopping by woods on a snowy evening. Robert Frost.—AdP—JoA-4—MaFw—PaF—RoIt
"A **store** is at the corner." See A walk in the city
Stories and storytelling
Aunt Sue's stories. L. Hughes.—HoD
Bedtime stories. L. Moore.—MoSm
"A boat, beneath a sunny sky." From Through the looking-glass. L. Carroll.—LiPc
Father Goose tells a story. A. Resnikoff.—CoOh
"I had a little hen, the prettiest ever seen." Mother Goose.—JoA-4
"I'll tell you a story." Mother Goose.—AlC—JoA-4
Lewis Carroll. E. Farjeon.—OpOx
Martha. W. De La Mare.—RoIt
True story. S. Silverstein.—SiW
The yarn of the Nancy Bell. W. S. Gilbert.—RoIt
Stories of the street. Leonard Cohen.—MoG
"The **stories** of the street are mine." See Stories of the street
Stork story. Mary Ann Hoberman.—HoR
Storks
Spirit of the wind. G. Okara.—AlPa
Stork story. M. A. Hoberman.—HoR
"The **storks** are coming now." See Spirit of the wind
"**Storm.**" See City thunder
The **storm** ("Against the stone breakwater") Theodore Roethke.—HiN
The **storm** ("In fury and terror") Elizabeth Jane Coatsworth.—CoPu
Storm at sea. Alexander Kotul'sky, tr. fr. the Russian by Miriam Morton.—MoM
Storm end. Jonathan Griffin.—MoT
A **storm** in childhood. T. Harri Jones.—MaFw
Storm on the island. Seamus Heaney.—HiN
Storms. See also Rain; Snow; Weather; Winds
"Am I to tell you next of the storms and stars of autumn." From The Georgics. Virgil.—MaFw
"An awful tempest mashed the air." E. Dickinson.—ThI
"Blow, winds, and crack your cheeks, rage, blow." From King Lear. W. Shakespeare.—MaFw
Brainstorm. H. Nemerov.—HiN
City thunder. R. Froman.—FrSp
Electrical storm. E. Bishop.—HaWr
"A fisherman discouraged by a storm." Chang Mann.—BaSs
Haying before storm. M. Rukeyser.—HaWr
Hurricane. A. MacLeish.—HiN
A hurricane at sea. M. Swenson.—HaWr
Instant storm. X. J. Kennedy.—KeO
Little exercise. E. Bishop.—HiN
A local storm. D. Justice.—HiN
Lucy Gray; or, Solitude. W. Wordsworth.—OpOx
Memory of a porch. D. Justice.—HiN
A nautical extravaganza. W. Irwin.—CoPt
Sailing to an island. R. Murphy.—ToM
The sailor's consolation. C. Dibden.—RoIt
Snow-bound. J. G. Whittier.—PaF
Lines from Snow-bound.—JoA-4 (sel.)—RoIt (sel.)
The snow-storm ("Announced by all the trumpets of the sky") R. W. Emerson.—PaF—RoIt
Snow storm ("What a night, the wind howls, hisses, and but stops") J. Clare.—MaFw (sel.)
Squall. J. Moore.—HiN
The storm ("Against the stone breakwater") T. Roethke.—HiN
The storm ("In fury and terror") E. J. Coatsworth.—CoPu
Storm at sea. A. Kotul'sky.—MoM
Storm end. J. Griffin.—MoT
A storm in childhood. T. H. Jones.—MaFw
Storm on the island. S. Heaney.—HiN
The story of Flying Robert. H. Hoffman.—LiS
Sudden storm. E. J. Coatsworth.—HoCs
Summer storm. J. R. Lowell.—RoIt
The tempest. J. T. Fields.—RoIt
There. R. Mezey.—MoT
Tornado. W. Stafford.—HaWr
"The winter storm." Buson.—AtM
The wreck of the Hesperus. H. W. Longfellow.—RoIt
A **story.** William Stafford.—CoPt
"A **story** is a special thing." See Reading
The **story** of Augustus who would not have any soup. Heinrich Hoffman.—LiS—OpOx
The **story** of fidgety Philip. Heinrich Hoffman.—OpOx
The **story** of Flying Robert. Heinrich Hoffman.—LiS
Story of Isaac. Leonard Cohen.—MoG
The **story** of Johnny Head-in-Air. Heinrich Hoffman.—OpOx
The **story** of little Suck-a-Thumb. Heinrich Hoffman.—LiS
Story of Reginald. Hubert Phillips.—CoOr

The **story** of Samuel Jackson. Charles Godfrey Leland.—CoPt
Story of the fowse or fox. David McCord.—McFm
The **story** of the zeros. Victor Hernandez Cruz.—AdPb
Storytelling. See Stories and storytelling
Stoutenburg, Adrien
Affinities.—MoT
Companions.—HaWr
Is is like is.—MoT
Ocean.—HaWr
Sky diver.—MoT
Suspense.—HaWr
Stow, Randolph
As he lay dying.—MaFw
"**Straight-backed** as a Windsor chair." See Schoolmistress
"The **straight** strokes of reeds." Ann Atwood.—AtM
Straight talk (from a surfer). Myra Cohn Livingston.—LiM
Strand, Mark
The collegiate angels. tr.—MaFw
"**Strange** but true is the story." See The sea turtle and the shark
Strange legacies. Sterling A. Brown.—AdPb
"**Stranger** pass by and waste no time." See Suffolk epitaph
The **stranger's** song. Thomas Hardy.—PlP
"The **strangest** bear I ever saw." See Bear with me and you may learn
"The **strangest** of adventures." See Lord Arnaldos
Strategies. Welton Smith.—AdPb
Strawberries
Cora punctuated with strawberries. G. Starbuck.—HiN
"I liked growing." K. Kuskin.—KuA
"The man in the wilderness asked of me." Mother Goose.—AlC
"A man in the wilderness."—RoIt
"A man in the wilderness asked me."—JoA-4
Millions of strawberries. G. Taggard.—UnGb
Strawberry fields forever. J. Lennon and P. McCartney.—MoG
Wild strawberries. R. Graves.—PaF
"**Strawberries** that in gardens grow." See Wild strawberries
Strawberry fields forever. John Lennon and Paul McCartney.—MoG
"**Strawberry** shortcake." Unknown.—EmN
"**Strawberry** shortcake, strawberry jam." Unknown.—EmN
"**Stream,** go hide yourself." See On a railroad right of way
Streamside exchange. J. P. Clark.—AlPa
"**Street** closed." Lois Lenski.—LeC
Street cries
Market women's cries, sels. J. Swift
Apples.—CoPi
Herrings.—CoPi
Onions.—CoPi
Street football. John Gay.—FlH
Street gangs
The Blackstone Rangers. G. Brooks.—AdPb
Gang. L. Lenski.—LeC
"**Street** lamp." See Meanlight
Street scene. Peter Suffolk.—CoPt
Street song. Dennis Lee.—LeA
"A **street** there is in Paris famous." See The ballad of bouillabaisse
Street window. Carl Sandburg.—SaT
Streets. See also Roads and trails
Alleyway. S. Quasimodo.—MaFw
"As I was standing in the street." Unknown.—BrM—CoOh—TrG
City street ("A blue-middied girl") F. Holman.—HoI
City street ("Honk-honk-honk") L. Lenski.—LeC
Glue. G. Burgess.—CoOh
Meanlight. R. Froman.—FrSp
125th street. L. Hughes.—HoCs
A piper. S. O'Sullivan.—CoPu
Stories of the street. L. Cohen.—MoG
Street scene. P. Suffolk.—CoPt
Street song. D. Lee.—LeA
The streets of Laredo. L. MacNeice.—ToM
Sunday street, downtown. R. Froman.—FrSp
Surgery. R. Froman.—FrSp
Water-front streets. L. Hughes.—HoD
"**Streets** are." See Surgery
"The **streets** are filled with mustached men." Karla Kuskin.—KuN
"The **streets** are quiet and empty." See Sunday in the city
The **streets** of Laredo. Louis MacNeice.—ToM
Strength
"I will walk with leg muscles." Unknown.—LeIb
Lineage. M. Walker.—AdB—AdPb
Magic formula. Unknown.—BiI
"The mightiest strong man on all the planet." J. Prelutsky.—PrC
String
String. R. Hoban.—HoE
The strings of time. T. Palmanteer.—AlW
"What is the opposite of *string.*" R. Wilbur.—WiO
String. Russell Hoban.—HoE
"**String-chewing** bass players." See Mingus
"**Strings** in the earth and air." See Chamber music
The **strings** of time. Ted Palmanteer.—AlW
"A **striped** Philistine with quick." See Requiem for a personal friend
"The **stripling** stranger strayed." Unknown.—EmN
"**Strolling** along." See Docks
Strong, George A.
The modern Hiawatha.—LiS
Strong, L. (Leonard) A. (Alfred) G. (George)
The knowledgeable child.—CoPi
The mad-woman.—CoPi
A memory.—CoPi
Old Dan'l.—CoPu

"A **strong** imagination from my youth has been combined." See The caulker
Strong men. Sterling A. Brown.—AdPb
Strong men, riding horses. Gwendolyn Brooks.—AdPb
"**Strong** men, riding horses, in the West." See Strong men, riding horses
A **strong** wind. Austin Clarke.—CoPi
The **stuck** horn. E. Merriam.—MeO
Study peace. LeRoi Jones.—AdPb
"**Stuff** of the moon." See Nocturne in a deserted brickyard
Stupid old myself. Russell Hoban.—HoE
"**Stupid** old myself today." See Stupid old myself
"The (**sturdy** clever muskrat)." See Ecology
Su Shih
Casual lines.—MaFw
Su Tung-p'o
On the birth of his son.—LiWw
Substitute. Aileen Fisher.—FiM
Suburban madrigal. John Updike.—PeS
Subway. Lois Lenski.—LeC
Subway deaf. Robert Froman.—FrSp
Subway ride. Lee Bennett Hopkins.—HoP
"**Subway** swinger." See Subway swinger (going)
Subway swinger (going). Virginia Schonborg.—HoP
The **subway** witnesses. Lorenzo Thomas.—AdPb
Subways
Dream voyage to the center of the subway. E. Merriam.—MeF
Subway. L. Lenski.—LeC
Subway deaf. R. Froman.—FrSp
Subway ride. L. B. Hopkins.—HoP
Subway swinger (going). V. Schonborg.—HoP
The subway witnesses. L. Thomas.—AdPb
"Subways are people." L. B. Hopkins.—HoP
Things to do if you are a subway. B. Katz.—HoCs—HoP
To nowhere. D. Ignatow.—HiN
The train runs late to Harlem. C. K. Rivers.—AdPb
Underground rumblings. J. S. Tippett.—HoP
"**Subways** are people." Lee Bennett Hopkins.—HoP
Succah. Elizabeth Wexler.—LaM
Success. See also Ambition; Fame; Service; Thrift
Henry's secret. D. Kilner.—OpOx
I may, I might, I must. M. Moore.—JoA-4
Robert Whitmore. F. M. Davis.—AdPb
"Success is counted sweetest." E. Dickinson.—RoIt
To get thine ends. R. Herrick.—RoIt
"**Success** is counted sweetest." Emily Dickinson.—RoIt
"**Such** a friend as my friend Thelma everyone has not." See My friend Thelma
Such is Holland. Petrus Augustus De Genestet, tr. fr. the Dutch by Adriaan J. Barnouw.—MaFw
Such stuff as dreams. Franklin P. Adams.—LiS
Suckling, John (about)
Brief lines in not so brief. O. Nash.—PlM
"**Sudden** and from horizon to horizon driven steady." See Storm end
"A **sudden** shower." Issa, tr. fr. the Japanese by Hanako Fukuda.—HaW
Sudden storm. Elizabeth Jane Coatsworth.—HoCs
"**Suddenly.**" See At the scorpions' ascent
Suddenly. David McCord.—McFm
"**Suddenly** all the fountains in the park." See The fountains
"**Suddenly** all the sky is hid." See Summer storm
"**Suddenly,** monotonously, the silence of the street is broken by the harsh rolling of a little drum." See Peep show
"**Suet** chunks and popcorn strings." See The outdoor Christmas tree
Suffer the children. Audre Lorde.—AdPb
Suffolk, Peter
Street scene.—CoPt
Suffolk epitaph. Unknown.—RoIt
Sugar
"Maple sugar." Unknown.—ClFc
"Sugar sacks should be shaken soundly." Unknown.—EmN
Sugarfields. B. Mahone.—AdPb
The **sugar-plum** tree. Eugene Field.—OpOx
"**Sugar** sacks should be shaken soundly." Unknown.—EmN
"**Sugar,** sugar." Unknown.—MoBw
Sugarfields. Barbara Mahone.—AdPb
"**Sugar's** sugar." Unknown.—EmN
Suggs, Sandra
"The most."—HoC
Suicide
But then. B. King.—CoPt
For black poets who think of suicide. E. Knight.—AdPb
Her story. N. L. Madgett.—AdPb
I break the sky. O. Dodson.—AdPb
Notes found near a suicide. F. Horne.—AdPb
Preface to a twenty volume suicide note. LeRoi Jones.—AdPb—PeS
Richard Cory. E. A. Robinson.—CoPt
Suicide note. L. Hughes.—HoD
Titwillow. From The Mikado. W. S. Gilbert.—RoIt
The unfortunate miller. A. E. Coppard.—CoPt
Suicide's note. Langston Hughes.—HoD
"**Sukey,** you shall be my wife." Mother Goose.—TucMgl
Sukkot (Feast of Tabernacles)
Succah. E. Wexler.—LaM
My succah. E. Bockstein.—LaM (sel.)
Sulk. Felice Holman.—HoI
"**Sullen** clouds are gathering fast over the black fringe." See The rainy day
Sullivan, A. M.
The chronometer.—JoA-4
Proprietor.—RoIt
Villanelle of the sea.—RoIt

"**Sumer** is icumen in." Unknown.—RoIt
Cuccu song.—MaFw
Cuckoo song.—LiS
"**Summa** is icumen in." See Baccalaureate
Summer. See also August; July; June; Seasons
April 23. N. Belting.—BeSc
Arabesque. F. Johnson.—AdPb
Arson. L. Moore.—MoSp
"As imperceptibly as grief." E. Dickinson.—PaF
"As my eyes." Unknown.—JoT
Ballade. W. E. Henley.—PaF
Before the summer downpour. S. Kolosova.—MoM
"Clouds of morning mist." Buson.—BeM
Cricket march. C. Sandburg.—SaT
Crisscross. C. Sandburg.—SaT
Dog-days. A. Lowell.—PaF
Exeunt. R. Wilbur.—HaWr—HiN
Farm boy after summer. R. Francis.—HiN
The hot day. M. Chute.—ChRu
"Hot time." A. Trias.—HoC
"Hotness." A. Copeman.—HoC
"If it's ever spring again." T. Hardy.—PlP
In fields of summer. G. Kinnell.—HaWr
In the mountains on a summer day. Li T'ai-po.—MaFw
It never looks like summer. T. Hardy.—PlP
"It's hot." A. Carrington.—HoC
"June's here." C. Martindale.—HoC
Knoxville, Tennessee. N. Giovanni.—AdB—AdM—AdPb
Late summer. Kinoshita Yūji.—MaFw
"Late summer evening." Shiki.—BeM
Like a summer bird. A. Fisher.—FiFo
May 14. N. Belting.—BeSc
Midsummer jingle. N. Levy.—CoPu
Monument. F. Holman.—HoI
"The most." S. Suggs.—HoC
My father paints the summer. R. Wilbur.—HiN
"O warmth of summer sweeping over the land." Unknown.—LeIb
On a summer's day. J. Keats.—PaF (sel.)
"On these summer days." Sung Hon.—BaSs
"Our flat is hot." L. Lenski.—LeC
Prelude. H. W. Longfellow.—PaF
Rain in summer. H. W. Longfellow.—PaF
Seasons. M. Chute.—ChRu
Shower bath. L. Lenski.—LeC
Sleep and poetry. J. Keats.—PaF (sel.)
So quickly came the summer. A. T. Pratt.—AlW
"A step-child beats straw." Issa.—HaW
"Summer." E. Hillery.—HoC
Summer. C. G. Rossetti.—PaF
Summer doings. W. Cole.—LaM
Summer festival. L. Lenski.—LeC
Summer goes. R. Hoban.—HoE
Summer is coming. Unknown.—RoIt
Summer is gone. Unknown.—CoPi
Summer music. M. Sarton.—HiN
Summer oracle. A. Lorde.—AdPb
Summer shower. D. McCord.—McFm
Summer song. W. C. Williams.—HaWr
Summer storm. J. R. Lowell.—RoIt
Summer: West Side. J. Updike.—PeS
Summertime and the living. R. Hayden.—AdPb—HiN
"Sweating." H. Linton.—HoC
Thank you. L. Breek.—MoM
The throstle. A. Tennyson.—RoIt
"A time." T. Chambers.—HoC
The time of roses. T. Hood.—RoIt
Two songs. E. Sitwell.—JoA-4
Vacation. F. Holman.—HoI
The visitor. M. Goldman.—HaWr
The waking. T. Roethke.—JoA-4
"Winter breaks." N. Belting.—BeSc
"**Summer.**" Edmund Hillery.—HoC
Summer. Christina Georgina Rossetti.—PaF
"The **summer** and autumn had been so wet." See Bishop Hatto
"**Summer** comes." See Magalu
Summer doings. William Cole.—LaM
"**Summer** ends now, now, barbarous in beauty, the stooks arise." See Hurrahing in harvest
Summer festival. Lois Lenski.—LeC
Summer goes. Russell Hoban.—HoE
"**Summer** goes, summer goes." See Summer goes
Summer grass. Carl Sandburg.—SaT
"**Summer** grass aches and whispers." See Summer grass
"**Summer** has reigned." See The olive tree
"**Summer** is a-coming in." Unknown.—RoIt
"**Summer** is all a green air." See Summer music
Summer is coming. Unknown.—RoIt
"**Summer** is coming. Summer is coming." See Summer is coming
"**Summer** is coming, summer is coming." See The throstle
Summer is gone. Unknown, tr. fr. the Irish by Sean O'Faolain.—CoPi
Summer morning. See Prairie
Summer music. May Sarton.—HiN
"**Summer** of 'sixty-three, sir, and Conrad was gone away." See Kentucky Belle
Summer oracle. Audre Lorde.—AdPb
Summer shower. David McCord.—McFm
Summer song. William Carlos Williams.—HaWr
Summer stars. Carl Sandburg.—AdP—SaT
Summer storm. James Russell Lowell.—RoIt
Summer: West Side. John Updike.—PeS
Summers, Hal
The rescue.—CoPt
"**Summer's** sun is warm and bright." See Pleasant changes
Summertime and the living. Robert Hayden.—AdPb—HiN
"**Summon** now the kings of the forest." See Mmenson
Summoned by bells, sel. John Betjeman
"Deal out again the dog-eared poetry books."—PlM
Sun
August 2. N. Jordan.—AdPb
Awake and asleep. R. Froman.—FrSp

Sun song. Langston Hughes.—AdM—HoD
"**Sun** suits suit." Mary Ann Hoberman.—HoN
"The **sun** that brief December day." See Snow-bound
"The **sun,** the moon, the stars, the seas, the hills and the plains." See The higher pantheism
The **sun** used to shine. Edward Thomas.—PlM
"The **sun** used to shine while we two walked." See The sun used to shine
"The **sun** was golden-shiny." See Spring morning
"**Sun,** you may send your haze gold." See Haze gold
Sun Yün Fêng
Riding at daybreak.—MaFw
"The **sunbeams** stream forward, dawn boys." Unknown, tr. fr. the Mescalero Apache by Pliny Earle Goddard.—JoT
Sund, Robert
"A bee thumps against the dusty window."—CoPu
"Star thistle, Jim Hill mustard, white tops."—CoPu
"Through a wide field of stubble."—CoPu
Sunday. See Days of the week—Sunday
Sunday afternoon. Dennis Levertov.—PeS
Sunday afternoon in St Enodoc church, Cornwall. John Betjeman.—PaP
Sunday in the city. Lois Lenski.—LeC
Sunday morning. Wayne Moreland.—AdPb
"**Sunday** morning and her mother's hands." See Birmingham 1963
Sunday morning: Lonely. Lucille Clifton.—ClS
Sunday morning song. Unknown.—AbM
Sunday night: Goodnight. Lucille Clifton.—ClS
Sunday sculpture. Bobbi Katz.—HoP
Sunday street, downtown. Robert Froman.—FrSp
"**Sunday** strollers along a sewage-choked Schuylkill." See To some millions who survive
"**Sundays** too my father got up early." See Those winter Sundays
Sundials
On a sundial. H. Belloc.—CoPu—LiWw
To a friend: Constructive criticism. The Emperor Trajan.—LiWw
Sunfish. David McCord.—McAa
"The **sunfish,** funny finny one." See Sunfish
Sung by a little girl to soothe a crying baby. Unknown, fr. the Iglulik Eskimo.—LeIb
Sung Hon
"On these summer days."—BaSs
Sung Sam Mun
"What shall I be."—BaSs
"The **sun's** beams are running out." See Songs of the ghost dance
Sunset. Lilian Moore.—MoSp
"**Sunset** and evening star." See Crossing the bar
The **sunset** city. Henry Sylvester Cornwell.—RoIt
"The **sunset** swept." See Valley song
Sunsets. Carl Sandburg.—SaT
Sunstrike. Douglas Livingstone.—ToM
"**Super-cool.**" See But he was cool
Supermarket. Lois Lenski.—LeC
"The **supermarket** is a place." See Supermarket
Supernatural. See Ghosts; Miracles; Witchcraft
Supernatural. Jerome Holland.—JoV
"**Supernatural** is only a space." See Supernatural
Superstink. Robert Froman.—FrSp
Superstitions
The beetle in the wood. B. H. Reece.—CoPt
"See a pin and pick it up." Mother Goose.—EmN—JoA-4
Supper
Early supper. B. Howes.—HiN
"How cold it is." Issa.—HaW
"If things were better." Issa.—HaW—LiWw
Supper with Lindsay. T. Roethke.—PlM
Supper with Lindsay. Theodore Roethke.—PlM
The **suppliant.** Georgia Douglas Johnson.—AdPb
Supplication to the rain god and the spirits of water. Unknown, tr. fr. the Aztec by Bernardino de Sahagún.—BiI
"**Suppose** the ceiling went outside." See The ceiling
"**Suppose** you were dreaming about your family." See Benign neglect/Mississippi, 1970
"**Surely** that moan is not the thing." See Fog-horn
"**Surely** the turkey." See Perfection
Surfing
Straight talk (from a surfer). M. C. Livingston.—LiM
Surgery
A correct compassion. J. Kirkup.—MaFw
Surgery. R. Froman.—FrSp
Surgical ward. W. H. Auden.—PeS
Surgery. Robert Froman.—FrSp
Surgical ward. W. H. Auden.—PeS
The **surprise** ("I had a pollywog with a tail") Marchette Chute.—ChRu
A **surprise** ("When the donkey saw the zebra") Malcolm Douglas.—CoOr
Surrender
The limits of submission. F. Nuur.—AdM—AlPa (sel.)
"Shango, I prostrate to you every morning." Unknown.—AlPa
The surrender speech of Chief Joseph. Unknown.—BiI
The surrender speech of Cuauhtémoc. Unknown.—BiI
Two voices in a meadow. R. Wilbur.—PeS
The **surrender** speech of Chief Joseph. Unknown, tr. fr. the Nez Percé by Arthur Chapman.—BiI
The **surrender** speech of Cuauhtémoc. Unknown, tr. fr. the Aztec by Ramírez of Otumba.—BiI
Surview. Thomas Hardy.—PlP

"The **sweet-voiced** quechol there, ruling the earth, has intoxicated my soul." See Song
"**Sweet** William, he married a wife." See Sweet William, his wife, and the sheepskin
Sweet William, his wife, and the sheepskin. Unknown.—RoIt
Sweet winds of love. Patricia Irving.—AlW
"**Sweet** winds of love, sweep not my plains." See Sweet winds of love
"**Sweeten** these bitter wild crabapples, Illinois." See Crabapples
The **sweetest** thing. Unknown, tr. by Ulli Beier.—AdM
Swenson, May
At breakfast.—PeS
Cat & the weather.—HaWr
The even sea.—HaWr
Hearing the wind at night.—HaWr
A hurricane at sea.—HaWr
Living tenderly.—AdP
Locked in. tr.—CoPt
Question.—JoA-4
Southbound on the freeway.—PeS
The watch.—CoPt—RoIt
The woods at night.—JoA-4
The word beautiful.—JoA-4
Swift, Jonathan
Apples. See Market women's cries
Herrings. See Market women's cries
Market women's cries, sels.
Apples.—CoPi
Herrings.—CoPi
Onions.—CoPi
On himself.—CoPi
Onions. See Market women's cries
Twelve articles.—LiWw
Swift, Jonathan (about)
On himself. J. Swift.—CoPi
Swimmers. Louis Untermeyer.—JoA-4 (sel.)
Swimming and diving. See also Bathing
At the pool. X. J. Kennedy.—KeO
The dive. C. B. Gould.—FlH
"Dolphin daughter." A. Fisher.—FiD
Easy diver. R. Froman.—FrSp
"The high-diver climbs to the ladder's top." J. Prelutsky.—PrC
Learner. Unknown.—CoOh
Learning to swim. M. Chute.—ChRu
The lifeguard. J. Dickey.—PeS
Minnow Minnie. S. Silverstein.—SiW
"Mother, may I go and swim." Unknown.—TrG
Muskrat. M. A. Hoberman.—HoLb
Swimmers. L. Untermeyer.—JoA-4 (sel.)
Upon boys diverting themselves in the river. T. Foxton.—OpOx
Written after swimming from Sestos to Abydos. Lord Byron.—FlH
"**Swimming** is an easy thing." See Learning to swim
Swinburne, Algernon Charles
Autumn in Cornwall.—PaP
A ballad of Bath.—PaP
The garden of Proserpine.—CoPu (sel.)
The higher pantheism in a nutshell.—LiS
Nephelidia.—LiS
White butterflies.—AdP
Swinburne, Algernon Charles (about)
Nephelidia. A. C. Swinburne.—LiS
Swineherd. Eiléan Ni Chuilleanáin.—CoPi
The **swing** ("Get on a swing and swing up high") Lois Lenski.—LeC
The **swing** ("How do you like to go up in a swing") Robert Louis Stevenson.—LiLc
The **swing** ("The wind blows strong and the swing rides free") Marchette Chute.—ChRu
"**Swing** dat hammer—hunh." See Southern road
"**Swing** high-a-low gently down." See Menominee lullaby
"**Swing** low, sweet chariot " Unknown.—BrW
A **swing** song. William Allingham.—RoIt
"**Swing,** swing." See A swing song
Swinging
Bump on your thumb. D. Lee.—LeA
Hammock. D. McCord.—McS
The swing ("Get on a swing and swing up high") L. Lenski.—LeC
The swing ("How do you like to go up in a swing") R. L. Stevenson.—LiLc
The swing ("The wind blows strong and the swing rides free") M. Chute.—ChRu
A swing song. W. Allingham.—RoIt
"**Swinging** down brightened roads." See Vacation
"**Swinging,** swaying grass." Issa, tr. fr. the Japanese by Harry Behn.—BeM
"**Swishing** one finger." See Friday: Mom is home—Payday
Switzerland
Thought of a Briton on the subjugation of Switzerland. William Wordsworth.—LiS
"**Sybil** of months, and worshipper of winds." See November
Sycamore, William (about)
The ballad of William Sycamore. S. V. Benét.—JoA-4—RoIt
Sycamore. Myra Cohn Livingston.—LiM
Sycamore trees
Sycamore. M. C. Livingston.—LiM
The **sycophantic** fox and the gullible raven. Guy Wetmore Carryl.—LiWw
Sylvie and Bruno concluded, sels. Lewis Carroll
"He stept so lightly to the land."—LiPc
"In stature the manlet was dwarfish."—LiPc
"King Fisher courted Lady Bird."—LiPc
The mad gardener's song.—OpOx
The gardener's song.—JoA-4
"He thought he saw an elephant."—LiPc
The pig tale.—LiPc
"There be three badgers on a mossy stone."—LiPc
What Tottles meant.—LiPc
Symmetries and asymmetries, sels. W. H. Auden
"Deep in earth's opaque mirror."—MaFw

Symmetries—*Continued*
"Leaning out over."—MaFw
Symons, Arthur
Amends to nature.—PaF
Symon's lesson of wisdom for all manner of children; or, how to become a bishop. Unknown.—OpOx
Sympathy. See also Friendship; Kindness; Love
At the wood's edge. Unknown.—BiI
Dream song. Unknown.—BiI
Requickening. Unknown.—BiI
Sympathy ("I know what the caged bird feels, alas") P. L. Dunbar.—AdPb
Sympathy ("Into his pool of silent sorrow") A. T. Pratt.—AlW
Sympathy ("I know what the caged bird feels, alas") Paul Laurence Dunbar.—AdPb
Sympathy ("Into his pool of silent sorrow") Agnes T. Pratt.—AlW
Synge, John M. (Millington)
In Glencullen.—CoPi—CoPu
Is it a month.—CoPi
Patch-Shaneen.—CoPi
A question.—CoPi
Synge, John M. (Millington) (about)
A memory. L. A. G. Strong.—CoPi

T

"T-shirts, shorts." See People in the city
"T. Timothy Ticklepitcher." Unknown.—EmN
"Ta ran, Ta ra." See Tarantula
Tabb, John Banister (Father Tabb)
Fascination.—CoOh
The fire-fly.—BrM
Hospitality.—BrM
An inconvenience.—BrM
The woodpecker.—BrM
The **table** and the chair. Edward Lear.—JoA-4—UnGb
Table deportment. Robert Froman.—FrSp
Table rules for little folks. Unknown.—OpOx
Table talk. Elizabeth Moody.—BrM
Tableau. Countee Cullen.—AdPb
Tables
"Alas, alas, for Miss Mackay." Mother Goose.—TucMgl
The table and the chair. E. Lear.—JoA-4—UnGb
Table deportment. R. Froman.—FrSp
The world. T. L. Peacock.—CoPu
Tabrar, Joseph
Dearly beloved brethren.—CoPu
Mary Ann.—CoPu
Tachibana Akemi
Poems of solitary delights.—MaFw (sel.)
Tadpoles. See Frogs; Toads; Tree toads
"Taffy was a Welshman, Taffy was a thief." Mother Goose.—AlC
Taggard, Genevieve
Millions of strawberries.—UnGb
Song for unbound hair.—RoIt
Tagore, Rabindranath
Baby's world.—MaFw
Paper boats.—MaFw (sel.)
The rainy day.—MaFw
"A **tail** behind, a trunk in front." See The elephant, or the force of habit
Tailor. Eleanor Farjeon.—OpOx
Tailors
"A carrion crow sat on an oak." Mother Goose.—JoA-4
"Four and twenty tailors." Mother Goose.—JoA-4
Tailor. E. Farjeon.—OpOx
Tails
Double-tail dog. S. Silverstein.—SiW
The gallivanting gecko. J. Prelutsky.—PrP
"Good morning, Mr Rabbit." Unknown.—EmN
"I had a little pig." Unknown.—EmN
Kitten capers. A. Fisher.—FiM
"The squirrel has a bushy tail." Unknown.—EmN
Tails. A. Fisher.—FiFo
The tale of a dog. J. S. Lambert, Jr.—BrM
Tails. Aileen Fisher.—FiFo
Takahama Kyoshi
"Against the broad sky."—MaFw
"In the old man's eyes."—MaFw
"On far hills."—MaFw
"The snake fled."—MaFw
"Take a wooden doll." See Can you can't
"Take a word like cat." Karla Kuskin.—KuN
"Take cake: a very easy rhyme for bake." See From the kitchen—Cake
"Take Haru, Natsu." See Japanese lesson
"Take off." Joanne Oppenheim.—HoP
"Take off your hat." See A Zulu lyric
Take one home for the kiddies. Philip Larkin.—CoPu
"Take the curious case of Tom Pettigrew." David McCord
Three limericks.—McS
The **taking** of life brings serious thoughts. Unknown, tr. fr. the Pima by Frank Russell.—BiI
The **taking** of the salmon. T. T. Stoddart.—FlH
Taking off ("The airplane taxis down the field") Unknown.—HoP
Taking off ("Barely did the dust settle") Ronald Rogers.—AlW
"Taking pity on this scrag-end of the city." See One kingfisher and one yellow rose
The **tale** of a dog. James Lambert, Jr.—BrM
The **tale** of Custard the Dragon. Ogden Nash.—UnGb
The **tale** of the hermit told. Alastair Reid.—CoPt
Tales of brave Ulysses. Eric Clapton and Martin Sharp.—MoG
A **talisman.** Marianne Moore.—HiN

Talking
"As Tommy Snooks and Bessy Brooks." Mother Goose.—AlC—JoA-4
Auk talk. M. A. Hoberman.—HoR
The battle. S. Silverstein.—SiW
Controlling the tongue. From The Canterbury tales—The manciple's tale. G. Chaucer.—OpOx
Gab. E. Merriam.—MeO
The hens. E. M. Roberts.—LiLc—UnGb
"I have a friend who keeps standing on her hands." K. Kuskin.—KuN
"If you talk too much, you are a swindler." Kim Sang-yong.—BaSs
It happened. M. C. Livingston.—LiM
"Jorridge and Porridge." L. A. Garnett.—BrM
Kitten talk. A. Fisher.—FiM
Little bush. E. M. Roberts.—LiLc
The lonely soul. R. E. G. Armattoe.—AlPa
The prater. M. Prior.—LiWw
Silent, but. . . . T. Shigeji.—MaFw
Speak gently. D. Bates.—LiS
Talking. M. Goode.—JoV
Tick-tock talk. D. McCord.—McAa—McS
A time to talk. R. Frost.—HiN
Tom. A. Fisher.—FiM
Wise nature. Unknown.—CoPu
Talking. Michael Goode.—JoV
Talking to his drum. Emerson Blackhorse ("Barney") Mitchell.—AlW
"Tall." See Washiri (Poet)
"Tall building." See Skyscratcher
"Tall people, short people." See People
"Tall timber stood here once, here on a corn belt farm along the Monon." See Improved farm land
"Tallest poet for his height." See Arroyo
"Tambourines." Langston Hughes.—HoD
Tan Taigi
"Winter withering."—MaFw
"Tangled over twigs." Onitsura, tr. fr. the Japanese by Harry Behn.—BeM
Taniusha
"A wondrous city is Moscow."—MoM
"Tank truck." See Mad
"A **(Tannen-baum).**" See Fable of the transcendent Tannenbaum
Taos Pueblo Indians. See Indians of the Americas—Taos Pueblo
"Taped to the wall of my cell are 47 pictures: 47 black." See The idea of ancestry
Tapir. Mary Ann Hoberman.—HoR
"The **tapir** has a tubby torse." See Tapir
Tapirs
Tapir. M. A. Hoberman.—HoR
Tarantella. Hilaire Belloc.—LiS
Tarantula. Mary Ann Hoberman.—HoR
Tarasova, Ana
"The weather is gloomy."—MoM
Target. R. P. Lister.—PeS
The **tarry** buccaneer. John Masefield.—CoPt
Tartary. Walter De La Mare.—OpOx
Tartuffe. Molière, tr. fr. the French by Richard Wilbur.—LiWw
Taste
Lorne Doone: Last cookie song. R. Hoban.—HoE
Raw carrots. V. Worth.—WoS
A taste of honey. K. D. Kuka.—AlW
Thumbs. S. Silverstein.—SiW
A **taste** of honey. King D. Kuka.—AlW
Tate, Allen
Mr Pope.—PlM
Tate, Nahum
While shepherds watched.—LaS
"While shepherds watched their flocks by night."—JoA-4
"While shepherds watched their flocks by night." See While shepherds watched
"A **tattering** of rain and then the reign." See Darkling summer, ominous dusk, rumerous rain
"Tattletale, teacher's pet." Unknown.—EmN
Tattoos
Blackie, the electric Rembrandt. T. Gunn.—MaFw
Tatya
"Open, open the gates."—MoM
Taught me purple. Evelyn Tooley Hunt.—PeS
Tauhid. Askia Muhammad Touré.—AdPb
Taunt song against a clumsy kayak paddler. Unknown, fr. North Greenland.—LeIb
Taunts. See Teasing
Taupin, Bernie
The king must die.—MoG
Taverns. See Inns and taverns
Taxes
Taxes. D. L. Lee.—AdB
Taxes. Don L. Lee.—AdB
Taxi driver. Lois Lenski.—LeC
Taxicabs
Dance of the infidels. A. Young.—AdPb
Taxi driver. L. Lenski.—LeC
Taxis. R. Field.—JoA-4
They call me. Y. Amichai.—MeP
Taxis. Rachel Field.—JoA-4
"Taxis below." See They call me
Taylor, Ann (Ann Gilbert)
The baby's dance.—OpOx
Meddlesome Matty.—OpOx
My mother.—OpOx
The notorious glutton.—OpOx
The pin.—OpOx
—and Taylor, Jane
The cow.—OpOx
"Lazy sheep, pray tell me why." See The sheep
The sheep.—OpOx
"Lazy sheep, pray tell me why."—TucMgl
Taylor, Bayard
Ode on a jar of pickles.—LiS
The promissory note.—LiS
The three songs.—CoPt
Taylor, Bert Leston (B. L. T., pseud.)
The dinosaur.—LiWw

Taylor, Bert Leston (B. L. T., pseud.) *—Continued*
Gentle Doctor Brown.—CoOh
Taylor, Cecil (about)
You are alms. J. W. Thompson.—AdPb
Taylor, Debra Jo
"There are."—HoC
Taylor, Jane
The gleaner.—OpOx
Greedy Richard.—OpOx
"I love (like) little pussy."—BlM—JoA-4
Pussy.—OpOx
Pussy. See "I love (like) little pussy"
The star.—LiS—OpOx
—See also Taylor, Ann, jt. auth.
Taylor, Jeffreys
The milkmaid.—RoIt
Tchernichovsky, Saul
The grave.—MeP
Man is nothing but.—MeP
Your people are drowning in blood.—MeP
Tea in a space-ship. James Kirkup.—ToM
Tea parties
"Oh dear me, Mother caught a flea." Mother Goose.—AlC
The party. R. Whittemore.—HiN
Tea in a space-ship. J. Kirkup.—ToM
Tea party. H. Behn.—LiLc
Tea party. Harry Behn.—LiLc
A **teacher** ("He hated them all one by one but wanted to show them") Reed Whittemore.—HiN
The **teacher** ("The teacher has quite curious ways") Annette Wynne.—BrM
"The **teacher** has quite curious ways." See The teacher
"**Teacher,** teacher made a mistake." Unknown.—EmN
Teachers and teaching. See also School
Academic. J. Reeves.—ToM
Chester. S. Silverstein.—SiW
Children are slaves. I. Velez.—JoV
Deborah Delora. Unknown.—CoOh
Dumbbell. W. Cole.—CoOh
The educators. D. M. Black.—ToM
"God made the teachers in the night." Unknown.—MoBw
Hear this. M. C. Livingston.—LiM
"If a Hottentot taught a Hottentot tot." Unknown.—EmN
"If to hoot and to toot, a Hottentot tot." Unknown.—EmN
"John Smith's a very guid man." Unknown.—JoA-4
Mr Beecher. N. M. Bodecker.—BoL
Mixed-up school. X. J. Kennedy.—KeO
On a school-teacher. Unknown.—LiWw
On Mauros the rhetor. Palladas.—LiWw
The pay is good. R. Kell.—ToM
The purist. O. Nash.—LiWw
Sands junior high school. A. Blackwell.—JoV
Schoolmaster. Y. Yevtushenko.—MaFw
A schoolmaster's admonition. Unknown.—OpOx
A schoolmaster's precepts. J. Penkethman.—OpOx
Schoolmistress. C. Sansom.—ToM
The special person. D. Lee.—LeA
"Tattletail, teacher's pet." Unknown.—EmN
A teacher ("He hated them all one by one but wanted to show them") R. Whittemore.—HiN
The teacher ("The teacher has quite curious ways") A. Wynne.—BrM
"Teacher, teacher made a mistake." Unknown.—EmN
The tooting tutor. Unknown.—BrM
"A tooter who tooted the flute."—EmN
The unhappy schoolboy. Unknown.—OpOx
The village schoolmaster. From The deserted village. O. Goldsmith.—RoIt
"Yonder comes the teacher." Unknown.—EmN
"**Teachers** now a days are utterly disgusting." See Sands junior high school
"**Teacups** and saucers." Unknown.—EmN
The **teakettle.** Volodya Lapin, tr. fr. the Russian by Miriam Morton.—MoM
Teapots. See Pottery
"**Tear** down the old." See Urban renewal
"A **tear** rolled down my cheek." Calvin O'John.—AlW
Tears
Goodbye and run. P. Irving.—AlW
"If teardrops were pearls." Unknown.—BaSs
"A tear rolled down my cheek." C. O'John.—AlW
Tears. A. Lopez.—AlW
Tears, idle tears. From The princess. A. Tennyson.—RoIt
"The weeping spreads." Unknown.—BiI
Tears. Alonzo Lopez.—AlW
Tears, idle tears. See The princess
"**Tears,** idle tears, I know not what they mean." See The princess—Tears, idle tears
"**Tears** of loneliness." See Tears
Teasdale, Sara
Moonlight.—CoPu
Night.—JoA-4—PaF
"She who could bind you."—CoPu
Teasing
"Ain't she sweet, ain't she sweet." Unknown.—EmN
"Apple core." Unknown.—EmN
"Ashes to ashes and dust to dust." Unknown.—EmN
"Bake a pudding, bake a pie." Unknown.—EmN
"Barbara, Barbara." Unknown.—EmN
"Betty's mad and I am glad." Unknown.—EmN
"Can't catch me." Unknown.—EmN
"Copycat, copycat." Unknown.—EmN
"Cry-baby, cry." Unknown.—EmN
"Do you like beer." Unknown.—EmN
"Do you like butter." Unknown.—EmN
"Do you like chicken." Unknown.—EmN
"Do you like jelly." Unknown.—EmN

Little Billee.—RoIt
Pocahontas.—RoIt
The sorrows of Werther.—LiWw
A tragic story. tr.—LiWw
Thank you. Lily Breek, tr. fr. the Russian by Miriam Morton.—MoM
"**Thank** you for the things we have." See November
"**Thank** you for your silence." See Acknowledgement
"**Thank** you, pretty cow, that made." See The cow
"**Thank** you, sun, for being there." See Thank you
Thankfulness. See also Thanksgiving day
"Blow, blow, thou winter wind." From As you like it. W. Shakespeare.—PaF—RoIt
"The lands around my dwelling." Unknown.—BiI—LaM
Pied beauty. G. M. Hopkins.—MaFw—RoIt
Prayer. Unknown.—BiI
A song of thanks. W. Cole.—CoOr
The story of little Suck-a-Thumb. H. Hoffman.—LiS
We thank Thee. R. W. Emerson.—LaM
Thanks anyhow. John Ciardi.—CiFs
"**Thanks** for the lovely time." See Concert
"**Thanks,** thanks, fair cousins, for your gift." Lewis Carroll.—LiPc
"**Thanks** to the human heart by which we live." See The human heart
Thanksgiving. Arthur Guiterman.—CoPu
Thanksgiving day. See also Thankfulness
A fable. O. Herford.—MaF
First Thanksgiving of all. N. B. Turner.—RoIt
Magic vine. Unknown.—JaP
November. L. Clifton.—ClE
Psalm 124, Bible, Old Testament
A psalm of thanksgiving.—MeP
Simon Soggs' Thanksgiving. W. A. Croffut.—CoPt
Thanksgiving. A. Guiterman.—CoPu
Thanksgiving day. L. M. Child.—RoIt
Thanksgiving day. Lydia Maria Child.—RoIt
"**Thanksgiving** dinner's sad and thankless." See Point of view
"**That** bottle of perfume that Willie sent." Unknown.—RoIt
"**That** broken star." See A Christmas package
That cat. Ben King.—RoIt
"**That** cat is crazy." Karla Kuskin.—KuN
That dark other mountain. Robert Francis.—HiN—PeS
"**That** God of ours, the Great Geometer." See Grace to be said at the supermarket
"**That** great tree covered with snow." See Cardinal
That head. Jerce Bullmer.—CoOr
"**That** hump of a man bunching chrysanthemums." See Old florist
"**That** king spent fifty years or more." See Citadels
That little black cat. D'Arcy Wentworth Thompson.—OpOx
Cure for a pussy cat.—RoIt
"**That** lonesome path that leads to nowhere." See That lonesome place
That lonesome place. Calvin O'John.—AlW
"**That** love is all there is." Emily Dickinson.—ThI
That mountain far away. Unknown, tr. fr. the Tewa by Herbert J. Spinder.—BiI
"**That** our earth mother may wrap herself." See Offering
"**That** red fox." See The trap
That sharp knife. Thomas Wolfe.—HiN
"**That** she was taken out of her mother, thanks be for that." Unknown, fr. the Ammassalik Eskimo.—LeIb
"**That** time." See Paul Robeson
"**That** time of year thou may'st in me behold." See Sonnets. William Shakespeare
That wind. Unknown, tr. fr. the Kiowa by James Mooney.—BiI
"That wind, that wind."—ClFc
"**That** wind, that wind." See That wind
"**That** winter love spoke and we raised no objection." See Jig
"**That** with this bright believing hand." See The impercipient
"**That's** Jack." See Jack
That's not. David McCord.—McAa
"**That's** not a grouse—a pheasant." See That's not
The **thaw** ("Icicles, which grow silently in the night") Jack Matthews.—HaWr
Thaw ("In time the snowman always dies") Walker Gibson.—CoPu
Thaw ("Over the land freckled with snow half-thawed") Edward Thomas.—MaFw
Thaw in the city. Lou Lipsitz.—HiN
Thaws
The thaw ("Icicles, which grow silently in the night") J. Matthews.—HaWr
Thaw ("In time the snowman always dies") W. Gibson.—CoPu
Thaw ("Over the land freckled with snow half-thawed") E. Thomas.—MaFw
Thaw in the city. L. Lipsitz.—HiN
Thaxter, Celia (Leighton)
The sandpiper.—OpOx—RoIt
Theatre mouse. Charles A. Wagner.—RoIt
Theatres
Pete the parrot and Shakespeare. D. Marquis.—PlM
Theatre mouse. C. A. Wagner.—RoIt
Theiner, George
A history lesson. tr.—MaFw
Theme in yellow. C. Sandburg.—HoH—LiLc—SaT
Theme one: The variations. August Wilson.—AdPb
Theme with variation. Myra Cohn Livingston.—LiM
"**Then** are the trackless copses alive with the trilling of birds." See The Georgics

"There is no frigate like a book." Emily Dickinson
A book.—RoIt
"There is no needle without piercing point." See Death
"There is not much that I can do." See At the railway station, Upway
"There is one that has a head without an eye." Christina Georgina Rossetti
A riddle.—OpOx
"There is only one horse on the earth." See Prologue to the family of man—Names
"There is something in the autumn that is native to my blood." See A vagabond song
"There is sweet music here that softer falls." See The lotos-eaters—Choric song
"There is the Succah, not yet covered." See Succah
"There it was, word for word." See The poem that took the place of a mountain
There lived a king. William Schwenck Gilbert.—CoPt
"There lived a king, as I've been told." See There lived a king
"There lived a sage in days of yore." See A tragic story
"There lived among the untrodden ways." Hartley Colderidge.—LiS
"There lived an old woman at Lynn." Unknown
Three wonderful old women.—OpOx
"There once was a grizzly bear." Unknown.—MoBw
"There once was a king." Unknown, tr. fr. the Danish by N. M. Bodecker.—BoI
"There once was a provident puffin." See The provident puffin
"There once was a willow, and he was very old." See The willow-man
"There once was a witch of Willowby wood." See The witch of Willowby wood
"There once was a young man named Hall." Unknown.—RoIt
"There was once a young man named Paul." Unknown.—MoBw
"There once was an ichthyosaurus." See The ichthyosaurus
"There shall be no more songs." See Black power
"There the black river, boundary to hell." See The Southern road
"There, there is no mountain within miles." See Nebraska
"There they are." See The Blackstone Rangers
"There was a Boy bedded in bracken." See Carol
"There was a boy in our town with long hair." See The long-haired boy
"There was a boy who skinned his knees." See Is this someone you know
"There was a boy whose name was Jim." See Jim, who ran away from his nurse, and was eaten by a lion
"There was a boy with a souped-up car." See Fast and far
"There was a cantankerous 'gator." See The cantankerous 'gator
"There was a crooked man." Mother Goose.—AlC—BlM
"There was a crooked man, and he went a crooked mile."—JoA-4
"There was a crooked man, and he went a crooked mile." See "There was a crooked man"
"There was a faith-healer of Deal." Unknown.—LiWw—RoIt
"There was a girl in our town." Unknown.—EmN
"There was a good grocer." See The unfortunate grocer
"There was a gray rat looked at me." See Rat riddles
"There was a great white wall—bare, bare, bare." See The smoked herring
"There was a high majestic fooling." See Laughing corn
"There was a jolly miller." See Love in a village
"There was a jolly miller once." See Love in a village—Song
"There was a lady loved a swine." Mother Goose.—MiMg
The lady and the swine.—CoOh
"There was a little girl." Henry Wadsworth Longfellow.—OpOx (sel.)—RoIt
"There was a little guinea-pig." See A guinea-pig song
"There was a little man, and he had a little gun." Mother Goose.—JoA-4
"There was a little turtle." See The little turtle
"There was a lofty ship, and she put out to sea." See The Golden Vanity
"There was a man, and he had nought." Mother Goose.—AlC
"There was a man and he stayed within." Mother Goose.—TucMg
"There was a man, and his name was Dob." See Chitterabob
"There was a man from Delaware." See A long hard day
"There was a man from Singapore." See Some sound advice from Singapore
"There was a man, now please take note." See The goat
"There was a man of Newington." Mother Goose.—AlC
"There was a man of Thessaly." See Alexander's song
"There was a man of Uriconium." See Uriconium
"There was a man who had a clock." See The sad tale of Mr Mears
"There was a man who lived in a house." See He lived, alas, in a house too big
"There was a man who lived in Perth." See And on some days I might take less

"**There** was an old woman as ugly as sin." See An old woman
"**There** was an old woman called Nothing-at-all." Mother Goose.—AlC
"**There** was an old woman had three sons." Mother Goose.—JoA-4
"**There** was an old woman, her name it was Peg." Mother Goose.—AlC
"**There** was an old woman in Surrey." Mother Goose.—OpOx—TucMgl
"**There** was an old woman named Towl." Unknown
Three wonderful old women.—OpOx
"**There** was an old woman sat spinning." Mother Goose.—AlC
"**There** was an old woman toss'd (tossed) up in a basket." Mother Goose.—AlC—JoA-4—MiMg
"**There** was an old woman who lived in a shoe." Mother Goose.—AlC—JoA-4
"**There** was an old woman who lived in a shoe (and all her grandchildren)." See The old woman who lived in a shoe
"**There** was one among us who rose." See Death of a friend
"**There** was one who was famed for the number of things." See An odd fellow
"**There** was such speed in her little body." See Bells for John Whiteside's daughter
"**There** was this Spike who simply could not fit." See Spike spoke spook
"**There** were five fellows." Clyde Watson.—WaF
"**There** were once two cats of Kilkenny." See The cats of Kilkenny
"**There** were three jovial Welshmen." Mother Goose.—AlC—JoA-4
"**There** were three sailors of Bristol city." See Little Billee
"**There** were three sisters fair and bright." See The riddling knight
"**There** were two men of holy will." See The marvellous bear shepherd
"**There**, where the skylark's." Kyorai, tr. fr. the Japanese by Harry Behn.—BeM
"**There** will be no Holy man crying out this year." See Jitterbugging in the streets
"**Therefore** all seasons shall be sweet to thee." See Frost at midnight
"**There's** a bench in the park." See Bench in the park
"**There's** a blue sky I like." See Like it should be
"**There's** a cat out there." See Alarm
"**There's** a certain illness within you." Arlene Blackwell.—JoV
"**There's** a certain slant of light." Emily Dickinson.—PaF—ThI
"**There's** a city that lies in the Kingdom of Clouds." See The sunset city
"**There's** a crevice in the granite." See Rabbit tracks
"**There's** a cross-eyed woman in our town." Unknown.—CoOh
"**There's** a family of wrens who lives upstairs." See Upstairs
"**There's** a fellow." See A ruffian
"**There's** a friend for little children." See Above the bright blue sky
"**There's** a glen in Aghadoe, Aghadoe, Aghadoe." See Aghadoe
"**There's** a grey wind wails on the clover." See Numerous Celts
"**There's** a hole in my bucket, dear Conrad, dear Conrad." Mother Goose, tr. fr. the German.—TucMg
"**There's** a hole in the bottom of the sea." See Do you want affidavits
"**There's** a humming in the sky." See Aeroplane
"**There's** a land that I see." See Free to be you and me
"**There's** a man who's been out sailing." See Cactus tree
"**There's** a patch of old snow in a corner." See A patch of old snow
"**There's** a star in the East on Christmas morn." See Rise up shepherd, and follow
"**There's** an autograph book in heaven." Unknown.—EmN
"**There's** black bug's blood." Unknown.—EmN
"**There's** dazzle." See Sunset
"**There's** more in words than I can teach." See Loving and liking
"**There's** more than one way to be right." Richard Wilbur.—WiO
"**There's** music in a hammer." Unknown.—RoIt
"**There's** no hiding place down there." See No hiding place
"**There's** not a hill in all the view." John Clare.—PaP
"**There's** one rides very sagely on the road." See Upon the horse and his rider
"**There's** something in a flying horse." See Peter Bell—The crescent boat
"**There's** somewhat on my breast, father." See The confession
"**There's** this that I like about hockey, my lad." John Kieran.—FlH
"**There's** this thing about Pandora's box." See Pandora
"**There's** this to remember about the gnu." See The gnu
"**These** are." John Vitale.—HoC
"**These** are the days when birds come back." Emily Dickinson.—PaF
"**These** buildings are too close to one." See Rudolph is tired of the city
These days. Charles Olsen.—MoT
"**These** fell miasmic rings of mist, with ghoulish menace bound." See Prejudice
"**These** few shoots cut from a mountain willow." Hong Nang, tr. fr. the Korean by Chung Seuk Park and ad. by Virginia Olsen Baron.—BaSs
"**These** men were kings, albeit they were black." See Black majesty
"**These** new night." See Ivory masks in orbit

"They've paid the last respects in sad tobacco." See Padraic O'Conaire, Gaelic storyteller
"The **thick** black pythons." See Pythons
"The **thief** in me is running a." See Zapata and the landlord
Thieves
The bushrangers. E. Harrington.—CoPt
"Crow Indian." Unknown.—ClFc
"Hickle them, pickle them." Mother Goose.—TucMgl
The highwayman's ghost. R. Garnett.—CoPt
"I knew a man." C. Watson.—WaF
"Johnny stole a penny once." Unknown.—CoOh
"Last night and the night before (a lemon and a pickle)." Unknown.—EmN
"Last night and the night before (twenty-four robbers)." Mother Goose.—AlC—EmN
"Little Jock Sanders of Dee." Unknown.—BoI
Paddy O'Rafther. S. Lover.—CoPi—CoPt
"Pinky Pauper picked my pocket." C. Watson.—WaF
"Policeman, policeman, don't take me." Mother Goose.—AlC—EmN
"The Queen of Hearts." Mother Goose.—JoA-4
The rain it raineth. Lord Bowen.—CoPu—LiWw
The rain.—RoIt
Small change. T. Ostrovskaya.—MoM
"Taffy was a Welshman, Taffy was a thief." Mother Goose.—AlC
"There was a man, and he had nought." Mother Goose.—AlC
"Tom, Tom, the piper's son (stole a pig)." Mother Goose.—AlC—JoA-4
"**Thin** streams." See The Shawangunks—early April
"The **thin** weary line of carriers." See Stanley meets Mutesa
A **thing** of beauty. John Keats.—RoIt
"A **thing** of beauty is a joy forever." See A thing of beauty
"The **thing** to draw with compasses." See Circles
Things to do if you are a subway. Bobbi Katz.—HoCs—HoP
Things to remember. James Reeves.—JoA-4
"**Think** of me early." Unknown.—EmN
"**Think** of one now." Unknown.—MoBw
"**Think** of pilgrims." See The pilgrimage
"**Think** of the storm roaming the sky uneasily." See Little exercise
Think tank. Eve Merriam.—MeO
"**Think** thinktank think." See Think tank
"**Think** you I am not fiend and savage too." See To the white fiends
Thinking in bed. Dennis Lee.—LeA
Thirst
"I am crying from thirst." A. Lopez.—AlW
Thirst. G. Cohoe.—AlW
Thirst. Grey Cohoe.—AlW
Thirteen ways of looking at a blackbird. Wallace Stevens.—MoT
"**Thirteen's** no age at all. Thirteen is nothing." See Portrait of a girl with comic book
"**Thirty** days hath September." Mother Goose.—JoA-4
"**Thirty** kopecks were missing." See Small change
Thirty-three triads. Unknown, tr. fr. the Irish by Thomas Kinsella.—CoPi
"**Thirty-two** times I went forth to my life." See On my birthday
"**Thirty** white horses." Mother Goose.—EmN—JoA-4
"**This** ae night, this ae night." See A lyke-wake dirge
"**This** afternoon, darling, when you were here." See Letter from a death bed
"**This** ancient hag." See Mexican market woman
"**This** boat that we just built is just fine." See Homemade boat
"**This** book is one thing." Unknown.—EmN
"**This** book you hold." See Introduction
"**This** boy think he bad to get." Cynthia Pass.—JoV
"**This** broken plate." See Memories
"**This** bug carries spots on his back." See Bug spots
"**This** cat." Karla Kuskin.—KuN
"**This** country might have." See Right on/white America
"**This** day is call'd the feast of Crispian." See King Henry V—King Henry's speech before Agincourt
This day is over. Calvin O'John.—AlW
"**This** dewdrop world." Issa.—AtM
"**This** evening, my love, even as I spoke vainly." See Sonnets of love and discretion
"**This** face you got." See Phizzog
"**This** fat woman in canvas knickers." See Tourist time
"**This** foggy night." See Ghost weather
"**This** guy on t.v." See The electric cop
This houre her vigill. Valentin Iremonger.—CoPi
"**This** house has been far out at sea all night." See Wind
"**This** is." See The cinquain
"**This** is a damned inhuman sort of war." See Unseen fire
"**This** is a free country." Unknown.—MoBw
"**This** is a game that Lewis Carroll played." See The game of doublets
"**This** is a lovely place to be." See At the library
"**This** is a silence." See Arabesque
"**This** is a white." See Imperial thumbprint
"**This** is a zither." Unknown.—EmN
"**This** is coyote's night." See Coyote's night
"**This** is father, short and stout." Mother Goose, tr. fr. the German.—TucMg
This is just to say. William Carlos Williams.—LiS—MaFw
"**This** is like a place." See Snowy night
"**This** is Mister Beers." See Mister Beers

"**This** is my last cry." See For Stephen Dixon
"**This** is my rock." David McCord.—JoA-4
"**This** is page one." Unknown.—MoBw
This is real. Ted Palmanteer.—AlW
"**This** is the." See The way that it's going
"**This** is the bridge." See The troll bridge
"**This** is the cat." Unknown.—BlM
"**This** is the forest primeval. The murmuring pines and the hemlocks." See Evangeline—Prologue to Evangeline
"**This** is the grave of Mike O'Day." See Epitaph
"**This** is the hour, said Santa Claus." See Santa and his reindeer
"**This** is the house that Jack built." Mother Goose.—JoA-4
The house that Jack built.—LiS
"**This** is the light of the mind, cold and planetary." See The moon and the yew tree
"**This** is the metre Columbian. The soft-flowing trochees, and dactyls." See The metre Columbian
"**This** is the Pentagon building." See Pentagonia
"**This** is the story of." See Brady's bend
"**This** is the surest death." See Mortality
"**This** is the urgency: live." See The second sermon on the warpland
"**This** is the weather the cuckoo likes." See Weathers
"**This** is the week when Christmas comes." See In the week when Christmas comes
This landscape, these people. Zulfikar Ghose.—ToM
"**This** little cow eats grass." See The five toes
"**This** little man lived all alone." Mother Goose.—TucMgl
This little morsel. See A child's day
"**This** little pig went to market." Mother Goose.—JoA-4
"**This** living hand, now warm and capable." See Lines supposed to have been addressed to Fanny Brawne
"**This** lovely flower fell to seed." See For my grandmother
"**This** man, this poet, said." See Spark of laurel
This morning. Jay Wright.—AbM
"**This** morning I jumped on my horse." See True story
"**This** morning I threw the windows." See This morning
"**This** morning, when he looked at me." See Black all day
This newly created world. Unknown, tr. fr. the Winnebago by Paul Radin.—BiI
"**This** piston's infinite recurrence is." See La marche des machines
"**This** porthole overlooks a sea." See Bendix
"**This** pretty bird, oh, how she flies and sings." See Upon the swallow
"**This** rose tree is not made to bear." See Envy
"**This** sacred lake." See Chad
"**This** skinny poem will introduce." See Introduction
"**This** small lodge is now alive." See Old man, the sweat lodge
"**This** started out as a." See Jumping rope
"**This** summer I shall." See Ambition
"**This** thing you see, bright ruse." See On her portrait
"**This** torment of love." See In which are described rationally the irrational effects of love
"**This** turtle moved his house across the street." See Turtle
"**This** unimportant." Bashō, tr. fr. the Japanese by Harry Behn.—BeM
This was a poet. See "This was a poet—It is that"
"**This** was a poet—It is that." Emily Dickinson
This was a poet.—PlM
"**This** was a rich morning." See Rich morning
"**This** was our valley, yes." See The dam
"**This** way, oh turn your bows." See The odyssey—The siren's song
Thistle-seed. Unknown, tr. fr. the Chinese by Isaac Taylor Headland.—JoA-4
"**Thistle-seed,** thistle-seed." See Thistle-seed
Thistles
My Aunt Dora. T. Hughes.—HuMf
"Theogenes, the Thessalonian thistle-sifter, sifting thistles." Unknown.—EmN
"Theophilus Thistle, the successful thistle-sifter." Unknown.—EmN
"Theophilus Thistledown, the successful thistle-sifter." Unknown.—EmN
Thistles. T. Hughes.—ToM
"T. Timothy Ticklepitcher." Unknown.—EmN
Thistles. Ted Hughes.—ToM
Thomas, D. M.
Eden.—HiN
Missionary.—ToM
Unknown shores.—ToM
Thomas, Dylan
"And death shall have no dominion."—ToM
Fern hill.—JoA-4—PaF—PeS
Poem in October.—PaF—ToM
A refusal to mourn the death, by fire, of a child in London.—ToM
Under Milkwood, sel.
"Johnnie Crack and Flossie Snail."—LiLc
Thomas, Dylan (about)
Dylan Thomas. S. Spender.—PlM
Dylan, who is dead. S. Allen.—AdPb
Fern hill. D. Thomas.—JoA-4—PaF—PeS
Poem in October. D. Thomas.—PaF—ToM
Thomas, Edward
Adlestrop.—MaFw—PaP
After rain.—HiN
Digging.—JoA-4—PaF
Haymaking.—PaP
If I should ever by chance.—OpOx
Lights out.—MaFw
Snow.—CoPu
The sun used to shine.—PlM
Thaw.—MaFw
What shall I give.—OpOx

"Will you come."—JoA-4
Thomas, Edward (about)
To E. T. R. Frost.—PlM
Thomas, Lorenzo
Onion bucket.—AdPb
The subway witnesses.—AdPb
Thomas, R. S.
A blackbird singing.—MaFw
Cynddylan on a tractor.—ToM
Death of a peasant.—MaFw
The evacuees.—ToM
Farm child.—CoPu—MaFw
For the record.—ToM
The hill farmer speaks.—ToM
January.—CoPu
Welsh landscape.—ToM
Thomas, Richard W.
Amen.—AdPb
Life after death.—AdPb
Martyrdom.—AdPb
Riots and rituals.—AdPb
To the new annex to the Detroit county jail.—AdPb
The worker.—AdPb
Thomas Hardy, poet. Mark Van Doren.—PlM
Thomas Hood. Edwin Arlington Robinson.—PlM
"**Thomas** is quiet." See Tom
Thomas Rymer. See True Thomas
"**Thomas** Thomas Tinkertoes." Clyde Watson.—WaF
"**Thomas** Tremble new-made me." See Inscription for a peal of eight bells
Thompson, D'Arcy Wentworth
Cure for a pussy cat. See That little black cat
That little black cat.—OpOx
Cure for a pussy cat.—RoIt
A very odd fish.—OpOx
Thompson, Edith Osborne
The monkeys.—BrM
Thompson, Francis
Ex ore infantium.—OpOx
To a snow-flake.—PaF
To a snowflake.—RoIt
To a snowflake. See To a snow-flake
Thompson, Glen
"The air is dirty."—JoV
Drums of freedom.—JoV
Hands.—JoV
Thompson, James W.
The yellow bird.—AdPb
You are alms.—AdPb
Thompson, Julius
To Malcom X.—AdM
Thompson, Larry
"Black is best."—AdB—AdM—AdPb
Thompson, Lulu E.
In Hardin county, 1809.—CoPt
Thompson, Philip (about)
The old pilot's death. D. Hall.—ToM
Thompson River Indians. See Indians of the Americas—Thompson River
Thomson, James
"Once in a saintly passion."—RoIt
Thoreau, Henry David
"I was born upon thy bank, river."—CoPu
My life has been the poem.—PlM
Thoreau, Henry David (about)
"I was born upon thy bank, river." H. D. Thoreau.—CoPu
My life has been the poem. H. D. Thoreau.—PlM
Thorley, Wilfrid
The harvest elves.—JaP
"**Those** awful words, Till death do part." See Early thoughts of marriage
"**Those** boys that ran together." Lucille Clifton.—AdPb
"**Those** days, the angry persons were the old." See Angry old men
"**Those** days when it was all right." See Letter to E. Franklin Frazier
"**Those** eager Little Leaguers." See Little League
"**Those** game animals, those long-haired caribou." Unknown, fr. Copper Eskimo.—LeIb
"**Those** moments, tasted once and never done." See Cornish cliffs
"**Those** mothers down there off the hill." See Seventh son
"**Those** my friendships most obtain." See Contentment
"**Those** rivers in that lost country." See Rivers
Those who go, not to return. Benjamin Galai, tr. fr. the Hebrew by Robert Mezey and Shula Starkman.—MeP
"**Those** who speak know nothing." See The philosophers—Lao-Tzu
Those winter Sundays. Robert Hayden.—AdPb
"**Thou** blossom bright with autumn dew." See To the fringed gentian
"**Thou** ill-form'd offspring of my feeble brain." See The author to her book
"**Thou** in whom the rhythm of life is hid." See The moon
"**Thou** seest me the meanest thing, and so I am indeed." See The book of Thel—The worm
"**Though** conscience void of all offence." See Praise
"**Though** days be dark." Unknown.—MoBw
"**Though** holly halos hang from many a nail." See A Christmas package
"**Though** it is New Year's eve." See Our cat
"**Though** knowledge must be got with pain." See For scholars and pupils
"**Though** not apparently, you choose it well." See Poet with sea horse
"**Though** the crocuses poke up their heads in the usual places." See Vernal sentiment
"**Though** the tribe holds a feast against me." See War song
"**Though** there is still quite a way to go." Unknown, tr. fr. the Korean by Chung Seuk Park and ad. by Virginia Olsen Baron.—BaSs
"**Though** they scold and nag and argue." Unknown.—MoBw

"**Though** three men dwell on Flannan isle." See Flannan isle
Thought. See also Mind
Awareness. D. L. Lee.—AdB—AdM
"Do not think." C. Freeman.—AdM
The little blue engine. S. Silverstein.—SiW
Silent, but. . . . Truboi Shigeji.—MaFw
Think tank. E. Merriam.—MeO
Thinking in bed. D. Lee.—LeA
What's my thought like. T. Moore.—LiWw
"When the rain raineth." Mother Goose.—TucMgl
A **thought.** Sasha Ukachev, tr. fr. the Russian by Miriam Morton.—MoM
The **thought-fox.** Ted Hughes.—HiN
Thought of a Briton on the subjugation of Switzerland. William Wordsworth.—LiS
Thoughtless guest. Valine Hobbs.—BrM
Thoughts at midnight. Thomas Hardy.—PlP
Thoughts of Phena. Thomas Hardy.—PlP
Thoughts while driving home. John Updike.—PeS
"A **thousand** doors ago." See Young
"A **thousand** hairy savages." Spike Milligan.—CoPu
"**Thousands** of sheep, soft-footed, black-nosed sheep, one by one." See Sheep
Three acres of land. Unknown.—RoIt
"**Three** big sailors had a tiny little boat." Mother Goose, tr. fr. the Spanish.—TucMg
Three birds flying. Eve Merriam.—MeO
"**Three** black boys." See Panther
"**Three** blind mice, see how they run." Mother Goose.—AlC
"**Three** children sliding on the ice." Mother Goose; also at. to John Gay.—AlC—JoA-4
"**Three** colts exercising in a six-acre." Joseph Campbell.—CoPi
"**Three** excellent qualities in narration." See Thirty-three triads
The **three** foxes. A. A. Milne.—OpOx
Three ghostesses. Unknown.—HoH—JaP
"**Three** gray geese in the green grass growing." Unknown.—EmN
Three hens. Henry Johnstone.—CoOr
The **three** hermits. William Butler Yeats.—MaFw
"**Three** jolly farmers." See Off the ground
The **three** kings. Rubén Dario, tr. by Lysander Kemp.—AbM
"**Three** little birches." Maya Nikogosian, tr. fr. the Russian by Miriam Morton.—MoM
"**Three** little ghostesses." See Three ghostesses
"**Three** little guinea pigs." Unknown, tr. fr. the Danish by N. M. Bodecker.—BoI
"**Three** little kittens." Mother Goose.—BlM
"**Three** little mice ran up the stairs. Unknown.—TrG
The **three** little pigs. Alfred Scott Gatty.—OpOx
"**Three** of us afloat in the meadow by the swing." See Pirate story
Three old brothers. Frank O'Connor.—CoPi
"**Three** old hermits took the air." See The three hermits
Three signs of spring. David McCord.—McS
The **three** songs. Bayard Taylor.—CoPt
Three spring notations on bipeds, sel. Carl Sandburg
Laughing child.—SaT
"**Three** strange men came to the inn." See A lady comes to an inn
"**Three** things there are more beautiful." See The beautiful
"**Three** wise men of Gotham." Mother Goose.—AlC—JoA-4
Three wise old women. Elizabeth T. Corbett.—OpOx
"**Three** wise old women were they, were they." See Three wise old women
"**Three** wishes." Karla Kuskin.—KuN
Three wishes. Unknown.—RoIt
Three wonderful old women. See "There lived an old woman at Lynn"
Three wonderful old women. See "There was an old woman named Towl"
"**Three** young rats with black felt hats." Mother Goose.—BlM—JoA-4
Thrift
"Melvin Martin Riley Smith." D. McCord.—McFm
The pin. A. Taylor.—OpOx
Portrait. E. Rodgers.—AdM
Sonnet IV. Unthrifty loveliness. W. Shakespeare.—MoG
Squirrel. M. A. Hoberman.—HoLb
The **throstle.** Alfred Tennyson.—RoIt
"**Through** a wide field of stubble." Robert Sund.—CoPu
"**Through** and through the inspired leaves." See The bookworms
"**Through** dawn's." See Through dawn's pink aurora
Through dawn's pink aurora. Phil George.—AlW
"**Through** every nook and every cranny." See Granny
"**Through** pine-black stilettos." See Shadows and song
"**Through** snowy woods and shady." See Seen by the waits
"**Through** the arch of the bridge." See Coca cola sunset
"**Through** the house what busy joy." See The first tooth
Through the looking-glass, sels. Lewis Carroll
The aged old man.—LiPc—LiS—OpOx
Ways and means.—RoIt
"A boat, beneath a sunny sky."—LiPc
"Child of the pure unclouded brow."—LiPc
"First, the fish must be caught."—LiPc
Humpty Dumpty's song.—OpOx
"In winter, when the fields are white."—LiPc
Jabberwocky.—JoA-4—LiPc—LiS—LiWw—OpOx—RoIt

Tintern Abbey
"Five years have past; five summers, with the length." From Lines composed a few miles above Tintern Abbey. W. Wordsworth.—PaP
"A **tiny** house." Karla Kuskin.—KuN
"**Tiny** man." Mother Goose, tr. fr. the Dutch—TucMg
"The **tiny** son of Marawambo." See Jungle incident
Tiny world. Jerome Holland.—JoV
"**Tip** top, tangle tongue." Unknown.—EmN
Tippett, James S. (Sterling)
Counting the days.—HoS
Trucks.—HoP—JoA-4
Tugs.—HoP
Underground rumbling.—HoP
Tired. Fenton Johnson.—AdPb
Tired Tim. Walter De La Mare.—JoA-4—LiLc
"'**Tis** dog's delight to bark and bite." Unknown.—BrM
'**Tis** midnight. Unknown.—LiWw
"'**Tis** midnight, and the setting sun." See 'Tis midnight
"'**Tis** of a rich merchant who in London did dwell." See Villikins and his Dinah
"'**Tis** sad to see the sons of learning." See He that never read a line
"'**Tis** spring; come out to ramble." See A Shropshire lad—The Lent lily
"'**Tis** sweet to kiss." Unknown.—MoBw
'**Tis** sweet to roam. Unknown.—LiWw
"'**Tis** sweet to roam when morning's light." See 'Tis sweet to roam
"'**Tis** the hour when white-horsed day." See Morning
'**Tis** the voice of the lobster. See Alice's adventures in wonderland—Alice's recitation
"'**Tis** the voice of the lobster, I heard him declare." See Alice's adventures in wonderland—Alice's recitation
"'**Tis** the voice of the sluggard: I heard him complain." See The sluggard
"'**Tis** time, I think, by Wenlock town." See A Shropshire lad
"**Tit** for tat." Unknown.—EmN
Tit for tat: A tale. John Aikin.—OpOx
Titmice. See Chickadees
Titwillow. See The Mikado
Tiutchev, Fyodor
"I am in the all, the all in me."—MoM
Tlingit Indians. See Indians of the Americas—Tlingit
To ——. William Stanley Braithwaite.—AdPb
To a captious critic. Paul Laurence Dunbar.—AbM
To a child dancing in the wind. William Butler Yeats.—CoPi
To a child five years old. Nathaniel Cotton.—OpOx
To a dark girl. Gwendolyn B. Bennett.—AdPb
To a fat lady seen from the train. Frances Cornford.—CoPu—LiS
To a fish of the brook. John Wolcot.—RoIt
To a friend. Vitaly Shlensky, tr. fr. the Russian by Miriam Morton.—MoM
To a friend: constructive criticism. Trajan, Emperor of Rome, tr. fr. the Roman by Dudley Fitts.—LiWw
To a lady in a phone booth. Phyllis McGinley.—LiWw
To a late poplar. Patrick Kavanagh.—CoPi
To a nightingale. John Keats.—PaF (sel.)
To a poet I knew. Johari Amini.—AdPb
To a poet who has had a heart attack. Richard Eberhart.—PlM
To a poet, who would have me praise certain bad poets, imitators of his and mine. William Butler Yeats.—CoPi—PlM
To a primrose. John Clare.—MaFw
To a reviewer who admired my book. See Pencil stubs
To a rogue. Joseph Addison.—CoPu
To a Saxon poet. Jorge Luis Borges, tr. by Norman Thomas di Giovanni.—PlM
To a single shadow without pity. Sam Cornish.—AdPb
To a slow walker and quick eater. Gotthold Ephraim Lessing.—LiWw
To a snow-flake. Francis Thompson.—PaF
To a snowflake.—RoIt
To a snowflake. See To a snow-flake
To a squirrel at Kyle-na-no. William Butler Yeats.—AdP—CoPu—LiLc—RoIt
To a war poet, on teaching him in a new country. D. J. Enright.—PlM
To a waterfowl. William Cullen Bryant.—RoIt
To a woman loved. Unknown, tr. fr. the Otomi by Angel Garibay.—BiI
To a woman who wants darkness and time. Gerald W. Barrax.—AdPb
To a young brother. Maria Jane Jewsbury.—OpOx
"**To** achieve a good life." Unknown, tr. fr. the Spanish.—MoBw
To all sisters. Sonia Sanchez.—AdPb
To an American poet just dead. Richard Wilbur.—PlM
To an oriole. Edgar Fawcett.—RoIt
"**To** Apis the boxer." See On Apis the prizefighter
"**To** assume a cat's asleep." See Half asleep
To Auden on his fiftieth. Richard Eberhart.—PlM
To autumn ("O autumn, laden with fruit, and stained") William Blake.—PaF
To autumn ("Season of mist and mellow fruitfulness") John Keats.—JoA-4—PaF
"**To** be born in the shadow of a mighty oak." See Lu Yün's lament
"**To** be in love." Gwendolyn Brooks.—PeS
"**To** be written after someone who has written." Unknown.—MoBw
To Beachey, 1912. Carl Sandburg.—SaT
"**To** become a chief's favorite." See Song
To Bobby Seale. Lucille Clifton.—AdM—AdPb

To the author of Hesperides and Noble Numbers. Mark Van Doren.—PlM
To the cedar tree. Unknown, tr. fr. the Kwakiutl by Frank Boas.—JoT
To the cuckoo. William Wordsworth.—RoIt
To the four courts, please. James Stephens.—CoPi
To the fringed gentian. William Cullen Bryant.—PaF
To the garden the world. Walt Whitman.—MoG
"**To** the garden the world anew ascending." See To the garden the world
To the ground hog. Kay Winters.—LaM
To the immortal memory of that noble pair, Sir Lucius Cary and Sir Henry Morison, sel. Ben Jonson
The noble nature.—RoIt
"It is not growing like a tree."—CoPu
"**To** the medicine man's house they have led me." Unknown, tr. fr. the Papago.—ClFc
To the memory of my beloved, the author, Mr William Shakespeare: and what he hath left us. Ben Jonson.—PlM (sel.)
To the mound of corpses in the snow. Uri Zvi Greenberg, tr. fr. the Hebrew by A. C. Jacobs.—MeP
To the new annex to the Detroit county jail. Richard W. Thomas.—AdPb
"**To** the prettiest girl in the world." Unknown.—MoBw
To the reader. Charles Baudelaire, tr. fr. the French by Roy Campbell.—MoG
To the river Duddon. Norman Nicholson.—PaP
To the shop. Unknown, tr. fr. the Welsh by Rose Fyleman.—JoA-4
To the terrestial globe. William Schwenck Gilbert.—LiWw
To the virgins, to make much of time. Robert Herrick.—LiS
To the white fiends. Claude McKay.—AdPb
To Theodora. Unknown.—OpOx
To Theon from his son Theon. C. A. Trypanis.—HiN
To Thomas Moore. Lord Byron.—PlM—RoIt
To Vietnam. Charlie Cobb.—AdPb
To W. H. Auden on his fiftieth birthday. Barbara Howes.—PlM
To Wallace Stevens. Daniel Berrigan.—PlM
"**To** you, my purse, and to none other wight." See To my empty purse
The **toad.** Kaye Starbird.—BrM
Toads. See also Frogs; Tree toads
The adventure of Chris. D. McCord.—McAa
As into the garden. A. E. Housman.—CoPt
"Croak, said the toad, I'm hungry, I think." Mother Goose.—TucMgl
A friend in the garden. J. H. Ewing.—OpOx
"Honorable Toad." Issa.—HaW
"I went to the toad that lies under the wall." Mother Goose.—MiMg
"The little red spiders." Unknown.—JoT
"Our Mr Toad." D. McCord.—JoA-4—McS
"Over a stone." K. Kuskin.—KuA
The skunk. A. Noyes.—BrM
The toad. K. Starbird.—BrM
Toadstools. See Mushrooms
The **toaster.** William Jay Smith.—BrM
"**Today.**" See January 3, 1970
"**Today.**" See May 8
"**Today.**" See Teeth
"**Today** in school we planted a tree." See Arbor day
"**Today** oh. Oh today oh. Oh today oh." See Sunday morning song
"**Today** they brought me a message: Wordsworth was dead." See Bells for William Wordsworth
Todd, Barbara Euphan
Sing a song of honey.—PaF
Todhunter, John
Aghadoe.—CoPi
Toe-play poems. See Finger-play poems
Toes
Baby toes. C. Sandburg.—LiLc—SaT
The five toes. Unknown.—JoA-4
Hiding. D. Aldis.—JoA-4
"In the tub we soak our skin." E. N. Horn.—CoPu
Moses. Unknown.—BrM
"Moses supposes his toeses are roses."—EmN
"The pobble who has no toes." E. Lear.—OpOx—UnGb
"**Together** we emerge with our rattles." See Emergence song
"**Toko** Waly my uncle, do you remember those distant nights when my head grew heavy against the patience of your back." See For Koras and Balafong
Tolkien, J. R. R.
The adventures of Tom Bombadil, sel.
Oliphaunt.—LiLc
Oliphaunt. See The adventures of Tom Bombadil
The **toll** taker. Patricia Hubbell.—HoCs
Tolson, Melvin B.
African China.—AdPb
PSI.—AdPb
The sea turtle and the shark.—AdP—AdPb
Tolstoy, Nikita
"Grandma snores."—MoM
"A pretty boat."—MoM
Tom. Aileen Fisher.—FiM
Tom and Joe. David McCord.—McAa
"**Tom** he was a piper's son." Mother Goose.—AlC
"**Tom** loves to be heard." See Tom and Joe
"**Tom** threw Tim three thumb tacks." Unknown.—EmN
"**Tom,** Tom, the piper's son (stole a pig)." Mother Goose.—AlC—JoA-4
"**Tom** was a bad boy." Unknown.—EmN
Tombs. See also Epitaphs
"Ah, are you digging on my grave." T. Hardy.—PlP
Alabama earth. L. Hughes.—HoD
An Arundel tomb. P. Larkin.—ToM

"A pant hunter, pantless, is panting for pants." Unknown.—EmN
"Pat's pa, Pete, poked to the pea patch." Unknown.—EmN
"Peter Piper pick'd a peck of peppers." Mother Goose.—EmN—HoMg—JoA-4
"Peter Prangle." Unknown.—BrM
"Peter Prangle, the prickly prangly pear picker."—EmN
"Prissy up the peach tree." Unknown.—EmN
Rabbit. M. A. Hoberman.—HoLb
"Red leather, yellow leather." Unknown.—EmN
"Robert Rowley rolled a round roll 'round." Unknown.—EmN
"Robert Rutter dreamt a dream." Unknown.—EmN
"Rubber baby-buggy bumpers." Unknown.—EmN
"Rush the washing, Russell." Unknown.—EmN
"A sailor went to sea." Unknown.—EmN
"S and Sh: Sea shells." Unknown.—EmN
The saplings. Unknown.—EmN
"Sarah saw a shot-silk sash shop." Unknown.—EmN
Say, did you say. Unknown.—BrM
Sea horse and sawhorse. X. J. Kennedy.—KeO
"The seething sea ceaseth." Unknown.—EmN
"She says she shall sew a sheet." Unknown.—EmN
"She sells sea shells at the sea shore." Unknown.—EmN
"She sells sea shells on the sea shell shore." Unknown.—EmN
She sells seashells. Unknown.—BrM
"She stood at the door." Unknown.—EmN
"Sheep shouldn't sleep in a shack." Unknown.—EmN
"Shining soldiers." Unknown.—EmN
Shut the shutter. Unknown.—BrM
"Silly Sally swiftly shooed seven silly sheep." Unknown.—EmN
"Sister Susie's sewing shirts for soldiers." Unknown.—EmN
The sitter and the butter and the better batter fritter. D. Lee.—LeA
"Six brave maids sat on six broad beds." Unknown.—EmN
"Six gray geese sat on the grass." Unknown.—EmN
"Six silly sisters selling silk to six sickly seniors." Unknown.—EmN
"Six sleek, slippery seals slipped silently ashore." Unknown.—EmN
"Sixty sticky thumbs." Unknown.—EmN
"So soon, so soon, so soon, said Sam." Unknown.—EmN
"Some shun sunshine." Unknown.—EmN
"Some snuff shop snuff." Unknown.—EmN
Song of the pop-bottlers. M. Bishop.—BrM
"The stripling stranger strayed." Unknown.—EmN
"Sugar sacks should be shaken soundly." Unknown.—EmN
"The sun shines on the shop signs." Unknown.—EmN
"Susan shineth shoes and socks." Unknown.—EmN
"Swan swam over the sea." Unknown.—EmN
"T. Timothy Ticklepitcher." Unknown.—EmN
"Theogenes, the Thessalonian thistle-sifter, sifting thistles." Unknown.—EmN
"Theophilus Thistle, the successful thistle-sifter." Unknown.—EmN
"Theophilus Thistledown, the successful thistle-sifter." Unknown.—EmN
"There's black bug's blood." Unknown.—EmN
"They say shoes and socks." Unknown.—EmN
"This is a zither." Unknown.—EmN
"Three gray geese in the green grass growing." Unknown.—EmN
"Tip top, tangle tongue." Unknown.—EmN
"Tom threw Tim three thumb tacks."—EmN
Tongue twister. D. Lee.—LeA
The tooting tutor. Unknown.—BrM
"A tooter who tooted the flute."—EmN
Toucans two. J. Prelutsky.—BrM—PrT
"Toy boat." Unknown.—EmN
A tree toad. Unknown.—BrM
"Truly rural." Unknown.—EmN
"Twin-screw steel cruisers." Unknown.—EmN
Two legs behind and two before. Unknown.—CoOh
Two witches. A. Resnikoff.—BrM—CoOh
"An undertaker undertook to undertake an undertaking." Unknown.—EmN
"What whim caused Whitney White to whittle." Unknown.—EmN
When a jolly young fisher. Unknown.—BrM
Which switch for Ipswich. Unknown.—BrM
"The wind ceaseth." Unknown.—EmN
"You've no need to light a night light." Unknown.—BrM
Zoo doings. J. Prelutsky.—PrT
"Tongue twisters twist tongues twisted." See My tang's tungled
Tongues
"Awake, arise, pull out your eyes." Mother Goose.—AlC
Can you copy. M. A. Hoberman.—HoR
My tang's tungled. Unknown.—BrM
"Tell tale, tit." Mother Goose.—AlC—EmN
To his little son Benedict from the Tower of London. J. Hoskyns.—OpOx
"Tonight." See Proposition
"Tonight at noon." Adrian Henri.—ToM
"Tonight is the night." See Hallowe'en
"Tonight I've watched." Sappho, tr. fr. the Greek by Mary Barnard.—ThI

"**Tonight** my children hunch." See It out-Herods Herod, pray you, avoid it
"**Tonight** the waves march." See Moonlight night: Carmel
"**Tonight** the wind gnaws." See Christmas landscape
"**Tonight** the winds begin to rise." See In memoriam
"**Tonite,** thriller was." See Beware, do not read this poem
A **tonversation** with baby. Morris Bishop.—LiWw
Tony Baloney. Dennis Lee.—LeA
"**Tony** Baloney is fibbing again." See Tony Baloney
Tony get the boys. D. L. Graham.—AdPb
Tony O. Colin Francis.—CoPu
Tony the turtle. E. V. Rieu.—BrM
"**Tony** was a turtle." See Tony the turtle
"**Too** dense to have a door." See The haystack
"**Too** many of the dead, some I knew well." See In the backs
Too polite. Ian Serraillier.—BrM
Tools
  "I want to laugh, I, because my sledge it is broken." Unknown.—LeIb
  "Long legs, crooked thighs." Mother Goose.—JoA-4
  Look: What am I. D. McCord.—McFm
Toomer, Jean
  Beehive.—AdPb
  Brown river, smile.—AdPb
  Five vignettes.—AdPb
  Georgia dusk.—AdPb
  The lost dancer.—AdPb
  Reapers.—AdPb
  Song of the son.—AdPb
"A **tooter** who tooted the flute." See The tooting tutor
Tooth trouble. David McCord.—McS
The **tooting** tutor. Unknown.—BrM
  "A tooter who tooted the flute."—EmN
"**Top.**" Unknown.—MoBw
"The **top** of the ridge is a cornfield." See Cornfield ridge and stream
Topsyturvey world. William Brighty Rands.—OpOx
Torn down from a glory daily. Anne Sexton.—HaWr
Tornado. William Stafford.—HaWr
"A **torrent.**" See Lacrimas or there is a need to scream
Tortoises. See Turtles
The **total** calm. Philip Booth.—HaWr
"The **tottering** wall has underground thoughts." See The wall
The **toucan.** Shel Silverstein.—SiW
Toucans
  The toucan. S. Silverstein.—SiW
  Toucans two. J. Prelutsky.—BrM—PrT
Toucans two. Jack Prelutsky.—BrM—PrT
Touch
  Touch. T. Gunn.—ToM
  "Touch me not, for I am fragile." P. Solomon.—JoV
Touch. Thom Gunn.—ToM
"**Touch** me not, for I am fragile." Phillip Solomon.—JoV
"**Tough** Captain Spud and his First Mate, Spade." See Captain Spud and his First Mate, Spade
Touré, Askia Muhammad
  Floodtide.—AdPb
  Ju Ju.—AdPb
  Tauhid.—AdPb
"**Touris',** white man, wipin' his face." See Song of the banana man
"A **tourist** came in from Orbitville." See Southbound on the freeway
Tourist time. F. R. Scott.—LiWw
"**Toward** calm and shady places." Unknown, tr. fr. the Chippewa.—ClFc
"**Toward** dawn I came awake hearing a crow." See The answer
"**Towards** the evening of her splendid day." See The fragment
The **tower** of Babel. Nathaniel Crouch.—OpOx
"**Towers.**" See View
"**Towery** city and branchy between towers." See Duns Scotus's Oxford
Towne, Charles Hanson
  The messed damozel.—LiS
Towns. See also Cities and city life; also names of towns, as Jerusalem
  Adlestrop. E. Thomas.—MaFw—PaP
  "Back in my home town." Issa.—BeM
  "Between two hills." C. Sandburg.—SaT
  In a town garden. D. Mattam.—CoPu
  "In Kamloops." D. Lee.—LeA
  Kahshe or Chicoutimi. D. Lee.—LeA
  People. L. Lenski.—HoCs
  Potom-ac town in February. C. Sandburg.—LiLc
  Seven wealthy towns. Unknown.—CoPu
  A time for building. M. C. Livingston.—HoCs
  "We are off to Timbuctoo." Mother Goose.—TucMg
  "Whose town did you leave." R. Wright
    Hokku poems.—AdPb
"**Toy** boat." Unknown.—EmN
Toys. See also Play; also names of toys, as Dolls
  Boating. M. Chute.—ChRu
  Dreidel song. E. Rosenzweig.—LaM
  The empty woman. G. Brooks.—PeS
  George. H. Belloc.—CoOh
  "Koala means the world to her." K. Kuskin.—KuN
  My lost Noah's ark. R. Hoban.—HoE
  My teddy bear. M. Chute.—ChRu
  "My teddy stands in the nook." Olga.—MoM
  "A tiny house." K. Kuskin.—KuN
  Upstairs. C. Sandburg.—SaT
  Us two. A. A. Milne.—OpOx
Tracey, Hugh
  Inspection. tr.—AlPa
  "Keep it dark." tr.—AlPa
  Modern concert song. tr.—AlPa

Song. tr.—AlPa
A Zulu lyric. tr.—AlPa
Tractor. Valerie Worth.—WoS
"The **tractor** rests." See Tractor
Tractors
Cynddylan on a tractor. R. S. Thomas.—ToM
New farm tractor. C. Sandburg.—SaT
Tractor. V. Worth.—WoS
Trades. See Occupations; also names of occupations, as Carpenters and carpentry
Tradja of Norway. Unknown, tr. fr. the Norwegian by Alice Dalgliesh and Ernest Rhys.—JoA-4
Trafalgar Square
London voluntary. W. E. Henley.—PaP
Traffic
City street. L. Lenski.—LeC
"Don't cross the street." L. Lenski.—LeC
Driving. M. C. Livingston.—HoP—LiM
Epitaph. Unknown.—RoIt
Freeway. M. C. Livingston.—LiM
The go-go goons. R. Froman.—FrSp
"J's the jumping Jay-walker." From All around the town. P. McGinley.—BrM
A left-handed poem. E. Merriam.—MeO
Motor cars. R. B. Bennett.—HoP
On a squirrel crossing the road in autumn, in New England. R. Eberhart.—JoA-4—RoIt
Pancho Villa. L. Lipsitz.—HiN
Reason. J. Miles.—HiN
Southbound on the freeway. M. Swenson.—PeS
Street scene. P. Suffolk.—CoPt
Traffic light. S. Silverstein.—SiW
Traffic light. Shel Silverstein.—SiW
"The **traffic** light simply would not turn green." See Traffic light
A **tragic** story. Adelbert von Chamisso, tr. fr. the German by William Makepeace Thackeray.—LiWw
The **tragical** history of Doctor Faustus, sel. Christopher Marlowe
"Ah, Faustus."—MaFw
Traherne, Thomas
Meditation.—RoIt
"**Trail** climbing." See Finding a poem
"The **train.**" Unknown, tr. fr. the Iteso by Gerhard Kubik.—AlPa
"The **train.** A hot July. On either hand." See In the fruitful flat land—Travelling home
Train ride. Dorothy Aldis.—HoP
The **train** runs late to Harlem. Conrad Kent Rivers.—AdPb
Trains. See Railroads
The **trains.** Rosemary Spencer.—HoP
Trains at night. Frances M. Frost.—HoP
Traitors
The renegade. D. Diop.—AlPa
Trajan, Emperor of Rome
To a friend: constructive criticism.—LiWw
Transplanting. Theodore Roethke.—HaWr
Transportation. See also names of modes of transportation, as Railroads
Marsupial transportation. T. Ireland.—BrM
The **trap.** William Beyer.—CoPt
"**Trapped** in a helmet." Bashō, tr. fr. the Japanese by Harry Behn.—BeM
Travel. See also Adventure and adventurers; Ocean; Seamen; Wayfaring life; also names of modes of travel, as Railroads
Airplane trip. B. Katz.—HoP
"Away and ago." D. McCord.—McAa
Beowulf's voyage to Denmark. Unknown.—MaFw (sel.)
"Exultation is the going." E. Dickinson.—ThI
"The first winter rain." Bashō.—AtM
Free will. W. Clark.—HiN
From a railway carriage. R. L. Stevenson.—OpOx
Go north, south, east and west, young man. S. Mulligan.—CoOr
Going somewhere. F. Holman.—HoI
"How many miles to Babylon." Mother Goose.—AlC—JoA-4
"How many miles to Boston town." Unknown.—EmN
"How many miles to Old Norfolk." C. Watson.—WaF
"I go by a Blue Goose bus." Unknown.—EmN
Lament for lost lodgings. P. McGinley.—LiS
The listeners. W. De La Mare.—HiN
The mountains of Mourne. P. French.—CoPi
October journey. M. Walker.—AdPb
Off to Yakima. L. F. Jackson.—BrM
On going to Hohokus (and why I live in New Jersey). J. Ciardi.—CiFs
"Over hill, over dale." From A midsummer night's dream. W. Shakespeare.—JoA-4
The path I must travel. E. B. Mitchell.—AlW
The person from Porlock. R. Graves.—PlM
Preferred vehicles. L. B. Jacobs.—HoP
Safari. M. Ridlon.—HoCs
"Sea way." S. Briody.—HoC—HoP
"Since wild geese flew south." Jo Myung-ri.—BaSs
"Singing through the forests." G. F. Saxe.—RoIt
Sky's nice. S. J. Johnson.—HoP
Song of the banana man. E. Jones.—ToM
"A stairway of light." A. Atwood.—AtM
The star. Jane Taylor.—LiS—OpOx
Subway swinger (going). V. Schonborg.—HoP
The swallow. L. Aikin.—OpOx
"Thomas Thomas Tinkertoes." C. Watson.—WaF
A time to talk. R. Frost.—HiN
To Henrietta, on her departure for Calais. T. Hood.—OpOx
Tourist time. F. R. Scott.—LiWw
Train ride. D. Aldis.—HoP
The trains. R. Spencer.—HoP
The traveling post office. A. B. Patterson.—CoPt
Traveling through the dark. W. Stafford.—CoPt—HiN—MaFw—MoT—PeS
Traveller's curse after misdirection. R. Graves.—HiN—LiWw

"**Trees** are the kindest things I know." See
 Trees
"The **trees** are undressing, and fling in many
 places." See Last week in October
"**Trees** growing, right in front of my window."
 See Pruning trees
"**Trees** in the old days used to stand." See
 Carentan O Carentan
"The **trees** inside are moving out into the
 forest." See The trees
"The **trees**' reflection." Ann Atwood.—AtM
"The **trees** turn." See Leaflight
"The **trees** walked." See Trees
"**Treetalk** and windsong are." See Sugarfields
Trelawny, Sir Johnathan (about)
 Song of the Western men. R. S. Hawker.—
 RoIt
Trench, Herbert
 Jean Richepin's song.—CoPi—CoPt
Trevelyan, R. C.
 Glaramara.—PaP
Trias, Amelia
 "Hot time."—HoC
"**Tribolite**, grapholite, nautilus pie." See Boston
 nursery rhymes—Rhyme for a geological
 baby
Trick or treat. Carson McCullers.—HoH
"**Trick** or treat, trick or treat." See Trick or
 treat
"A **trick** that everyone abhors." See Rebecca,
 who slammed doors for fun and perished
 miserably
Tricking. Dennis Lee.—LeA
Trifles. See Little things, Importance of
Trilles, P.
 Prayer before the dead body. tr.—AlPa
 Song for the sun that disappeared behind the
 rainclouds. tr.—AlPa
Trinity Place ("The grave of Alexander
 Hamilton is in Trinity yard at the end of
 Wall street") Carl Sandburg.—SaT
Trinity Place ("With light enough on clean
 fresh-fallen snow") David McCord.—McAa
Trio. Edwin Morgan.—ToM
Triolet ("I love you, my Lord") Paul T.
 Gilbert.—CoPu
Triolet ("I wish I were a jelly fish") Gilbert
 Keith Chesterton.—LiLc
Triolet against sisters. Phyllis McGinley.—LiWw
Triolets
 "The birds in the feeder." D. McCord
 Two triolets.—McS
 "It's a foggy day." D. McCord
 Two triolets.—McS
 Triolet ("I love you, my Lord") P. T.
 Gilbert.—CoPu
 Triolet ("I wish I were a jelly fish") G. K.
 Chesterton.—LiLc
 Triolet against sisters. P. McGinley.—LiWw
"**Trip** upon trenchers, and dance upon dishes."
 Mother Goose.—AlC
"**Trōchĕe** trĭps frŏm lŏng tŏ shŏrt." See
 Metrical feet
The **troll** bridge. Lilian Moore.—MoSm

Troll trick. B. J. Lee.—JaP
The **tropics** in New York. Claude McKay.—
 AdPb—RoIt
"**Trot**, trot, trot." Mother Goose, tr. fr. the
 German.—TucMg
Troubadours. See Minstrels and troubadours
The **trouble-lover.** Unknown, tr. fr. the Yoruba
 by S. A. Babalola.—AlPa
The **trouble** was simply that. David McCord.—
 McFm
"The **trouble** with a dinosaur." X. J.
 Kennedy.—KeO
Troubled woman. Langston Hughes.—HoD
Troupe, Quincy
 Dirge.—AdPb
 For Malcolm who walks in the eyes of our
 children.—AdPb
 In Texas grass.—AdPb
 Poem for friends.—AdPb
 A sense of coolness.—AdPb
"**Trousers** of wind and buttons of hail." See The
 worthless lover
The **trout.** John Montague.—CoPi
"A **trout** leaps high." Onitsura, tr. fr. the
 Japanese by Harold G. Henderson.—MaFw
Trowbridge, John Townsend
 Darius Green and his flying machine.—OpOx
Trucks
 Baby. L. Hughes.—HoD
 Country trucks. M. Shannon.—HoP
 A fire-truck. R. Wilbur.—HiN
 Greedy. R. Froman.—FrSp
 Mad. R. Froman.—FrSp
 Pancho Villa. L. Lipsitz.—HiN
 A rumble. V. Schonborg.—HoP
 Stop. R. Wilbur.—HaWr
 Trucks. J. S. Tippett.—HoP—JoA-4
 Winter weather. C. Sandburg.—SaT
Trucks. James S. Tippett.—HoP—JoA-4
"**True.**" Karla Kuskin.—KuA
"**True** friends are like diamonds." Unknown.—
 EmN
The **true** import of present dialogue, black vs.
 Negro. Nikki Giovanni.—AdPb
"**True**: nor love or loving is ultimate." See A
 taste of honey
True story. Shel Silverstein.—SiW
True Thomas. Unknown.—CoPt
 Thomas Rymer.—MaFw
"**True** Thomas lay on Huntlie bank." See True
 Thomas
"**True** to your might winds on dusky shores."
 See On the death of William Edward
 Burghardt Du Bois by African moonlight
 and forgotten shores
Truly my own. Vanessa Howard.—JoV
"**Truly** rural." Unknown.—EmN
"**Truly** the light is sweet." See Ecclesiastes—
 The light is sweet
Trumpets
 From jazz for five. J. Smith.—ToM (sel.)
 How high the moon. L. Jeffers.—AdPb
 Where shall I be. Unknown.—BrW
The **truth.** Ted Joans.—AdB

"The **truth** I do not stretch or shove." See The dog
The **truth** is quite messy. William J. Harris.—AdB
Truth the best. Elizabeth Turner.—OpOx
Truthfulness and falsehood
He thinks of those who have spoken evil of his beloved. W. B. Yeats.—CoPi
"Liar, liar." Unknown.—EmN
Lying. T. Moore.—CoPi
Lying on things. D. Lee.—LeA
Matilda, who told lies, and was burned to death. H. Belloc.—CoPt—OpOx
Mendax. Unknown.—CoPu
My ace of spades. T. Joans.—AdB
A nautical extravaganza. W. Irwin.—CoPt
"No matter how he ties." S. Aleksandrovsky.—MoM
Tony Baloney. D. Lee.—LeA
True story. S. Silverstein.—SiW
True Thomas. Unknown.—CoPt
Thomas Rymer.—MaFw
The truth. T. Joans.—AdB
The truth is quite messy. W. J. Harris.—AdB
Truth the best. E. Turner.—OpOx
Who. S. Silverstein.—SiW
"**Try** as you may to banish from your mind." See The death of Keats
Trypanis, C. A.
To Theon from his son Theon.—HiN
Tsaro-Wiwa Ken
Night encounter.—AlPa
Voices.—AlPa
Tsimshian Indians. See Indians of the Americas—Tsimshian
Tsuboi Shigeji
Silent, but. . . . —MaFw
Tsumori Kunimoto
"The wild geese returning."—AdP
Tsyganok, Tanya
Something peaceful.—MoM
Ttimba. Unknown, tr. fr. the Luganda by W. Moses Serwadda.—SeS
Tu Fu
South wind.—MaFw
To Pi Ssu Yao.—PlM
Tubman, Harriet (about)
Cross over the river. S. Cornish.—AdM
Tuesday all day: Rain. Lucille Clifton.—ClS
Tugs. James S. Tippett.—HoP
Tule Indians. See Indians of the Americas—Tule
"The **tumblers** of the rapids go white, go green." See The people, yes—Niagara
Tumbleweed. Ramona Carden.—AlW
Tumbleweeds
Tumbleweed. R. Carden.—AlW
Tumbling. Unknown.—OpOx
Tuning up. Felice Holman.—HoI
Tupi Indians. See Indians of the Americas—Tupi
Turkeys
A black November turkey. R. Wilbur.—HiN
Perfection. F. Holman.—HoI
Point of view. S. Silverstein.—SiW
The skeleton walks. X. J. Kennedy.—KeO
Turkeys observed. S. Heaney.—MaFw
"Widdy widdy wurkey." Mother Goose.—TucMg
Turkeys observed. Seamus Heaney.—MaFw
"**Turn** to the next page and see a man." Unknown.—MoBw
Turner, Charles Tennyson
Julius Caesar and the honey-bee.—RoIt
Turner, Elizabeth
The canary.—OpOx
How to write a letter.—OpOx
Truth the best.—OpOx
The two little Miss Lloyds.—OpOx
Turner, Nancy Byrd
First Thanksgiving of all.—RoIt
"Old Quin Queeribus."—BrM
Turner, Nat (about)
Remembering Nat Turner. S. A. Brown.—AdPb
Turner, W. (Walter) J. (James)
Silence.—PaF
"**Turning** and turning in the widening gyre." See The second coming
Turnips
"If a man who turnips cries." S. Johnson.—MiMg
"My aunt kept turnips in a flock." R. Jarrell.—LiWw
Peter Rabbit. D. Lee.—LeA
Turtle ("This turtle moved his house across the street") David McCord.—McFm
The **turtle** ("The turtle's always been inclined") Jack Prelutsky.—PrT
Turtle soup. See Alice's adventures in wonderland
Turtles
The bagpipe who didn't say no. S. Silverstein.—SiW
The emancipation of George Hector. M. Evans.—AbM
The giant tortoise. E. Lucie-Smith.—CoPu
"The house of snail upon his back." K. Kuskin.—KuN
"In the beginning there was no earth." N. Belting.—BeWi
The little turtle. V. Lindsay.—LiLc—RoIt
Living tenderly. M. Swenson.—AdP
Over the water. Unknown.—BiI
The sea turtle and the shark. M. B. Tolson.—AdP—AdPb
"Snee A-P snap." Unknown.—EmN
Tony the turtle. E. V. Rieu.—BrM
Turtle ("This turtle moved his house across the street") D. McCord.—McFm
The turtle ("The turtle's always been inclined") J. Prelutsky.—PrT
Turtle soup. From Alice's adventures in wonderland. L. Carroll.—LiPc—LiS
Who am I (II). M. A. Hoberman.—HoLb
"The **turtle's** always been inclined." See The turtle

Tusiani, Joseph
The little animal.—RoIt
"The **tusks** that clashed in mighty brawls." See On the vanity of earthly greatness
Tutankh-Amen, King of Egypt (about)
"King Tut." X. J. Kennedy.—KeO—LiWw
The **twa** corbies. Unknown.—CoPt—MaFw
"'**Twas** a Friday morn when we set sail." See The mermaid
"'**Twas** Euclid, and the theorem pi." See Plane geometry
"'**Twas** ever thus." Henry Sambrooke Leigh.—LiS
"'**Twas** ever thus from childhood's hour." See Disaster
"'**Twas** in heaven pronounced and 'twas muttered in hell." See A riddle
"'**Twas** in the middle of the night." See Mary's ghost
"'**Twas** in the moon of winter-time when all the birds had fled." See The Huron Indian carol
"'**Twas** just behind the woodshed." See My first cigar
"'**Twas** midnight in the schoolroom." See The A B C
"'**Twas** more than a million years ago." See Annabel Lee
"'**Twas** on the shores that round our coast." See The yarn of the Nancy Bell
"'**Twas** out in California in the days of forty-nine." See How Bill went East
"'**Twas** sung of old in hut and hall." See Birthday verses written in a child's album
"'**Twas** the first day of the springtime." See Snowman
"'**Twas** the night before Christmas, when all through the house." See A visit from St Nicholas
"**Tweedle-dum** and Tweedle-dee." Mother Goose.—AlC
Twelfth night
"Now, now the mirth comes." R. Herrick.—MaF
Twelfth night. Unknown.—JoA-4
Twelfth night carol. Unknown.—RoIt
Twelfth night, sel. William Shakespeare
Sweet-and-twenty.—MoG
Twelfth night. Unknown, tr. fr. the Italian by Rose Fyleman.—JoA-4
Twelfth night carol. Unknown.—RoIt
Twelve articles. Jonathan Swift.—LiWw
The **twelve** days of Christmas. Mother Goose.—JoA-4
12 gates to the city. Nikki Giovanni.—AdPb
"**Twelve** hundred million men are spread." Rudyard Kipling.—CoPu
"**Twelve** huntsmen with horns and hounds." Mother Goose.—AlC
"**Twelve** o'clock—a misty night." See The highwayman's ghost
12 October. Myra Cohn Livingston.—LiM
"**Twelve** pears hanging high." Unknown.—EmN
"**Twelve** stories high." See Home in the sky
Twerüre. Unknown, tr. fr. the Luganda by W. Moses Serwadda.—SeS
Twice shy. Seamus Heaney.—HiN
Twilight at the zoo. Alex Rodger.—HiN
"**Twilight** glitters on the fragmented glass." See Judeebug's country
Twilight piece. Chaim Nachman Bialik, tr. fr. the Hebrew by Robert Friend.—MeP
Twilight's feet. Agnes T. Pratt.—AlW
Twin lakes hunter. A. B. Guthrie, Jr.—CoPt
"**Twin-screw** steel cruiser." Unknown.—EmN
"**Twinkle,** twinkle, little bat." See Alice's adventures in wonderland—The mad hatter's song
"**Twinkle,** twinkle, little star." See The star
"**Twinkle,** twinkle, little star." Paul Dehn.—LiS
Twins
Betwixt and Between. H. Lofting.—BrM
"Here are the twins." S. Silverstein.—CoOh
Twins ("Here's a baby. Here's another") L. F. Perkins.—CoOr
The twins ("In form and feature, face and limb") H. S. Leigh.—BrM—RoIt
The two little Miss Lloyds. E. Turner.—OpOx
Twins ("Here's a baby. Here's another") Lucy Fitch Perkins.—CoOr
The **twins** ("In form and feature, face and limb") Henry Sambrooke Leigh.—BrM—RoIt
"**Twirl** about, dance about." See Dreidel song
"**Twirling** your blue skirts, travelling the sward." See Blue girls
The **twist.** Edward Brathwaite.—AbM
"**Twist** me a crown of windflowers." See A crown of windflowers
"**Twitching** in the cactus." See Deathwatch
"**2** and 2 are 4." Unknown.—EmN
"**2** big U R." Unknown.—EmN
"**Two** black heifers and a red." See Drinking time
Two boxes. Shel Silverstein.—SiW
"**Two** boxes met upon the road." See Two boxes
"**Two** boys uncoached are tossing a poem together." See Catch
"**Two** brothers we are." Unknown.—EmN
"**Two** bubbles found they had rainbows on their curves." See Bubbles
"**Two** cats were sitting in a tree." Unknown, tr. fr. the Danish by N. M. Bodecker.—BoI
"**Two** days." Michael De Veaux.—HoC
Two dedications. Gwendolyn Brooks.—AdPb (sel.)
"**2** good." Unknown.—MoBw
"**Two** heads I have, and when my voice." Unknown.—EmN
"The **two-horned** black rhinoceros." Jack Prelutsky.—PrP
"**Two** horses race into the ring." Jack Prelutsky.—PrC
"**Two** hundred lines a day." Martial, tr. fr. the Latin by Rolfe Humphries.—PlM
224 stoop. Victor Hernandez Cruz.—AdB

"**Two** hundred twenty thousand, five hundred twenty-three." See We all have thought a lot about you
Two lean cats. Myron O'Higgins.—AdPb
Two legs behind and two before. Unknown.—CoOh
"**Two** legs sat on three legs." Mother Goose.—JoA-4
"**Two** little clouds one April day." See April
Two little kittens. Unknown.—OpOx
"**Two** little kittens, one stormy night." See Two little kittens
"**Two** little mice went tripping down the street." See Well, I never
The **two** little Miss Lloyds. Elizabeth Turner.—OpOx
"**Two** lookers." Unknown.—EmN
Two men. Edwin Arlington Robinson.—LiWw
"The **two** Miss Lloyds were twins, and dressed." See The two little Miss Lloyds
Two mornings. Lawrence McGaugh.—AdPb
Two mothers. Ira Sheyanova, tr. fr. the Russian by Miriam Morton.—MoM
"**Two** n's, two o's, an l, and a d." Unknown.—EmN
"**Two** roads diverged in a yellow wood." See The road not taken
Two-room flat. Lois Lenski.—LeC
Two sad tales. Unknown.—CoOh
"**2** skinny." Unknown.—MoBw
Two songs, sels. Edith Sitwell.—JoA-4
"The clouds are bunched roses"
"In summer when the rose-bushes"
Two Spanish gypsy lullabies. Unknown.—MaFw
"**Two** statesmen met by moonlight." See What the moon saw
"**Two** things fly in the dark of the night." See Night travel
The **two** travellers. C. J. Boland.—CoPi
"**Two** voices are there: one is of the deep." See A sonnet on Wordsworth
"**Two** voices are there; one is of the sea." See Thought of a Briton on the subjugation of Switzerland, 1807-1807
Two voices in a meadow. Richard Wilbur.—PeS
Two witches. Alexander Resnikoff.—BrM—CoOh
"'**Twould** ring the bells of Heaven." See The bells of Heaven
Tynan, Katharine (Katharine Tynan Hinkson)
August weather.—PaF
Slow spring.—PaF
Winter.—PaF
Tyson's corner. Primus St John.—AdPb

U

"**U** bet u wer." See To a poet I knew
U name this one. Carolyn M. Rodgers.—AdPb
"**U** R 2 good." Unknown.—EmN
U Tam'si, Tchicaya
The belly remains.—AlPa (sel.)
Bow harp.—AlPa
Cradlesong.—AlPa (sel.)
Marine nocturne.—AlPa
Obolus.—AlPa (sel.)
Uejima Onitsura. See Onitsura
UFOs
Unidentified flying object. R. Hayden.—HiN
Ugliness
Disgrace. Unknown.—AbM
An old woman. C. H. Ross.—OpOx
Uhrman, Celia
The plane.—HoP
Ukachev, Sasha
A thought.—MoM
Ukraine
The grave. S. Tchernichovsky.—MeP
Ulivfak's song of the caribou. Unknown, fr. Caribou Eskimo.—LeIb
Ultima ratio regum. Stephen Spender.—PeS—ToM
Ulysses (about)
Odysseus. C. Guri.—MeP
Tales of brave Ulysses. E. Clapton and M. Sharp.—MoG
Umamina. B. W. Vilakazi, tr. by R. M. Mfeka and ad. by Peggy Rutherfoord.—AlPa (sel.)
Umbilical. Eve Merriam.—MeF
The **umbrella** brigade. Laura E. Richards.—JoA-4
Umbrellas
The elf and the dormouse. O. Herford.—JaP—UnGb
The gingham umbrella. L. E. Richards.—CoOr
"I left home without my umbrella." Kim Jae.—BaSs
"In the storm of life you may need an umbrella." Unknown.—EmN
Little snail. H. Conkling.—JoA-4
"The rain it raineth." Lord Bowen.—CoPu—LiWw
The rain.—RoIt
"Slanting, windy rain. . . . " Buson.—BeM
The story of Flying Robert. H. Hoffman.—LiS
Sudden storm. E. J. Coatsworth.—HoCs
Tuesday all day: Rain. L. Clifton.—ClS
The umbrella brigade. L. E. Richards.—JoA-4
The **umpire.** Walker Gibson.—FlH
"**Un,** deux, trois, j'irai dans le bois." Mother Goose.—JoA-4
Uncle. Harry Graham.—CoOr
Uncle Bull-boy. June Jordan.—AdPb
Uncle Death. Walter Clark.—HiN
Uncle Roderick. Norman MacCaig.—ToM
Uncle Simon and Uncle Jim. Artemus Ward.—BrM
"**Uncle** Simon he." See Uncle Simon and Uncle Jim
"**Uncle,** whose inventive brains." See Uncle
Uncles
Bobby's first poem. N. Gale.—CoPu
Giant snail. X. J. Kennedy.—KeO
Incidents in the life of my Uncle Arly. E. Lear.—LiWw—RoIt

I've got a home in that rock. R. R. Patterson.—AdM—AdPb
My Uncle Dan. T. Hughes.—CoOh—HuMf
My Uncle Jehoshaphat. L. E. Richards.—OpOx
My Uncle Mick. T. Hughes.—HuMf
"Nobody loses all the time." E. E. Cummings.—LiWw—MaFw
On Tuesdays I polish my uncle. D. Lee.—LeA
Uncle. H. Graham.—CoOr
Uncle Roderick. N. MacCaig.—ToM
Uncle Simon and Uncle Jim. A. Ward.—BrM
"Uncles are brothers to fathers." M. A. Hoberman.—HoN
Waking up uncle. X. J. Kennedy.—KeO
"**Uncles** are brothers to fathers." Mary Ann Hoberman.—HoN
Undefeated. Robert Froman.—FrSp
Under a hat rim. Carl Sandburg.—SaT
"**Under** a maple tree." See Dog
"**Under** a small, cold." Ransetsu, tr. fr. the Japanese by Harry Behn.—BeM
"**Under** a splintered mast." See A talisman
"**Under** a spring mist." Teitoku, tr. fr. the Japanese by Harry Behn.—BeM
"**Under** a toadstool." See The elf and the dormouse
Under Ben Bulben. William Butler Yeats.—PlM (sel.)
Under Milk Wood, sel. Dylan Thomas
"Johnnie Crack and Flossie Snail."—LiLc
"**Under** my window." See Letter in winter
"**Under** the bubbles." See The fishes of Kempenfelt bay
"**Under** the dark is a star." See Sleeping outdoors
"**Under** the field." See An old man's herd—On the Friday before Christmas
Under the goal posts. Arthur Guiterman.—FlH
"**Under** the greenwood tree." See As you like it
"**Under** the hot lights." See Hockey
"**Under** the rabbit there, I saw a tree." See Mr Mixup tells a story
"**Under** the sun." See Song of the rain
Under the white pine. David McCord.—McFm
"**Under** the wide and starry sky." See Requiem
"**Under** the willow." Issa, tr. fr. the Japanese by Lewis Mackenzie.—MaFw
"**Under** this stone, reader, survey." See On Sir John Vanbrugh, architect
Underground rumbling. James S. Tippett.—HoP
Underhill, Ruth
Come all. tr.—BiI
"In the night." tr.—BiI
Song of encouragement. tr.—BiI
Song of the deer. tr.—BiI
Song of the hunter. tr.—BiI
"**Underneath** the tree on some." See Like they say
"**Understand** too late? Of course we can." See Poem for Gerard
"An **undertaker** undertook to undertake an undertaking." Unknown.—EmN
Underwood, Edna Worthley
Evening in Haiti. tr.—AbM
Phantoms of the steppe. tr.—AbM
"**Une** fill' a batty." Mother Goose.—JoA-4
Unearned increment. Christopher Morley.—LiWw
The **unending** sky. John Masefield.—MaFw
The **unfortunate** grocer. Laura E. Richards.—CoOr
The **unfortunate** miller. A. E. Coppard.—CoPt
"**Unhappy** country, what wings you have. Even here." See Eagle valor, chicken mind
The **unhappy** schoolboy. Unknown.—OpOx
The **unicorn.** Shel Silverstein.—SiW
Unicorns
"The lion and the unicorn." Mother Goose.—AlC—JoA-4
The unicorn. S. Silverstein.—SiW
Unidentified flying object. Robert Hayden.—HiN
United States. See also America; also names of states, as New Hampshire
I hear America singing. W. Whitman.—RoIt
I, too. L. Hughes.—HoD—RoIt
"I, too, sing America."—AdPb
Islands in Boston harbor. D. McCord.—McFm
United States—History. See also America; Frontier and pioneer life; Indians of the Americas
Atlantic Charter. From The island: 1620-1942. F. B. Young.—JoA-4
United States—History—Civil war
Battle-hymn of the Republic. J. W. Howe.—RoIt
The blue and the gray. F. M. Finch.—RoIt
Kentucky Belle. C. F. Woolson.—CoPt
October 16: The raid. L. Hughes.—AdB—AdPb
United States—History—Modern
Lines. H. Martin.—AdPb
United States—History—Reconstruction
An old woman remembers. S. A. Brown.—AdPb
United States—History—Revolution
"Yankee Doodle went to town." Unknown.—JoA-4
United States—History—Vietnamese war
A bummer. M. Casey.—MoT
The children of Vietnam. O. Teitelman.—MoM
Containing communism. C. Cobb.—AdPb
Counting small-boned bodies. R. Bly.—MoT
Gods in Vietnam. E. Redmond.—AdPb
Junglegrave. S. E. Anderson.—AdPb
A Negro soldier's Viet Nam diary. H. Martin.—AdPb
Photographs: A vision of massacre. M. S. Harper.—AdPb
To Vietnam. C. Cobb.—AdPb
Vietnam. C. Major.—AdPb
Vietnam #4. C. Major.—AdB—AdPb

Universe. See World
"**Unkind** fate sent the Porlock person." See The person from Porlock
The **Unknown** Citizen. W. H. Auden.—PeS
Unknown shores. D. M. Thomas.—ToM
"**unmooooooooooooinng.**" See The stuck horn
Unseen fire. R. N. Currey.—ToM
Unselfishness. Harry Graham.—CoOr
Untermeyer, Louis
  Caliban in the coal mines.—PeS
  Last words before winter.—JoA-4
  Questions at night.—UnGb
  Swimmers.—JoA-4 (sel.)
"**Unthrifty** loveliness, why dost thou spend." See Unthrifty loveliness (Sonnet IV)
Until then. Phil George.—AlW
Until they have stopped. Sarah E. Wright.—AdPb
"**Until** they have stopped glutting me with slop from." See Until they have stopped
Untitled ("Go, my child") Alonzo Lopez.—AlW
Untitled ("I've built myself a stairway") Agnes T. Pratt.—AlW
Untitled requiem for tomorrow. Conyus.—AdPb
"**Unto** the death gois all Estatis." See Lament for the makers
Unusual shoelaces. X. J. Kennedy.—KeO
"**Unwarned** by any sunset light." See Snow-bound—Lines from Snow-bound
"**Unwinding** the spool of the morning." See Invocation
Up and down. N. M. Bodecker.—BoL
"**Up** and down Pie street." Mother Goose.—AlC
"**Up** and down the city road." See Pop goes the weasel
Up from down under. David McCord.—JoA-4
"**Up** he is, at the break of dawn." See The leprechaun
"**Up** in the attic row on row." See Stark boughs on the family tree
"**Up** in the mountains, it's lonesome all the time." See The mountain whippoorwill
"**Up** on the penthouse roof." See Penthouse
"**Up** rose the sun again, again the sun set." See Twilight piece
"**Up** stairs." See Up and down
"**Up** the airy mountain." See The fairies
"**Up** the ladder, down the ladder." Unknown.—EmN
"**Up** the river." Unknown.—MoBw
"**Up** there at the window." See Two-room flat
"**Up** three." See Public library
"**Up,** up, ye dames, and lasses gay." See Hunting song
"**Up** where the world grows cold." See A North Pole story
An **upbraiding.** Thomas Hardy.—PlP
Updike, John
  Bendix.—PeS
  Hoeing.—MoT
  May.—JoA-4
  Mosquito.—MaFw
  October.—JoA-4
  Sonic boom.—PeS
  Suburban madrigal.—PeS
  Summer: West Side.—PeS
  Telephone poles.—MaFw
  Thoughts while driving home.—PeS
  Wash.—MoT
  Winter ocean.—CoPu
"The **upland** farmers have all gone." See Above Penmaenmawr
Upon a snail. John Bunyan.—OpOx
Upon an image from Dante. Sacheverell Sitwell.—PaP
Upon boys diverting themselves in the river. Thomas Foxton.—OpOx
Upon his Julia. Robert Herrick.—LiS
Upon Julia's clothes. Robert Herrick.—LiS
Upon leaving the parole board hearing. Conyus.—AdPb
"**Upon** the hill there is a mill." Unknown.—EmN
Upon the horse and his rider. John Bunyan.—OpOx
Upon the swallow. John Bunyan.—OpOx
Upon the weathercock. John Bunyan.—OpOx
"**Upon** this cake of ice is perched." See The puffin
Upright. Robert Froman.—FrSp
"**(Ups)** Earth July 1975." See Wooden ships
Upstairs ("I too have a garret of old playthings") Carl Sandburg.—SaT
Upstairs ("There's a family of wrens who live upstairs") Shel Silverstein.—SiW
"**Upstairs** on the third floor." See Bottled: New York
"**Upstood** upstaffed." See Christophe
"**Upton** Weller." See Mr Weller
"**Uptown,** downtown." Clyde Watson.—WaF
"**Uptown** on Lenox avenue." See Prime
Upward going. Unknown, tr. fr. the Tewa by Herbert J. Spinder.—BiI
Urban renewal. See also Cities and city life
  "High-rise project." L. Lenski.—LeC
  Rehabilitation. L. Lenski.—LeC
  Urban renewal. L. Lenski.—LeC
Urban renewal. Lois Lenski.—LeC
Urbanity. Eve Merriam.—MeF
Uriconium. James Reeves.—JoA-4
Us ("For so long") Julius Lester.—AdPb
Us ("Me and him") Shel Silverstein.—SiW
Us two. A. A. Milne.—OpOx
Utah
  Utah. A. Stevenson.—HiN
Utah. Anne Stevenson.—HiN
Ute-Navajo Indians. See Indians of the Americas—Ute-Navajo
Utitraq's song. Unknown, fr. Baffin island.—LeIb
Utopia
  Tony O. C. Francis.—CoPu

V

"**Vacant** lot full of." See Humbleweeds
Vacation
Leavetaking. E. Merriam.—LaM
Vacation. F. Holman.—HoI
"Vacation, vacation." Unknown.—MoBw
Vacation. Felice Holman.—HoI
"**Vacation** is over." See Leavetaking
"**Vacation,** vacation." Unknown.—MoBw
A **vagabond** song. Bliss Carman.—RoIt
Vagabonds. See Gipsies
"The **vagrant** visitor erstwhile." See Out into Essex
Valentine ("I got a valentine from Timmy") Shel Silverstein.—LaM
Valentine ("I'll make a card for my valentine") Marchette Chute.—ChRu
A **valentine** for a lady. Lucilius, tr. fr. the Roman by Dudley Fitts.—LiWw
Valentine, Saint. See Saint Valentine's day
Valentines. See Saint Valentine's day
"**Valentines,** I like them fine." M. A. Hoberman.—HoN
"**Valley** floors." See A collage for Richard Davis—two short forms
The **valley** of men. Uri Zvi Greenberg, tr. fr. the Hebrew by Robert Mezey and Ben Zion Gold.—MeP
Valley song. Carl Sandburg.—SaT
"The **valley** was swept with a blue broom to the west." See Santa Fe sketch
Van Doren, Mark
"The child at winter sunset."—HiN
"The fields of November."—HaWr
The first snow of the year.—HiN
King wind.—HiN
Only for me.—HiN
Single majesty.—RoIt
Spring thunder.—HaWr
Thomas Hardy, poet.—PlM
To the author of Hesperides and Noble Numbers.—PlM
Will you, won't you.—HiN
Van Doren, Mark (about)
A ballad of remembrance. R. Hayden.—AdPb
Vanity. See Pride and vanity
"**Vanity,** saith the preacher, vanity." See The bishop orders his tomb at Saint Praxed's church
Vapor trail reflected in the frog pond. Galway Kinnell.—PeS
Variation on a sentence. Louise Bogan.—RoIt
Variations on a theme by William Carlos Williams. Kenneth Koch.—LiS
Vasko, Popa
Donkey.—MoT
Vaticide. Myron O'Higgins.—AdPb
Vaughan, Henry
The morning watch. See The Silex Scintillans
The shower.—CoPu—MaFw
The Silex Scintillans, sel.
The morning watch.—MoG
A **vegetable,** I will not be. Donna Whitewing.—AlW
Vegetables. See also Gardens and gardening; also names of vegetables, as Potatoes
Akanyonyi. Unknown.—SeS
"Do you carrot all for me." Unknown.—EmN
Green with envy. E. Merriam.—MeO
"Pat's pa, Pete, poked to the pea patch." Unknown.—EmN
"Peter Piper picked a peck of pickled peppers." Mother Goose.—EmN—HoMg—JoA-4
Raw carrots. V. Worth.—WoS
A vegetable, I will not be. D. Whitewing.—AlW
Vegetables. S. Silverstein.—CoOr
The watercress seller. T. Miller.—OpOx
Vegetables. Shel Silverstein.—CoOr
Vegetarians
Natural history. W. J. Smith.—LiWw
Velez, Isabel
Children are slaves.—JoV
If I were president.—JoV
Velvet shoes. Elinor Wylie.—AdP—PaF—RoIt
Venders. See Peddlers and venders
"**Venerable** mother toothache." See A charm against toothache
"**Vera** had a little light." Unknown.—EmN
Vermont
Indian summer: Vermont. A. Stevenson.—HiN
On being chosen poet of Vermont. R. Frost.—PlM
Vern. Gwendolyn Brooks.—HoCs
Vernal sentiment. Theodore Roethke.—CoPu
Verse written in the album of mademoiselle. Pierre Dalcour, tr. fr. the Creole by Langston Hughes.—AbM
Verses. William Cowper.—RoIt
Verses expressing the feelings of a lover. Juana Inez De la Cruz, tr. fr. the Mexican by Judith Thurman.—ThI (sel.)
Very much afraid. Unknown, ad. by John Bierhorst from the collections of Francis Densmore.—BiS
A **very** odd fish. D'Arcy Wentworth Thompson.—OpOx
"**Very** old are the woods." See All that's past
"A **very** West-of-Wessex girl." See The West-of-Wessex girl
Vesey, Paul. See Allen, Samuel
Vespers. A. A. Milne.—LiS—OpOx
The **vesture** of the soul. George William Russell.—CoPi
Vet's rehabilitation. Ray Durem.—AdPb
Vicars
"An indolent vicar of Bray." Unknown.—RoIt
The poet of Bray. J. Heath-Stubbs.—PlM
Vice versa verse. Mary Ann Hoberman.—HoLb
Victory
Conquerors. H. Treece.—ToM
Overheard in the Louvre. X. J. Kennedy.—LiWw
They will appear. Unknown.—BiI

Voth, H. R.
"The day has risen." tr.—BiI
"There." tr.—BiI
Voyages. See Adventure and adventurers; Seamen; Travel
The **vulture** ("The vulture eats between his meals") Hilaire Belloc.—OpOx
Vulture ("The vulture's very like a sack") X. J. Kennedy.—KeO
"The **vulture** eats between his meals." See The vulture
Vultures
The vulture ("The vulture eats between his meals") H. Belloc.—OpOx
Vulture ("The vulture's very like a sack") X. J. Kennedy.—KeO
"The **vulture's** very like a sack." See Vulture

W

W., T. S.
Hints on pronunciation for foreigners.—MaFw
W. W. LeRoi Jones.—AdPb
Wabanaki Indians. See Indians of the Americas—Wabanaki
Wagner, Charles A.
Theatre mouse.—RoIt
Wagner, Günter
Prayer of warriors. tr.—AlPa
Wagner, Joel
"Baseball."—HoC
Wagoner, David
Staying alive.—MoT
The words.—MoT
"A **wagonload** of radishes on a summer morning." See Prairie—Summer morning
Wags and purrs. Aileen Fisher.—FiM
Wailing song. Unknown, tr. fr. the Fox by Truman Michelson.—BiI
Wain, John
Au jardin des plantes.—MaFw
Waiting
Day before Christmas. M. Chute.—HoS—LaM
The gathering time. D. Whitewing.—AlW
"I am waiting." M. Goode.—JoV
To a lady in a phone booth. P. McGinley.—LiWw
Waiting ("Dreaming of honeycombs to share") H. Behn.—JoA-4
Waiting ("Fireplug") R. Froman.—FrSp
Waiting ("Hurry, say the voices") A. Fisher.—FiFo
Waiting ("I wait with a pencil in my hand") J. Kirkup.—MaFw
Waiting both. T. Hardy.—PlP
Waiting ("Dreaming of honeycombs to share") Harry Behn.—JoA-4
Waiting ("Fireplug") Robert Froman.—FrSp
Waiting ("Hurry, say the voices") Aileen Fisher.—FiFo
Waiting ("I wait with a pencil in my hand") James Kirkup.—MaFw
"**Waiting** at night for her where once she came." See The Muse
Waiting both. Thomas Hardy.—PlP
Wake, Clive
Defiance against force. tr.—AlPa
—See also Reed, John, jt. auth.
"**Wake.**" See Snowy morning
"**Wake** ev'ry breath." William Billings.—LaS
"**Wake:** the silver dusk returning." See A Shropshire lad—Reveille
Wake-up niggers. Don L. Lee.—AdPb
"**Wake** up, O world; O world, awake." See The lost zoo—The wakeupworld
Wake-up poems. See also Morning
"Awake, arise, pull out your eyes." Mother Goose.—AlC
"Bums, on waking." J. Dickey.—MoT
Corinna's going a-Maying. R. Herrick.—MaF
Get up, get up. Unknown.—CoPu
Janet waking. J. C. Ransom.—HiN—PeS
A morning song. From Cymbeline. W. Shakespeare.—JoA-4
Reveille. From A Shropshire lad. A. E. Housman.—RoIt
Ripeness. R. Whitman.—MoT
Sister awake. T. Bateman.—MaF
"Softly, drowsily. From A child's day. W. De La Mare.—JoA-4
Time to rise. R. L. Stevenson.—OpOx
The wakeupworld. From The lost zoo. C. Cullen.—JoA-4
Waking. A. Higgins.—CoPu
The wrong start. M. Chute.—ChRu
Wakerfield, Samuel
All hail to the morning.—LaS
The **wakeupworld.** See The lost zoo
Waking ("I said to myself one morning") Anne Higgins.—CoPu
The **waking** ("I strolled across") Theodore Roethke.—JoA-4
Waking up uncle. X. J. Kennedy.—KeO
Waldrop, Keith
Dog with schoolboys. tr.—CoPu
Wales
Wales. N. Nicholson.—PaP
Welsh landscape. R. S. Thomas.—ToM
The whales of Wales. X. J. Kennedy.—KeO
Wales. Norman Nicholson.—PaP
"**Wales** England wed; so I was bred. 'Twas merry London gave me breath." See An autobiography
Waley, Arthur
The eastern gate. tr.—MaFw
Fighting south of the ramparts. tr.—MaFw
Getting up early on a spring morning. tr.—MaFw
The herdboy. tr.—MaFw
Hot cakes. tr.—MaFw
In the mountains on a summer day. tr.—MaFw
The little cart. tr.—MaFw

War songs, sels. Unknown, tr. fr. the Chippewa by H. R. Schoolcraft.—BiI
"From the place of the south"
"I cast it away"
"On the front part of the earth"
"**War** war." See April 4, 1968
"**Warbler,** wipe your feet." Issa, tr. fr. the Japanese by Harry Behn.—BeM
Ward, Artemus
Uncle Simon and Uncle Jim.—BrM
"The **warm** of heart shall never lack a fire." Elizabeth Jane Coatsworth.—CoPu
"The **warm** sun gone now." See Rain in the city
"The **warm** sun is failing, the bleak wind is wailing." See Autumn
Warning ("Inside everybody's nose") Shel Silverstein.—SiW
Warning ("When I am an old woman I shall wear purple") Jenny Joseph.—ToM
Warning to children. Robert Graves.—MaFw
Warnings
Alarm. D. McCord.—McAa
Beware. L. Blair.—JaP
"Crow Indian." Unknown.—ClFc
Punta De Los Lobos Marinos. M. C. Livingston.—LiM
Warning ("Inside everybody's nose") S. Silverstein.—SiW
Warning ("When I am an old woman I shall wear purple") J. Joseph.—ToM
Warning to children. R. Graves.—MaFw
The **warrior** bards. Henry Treece.—PlM
Warships. See also Naval battles
The Armada, 1588. J. Wilson.—OpOx
I've got to know. W. Guthrie.—PeS
Old Ironsides. O. W. Holmes.—RoIt
Was a man. Philip Booth.—HiN
"**Was** a man, was a two——." See Was a man
"**Was** I clever enough? Was I charming." See Thoughts while driving home
"**Was** I surprised." See Uncle Death
"**Was** it a little baby." See A tonversation with baby
"**Was** it the proud full sail of his great verse." See Sonnets. William Shakespeare
Wash. John Updike.—MoT
"The **wash** is hanging on the line." See Windy wash day
Washed in silver. James Stephens.—RoIt
"**Washing** on the line." See Dance
Washing windows. Barry Spacks.—HiN
Washington, Booker T. (about)
Alabama earth. L. Hughes.—HoD
Booker T. and W. E. B. D. Randall.—AbM
Washington, Dinah (about)
To Dinah Washington. E. Knight.—AdPb
Washington, George (about)
George Washington. S. Silverstein.—LaM
Which Washington. E. Merriam.—LaM
Washiri (poet). Kattie M. Cumbo.—AdB
"**Wasn't** that a mighty day." Unknown.—LaS
The **wasp.** William Sharp.—JoA-4
Wasps. See also Hornets
"There was an old man of St Bees." W. S. Gilbert.—RoIt
The wasp. W. Sharp.—JoA-4
The wasps' nest. G. MacBeth.—MaFw
Winter nests. A. Fisher.—FiFo
Yellow jacket. D. McCord.—McAa
The **wasps'** nest. George MacBeth.—MaFw
"**Wassail,** wassail all over the town." See The Kentucky wassail song
Watanabe Suiha
"The noisy cricket."—MaFw
The **watch.** May Swenson.—CoPt—RoIt
"**Watch** the net drift. Grey tides." See How to catch tiddlers
"A **watched** clock never moves, they said." See The slow starter
Watches. See Clocks and watches
"**Watching** a petal." Kubutsu, tr. fr. the Japanese by Harry Behn.—BeM
"**Watching** hands transplanting." See Transplanting
Watching post. C. Day-Lewis.—ToM
Watching the wrecking crane. Bobbi Katz.—HoP
Water. See also Waterfalls; Weather; Wells; also names of streams and rivers
Appoggiatura. D. J. Hayes.—AdPb
Aqalàni. Unknown.—BiI
"As I went over the water." Mother Goose.—AlC
"At the first sign of my horse's fright." Unknown.—BaSs
Cold water. D. Hall.—HiN
"From the middle." Unknown.—ClFc
The full heart. R. Nichols.—CoPu
"I tremble with each breath of air." Unknown.—EmN
Jack and Jill went up the hill." Mother Goose.—AlC—JoA-4
Lazy Jane. S. Silverstein.—SiW
The noise of waters. From Chamber music. J. Joyce.—RoIt
Chamber music (XXXV).—MaFw
Prairie waters by night. C. Sandburg.—SaT
"Runs as smooth as any rhyme." Unknown.—EmN
"Springs do not freeze in the cold of winter." N. Belting.—BeWi
"The straight strokes of reeds." A. Atwood.—AtM
Sunstrike. D. Livingstone.—ToM
"Under a spring mist." Teitoku.—BeM
"The water bug is dipping." Unknown.—ClFc
"The winter storm." Buson.—AtM
The **water** babies, sels. Charles Kingsley
The little doll.—OpOx
The tide river.—OpOx—RoIt
Young and old.—OpOx
The old song.—RoIt
Water baby. Calvin O'John.—AlW
"The **water** bug is dipping." Unknown, tr. fr. the Yuma.—ClFc

Water-front streets. Langston Hughes.—HoD
Water mills. See Mills
"**Water** poured into tumblers." See A thought
"The **water** ran off, the earth dried, the lakes were at rest, all was silent." See Over the water
The **watercress** seller. Thomas Miller.—OpOx
"**Waterfall,** only." Issa, tr. fr. the Japanese by Harry Behn.—BeM
Waterfalls
The cataract of Lodore. R. Southey.—LiS—OpOx
"Waterfall, only." Issa.—BeM
Watering the horse. Robert Bly.—HiN
Waterloo, Battle of, 1815
Chorus of the years. From The dynasts. T. Hardy.—PlP
Watermaid. Christopher Okigbo.—AlPa
The **watermelon.** Liuda Alaverdoshvili, tr. fr. the Russian by Miriam Morton.—MoM
Watermelons
"As I went the country road." Unknown.—EmN
"On the hill there is a green house." Unknown.—EmN
The watermelon. L. Alaverdoshvili.—MoM
"**Waters** above, eternal springs." See The shower
Watkins, Vernon
The collier.—MaFw—ToM
The death of Keats.—PlM
Watson, Clyde
"Apples for the little ones."—WaF
"Belly & Tubs went out in a boat."—WaF
"Bimbo, bombo, tomkin pie."—WaF
"Country bumpkin."—WaF
"Dilly dilly piccalilli."—WaF
"Ding, dong."—WaF
"Happy birthday, silly goose."—WaF
"Here's a song of Tinker & Peter."—WaF
"How many miles to Old Norfolk."—WaF
"Huckleberry, gooseberry, raspberry pie."—WaF
"I knew a man."—WaF
"Knickerbocker knockabout."—WaF
"Knock. Knock. Anybody there."—WaF
"Let the fall leaves fall."—WaF
"Little Martha piggy-wig."—WaF
"Miss Quiss."—WaF
"Mister Lister sassed his sister."—WaF
"Nanny banny bumblebee."—WaF
"Oh my goodness, oh my dear."—WaF
"Penny candy."—WaF
"Pinkey Pauper picked my pocket."—WaF
"The rain falls down."—WaF
"Ride your red horse down Vinegar lane."—WaF
"Rock, rock, sleep, my baby."—WaF
"See saw."—WaF
"The sky is dark, there blows a storm."—WaF
"Soft falls the snow."—WaF
"Somersault & pepper-upper."—WaF
"There were five fellows."—WaF
"Thomas Thomas Tinkertoes."—WaF
"Uptown, downtown."—WaF
Watson, Sir William
Song.—JoA-4
Watton, Joan
Requiem of a war-baby.—CoPi
Watts, Isaac
Against idleness and mischief.—LiS—OpOx
Against quarrelling and fighting.—OpOx
Cradle hymn.—OpOx
Hush, my babe.—LaS
For the Lord's day evening.—OpOx
Hush, my babe. See Cradle hymn
Our saviour's golden rule.—OpOx
The sluggard.—LiS—OpOx
Watts ("From what great sleep") Alvin Saxon.—AdPb
Watts ("Must I shoot the") Conrad Kent Rivers.—AdB—AdPb
The **wave.** David McCord.—McFm
Waves. See Ocean
"The **waves** are so cold." Bashō, tr. fr. the Japanese by Harry Behn.—BeM
"The **waves** of life flow on forever." Unknown.—MoBw
Wavvuuvuumira. Unknown, tr. fr. the Luganda by W. Moses Serwadda.—SeS
Waxman, Meyer
Born without a star. tr.—MeP
Waxwings
Cedar waxwing. W. H. Matchett.—HaWr
The **way.** Edwin Muir.—JoA-4
"The **way** a crow." See Dust of snow
"The **way** at night these piping peepers." See The peepers in our meadow
"**Way** back here and out of sight." Unknown.—EmN
"**Way** down South in Dixie." See Song for a dark girl
"'**Way** high up the Mogollons." See The glory trail
"The **way** I read a letter's—this." Emily Dickinson.—ThI
"**Way** out there." Felice Holman.—HoI
Way out West. LeRoi Jones.—AdPb
The **way** that it's going. Myra Cohn Livingston.—LiM
The **way** through the woods. See Rewards and fairies
"**Way** up in my tree I'm sitting by my fire." See Gypsy eyes
"**Way** up on the hill." Unknown.—MoBw
"**Way** way way way way." See Lullaby
Ways and means. See Through the looking-glass—The aged aged man
Ways of winding a watch. Eve Merriam.—MeF
"**Ways** to learn to be." See On re-reading the complete works of an elder poet
We all have thought a lot about you. John Ciardi.—CiFs
"**We** all look on with anxious eyes." See When father carves the duck
"**We** are all in the dumps." See "We're all in the dumps"

We three kings. John Henry Hopkins.—LaS
"**We** three kings of Orient are." See We three kings
"**We** used to gather at the high window." See When Mahalia sings
"**We** waited for an omnibus." See Walking song
"**We** walk back from the movies." See Frightened flower
We walk the way of the new world. Don L. Lee.—AdPb
" . . . **We** want." LeRoi Jones.—AdB
"**We** watch through the shop-front while." See Blackie, the electric Rembrandt
We wear the mask. Paul Laurence Dunbar.—AdPb
"**We** wear the mask that grins and lies." See We wear the mask
"**We** weep." See On the death of Atahualpa
"**We** went down to the river's brink." See Explanation, on coming home late
"**We** were alone and did your life." See To children
"**We** were as tough as our glasses." See Tyson's corner
"**We** were camped on the plains at the head of the Cimarron." See The Zebra Dun
"**We** were crowded in the cabin." See The tempest
"**We** were going single file." See A bummer
We were not like dogs. Uri Zvi Greenberg, tr. fr. the Hebrew by Robert Mezey.—MeP
"**We** were not like dogs among the Gentiles . . . they pity a dog." See We were not like dogs
"**We** were together." See Song of an old man about his wife
"**We** wish you a merry Christmas." Unknown.—RoIt
"The **weak** scattered rays of yellow sun." See New York skyscrapers
Wealth
"Bring out your hair ornaments." Unknown.—LeIb
"The fairies have never a penny to spend." R. Fyleman.—OpOx
Florida road workers. L. Hughes.—PeS
Had I a golden pound. F. Ledwidge.—CoPi
Handfuls of wind. Y. Mar.—MeP
Hope to keep. A. T. Pratt.—AlW
If I should ever by chance. E. Thomas.—OpOx
"If you talk too much, you are a swindler." Kim Sang-yong.—BaSs
"Melvin Martin Riley Smith." D. McCord.—McFm
My nickel. L. Lenski.—LeC
Not mine. M. C. Livingston.—LiM
"Old mother witch fell in a ditch." Unknown.—EmN
On being too right to be polite. J. Ciardi.—CiFs
The pack rat. J. Prelutsky.—PrP
The poor man. Unknown.—FlH
The ruined maid. T. Hardy.—PlP
A sense of property. A. Thwaite.—ToM
"Sukey, you shall be my wife." Mother Goose.—TucMgl
There lived a king. W. S. Gilbert.—CoPt
"This is my rock." D. McCord.—JoA-4
Timbuctu. E. Brathwaite.—ToM
"Tomorrow belongs to God." A. M'Baye.—AlPa
The woman of three cows. Unknown.—CoPi
Weapons. See Arms and armor; also names of weapons, as Guns
"**Wear** it." See Color
"**Wear** modest armour; and walk quietly." See Advice to a knight
"**Wearied** arm and broken sword." See Pocahontas
"**Weary** men, what reap ye?—Golden corn for the stranger." See The famine year
"**Weary** was when coming on a stream." See Aswelay
"The **weary** year his race now having run." See Sonnet
Weasel. Aileen Fisher.—FiFo
Weasels
Don't ever seize a weasel by the tail. J. Prelutsky.—BrM
Weasel. A. Fisher.—FiFo
Weather. See also Clouds; Dew; Fog; Mist; Rainbows; Seasons; Snow; Storms; Weather vanes; Winds
August weather. K. Tynan.—PaF
Cat & the weather. M. Swenson.—HaWr
A dog and a cat. Mother Goose.—BlM
"A dog and a cat went out together."—TucMgl
A hot weather song. D. Marquis.—CoPu
The kayak paddler's joy at the weather. Unknown.—LeIb
Man is a fool. Unknown.—RoIt
"One misty moisty morning." Mother Goose.—AlC—JoA-4
Paddler's song on bad hunting weather. Unknown.—LeIb
Prayer for fine weather. S. Leslie.—CoPi
Showers, clearing later in the day. E. Merriam.—MeF
Suddenly. D. McCord.—McFm
Texas norther. M. C. Livingston.—LiM
"This little man lived all alone." Mother Goose.—TucMgl
To the ground hog. K. Winters.—LaM
Weather chant. Unknown.—LeIb
Weather ear. N. Nicholson.—ToM
Weather incantation ("Clouds, clouds") Unknown.—LeIb
Weather incantation ("Only come, only come") Unknown.—LeIb
Weather report. L. Moore.—MoSp
Weathers. T. Hardy.—PlP
Weather chant. Unknown, fr. Aivilik Eskimo.—LeIb
Weather ear. Norman Nicholson.—ToM
Weather incantation ("Clouds, clouds") Unknown, fr. the Copper Eskimo.—LeIb

Weather incantation ("Only come, only come") Unknown, fr. the Copper Eskimo.—LeIb
"The **weather** is gloomy. Ana Tarasova, tr. fr. the Russian by Miriam Morton.—MoM
Weather report. Lilian Moore.—MoSp
Weather vanes
The four letters. F. Reeves.—JoA-4
"I saw a gnome." H. Behn.—JaP
Weatherly, Tom
Arroyo.—AdPb
Canto 4.—AdPb
Canto 5.—AdPb
Canto 7.—AdPb
First Monday Scottsboro Alabama.—AdPb
Imperial thumbprint.—AdPb
Weathers. Thomas Hardy.—PlP
Weavers and weaving
The ballad of the harp-weaver. E. St V. Millay.—CoPt—RoIt
"I see a star." A. Lopez.—AlW
Song of the sky loom. Unknown.—MoT
Weber, Richard
For the moment.—CoPi
Stephen's green revisited.—CoPi
"**Wed** flowers bloob." See Llude sig kachoo
Weddings. See Brides and bridegrooms; Marriage
Wednesday night prayer meeting. Jay Wright.—AdPb
Wednesday noon: Adventure. Lucille Clifton.—ClS
"**Wednesdays** at the bone orchard deliveries." See Memo
"A **wee** bird sat upon a tree." Unknown, tr. fr. the Scottish by Norah and William Montgomerie.—JoA-4
Wee Davie Daylicht. Robert Tennant.—OpOx
"**Wee** Davie Daylicht keeks owre the sea." See Wee Davie Daylicht
Wee Willie Gray. Robert Burns.—OpOx
"**Wee** Willie Gray, and his leather wallet." See Wee Willie Gray
"**Wee** Willie Winkie runs through the town." See Willie Winkie
"**Wee** Willie Winkie runs through the town." Mother Goose.—JoA-4
Weeds
Bird gardens. A. Fisher.—FiFo
Humbleweeds. R. Froman.—FrSp
"A man of words and not of deeds." Mother Goose.—AlC
My Aunt Dora. T. Hughes.—HuMf
Plants and planting. L. Lenski.—LeC
Song of weeds. M. W. Kumin.—JoA-4
Undefeated. R. Froman.—FrSp
Weeds. C. Sandburg.—SaT
Weeds: A hex. E. Merriam.—MeO
Weeds. Carl Sandburg.—SaT
Weeds: a hex. Eve Merriam.—MeO
A **week** after the first Sputnik. Unknown, tr. fr. the Russian by Miriam Morton.—MoM
Weeksville women. Elouise Loftin.—AdPb
"**Weep** not, weep not." See Go down death
"The **weeping** spreads." Unknown, tr. fr. the Aztec by Miguel León-Portilla.—BiI
Weilerstein, Sadie Rose
For a good and sweet New Year.—LaM
Welburn, Ron
"Avoidances."—AdPb
Cecil county.—AdPb
Eulogy for populations.—AdPb
Welchmen. See Welshmen
Welcome here. Unknown.—LaS
"**Welcome** here, welcome here, all be alive and be of good cheer." See Welcome here
"**Welcome,** pale primrose, starting up between." See To a primrose
"**Welcome** Robin with thy greeting." See Robin Redbreast
"**Welcome** to you rich autumn days." See Rich days
We'll go to the sea no more. Unknown, tr. fr. the Scottish.—JoA-4
"**Well,** here we go again." See Time to practice
"**Well** I never." Mother Goose, tr. fr. the Spanish by Rose Fyleman.—AlC—JoA-4
"**Well** I woke up this mornin' it was Christmas day." See Adrian Henri's talking after Christmas blues
"**Well,** it happened." See It happened
Well met. Abbie Huston Evans.—CoPu
"**Well,** old spy." See Award
"**We'll** see what we'll see." See The people, yes—Proverbs
"**Well,** son, I'll tell you." See Mother to son
Well, welcome, now that you're here. John Ciardi.—CiFs
Well, yes. Robert Froman.—FrSp
Wells, Peter
How foolish.—BrM
Wells cathedral
The Mendip hills over Wells. H. Alford.—PaP
Wells
"As round as an apple, as deep as a cup." Mother Goose.—JoA-4
Aunt Eliza. H. Graham.—LiWw
"Riddle me, riddle me, riddle me." Unknown.—EmN
The star in the pail. D. McCord.—McS
Welsh landscape. R. S. Thomas.—ToM
Welsh nursery rhymes. See Nursery rhymes—Welsh
Welshmen
"Taffy was a Welshman, Taffy was a thief." Mother Goose.—AlC
"There were three jovial Welshmen." Mother Goose.—AlC—JoA-4
"**Wendy** put her black eyes on me." See Sweeping Wendy, study in fugue
"**We're** all in the dumps." Mother Goose.—AlC
In the dumps.—RoIt
"We are all in the dumps."—MiMg
"**We're** an African people." See African poems
"**We're** related—you and I." See Brothers
Were you on the mountain. Unknown, tr. fr. the Irish by Douglas Hyde.—CoPu
Were you there. Unknown.—BrW

"**Were** you there when they crucified my Lord." See Were you there
"**Werther** had a love for Charlotte." See The sorrows of Werther
Wesley, Charles
"Gentle Jesus, meek and mild."—OpOx
West, Paul
The cumberbunce.—CoOh
The **West-of-Wessex** girl. Thomas Hardy.—PlP
"The **west** ridge is an old ridge." See The west ridge is menthol cool
The **west** ridge is menthol cool. D. L. Graham.—AdPb
The **west** wind. John Masefield.—PaP—RoIt
"**Western** wind, when will thou blow." See The lover in winter plaineth for the spring
Westminster bridge
Composed upon Westminster bridge. W. Wordsworth.—PaP
Westwood, Thomas
Spring night.—RoIt
Wet. Lilian Moore.—MoSp
"**Wet** almond-trees, in the rain." See Bare almond-trees
"A **wet** sheet and a flowing sea." Allan Cunningham.—RoIt
"**Wet** wet wet." See Wet
Wexler, Elizabeth
Succah.—LaM
"**Wha** lies here." Unknown.—CoPu
Johnny Dow.—LiWw
Whack fol the diddle. Peadar Kavanagh.—CoPi
The **whale** ("There was a most monstrous whale") Theodore Roethke.—CoOr—CoPu
Whale ("A whale is stout about the middle") Mary Ann Hoberman.—HoR
Whale food. Lilian Moore.—MoSm
"A **whale** is stout about the middle." See Whale
"A **whale** liked to eat portions double." See Whale food
Whalers. See Whales and whaling
Whales and whaling
The caulker. M. A. Lewis.—CoPt
For a coming extinction. W. S. Merwin.—MoT
The harpooning. T. Walker.—HaWr
"I'm swimming around in the sea, see." K. Kuskin.—KuA
Melinda Mae. S. Silverstein.—SiW
The powerful eyes o' Jeremy Tait. W. Irwin.—CoPt
The whale ("There was a most monstrous whale") T. Roethke.—CoOr—CoPu
Whale ("A whale is stout about the middle") M. A. Hoberman.—HoR
Whale food. L. Moore.—MoSm
The whales off Wales. X. J. Kennedy.—KeO
"Who is my equal or can compare with me." Unknown.—ClFc
Why Noah praised the whale. J. Ciardi.—CiFs
"**Whales** have calves." See The guppy
The **whales** off Wales. X. J. Kennedy.—KeO
"**Whan** that Aprille with his shoures soote." See The Canterbury tales—The prologue
What a beautiful word. William Cole.—CoOr
"**What** a day." Shel Silverstein.—SiW
"**What** a delight it is." See Poems of solitary delights
"**What** a night in November." See On one who lived and died where he was born
"**What** a night, the wind howls, hisses, and but stops." See Snow storm
"**What** a wonderful bird the frog are." See The frog
"**What** am I bid? What am I bid." See Auctioneer
What are heavy. Christina Georgina Rossetti.—OpOx
"**What** are heavy? Sea sand and sorrow." See What are heavy
What are little boys made of . . . (love and care). Elaine Laron.—ThF
"**What** are little boys made of, made of." See What are little boys made of . . . (love and care)
"**What** are little boys made of, made of." Mother Goose.—AlC—EmN—JoA-4
"**What** are pockets for." David McCord.—McAa
What became of them. Unknown.—OpOx
"**What** can I give Him." See Carol ("In the bleak mid-winter")
"**What** cannot be committed to memory, this can save." See Photograph
"**What** can't be cured." Unknown.—RoIt
"**What** care I for the leagues o' sand." See The mither's lament
What color is black. Barbara Mahone.—AdM
"**What** desperate nightmare rapts me to this land." See Legacy: My South
"**What** do hens say." See Near and far
"**What** do I smell." See Smells
"**What** do I smell as I go marching." See Bakery shop
"**What** do you do when you're up in a tree." See Riddle
"**What** do you know? It's going to snow." See Questions, questions, questions
"**What** does little birdie say." See Sea dreams—Cradle song
"**What** does the bee do." Christina Georgina Rossetti.—OpOx
"**What** does the cracker." See Self
"**What** does the pelican." See The pelican
"**What** does the zoo-keeper do, do, do." See Zoo-keeper
"**What** eyes, what a nose." Unknown, tr. fr. the Spanish.—MoBw
What flower is this. Unknown.—EmN
"**What** God gives, and what we take." See A grace for children
"**What** goes over hill and vale." Unknown.—EmN
"**What** happened to Joey on our block." See Of kings and things
"**What** happens to a dream deferred." See Dream deferred

"**What** shall we do for timber." See Kilcash
"**What** shoemaker makes shoes without leather." Unknown.—EmN
Riddle.—RoIt
"**What** sings morning, noon, and night." Unknown.—EmN
"**What** splendid names for boys there are." See Boys' names
"**What,** still alive at twenty two." Hugh Kingsmill.—LiS
"**What** stirred the breath." See As I float
"**What** stories are mixed together." See Mingled yarns
What the moon saw. Vachel Lindsay.—LiWw
"**What** there is of me to see." Karla Kuskin.—KuA
What they said. Unknown.—JaP
"**What** this that came." See I'm no animal
"**What** time is it, said the one." See The chronometer
"**What** time of night it is." See Night rain
What Tottles meant. See Sylvie and Bruno concluded
"**What** was the name you called me." See Evening waterfall
"**What** was your war record, Prytherch." See For the record
"**What** way does the wind come? What way does he go." See Address to a child during a boisterous winter evening
"**What** were we playing? Was it prisoner's base." See Running
"**What** were you carrying, Pilgrims, Pilgrims." See The island—Atlantic Charter: 1620-1942
"**What** whim caused Whitney White to whittle." Unknown.—EmN
"**What** will I be married in." Unknown.—EmN
"**What** will I wear on my feet." Unknown.—EmN
"**What** will my house be." Unknown.—EmN
"**What** will my husband be." Unknown.—EmN
"**What** will you find at the edge of the world." See Landscape
What witches do. Leland B. Jacobs.—HoH
"**What** wondrous life is this I lead." See The garden
"**What** wondrous love is this." See Wondrous love
"**What** wondrous pretty things I've seen." See Young Master's account of a puppet show
"**What** would it be." See Query
"**What** would you like to be." See Interview
"**What** you gonna call yo' pretty little baby." Unknown.—LaS
"**What'd** you get, black boy." See Mr Roosevelt regrets
"**Whatever** is inside that sheet." See A-ha
"**Whatever** one toucan can do." See Toucans two
"**Whatever** you have to say, leave." See These days
"**Whatever** you think." See December 24: A tree in an elevator
What's black power. Londel Baez.—JoV
"**What's** for rabbits." Aileen Fisher.—FiFo
"**What's** greater, pebble or pond." See Once more, the round
"**What's** he waiting for." See Game for autumn
"**What's** in the cupboard." Mother Goose.—JoA-4
What's in the sack. Shel Silverstein.—SiW
"**What's** in the sack? What's in the sack." See What's in the sack
What's my thought like. Thomas Moore.—LiWw
"**What's** that, over a distance." See Thirst
"**What's** the good of breathing." See The frost pane
"**What's** the news of the day." Mother Goose.—AlC—MiMg
"**What's** the use, said the rooster." Unknown.—EmN
What's their names. Mary Ann Hoberman.—HoR
"**What's** your name (John Brown)." Unknown.—EmN
"**What's** your name (Pudding-and-Tame)." Unknown.—EmN
Wheat
Nebraska. J. Swan.—HaWr
The **wheatear** and the snowbird. Unknown, fr. West Greenland.—LeIb
Wheelbarrows
The red wheelbarrow. W. C. Williams.—MaFw—MoT
"**Wheelless.**" See Blast off
Wheelock, John Hall
Afternoon: Amagansett beach.—HaWr
The answer.—HaWr
The beetle in the country bathtub.—HaWr
Dismal observations.—PlM
Secret intimations.—CoPu
Wheels. See Bicycles and bicycling
"The **wheels** of the bus go round and round." Unknown.—HoP
"**When.**" See The past poem
"**When.**" See The right time
"**When** a cat is asleep." Karla Kuskin.—KuN
"**When** a cuckoo sings." Bashō, tr. fr. the Japanese by Harry Behn.—BeM
"**When** a friend calls to me from the road." See A time to talk
When a jolly young fisher. Unknown.—BrM
"**When** a jolly young fisher named Fisher." See When a jolly young fisher
"**When** a shadow appeared on the water." Unknown, tr. fr. the Korean by Chung Seuk Park and ad. by Virginia Olsen Baron.—BaSs
"**When** a task is once begun." Unknown.—MoBw
When . a . y and I . a told . a . . i e they'd seen a." Lewis Carroll.—LiPc
"**When** Alexander Pope strolled in the city." See Mr Pope
"**When** all the world is young, lad." See Water babies—Young and Old—The old song

"When all your friends have deserted you." Unknown.—EmN
"When an elf is as old as a year and a minute." See The seven ages of elf-hood
"When as in silks my Julia goes." See Upon Julia's clothes
"When as the mildest month." See The rose
"When at break of day at a riverside." See Piano and drums
"When at home alone I sit." See The little land
"When Barney was one." Unknown.—EmN
"When Bill gives me a book, I know." See The Christmas exchange
"When black people are." A. B. Spellman.—AdPb
"When Blackie." See Substitute
"When cats run home and light is come." See Song: The owl
"When cherry trees bloom." Jōsō, tr. fr. the Japanese by Harry Behn.—BeM
"When C. J. G. Arden goes out in the garden." See To his godson, Gerald C. A. Jackson
"When darkness covers the mountain village." Chun Keum, tr. fr. the Korean by Chung Seuk Park and ad. by Virginia Olsen Baron.—BaSs
"When distant lands divide us." Unknown.—EmN
"When egg and I sit down to tea." See The friends
"When everything has drawn to a close." Karla Kuskin.—KuA
When father carves the duck. Ernest V. Wright.—RoIt
"When first glow of early dawn." See Talking to his drum
"When folks like you are far away." Unknown.—MoBw
"When foxes eat the last gold grape." See Escape
"When Francis preached love to the birds." See Saint Francis and the birds
"When gardens shone with flowery pride." See On a little boy's endeavouring to catch a snake
"When George the Third was reigning a hundred years ago." See A ballad for a boy
"When George's grandmamma was told." See George
"When God said." See The creation of man
"When God set about to create heaven." See Genesis
"When gold you carry, camel." See Timbuctu
"When good King Arthur ruled this land." Mother Goose.—AlC—JoA-4
"When grandma visits you, my dears." See Advice to grandsons
When happy little children play. John Ciardi.—CiFs
"When happy little children run." See When happy little children play
"When have you done with my letters." See Requiem for a black girl
"When he killed the Mudjokivis." See The modern Hiawatha
"When I." See The rebel
"When I." See The watch
"When I a verse shall make." See The prayer to Ben Jonson
"When I am an old woman I shall wear purple." See Warning
"When I am gone out of your mind." Unknown.—MoBw
"When I am grown to man's estate." See Looking forward
"When I am hearing music." See Listening to music
"When I am living in the midlands." See The south country
When I am me. Felice Holman.—HoI
"When I am seven." See Friday: Waiting for mom
"When I asked for him at Entoto, he was towards Akaki." See Household song
When I awoke. Raymond Richard Patterson.—AdPb
"When I awoke, she said." See When I awoke
When I brought the news. J. P. Donleavy.—CoPt
"When I can count the numbers far." See Numbers
"When I carefully consider the curious habits of dogs." See Meditatio
"When I catch sight of your fair head." Louise Labe, tr. fr. the French by Judith Thurman.—ThI
"When I consider how my light is spent." See On his blindness
"When I fall asleep, and even during sleep." See Baudelaire
"When I gaze at the sun." See A moment please
"When I get sick I have to go." See Doctor
"When I get to be a composer." See Daybreak in Alabama
"When I go out to trick or treat." See Creepy
"When I hear the old men." See A song of greatness
"When I heard dat." See When I heard dat white man say
When I heard dat white man say. Zack Gilbert.—AdPb
"When I heard the learn'd astronomer." Walt Whitman.—RoIt
"When I kiss Eve." See Eden
"When I look at cows and think." See Cows
When I peruse the conquer'd fame. Walt Whitman.—CoPu
"When I peruse the conquer'd fame of heroes and the victories of mighty generals, I do not envy the generals." See When I peruse the conquer'd fame
"When I play on my fiddle in Dooney." See The fiddler of Dooney
"When I put her out, once, by the garbage pail." See The geranium

"**When** night folds its curtain." Unknown.—EmN
"**When** night stirred at sea." See The planter's daughter
"**When** nightingales burst." Jurin, tr. fr. the Japanese by Harry Behn.—BeM
"**When** Noah, perceiving 'twas time to embark." See The dog's cold nose
"**When** nothing is left to say." Unknown.—MoBw
"**When** on the coral-red steps of old brownstones." See Summer: West Side
"**When** on this page." Unknown.—EmN
"**When** on this page your eyes do bend." Unknown.—MoBw
"**When** Pat came o'er the hills his colleen for to see." See The whistling thief
"**When** people's ill, they come to I." See On Dr Lettson, by himself
"**When** periwigs came first in wear." See The bald cavalier
"**When** Robin Hood and Little John." See The death of Robin Hood
"**When** Robin Hood was about twenty years old." See Robin Hood and Little John
"**When** she was little." See Poem for Flora
"**When** singing songs of scariness." See The worst
"**When** Sir Joshua Reynolds died." See Sir Joshua Reynolds
"**When** ski-ing in the Engadine." See Patience
"**When** Solomon was reigning in his glory." See Solomon and the bees
When Sue wears red. Langston Hughes.—JoA-4
"**When** Susanna Jones wears red." See When Sue wears red
"**When** the." See August 2
"**When** the." Vanessa Fraser.—HoC
"**When** the acorn tumbles down." See The fieldmouse
"**When** the cock crows." See The lazy man
"**When** the corn stands yellow in September." See Harvest
"**When** the cupboard's empty." See Hungry
"**When** the day is cloudy." Unknown, tr. fr. the Crow by Robert H. Lowie.—JoT
"**When** the day is over." See This day is over
"**When** the donkey saw the zebra." See A surprise
"**When** the dusk of twilight's falling." Unknown.—MoBw
"**When** the earth is turned in spring." See The worm
"**When** the golden sun is setting (and your feet)." Unknown.—EmN
"**When** the golden sun is setting (and your mind)." Unknown.—EmN
"**When** the golden sun is sinking." Unknown.—MoBw
"**When** the grass was closely mown." See The dumb soldier
"**When** the green woods laugh with the voice of joy." See Laughing song
"**When** the hamlet hailed a birth." See Mady Judy
"**When** the jet sprang into the sky." See Geography lesson
"**When** the Lord turned again the captivity of Zion." See Psalms—Psalm 126—The Lord hath done great things for us
"**When** the master lived a king and I a starving hutted slave beneath the lash, and." See On listening to the spirituals
"**When** the mole goes digging." See The mole
"**When** the moon." See Autumn ghost sounds
"**When** the morning sun is on the trumpet-vine blossoms, sing at the kitchen pans." See Prairie—Songs
"**When** the neat white." See Duck
"**When** the night winds sigh." See Elves' song
"**When** the rain comes tumbling down." See The story of Flying Robert
"**When** the rain raineth." Mother Goose.—TucMgl
"**When** the ripe pears droop heavily." See The wasp
"**When** the sky to the North darkens." See Sadness
"**When** the sweet showers of April fall and shoot." See The Canterbury tales—The prologue
"**When** the tea is brought at five o'clock." See Milk for the cat
"**When** the voices of children are heard on the green." See Nurse's song
"**When** the waters are calm." See The spirit will appear
"**When** the wind blows." See Wind song
"**When** the wind blows loud and fearful." See The beggar boy
"**When** the wind is blowing hard." See Like a giant in a towel
"**When** the wind is in the thrift." See By the saltings
"**When** the winds of March are wakening." See Finding fairies
"**When** the world is all against you." See The optimist
"**When** the young dawn spread in the eastern sky." See The odyssey—The boar hunt
"**When** they bring me a plate." See Tricking
"**When** they brought my father to the mound of corpses." See To the mound of corpses in the snow
"**When** they shot Malcolm Little down." See At that moment
"**When** things began to happen to our favorite spot." See To T. S. Eliot of his sixtieth birthday
"**When** this is all over, said the swineherd." See Swineherd
"**When** three hens go a-walking, they." See Three hens
"**When** three hens go out to feed." Mother Goose, tr. fr. the French.—TucMg
When thy king is a boy. Ed Roberson.—AdPb (sel.)

"**When** Tim was six or seven or eight." See Tim
"**When** Uncle Devereux died." See Dunbarton
"**When** walking in a tiny rain." See Vern
"**When** we are going toward someone we say." See Simple song
When we grow up. Shelley Miller.—ThF
"**When** we grow up will I be pretty." See When we grow up
"**When** white people speak of being uptight." See The dancer
"**When** will I be married." Unknown.—EmN
"**When** winter scourged the meadow and the hill." See Ice
"**When,** with my little daughter Blanche." See Presence of mind
"**When** you are married." Unknown.—EmN
When you are old. William Butler Yeats.—MaFw
"**When** you are old and cannot see." Unknown.—EmN
"**When** you are old and grey and full of sleep." See When you are old
"**When** you are twenty and able to dress." Unknown.—EmN
"**When** you bake your first cherry pie." Unknown.—MoBw
"**When** you fall down." Unknown.—MoBw
"**When** you get big, my beautiful calf." See Baby giraffe
"**When** you get married." See "When you get married and live in a shanty"
"**When** you get married (and drive a truck)." Unknown.—MoBw
"**When** you get married (and have a set of twins)." Unknown.—EmN
"**When** you get married (and have 8 or 9)." Unknown.—MoBw
"**When** you get married (and have 24)." Unknown.—MoBw
"**When** you get married (and live in a flat)." Unknown.—MoBw
"**When** you get married (and live in New York)." Unknown.—MoBw
"**When** you get married (and live on a hill)." Unknown.—MoBw
"**When** you get married (and live upstairs)." Unknown.—MoBw
"**When** you get married (and your husband gets cross)." Unknown.—EmN
"**When** you get married (and your husband is cross, come over to my house)." Unknown.—MoBw
"**When** you get married (live at your ease)." Unknown.—EmN
"**When** you get married and live in a shanty." Unknown.—EmN
"When you get married."—MoBw
"**When** you get old and blind." Unknown.—EmN
"**When** you grow up and have a car." Unknown.—MoBw
"**When** you have a boyfriend." Unknown, tr. fr. the Spanish.—MoBw
"**When** you hear thunder without rain." See Efon (Buffalo)
"**When** you intend to get married." Unknown, tr. fr. the Spanish.—MoBw
"**When** you look before you go." See Windows
"**When** you say yes." Unknown, tr. fr. the Spanish.—MoBw
"**When** you show me." See Colors for mama
"**When** you spit from the twenty-sixth floor." See My hobby
"**When** you stand before the sink." Unknown.—MoBw
"**When** you stand upon the stump." Unknown.—MoBw
"**When** you turn the corner." See Final curve
"**When** you were." See For Angela
"**When** your eyes gaze seaward." See Golden moonrise
"**When** you're courting." Unknown.—MoBw
"**When** you're in the country." Unknown.—EmN
"**When** you're lying awake with a dismal headache and repose is tabooed by anxiety." See Iolanthe—Lord chancellor's song
"**When** you're sailing in strange harbors, Cutty Sark, Cutty Sark." See The clipper Dunbar to the clipper Cutty Sark
"**When** you're sitting all alone." Unknown.—MoBw
"**When** you're up to your neck in hot water." Unknown.—MoBw
"**When** you're washing dishes." Unknown.—MoBw
"**Whenas** in perfume Julia went." See Herrick's Julia
"**Whence** does he spring." See Song
"**Whence** the beginning." See Question
"**Whenever** I eat, I eat the pain of your love, mistress." See Love song of a young man
"**Whenever** I see the ocean." Issa, tr. fr. the Japanese by Hanako Fukuda.—HaW
"**Whenever** Richard Cory went down town." See Richard Cory
"**Whenever** the days are cool and clear." See The sandhill crane
"**Whenever** the moon and stars are set." See Windy nights
"**Whenever** the stars are out of sight." Ruth Harnden.—HoP
"**Whenever** you may meet a skunk." See The skunk
"**Where.**" See Ruby-throated hummingbird
"**Where.**" Karla Kuskin.—KuN
Where. Walter De La Mare.—CoPu
"**Where** are the men with the strength to be men." See His answer to the critics
"**Where** are the people going." See Going
"**Where** are they? Where are thy wise men." See Isaiah—From the prophecy against Egypt
"**Where** are we to go when this is done." See Sonnet
"**Where** are you going." See Mittens for kittens

Whispering
"Goldfish whisper." M. C. Livingston.—LiM
"Whispers." M. C. Livingston.—JoA-4—LiLc
"**Whispers.**" Myra Cohn Livingston.—JoA-4—LiLc
"**Whispers** of maroon came on the little river." See Maroon with silver frost
Whistle. David McCord.—McFm
"**Whistle,** daughter, whistle." Mother Goose.—HoMg
Whistles. See also Whistling
Whistle. D. McCord.—McFm
Whistling. See also Whistles
"Whistle, daughter, whistle." Mother Goose.—HoMg
The whistling thief. Unknown.—CoPt
The **whistling** thief. Unknown.—CoPt
White, E. B.
A classic waits for me.—LiS
"I marvel at the ways of God."—LiWw
White, J. E. Manchip
Hymn to the sun. tr.—AbM
White, Joseph
Black is a soul.—AdPb
White (color)
The polar bear. J. Prelutsky.—PrT
"There's more than one way to be right." R. Wilbur.—WiO
"**White.**" See White people
"**White** and wise and old." Buson, tr. fr. the Japanese by Harry Behn.—BeM
White butterflies. Algernon Charles Swinburne.—AdP
White Christmas. W. R. Rodgers.—CoPi
"The **white** cock's tail." See Ploughing on Sunday
"A **white** crow flies from the fairyland." See An enjoyable evening in the village near the lake
"**White** horses galloping on the sand." See The black cliffs, Ballybunion
The **white** house. Claude McKay.—AdPb
"The **white** house is silent." See Arriving in the country again
"The **white** lady has asked me to dance." See Fourth dance poem
White man and black man are talking. Michael Goode.—JoV
"The **white** man drew a small circle in the sand." See The people, yes—Circles
"The **white** man has brought his war to the beach." See War chant
"The **white** man is." See 12 gates to the city
"**White** men's children spread over the earth." See The riddle
"**White** moon comes in on a baby face." See Baby face
"**White** mountains, seen also." Issa, tr. fr. the Japanese by Hanako Fukuda.—HaW
White people. David Henderson.—AdPb
"**White** plus white equals one." See The new math
The **white** rabbit's verses. See Alice's adventures in wonderland—"They told me you had been to her"
"**White** sheep, white sheep." See Clouds
"**White** sky, over the hemlocks bowed with snow." See The buck in the snow
"**White** storks spend their winters." See Stork story
"A **white** terrace stretching far over the sea." See Evening in Haiti
The **white** window. James Stephens.—JoA-4
"**White** women have you heard." See Montgomery
Whitewing, Donna
August 24, 1963—1:00 A.M.—Omaha.—AlW
Can you can't.—AlW
Cry silent.—AlW
The gathering time.—AlW
Love song.—AlW
A vegetable, I will not be.—AlW
Why is happy.—AlW
"**Whither,** midst falling dew." See To a waterfowl
Whitman, Ruth
Do fishes go to school.—RoIt
Ripeness.—MoT
Whitman, Walt
Cavalry crossing a ford.—CoPu
The dalliance of the eagles.—CoPu
The first dandelion.—RoIt
Give me the splendid silent sun.—JoA-4 (sel.)—RoIt
I hear America singing.—RoIt
"I think I could turn and live with animals." See Song of myself
Miracles. See Song of myself
O captain, my captain.—RoIt
The ox-tamer.—RoIt
The runner.—FlH
"Sea of stretch'd ground-swells." See Song of myself
Shut not your doors.—PlM
Song of myself, sels.
"I think I could turn and live with animals."—RoIt
Miracles.—JoA-4—MaFw—RoIt
"Sea of stretch'd ground-swells."—MoG
What is the grass.—RoIt
To the garden the world.—MoG
"What is the grass." See Song of myself
"When I heard the learn'd astronomer."—RoIt
When I peruse the conquer'd fame.—CoPu
Whitman, Walt (about)
A classic waits for me. E. B. White.—LiS
Old Walt. L. Hughes.—PlM
A pact. E. Pound.—PlM
Shut not your doors. W. Whitman.—PlM
Sincere flattery of W. W. (Americanus). J. K. Stephen.—LiS
Song of myself, sels. W. Whitman
"I think I could turn and live with animals."—RoIt
Miracles.—JoA-4—MaFw—RoIt

Why ("Why does the clock") Lilian Moore.—MoSm
"**Why** are all the dogs so nervous." See Songs for the television shows I would like to see
"**Why** did I forget the chocolate." See Chocolate
"**Why** didn't you say you was promised, Rose-Ann." See Rose-Ann
"**Why** do you lie with your legs ungainly huddled." See The dug-out
"**Why** do you lose things this way." See Big question
"**Why** do you rush through the field in trains." See The fat white woman speaks
"**Why** do your warships sail on my waters." See I've got to know
"**Why** does the clock." See Why
"**Why** don't I send my books to you." Martial, tr. fr. the Latin by Rolfe Humphries.—PlM
"**Why** don't we rock the casket here in the moonlight." See The pale blue casket
"**Why** flyest thou away with fear." See To a fish of the brook
"**Why** go to Saint-Juliot? What's Juliot to me." See A dream or no
"**Why** is a pump like Viscount Castlereagh." See What's my thought like
Why is happy. Donna Whitewing.—AlW
"**Why** mourns the dove." See The mourning dove
Why Noah praised the whale. John Ciardi.—CiFs
"**Why** should this flower delay so long." See The last chrysanthemum
"**Why** should you envy the fish." Yi Jung-bo, tr. fr. the Korean by Chung Seuk Park and ad. by Virginia Olsen Baron.—BaSs
Why the sky is blue. John Ciardi.—CiFs
"**Why** then, why there." See Elegy for J. F. K.
"**Why** this girl has no fear." See Carmen
"**Why**, who makes much of a miracle." See Song of myself—Miracles
"**Why** will they never speak." See The grandfathers
"**Why** would I want." William J. Harris.—AdPb
"The **wicked** little Kukook." Unknown, fr. South Greenland.—LeIb
"A **wicked** witch." See Poison ivy
Wicked witch's kitchen. X. J. Kennedy.—KeO
"The **widdly,** waddly walrus." See The walrus
"**Widdy** widdy wurkey." Mother Goose, tr. fr. the German.—TucMg
The **widow** of Drynam. Patrick MacDonogh.—CoPi
Wiegrabe, P.
Longing for death. tr.—AlPa
The **wife** of Llew. Francis Ledwidge.—CoPi
"**Wiggle** to the laundromat." Dennis Lee.—LeA
"The **wiggling,** wriggling, jiggling juggler." Jack Prelutsky.—PrC
Wilbur, Richard
"Because what's *present* doesn't last."—WiO
A black November turkey.—HiN
Boy at the window.—PeS
A Christmas hymn.—ToM
Digging for China.—HiN
Exeunt.—HaWr—HiN
A fire-truck.—HiN
For K. R. on her sixtieth birthday.—PlM
He was.—HiN
Juggler.—HiN
Mind.—HiN
Museum piece.—LiWw
My father paints the summer.—HiN
"Not to have any *hair* is called."—WiO
"The opposite of a *cloud* could be."—WiO
"The opposite of a *hole's* a heap."—WiO
"The opposite of a king, I'm sure."—WiO
"The opposite of *doughnut?* Wait."—WiO
"The opposite of *fast* is *loose.*"—WiO
"The opposite of *foot* is *what.*"—WiO
"The opposite of *junk* is *stuff.*"—WiO
"The opposite of *making faces.*"—WiO
"The opposite of *opposite.*"—WiO
"The opposite of *post,* were you."—WiO
"The opposite of *spit,* I'd say."—WiO
"The opposite of *squash?* Offhand."—WiO
"The opposite of *standing still.*"—WiO
"The opposite of *tiller?* Well."—WiO
"The opposite of *trunk* could be."—WiO
"The opposite of *well* is *sick.*"—WiO
"The opposites of *earth* are two."—WiO
Running.—HiN
Seed leaves.—HiN
Stop.—HaWr
Tartuffe. tr.—LiWw (sel.)
"There's more than one way to be right."—WiO
To an American poet just dead.—PlM
Two voices in a meadow.—PeS
"What is the opposite of a *prince.*"—WiO
"What is the opposite of a *shoe.*"—WiO
"What is the opposite of *actor.*"—WiO
"What is the opposite of *ball.*"—WiO
"What is the opposite of *bat.*"—WiO
"What is the opposite of *cheese.*"—WiO
"What is the opposite of *Cupid.*"—WiO
"What is the opposite of *doe.*"—WiO
"What is the opposite of *fleet.*"—WiO
"What is the opposite of *flying.*"—WiO
"What is the opposite of *fox.*"—WiO
"What is the opposite of *hat.*"—WiO
"What is the opposite of *July.*"—WiO
"What is the opposite of *mirror.*"—WiO
"What is the opposite of *nuts.*"—WiO
"What is the opposite of *penny.*"—WiO
"What is the opposite of *riot.*"—WiO
"What is the opposite of *string.*"—WiO
"What is the opposite of *two.*"—WiO
"A **wild-bear** chase, didst never see." See The bear hunt
"The **wild** beauty of an eagle, once born to virgin sky." See The folding fan
Wild boar. Shel Silverstein.—SiW
The **wild** flower and the rose. David Nikogosian, tr. fr. the Russian by Miriam Morton.—MoM

Handfuls of wind. Y. Mar.—MeP
The hawk. A. Fisher.—FiFo
Hearing the wind at night. M. Swenson.—HaWr
Heat. H. D.—PaF
I am Chicago. From The windy city. C. Sandburg.—SaT
"I called to the wind." Kyorai.—BeM
It was the wind. Unknown.—BiI
King wind. M. Van Doren.—HiN
The kite. H. Behn.—JoA-4
Like a giant in a towel. D. Lee.—LeA
Little wind. K. Greenaway.—JoA-4
"Mad coyote." Unknown.—JoT
March. L. Clifton.—ClE
Maybe the birds. J. Jordan.—MoT
Mid-country blow. T. Roethke.—CoPu
"The moon's the north wind's cooky." V. Lindsay.—JoA-4—LiLc—UnGb
Nebraska. J. Swan.—HaWr
Night and a distant church. R. Atkins.—AdPb
The night-wind. E. Brontë.—PaF
Night wind in fall. W. R. Moses.—HiN
"The north wind doth blow." Mother Goose.—AlC—JoA-4
"North wind dresses her daughter winds." N. Belting.—BeWi
North wind in October. R. Bridges.—PaF
November. J. Clare.—PaF
Ode to the west wind. P. B. Shelley.—PaF
Off and away. R. Froman.—FrSp
Pearl cobwebs. From Smoke and steel. C. Sandburg.—SaT
A piece of sky. F. Holman.—HoI
Pines. A. Fisher.—FiFo
Saying. A. R. Ammons.—MoT
Secret intimations. J. H. Wheelock.—CoPu
Small song. A. R. Ammons.—CoPu
Songs of the ghost dance. Unknown.—BiI
South wind. Tu Fu.—MaFw
Spirit of the wind. G. Okara.—AlPa
Squall. J. Moore.—HiN
A strong wind. A. Clarke.—CoPi
Sweet and low. From the princess. A. Tennyson.—JoA-4—OpOx—RoIt
"Ten years it took." Song Soon.—BaSs
Texas norther. M. C. Livingston.—LiM
That wind. Unknown.—BiI
"That wind, that wind."—ClFc
To a child dancing in the wind. W. B. Yeats.—CoPi
"Tonight the winds begin to rise." From In memoriam. A. Tennyson.—PaF
"The trees' reflection." A. Atwood.—AtM
Tumbleweed. J. Carden.—AlW
The unfortunate miller. A. E. Coppard.—CoPt
The west wind. J. Masefield.—PaP—RoIt
"What goes over hill and vale." Unknown.—EmN
"Who are you." K. Kuskin.—KuA
"Who has seen the wind." C. G. Rossetti.—JoA-4—LiLc—RoIt
The wind.—OpOx
Whooo. L. Moore.—MoSm
The wind ("I can get through a doorway without any key") J. Reeves.—CoPu
The wind ("I come to work as well as play") Unknown.—RoIt
The wind ("I saw you toss the kites on high") R. L. Stevenson.—JoA-4—RoIt
Wind ("This house has been far out at sea all night") T. Hughes.—MaFw—ToM
The wind ("The wind stood up, and gave a shout") J. Stephens.—CoPi—CoPu
Wind and silver. A. Lowell.—CoPu
The wind and the moon. G. MacDonald.—LiLc (sel.)
The wind blew words. T. Hardy.—PlP
The wind blows from the sea. Unknown.—BiI
"The wind blows grey." Naitō Meisetsu.—MaFw
"The wind ceaseth." Unknown.—EmN
Wind horses. C. Sandburg.—SaT
The wind in a frolic. W. Howitt.—OpOx
"Wind is a ghost." N. Belting.—BeWi
The wind is round. H. Moss.—HaWr
"Wind last night blew down." Unknown.—BaSs
"The wind of autumn." Issa.—HaW
Wind poem. Ryojirô Yamanaka.—MoT
Wind song ("Long ago I learned how to sleep") C. Sandburg.—SaT
Wind song ("When the wind blows") L. Moore.—UnGb
Wind song ("Wind now commences to sing") Unknown.—BiI
"The wind, tapped like a tired man." E. Dickinson.—ThI
"The winds are people dwelling." N. Belting.—BeWi
Winds of the windy city. From The windy city. C. Sandburg.—SaT
Windy nights. R. L. Stevenson.—OpOx
Windy wash day. D. Aldis.—JoA-4
The youth and the northwind. J. G. Saxe.—CoPt
The **wind**. See "Who has seen the wind"
The **wind** ("I can get through a doorway without any key") James Reeves.—CoPu
The **wind** ("I come to work as well as play") Unknown.—RoIt
The **wind** ("I saw you toss the kites on high") Robert Louis Stevenson.—JoA-4—RoIt
Wind ("This house has been far out at sea all night") Ted Hughes.—MaFw—ToM
The **wind** ("The wind stood up, and gave a shout") James Stephens.—CoPi—CoPu
Wind and silver. Amy Lowell.—CoPu
The **wind** and the moon. George MacDonald.—LiLc (sel.)
"**Wind** around the corner." See Blow up
"The **wind** billowing out the seat of my britches." See Child on top of a greenhouse
"**Wind,** bird, and tree." See The words
The **wind** blew words. Thomas Hardy.—PlP

"Winifred Waters sat and cried." See Winifred Waters
Winkelman Von Winkel. Clara Odell Lyon.—CoOr
"Winkelman Von Winkel is the wisest man alive. See Winkelman Von Winkel
Winnebago Indians. See Indians of the Americas—Winnebago
"Winslow Metter." See Mr Metter
Winter. See also December; January; March; Seasons; Snow
 After the winter. C. McKay.—AdPb
 After winter. S. A. Brown.—AdPb
 Ancient music. E. Pound.—LiS—MaFw
 "And in the frosty season, when the sun." From The prelude. W. Wordsworth.—PaF
 The beggar man. L. Aikin.—OpOx
 Birds at winter nightfall. T. Hardy.—CoPu—JoA-4—PlP
 Blossom themes. C. Sandburg.—MaFw—SaT
 "Blow, blow, thou winter wind." From As you like it. W. Shakespeare.—PaF—RoIt
 Blue horses. E. Roberson.—AdPb
 Cardinal. J. Harrison.—HaWr
 Carrying food home in winter. M. Atwood.—MoT
 "The child at winter sunset." M. Van Doren.—HiN
 Christmas landscape. L. Lee.—MaFw
 Christmas time. L. B. Hopkins.—HoS
 "Cloudy days." A. Coor.—HoC
 Cold morning. F. Holman.—HoI
 A collage for Richard Davis—two short forms. De Leon Harrison.—AdPb
 The darkling thrush. T. Hardy.—PaF—PlP—RoIt
 December. A. Fisher.—HoS
 Depression before spring. W. Stevens.—HaWr
 Dirge for the year. P. B. Shelley.—PaF
 February—It's an ill wind. F. Holman.—HoI
 "The first winter rain." Bashō.—AtM
 Flight. L. Moore.—MoSp
 The frost pane. D. McCord.—JoA-4
 Glass world. D. Donnelly.—HiN
 Hot cakes. S. Hsi.—MaFw
 How still, how happy. E. Brontë.—PaF
 "How still, how happy! Those are words."—PaP
 Ice. C. G. D. Roberts.—CoPu
 "Ice cold." D. Adams.—HoC
 "Icicles are the walking sticks of the winter winds." N. Belting.—BeWi
 The idle flowers. R. Bridges.—JoA-4
 In the farmhouse. G. Kinnell.—HaWr
 In winter sky. D. McCord.—McFm
 "It's a foggy day." D. McCord
 Two triolets.—McS
 Journey. M. Chute.—ChRu
 Langdale: Nightfall, January 4th. M. Roberts.—PaP
 Last words before winter. L. Untermeyer.—JoA-4
 Letter in winter. R. R. Patterson.—AdPb
 Logs of wood. C. Causley.—CaF
 Morning. C. S. Calverley.—RoIt
 The new muffler. M. Chute.—ChRu
 "Now winter nights enlarge." T. Campion.—MaFw—RoIt
 Old Dan'l. L. A. G. Strong.—CoPu
 Old winter. T. Noel.—RoIt
 Out skiing. L. Shakhovich.—MoM
 Perfection. G. Ost'or.—MoM
 Robin Redbreast. Unknown.—RoIt
 Seasons. M. Chute.—ChRu
 The shawangunks—early April. L. Moore.—MoSp
 Sheep in winter. J. Clare.—MaFw
 Shine out fair sun. Unknown.—MaFw
 Sick in winter. R. Hoban.—HoE
 Sing a song of honey. B. E. Todd.—PaF
 "The sky is low, the clouds are mean." E. Dickinson.—PaF
 "The snow." T. Batchelor.—HoC
 Snowflakes. D. McCord.—McS
 "Something told the wild geese." R. Field.—JoA-4
 Somewhere around Christmas. J. Smith.—MaFw
 A song of winter. Unknown.—CoPi
 Sonnet. E. Spenser.—PaF
 The sorceress. L. Pagharskaya.—MoM
 Spanish music in winter. Unknown.—MeP (sel.)
 A spell before winter. H. Nemerov.—HaWr
 Star-talk. R. Graves.—PaF
 Stop. R. Wilbur.—HaWr
 Thaw. E. Thomas.—MaFw
 "There's a certain slant of light." E. Dickinson.—PaF—ThI
 Those winter Sundays. R. Hayden.—AdPb
 The total calm. P. Booth.—HaWr
 "A tree with no leaves." J. Gonzalez.—JoV
 Twin lakes hunter. A. B. Guthrie, Jr.—CoPt
 "Under a small, cold." Ransetsu.—BeM
 Weather report. L. Moore.—MoSp
 "A wee bird sat upon a tree." Unknown.—JoA-4
 Wet. L. Moore.—MoSp
 "When icicles hang by the wall." From Love's labour's lost. W. Shakespeare.—JoA-4—RoIt
 Winter.—PaF
 Willow yellow. L. Moore.—MoSp
 "The wind blows grey." Naitō Meisetsu.—MaFw
 "Winter." M. Hicks.—HoC
 Winter ("Bread and milk for breakfast") C. G. Rossetti.—RoIt
 Winter ("The frost is here") A. Tennyson.—PaF
 Winter ("Now the snow") W. C. Williams.—HiN
 Winter ("Now winter as a shrivelled scroll") K. Tynan.—PaF
 Winter alphabet. E. Merriam.—MeO
 Winter birds. A. Fisher.—FiFo—LaM
 "Winter breaks." N. Belting.—BeSc

"Faith, I wish I were a leprechaun." M. Rittor.—JaP
Fish story. R. Armour.—FlH
Give me the splendid silent sun. W. Whitman.—JoA-4 (sel.)—RoIt
The hawk. A. Fisher.—FiFo
He wishes for the cloths of Heaven. W. B. Yeats.—JoA-4
Helga. C. Sandburg.—SaT
"I do not wish I were a cat." K. Kuskin.—KuN
"I want you to live as long as you want." Unknown.—EmN
"I wish." L. Moore.—MoSm
"I wish I was a head of cabbage." Unknown.—EmN
"I wish I were a china cup." Unknown.—EmN
"I wish you a merry Christmas." Mother Goose.—TucMgl
"I wish you health." Unknown.—EmN
"I wish you love." Unknown.—EmN
"I wish you luck, I wish you joy." Unknown.—EmN
"If Cupid shoots." Unknown.—EmN
If I was president. M. Cowan.—JoV
"If *ifs* and *ands.*" Unknown.—EmN
"If wishes were horses." Mother Goose.—AlC—EmN
"The jazz world." M. Gill.—JoV
Jerusalem. Judah Halevi.—MeP
The kayak paddler's joy at the weather. Unknown.—LeIb
Lester. S. Silverstein.—SiW
"Let there always be a sky." K. Barannikov.—MoM
Magic song for him who wishes to live. Unknown.—LeIb
Margaret. C. Sandburg.—SaT
"May all your life be as bright." Unknown.—EmN
"May the angels round." Unknown.—EmN
"May the larkspur with its eye of blue." Unknown.—EmN
"May you be happy." Unknown.—EmN
"May you grow fair." Unknown.—EmN
"May your life be like arithmetic." Unknown.—EmN
"May your wing of happiness." Unknown.—EmN
O to be a dragon. Marianne Moore.—JoA-4
An old woman of the roads. P. Colum.—RoIt
The pedlar's caravan. W. B. Rands.—OpOx
Poem for Flora. Nikki Giovanni.—AdM—AdPb—NeA
A pony. A. Fisher.—FiFo
Presents. M. Chute.—BrM
Runover rhyme. D. McCord.—McFm—McS
"Sea way." S. Briody.—HoC—HoP
Songs for television shows I would like to see. R. Hoban.—HoE
Tartary. W. De La Mare.—OpOx
Three wishes. Unknown.—RoIt
"Three wishes three." K. Kuskin.—KuN
Triolet. G. K. Chesterton.—LiLc
"When you are twenty and able to dress." Unknown.—EmN
Wish. M. A. Hoberman.—HoR
"Wish I was in Arkansas." Unknown.—EmN
Wishes of an elderly man. W. Raleigh (1861-1922).—CoPu—LiWw
Wishing. W. Allingham.—OpOx
"The wolves are howling." Unknown.—ClFc

Wishes of an elderly man. Walter Raleigh (1861-1922).—CoPu—LiWw
"The **wishes** on this child's mouth." See Helga
Wishing. William Allingham.—OpOx
The **witch.** Eleanor Farjeon.—CoOr
Witch goes shopping. Lilian Moore.—MoSm
The **witch** of Willowby wood. Rowena Bastin Bennett.—LaM (sel.)
"**Witch** rides off." See Witch goes shopping
"The **witch.** The witch. Don't let her get you." See The witch
Witch ways. Unknown.—JaP
Witch, witch. Rose Fyleman.—JaP
"**Witch,** witch, where do you fly." See Witch, witch

Witchcraft
Adventures of Isabel. O. Nash.—NeA
April 30. N. Belting.—BeSc
Bedtime stories. L. Moore.—MoSm
Beware. L. Blair.—JaP
"Bittersweet." I. O. Eastwick.—JaP
Dear country witch. L. Moore.—MoSm
Eight witches. B. J. Lee.—HoH
Fog. L. Moore.—MoSm
Hitchhiker. D. McCord.—McAa—McS
"I never saw." L. Moore.—MoSm
If you've never. E. M. Fowler.—HoH
Knitted things. K. Kuskin.—LaM (sel.)
Little Ugh. L. Moore.—MoSm
Mr Macklin's visitor. D. McCord.—McAa
Molly Means. M. Walker.—CoPt
My Aunt Flo. T. Hughes.—HuMf
"Old mother witch fell in a ditch." Unknown.—EmN
On Halloween. N. W. Walter.—HoH
"Once upon a time." Issa.—BeM
Pamela. D. McCord.—McFm
Poison ivy. K. Gallagher.—JaP
The quiet child. R. Field.—NeA
The skeleton walks. X. J. Kennedy.—KeO
Two witches. A. Resnikoff.—BrM—CoOh
What they said. Unknown.—JaP
What witches do. L. B. Jacobs.—HoH
Wicked witch's kitchen. X. J. Kennedy.—KeO
The witch. E. Farjeon.—CoOr
Witch goes shopping. L. Moore.—MoSm
The witch of Willowby wood. R. B. Bennett.—LaM (sel.)
Witch ways. Unknown.—JaP
Witch, witch. R. Fyleman.—JaP
Witches. Linden.—LaM
Witch's broom notes. D. McCord.—McAa
The witch's garden. L. Moore.—MoSm
The witch's house. L. Benét.—RoIt

Witchcraft—*Continued*
The witch's song. L. Moore.—HoH—MoSm
Witches. See Witchcraft
Witches. Linden.—LaM
"The **witches** don their pointed hats." See What witches do
"The **witches** fly." See On Halloween
Witch's broom notes. David McCord.—McAa
"**Witch's** daughter." See Little Ugh
The **witch's** garden. Lilian Moore.—MoSm
The **witch's** house. Laura Benét.—RoIt
The **witch's** song. Lilian Moore.—HoH—MoSm
"**With** a c and a si and a constanti." Unknown.—EmN
"**With** a twitching nose." Richard Wright
Hokku poems.—AdPb
"**With** a violin in the alley grandfather and son disappeared." See Beyond melody
"**With** a whispering." Boncho, tr. fr. the Japanese by Harry Behn.—BeM
"**With** all sorts of things we are crammed." See We, the young
"**With** Anne gone." See For Anne
"**With** deep affection." See The Shandon bells
"**With** flintlocked guns and polished stocks." See In Hardin county, 1809
"**With** his apology." Karai Senryū, tr. fr. the Japanese by Geoffrey Bownas and Anthony Thwaite.—MaFw
With his mouth full of food. Shel Silverstein.—SiW
"**With** legs so short and far apart." See A duck
"**With** light enough on clean fresh-fallen snow." See Trinity place
"**With** many a scowl." See Troll trick
With my God, the smith. Uri Zvi Greenberg, tr. fr. the Hebrew by Robert Mezey and Ben Zion Gold.—MeP
"**With** my harp against my knee." Kim Chang-up, tr. fr. the Korean by Chung Seuk Park and ad. by Virginia Olsen Baron.—BaSs
"**With** my multi-colored balloon." See Multi-colored balloon
"**With** older eyes than any Roman had." See Thomas Hardy, poet
"**With** rejoicing mouth." Unknown, tr. fr. the Spanish by John Bierhorst.—BiI
"**With** rue my heart is laden." See A Shropshire lad
"**With** songs and dances—a celebration." See A celebration
"**With** the last whippoorwill call of evening." See Birmingham
"**With** their lithe long strong legs." See Bullfrog
"**With** troubled heart and trembling hand I write." See In memory of my dear grandchild Anne Bradstreet
"**With** two 60's stuck on the scoreboard." See Foul shot
"**With** walloping tails, the whales off Wales." See The whales off Wales
"**With** what a glory comes and goes the year." See Autumn

Wither, George
For scholars and pupils.—OpOx
Our joyful feast.—RoIt
A rocking hymn.—OpOx
"**Within** a thick and spreading hawthorn bush." See The thrush's nest
"**Within** my bowl there lies." See Song of encouragement
"**Within** the city." See The park
"**Within** the curved edge of quarter moon." See The path I must travel
"**Within** this black hive to-night." See Beehive
"**Within** this book so pure and white." Unknown.—EmN
"**Within** this tomb a patriot lyes." See Epitaph
Without ceremony. Thomas Hardy.—PlP
"**Without** expectation." See Summer oracle
Without name. Pauli Murray.—AdPb
Without, not within her. Thomas Hardy.—PlP
"**Without** warning." Sappho, tr. fr. the Greek by Mary Barnard.—ThI
Witness. Eve Merriam.—MeF
The **witnesses.** Clive Sansom.—MaFw (sel.)
Wives. See Married life
"The **wizard** of the woods is he." See The woodpecker
Wizards
"Bellowed the ogre." L. Moore.—MoSm
"I never saw." L. Moore.—MoSm
Lost and found. L. Moore.—MoSm
Wizzle. David McCord.—McAa
"**Woke** up, it was Chelsea morning." See Chelsea morning
Wolcot, John
To a fish of the brook.—RoIt
"A **wolf.**" Unknown, tr. fr. the Teton Sioux by Frances Densmore.—JoT
The **wolf** and the dog. Carmen Rosario.—JoV
Wolfe, Ffrida
Choosing shoes.—BrM
Wolfe, Humbert
Autumn.—PaF
The blackbird.—JoA-4
"When lads have done with labor."—LiS
Wolfe, Mary Claire
"The park."—HoC
Wolfe, Thomas
Ben.—HiN
That sharp knife.—HiN
Wolves
The builders. S. H. Hay.—LiWw
Day of the wolf. K. Wilson.—HaWr
"A hungry wolf is in the street." Irina.—MoM
"A lone wolf I am." Unknown.—ClFc
A North Pole story. M. B. Smedley.—OpOx
"A wolf." Unknown.—JoT
The wolf and the dog. C. Rosario.—JoV
"The wolves are howling." Unknown.—ClFc
"The **wolves** are howling." Unknown, tr. fr. the Clayquot.—ClFc
Woman. Elouise Loftin.—AdPb
A **woman** driving. Thomas Hardy.—PlP

"**Woman,** lay on my forehead your perfumed hands, hands softer than fur." See Night of Sine
A **woman** mourned by daughters. Adrienne Rich.—HiN
"**Woman** much missed, how you call to me, call to me." See The voice
The **woman** of three cows. Unknown, tr. fr. the Irish by James Clarence Mangan.—CoPi
"A **woman** who lived." See The moon
Woman with girdle. Anne Sexton.—HiN
"**Woman,** you'll never credit what." See The shepherd's tale
A **woman's** complaint. Unknown, tr. fr. the Aztec by Miguel León-Portilla.—BiI
Women—Portraits. See People—Portraits—Women
"**Women** who never have to hoe." See Awo
Women's liberation
"I am waiting to hear from the president, to ask." V. Bryant.—JoV
Wonder. Langston Hughes.—HoD
"**Wonderful** bears that walked my room all night." See Bears
Wonderful New York. Christopher Meyer.—JoV
"A **wondrous** city is Moscow." Tanivsha, tr. fr. the Russian by Miriam Morton.—MoM
Wondrous love. Unknown.—LaS
Wonodi, Okogbule
The immigrant.—AlPa
Lament of the exiles.—AlPa
Won't you. Shel Silverstein.—SiW
"**Won't** you plant your seeds with care." Mother Goose, tr. fr. the French.—TucMg
Woo Tahk
"I hold a rod in one hand."—BaSs
Wood, Robert Williams
The puffin.—CoOh
Wood, William
"My little parrot seemed to live."—CoPu
Wood
Kilcash. Unknown.—CoPi
Logs of wood. C. Causley.—CaF
Recycled. L. Moore.—MoSp
Woodchucks
Ground hogs. M. Pomeroy.—CoPu
"How much wood would a woodchuck chuck." Mother Goose.—EmN—JoA-4
To the groundhog. K. Winters.—LaM
"Who (is knocking)." Unknown.—BoI
Wooden ships. David Crosby, Paul Kantner, and Stephen Stills.—MoG
The **woodman's** dog. William Cowper.—CoPu—JoA-4
The **woodpecker.** John Banister Tabb.—BrM
Woodpeckers
Like they say. R. Creeley.—CoPu
"When cherry trees bloom." Jōsō.—BeM
The woodpecker. J. B. Tabb.—BrM
Woods. See Forests and forestry
"The **woods** are full of fairies." See The child and the fairies
The **woods** at night. May Swenson.—JoA-4
"The **woods** decay, the woods decay and fall." See After many a summer
Woodstock, New York
Woodstock. J. Mitchell.—MoG
Woodstock. Joni Mitchell.—MoG
"**Woody** says, Let's *make* our soap." See Social studies
"**Wool** white horses and their heads sag and roll." See Sky talk—Rolling clouds
Woolsey, Sarah Chauncy. See Coolidge, Susan
Woolson, Constance Fennimore
Kentucky Belle.—CoPt
Woowooto. Unknown, tr. fr. the Lugando by W. Moses Serwadda.—SeS
The **word** beautiful. May Swenson.—JoA-4
Word bird. Eve Merriam.—MeF
A **word** of encouragement. J. R. Pope.—CoPu
A **word** or two on Levinia. David McCord.—McAa
Word poem. Nikki Giovanni.—AdB—AdPb
"**Wordless** words." Karla Kuskin.—KuN
Words
"At noontime." Sappho.—ThI
Basket. C. Sandburg.—SaT
"Because what's *present* doesn't last." R. Wilbur.—WiO
Blum. D. Aldis.—LiLc
Booteries and fluteries and flatteries and things. N. M. Bodecker.—BoL
Chester. S. Silverstein.—SiW
Coal. A. Lorde.—AdPb
"Cow sounds heavy." K. Kuskin.—KuN
Euphemistic. E. Merriam.—MeO
Floccinaucinihilipilification. E. Merriam.—MeO
For a wordfarer. R. Humphries.—PlM
The game is doublets. D. McCord.—McFm
Gloss. D. McCord.—LiWw
"A grandfather poem." W. J. Harris.—AdM—AdPb
"Hello's a handy word to say." M. A. Hoberman.—HoN
Jabberwocky. From Through the looking-glass. L. Carroll.—JoA-4—LiPc—LiS—LiWw—OpOx—RoIt
Like you as it. D. McCord.—McAa
"Little girl, be careful what you say." C. Sandburg.—MaFw—SaT
The little star. Unknown.—LiS
Lmntl. D. McCord.—McFm
The look and sound of words. D. McCord.—McFm
Magic words. Unknown.—LeIb
"A man of words and not of deeds." Mother Goose.—AlC
Metaphor man. E. Merriam.—MeO
More or less. D. McCord.—McFm
"Not to have any *hair* is called." R. Wilbur.—WiO
A number of words. E. Merriam.—MeF
Only. D. McCord.—McAa
"The opposite of a *cloud* could be." R. Wilbur.—WiO

Words—*Continued*
"The opposite of a *hole's* a *heap.*" R. Wilbur.—WiO
"The opposite of a *king.* I'm sure." R. Wilbur.—WiO
"The opposite of *doughnut?* Wait." R. Wilbur.—WiO
"The opposite of *fast* is *loose.*" R. Wilbur.—WiO
"The opposite of *foot* is what." R. Wilbur.—WiO
"The opposite of *junk* is *stuff.*" R. Wilbur.—WiO
"The opposite of *making faces.*" R. Wilbur.—WiO
"The opposite of *opposite.*" R. Wilbur.—WiO
"The opposite of *post,* were you." R. Wilbur.—WiO
"The opposite of *spit,* I'd say." R. Wilbur.—WiO
"The opposite of *squash?* Offhand." R. Wilbur.—WiO
"The opposite of *standing still.*" R. Wilbur.—WiO
"The opposite of *tiller?* Well." R. Wilbur.—WiO
"The opposite of *trunk* could be." R. Wilbur.—WiO
"The opposite of *well* is *sick.*" R. Wilbur.—WiO
"The opposites of *earth* are two." R. Wilbur.—WiO
Pome. D. McCord.—McAa
Primer lesson. C. Sandburg.—SaT
The reason. M. Chute.—ChRu
Rhyme for a simpleton. Unknown.—RoIt
Spike spoke spook. D. McCord.—McAa
Stop playing. Z. Shneour.—MeP
Sympathy. A. T. Pratt.—AlW
"Take a word like *cat.*" K. Kuskin.—KuN
"There's more than one way to be right." R. Wilbur.—WiO
Tom and Joe. D. McCord.—McAa
"We are little airy creatures." Unknown.—EmN
What a beautiful word. W. Cole.—CoOr
"What is the opposite of a *prince.*" R. Wilbur.—WiO
"What is the opposite of a *shoe.*" R. Wilbur.—WiO
"What is the opposite of *actor.*" R. Wilbur.—WiO
"What is the opposite of *ball.*" R. Wilbur.—WiO
"What is the opposite of *bat.*" R. Wilbur.—WiO
"What is the opposite of *cheese.*" R. Wilbur.—WiO
"What is the opposite of *Cupid.*" R. Wilbur.—WiO
"What is the opposite of *doe.*" R. Wilbur.—WiO
"What is the opposite of *fleet.*" R. Wilbur.—WiO
"What is the opposite of *flying.*" R. Wilbur.—WiO
"What is the opposite of *fox.*" R. Wilbur.—WiO
"What is the opposite of *hat.*" R. Wilbur.—WiO
"What is the opposite of *July.*" R. Wilbur.—WiO
"What is the opposite of *mirror.*" R. Wilbur.—WiO
"What is the opposite of *nuts.*" R. Wilbur.—WiO
"What is the opposite of *penny.*" R. Wilbur.—WiO
"What is the opposite of *riot.*" R. Wilbur.—WiO
"What is the opposite of *string.*" R. Wilbur.—WiO
"What is the opposite of *two.*" R. Wilbur.—WiO
"Whispers." M. C. Livingston.—JoA-4—LiLc
"Who needs a poet." M. C. Livingston.—LiM
The wind blew words. T. Hardy.—PlP
Word bird. E. Merriam.—MeF
A word or two on Levinia. D. McCord.—McAa
"Wordless words." K. Kuskin.—KuN
"Words." Unknown.—MoBw
Words ("I like to listen to the sound") M. Chute.—ChRu
The words ("Wind, bird, and tree") D. Wagoner.—MoT
"X." M. A. Hoberman.—HoN
"Yes." M. A. Hoberman.—HoN
"Words." Unknown.—MoBw
Words ("I like to listen to the sound") Marchette Chute.—ChRu
The **words** ("Wind, bird, and tree") David Wagoner.—MoT
Words spoken by a mother to her newborn son as she cuts the umbilical cord. Unknown, tr. fr. the Aztec by Bernardino de Sahagún.—BiI
Wordsworth, Dorothy
Address to a child during a boisterous winter evening.—OpOx
The cottager to her infant.—OpOx
Loving and liking.—OpOx
Wordsworth, William
Alice Fell: or, Poverty.—LiS
"All at once, behold." See The excursion
"And in the frosty season, when the sun." See The prelude
"Bright was the summer's noon when quickening steps." See The prelude
Composed on a May morning, 1838.—PaF
Composed upon Westminster bridge.—PaP
The crescent boat. See Peter Bell
Daffodils.—JoA-4
"I wandered lonely as a cloud."—LiS
The excursion, sel.
"All at once, behold."—PaP

"Five years have past; five summers, with the length." See Lines composed a few miles above Tintern Abbey
The human heart.—RoIt
"I wandered lonely as a cloud." See Daffodils
Intimations of immortality.—PaF (sel.)
I've watched you now.—RoIt
The kitten and the falling leaves. See The kitten playing with the falling leaves
The kitten playing with the falling leaves.—UnGb
The kitten and the falling leaves.—RoIt
Lines composed a few miles above Tintern Abbey, sel.
"Five years have past; five summers, with the length."—PaP
Lines written in early spring.—RoIt
London, 1802.—PlM
Lucy Gray; or, Solitude.—OpOx
March. See Written in March
My heart leaps up.—JoA-4—RoIt
"One summer evening (led by her) I found." See The prelude
The pet lamb.—OpOx
Peter Bell, sel.
The crescent boat.—RoIt
The prelude, sels.
"And in the frosty season, when the sun."—PaF
"Bright was the summer's moon when quickening steps."—PaP
"One summer evening (led by her) I found."—MaFw
Resolution and independence.—LiS (sel.)—MaFw (sel.)—PlM (sel.)
"She dwelt among the untrodden ways."—LiS
"A slumber did my spirit seal."—MaFw
The solitary reaper.—RoIt
Stay near me.—RoIt
Thought of a Briton on the subjugation of Switzerland.—LiS
To my sister.—PaF (sel.)
To the cuckoo.—RoIt
We are seven.—LiS—OpOx—RoIt
Written in March.—RoIt
March.—JoA-4
Written in the album of a child.—OpOx
Wordsworth, William (about)
"All at once, behold." From The excursion. W. Wordsworth.—PaP
Bells for William Wordsworth. D. Moraes.—PlM
I've watched you mow. W. Wordsworth.—RoIt
The lost leader. R. Browning.—PlM
Only seven. H. S. Leigh.—LiS
The prelude, sels. W. Wordsworth
"And in the frosty season, when the sun."—PaF
"Bright was the summer's moon when quickening steps."—PaP
"One summer evening (led by her) I found."—MaFw
Resolution and independence. W. Wordsworth.—LiS (sel.)—MaFw (sel.)—PlM (sel.)
A sonnet on Wordsworth. J. K. Stephen.—PlM
A sonnet.—LiS
Stay near me. W. Wordsworth.—RoIt
"There lived among the untrodden ways." H. Coleridge.—LiS
To the river Duddon. N. Nicholson.—PaP
Work
After working. R. Bly.—HaWr
Bang-klang. S. Silverstein.—SiW
The chickens. Unknown.—RoIt
Five little chickens.—UnGb
Contemporary nursery rhyme. Unknown.—LiS
"Ding, dong." C. Watson.—WaF
Donkeys. Edward Field.—RoIt
Dress me, dear mother. A. Shlonsky.—MeP
"Even butterflies." Issa.—HaW
The father and his children. Unknown.—OpOx
"The garden of a London house." B. Jones.—MaFw
The gleaner. Jane Taylor.—OpOx
The hands of toil. J. R. Lowell.—RoIt
"Hey there, white seagull." Kim Kwang-wuk.—BaSs
I have seen black hands. R. Wright.—AdPb
I hear America singing. W. Whitman.—RoIt
"I meant to do my work today." R. Le Gallienne.—JoA-4—UnGb
"I'm a navvy, you're a navvy." Mother Goose.—TucMgl
The line-gang. R. Frost.—MaFw
"Mom has a job." L. Lenski.—LeC
My father. T. Hughes.—HuMf
Myself my slogan. A. Higo.—AlPa
A Negro labourer in Liverpool. D. Rubadiri.—AlPa
Not yet enough. Unknown.—AlPa
The old man who lived in the woods. Unknown.—RoIt
Pastures of plenty. W. Guthrie.—PeS
People who must. C. Sandburg.—SaT
The queens' rhyme. I. Serraillier.—BrM
Sisyphus. R. J. Burdette.—CoPt
Six ten sixty-nine. Conyus.—AdPb
"A stepchild beats straw." Issa.—HaW
Walkers with the dawn. L. Hughes.—HoD
Washing windows. B. Spacks.—HiN
Work. F. Johnson.—AdPb
Work is love. Unknown.—RoIt
"Work never killed anyone." Unknown.—MoBw
Work song. Unknown.—AbM
The worker. R. W. Thomas.—AdPb
Work is love. Unknown.—RoIt
"**Work** is love made visible." See Work is love
"**Work** never killed any one." Unknown.—MoBw
Work song. Unknown, tr. by Harold Courlander.—AbM

Worth, Valerie
Aquarium.—WoS
Cat.—WoS
"Chairs."—WoS
Clock.—WoS
Coins.—WoS
Cow.—WoS
"Crickets."—WoS
Daisies.—WoS
Dog.—WoS
Duck.—WoS
Fence.—WoS
Frog.—WoS
Grass.—WoS
Hollyhocks.—WoS
Jewels.—WoS
Marbles.—WoS
Pebbles.—WoS
Pie.—WoS
Pig.—WoS
Porches.—WoS
Raw carrots.—WoS
Sun.—WoS
Tractor.—WoS
Zinnias.—WoS
The **worthless** lover. Unknown, tr. fr. the Amhara by Sylvia Pankhurst.—AlPa
Wotton, Sir Henry
The character of a happy life.—RoIt
"**Would** it had been the man of our wish." See In the room of the bride-elect
"**Would** you like to buy a dog with a tail at either end." See Double-tail dog
"**Would** you like to hear." See The battle
"**Would** you like to know who my friends are." Yun Sun-do, tr. fr. the Korean by Chung Seuk Park and ad. by Virginia Olsen Baron.—BaSs
"**Would'st** be happy, little child." See To Theodora
Wrath. John Hollander.—LiWw
The **wreck** of the Hesperus. Henry Wadsworth Longfellow.—RoIt
The **wreck** of the Julie Plante. William Henry Drummond.—CoPt
The **Wrekin.** See Adbaston
The **wren.** Unknown.—OpOx
Wrens
"Jenny Wren fell sick." Mother Goose.—JoA-4
People of the eaves, I wish you good morning. C. Sandburg.—SaT
"The razor-tailed wren." S. Silverstein.—SiW
Upstairs. S. Silverstein.—SiW
The wren. Unknown.—OpOx
The wrens. A. Fisher.—FiFo
The **wrens.** Aileen Fisher.—FiFo
"The **wrens** have trouble like us, the house of a wren will not run itself." See People of the eaves, I wish you good morning
"The **wrens** who rent our birdhouse." See The wrens
"The **wretched** lost rejected lover." See For the moment
Wright, Bruce McM.
The African affair.—AdPb
Wright, Ernest V. (Vincent)
When father carves the duck.—RoIt
Wright, James
Arriving in the country again.—CoPu
A blessing.—MaFw
Wright, Jay
Death as history.—AdPb
The homecoming singer.—AdPb
An invitation to Madison county.—AdPb
This morning.—AbM
Wednesday night prayer meeting.—AdPb
Wright, Judith
The cicadas.—MaFw
Egrets.—AdP—HiN—JoA-4
Eve to her daughters.—ToM
Legend.—CoPt—MaFw
Wright, Richard
Between the world and me.—AdPb
"The crow flew so fast"
Hokku poems.—AdPb
"I am nobody"
Hokku poems.—AdPb
I have seen black hands.—AdPb
"In the falling snow"
Hokku poems.—AdPb
"Keep straight down this block"
Hokku poems.—AdPb
"Make up your mind, snail"
Hokku poems.—AdPb
"The spring lingers on"
Hokku poems.—AdPb
"Whose town did you leave"
Hokku poems.—AdPb
"With a twitching nose"
Hokku poems.—AdPb
Wright, Sarah E.
To some millions who survive Joseph E. Mander, Senior.—AdPb
Until they have stopped.—AdPb
"A **wrinkled,** crabbed man they picture thee." See Winter portrait
"**Write** about a radish." Karla Kuskin.—KuN
"**Write** in your book." Unknown, tr. fr. the Spanish.—MoBw
Writers and writing. See also Books and reading; Poets and poetry; also names of authors, as Lear, Edward (about)
August 24, 1963—1:00 A.M.—Omaha. D. Whitewing.—AlW
The author to her book. A. Bradstreet.—ThI
"By hook or by crook." Unknown.—EmN
A considerable speck. R. Frost.—AdP
Digging. S. Heaney.—ToM
Dorset. J. Betjeman.—ToM
Fame. W. S. Landor.—CoPu
"I might repeat in every line." S. Aleksandrovsky.—MoM
"It tickles me." Unknown.—EmN
"Let the fall leaves fall." C. Watson.—WaF
"My pen is poor." Unknown.—EmN
Opportunity. H. Graham.—LiWw
Pangur Bán. Unknown.—CoPi

Writers and writing—*Continued*
The piper. W. Blake.—LiLc—OpOx
Happy songs.—UnGb
"Some write for pleasure." Unknown.—EmN
A song of thanks. W. Cole.—CoOr
To a captious critic. P. L. Dunbar.—AbM
"Way back here and out of sight." Unknown.—EmN
"When on this page." Unknown.—EmN
"Write about a radish." K. Kuskin.—KuN
The **writing** of Hezekiah King of Judah, when he had been sick, and was recovered by his sickness. See Isaiah
Written after swimming from Sestos to Abydos. Lord Byron.—FlH
Written in March. William Wordsworth.—RoIt
March.—JoA-4
Written in the album of a child. William Wordsworth.—OpOx
The **wrong** start. Marchette Chute.—ChRu
"**Wyatt** Earp." See Speaking of television—The importance of being Western
Wylie, Elinor
The eagle and the mole.—RoIt
Escape.—JoA-4
Love to Stephen.—PlM
Velvet shoes.—AdP—PaF—RoIt
Wynken, Blynken, and Nod. Eugene Field.—OpOx
"**Wynken,** Blynken, and Nod one night." See Wynken, Blynken, and Nod
Wynne, Annette
Fairy shoes.—JaP
The teacher.—BrM
Wynne, John Huddlestone
The horse and the mule.—OpOx
Time.—OpOx

X

"**X.**" Mary Ann Hoberman.—HoN
"**X-man.**" Unknown.—MoBw
Xmas time. Walta Karsner.—CoPu

Y

"**Ya-che-ma,** he comes." See Nespelim man
The **yachts.** William Carlos Williams.—FlH—MaFw—PeS
The **yak** ("As a friend to the children commend me the yak") Hilaire Belloc.—JoA-4—OpOx
Yak ("The long-haired yak has long black hair") William Jay Smith.—CoOr
The **yak** ("There was a most odious yak") Theodore Roethke.—LiLc
"A **yak** who was new to the zoo." David Ross.—RoIt
Yaks
The yak ("As a friend to the children commend me the yak") H. Belloc.—JoA-4—OpOx
Yak ("The long-haired yak has long black hair") W. J. Smith.—CoOr
The yak ("There was a most odious yak") T. Roethke.—LiLc
"A yak who was new to the zoo." D. Ross.—RoIt
Yale
The snail at Yale. N. M. Bodecker.—BoL
Yana Indians. See Indians of the Americas—Yana
Yang Ung-jeung
"How I'd like to live."—BaSs
"**Yankee** Doodle went to town." Unknown.—JoA-4
"**Yap** yawp palaver prattle." See Gab
Yaqui Indians. See Indians of the Americas—Yaqui
Yardbird's skull. Owen Dodson.—AdPb
The **yarn** of the Loch Achray. John Masefield.—CoPt
The **yarn** of the Nancy Bell. William Schwenck Gilbert.—RoIt
"**Ye** are the temples of the Lord." See The exhortation of a father to his children
Ye carpette knights. Lewis Carroll.—LiPc
"**Ye** distant spires, ye antique towers." See On a distant prospect of Eton college
Ye hasten to the grave. Percy Bysshe Shelley.—MoG
"**Ye** hasten to the grave: What seek ye there." See Ye hasten to the grave
"**Ye** nations all, on ye I call." See The babe of Bethlehem
Year. See also New Year
Autumn. H. W. Longfellow.—PaF
A calendar. S. Coleridge.—UnGb
Dirge for the year. P. B. Shelley.—PaF
End of a year. P. Hubbell.—LaM
The garden year. S. Coleridge.—RoIt
A calendar.—UnGb
The months.—OpOx
The new year. D. M. Mulock.—RoIt
November. H. Coleridge.—PaF
The old year. J. Clare.—RoIt
Slow spring. K. Tynan.—PaF
The year. C. Patmore.—RoIt
The **year.** Coventry Patmore.—RoIt
"The **year** is withering; the wind." See Dry season
"The **year** lies fallen and faded." See Autumn in Cornwall
"The **year's** at the spring." See Pippa passes—Pippa's song
The **year's** awakening. Thomas Hardy.—PlP
Yeatman, R. J. and Sellar, W. C.
How I brought the good news from Aix to Ghent (or vice versa).—LiS
Yeats, William Butler
Adams's curse.—CoPi
All things can tempt me.—CoPi

"**You** should have heard the old men cry." See The one who stayed
"**You** should never squeeze a weasel." See Don't ever seize a weasel by the tail
"**You** smiled." Calvin O'John.—AlW
"**You** spotted snakes." See A midsummer night's dream
"**You** sprouted from sand." See Navajo children, Canyon de Chelly, Arizona
"**You** strange, astonished-looking, angle-faced." See The man and the fish
"**You** take a bath and sit there bathing." See Poems in praise of practically nothing
"**You** think all pies are round." Unknown.—MoBw
"**You** think you're cute." Unknown.—MoBw
"**You** think you're smart." Barry Jackson.—MoBw
"**You** thought the leaden winter." See Tales of brave Ulysses
You too. Patricia Irving.—AlW
"**You**: trapped in the homeland of the Chosen People." See National thoughts
"**You** use it between your head and your toes." Unknown.—EmN
"**You** used to be behind before." Unknown.—MoBw
"**You** wake up feeling." See Ripeness
"**You** walk it in the winter." See The Malibu
"**You** walked as if in snow. And you walked in snow." See Blue and red poem
"**You** want to integrate me into your anonymity." See Black Narcissus
"**You** were my friend." Unknown.—MoBw
"**You** were the sort that men forget." Thomas Hardy.—PlP
"**You** weren't even a." See To L.
"**You** who bow you who mourn." See Defiance against force
"**You** who descend river by river." See Giraffe
"**You** who desired so much—in vain to ask." See To Emily Dickinson
"**You**, whose day it is." Unknown, tr. fr. the Nootka by Frances Densmore.—JoT
"**You** whose flesh, now dust and planet." See To a Saxon poet
"**You** will always find me." Unknown, tr. fr. the Makah.—ClFc
"**You** will ask how I came to be eavesdropping, in the first place." See Confession overheard in a subway
"**You** will be aware of an absence, presently." See For a fatherless son
"**You** wouldn't believe her name." See Sophie Schnitter
"**Youd** better not." See Not again
Young, Al
A dance for militant dilettantes.—AdPb
Dance of the infidels.—AdPb
The dancer.—AdPb
For poets.—AdPb
Kiss.—AdPb
Loneliness.—AdPb
The move continuing.—AdPb
Myself when I am real.—AdPb
Yes, the secret mind whispers.—AdPb
Young, Andrew
The haystack.—CoPu
Mist.—MaFw
Young, Douglas
Last laugh.—CoPu
Young, Francis Brett
Atlantic Charter. See The island: 1620-1942
The island: 1620-1942, sel.
Atlantic Charter.—JoA-4
Young. Anne Sexton.—HiN—ToM
Young Africa's plea. Dennis Osadebay.—AlPa
Young and old. See The water babies
"A **young** Apollo, golden-haired." See Youth
Young Beichan. Unknown.—MaFw
The **young** Cossack. Andrei Kamensky, tr. fr. the Russian by Miriam Morton.—MoM
A **young** lady of Spain. See "There was a young lady of Spain"
Young lady's song of retor. Unknown, fr. the Ammassalik Eskimo.—LeIb
"A **young** man going to war." Unknown, tr. fr. the Cheyenne-Arapaho by Frances Densmore.—JoT
A **young** man's epigram on existence. Thomas Hardy.—PlP
Young Master's account of a puppet show. John Marchant.—OpOx
"**Young** men riding in the street." See Image from d'Orlean
"**Young** niggers." See Dedication to the final confrontation
The **young** ones, flip side. James A. Emanuel.—AbM
Young poet. Myron O'Higgins.—AdPb
"The **young** poet Eumenes." See The first step
"**Young** Roger came tapping at Dolly's window." Mother Goose.—AlC
Young sea. Carl Sandburg.—SaT
Young soul. LeRoi Jones.—MoT
Young training. Lawrence McGaugh.—AdPb
"**Your** album is a garden." Unknown.—MoBw
"**Your** being has caused." See Love song
Your cat and mine. Aileen Fisher.—FiM
"**Your** clear eye is the one absolutely beautiful thing." See Child
"**Your** death has taken me by surprise." See Lament
"**Your** dog? What dog? You mean it?—that." See Susie's new dog
"**Your** door is shut against my tightened face." See The white house
Your eyes have their silence. Gerald W. Barrax.—AdPb
"**Your** eyes have their silence in giving words." See Your eyes have their silence
"**Your** father and I, my penguin chick." See Penguin chick
"**Your** father is a baker." Unknown.—MoBw
"**Your** father's gone, my bald headmaster said." See The lesson
Your hands. Angelina Weld Grimké.—AdPb

"**Your** heart is not a plaything." Unknown.—EmN
"**Your** house is so classy." Unknown.—MoBw
"**Your** little hands." Samuel Hoffenstein.—LiWw
"**Your** midriff sags toward your knees." See Woman with girdle
"**Your** mother." Sam Cornish.—AdM
Your people are drowning in blood. Saul Tchernichovsky, tr. fr. the Hebrew by Robert Mezey and Shula Starkman.—MeP
"**Your** people are drowning in blood and you're making poems." See Your people are drowning in blood
You're. Sylvia Plath.—HiN
"**You're** a joy to behold." Unknown.—MoBw
"**You're** a lucky one, Joey." See Joey Kangaroo
"**You're** in the mood for freaky food." See Wicked witch's kitchen
You're nothing but a Spanish colored kid. Felipe Luciano.—AdPb
"**Yours** till a man-eater eats a woman." Unknown.—MoBw
"**Yours** till Brussels sprouts." Unknown.—MoBw
"**Yours** till Buffalo Bill." Unknown.—MoBw
"**Yours** till China gets Hungary." Unknown.—EmN
"**Yours** till day breaks." Unknown.—MoBw
"**Yours** till Gaza strips." Unknown.—MoBw
"**Yours** till ice skates." Unknown.—MoBw
"**Yours** till lemon drops." Unknown.—MoBw
"**Yours** till lip sticks." Unknown.—MoBw
"**Yours** till my breath comes in pants." Unknown.—MoBw
"**Yours** till Niagara falls." Unknown.—EmN
"**Yours** till potato chips, the ferry slips, and the comic strips." Unknown.—MoBw
"**Yours** till Russia takes down the Iron Curtain." Unknown.—MoBw
"**Yours** till the cereal bowls." Unknown.—MoBw
"**Yours** till the foot of Main street." Unknown.—MoBw
"**Yours** till the Iron Curtain rusts." Unknown.—MoBw
"**Yours** till the ocean waves at you." Unknown.—EmN
"**Yours** till the pencil case is solved." Unknown.—MoBw
"**Yours** till the river wears rubber pants." Unknown.—EmN
Youth. See also Boys and boyhood; Childhood recollections; Girls and girlhood; Youth and age
  Fifteen. W. Stafford.—PeS
  Great-aunts. S. O'Críadain.—CoPi
  Hoeing. J. Updike.—MoT
  Pastoral. W. C. Williams.—PeS
  Sweet and twenty. From Twelfth night. W. Shakespeare.—MoG
  We real cool. G. Brooks.—AbM—AdPb
  Young. A. Sexton.—HiN—ToM
  The young ones, flip side. J. A. Emanuel.—AbM
  Youth ("We have tomorrow") L. Hughes.—HoD—JoA-4
  Youth ("A young Apollo, golden-haired") F. Cornford.—CoPu
  The youth and the northwind. J. G. Saxe.—CoPt
Youth and age. See also Birthdays; Childhood recollections; Old age; Youth
  Adventures with my grandfather. A. Marx.—RoIt
  Blue and red poem. A. Gilboa.—MeP
  Brown penny. W. B. Yeats.—CoPi
  Changed. C. S. Calverley.—RoIt
  "The fairies have never a penny to spend." R. Fyleman.—OpOx
  Fast and slow. J. Ciardi.—CiFs
  The first snow of the year. M. Van Doren.—HiN
  Glimpses # xii. L. McGaugh.—AdB (sel.)
  Going where. P. Irving.—AlW
  "I have lived up half my life already." Yi Myung-han.—BaSs
  "I like you, bamboo." Kim Kwang-wuk.—BaSs
  "I remember, I remember." T. Hood.—RoIt
  In honor of a king who acquired several young wives. Unknown.—AlPa
  July 31. N. Jordan.—AdPb
  "Let me ask you, Mind." Unknown.—BaSs
  Lewis Carroll. E. Farjeon.—OpOx
  Love and age. From Gryll Grange. T. L. Peacock.—RoIt
  Moment of visitation. G. Davidson.—RoIt
  My early home. J. Clare.—RoIt
  My heart leaps up. W. Wordsworth.—JoA-4—RoIt
  My lost youth. H. W. Longfellow.—RoIt
  Niño leading an old man to market. L. Nathan.—HiN
  Old black men. G. D. Johnson.—AdPb
  Old black men say. J. A. Emanuel.—AdM—AdPb
  "Old man weighed down with a bundle on your head." Chung Chui.—BaSs
  The old man's comforts and how he gained them. R. Southey.—LiS—OpOx
  One, two, three. H. C. Bunner.—RoIt
  Points of view. A. Lowell.—CoPu
  Politics. W. B. Yeats.—CoPi
  Sing me a song. R. L. Stevenson.—RoIt
  Ulifak's song of the caribou. Unknown.—LeIb
  We, the young. M. Gurvich.—MoM
  When you are old. W. B. Yeats.—MaFw
  "You are old, Father William, the young man said." From Alice's adventures in wonderland. L. Carroll.—LiPc
    Father William.—LiS
    You are old, Father William.—OpOx
  Young and old. From The water babies. C. Kingsley.—OpOx
    The old song.—RoIt
Youth ("We have tomorrow") Langston Hughes.—HoD—JoA-4

Youth ("A young Apollo, golden-haired") Frances Cornford.—CoPu
The **youth** and the northwind. John Godfrey Saxe.—CoPt
"**Youth** cocks his hat and rides up the street." See Points of view
"**You've** heard how a green thumb." See My Aunt Dora
"**You've** no need to light a night light." Unknown.—BrM
Yüan Chēn (about)
On hearing some one sing a poem by Yüan Chēn. Po Chü-i.—PlM
Yüan Mei
By chance I walk.—MaFw
Chopsticks.—MaFw
Standing at the foot of the steps at night.—MaFw
"**Yucca.**" See In my mother's house
Yucca
"Yucca." From In my mother's house. A. N. Clark.—JoA-4
Yuletide in a younger world. Thomas Hardy.—PlP
Yuma Indians. See Indians of the Americas—Yuma
Yun Sun-do
"Is that a cuckoo singing."—BaSs
"Would you like to know who my friends are."—BaSs

Z

Zachary Zed. James Reeves.—CoOh
"**Zachary** Zed was the last man." See Zachary Zed
Zalka Peetruza. Ray Garfield Dandridge.—AdPb
Zapata and the landlord. A. B. Spellman.—AdPb
Zebra ("The eagle's shadow runs across the plain") Isak Dinesen.—AdP
The **zebra** ("The zebra is undoubtedly") Jack Prelutsky.—PrT
The **Zebra** Dun. Unknown.—CoPt
"The **zebra** is undoubtedly." See The zebra
"**Zebra** starts with Z—just look." Mary Ann Hoberman.—HoN
Zebras
The new one. M. C. Livingston.—LiM
A surprise. M. Douglas.—CoOr
Zebra ("The eagle's shadow runs across the plain") I. Dinesen.—AdP
The zebra ("The zebra is undoubtedly") J. Prelutsky.—PrT
"Zebra starts with Z—just look." M. A. Hoberman.—HoN
Zebu. Flavien Ranaivo, tr. by John Reed and Clive Wake.—AbM
Zebus
Zebu. F. Ranaivo.—AbM
Zoo doings. J. Prelutsky.—PrT
"**Zee** hat comes from gay Paree." Unknown.—MoBw
"**Zero.**" See The story of the zeros
Zinnias
Zinnias. V. Worth.—WoS
Zinnias. Valerie Worth.—WoS
"**Zinnias,** stout and stiff." See Zinnias
Zinoviev, Kolya
The shore of the universe.—MoM
Zodiac, Signs of
Signs of the zodiac. D. McCord.—LiWw
The **zoo.** Boris Pasternak, tr. fr. the Russian by Lydia Pasternak.—MaFw
Zoo doings. Jack Prelutsky.—PrT
Zoo-keeper. Lois Lenski.—LeC
"The **zoo** lies in the parkland thickets." See The zoo
Zoogeography. Mary Ann Hoberman.—HoR
Zoos
Anthropoids. M. A. Hoberman.—HoR
At the zoo ("First I saw the white bear, then I saw the black") W. M. Thackeray.—OpOx
At the zoo ("I like the zebra") A. Fisher.—FiFo
The bear. L. Lenski.—LeC
Boy in the Roman zoo. A. MacLeish.—HiN
Conversation with a giraffe at dusk in the zoo. D. Livingstone.—ToM
"East is east and west is west." Unknown.—CoOh
Giraffe. C. McCullers.—HoCs
The gnu family. I. Orleans.—BrM
"I found a silver dollar." D. Lee.—LeA
Making friends. V. Lapin.—MoM
"Mr Zookeeper." L. B. Hopkins.—HoCs
The monkeys. E. O. Thompson.—BrM
Some natural history. D. Marquis.—LiWw
"Spangled pandemonium." P. Brown.—CoOr
Twilight at the zoo. A. Rodger.—HiN
The zoo. B. Pasternak.—MaFw
Zoo doings. J. Prelutsky.—PrT
Zoo-keeper. L. Lenski.—LeC
Zoogeography. M. A. Hoberman.—HoR
Zorach, William
Look, the sea.—AdP
"**Zounds,** gramercy, and rootity-toot." See Speaking of television—Robin Hood
A **Zulu** lyric. Unknown, tr. fr. the Zulu by Hugh Tracey.—AlPa
Zuni Indians. See Indians of the Americas—Zuni

DIRECTORY OF PUBLISHERS AND DISTRIBUTORS

ATHENEUM. Atheneum Publishers, 122 E. 42 St, New York 10017

BOBBS-MERRILL. The Bobbs-Merrill Company, Inc, 433 W 62 St, Indianapolis, Indiana 46206

CROWELL. Thomas Y. Crowell Company, 666 Fifth Av, New York 10019

DELACORTE. Delacorte Press/Dell Publishing Company, Inc, 1 Dag Hammarskjold Plaza, 24 SE 47 St, New York 10017

DIAL. The Dial Press (subsidiary of Dell), 1 Dag Hammarskjold Plaza, 24 SE 47 St, New York 10017

DODD. Dodd, Mead and Company, 79 Madison Av, New York 10016

DOUBLEDAY. Doubleday Publishing Company, Garden City, New York 11530

DUTTON. E. P. Dutton and Company, Inc, 20 Park Av S, New York 10003

FARRAR. Farrar, Straus, and Giroux, Inc, 19 Union Sq W, New York 10003

FOUR WINDS. Four Winds Press, Scholastic Book Services, 50 W 44 St, New York 10036

GARRARD. Garrard Publishing Company, 1607 N Market St, Champaign, Ill. 61820

GOLDEN GATE. Golden Gate Junior Books, 6922 Hollywood Blvd, Los Angeles, Calif. 90028

GOLDEN PRESS. Golden Press, Inc, 850 Third Av, New York 10022

GROSSET. Grosset and Dunlap, Inc, 51 Madison Av, New York 10010

HARCOURT. Harcourt Brace Jovanovich, Inc. 757 Third Av, New York 10017

HARPER. Harper and Row, Publishers, 10 E 53 St, New York 10022

HOLT. Holt, Rinehart and Winston, 383 Madison Av, New York 10017

HOUGHTON. Houghton Mifflin Company, 2 Park St, Boston 02107

KNOPF. Alfred A. Knopf, Inc, 201 E 50 St, New York 10022

LIPPINCOTT. J. B. Lippincott Company, East Washington Sq, Philadelphia 19105

LITTLE. Little, Brown and Company, 34 Beacon St, Boston 02106

MCCALL. McCall Books, Saturday Review Press, 230 Park Av, New York 10017

MCGRAW-HILL. McGraw-Hill Book Company, 1221 Av of the Americas, New York 10020

MACMILLAN. The Macmillan Publishing Company, Inc, 866 Third Av, New York 10022

MORROW. William Morrow and Company, Inc, 105 Madison Av, New York 10016

OXFORD. Oxford University Press, Inc, 200 Madison Av, New York 10016

SCRIBNER. Charles Scribner's Sons, 547 Fifth Av, New York 10017

SIMON. Simon and Schuster, Inc, 630 Fifth Av, New York 10020

VIKING. The Viking Press, Inc, 625 Madison Av, New York 10022

WALCK. Henry Z. Walck, Inc, 750 Third Av, New York 10017

WALKER. Walker and Company, 720 Fifth Av, New York 10019

WATTS. Franklin Watts, Inc, 730 Fifth Av, New York 10019

WORLD. The World Publishing Company, 110 E 59 St, New York 10022